General Equilibrium Modeling and Economic Policy Analysis

General Equilibrium Modeling and Economic Policy Analysis

Lars Bergman, Dale W. Jorgenson
and Erno Zalai

Basil Blackwell

Library of Congress Cataloging in Publication Data
A CIP catalogue record for this book is available from the Library of Congress.
ISBN: 1-55786-027-0

British Library Cataloguing in Publication Data
A CIP catalogue record for this book is available from the British Library.

Typeset in 10 on 11½ pt Times by Keytec, Bridport, Dorset
Printed in Great Britain by Billing & Sons Ltd, Worcester

Contents

List of Contributors   vii

Preface   x

PART I Introduction

1 The Development of Computable General Equilibrium   3
  Modeling
  Lars Bergman

PART II Finance and Taxation

2 A Framework for Evaluating Tax Capitalization Effects in   33
  Asset Markets
  Jonas Agell

3 Tax Policy and US Economic Growth   58
  Dale W. Jorgenson and Kun-Young Yun

4 Indeterminacy in Applied Intertemporal General   111
  Equilibrium Models
  Timothy J. Kehoe and David K. Levine

5 An Applied General Equilibrium Model of the Asset   149
  Markets in Sweden
  Lars Werin

PART III International Trade

6 The Common Agricultural Policy of the European   195
  Community and the World Economy: A General
  Equilibrium Analysis
  Jean Marc Burniaux and Jean Waelbroeck

7 Foreign Exchange Retention and Trade Incentives: A 218
General Equilibrium Evaluation for Yugoslavia
Mathias Dewatripont, Wafik Grais and Gilles Michel

8 A Decade of Applied General Equilibrium Modelling for 241
Policy Work
Alan A. Powell and Tony Lawson

9 Applied General Equilibrium Modelling in the Australian 291
Industries Assistance Commission: Perspectives of a
Policy Analyst
David P. Vincent

PART IV Economic Planning
10 General Equilibrium Approaches to Energy Policy 351
Analysis in Sweden
Lars Bergman and Stefan Lundgren

11 Two Alternative Disequilibrium Models for a Planned 383
Economy
Wojciech Charemza and Vladimir Dlouhý

12 Computable General Equilibrium Models for Socialist 405
Economies
Péter Kis, Sherman Robinson and Laura D. Tyson

13 Modelling and its Environment in Hungarian Medium- 431
term Planning
Zsolt Ámon and István Ligeti

Index 460

Contributors

Dr Jonas Agell
Department of Economics
Uppsala University
PO Box 513
S-751 20 Uppsala
SWEDEN

Dr Zsolt Ámon, Division Head
Department of Economics
National Planning Office
PO Box 610
H-1370 Budapest
HUNGARY

Prof. Lars Bergman
Department of Economics
Stockholm School of Economics
PO Box 6501
S-113 83 Stockholm
SWEDEN

Dr Jean Marc Burniaux,
Administrator
Growth Studies Division
Economic and Statistics
Department
OECD
2 rue André-Pascal
75 775 Paris Cédex 16
FRANCE

Dr Wojciech Charemza
Department of Economics
University of Leicester
University Road
Leicester LE1 7RH
UNITED KINGDOM

Prof. Mathias Dewatripont
Department of Applied
Economics
Free University of Brussels
PO Box 140
50 Avenue Roosevelt
B-1050 Brussels
BELGIUM

Dr Vladimir Dlouhý
Institute of Forecasting
Czechoslovakian Academy of
Sciences
Opletalova 19
110 00 Prague
CZECHOSLOVAKIA

Dr Wafik Grais
The World Bank
1818 H Street NW
Washington, DC 20433
USA

Prof. Dale W. Jorgenson
Department of Economics
Harvard University
Littauer Center 122
Cambridge, MA 02138
USA

Prof. Timothy J. Kehoe
Department of Economics
University of Minnesota
Minneapolis, MN 55455
USA

Dr Péter Kis
Institute of Economic Planning
National Planning Office
Roosevelt ter 7–8
H-1370 Budapest
HUNGARY

Mr Tony Lawson
Industries Assistance Commission
PO Box 80
Belconnen, ACT 2616
AUSTRALIA

Prof. David K. Levine
Department of Economics
University of California, Los
Angeles
Los Angeles, CA 90024
USA

Mr István Ligeti, Head
Department of Methodology
Development
National Planning Office
PO Box 610
H-1370 Budapest
HUNGARY

Dr Stefan Lundgren
Department of Economics
Stockholm School of Economics
PO Box 6501
S-113 83 Stockholm
SWEDEN

Dr Gilles Michel
The World Bank
1818 H Street NW
Washington, DC 20433
USA

Prof. Alan A. Powell, Director
Impact Project
University of Melbourne
153 Barry Street
Carlton, Vic. 3053
AUSTRALIA

Prof. Sherman Robinson
Department of Agriculture and
Resource Economics
University of California
207 Giannini Hall
Berkeley, CA 94720
USA

Prof. Laura D. Tyson
Department of Economics
University of California
Berkeley, CA 94720
USA

Mr David P. Vincent, Chief
Economist
Centre for International
Economics
GPO Box 2203
Canberra, ACT 2601
AUSTRALIA

Prof. Jean Waelbroeck
Department of Applied
Economics
Free University of Brussels
PO Box 140
50 Avenue Roosevelt
B-1050 Brussels
BELGIUM

Prof. Lars Werin
Department of Economics
University of Stockholm
Universitetsvagen 10A
S-106 91 Stockholm
SWEDEN

Prof. Kun-Young Yun
College of Business and
Economics
Yonsei University
Seoul 120
KOREA

Prof. Erno Zalai
Department of National
Economic Planning
Karl Marx University of
Economics
Dimitrov ter 8
H-1093 Budapest
HUNGARY

Preface

This book reports the proceedings of the 1986 IIASA Task Force Meeting on Applied General Equilibrium Modeling, held at the International Institute for Applied Systems Analysis (IIASA), Laxenburg, Austria, on August 25-9. The Task Force Meeting was preceded by an International Summer School on Applied General Equilibrium Modeling, also held at IIASA. Both of these activities were planned and implemented by an international organizing committee consisting of Dale W. Jorgenson, Harvard University (Chairman), Lars Bergman, Stockholm School of Economics, and Erno Zalai, Karl Marx University of Economics, Budapest.

The program of the 1986 IIASA Task Force Meeting was designed to achieve three major objectives. First, survey papers were commissioned to summarize major areas of policy application. Second, panel discussions involving modelers and policy makers were conducted to review experiences in the interaction between the two groups. Third, contributed papers on new and promising areas of policy analysis, especially by younger investigators, were solicited from a broad range of academic and policy-making institutions known to be active in general equilibrium modeling.

The Task Force Meeting attracted almost 80 participants from 23 countries. These included many of the centrally planned economies of Eastern Europe – Bulgaria, Czechoslovakia, the German Democratic Republic, Hungary, Poland, the USSR and Yugoslavia. Also included were a substantial number of Western European countries – Austria, Belgium, Denmark, the Federal Republic of Germany, France, the Netherlands, Norway, Spain, Sweden and the UK. Finally, the conference included participants from several countries outside Europe – Australia, Cameroon, Canada, Japan, Kuwait and the USA.

Policy applications of general equilibrium modeling have undergone explosive growth in the past decade and a half. The distinguishing characteristic of the general equilibrium approach is a focus on economy-wide resource allocation. This focus has made the approach a highly attractive vehicle for economic planning and policy analysis. The papers in this volume provide a representative selection of the numerous and varied applications of general equilibrium modeling to economic policy analysis presented at the Task Force Meeting. Applications include market economies, both large and small, and centrally planned economies.

An overview of previous research on general equilibrium modeling is presented by Bergman in his introductory essay to the volume. Bergman outlines four basic approaches to the construction of general equilibrium models. General equilibrium modeling was originated by the late Leif Johansen in his 1960 doctoral dissertation, "A multisectoral study of economic growth", at the University of Oslo in Norway. Johansen's multisectoral growth (MSG) model was taken over by the Norwegian Ministry of Finance in the 1970s and has become the primary framework for long-term macroeconomic planning and forecasting in Norway. The focus of recent applications has been Norwegian energy policy.

The MSG model provided the immediate inspiration for the development of computable general equilibrium (CGE) models by Peter Dixon, Tony Lawson and Alan Powell at the University of Melbourne in Australia and David Vincent, then at the Australian Industries Assistance Commission and now at the Centre for International Economics in Canberra. Powell and Lawson describe the results of a decade of experience with the application of general equilibrium modeling in Australia in chapter 8 of this volume. Vincent presents the perspective of the Industries Assistance Commission on this experience in chapter 9.

A second approach to general equilibrium modeling described by Bergman in his introductory chapter focuses on efficiency and income distribution effects of tax and trade policies. John Shoven and John Whalley and their collaborators have developed a series of models of the US economy for the analysis of tax policy. Recent tax policy modeling has focused on intertemporal aspects of tax policy analysis. These newer developments are presented in this volume by Jorgenson and Kun-Young Yun in chapter 3 and Kehoe and Levine in chapter 4.

A distinctive feature of the intertemporal equilibrium model of the US economy presented by Jorgenson and Yun is the econometric estimation of the parameters. As Bergman points out in his introduction to the volume, the approach to general equilibrium modeling employed by Shoven, Whalley and other tax policy modelers has been based on two steps. First, parameters are selected from those available in the published literature. Second, the general equilibrium model containing these parameters is "calibrated" to a single data point. The econometric approach employed by Jorgenson and Yun requires a complete time series of national accounting data.

Kehoe and Levine have analyzed the problem of uniqueness of intertemporal equilibrium in a family of tax policy models introduced by Alan Auerbach and Lawrence Kotlikoff. These models employ an overlapping generations representation of consumer behavior, so that the existence of a unique intertemporal equilibrium corresponding to each tax policy is not assured. Kehoe and Levine demonstrate the value of general equilibrium theory in characterizing the set of possible equilibria for the class of models developed by Auerbach and Kotlikoff.

The first section of this book is devoted to applications of general equilibrium models to finance and taxation. In chapter 2 Jonas Agell presents a framework for the analysis of tax capitalization effects, based on the capital asset model commonly used in finance. In chapter 5 Lars Werin applies a related model to the analysis of impacts of alternative methods for financing a government deficit. Both models employ data for markets for real and financial assets in Sweden. Chapter 3 by Jorgenson and Yun and chapter 4 by Kehoe and Levine deal with tax policy models for the USA.

The second section of the book is devoted to applications of general equilibrium models to international trade policy. Jean Marc Burniaux and Jean Waelbroeck present an analysis of the impact of the Common Agricultural Policy of the European Economic Community in chapter 6. In chapter 7 Mathias Dewatripont, Wafik Grais and Gilles Michel discuss the impact of retention of foreign exchange on incentives to export in Yugoslavia. Chapter 8 by Powell and Lawson and chapter 9 by Vincent discuss Australian experience with general equilibrium modeling of the impact of trade policies.

The third and final section of the volume is devoted to economic planning in both market-oriented and centrally planned economies. In chapter 10 Bergman and Stefan Lundgren present an approach to energy policy analysis that combines a CGE model of the Swedish economy with an activity analysis model of the energy sector. The activity analysis framework provides a vehicle for the introduction of detailed information about alternative energy technologies. This framework exemplifies the final approach to general equilibrium modeling analyzed by Bergman in his introduction to the volume. This approach is based on optimizing models originally employed in development planning.

In chapter 11 Wojciech Charemza and Vladimír Dlouhý discuss alternative disequilibrium models of a centrally planned economy. Disequilibrium results from fixed prices; the alternative models represent alternative approaches to dealing with the resulting imbalances between demands and supplies of goods and factors. Finally, in chapter 12 of the volume Péter Kis, Sherman Robinson and Laura Tyson present a CGE model constructed under World Bank auspices in support of the seventh Hungarian Five Year Plan and, in chapter 13, Zsolt Ámon and István Ligeti discuss the environment for application of this model in Hungary and compare the CGE approach with earlier models used to support central planning in Hungary. These earlier models, like models employed in development planning, were based on optimization.

For this brief review we can conclude that general equilibrium modeling is a well-established approach to the analysis of the impact of economic policies. This approach has been successfully implemented in many different countries and in a variety of institutional settings. The policies considered have included economic planning, trade, tax and budget policies that affect an entire economy, and sector-specific policies, such as energy policies, that have an economy-wide impact.

Despite the high costs of full-scale implementation of the applied general equilibrium approach, this approach has been widely adopted by policy analysts. It has displaced such alternative methodologies as macroeconometric modeling and input–output analysis in many areas of application. It has also displaced economy-wide optimization models in economic planning for developing countries. This volume demonstrates that the possibilities for utilizing general equilibrium models in centrally planned economies have also been clearly recognized.

We are indebted to the Ford Foundation for its generous support of the 1986 IIASA Task Force Meeting and the associated International Summer School. Needless to say, the Foundation is not to be held responsible for any deficiencies in this proceedings volume. We are also grateful to Shanta Deverajan of Harvard University and Sherman Robinson of the University of California, Berkeley, for serving together with Bergman and Zalai on the faculty of the International Summer School. Finally, we would like to express our appreciation to Alan MacDonald of IIASA's US National Member Organization for his help with the administrative arrangements and Ms Agnetta Newton and her very efficient staff at IIASA Conference Services in Laxenburg for their assistance with the Task Force Meeting.

Lars Bergman
Dale W. Jorgenson
Erno Zalai

PART I

Introduction

1

The Development of Computable General Equilibrium Modeling

Lars Bergman

1 Introduction

The notion of general equilibrium is one of the basic ideas of economics. Formalized analyses of general equilibrium systems have provided fundamental insights into the factors determining the allocation of resources and the distribution of incomes in market economies. With the development of "computable general equlibrium" (CGE) models general equilibrium theory has become an operational tool in empirically oriented economic analysis.

The purpose of this survey is to review briefly the development of this field of economic modeling. In doing this I will focus on a number of distinct and basic approaches rather than trying to make a complete account of individual models. Thus I will discuss only a few specific models and use each one of these as a point of departure for a somewhat more general discussion of particular problems in the CGE modeling. Needless to say this means that several outstanding contributions to CGE modeling will be left out of this survey.

The exposition is organized in the following way. In section 2 I briefly discuss the main characteristics and uses of CGE models. This discussion is an introduction to section 3 in which four lines of development of CGE modeling are dealt with at some length. In section 4, finally, some comments on recent developments in CGE modeling are made.

2 The Main Characteristics and Uses of Computable General Equilibrium Models

Although the label "computable general equilibrium" conveys an intuitive message, there is no precise definition of a CGE model. Yet the class of numerical multisectoral economic models usually referred to as "CGE models" has a set of common and distinct features. One of these is that both quantities and relative prices are endogenously determined within the models. In this respect CGE models differ sharply from input–output and programming models used for development planning purposes.

Another feature is that CGE models in general can be numerically solved for market clearing prices on all product and factor markets.[1] Moreover, CGE models are generally focused on the real side of the economy, although financial instruments and financial markets are included in some models (see for instance Feltenstein, 1984).

With few exceptions CGE models are aimed at elucidating equilibrium resource allocation patterns rather than business cycle phenomena, and the mechanisms by which policy measures affect the economy rather than the exact outcome of a certain government intervention. In other words it seems that the aim of Adelman and Robinson to build "a realistic structural model, not a reduced form forecasting model" (Adelman and Robinson, 1978, p. 6) is shared by most CGE modelers. As a consequence most CGE models are intended for quantitative comparative statics[2] analyses of the impact of nonmarginal changes in conditions which are exogenous to the modeled economy. Typically these analyses take the form of comparisons across different second-best resource allocation patterns.

In spite of their multisectoral character, CGE models generally provide a very aggregated representation of the economy.[3] Hence, if the label "general equilibrium model" is reserved for models of the interaction of the microunits in the economy, a CGE model is not a general equilibrium model. Yet the design of CGE models typically has a strong flavor of Walrasian general equilibrium theory.[4]

Thus, in a standard CGE model all product and factor markets are taken to be fully competitive and excess demand functions are homogeneous of degree zero in prices and satisfy Walras's law. Moreover, household product demand and factor supply functions are specified to be consistent with utility maximization subject to a budget constraint, while the product supply and factor demand functions of the producers in the same spirit are specified to be consistent with profit maximization subject to technology constraints.

Within this general modeling framework, however, there is a lot of variety. For instance, there are both one-country and multicountry CGE models. Models in the former class are generally intended for analysis of resource allocation and income distribution issues within a national economy faced with exogenously given world market conditions, while those in the latter category are typically aimed at elucidating the corresponding issues in a regional or global perspective.

Moreover CGE models differ significantly with respect to the level of aggregation as well as to the emphasis in the representation of the modeled economy. Thus, in some models the representation of production and technical change is rather elaborate, while a disaggregated household sector and a detailed treatment of the tax and transfer system are the main features of other CGE models. It should also be mentioned that some CGE models can be characterized as large or even very large, multipurpose models, while another rapidly growing category comprises CGE models that are especially designed and used for analysis of a particular problem in a particular context.

These dissimilarities between existing CGE models of course reflect the simple fact that different models are intended for a number of different specific purposes. As I have already indicated, however, most CGE models are intended for some kind of numerical comparative statics analysis of changes in exogenous conditions. The natural and often raised question then is why numerical rather than analytical models are chosen in these instances. The answer emerging from the literature on CGE models is that there is not really a choice between numerical and analytical models. Instead, the numerical models should be seen as complements to and extensions of the analytical models. Thus the usefulness of CGE models is emphasized in two types of situation.

In the first the reason for using a numerical model is that analytical solutions are difficult or impossible to obtain. Normally this is due to the size or complexity of the model which is regarded as relevant and adequate in the analysis of a specific issue. Using a CGE model then might make it possible to gain useful insights into the economic problem under study. A related case obtains when analytical results are indeterminate; a CGE model can yield determinate results in relevant special cases.

The second type of situation in which a CGE model is regarded as a useful extension of analytical models is when the order of magnitude of various effects definitely matters. For instance, on the basis of analytical results it can be established that taxes other than lump-sum taxes cause dead-weight losses, but from the practical policy point of view the magnitude of these losses, as well as the differences in this respect across different tax system designs, are quite important. Thus CGE models can be regarded as tools for adding quantitative information to qualitative results.

Occasionally it is pointed out that the results obtained in simulations with numerical models all refer to special cases and thus are less general than results obtained from analytical models. However, although this is certainly true, it is not always a real limitation. In fact it is sometimes argued that CGE models are particularly useful just because they reflect the actual structure of the economy, and that the comparative statics results obtained from CGE models do reflect the existing distortions in the economy.

3 The Development of Computable General Equilibrium Modeling

With this general background I will now turn to a somewhat more detailed description of the development of CGE modeling. I have identified four basic approaches and each one of these is dealt with in a separate subsection. The first, in my exposition as well as in a chronological order of the four approaches to be discussed, originates from the late Leif Johansen's so-called multisectoral growth (MSG) model. The second is largely due to Arnold C. Harberger, Herbert E. Scarf, John B. Shoven and John Whalley. It is represented by a number of CGE models aimed at elucidating efficiency and income distribution effects of trade or tax and transfer policies. The third is essentially due to Dale W. Jorgenson and can be characterized as an econometric approach to CGE modeling. The fourth approach is due to Victor Ginsburgh and Jean Waelbroeck and can be characterized as an extension of activity analysis and linear programming modeling.

3.1 The various models

3.1.1 Johansen's multisectoral growth model

I believe that by now it is commonly agreed that CGE modeling began with Leif Johansen's doctoral dissertation "A multi-sectoral study of economic growth" (Johansen, 1960). As the title suggests, Johansen's study was intended to be a contribution to the analysis of economic growth in Norway. In particular his aim was to shed light on some sectoral aspects of economic growth, i.e. phenomena such as the sectoral reallocation of labor and capital, changes in sectoral terms of trade etc. in the process of economic growth. The basic tool in this analysis was a disaggreated numerical model which later has become known as the "MSG model".

Since Johansen's model is the natural point of departure in a discussion about the development of CGE modeling, it is worthwhile to briefly consider the structure of that model. Thus I will give a short description of the main building blocks in the MSG model and particularly point out how it differs from CGE models of more recent vintage.

The MSG model was essentially a model of a closed economy; the only endogenous foreign trade is import of certain inputs which could not be produced domestically. The rest of Norway's foreign trade was treated as exogenously determined (positive or negative) final demand and added to the exogenously determined demand for public consumption and net investment purposes. On the resource side, the aggregate supply of capital and labor, as well as the rate of technical change, was exogenously determined. As a consequence of these features relative product and factor prices were determined largely by domestic conditions in the MSG model.

In the original version of the MSG model, there were 20 "real" production sectors, each one using the other sectors' outputs as inputs in its own production process. In addition there were two "book-keeping" sectors, i.e. artificial sectors with the role of defining certain aggregated commodity groups. The assumptions about the technological constraints on the sectoral level can be summarized by the following three equations, where X_i is gross outputs in sector i, X_{ij} the use of sector i outputs in sector j, N_i the use of labor in sector i, K_i the use of capital in sector i and M_i the use of so-called complementary imports in sector i.

The parameters a_{ij} and m_i are Leontief-type fixed input coefficients for domestically produced and imported inputs respectively, while the parameters u_i and v_i are the output elasticities for labor and capital respectively, in the value-added process. As t is a time index, the parameter g_i represents the rate of annual (neutral) technical change.

$$X_i = A_i N_i^{u_i} K_i^{v_i} \exp(g_i t) \qquad i = 1, \ldots, 20$$

$$X_{ij} = a_{ij} X_j \qquad i = 1, \ldots, 22 \qquad j = 1, \ldots, 22$$

$$M_i = m_i X_i \qquad i = 1, \ldots, 22$$

Thus, interindustry deliveries were determined as in the input–output model, whereas value-added deliveries were determined in accordance with Cobb–Douglas production functions.[5] In other words the possibilities for input substitution on the sectoral level were confined to the value-added process.

Later versions of the MSG model, as well as other CGE models, have included less restrictive technology assumptions. From Johansen's point of view the above assumptions were a compromise between what was desirable and what was possible.[6] In fact, all parameters in the equations above can be estimated on the basis of one single input–output table.

Another set of particular features of the MSG model reflects the fact that Johansen wanted the model to be a tool for long-term economic planning and forecasting.[7] The long-term perspective was the prime motivation for assuming full utilization of available resources, but the emphasis on the model's forecasting ability also led to a formulation which was not fully consistant with Walrasian general equilibrium theory. However, this did not seem to bother Johansen very much; apparently he did not believe that a model entirely based on Walrasian general equilibrium theory could explain the resource allocation pattern in a real world economy. Thus Johansen's vision of the "true and complete" model was something much more elaborate than the MSG model. In orther words the MSG model was taken as a crude approximation of a complex but largely unknown "true model".

This general attitude was most visible in the treatment of the remuneration of labor and capital in the MSG model. Thus, in spite of the fact that only one type of labor was identified in the model, wage rates differed across sectors in accordance with an exogenously given wage structure. Moreover, although aggregate capital was assumed to be homogeneous and fully mobile, the rate of return on capital was not equalized across sectors in the MSG model.

In other words the wage rate paid in sector j, W_j was determined by

$$W_j = w_j W \qquad j = 1, 2, \ldots, 20$$

where W is an index of the overall real wage level in the economy and w_j is a sector-specific constant.[8] In the same spirit the "user cost of capital" in sector j, Q_j, was determined by

$$Q_j = P_{kj} (d_j + r_j R) \qquad j = 1, 2, \ldots, 20$$

where R is an index of the overall rate of return on capital in the economy, r_j is a sector-specific constant, d_j is the rate of depreciation in sector j and P_{kj} is the price of the aggregate of capital goods used in sector j.

The underlying assumption behind this formulation was that the observed intersectoral wage and profit differentials reflected persistent phenomena such as intersectoral differences with respect to composition of the labor force, working conditions, uncertainty of future prospects and degree of monopolization, i.e. factors that could not easily be incorporated in the MSG model.

With this background one can say that Johansen's approach was to depict a complex economic system by means of a simple model in which *ad hoc* constraints were added in order to account for important aspects of the real world. Similar approaches have been adopted by several other CGE modelers, while others to a larger extent have emphasized consistency between the model and general equilibrium (and international trade) theory. In fact, "consistency with standard general equilibrium theory" seems to be a dimension along which CGE models could reasonably be classified.

Turning next to the demand side of the MSG model, I have already pointed out that the commodity demands for public consumption, net investment and net export purposes[9] were exogenously determined. Thus, household consumption was the only truly endogenous final demand component in the MSG model. Later CGE models are very different from this point of view. In particular the foreign trade is endogenously determined in most CGE models, although most of them also differ from the MSG model with respect to the level of aggregation of the household sector. Thus, in the MSG model there is only one type of household,[10] whereas several types of households are identified in many CGE models of more recent vintage. However, one common feature of the MSG model and all other CGE models is that the household demand functions are derived on the assumption of utility maximization under a budget constraint on the part of the representative household.[11]

Two more comments about the MSG model should be made. The first is that the specification of the MSG model was entirely non-stochastic; the structural relations implied by the model were simply assumed to be correct. Thus, most parameters of the model were estimated on the basis of one single observation of the allocation of resources across the sectors covered by the model. Of course this is not very satisfactory, but lack of suitable data effectively ruled out a full stochastic specification and utilization of econometric techniques for parameter estimation. Johansen's approach to parameter estimation has later been reinvented and christened the "reference equilibrium method". However, as will be clear later, stochastically specified CGE models have also been developed. Thus, the method used for parameter estimation can also be used as a criterion for classification of CGE models.

The final comment on the MSG model is related to the procedure for obtaining numerical solutions. The method adopted by Johansen essentially amounts to specifying log-linear approximations to the general equilibrium solution and then solving the resulting linear equations for changes in the endogenous variables as functions of changes in the exogenous variables. This means that the solution describes the relative rates of change of endogenous variables from an initial, and known, allocation of resources.

From a technical point of view Johansen's method has advantages as well as disadvantages. One advantage of the method is that it is simple and relatively cheap to apply. This is of course important in the case of large-scale models. A disadvantage is that the results are affected by approximation errors, and these errors tend to increase with the magnitude of changes in exogenous variables. Considerable efforts have been spent on the development of more efficient and precise methods for finding solutions to CGE models. That work involves elaborations of Johansen's method as well as the development of algorithms capable of directly solving the model in its nonlinear form. I will briefly comment on that work later, and close this subsection by noting that existing CGE models can also be classified on the basis of the method used for obtaining numerical solutions.

3.1.2 *Extensions of Johansen's approach*

Although Johansen's MSG model can be regarded as the first CGE model, not all CGE modelers have taken the MSG model as their point of departure. In particular, the Harberger–Scarf–Shoven–Whalley approach to CGE modeling (discussed later) seems to have been initiated and developed quite independently of, although somewhat later than, Johansen's work in this field. However, there is a significant branch of CGE modeling within which the individual models should be regarded as extensions and elaborations of the MSG models.[12] In the following I will briefly comment on the line of development represented by these models.

Later versions of the multisectoral growth model   The obvious point of departure then is the further development of the MSG model itself. This work, which is summarized by Longva, Lorentsen and Olsen (1985), includes an increase in the number of sectors, more extensive application of econometric methods for parameter estimation, less restrictive assumptions about the technological constraints as well as sector models partly based on engineering data. However, to a large extent the exogenous treatment of foreign trade is retained also in later versions of the MSG model.

In spite of the extensive development of the MSG model one can say that a rather conservative strategy has been adopted in this work. In fact it seems reasonable to conclude that the impact of the MSG model on the development of CGE modeling almost entirely stems from Johansen's original formulation.

However, the continuing use of the MSG model within the Norwegian economic planning system[13] has become an often cited example of the potential usefulness of this kind of modeling approach. It may also be the case that conservative strategy in terms of model development has been a consequence of, and perhaps a necessary condition for, the many administrative uses of the MSG model.

The ORANI model   The close relation to practical economic planning and policy evaluation is a feature that the "MSG project" shares with the Australian so-called IMPACT project. This project is located at the University of Melbourne but is sponored by a number of Australian government agencies, in particular the Industries Assistance Commission. Within the IMPACT project an MSG-type model called ORANI has been developed. Of all the widely known models in the CGE catagory, ORANI is the one that most resembles the MSG model. This is true with respect to both the general specification of the model and, as mentioned above, its heavy orientation towards practical application. The chapters by Powell and Lawson and Vincent in this volume provide interesting perspectives on the development and utilization of the ORANI model.

Like the MSG model the ORANI model is essentially a model of the sectoral allocation of capital and labor as well as of the distribution of sectoral outputs between different uses. Moreover, like the MSG model ORANI does not treat the distribution of disposable income across different types of households. Another feature worth mentioning is that ORANI is numerically solved by means of an elaborated version of Johansen's original linearization technique. A comprehensive description of ORANI is given by Dixon et al. (1982). In the following I will only point out the essential differences between the MSG model and ORANI, thus indicating how and to what extent the ORANI model has contributed to the development of CGE modeling.

First, ORANI represents a significant increase in size; compared with all other CGE models ORANI is really a large-scale model. Thus in standard applications it explicitly treats 113 producing sectors, 115 domestically produced commodity categories and an equal number of imported commodity categories, nine types of labor, seven types of agricultural land and 113 types of (industry-specific) capital. In so-called special purpose versions, designed to elucidate specific policy problems, there is a quite significant amount of additional detail. Thus, in ORANI-MILK, designed for analysis of assistance arrangements for the Australian dairy industry, a large number of dairy products originating in different regions of the Australian economy as well as a detailed representation of the initially existing system of taxes and subsidies were incorporated. In other words ORANI, and in particular the special purpose versions of ORANI, are designed for a numerical second-best comparative statics on a very disaggregated level.

Another and perhaps more basic difference between the MSG model and the ORANI model is that the latter treats the economy as a truly open economy. This is certainly an extension of Johansen's approach. However, although the Heckscher–Ohlin model of international trade theory might seem to be the natural point of departure for the design of a CGE model of a "small open economy", the treatment of foreign trade in ORANI, as well as in most other open-economy CGE models,[14] rests on the so-called "Armington assumption".[15] Thus the small economy is assumed to have some market power rather than being a price-taker on international markets for tradeables.

The essential reason for this is no doubt the well-known specialization properties of models with parametric prices on tradeables, constant returns to scale production functions and more tradeable goods than primary factors. In view of empirical observations of the real world, model builders, and even more users of the results, are not prepared to accept the extreme specialization implied by the standard theoretical model.

Both the MSG model, particularly the later versions, and the ORANI model represent very significant efforts to design practically useful tools with a solid base in economic theory. For an outsider it is of course difficult to judge the degree of success in these ventures. However, the fact that both projects continue to exist and seemingly expand does suggest a reasonable degree of success.

A striking feature of several comments made by users of the models is that the model to a large extent is used as a pedagogical device; the numerical results from model simulations have forced the analysts to revise some of their hypotheses and, in view of the general equilibrium effects revealed by the model, broaden their perspective. Moreover, there does not seem to be any case in which the conclusions of an analysis carried out entirely within a government agency are based on model results; for good or bad the model is used as a complement to rather than as a substitute for other methods of analysis.

3.1.3 Computable general equilibrium models of developing countries

Another branch of CGE modeling originating from Johansen's MSG model is focused on developing countries. The work along these lines was initiated in the early 1970s and was for a long time almost entirely carried out at, or at least for, the World Bank. The first major study was presented in the book by Irma Adelman and Sherman Robinson *Income Distribution Policy in Developing Countries: A Case Study of Korea* (Adelman and Robinson 1978). As the title suggests, income distribution issues were of major concern in this study. The emphasis on this aspect of economic development remains a typical feature of most models in this branch of CGE modeling, although a number of studies have dealt with trade policy and other aspects of economic policy in a developing country.

Like the studies based on the ORANI model the Adelman–

Robinson study was very detailed. Thus their model contained 29 producing sectors and in each sector there were four firm size categories. Moreover there were six labor skill categories and 15 household types. In addition a large number of policy instruments were included. The basic modeling strategy was to incorporate essentially all mechanisms through which the distribution of income would be affected within a time horizon of ten years under the prevailing institutional framework. Thus the model incorporated inflation and rationing as well as rigidities in the functioning of product and factor markets. In terms of theoretical basis and derivation of the structural relations one can say that the Adelman–Robinson model had both Walrasian and "structuralist" features. Thus, like the MSG model the Adelman–Robinson model was far from a fully fledged Walrasian general equilibrium model.

However, it is worth pointing out that while both the MSG model and the ORANI model were linearized and solved for the relative rates of change of the endogenous variables at a certain point in time, the Adelman–Robinson model was solved directly in terms of the levels of the endogenous variables. Apart from the possible computational advantages, this made it possible to incorporate an explicit time dimension in the model. Thus the model was specified as a static within-period model linked to a dynamic intertemporal-adjustment model. The underlying feature of reality which could then be captured was that the adjustment possibilities of firms and households were considered to be a lot more limited within periods than between periods.

Development economics has become the field of economic research in which the CGE models have been used most extensively. Thus, a recent bibliography of CGE models applied to developing countries contained around 200 titles (Devarajan, Lewis and Robinson, 1986). However, apart from the already mentioned emphasis on income distribution issues, this branch of CGE modeling has developed along quite different lines from those suggested by the Adelman–Robinson study.

Accordingly, one overall tendency is that more recent models tend to be quite a lot smaller and less detailed than the Adelman–Robinson model. Moreover, recent CGE models in this category are often aimed at elucidating the impact of one specific type of policy measure (such as trade policy) on the allocation of resources and distribution of income, rather than explaining the determination and evolution of these phenomena as a function of the simultaneous operation of a large number of factors. It also seems to be true that later CGE models of developing countries exhibit a considerably higher degree of consistency with neoclassical economic theory than the Adelman–Robinson model does.

The widespread use of CGE models for analysis of economic development problems suggests that CGE modeling has become an established methodological approach. Moreover, the widespread use of CGE models in developing countries has stimulated, or even forced, improvements in national accounting techniques as well as integration of the national income accounts, the input–output accounts and the national product accounts into a consistent social accounting matrix (SAM) framework. The typical modeling strategy in many of the studies in this category is to compile a SAM, carry out simple multiplier analysis and, finally, construct a CGE model aimed at identifying and measuring possible changes in the entries of the SAM when conditions exogenous to the economy change.

Again it is difficult for an outsider to judge the practical importance of the development studies based on CGE models. However, compared with the MSG and ORANI projects, CGE modeling of economic development typically seems to have a slightly stronger academic flavor. Also, CGE modeling has apparently made a contribution to development economics by explicitly bringing in a quantitative general equilibrium perspective on development problems and by providing a framework for empirical testing of certain propositions in development economics.

3.2 The Harberger–Scarf–Shoven–Whalley approach

This approach to CGE modeling began with three distinct scientific contributions. The first is Arnold Harberger's studies in the early 1960s on the incidence of taxation within the frame of a numerical two-sector model (Harberger, 1962). The second is Herbert Scarf's computer algorithm for numerical determination of the equilibrium of a Walrasian system (Scarf, 1967). The third is the work of John Shoven and John Whalley on the proof of existence of, and computational procedure for finding, a general equilibrium with taxes (Shoven and Whalley, 1973).

The models in the Harberger–Scarf–Shoven–Whalley tradition differ from the MSG and ORANI models in basically three respects. First there is a difference in terms of the level of aggregation of the household sector. Thus a typical model in the Harberger–Scarf–Shoven–Whalley tradition explicitly incorporates two or more types of households and for that reason a specification of the initial endowments and the determination of the budget constraint of each type of household. But in ORANI and the MSG model there is only one type of houeshold and the budget constraint of the single household sector is implicitly determined by Walras's law. In particular this means that the tax and transfer system is not explicitly treated in these models.

The second basic difference is related to the type of applications the models are intended for. Thus, the MSG and ORANI models essentially are aimed at elucidating the impact of changes in exogenous conditions on the allocation of resources in the economy, while income distribution aspects are neglected or treated in a superficial way. Moreover, model results are frequently presented in a multi-dimensional fashion, emphasizing variables such as gross domestic product (GDP), the sectoral allocation of output and employment etc.

The Harberger–Scarf–Shoven–Whalley models, however, are to a large extent aimed at evaluating policy changes in terms of both efficiency and income distribution effects. Moreover, these effects are usually expressed in terms of one-dimensional welfare measures such as Hicksian compensating or equivalent variations. Although the practical importance of this difference may seem insignificant, it clearly indicates that the Harberger–Scarf–Shoven–Whalley models have their roots in applied welfare economics, while the models dealt with in the previous section to a large extent originate from the literature on economic planning and input–output analysis.

The third basic difference is related to the way in which Walrasian general equilibrium theory is incorporated in the models. As I mentioned above Johansen seemingly regarded the MSG model as an approximation to a significantly more complex, but largely unknown, "true" model. This led to the incorporation of features of the real world which in a strict sense were inconsistent with Walrasian general equilibrium theory. For instance, in the MSG model aggregate capital was homogeneous and fully mobile, but differently remunerated across sectors.

The Harberger–Scarf–Shoven–Whalley models, however, to a very large extent can be regarded as numerical counterparts of Walrasian general equilibrium models. However this does not necessarily reflect a basically different view on the functioning of real world economies. Instead it reflects the view that CGE modeling is an extension of thoeretical general equilibrium analysis; the numerical model is a tool for adding quantitative estimates to the insights already gained from qualitative models. Consequently, according to this view, the numerical model has to be entirely consistent with an explicit theoretical model; incorporating *ad hoc* assumptions may make model results more "realistic" but also difficult or impossible to interpret.

Without going into details it is still useful to consider briefly a highly stylized version of a CGE model in the Harberger–Scarf–

Shoven–Whalley tradition. The exposition is directly based on Shoven and Whalley (1984). It is a static general equilibrium model of a two-good two-factor two-consumer closed economy. The factors of production are "capital" and "labor", and there is a "rich" household which owns all capital, and a "poor" household which owns all the labor. The technological constraints are represented by constant returns to scale constant elasticity of substitution (CES) production functions. Thus, labor input L_i and capital input K_i in sector i yield output Q, in accordance with

$$Q_i = A_i(d_i L_i^{r_i} + (1 - d_i)K_i^{r_i})^{1/r_i} \qquad i = 1, 2$$

With factor prices P_L and P_K, and assuming profit maximization behavior on the part of the producers, these production functions yield a set of factor demand equations

$$L_i = L_i\,(P_L, P_K, Q_i) \qquad i = 1, 2$$
$$K_i = K_i\,(P_L, P_K, Q_i) \qquad i = 1, 2$$

with standard properties. It should be noted that factor prices are taken to be equal across sectors in accordance with the discussion above.

It should also be noted that, as a consequence of the CES specification of the production functions, the factor demand functions above have only three parameters: the scale factor A_i, the substitution parameter r_i and the distribution parameter d_i. With extraneous information on the value of one of these parameters, one single observation on equilibrium prices and quantities is sufficient to identify the remaining two parameters. Thus, compared with the Cobb–Douglas specification of technology of the MSG model, the CES specification used in most Harberger–Scarf–Shoven–Whalley CGE models offers one degree of freedom to utilize econometric estimates of crucial elasticity parameters. However, it is still a typical feature of these models that very restrictive assumptions about factor substitution possibilities are imposed a priori. Clearly this is a feature that limits the empirical applicability of this kind of CGE model.

The household demand functions of the model are derived from CES utility functions and standard assumptions about utility maximization subject to a budget constraint. The budget constraints of the two types of households are defined by the initial factor endowments and the endogenous factor prices so that the household demands can be written as functions of the good prices P_1 and P_2 and factor prices P_L and P_K. With this background, and assuming that the inelastic supplies of capital and labor are K^* and L^* respectively , the entire model can be summarized in six equations:

two factor market equilibrium conditions, two product market equilibrium conditions and two zero-profit conditions:

$$K_1(P_L, P_K, Q_1) + K_2(P_L, P_K, Q_2) = K^*$$

$$L_1(P_L, P_K, Q_1) + L_2(P_L, P_K, Q_2) = L^*$$

$$X_1(P_1, P_2, P_L, P_K) + X_1(P_1, P_2, P_L, P_K) = Q_1$$

$$X_2(P_1, P_2, P_L, P_K) + X_2(P_1, P_2, P_L, P_K) = Q_2$$

$$P_K K_1(P_L, P_K, Q_1) + P_L L_1(P_L, P_K, Q_1) = P_1 Q_1$$

$$P_K K_2(P_L, P_K, Q_2) + P_L L_2(P_L, P_K, Q_2) = P_2 Q_2$$

As all supply and demand relations are homogeneous of degree zero in prices, only relative prices can be determined. In order to normalize the level of prices in the model, the condition that the sum of product and factor prices should add up to unity is generally imposed. Since one of the market equilibrium conditions is redundant by Walras's law this means that the model has an equal number of endogenous variables and independent equations, and equilibrium relative prices and output levels can be determined. Once that is done, factor demand by sector and product demand by household type can also be determined.

In contrast with the MSG model, Harberger–Scarf–Shoven–Whalley models are solved directly in the levels of the endogenous variables. Initially numerical solutions were determined by means of Scarf's algorithm (Scarf, 1967; Scarf and Hansen, 1973), but later faster variants of Scarf's algorithm, especially due to Merrill (1972), or Newton-type local linearization techniques have become more commonly used. However, in order to make the model useful for policy simulation it is not sufficient to determine the first-best general equilibrium corresponding to a given set of endowments, preferences and technological constraints. It is also necessary to determine the second-best general equilibrium, if such an equilibrium exists, resulting from the imposition of distortions such as taxes.

Making use of Scarf's algorithm, Shoven and Whalley were able to prove the existence of a general equilibrium with taxes and to design a computational procedure for finding such an equilibrium (Shoven and Whalley, 1972). Initially the applicability of their method was limited in the sense that the analysis had to be confined to one tax at a time. But in Shoven and Whalley (1973) a refined method capable of dealing simultaneously with several taxes was developed.

The Shoven–Whalley method has been applied in a number of studies of the efficiency and income distribution effects of taxation. An example of a large-scale application is that of Piggott and Whalley

(1977) in which the tax and subsidy system of the UK was analyzed by means of a 33 product and 100 households CGE model. Due to the disaggregated representation of the household sector, with households classified by income, occupation and family size, the model enabled the authors to elucidate the income distribution consequences of a series of hypothetical tax changes.

A survey of this field of CGE modeling can be found in Shoven and Whalley (1984), while Fullerton, Henderson and Shoven (1984) and Mieszkowski (1984) provide quite positive evaluations of what has been accomplished. Contrary to the MSG and ORANI projects, the work along the lines discussed in this section has led to the development of several different models, more or less focused on a distinct set of policy issues. The models have to a large extent been applied in empirical studies aimed at evaluating actual or proposed changes in national tax or international trade policies.

Before leaving the Harberger–Scarf–Shoven–Whalley approach and turning to the econometric approaches to CGE modeling, a few words should be said about the way in which the parameters of the structural equations of these models are usually estimated. As I mentioned above, the extensive use of CES production and utility functions means that it is possible to identify all parameters of the model on the basis of a set of extraneous elasticity estimates and one single observation of a general equilibrium in the economy. Thus by constructing a "reference equilibrium" and relying on literature surveys it is in principle possible to develop a CGE model without doing any original econometric work.

Since the so-called "reference equilibrium" or "calibration" method is extensively used in CGE modeling, there is clearly an issue about the empirical relevance of CGE models. I will come back to this issue in the ensuing section. Here I will briefly comment on a significant difference between Johansen's application of the "calibration" method and the way that method has been applied by CGE modelers in the Harberger–Scarf–Shoven–Whalley tradition. The difference has to do with the construction of the "reference equilibrium".

Johansen, on the one hand, to a large extent relied on available input–output, factor income, employment and capital stock statistics when he constructed the base year statistical representation of the commodity and factor service flows covered by the MSG model. Thus, rather than adjusting the data he adjusted the specification of the model. As a consequence the observed intersectoral wage and profit differentials were taken as persistent features of the economy and incorporated as exogenous constraints on the factor price formation in the model.

CGE modelers in the Harberger–Scarf–Shoven–Whalley tradition, on the other hand, tend to adjust the data rather than the model (see Whalley and Mansur, 1984). Thus the units of capital and labor inputs are chosen in such a way that the remuneration rates to these factors are equalized across the sectors. Among other things this means that the results obtained in model simulations cannot readily be interpreted in terms of the aggregates identified in standard national accounting.

3.3 Econometric approaches to computer general equilibrium modeling

As I mentioned in the previous section the common practice with respect to parameter estimation in CGE models is to use simple calibration procedure method. In order to discuss the "econometric" approach to CGE modeling it is useful to be somewhat more precise about the specific assumptions implied by the "calibration method", as well as about the method's limitations. To do this we consider the following general specification of a CGE model, where $(Y_1, \ldots, Y_n)$ is a vector of endogenous variables, X is a vector of exogenous variables, B is a vector of m unknown parameters and e is a vector of stochastic disturbances:

$$F_i(Y_1, \ldots, y_n; X, B, e) = 0 \qquad i = 1, 2, \ldots, n$$

The "calibration method" amounts to setting all components of e identically equal to zero and solving for the vector B on the basis of a single realization of $Y_1, \ldots, Y_n$ and X. However, to the extent that B has more than n components, extraneous information is needed in order to determine $m - n$ of the unknown parameters. This is, the "calibration method" implies the extremely strong assumption that the observed values of the endogenous variables are determined only by the factors explicitly included in the model.

Needless to say this method has several serious limitations. One is that in order to keep the number of parameters to be estimated sufficiently low, the representation of preferences and technology to a large extent has to be based on CES or Cobb–Douglas functions, i.e. functional forms with a small number of parameters. But this also implies that very restrictive assumptions about the underlying preferences and technological constraints have to be accepted. Thus, even though the CGE model approach has the potential of providing numerical estimates of various comparative statics effects, the actual measurements may be too constrained by such a priori restrictions to be of any significant value. Another serious limitation resulting from the "calibration method" for parameter estimation is that no measure of the accuracy of the model and its predictions is obtained.

The obvious way to overcome these limitations, and thus increase the empirical relevance and usefulness of CGE models, is to use a stochastic specification model and to estimate the parameters of the model by means of econometric methods. However, there are significant difficulties associated with such an approach. In particular the dimensionality of any reasonably disaggregated model causes serious degrees-of-freedom problems, especially if restrictive assumptions about the structure of preferences and technonlogies are to be avioded. In addition the simultaneous estimation of a general equilibrium model requires quite sophisticated econometric techniques (see for instance Lau, 1984, and Whalley and Mansur, 1984).

The difficulties associated with full stochastic specification of a CGE model call for a somewhat less ambitious approach. One alternative, then, is to implement stochastically specified submodels of production and/or consumption and to use these models as building blocks in a general equilibrium model. That approach has for instance been adopted in the development of later versions of the MSG model. However, the first example of this type of econometric approach to CGE modeling is due to Hudson and Jorgenson (1975) and the subsequent work along these lines to large extent is due to Dale W. Jorgenson.[16]

The Hudson–Jorgenson model was basically aimed at highlighting the long-run economic impact of a set of energy policy strategies for the USA. The core of the model was a nine-sector (five energy and four nonenergy sectors) two-stage production model. In the first stage of the so-called KLEM model sectoral output was taken as a function of the inputs of capital and labor services, an aggregate of the five energy inputs and an aggregate of the four nonenergy inputs. At the second stage the compositions of the two aggregates in terms of the individual energy and nonenergy inputs respectively were determined within two separate submodels.

At each stage of the production model the substitutability of the different factors of production was represented by econometrically estimated constant returns to scale price possibility frontiers. As these were specified as so-called translog price possibility frontiers, no a priori constraints on the pattern of partial elasticities of substitution were imposed. Thus, unlike CGE models where the technological constraints are represented by CES or Cobb–Douglas production functions, neither complementarity between two types of inputs nor different partial elasticities of substitution between different pairs of inputs were ruled out by the specifications of the model.

The main function of the production model was to generate sectoral output prices as well as a complete set of input–output coefficients. However, in order to solve the production model for equilibrium output prices, the prices of capital and labor services, as well as the prices of imported inputs, had to be determined. The latter set of prices were simply taken to be exogenously determined, while the prices of capital and labor services were determined within a Klein–Goldberger type of macroeconometric model with explicit factor market equilibrium conditions. By the so-called nonsubstitution theorem the sectoral output prices, and therefore the input–output coefficients, thus determined by the production model were independent of the sectoral output levels as long as the capital and labor services prices were kept constant. As a result sectoral output levels were linear functions of the final demand levels in the usual input–output fashion. However, while there is only one set of input–output coefficients in a standard Leontief model, there was one set of input–output coefficients for each set of capital, labor and import prices in the Hudson–Jorgenson model.

In order to build a complete model the nine-sector production model was linked to the macroeconometric model. Thus the aggregate consumption and investment expenditures determined within the macroeconometric model were taken as constraints on the solution of the nine-sector production model. Technically this was done by means of a fairly simple household demand model and a set of assumptions about the sectoral composition of investment and government demand. In this way the allocation of resources as well as the determination of product and factor prices could be modeled. Moreover the model could be used for year-by-year projections of the development of the US economy on the nine-sector level under alternative assumptions about the national energy policies.

However, the Hudson–Jorgenson model was not a complete general equilibrium model. For instance, there was no endogenous mechanism ensuring that the aggregated demand for capital services by the nine production sectors at the given prices did not exceed the supply of capital services determined within the macoeconometric model, and the same applies to the demand for labour services. Moreover, imports were used as inputs in sectoral production processes but not in the aggregated production function. This means that, for instance, an increase in international oil prices affected capital and labor service prices only indirectly through the rate of saving and capital accumulation. It should also be emphasized that the level of net exports was essentially exogenously determined in the Hudson–Jorgenson model.

Subsequent work in this field by Jorgenson and his associates does not seem to have led to any major revision of the basic structure of the original Hudson–Jorgenson model. However, both the production and the household consumption submodels have been significantly elaborated. Thus, the production submodel has been disaggregated to the 35-sector level as well as elaborated to incorporate price-endogenous technical change (see for instance Jorgenson, 1984a, b). As is demonstrated by Jorgenson (1982) the production model has also been elaborated to incorporate detailed engineering data describing the technological constraints of the energy sector.

Later developments of the household consumption model include replacement of the simple Cobb–Douglas utility function by a translog indirect utility function to represent the preferences of the aggregated household sector. The parameters of the aggregate consumer model are estimated on the basis of time-series and cross-section data, where the latter set of data include socioeconomic attributes of different types of households. Moreover, the number of commodity groups identified in the model has been increased significantly.

The novel feature of this work is that the model of aggregate comsumer behavior is based on the theory of exact aggregation development by Jorgenson, Lau and Stoker (see Jorgenson, 1984a, b; Jorgenson and Slesnick, 1985; and the references given in those volumes). Using this approach it is possible to recover systems of individual demand functions uniquely from systems of aggregate demand functions. By requiring that individual demand functions are integrable, individual indirect utility and expenditure functions, as well as individual welfare measures based on these functions, can be defined. Needless to say this significantly increases the possibilities of carrying out empirical analysis of the efficiency and income distribution consequences of different policy measures.

Another example of the econometric approach to CGE modeling is provided by Jorgenson and Yun (1986). This is a highly aggregated intertemporal general equilibrium model, aimed at elucidating and measuring welfare losses due to tax-induced inefficiencies in the allocation of capital in the US economy. As I mentioned in the introduction, most CGE models are static or, in some cases, designed as a series of partially linked static models. Consequently the work of Jorgenson and Yun represents an important extension of CGE modeling. It is also interesting to note that Johansen's original aim was to shed light on the process of economic growth, and how different economic policies could affect that process, rather than on the atemporal allocation of resources. However, the multisectoral perspective was emphasized in the MSG model as well as in the mainstrean of CGE modeling, and from this point of view the Jorgenson–Yun model is somewhat limited.

To sum up it seems that the econometric approach to CGE modeling has the potential of significantly increasing the empirical relevance of CGE models, both by allowing for less restrictive parameterizations of production (or cost) and preference functions and by more efficient utilization of available data in connection with parameter estimation. Needless to say work along these lines is very promising in terms of making general equilibrium theory an operational tool in practically oriented economic analysis. However, it still remains to integrate econometrically estimated production and consumption models within a consistent general equilibrium framework, and to evaluate how well a model based on the notions of Walrasian general equilibrium theory can explain relative price determination and resource allocation patterns in a real world market economy.

3.4 Activity analysis approaches to computable general equilibrium modeling

A quite different approach to CGE modeling is represented by the so-called "activity analysis general equilibrium" (AGE) models developed by Victor Ginsburgh and Jean Waelbroeck as well as by Alan S. Manne. Peter B. Dixon has also contributed to the development in the field of AGE modeling. It is a matter of definition whether AGE models should be regarded as a variant of CGE models or as an alternative to CGE models. In any case the development in this particular field of economic modeling should not be left out of this survey.

The origin of the AGE modeling tradition is the linear programming type of planning model that, in various versions, was extensively used in the 1960s and 1970s, and much of the work on AGE models seems to have been initiated by the critique of these linear programming models.[17] The thrust of this critique, and the response to it, can be summarized by using a stylized version of a standard planning model. Thus, consider the following model of a one-consumer economy where the vectors x, y and w represent comsumption, production and initial endowment respectively. The comsumption vector x belongs to the convex consumption set X, while the production vector y belongs to the convex set Y. Preferences are represented by the concave utility function $U(x)$.

Using this planning model is equivalent to looking for an allocation of resources which solves the problem

$$\max U(x)$$

$$\text{subject to } x - y - w \leq 0 \quad \text{and} \quad x \in X, y \in Y$$

On the basis of a theorem by Karlin (1959), the solution to this problem, x^* and y^*, and the dual prices p^* associated with the inequality constraint, are consistent with a competitive equilibrium.

For various reasons this property of the planning model contributed significantly to its popularity and widespread use. However, in practical applications with the planning model the availability and cost efficiency of linear programming (as opposed to nonlinear and integer programming) algorithms led to a linear specification of the utility function.

As is well known, however, only n of the $2n$ consumption and production variables will attain nonzero values in an optimal solution to an n-commodity linear programming planning model. This will also hold if n export, n import and n investment activities are included in the model. Thus an open-economy intertemporal version of the planning model would produce solutions implying extreme specialization in production and intertemporal consumption patterns. Superficially this somewhat disturbing result is due to the linear specification of the model. The real problem, however, is that economic theory offers too few constraints on the resource allocation problem in question. In view of this, and the desire to obtain "realistic" solutions, modelers invented additional restrictions.

This may have made model solutions more attractive from the user's point of view, but at the same time the possibility of interpreting the results in terms of a competitive equilibrium was destroyed. Not surprisingly these practices met with quite strong criticism; in fact it can be argued that the increasingly bad reputation of linear programming models paved the way for the modeling approaches discussed earlier in this chapter. However, the development of AGE models has, at least to some extent, restored linear programming as a tool for economy-wide modeling.

The main contributions are due to Victor Ginsburgh and Jean Waelbroeck (1981, 1984). The basic idea in their work is to generate additional restrictions to the linear program on the basis of economic theory rather than on the basis of *ad hoc* assumptions. Thus in an AGE model specified along the lines suggested by Ginsburgh and Waelbroeck the assumption about constant marginal utility of comsumption, implied by the linear utility function, is abolished. Instead a conventional, but piecewise linearized, concave utility function is incorporated. This leads to a set of economically meaningful additional linear constraints in the model.

The most significant general contribution resulting from this work is that a consistent procedure for implementing general equilibrium models based on engineering or other types of microdata has been demonstrated. Moreover, it has been shown that numerically implemented general equilibrium models can be solved by means of a linear programming algorithm, i.e. a very accessible type of computer code. Nevertheless it seems that AGE modeling is a side track, and that future developments of numerical economic models are more likely to build on the approaches discussed in the preceding sections.

4 Recent Developments in Computable General Equilibrium Modeling

In view of the developments in recent years, CGE modeling is a rapidly growing field in economics. It is beyond the scope of this survey to give a comprehensive description of the work by the "second generation" CGE modelers. Instead I will just indicate a few contributions and lines of development that seem especially interesting. In particular I will indicate how the contributions presented in this volume fit into the general trends of development in CGE modeling. Before that, however, it is necessary to say a few words about the recent development of computer software suitable for handling CGE models.

As I have indicated above, Johansen's original MSG model was solved by means of a simple linearization technique. At the time that seemed to be the only real possibility. Moreover for Johansen the development of a suitable method for finding numerical solutions to the model was an integrated part of the modeling work. Today the situation is quite different. The development of computer codes for handling CGE models has become a speciality of its own. Thus today a CGE modeler, without much knowledge in programming, can easily employ user-friendly codes such as GAMS (Brooke, Kendrick and Meeraus, 1988), HERCULES (Drud and Kendrick, 1986), SCLP (Mathiesen, 1985) or MPS/GE (Rutherford, 1986). In view of this development, CGE modeling has become a highly accessible tool for economic analysis.

Another feature of the recent developments in CGE modeling is that a broader spectrum of theoretical concepts has been incorporated in the models. One often cited example is Harris (1984) in which economies of scale as well as imperfect competition were incorporated in a CGE model of the Canadian economy. Another example is the model by Auerbach, Kotlikoff and Skinner (1983) in which the notion of overlapping generations was incorporated. Work along these lines has induced theoretical work such as the work by Kehoe and Levine discussed in chapter 4. A step towards integration of asset markets and uncertainty in a CGE framework was taken by Agell (chapter 2) while a related approach is presented by Weril (chapter 5).

However, the most striking feature of the development in CGE modeling is that models of this kind are used for analysis and evaluation of a wide range of specific policy proposals. This volume provides several examples of this development. Thus Jorgenson and Yun use a dynamic CGE model for an evaluation of the impact of the 1986 Tax Reform Act on US economic growth (chapter 3). Burniaux and Waelbroeck in chapter 6 analyze the impact of the Common Agricultural Policy of the European Community on the world economy using a multiregion CGE model. In chapter 7 by Dewatripont, Grais and Michel the incentive structure implied by a foreign trade regime for Yugoslavia, in which import rationing and foreign exchange retention are combined, is analyzed by means of a CGE model. In chapter 10 Bergman and Lundgren evaluate two specific energy policy proposals by means of CGE models of the Swedish economy.

A particular kind of application is to use the CGE modeling approach in analyses of socialist economies. This topic is dealt with in chapter 12 by Kis, Robinson and Tyson. Additional perspectives on economic modeling in Hungary are given in chapter 13 by Ámon and Ligeti. An alternative approach to modeling a planned economy is described in chapter 11 by Charemza and Dlouhý. Needless to say CGE modeling is not a universal tool for empirical economic analysis, but this survey and the chapters in this volume suggest that the method has become widely used.

Notes

I am grateful to Erik Offerdal for the comments on an earlier version of this chapter, and to the Energy Research and Development Council for financial support.
1   However, rigidities in the adjustment of relative prices are assumed in many applications.
2   In some cases CGE models are designed for comparative dynamics analysis. See for instance Dervis, de Melo and Robinson (1982) and Jorgenson and Yun (1986).
3   The only exception to this rule is the so-called ORANI model which I will discuss at some length in the next section.
4   As I discuss in some detail in section 3, however, there is a lot of difference across CGE models from this point of view; some models are close to numerical counterparts to textbook general equilibrium models, while others to a large extent incorporate other types of assumptions.
5   With two exceptions, agriculture and fishing, constant returns to scale were assumed in all sectors.
6   The first comment on this general problem can be found already on page 1 in Johansen's book. It reads: "The model presented in this study is in many respects unsatisfactory when judged from a purely theoretical point

of view. It is, however, constructed with an eye to the possibility of being implemented by existing statistics. Without this possibility the model would hardly be very interesting." Although the availability of relevant statistical data is better in the 1980s this comment is probably valid for most CGE models.

7 Noting the habit of carrying out quantitative analyses with the purpose of illustrating a certain method or model, Johansen characterized his own study in the following way: "The data and the quantitative analysis do serve the purpose of illustrating the method and the model. But, at the same time, if I were required to make decisions and take actions in connection with relationships covered by this study, I would (in the absence of more reliable results, and without doing more work) rely to a great extent on the data and the results presented in the following chapters. Thus, the quantitative analysis does not solely serve the purpose of illustrating a method. I do believe that the numerical results also give a rough description of some important economic relationships in the Norwegian reality".

8 It should perhaps be pointed out that as the variable W was taken as the numeraire of the price system and set equal to unity and the model was formulated in terms of relative rates of change this equation did not appear explicitly in Johansen's original description of the MSG model.

9 Except for so-called "complementary imports".

10 One obvious consequence of this is that the MSG model was not well suited for analysis of problems in which the distribution of disposable income across different households is an important aspect. A somewhat technical consequence is that there was no need to represent the tax and transfer system explicitly in the model.

11 It should perhaps be mentioned that the constant elasticity type of demand equations that Johansen used in the numerical calculations did not identically satisfy the budget constraint, a fact of which Johansen was fully aware.

12 A survey of the extensions and applications of the MSG model is given by Bergman (1985).

13 An interesting description is given by Schreiner and Larsen (1985).

14 Norman and Haaland (1987) is an important exception.

15 The "Armington assumption" refers to Armington (1969) in which commodities with the same statistical classification but a different country of origin were treated as qualitatively different goods.

16 For a survey of the current status of the work, see Jorgenson (1984a, b).

17 This critique was efficiently formulated by Taylor (1975).

References

Adelman, I., and S. Robinson (1978) *Income Distribution Policy in Developing Countries*, Oxford: Oxford University Press.

Armington, P. (1969) "A Theory of Demand for Products Distinguished by Place of Production", *IMF Staff Papers*, 16, 159–78.

Auerbach, A. J., L. J. Kotlikoff and J. Skinner (1983) "The Efficiency Gains from Dynamic Tax Reform", *International Economic Review*, 24, 81–100.

Bergman, L. (1985) "Extensions and Applications of the MSG-model: A Brief Survey", in F. Forsund (ed). *Production, Multi-Sectoral Growth and Planning*, Amsterdam: North-Holland, pp. 127–61.

Brook, A., D. Kendrick and A. Meeraus (1988) *GAMS. A User's Guide*, Redwood City, CA: Scientific Press.

Christensen, L. R., D. W. Jorgenson and L. J. Lau (1971) "Conjugate Duality and the Transcendental Logarithmic production Function", *Econometrica*, 39 (4), July, 255–6.

——, ——, —— (1973) "Transcendental Logarithmic Production Frontiers", *Review of Economics and Statistics*, 55 (1), February, 28–45.

——, ——, —— (1975) "Transcendental Logarithmic Utility Functions", *American Economic Review*, 65 (3), June, 367–83.

Dervis, K., J. de Melo and S. Robinson (1982) *General Equilibrium Models for Development Policy*, Cambridge: Cambridge University Press.

Devarajan, S., J. D. Lewis and S. Robinson (1986) "A Bibliography of Computable General Equilibrium (CGE) Models Applied to Developing Countries", Berkeley, CA: Division of Agriculture and Natural Resources, University of California, Berkeley, Working Paper No. 400.

Dixon, P. B. (1975) *The Theory of Joint Maximization*, Amsterdam: North-Holland.

——, B. R. Parmenter, J. Sutton and D. P. Vincent (1982) *ORANI: A Multisectoral Model of the Australian Economy*, Amsterdam: North-Holland.

Drud, A., and D. Kendrick (1986) "HERCULES. A System for Large Economywide Models", unpublished paper.

Feltenstein, A. (1984) "Money and Bonds in a Disaggregated Open Economy", in H. E. Scarf and J. B. Shoven (eds), *Applied General Equilibrium Analysis*, Cambridge: Cambridge University Press, pp. 209–42.

Forsund, F. R., M. Hoel and S. Longva (eds) (1985) *Production, Multisectoral Growth and Planning*, Amsterdam: North-Holland.

Fullerton, D., Y. K. Henderson and J. B. Shoven (1984) "A Comparison of Methodologies in Empirical General Equilibrium Methods of Taxation", in H.E. Scarf and J.B.Shoven (eds), *Applied General Equilibrium Analsyis*, Cambridge: Cambridge University Press, pp. 367–410.

Ginsburgh, V. A., and J. L. Wealbroeck (1981) *Activity Analysis and General Equilibrium Modeling*, Amsterdam: North-Holland.

——, —— (1984) "Planning Models and General Equilibrium Activity Analysis", in H. E. Scarf and J. B. Shoven (eds), *Applied General Equilibrium Analysis*, Cambridge: Cambridge University Press, pp. 415–39.

Harberger, A. C. (1962) "The Incidence of the Corporate Income Tax", *Journal of Political Economy*, 70 (3), June, 215–40.

Harris, R. (1984) "Applied General Equilibrium Analysis of Small Open Economies with Scale Economies and Imperfect Competition", *American Economic Review*, 74, December, 1016–31.

Hudson, E. A., and D. W. Jorgenson (1975) "U.S. Energy Policy & Economic Growth 1975–2000", *Bell Journal of Economics and Management Science*, 5 (2) Autumn, 461–514.

Johansen, L. (1960) *A Multi-sectoral Study of Economic Growth*, Amsterdam: North-Holland.

Jorgensen, D. W. (1982) "Econometric and Process Analysis Models for Energy Policy Assessments", in R. Amit and M. Ariel (eds), *Perspectives* on *Resource Policy Modeling: Energy and Minerals*, Cambridge, MA: Ballinger, pp. 9–62.

——, (1984a), "Econometric Methods for Applied General Equilibrium Analysis", in H. E. Scarf and J. B. Shoven (eds), *Applied General Equilibrium Analysis*, Cambridge: Cambridge University Press, pp. 139–203.

——, (1984b) "An Econometric Approach to General Equilibrium Analysis", Chung-Hua Series of Lectures by Invited Eminent Economists No. 7, The Institute of Economics, Academia Sinica, Nankang, Taipei, Taiwan.

——, and J. J. Laffont (1974) "Efficient Estimation of Nonlinear Simultaneous Equations with Additive Disturbances", *Annals of Social and Economic Measurement*, 3 (4), October, 615–40.

——, and D. T. Slesnick (1985) "General Equilibrium Analysis of Economic Policy", in C. Piggott and J. Whalley (eds), *New Developments in Applied General Equilibrium Analysis*, Cambridge: Cambridge University Press, pp. 293–370.

——, and K.-Y. Yun (1986) "The Efficiency of Capital Allocation", *Scandinavian Journal of Economics*, 88 (1), 85–107.

Karlin, S. (1959) *Mathematical Methods and Theory in Games, Programming and Economics*, London: Pergamon.

Lau, L. J. (1984) "Comment", on A. Mansur and J. Whalley, "Numerical Specification of Applied General Equilibrium Models: Estimation, Calibration and Data", in H. E. Scarf and J. B. Shoven, (eds), *Applied General Equilibrium Analysis*, Cambridge: Cambridge University Press, pp. 127–37.

Longva, S., L. Lorentsen and O. Olsen (1985) "The Multi-sectoral Growth Model MSG-4. Formal Structure and Empirical Characteristics", in F. R. Forsund, M. Hoel and S. Longva (eds), *Production, Multi-sectoral Growth and Planning*, Amsterdam: North-Holland, pp. 187–240.

Mathiesen, L. (1985) "Computation of Economic Equilibria by a Sequence of Linear Complementarity Problems", *Mathematical Programming Study*, 23, 144–62.

Merrill, O. H. (1972) "Applications and Extensions of an Algorithm that Computes Fixed Points of Certain Upper Semi-continuous Point to Set Mapping", Ph.D. dissertation, Department of Industrial Engineering, University of Michigan, Ann Arbor, MI.

Mieszkowski, P. (1984) "Comment" on D. Fullerton et al., "A Comparison of Methodologies in Empirical General Equilibrium Models of Taxation", in H. E. Scarf and J. B. Shoven (eds), *Applied General Equilibrium Analysis*, Cambridge: Cambridge University Press, pp.410–14.

Norman, V. D., and J. Haaland (1987) "VEMOD – a Ricardo–Viner–Heckscher–Ohlin–Jones Model of Factor Price Determination", *Scandinavian Journal of Economics*, 89 (3), 251–70.

Piggott, J., and J. Whalley (1977) "General Equilibrium Investigation of U.K. Tax-subsidy Policy: Progress Report", in M. J. Artis and A. R. Nobay (eds), *Studies in Modern Economic Analysis*, Oxford: Blackwell, pp. 259–99.

——, —— (1985) *New Developments in Applied General Equilibrium Analysis*, Cambridge: Cambridge University Press.

Rutherford, T. F. (1986) *MPS/GE User's Manual*, Bergen: Centre for Applied Research.

Scarf, H. E. (1967) "On the Computation of Equilibrium Prices", In W. J. Feliner (ed.), *Ten Economic Studies in the Tradition of Irving Fisher*, New York: Wiley.

——, and T. Hansen (1973) *The Computation of Economic Equilibria*, New Haven, CN: Yale University Press.

——, and J. B. Shoven (1984) *Applied General Equilibrium Analysis*, Cambridge: Cambridge University Press.

Schreiner, P., and K. A. Larsen (1985) "On the Introduction and Application of the MSG-model in the Norwegian Planning System", in F.R. Forsund, M. Hoel and S. Longva (eds), *Production, Multi-sectoral Growth and Planning*, Amsterdam: North-Holland, pp. 241–70.

Shoven, J. B and J. Whalley (1972) "A General Equilibrium Calculation of the Effects of Different Taxation of Income from Capital in the US", *Journal of Public Economics*, 9, 281–321.

——, —— (1973) "General Equilibrium with Taxes: A Computation Procedure and an Existence Proof", *Review of Economics Studies*, 60, October, 475–90.

——, —— (1984) "Applied General Equilibrium Models of Taxation and Trade: An Introduction and Survey", *Journal of Economic Literature*, 22, September, 1007–51.

Taylor, L. (1975) "Theoretical Foundation and Technical Implications", in C. Blitzer, P. Clark and L. Taylor (eds), *Economy-wide Models and Development Planning*, Oxford: Oxford University Press.

Whalley, J. and A. Mansur (1984) "Numerical Specifications of Applied General Equilibrium Models: Estimation Calibration and Data", in H. E. Scarf and J. B. Shoven, (eds), *Applied General Equilibrium Analysis*, Cambridge: Cambridge University Press, pp. 69–127.

PART II
Finance and Taxation

2

A Framework for Evaluating Tax Capitalization Effects in Asset Markets

Jonas Agell

1 Introduction

The short-term effects of tax changes on the valuation of the capital assets of the economy are issues of obvious interest to public finance economists as well as tax reformers in the Western industrialized countries. First, since tax induced windfall gains and losses may imply distributional outcomes violating the normative principle of horizontal equity, examining the potential for short-term tax capitalization effects in asset markets is an essential ingredient when assessing tax reform proposals (Feldstein, 1976). Second, the relationship between asset prices and investment stressed in the q theory of investment (Tobin, 1969; Hayashi, 1982) suggests that the response of asset prices to tax changes can be used as a vehicle for inferring the longer-term tax effects on capital accumulation in different production sectors (Summers, 1985).

This paper presents a framework for quantitative evaluation of the extent of tax capitalization effects in asset markets. The proposed model incorporates the tax-adjusted capital-asset pricing model (tax-CAPM) of Brennan (1970) into a Brainard and Tobin (1968) accounting framework identifying the assets and liabilities of different agents of the economy. The sources of risk facing investors are explicitly recognized, and the provisions of the tax system at both the corporate and personal levels are specified, recognizing the risk-sharing facilities provided by the tax system as well as various inflation-induced asymmetries of the existing tax code.

The resulting model of general asset market equilibrium is parameterized and calibrated in order to replace a benchmark data set, constructed using 1980 Swedish asset market data. Since no linear approximations are involved, the numerical framework can be used to examine the impact of nonmarginal tax changes on portfolio choice and asset markets. In order to illustrate the kind of policy experiments that can be considered, the present paper uses the model to examine the capitalization effects in asset markets when indexing the tax system. Apart from demonstrating the workings of the model, this application permits us to address questions raised in recent literature discussing the joint effects of nominal tax systems and inflation on asset markets (see for instance Feldstein, 1980a, b, c; Hendershott and Hu, 1981; Summers, 1981a, b; Ebrill and Possen, 1982a, b; Poterba, 1984). Here, we shall see how using a computable general equilibrium representation of asset markets, incorporating potentially important wealth effects and complementary relationships among assets, provides new insights to issues discussed in earlier literature.

This paper differs from earlier work on the effects of tax policy on portfolio choice and asset markets. First, whereas the tax-CAPM provides a useful characterization of the equilibrium structure of after-tax rates of return on different financial assets, this paper incorporates an expected utility formulation of individual asset demands into a balance sheet framework of the economy. This allows us to go "behind" the pricing relations of the tax-CAPM to investigate the implications of existing taxes and individual optimizing behavior for variables such as the distribution of wealth and risk across investors, the distribution of government tax revenue, the incentives to accumulate physical capital in different production sectors, etc. Second, the use of quantitative computational methods – borrowed from the rapidly expanding literature on applied general equilibrium modeling (Johansen, 1960; Shoven and Whalley, 1972; etc.) – is so far rarely encountered in the finance literature.

The paper is organized in the following manner. Section 2 outlines the basic modeling approach. Section 3 presents a small-scale asset market model structured along the lines discussed in the second section. This particular version of a computable financial sector equilibrium model is aimed neither at describing the complex patterns of ownership, government regulations and diversity of financial instruments that characterize the financial sector, nor to give an accurate forecast of the actual capitalization effects when changing tax regime. Instead, the aim is to demonstrate how the analytical tools of monetary economics and capital asset pricing theory can be used to provide quantitative answers to questions of tax policy design. Section 4 uses a Swedish benchmark data set to parameterize and calibrate the model. Section 5 employs the numerical model to simulate the effects of indexing the nominalistic Swedish tax system. Some concluding comments are provided in section 6.

2 The Analytical Setting

The proposed framework is developed using four distinct building blocks. The first is a capital accounting framework developed along the lines of Brainard and Tobin (1968) and Tobin (1969). A generalized version is shown in table 2.1. Rows denote the assets and liabilities of the hypothetical economy of the table; columns represent the different sectors owning the assets in question. The potential menu of assets includes both financial assets such as corporate shares and different debt instruments, and physical assets such as stocks of productive capital in production sectors. Also, a fully specified economy-wide balance sheet accounts for the existence of nonmarketable assets such as human health and implicit debts in the form of future expected tax payments used to finance payment of principal and interest on government debt (Barro, 1974). The ownership sectors include households, financial intermediaries, businesses, foreign investors, the central bank, central and local government etc. The net wealth position of each investor is given by vertical summation of the elements of the respective columns. Adding across a row yields the net supply of a given asset to the economy.

Table 2.1 The capital accounting framework

Assets and liabilities	Ownership sectors[a]					
	1	2	.	.	.	k
1						
2						
.						
.						
.						
l						
Net worth						

[a]Includes central and local government, the rest of the world etc.

In order to turn the book-keeping identities of the balance sheet into a framework for economic analysis, we also need assumptions concerning the behavior of the various agents appearing in the capital account. In macroeconomic models of portfolio balance, postulated asset demand functions assumed to satisfy standard "adding-up" conditions are typically employed (e.g. Tobin, 1969). Here, I will impose additional structure on asset demands by deriving them from basic microeconomic principles. Thus, the second important building block is the assumption that the asset demand functions of financial investors are derived from maximization of expected utility.

The third building block is explicit modeling of different types of asset risk facing investors. This is especially important in an analysis focusing on tax aspects, since existing tax systems typically provide different degrees of loss offset depending on the type of loss incurred. For instance, a significant part of risk associated with holdings of long-term financial assets is related to the volatility of asset prices ("capital" risk) rather than to random income flows ("income" risk). As the corporate income tax absorbing part of the income risk confronting corporate equity investors is generally higher than the effective capital gains tax shouldering part of the capital risk facing investors in the corporate share market, tax policy analysis incorporating only the former type of risk is likely to underestimate the distortionary effects of taxes on asset choice and risk taking (Bulow and Summers, 1984).

The theory of portfolio choice with taxes as developed since the pioneering article by Domar and Musgrave (1944) has examined the implications of idealized tax systems for individual portfolio choice.[1] Here, our aim is instead to evaluate the effects on portfolio choice and asset markets of the existing tax system, with its diverse treatment of different assets and investors and complicated mixture of nominal and real principles of income measurement. Thus, the final building block is the incorporation of a variety of special features of the actual system of corporate and personal capital income taxation into the model.

After incorporating the derived asset demands into the balance sheet and assigning a random investor specific post-tax rate of return to each asset, the general equilibrium problem for the economy's asset market can be formulated as follows: is there an equilibrium vector of random rates of return such that – at the microlevel – each investor has chosen an optimal composition of net wealth – at the macrolevel – is compatible with clearing markets for all marketable assets. If such an equilibrium vector exists, and is stable as well as unique, meaningful comparative statics experiments can be performed.

Underlying this modeling strategy is an analytical short-cut frequently adopted in financial and monetary economics: the focus is on the determination of the stock equilibrium of financial markets, whereas "real" variables such as production and profitability of physical capital in production sectors are treated as exogenous, although possibly random (as in this paper), throughout the analysis. This separation of economic decisions has one obvious drawback. By examining temporary asset market equilibrium. I implicitly impose static expectations on investors. In a complete intertemporal model of asset model equilibrium, forward-looking investors would price financial assets while accounting for the dynamic interactions between asset prices and capital formation in production sectors.[2]

3 An Applied Equilibrium Asset Market Model

This section outlines a small-scale asset market model structured along the lines discussed in the previous section. As the details of the model have been presented elsewhere (see Agell, 1986), the general characteristics of the model can be briefly described as follows.

Institutional setting and level of aggregation In order to facilitate interpretation and exposition, two guiding principles underlie the analytical framework. First, the level of asset and investor aggregation is high, emphasizing a few important aggregates. Thus the aggregate balance sheet of the economy incorporates six sectors, four financial assets and two underlying stocks of sector-specific productive capital. The financial claims issued by production sectors are held by two different types of households (wealthy and nonwealthy households) and by an institutional investor whose empirical counterpart is a heterogeneous aggregate of financial institutions such as banks, pension funds, insurance companies etc. There is also a government sector issuing long- and short-term debt instruments. Second, the model tells an essentially Walrasian story of tax-induced asset market adjustments, emphasizing the portfolio choice of nonrationed agents, which eliminates the need for specifying *ad hoc* rationing schemes.

Heterogeneous stocks of physical capital A distinction is made between the predetermined stock of physical capital in the corporate and housing sector, respectively.[3] It is also recognized that corporate capital in reality is a heterogeneous aggregate of machinery, structures and inventories – all of which are treated differently for tax purposes and characterized by different economic lifetimes – by assuming that corporate capital is of the "sandwich" variety proposed by Feldstein and Summers (1978). Consequently, each unit of corporate capital is modeled as a mix of machinery, structures and inventories.

Treatment of housing assets The housing sector is treated as a separate production sector. The output of the sector is sold on the market for housing services, and the thereby established rent level defines the exogenously given pre-tax real rate of return on housing capital. The equity capital of the housing sector consists of financial claims on the underlying real property. The stock demand for these "housing certificates" is based on traditional portfolio considerations.[4]

Behavioral functions By assuming that preference orderings exhibit constant relative risk aversion and that asset returns are joint normally distributed, convenient closed-form expressions are derived for the asset demands of investors. Ideally, a complete analysis of asset market equilibrium should also explicitly incorporate derived debt–equity and payout decisions of production sectors. However, recognizing the absence of any generally accepted theory of optimal capital structure and dividend decision of firms, we will simply follow the conventional procedure of assuming that production sectors aim at certain "target" ratios (assumed fixed throughout the short-term horizon of our analysis) for dividend payments and debt financing. This is modeled by letting production sectors issue new debt instruments at a rate corresponding to the general inflation rate.

Stochastic modeling Production technologies and the relative prices of produced goods and housing services within the housing and corporate sectors are assumed to be stochastic, causing income uncertainty. This is recognized by defining the pre-tax real rates of return to physical capital in these sectors as two random variables. The other type of uncertainty, capital uncertainty, is investors' uncertainty concerning the rate of change of the market values of the model's long-term assets. In the present static asset market framework, this type of risk is incorporated simply by letting the exogenously given rates of nominal price increase of the long-term assets be random variables. Since we assume three types of long-term assets traded in financial markets, the model incorporates five random variables in total. They are conveniently summarized by the five-dimensional vector $\widetilde{A}$, assumed to follow a multivariate normal distribution $N[E(\widetilde{A}), V(\widetilde{A})]$, where the vector $E(\widetilde{A})$ contains the means of random exogenous variables and $V(\widetilde{A})$ is a symmetric 5×5 covariance matrix of full rank. Finally, it is assumed that the model's short-term debt instruments are riskless.[5]

Heterogeneous expectations The basic Sharpe–Lintner–Mossin capital asset pricing model typically assumes that investors make identical, and correct, assessments of the distribution functions of stochastic variables. The assumption of homogeneous expectations implies that investors will hold identical portfolios in the absence of taxes and transaction costs. This unrealistic prediction has led to the development of alternative models that, by allowing for the possibility of heterogeneous probability beliefs of investors, suggest that investors may hold nonuniform portfolios.[6] Here, we will follow the latter approach and assume that, because of incomplete information, each investor j has to form subjective judgments $E_j(\widetilde{A})$ and $V_j(\widetilde{A})$ concerning the true vector of means and the matrix of covariances of random exogenous variables.

Tax modeling As already mentioned, a main thrust of the present analysis is the incorporation of a realistic specification of the Swedish tax system[7] into a consistent asset market framework. The corporate tax system is modeled recognizing tax incentives such as accelerated depreciation and initial investment allowances, while our specification of the tax system at the investor level includes both taxes on investment income – capital gains taxes on an accrual-equivalent basis (Bailey, 1969), taxes on dividends and interest income – and wealth taxes. Furthermore, various inflation-induced distortions of the Swedish tax system are incorporated. These are, first, the use of first-in–first-out (FIFO) inventory accounting and historic cost depreciation when calculating taxable corporate income, second, the taxation of nominal capital gains on corporate shares and, finally, the deductibility of nominal interest expenses and the taxation of nominal interest income. The progressivity of the tax system is modeled by simply assigning the two representative household investors to different tax brackets. Finally, the risk sharing provided by the tax system is modeled in detail, with due regard to the fact that different taxes provide different risk-sharing facilities.

Differential tax incidence The simulation experiments rely on the concept of differential tax incidence: any reduction in government expected tax revenue caused by changes in the system of capital taxation will be compensated for by raising an equivalent amount from a nondistortionary tax on total private wealth.[8]

Government risk sharing Underlying the specification of government risk sharing through the tax system are two simplifying assumptions. First, we assume that the tax law allows full loss offset. Due to the limitations of the loss carry-over clauses of existing tax systems, this is obviously not an exact description of reality. Second, the present study treats risk passed on to the government as if it were no longer shouldered by private investors.[9]

Small open economy There is no explicit modeling of external capital flows and the links between domestic and international asset markets. However, the spirit of a small open economy is retained by a particular choice of numeraire in the numerical applications. Thus, it is assumed that the nominal interest rate on short-term debt instruments is determined exogenously – a situation which applies to a small open economy facing perfectly mobile short-term capital flows.

Table 2.2 summarizes the structure of our simple version of a financial sector general equilibrium model. First, there are four wealth restrictions. At each instant, financial institutions and wealthy and nonwealthy households maximize expected utility by choosing asset portfolios subject to the constraint that the market value of their respective wealth portfolios must not exceed the current market value of their initial endowments (equations b – d). The β_is and μ_is appearing in these equations simply define the economy's initial wealth distribution. These individual restrictions have a correspondence at the macrolevel, implying that the value of total privately owned wealth must not exceed the value of the initial stock (equation a).

Table 2.2 The model

Wealth definitions

$$W = q_C(1 - b_{SD} - q_{LD}b_{LD})K_C + q_H(1 - h_{SD} - q_{LD}h_{LD})K_H \quad \text{(a)}$$
$$+ q_{LD}(K_H h_{LD} + K_C b_{LD} + LD_G) + K_H h_{SD} + K_C b_{SD} + SD_G$$

$$W_{H1} = \alpha_S q_C(1 - b_{SD} - q_{LD}b_{LD})K_C + \alpha_H q_H(1 - h_{SD} - q_{LD}h_{LD})K_H \quad \text{(b)}$$
$$+ \alpha_{LD}q_{LD}(K_H h_{LD} + K_C b_{LD} + LD_G)$$
$$+ \alpha_{SD}(K_H h_{SD} + K_C b_{SD} + SD_G)$$

$$W_{H2} = \mu_S q_C(1 - b_{SD} - q_{LD}b_{LD})K_C + \mu_H q_H(1 - h_{SD} - q_{LD}h_{LD})K_H \quad \text{(c)}$$
$$+ \mu_{LD}q_{LD}(K_H h_{LD} + K_C b_{LD} + LD_G)$$
$$+ \mu_{SD}(K_H h_{SD} + K_C b_{SD} + SD_G)$$

$$W_I = W - W_{H1} - W_{H2} \quad \text{(d)}$$

Asset market equilibrium

$$\sum_{j=H1}^{I} S_j^*[E(R_j), V(R_j), C_j]W_j = q_C K_C(1 - b_{SD} - q_{LD}b_{LD}) \quad \text{(e)}$$

$$j \equiv H1, H2, I; \; S_j^*(.) \geqslant 0$$

$$\sum_{j=H1}^{I} O_j^*[E(R_j), V(R_j), C_j]W_j = q_H K_H(1 - h_{SD} - q_{LD}h_{LD}) \quad \text{(f)}$$

$$j \equiv H1, H2, I; \; O_j^*(.) \geqslant 0$$

$$\sum_{j=H1}^{I} LD_j^*[E(R_j), V(R_j), C_j]W_j = q_{LD}(K_H h_{LD} + K_C b_{LD} + LD_G) \quad \text{(g)}$$

$$j \equiv H1, H2, I; \; LD_j^*(.) \geqslant 0$$

Table 2.2 (*cont.*)

$$\sum_{j=\text{H1}}^{\text{I}} \text{SD}_j^*[E(R_j),\ V(R_j),\ C_j]W_j = K_\text{H}h_\text{SD} + K_\text{C}b_\text{SD} + \text{SD}_\text{G} \tag{h}$$

$j \equiv \text{H1, H2, I}$

Elements of $E(R_j)$ and $V(R_j)$

$$E(R_{ij}) = f[E_j(\widetilde{A}),\ \ldots] \tag{i}$$

$$\text{cov}(R_{ij},\ R_{kj}) = g[V_j(\widetilde{A}),\ \ldots] \tag{j}$$

Equal revenue requirement

$$\text{GR} = \text{E}\,\widetilde{T}^{\,C}(.) + \sum_{j=\text{H1}}^{\text{I}} \sum_{i=\text{SD}}^{\text{S}} \text{E}\,\widetilde{T}_{ij}(.) \tag{k}$$

$j \equiv \text{H1, H2, I};\ i \equiv \text{S, O, LD, SD}$

W_j	net wealth of investor j where j is wealthy households (H1), nonwealthy households (H2), financial institutions (I)
$K_\text{C},\ K_\text{H}$	physical stock of capital valued at replacement cost of corporate (C) and housing (H) sector
$\alpha_i,\ \mu_i$	wealthy and nonwealthy households' initial share of asset i where i is corporate shares (S), housing certificates (H), long-term debt (LD), short-term debt (SD)
q_i	Tobin's q of the equity of production sector i; $i \equiv$ C, H
q_LD	Tobin's q of long-term debt
$b_\text{LD},$ b_SD	proportions of long- and short-term debt financing in corporate sector
$h_\text{LD},$ h_SD	proportions of long- and short-term debt financing in housing sector
$\text{SD}_\text{G},$ LD_G	accounting value of short- and long-term government debt
$S_j^*(.)$	optimal portfolio fraction of corporate shares in portfolio of investor j
$O_j^*(.)$	optimal portfolio fraction of housing certificates in portfolio of investor j
$\text{LD}_j^*(.)$	optimal portfolio fraction of long-term debt in portfolio of investor j
$\text{SD}_j^*(.)$	optimal portfolio fraction of short-term debt in portfolio of investor j
GR	total expected government revenue from capital taxation
$\widetilde{T}^{\,C}(.)$	total random government revenue from the corporate income tax
$\widetilde{T}_{ij}(.)$	total random government revenue from the taxation of the jth investor's holdings of the ith asset

Equations (e) – (h) are the equilibrium conditions for the financial markets of the economy. Four different financial assets are distinguished, held by investors as claims against the government and the two production sectors. The equity of the corporate sector is ordinary shares, whereas the equity claims of the housing sector consist of special housing certificates, entitling their owner to the right of disposition of the residual cash flow of that sector. There are two types of marketable debt, the first being a simple period bond with a variable nominal interest rate, and the second being a consol with a fixed nominal coupon. These debt instruments are supplied both by the production sectors and the government, implying that government and private debt instruments of the same duration are treated as perfect substitutes.

For each market, the right-hand side of the equality sign specifies the supply conditions, while the left-hand side gives a general representation of the optimal portfolio demands of investors. The supply of corporate shares (equation e) is given by the predetermined stock of physical corporate and the corporate sector's choice of capital structure. It is assumed, by appropriate choice of accounting units, that each unit of corporate capital commands a replacement cost of SEK 1. Since the total stock of corporate capital consists of K_C such units, and each unit has been financed by short- and long-term debt according to the financial "target" ratios b_{SD} and b_{LD}, respectively, it follows that $K_C(1 - b_{SD} - b_{LD})$ is the equity once subscribed to by corporate shareholders. However, the current market values of corporate equity and long-term debt instruments may diverge from the current replacement value of the underlying capital stock. Consequently, we introduce the variables q_C and q_{LD} defining the market prices of corporate shares and long-term debt relative to the reproduction cost of physical corporate capital. Recognizing that changes in q_{LD} generate equivalent capital gains or losses to equity holders, the stock market value of corporate shares becomes $q_C(1 - b_{SD} - q_{LD}b_{LD})K_C$.

The residential real estate sector is modeled in a manner paralleling the treatment of the corporate sector. Thus the supply of housing certificates (equation f) can be rationalized in a way similar to the supply of corporate shares. The supply of long-term debt instruments (equation g) is the sum of debt issued by the government and production sectors. Finally, there is no q variable for short-term debt instruments (equation h). The outstanding volume of short-term debt is turned over in each period, so the book-keeping value of short-term debt instruments must coincide with their current market value.

Let us next turn to the demand side of the specification of the asset demand functions of households and financial institutions. First, let R_j be an investor-specific vector of rates of return, incorporating as its elements the random real after-tax rate of return on each of the financial assets available to the jth investor. Then, assuming that investors' utility functions are of the constant relative risk aversion variety, the asset demands of investors maximizing expected utility in a world with continuous and costless portfolio readjustments will be linearly homogeneous in net wealth and will incorporate as additional arguments (a) the Arrow–Pratt measure C_j of relative risk aversion, (b) the vector $E(R_j)$ of expected after-tax rates of return and (c) the elements of the covariance matrix $V(R_j)$ of random after-tax returns.[10]

Non-negativity constraints are imposed on the asset demands for corporate shares, housing certificates and long-term debt, whereas investors are permitted to hold negative amounts of short-term debt. Thus, although the net supply of short-term debt is given by the financing decisions of production sectors and the government, we allow for internally generated debt holdings within the aggregate of private investors. Since investors respect their wealth constraints, Walras's law applies and one of the market excess demands is a linear combination of the asset demands on the three remaining markets. Consequently, the model can only determine a set of relative rates of return; all market-determined rates of return must be expressed in terms of numeraire.

For each investor, the elements of the vector $E(R_j)$ and the covariance matrix $V(R_j)$ are specified recognizing the details of the Swedish tax system, different sources of risk facing investors etc. For our present purpose, it is sufficient to introduce equations (i) and (j) as simple general representations of the expressions for means, variances and covariances of return derived elsewhere (see Agell, 1986). The explanatory variables include elements from the first and second moments of the subjective joint distributions $N[E_j(\widetilde{A}), V_j(A)]$ of the exogenous stochastic variables of the model, variables related to the financial decisions of production sectors (divided payout ratio, debt–equity mixes), the general inflation rate and tax parameters summarizing the relevant aspects of the personal and corporate tax system. The means, variances and covariances of returns also depend on the q variables of the model – changes in the market valuation of long-term assets will alter the risks and expected returns confronting investors.

Finally, equation (k) defines the government budget constraint. The left-hand side variable GR is the government's exogenously given revenue requirement from taxes on capital income, while the right-hand side specifies the different sources of tax revenue. As the present framework explicitly incorporates uncertainty, the yield requirement equation is defined in terms of the means of random tax proceeds. Thus, we will calculate equilibria for alternative regimes of capital taxation, where induced losses in government tax revenue compared with the expected revenue under the present system of nominal income taxation is recovered by the introduction of a nondistortionary tax on total private net wealth.

The model can be interpreted in terms of an unregulated capital market, where all rates of return, except the numeraire, are determined simultaneously. For given values of parameters and exogenous variables (including the elements of the tax vector, the subjectively perceived vectors and matrices of means, variances and covariances of the random exogenous variables), the model is solved for – assuming the existence of a unique solution – first, the means, variances and covariances of the equilibrium real after-tax returns on the assets of the economy, second, the net wealth and portfolio composition of investors, third, government-expected revenue from different taxes (including the required rate of the compensating wealth tax) and, finally, the prices of corporate shares, housing certificates and long-term debt. Given this solution, we can solve in a recursive manner for the allocation of risk bearing, wealth and capital income among investors. The numeraire is the real rate of interest on short-term debt. The natural interpretation of this particular choice of numeraire refers (as mentioned above) to the exogeneity of the real rate of interest in a small open economy which is fully integrated with the world market for short-term capital.

4 A Numerical Application of the Model

Incorporating the wealth restrictions (a)–(d) and the derived elements of $E(R_j)$ and $V(R_j)$ into the market equilibrium conditions (e)–(g) produces a system of equations in three-dimensional (q_C, q_H, q_{LD}) space. The nonlinearities of the model preclude finding an explicit analytical solution for q_C, q_H and q_{LD}. Consequently, a numerical solution method has to be used.[11]

When the model is implemented numerically, the first task is to assemble a data set defining the initial "benchmark" equilibrium of the model. The benchmark equilibrium data set can obviously be constructed using either an "invented" data set or data derived from empirical sources. Here, the latter approach is followed, and the model is parameterized using Swedish asset market data for 1980 (see Agell, 1986). However, despite the fact that the numerical model has certain characteristics in common with the real world, the analogy cannot for obvious reasons be stretched very far. Thus, the usual caveats of the applied general equilibrium literature apply.[12]

The benchmark data set include values of, first, the different tax rates appearing in the model, second, exogenous variables such as capital stocks valued at replacement costs, target borrowing rates of production sectors, value and maturity structure of government debt etc., third, the parameters of initial wealth distribution, fourth, the numeraire and, finally, intial equilibrium values of the q variables of the model.

The values of the coefficient of relative risk aversion C_j and the elements of the subjective distributions $N[E_j(\widetilde{A}), V_j(\widetilde{A})]$ of random exogenous variables are set using several external sources of information. First, the parameter of relative risk aversion is set equal to six for each investor – an assumption based on recent results obtained by Friend and Hasbrouck (1982).[13] Second, structure is imposed on each subjective covariance matrix $V_j(\widetilde{A})$ by determining the correlation coefficients of return among the model's risky assets using Swedish annual data on asset yields for the period 1960–79. Third, the means of random exogenous variables included in $E_j(\widetilde{A})$ are set (a) using historical data on the average pre-tax real rate of return to corporate capital, (b) using an imputed value for the marginal product of housing capital and (c) assuming that the subjective means of random asset inflation in stationary equilibrium equal the average 10 percent rate of change of the Swedish consumer price index for the years 1978–80.

Using this additional information the model is calibrated by solving it backwards for the subjective variances of asset inflation included in each matrix $V_j(\widetilde{A})$ that make the model replicate the benchmark vaues for the endogenous variables. Then the model is set for policy analysis. Assuming a particular tax change, a new equilibrium solution is calculated using the already inferred values of the subjective variances of asset inflation as inputs in the new simulation. Table 2.3 provides a summary statement of the equilibrum values of some of the endogenous variables in the 1980 benchmark economy. Since the benchmark data set has been adjusted for reasons of internal consistency, the results of the table are not an exact replication of the Swedish financial sector in 1980. Nevertheless, they share the same basic characteristics as the actual outcome.

The value of the stock exchange is only 23 percent of the equity value of the residential real estate sector (which in the present application is assumed to consist of the economy's stock of owner-occupied housing). This reflects the contemporaneous decline in real share prices and increase in real estate values that occurred during the 1970s, with 1979 marking the final year of these price developments. Related information is conveyed in the Tobin's q variables of the housing and corporate production sectors (defined as the ratio of total market value of outstanding financial instruments – including equity *and* debt – to the replacement value of the underlying capital

Table 2.3 The 1980 reference economy

	Value		
Value of stock exchange	SEK 75.7 billion		
Value of housing equity	SEK 327.6 billion		
Tobin's q of corporate sector	0.69		
Tobin's q of housing sector	1.18		

	Wealthy households	Nonwealthy households	Institutions
Expected after-tax real rate of return on corporate shares	0.025	0.046	0.063
Expected after-tax real rate of return on housing equity	0.027	0.038	–
Expected after-tax real rate of return on long-term debt	–	–	0.035
Expected after-tax real rate of return on short-term debt	−0.072	−0.032	0.015
Distribution of private wealth	0.286	0.3	0.414
Distribution of real after-tax capital income	−0.015	0.219	0.796
Distribution of private after-tax risk	0.457	0.312	0.231

stock). The values of the q variables will at any given instant be taken as an indication of the incentives to accumulate new physical capital in production sectors.[14] Then it can be expected that the calculated q values constitute a substantial disincentive to investments in physical corporate capital and a corresponding incentive to the accumulation of housing capital.[15]

The expected equilibrium real after-tax rates of return indicate the considerable discrepancies in the tax treatment across assets and portfolio investors. An expected general inflation rate of 10 percent, nominal taxation of interest income and wealth taxes produce an *ex ante* real after-tax rate of return of −7.2 percent on wealthy households' holdings of short-term debt instruments, while the safe real rate of return obtained by financial institutions (assumed to be tax exempt) is 1.5 percent. The expected equilibrium real rate of return on long-term debt (held only by financial institutions) is 3.5 percent, indicating an upward-sloping yield curve. This maturity-related risk premium is explained by the capital risk associated with holdings of long-term bonds. The expected real rate of return on corporate shares after payment of corporate income taxes is 6.3 percent. After taxation of dividends, nominal capital gains and personal wealth, the expected after-tax return on wealthy households' holdings of corporate shares is 2.5 percent. Finally, the expected rate of return on portfolio investments in owner-occupied housing is calculated recognizing the existence of government interest subsidies to owner-occupiers, capital gains taxes, taxation of imputed income of owner-occupied homes, deductibility of mortgage interest expenses and wealth taxes.

The capital income share of tax-exempt financial institutions is far larger than their share of total private wealth. This is primarily due to the combined effect of inflation and full taxation of nominal interest receipts on the real income of household investors (note that the share of wealthy households is negative). The wealth ownership share of nonwealthy households is slightly larger than the share of their wealthier counterparts, a circumstance stemming from the fact that total holdings of short-term debt and owner-occupied homes are skewed toward less wealthy households. The distribution of private risk taking is inversely related to the institutional investors' large holdings of relatively safe short- and long-term bonds and by household investors' relatively large holdings of risky assets such as corporate shares and residential real estate.

5 The Effects of Indexing the Tax System

The potentially detrimental effects of the combination of relatively high inflation rates and basically nominal systems of capital taxation has aroused much concern in many Western industrialized countries. For instance, many academic economists have argued that the appearance of unexpected inflation in economics with nominal systems of income taxation induces households and financial institutions to transfer wealth from financial markets to the markets for "real" assets. The ensuing short-run market adjustments are reflected in the form of rising relative prices of residential real estate and consumer durables, while the value of corporate shares and long-term bonds declines (Feldstein, 1980a, b, c; Summers, 1981a, b; Ebrill and Possen, 1982a, b etc.). These tax-induced revaluations of the economy's stock of productive capital are said to stimulate investments in less productive residential capital and to crowd out productive investments in corporate capital. The purpose of the present section is to evaluate this claim using our applied equilibrium asset market model.

The 1980 benchmark equilibrium serves as our norm of comparison when the effects on portfolio choices and asset markets of an unanticipated switch to an inflation-neutral tax system are examined. At the personal level, the tax change involves taxing only real interest income, allowing deductions for tax purposes for only real interest

Table 2.4 Effects of indexing the personal and corporate income tax

Percentage change compared with 1980 reference economy

Value of stock exchange	−40.6
Value of housing equity	−57
Tobin's q of corporate sector	− 8.7
Tobin's q of housing sector	−38.1
Expected revenue from corporate income tax	+23.9
Expected revenue from total distortionary taxes on personal and corporate capital income	−38.3

Equilibrium values of selected endogenous variables

	Share of wealthy households	Share of nonwealthy households	Share of institutions
Wealth distribution	0.228 (0.286)	0.252 (0.300)	0.52 (0.414)
Distribution of real after-tax capital income	0.144 (−0.015)	0.287 (0.219)	0.569 (0.796)
Distribution of private risk	0.163 (0.457)	0.209 (0.312)	0.628 (0.231)

The required compensating lump-sum tax rate on total private wealth is 0.6 percent.
Figures in parentheses denote benchmark values.

expenses and taxing (or allowing deduction for) only that part of realized capital gains (losses) on corporate shares and residential real estate that constitutes a real capital gain (loss). The tax change at the corporate level includes three modifications of the existing tax code: (a) FIFO inventory accounting is replaced by the last-in–first-out (LIFO) inventory valuation method; (b) the historic cost method of depreciation for tax purposes is replaced by replacement cost depreciation: (c) deductions are permitted for only real interest expenses on corporate debt. Finally, the government compensates for any revenue losses induced by this indexing scheme by introducing a uniform lump-sum tax on total privately owned wealth valued at the new equilibrium asset prices.

The new equilibrium solution is reported in table 2.4. At the macrolevel, the value of the corporate share market declines by 40 percent, while the market value of housing equity declines by 57 percent. These price adjustments may appear dramatic. However, compared with the changes in asset prices in recent years they are modest. For example, from July 1980 to July 1983, the Swedish stock market value rose by 80 percent in real terms.

In order to examine how the valuation in financial markets of the economy's total stocks of productive capital is altered, we must also account for the capitalization effects in the markets for debt instruments. Since these turn out to be modest (the effective real rate of interest on long-term bonds increases from 3.5 to 3.6 percent, indicating a somewhat steeper slope of the yield curve), the changes in the Tobin's q variables are less drastic than the corresponding revaluations of equity instruments. The ratio of the two q variables increases by 48 percent (an increase from 0.58 to 0.86), which suggests that the present Swedish tax system compared with a norm of inflation-neutral treatment of different assets worsens the relative incentives to invest in physical capital in the corporate sector.

The reduced equity values of the housing and corporate sectors reduce the value of net wealth of portfolio investors. The wealth of the aggregate of household investors decreases by 36 percent, while the percentage decline in the value of wealth of financial institutions is 3.9 percent. Turning to the distribution of expected real after-tax capital income, households increase their share at the expense of financial institutions. Thus, the income share of wealthy households increases from −0.015 to 0.144, the share of nonwealthy households is raised from 0.219 to 0.287 and the share of financial institutions decreases from 0.796 to 0.569. Household investors also reduce their share of private risk taking, with the largest percentage decline benefiting the wealthy households because of a sharply reduced fraction of corporate shares included in their portfolios.

Indexing the corporate income tax leads to an increase in the expected revenue from the corporate income tax. This is because abolishing the deductibility of nominal interest expenses on corporate debt gives a larger gain to the government than the loss associated with introducing LIFO inventory valuation and replacement cost depreciation on investments in machinery and buildings.[16] However, the expected total revenue from distortionary taxes (i.e. the taxes existing already in the benchmark economy) decreases – the negative net effect of indexing the personal income tax dominates the positive effect of indexing the corporate income tax. This expected revenue loss is compensated for by raising an equivalent amount from a uniform lump-sum tax on all privately owned wealth valued at post-reform asset prices. In this case, the required tax rate turns out to be 0.6 percent.

Using the comparative statics results of table 2.4 as a frame of reference, the underlying economic adjustment mechanism can be sketched as follows. The initial impact of indexing the tax system and introducing a compensating lump-sum tax on private wealth is to alter the structure of after-tax real rates of return. The real rate of return on short-term debt instruments expected by household investors increases, and the expected return on housing equity decreases (the loss of tax deductibility of interest expenses on mortgage debt outweighs the abolished taxation of nominal capital gains on residential real estate). The expected return on household investors' holdings of corporate shares is approximately unaltered (the expected increase in corporate tax payments is countered by the elimination of purely nominal capital gains on corporate shares from the personal tax base), while the expected yield on corporate equity held by financial institutions is slightly reduced.

These first-round adjustments alter the optimal asset choices of investors. This is reflected by excess supplies in the corporate and housing equity markets, and excess demand in the markets for interest-bearing (and previously nominally taxed) assets. Since the nominal short-term rate of interest is exogenously given by the requirement of interest parity with the rest of the world. the burden of the necessary yield adjustments is shifted to the equity markets of the economy (the covariance structure of real rates of return implies that short- and long-term debt instruments are close enough substitutes to prevent substantial changes in the effective long-term bond yield). Thus the prices of corporate and housing equity instruments in financial markets are adjusted downwards.

These revaluations initiate dampening mechanisms working in the direction of restoring general asset market equilibrium. First, the lowered valuation of corporate equity causes a rise in the effective corporate equity yield, which makes financial institutions attempt to substitute corporate shares for their initial holdings of short- and long-term debt. The asset substitution between corporate shares and long-term debt creates excess supply in the bond market, which in turn raises the effective long-term interest rate; the substitution between corporate shares and short-term debt reduces the disequilbria in the markets for corporate shares and short-term debt. Second, the capitaliztion effects in equity markets in general and the residential real estate market in particular creates wealth effects which further constrain the excess demand for short-term debt. Finally, the rather drastic fall in the value of housing equity tends in itself to reduce the disequilibrium in the housing equity market, since the induced increase in the effective yield on housing equity soon turns the excess supply of housing equity of nonwealthy households into an excess demand countering the excess supply on behalf of wealthy households (the loss of tax deductibility of nominal interest expenses is the most costly for wealthy – high tax – households; consequently, they require a greater increase in the yield on housing equity than do the nonwealthy households before they are content with holding the given stock).

Since an examination of the consequences of indexing the overall tax system is equivalent to investigating the effects of a sudden change in the inflation rate from 10 percent (the benchmark equilibrium inflation rate) to 0 percent, it is clear that the results of table 2.4 do not support the claim of Feldstein and others that the combination of inflation and nominalistic tax systems leads to financial crowding out of corporate investments. Instead, our simulation analysis provides support for the antithesis that the combination of increased inflation and a nominal income tax system increases real corporate share prices. Thus, to the extent that there are unemployed resources in the economy, we would even expect the interaction between inflation and the tax system to crowd in physical investments in both the housing and corporate production sectors.

The explanation for these contradictory results is straightforward and related to different modeling approaches. Thus, whereas the present analysis incorporates an explicit treatment of optimal portfolio choice into a general equilibrium model of asset markets, the "tax-inflation" hypothesis referred to above is typically based on partial equilibrium modeling of individual asset markets or simple two-asset models of asset market equilibrium. The advantage of a general equilibrium formulation is that it allows us to incorporate both wealth effects across markets and complementarity relationships among assets. In particular, an inflation-induced increase in the value of housing assets will in our framework initiate positive wealth effects, which in turn have positive spillover effects on the stock market.

Also, underlying our 1980 benchmark equilibrium is the empirical observation that the returns on corporate shares and residental real estate are negtively correlated, indicating that household investors will invest in real estate simply to hedge the risk of any given position in corporate shares. But then, in our multi-asset framework, an inflation-induced increase in the after-tax return on owner-occupied homes will actually stimulate demand for a hedged package including real estate *and* corporate shares. In contrast, underlying partial equilibrium stock market models is a simple two-asset economy where increases in the exogenously given return on the alternative asset necessarily reduces desired shareholdings. Thus use of partial equilibrium asset market models precludes the possibility of complementary relationships among assets – assets must be gross substitutes simply by the construction of the model.

6 Conclusions

The rapidly growing literature on computable general equilibrium modeling has focused on the effects of various policy measures on the "real" side of the economy: What are the effects of tax policy on the sectoral allocation of production and production factors? How do tariffs and taxes on international trade affect welfare? etc. In answering these questions, asset markets and the behavior of portfolio investors are treated as a veil that can safely be ignored. In this paper, matters have been turned the other way round. Thus, while using the methodology of the computable general equilibrium literature, I have presented a model of the financial sector which treats the allocation of production across sectors as exogenously given.

This simplification has allowed us to explore the short-term effects of fiscal policy on the distribution of wealth and risk bearing and the incentives to invest in production sectors. However, although the analytical framework is parameterized and calibrated to replicate a 1980 Swedish benchmark data set, the quantitative simulation experiments of section 5 have only limited predictive value. Instead, the basic lesson is rather one of reasoning and clarification. Thus the numerical framework serves as a consistent framework when discussing tax policy issues, but in its present form it is not suitable for forecasting the likely magnitudes of tax-induced capitalization effects in asset markets.

It is straightforward to extend the computable asset market model in a number of different ways. For instance, the numerical implementation of the model is based on the deterministic calibration method used in the applied general equilibrium literature. Obviously, this procedure is less satisfactory in the sense that it gives no guidance concerning the model's empirical applicability and usefulness for policy evaluation purposes. This deficiency can only be remedied by an econometric approach permitting statistical tests of key parameter values and functional forms.[17] In particular, with access to cross-sectional microdata on household wealth composition, the asset demands of different types of households could be estimated as functions of household-specific characteristics such as age, wealth, family composition etc. (King and Leape, 1984; Agell and Edin, 1989). Also, the accounting framework underlying the analytical model can easily accommodate the introduction of additional assets and investors. Thus there are no conceptual problems preventing us from a more realistic treatment of international capital flows, a disaggregated treatment of domestic financial institutions etc.

Finally, we may note that the most important item on the research agenda requires a much more substantial effort: how is one to proceed in order to construct a computable general equilibrium model, based on solid microeconomic principles, where financial markets *interact* with the "real" side of the economy? This question is obviously closely related to the long-standing issue in macroeconomics of how to integrate monetary theory and value theory. Although still suffering from an oversimplified treatment of production and capital formation, future exploration of recent developments in financial economics (Cox, Ingersoll and Ross, 1985) could provide very interesting tools for quantitative policy analysis

Notes

1 See Sandmo, 1985, for a comprehensive survey of the literature.
2 The integration of real and financial markets is an area of recent research interests. See Goulder and Summers (1987) for a tax policy model incorporating a deterministic *q* theory of investment in a multisector production economy, and Cox, Ingersoll and Ross (1985) for a framework integrating recent continuous-time models of asset pricing and stochastic growth theory.
3 For similar generalizations of the Brainard and Tobin balance sheet approach to the case of heterogeneous sector-specific stocks of physical capital, see Smith and Starnes (1979) and Ebrill and Possen (1982b).
4 For other work adopting this portfolio treatment of the demand for housing capital in general, and owner-occupied housing in particular, see Ebrill and Possen (1982a), Poterba (1984) and Summers (1981b).
5 This particular choice of safe asset can be rationalized along the lines proposed by Hicks (1946) and Stiglitz (1970) emphasizing the capital

uncertainty confronting investors investing in long-term assets while having a short-run consumption horizon. Thus, an individual paying attention only to next-period consumption will find a one-period bond safe, whereas long-term assets – due to the possibility of revaluations one period from now - are risky.

6 For an early contribution, see Lintner (1969).

7 The Swedish system of personal and corporate capital taxation shares the same basic characteristics as the tax systems of other Western industrialized countries. Consequently, the tax treatment of different portfolio assets depends on whether the yield occurs as dividend yield, income in kind or capital gain. Also, as the tax code is based on purely nominal concepts, the effective tax rates on various asset yields will be sensitive to the rate of inflation. See King and Fullerton (1984) for further details.

8 As noted by Stiglitz (1969), the precise meaning of differential tax incidence is ambiguous in an uncertainty context, where taxes with the same expected yield may differ in the distribution of revenue across different states of the world.

9 This assumption is equivalent to assuming that the government uses the stochastic revenue from capital taxation to finance spending on a public good, which enters private investors' utility function in an additively separable way. See, for example, Atkinson and Stiglitz (1980, ch. 4).

10 See for instance Friedman and Roley (1979) for a derivation of the relevant algebraic function.

11 In the numerical applications, I compute an equilibrium point for the model using a version of Powell's hybrid method included in the International Mathematical and Statistical Library. One potential problem with this procedure is, of course, that the solution algorithm only establishes a locally valid equilibrium point; we cannot exclude the theoretical possibility of multiple equilibria. However, repeated tests (which involved trying different initial values for the computational procedures) have not located any case of nonuniqueness in the region of economically meaningful solutions.

12 In particular, the idea of constructing a benchmark data set for a general equilibrium model using empirical data derived from an economy characterized by disequilibrium adjustments in many markets is not without problems. However, it is a slight comfort that imposing equilibrium conditions on empirical asset market data is probably more easily justified than when dealing with data from income and production accounts.

13 The numerical value of Arrow–Pratt's measure of relative risk aversion is an unsettled empirical question. The analysis of Pindyck (1984) suggests a value of C_j around 5 or 6 and indirect evidence of Grossman and Shiller (1981) indicates a value in the neighborhood of 4, whereas the estimates of Friend and Blume (1975) imply a value of at least 2.

14 Formally, the q theory of investment suggests that investment is a function of the unobservable "marginal q" (the shadow price of investment in a dynamic investment model incorporating installation costs) rather than the "average q" measured in financial markets. A derivation of the exact relationship between marginal and average q is given by Hayashi (1982), who also establishes under what set of assumptions q equals marginal q.

15 Here, I implicitly adopt the view that the equilibrium value of Tobin's q –

inducing zero net investments – is equal to unity in both production sectors. This is not to deny the short-run relevance of the tax capitalization hypothesis developed by Bergström and Södersten (1976), King (1977) and Auerbach (1979) in order to explain why q for the corporate sector may differ from unity for tax reasons. However, recognizing the potential for firms to engage in arbitrage in physical capital as soon as market values quoted in the stock exchange differ from replacement values of the underlying stocks of capital, it seems likely that strong forces work in the direction of equilibrating corporate q at a value of unity in the long run. See Gordon and Bradford (1980) for empirical evidence supporting this view.

16 The reason is that the representative firm's real gain from nominal interest deductions (assuming unchanged behavior of the firm) is a linear function of the expected inflation rate, while it can be shown that the real loss associated with historic cost depreciation is an increasing strictly concave function of the inflation rate. This implies that at low rates of inflation the real loss of depreciation allowances will dominate the gains from nominal interest deductions; consequently, indexing the corporate income tax will then decrease tax payments. However, as the inflation rate rises, the real gain from nominal interest deductions will eventually overtake the accumulated real losses of historic cost depreciation, which in turn implies that indexation now leads to increased expected tax payments. See Hasbrouck (1983) and Agell (1986) for further analysis.

17 Mansur and Whalley (1984) provide a good exposition of alternative econometric methods for estimating the unknown parameters of applied general equilibrium models. However, the complexities of the econometric approach have so far made most researchers prefer the deterministic calibration procedure (but see Jorgenson and Yun, 1986a, b, for an exception).

References

Agell, J. (1986) *The Effects of Capital Taxation: An Equilibrium Asset Market Approach*, Stockholm: Almqvist & Wiksell International.

——and P.-A. Edin (1989) "Marginal Taxes and the Asset Portfolios of Swedish Households", Stockholm: Trade Union Institute for Economic Research, Working Paper No. 58.

Atkinson, A., and J. Stiglitz (1980) *Lectures on Public Economics*, New York: McGraw-Hill.

Auerbach, A. (1979) "Share Valuation and Corporate Equity Policy", *Journal of Public Economics*, 11, 291–305.

Bailey, M. J. (1969) "Capital Gains and Income Taxation", in A. Harberger and M. J. Bailey (eds), *The Taxation of Income from Capital*, Washington, DC: Brookings Institution.

Barro, R. (1974) "Are Government Bonds Net Worth?", *Journal of Political Economy*, 82, 1095–117.

Bergström, V. and J. Södersten (1976) "Double Taxation and Corporate

Capital Cost", Stockholm: Industrial Research Institute, Working Paper No. 9.

Brainard, W., and J. Tobin (1968) "Pitfalls in Financial Model Building", *American Economic Review*, 58, 99–122.

Brennan, M. (1970) "Taxes, Market Valuation, and Corporate Financial Policy", *National Tax Journal*, 23, 417–27.

Bulow, J., and L. Summers (1984) "The Taxation of Risky Assets", *Journal of Political Economy*, 92, 20–39.

Cox, J., J. Ingersoll and S. Ross (1985) "An Intertemporal General Equilibrium Model of Asset Prices", *Econometrica*, 53, 363–84.

Domar, E., and R. Musgrave (1944) "Proportional Income Taxation and Risk-taking", *Quarterly Journal of Economics*, 58, 388–422.

Ebrill, L. P., and U. M. Possen (1982a) "Inflation and the Taxation of Equity in Corporations and Owner-occupied housing", *Journal of Money, Credit and Banking*, 14, 33–47.

—— and —— (1982b) "The Interaction of Taxes and Inflation in a Macroeconomic Model", *Quarterly Journal of Economics*, 97, 231–50.

Feldstein, M. (1976) "Toward a Theory of Tax Reform", *Journal of Public Economics*, 6, 77–104.

—— (1980a) "Inflation, Tax Rules, and the Stock Market", *Journal of Monetary Economics*, 6, 309–31.

—— (1980b) "Inflation and the Stock Market", *American Economic Review*, 70, 839–47.

—— (1980c) "Inflation, Tax Rules, and the Prices of Land and Gold", *Journal of Public Economics*, 14, 309–17.

—— and L. Summers (1978) "Inflation, Tax Rules, and the Long-term Interest Rate", *Brookings Papers on Economic Activity*, 61–109.

Friend, I., and M. Blume (1975) "The Demand for Risky Assets", *American Economic Reviews*, 65, 900–22.

—— and J. Hasbrouck (1982) "The Effect of Inflation on the Profitability and Valuation of US Corporations", in M. Sarnat and G. Szegö (eds), *Saving Investment, and Capital Markets in an Inflationary Economy*, Cambridge, MA: Ballinger.

Friedman, B., and V. Roley (1979) "A Note on the Derivation of Linear Homogeneous Asset Demand Functions", mimeo, Department of Economics, Harvard University.

Gordon, R. H., and D. Bradford (1980) "Taxation and the Stock Market Valuation of Capital Gains and Dividends", *Journal of Public Economics*, 14, 109–36.

Goulder, L., and L. Summers (1987) "Tax Policy, Asset Prices, and Growth: A General Equilibrium Analysis", National Bureau of Economic Research, Working Paper No. 2128.

Grossman, S., and R. Shiller (1981) "The Determinants of the Variability of Stock Market Prices", *American Economic Review*, 71, 222–7.

Hasbrouck, J. (1983) "The Impact of Inflation upon Corporate Taxation", *National Tax Journal*, 36, 65–81.

Hayashi, F. (1982) "Tobin's Marginal q and Average q: A Neoclassical Interpretation", *Econometrica*, 50, 213–24.

Hendershott, P. and C. Hu (1981) "Inflation and Extraordinary Returns to Owner-occupied Housing", *Journal of Macroeconomics*, 3, 177–203.

Hicks, J. (1978) *Value and Capital*, 2nd edn, Oxford: Oxford University Press.

Johansen, L. (1960) *A Multi-sectoral Study of Economic Growth*, Amsterdam: North-Holland.

Jorgenson, D., and K.-Y. Yun (1986a) "The Efficiency of Capital Allocation", *Scandinavian Journal of Economics*, 88 (1), 85–107.

—— and —— (1986b) "Tax Policy and Capital Allocation", *Scandinavian Journal of Economics*, 88 (2) 355–77.

King, M. (1977) *Public Policy and the Corporation*, London: Chapman and Hall.

—— and D. Fullerton (eds) (1984) *The Taxation of Income from Capital: A Comparative Study of the US., UK, Sweden and West-Germany*, Chicago, IL: University of Chicago Press.

—— and J. Leape (1984) "Wealth and Portfolio Composition: Theory and Evidence", London: Economic and Social Research Programme in Taxation, Incentives, and the Distribution of Income, Research Report No. 68.

Lintner, J. (1969) "The Aggregation of Investor's Diverse Judgements and Preferences in Purely Competitive Security Markets", *Journal of Financial and Quantitative Analysis*, 4, 347–400.

Mansur, A., and J. Whalley (1984) "Numerical Specification of Applied General Equilibrium Models: Estimation, Calibration and Data", in H. Scarf and J. Shoven (eds), *Applied General Equilibrium Analysis*, Cambridge: Cambridge University Press.

Pindyck, R. (1984) "Risk, Inflation, and the Stock Market", *American Economic Review*, 74, 335–51.

Poterba, J. (1984) "Tax Subsidies to Owner-occupied Housing: An Asset-market Approach", *Quarterly Journal of Economics*, 99, 729–52.

Sandmo, A. (1985) "The Effects of Taxation on Savings and Risk-taking", in A. Auerbach and M. Feldstein (eds), *Handbook of Public Economics*, Amsterdam: North-Holland.

Shoven, J., and J. Whalley (1972) "A General Equilibrium Calculation of the Effects of Differential Taxation of Income from Capital in the US', *Journal of Public Economics*, 1, 281–321.

Smith, G., and W. Starnes (1979) "A Short-run Two-sector Model with Immobile Capital", *Journal of Money, Credit and Banking*, 11, 47–67.

Stiglitz, J. (1969) "The Effects of Income, Wealth and Capital Gains Taxes on Risk-taking," *Quarterly Journal of Economics*, 83, 262-83.

—— (1970) "A Consumption-oriented Theory of the Demand for Financial Assets and the Term Structure of Interest Rates", *Review of Economic Studies*, 37, 321–51.

Summers, L. (1981a) "Taxation and Corporate Investment: A q-theory Approach", *Brookings Papers on Economic Activity*, 67–127.

—— (1981b) "Inflation, the Stock Market, and Owner-occupied Housing", *American Economic Review*, 71, 429–34.

—— (1985) "The Asset Price Approach to the Analysis of Capital Income Taxation, in G. Feiwel (ed.), *Issues in Contemporary Macroeconomics and Distribution*, London: Macmillan.

Tobin, J. (1969) "A General Equilibrium Approach to Monetary Theory", *Journal of Money, Credit, and Banking*, 1, 15–29.

3

Tax Policy and US Economic Growth

Dale W. Jorgenson and Kun-Young Yun

1 Introduction

The purpose of this paper is to evaluate the impact of the Tax Reform Act of 1986 on US economic growth. We also analyze the potential impact of proposals for tax reform that figured prominently in the debate leading up to the the 1986 tax reform. First we consider in detail proposals advanced by the Department of the Treasury and by President Ronald Reagan since these proposals were instrumental in shaping the final legislation.[1] Second, we assess the potential impact of a number of hypothetical tax reform proposals that embody notions of neutrality in the treatment of different kinds of income. The results of this analysis are useful in suggesting fruitful directions for further tax reform.

Harberger (1962, 1966) has argued that the US tax system leads to a loss of efficiency in the allocation of resources, since it fails to impose a uniform tax rate on the capital used in competing economic activities. There have been wide gaps between the rates of return on investment before and after taxes for assets employed in different sectors and among assets in different durability categories. However, the argument that the efficiency of capital allocation requires a uniform tax rate holds only under the restrictive assumption that the allocation of capital is separable from the allocation of other resources in production and consumption. In a more general setting, the uniformity of tax treatment of different kinds of income from capital is neither necessary nor sufficient for efficient resource allocation.[2]

Harberger's analysis of the impact of tax policy on the efficiency of capital allocation is limited to the allocation of a given capital stock.[3] However, saving behavior may be affected by changes in tax policy, so that the capital stock must be determined endogenously in order to assess the economic impact of tax reform.[4] In addition, the notion of efficiency in the allocation of resources must be extended to encompass intertemporal allocations. The absence of tax distortions in the intertemporal allocation of resources requires that income from capital should not be taxed at all. A possible approach to eliminating taxes on capital income is to replace corporate and individual income taxes on capital with taxes on labor income. An alternative approach is to replace income taxes by tax on consumption expenditures.[5]

The argument for eliminating capital income taxes ignores the fact that distortions in resource allocation resulting from these taxes must be replaced by other tax-induced distortions. For example, labor income accounts for roughly 60 percent of US private national income and a very substantial proportion of US tax revenues. The taxation of labor income has received much less attention than the taxation of capital income. However, it is well established that, even though the price elasticity of labor supply is very low, there is a substantial substitution effect that is similar in magnitude but opposite in sign to the income effect of a change in the wage rate.[6] It is the substitution effect, not the total price effect, that is relevant to the impact of a tax on labor income on economic efficiency. The taxation of labor income has important implications for economic efficiency through its effect on the choice between labor and leisure.

Major tax legislation like the Tax Reform Act of 1986 can produce substantial alterations in the rate of accumulation of capital and the allocation of capital among sectors and different types of assets. An assessment of the impact of tax reform depends not only on the changes in tax policy but also on the elasticities of substitution along all the relevant margins. The intertemporal margin, involving the allocation of resources between present and future consumption, is essential to the evaluation of the consequences of tax reform involving changes in the treatment of income from capital. We conclude that a fully dynamic model of the economy is required for measuring the impact of the tax reform on economic welfare.

In order to evaluate the economic impact of alternative tax reform proposals – the Treasury proposal, the President's proposal and the Tax Reform Act of 1986 – we employ a dynamic general equilibrium model. This model provides a highly schematic representation of the US economy. A single representative producer employs capital and labor services to produce outputs of consumption and investment goods. We have simplified the representation of technology by introducing a single stock of capital at each point in time. This capital is perfectly malleable and is allocated so as to equalize after-tax rates to equity in the corporate, noncorporate and household sectors.

Our model also incorporates a representative consumer that supplies labor services, demands consumption goods and makes choices between consumption and saving. This model of consumer behavior is based on an intertemporally additive utility function that depends on levels of full consumption in all time periods. Full consumption is an aggregate of consumption goods, household capital services and leisure. To simplify the representation of preferences we endow the representative consumer with an infinite lifetime and perfect foresight about future prices. We have fitted econometric models of producer and consumer behavior to data for the US economy covering the period 1947–86.[7]

In our model the equilibrium of the US economy is characterized by an intertemporal price system that clears the markets for all four commodity groups included in the model – labor and capital services and consumption and investment goods. Equilibrium at each point in time links the past and the future through markets for investment goods and capital services. Assets are accumulated as a result of past investments, while the price of an asset must be equal to the present value of future capital services. The time path of consumption must satisfy the conditions for intertemporal optimality of the household sector under perfect foresight.[8] Similarly, the time path of investment must satisfy requirements for the accumulation of assets by both business and household sectors.

The government sector of the US economy raises revenues through taxes on income from capital and labor services. Corporate capital income is taxed at both corporate and individual levels, noncorporate capital income is taxed only at the individual level and household capital income is not subject to income taxation. In addition, the government sector imposes sales taxes on the production of consumption and investment goods and property taxes on assets held by the business and household sectors. Taxes insert wedges between demand and supply prices for investment and consumption goods and for capital and labor services. These tax wedges distort private decisions and lead to losses in efficiency.

In order to evaluate alternative tax policies, we first consider the intertemporal equilibrium associated with each policy. Under perfect foresight there is a unique transition path to balanced growth equilibrium corresponding to any tax policy and any initial level of capital. The growth path of the US economy consists of a plan for consumption of goods and leisure at every point in time by the representative consumer and a plan for production of investment and consumption goods from capital and labor services at any point in time by the representative producer. These plans are brought into consistency by the intertemporal price system.

Associated with each tax policy and the corresponding intertemporal equilibrium is a level of welfare for the representative consumer. This level of welfare can be interpreted as a measure of economic efficiency corresponding to the potential level of welfare for society as a whole. The actual level of welfare also depends on the distribution of welfare among consuming units. To evaluate changes in tax policy in terms of efficiency we translate changes in potential welfare into an equivalent change in private national wealth. We first consider the time path of the price of full consumption associated with current tax policy. We then evaluate the difference in wealth required to attain levels of potential welfare before and after the change in tax policy at prices prevailing before the policy change.

The arrangement of this paper is as follows. In section 2, we summarize the 1986 tax reform, the Treasury proposal and the President's proposal in terms of changes in tax rates, the treatment of deductions from income for tax purposes, the availability of tax credits and provisions for indexing taxable income for inflation. In section 3, we analyze the tax burdens on capital income under four alternative tax policy regimes: the tax law in effect prior to the 1986 tax reform, the Treasury proposal, the President's proposal and the Tax Reform Act of 1986. We utilize the concept of an effective tax rate, which summarizes the statutory tax rates and the provisions of a given tax law that affect the definition of taxable income. We also employ the notion of a tax wedge, defined in terms of differences in tax burdens imposed on different types of income.

In section 4 of the paper we analyze the impact of each of the alternative tax policies on US economic growth. We evaluate the effects of changes in tax policy on economic efficiency by measuring the corresponding changes in potential economic welfare. The reference level of welfare, which serves as the basis of comparison among alternative tax policies, is the level attainable by the US economy under the tax law in effect prior to the 1986 tax reform. We also analyze the losses in efficiency associated with tax wedges between different kinds of capital income. These tax wedges are the consequences of the corporate and personal income taxes, property taxes and sales taxes on investment goods.

Section 5 provides a summary of the paper and presents our main conclusions. Our conclusions are, first, that much of the potential gain in welfare from the 1986 tax reform was dissipated through failure to index the income tax base for inflation. At rates of inflation near zero the loss is not substantial. However, at moderate rates of inflation like those prevailing for the past decade, the loss is highly significant. Second, the greatest welfare gains would have resulted from integrating the income from household assets into the tax base while reducing the tax rates on capital income in the business sector. This approach to tax policy played a minor role in the debates leading up to the Tax Reform Act of 1986. Third, the potential welfare gains from an income-based tax system, reconstructed along these lines, would have exceeded those from a consumption-based tax system.

2 The 1986 Tax Reform

When the Reagan Administration took office in 1981, there was widespread concern about the slowdown in US economic growth. Federal tax policy was viewed by the new Administration as a major barrier to improved economic performance. Tax reform proposals by the Administration received overwhelming support from the Congress with the enactment of the Economic Recovery Tax Act (ERTA) of 1981.[9] The 1981 Tax Act combined sizable enhancement in investment incentives with substantial reductions in statutory tax rates for individuals and corporations.

The 1981 Tax Act introduced multiyear cuts in statutory tax rates at both individual and corporate levels with the aim of improving incentives "to work, save, and invest, consistent with the goal of eliminating the Federal budget deficit by 1984" (Joint Committee on Taxation, 1981). Prior to the 1981 Tax Act statutory tax rates under the individual income tax ranged from 14 to 70 percent of taxable income over 14 tax brackets. However, important categories of income were excluded from the tax base. For example, only 40 percent of capital gains were included in income for tax purposes, so that the top rate for capital gains taxation was only 28 percent. There were four statutory tax brackets for corporate income with a top rate 46 percent.

The 1981 Tax Act cut the statutory tax rates for individuals by 23 percent over the years 1982–4 – 10 percent in 1982, another 10 percent in 1983 and a final 5 percent in 1984.[10] As a consequence of the multiyear reductions in statutory tax rates, the range of marginal tax rates for individuals was narrowed from 14–70 percent of taxable income to 11–50 percent. The 1981 Act also reduced corporate tax rates for the lowest two income brackets from 17 to 15 percent and from 20 to 18 percent over the years 1982–3.

2.1 The 1986 Tax Law

In describing the key features of the Tax Reform Act of 1986, we find it useful to begin with a description of the pre-existing tax law in order to provide a basis for comparison. We refer to this law as the 1986 Tax Law since it remained in force until the end of calendar year 1986. To provide additional perspective on the objectives of the

1986 tax reform, we also characterize two alternative tax reform proposals presented by the Department of the Treasury and the President. We summarize the statutory tax rates under the 1986 Tax Law, the Treasury and the President's proposals and the 1986 Tax Reform Act in table 3.1. We summarize the definition of income for tax purposes in table 3.2.

The second column in table 3.1 gives average marginal tax rates for different types of income under the 1986 Tax Law for 0, 6 and 10 percent annual inflation rates. The tax rate on each type of income is a weighted average of marginal tax rates paid by taxpayers in all income tax brackets. Average tax rates on different types of income reflect differences in the distribution of each type of income over the tax brackets. We present rates for income in the form of dividends and other distributions on corporate and noncorporate equity, for capital gains accruing on corporate and noncorporate equity and for interest on corporate, noncorporate, household and government debt.[11]

We also give the average marginal tax rate on labor income, the average marginal tax rate on income under the corporate income tax and the average tax rate under the individual income tax. All tax

Table 3.1 Tax rates

	1986 law	Treasury proposals	President's proposals	1986 Act
Average marginal tax rates of individual capital income				
0% annual inflation				
TEQ	0.2555	0.2261	0.2240	0.2029
TEM	0.2934	0.2427	0.2572	0.2494
TGQ	0.0303	0.0596	0.0325	0.0562
TGM	0.0293	0.0607	0.0322	0.0624
TDQ	0.1533	0.1452	0.1532	0.1285
TDM	0.1971	0.1805	0.1912	0.1670
TDH	0.2717	0.2252	0.2387	0.2310
TDG	0.2205	0.1868	0.1970	0.1852
6% annual inflation				
TEQ	0.2559	0.2261	0.2240	0.2033
TEM	0.2934	0.2427	0.2572	0.2494
TGQ	0.0303	0.0596	0.0600	0.0562
TGM	0.0293	0.0607	0.0643	0.0624
TDQ	0.1730	0.1452	0.1532	0.1434
TDM	0.2151	0.1805	0.1912	0.1807
TDH	0.2722	0.2252	0.2387	0.2314
TDG	0.2260	0.1868	0.1970	0.1894

Table 3.1 (*cont.*)

	1986 Law	Treasury proposals	President's proposals	1986 Act
Average marginal tax rates of individual capital income				
10% annual inflation				
TEQ	0.2560	0.2261	0.2240	0.2034
TEM	0.2934	0.2427	0.2572	0.2494
TGQ	0.0303	0.0596	0.0600	0.0562
TGM	0.0293	0.0607	0.0643	0.0624
TDQ	0.1806	0.1452	0.1532	0.1492
TDM	0.2222	0.1805	0.1912	0.1861
TDH	0.2724	0.2252	0.2387	0.2315
TDG	0.2282	0.1868	0.1970	0.1910

Marginal tax rates of labor income, corporate income and average personal tax rates

	1986 Law	Treasury proposals	President's proposals	1986 Act
TLM	0.2967	0.2512	0.2536	0.2517
TQ	0.5084	0.4006	0.4006	0.3847
TAP	0.1315	0.1203	0.1223	0.1233

Tax rates held constant across the alternative tax policies
TPQ = 0.0100   TPM = 0.0096   TPH = 0.0100
TC = 0.0579   TI = 0.0579
TT = 0.0229
TW = 0.0006

We set TEH = TEM and TGH = 0.
TEQ, TEM, TEH, average marginal tax rates of individual income accruing to corporate, noncorporate and household equities, respectively.
TGQ, TGM, TGH, average marginal tax rates of capital gains accruing to corporate, noncorporate and household equities, respectively.
TDQ, TDM, TDH, TDG, average marginal tax rates of interest income accruing to corporate, noncorporate, household and government debts, respectively.
TLM, average marginal tax rate of labor income.
TQ, corporate income tax rate (Federal + state and local).
TAP, average tax rate of individual income; the Treasury proposal, the President's proposal, and the 1986 Tax Reform Act are assumed to reduce TAP by 8.5 percent, 7.0 percent, and 6.2 percent, respectively.
TPQ, TPM, TPH, property tax rates of corporate, noncorporate and household assets, respectively.
TC, TI, sales tax rates of consumption and investment goods.
TT, rate of personal nontaxes.
TW, effective rate of wealth taxation.

rates include taxes levied at both Federal levels and state and local levels and take into account the deductibility of state and local taxes at the Federal level. In projecting US economic growth under the 1986 Tax Law we take the average marginal tax rates on each type of

Table 3.2 Indexing and deduction of capital incomes

	1986 Law	Treasury proposals	President's proposals	1986 Act
Indexing				
DC	0.0	1.0	0.0 (1.0)[a]	0.0
DI	0.0	INF/(0.06 + INF)	0.0	0.0
HDI	0.0	0.0	0.0	0.0
Deduction of capital income				
DD	0.0	0.5	0.1	0.0
ICDD	0.85	0.50	0.90	0.80
IRCR	0.0	1.0	1.0	0.0
DHI	1.0	1.0	1.0	1.0
Inclus	0.4	1.0	0.5 (1.0)[a]	1.0
Deduction of state and local taxes				
DSLI	1.0	0.0	0.0	1.0
DSLQ	1.0	1.0	1.0	1.0
DSLM	1.0	1.0	1.0	1.0
DSLH	1.0	0.0	0.0	1.0

DC, indexing of long-term capital gains; DC = 1.0 for complete indexing.
DI, indexing of interest income and interest expenses of the corporate and noncorporate sectors; DI = 1.0 for complete indexing.
HDI, indexing of household interest payment.
DD, deduction of dividend paid for corporate tax purposes.
ICDD, deduction of intercorporate dividends received.
IRCR, fraction of accrual-based taxation of life insurance company's inside build-up.
DHI, deduction of household interest expenses.
Inclus, fraction of long-term capital gains taxed as ordinary income.
DSLI, deduction of state and local income taxes.
DSLQ, deduction of state and local other taxes, corporate.
DSLM, deduction of state and local other taxes, noncorporate.
DSLH, deduction of state and local other taxes, household.
INF, annual rate of inflation.
[a]Beginning in 1991, instead of excluding 50 percent of long-term capital gains, taxpayers will have the option of 100 percent inclusion and complete indexing. We assume that if inflation is higher than 6 percent taxpayers choose indexing.

income and the average individual income tax rate as fixed. Tax revenues received by the government are generated by applying these tax rates to streams of income generated endogenously within our model of US economic growth.

Prior to the 1981 Tax Act, the time period for capital cost recovery was based on the "useful life" of an asset. Under the 1981 Tax Act useful lifetimes were replaced by a highly simplified system of "tax lifetimes". The purpose of the new system was to reduce the burden of taxation on income from capital with the aim of promoting a higher level of capital formation. Tax lifetimes were considerably shorter than the corresponding useful lives and resulted in more rapid recovery of capital costs. Investment outlays on producers' durable equipment could be recovered over a five-year tax lifetime. A three-year lifetime was applied to automobiles, light trucks, special tools and property used in connection with research and experimentation. Lifetimes of ten and 15 years were employed for public utility property. Structures were also assigned a tax lifetime of 15 years.

The 1981 Tax Act provided three statutory schedules for capital consumption allowances for each category of investment expenditures on producers' durables: the first for property placed in service during the years 1981–4, the second for property placed in service in 1985 and the third for property placed in service after 1985. These three schedules provided for a gradual increase in the rates at which capital costs could be recovered. For structures the 1981 Tax Act provided a single schedule for capital cost recovery.

Prior to the 1981 Tax Act, a 10 percent investment tax credit was allowed for assets with a useful life of seven years or more. Two-thirds of the regular credit was allowed for assets with a useful life of five to six years and one-third of the credit for assets with a useful life of three to four years. The 1981 Tax Act made the investment tax credit more generous by allowing the 10 percent credit for assets with five-year, ten-year and 15-year tax lifetimes. The tax credit was applied to tangible property included in buildings such as elevators, but the structural components of buildings were excluded. The 1981 Tax Act permitted 60 percent of the regular credit for assets with a tax lifetime of three years. In addition to shortening capital recovery periods and liberalizing the investment tax credit, the 1981 Tax Act reduced the burden of taxation on capital by lowering individual income tax rates and introducing so-called "safe harbor" leasing rules.

The 1981 Tax Act involved tax reductions across the board and created the prospect of rising Federal deficits. Only one year after the 1981 Tax Act the Congress passed the Tax Equity and Fiscal Responsibility Act of 1982 (TEFRA), which repealed the provisions of the 1981 Act for phasing in more accelerated cost recovery system for property placed in service in 1985 and after. In addition, the 1982 Tax Act reduced the capital cost to be amortized over the tax lifetime of the asset by 50 percent of the investment tax credit. After a transitional period, the 1982 Tax Act repealed the safe harbour leasing provisions on January 1, 1984. In table 3.3 we present

economic depreciation rates for each of 51 classes of assets distinguished in the US national income and production accounts. We also
gave statutory rates of the investment tax credit and tax lifetimes
under the 1986 Tax Law, the Treasury and President's proposals and
the Tax Reform Act of 1986.[12] In table 3.4, column 1, we present
average rates of the investment tax credit and the present values of
capital consumption allowances for short-lived and long-lived business
assets under the 1986 Tax Law, prior to the enactment of the Tax
Reform Act of 1986. Short-lived assets include all types of producers'
durable equipment employed in the business sector. Long-lived assets
include residential and nonresidential structures, land and inventories.

2.2 The Treasury proposal

The tax reforms of the early 1980s substantially reduced the burden
of taxation on capital income. However, these reforms also introduced important non-neutralities in the taxation of income from
different sources. Differences in the tax treatment of different types
of assets gave rise to concerns in Congress about the fairness of the
tax system and the impact of tax-induced distortions on the efficiency
of capital allocation. In the State of the Union Address in January
1984 President Reagan announced that he had requested a plan for
further tax reform from the Department of the Treasury.

In November 1984 the Treasury Department presented a tax
reform plan that became known as the Treasury proposal. A principal
objective of the Treasury plan was to reduce statutory tax rates at
both individual and corporate levels. However, the Treasury plan was
intended to be "revenue neutral", so as to produce the same revenue
as the existing tax system.[13] Lower statutory tax rates were to be
offset by eliminating a wide range of tax preferences, greatly
broadening the tax base. In addition, the plan had the objective of
introducing greater neutrality in the tax treatment of different types
of assets. The Treasury proposed to offset the decreased progressivity
of the rate structure by curtailing tax preferences heavily used by high
income taxpayers and reducing the tax burden for low income earners
through increased personal exemptions and zero bracket amounts for
household heads.

Under the 1986 Tax Law the rate structure for the individual
income tax consisted of 14 separate tax brackets with statutory tax
rates ranging from 11 to 50 percent of taxable income. Corporate
income was taxed under a graduated rate structure with a top rate of
46 percent. The Treasury plan proposed to replace the 14 individual
income tax brackets with three broader brackets. Individual income

Table 3.3 Tax lives, investment tax credit, and economic rate of depreciation

Asset	DEL	ITC85	BEA	LAW86	TREAS	PRESID	ACT86
1	0.138	0.10	12.0	5.0	17.0	7.0	5.0
2	0.118	0.10	14.0	5.0	17.0	7.0	7.0
3	0.092	0.10	18.0	5.0	17.0	7.0	7.0
4	0.052	0.10	32.0	10.0	25.0	10.0	15.0
5	0.206	0.10	8.0	10.0	25.0	10.0	10.0
6	0.145	0.10	9.0	5.0	12.0	6.0	7.0
7	0.163	0.10	8.0	5.0	12.0	6.0	5.0
8	0.118	0.10	14.0	5.0	17.0	7.0	7.0
9	0.172	0.10	10.0	5.0	12.0	6.0	5.0
10	0.150	0.10	11.0	5.0	12.0	6.0	7.0
11	0.123	0.09	16.0	5.0	17.0	7.0	5.0
12	0.103	0.10	16.0	5.0	17.0	7.0	7.0
13	0.123	0.10	16.0	5.0	17.0	7.0	7.0
14	0.273	0.10	8.0	5.0	8.0	5.0	5.0
15	0.165	0.10	10.0	5.0	12.0	6.0	5.0
16	0.110	0.10	15.0	7.0	17.0	7.0	10.0
17	0.050	0.10	33.0	7.0	17.0	7.0	10.0
18	0.165	0.10	10.0	5.0	17.0	7.0	5.0
19	0.183	0.10	9.0	5.0	17.0	7.0	5.0
20	0.254	0.07	9.0	5.0	8.0	5.0	5.0
21	0.333	0.06	10.0	3.0	5.0	4.0	5.0
22	0.183	0.10	16.0	5.0	12.0	6.0	7.0
23	0.061	0.10	27.0	5.0	25.0	10.0	10.0
24	0.055	0.10	30.0	5.0	25.0	7.0	7.0
25	0.135	0.10	12.0	7.0	12.0	6.0	7.0
26	0.180	0.10	9.0	5.0	12.0	6.0	5.0
27	0.147	0.10	11.0	5.0	12.0	6.0	5.0
28	0.036	0.03	31.0	19.0	63.0	28.0	31.5
29	0.056	0.00	16.0	19.0	63.0	28.0	31.5
30	0.025	0.00	36.0	19.0	63.0	28.0	31.5
31	0.022	0.00	40.0	19.0	63.0	28.0	31.5
32	0.026	0.07	34.0	10.0	17.0	7.0	15.0
33	0.019	0.00	48.0	19.0	63.0	28.0	31.5
34	0.019	0.00	48.0	19.0	63.0	28.0	31.5
35	0.023	0.00	48.0	19.0	63.0	28.0	31.5
36	0.025	0.00	32.0	19.0	63.0	28.0	31.5
37	0.047	0.10	30.0	10.0	17.0	7.0	15.0
38	0.037	0.00	38.0	19.0	63.0	28.0	31.5
39	0.017	0.10	54.0	5.0	38.0	10.0	7.0
40	0.023	0.08	40.0	10.0	38.0	10.0	15.0
41	0.023	0.10	40.0	15.0	38.0	10.0	20.0
42	0.023	0.06	40.0	10.0	38.0	10.0	20.0
43	0.045	0.10	38.0	5.0	38.0	10.0	5.0
44	0.045	0.10	40.0	5.0	38.0	10.0	15.0
45	0.024	0.00	38.0	19.0	63.0	28.0	20.0

Table 3.3 (*cont.*)

Asset	DEL	ITC85	BEA	LAW86	TREAS	PRESID	ACT86
46	0.056	0.10	16.0	5.0	38.0	7.0	7.0
47	0.056	0.10	16.0	5.0	38.0	7.0	7.0
48	0.023	0.00	40.0	19.0	63.0	28.0	31.5
49	0.024	0.10	38.0	5.0	38.0	10.0	7.0
50	0.250	0.10	6.0	5.0	12.0	6.0	7.0
51	0.013	0.00		19.0	63.0	28.0	27.5

DEL, economic depreciation rate; ITC85, investment tax credit, 1985; BEA, Bureau of Economic Analysis lifetime; LAW86, 1986 Tax Law, tax lifetime; TREAS, Treasury proposal, tax lifetime; PRESID, the President's proposal, tax lifetime; ACT86, the 1986 Tax Reform Act, tax lifetime.

was to be taxed at statutory rates of 15, 25 and 35 percent. The reduction of statutory income tax rates was expected to lower the average marginal tax rate of individuals by 20 percent and the average individual tax rate by 8.5 percent.

Table 3.1 shows the effect of the Treasury plan on average marginal tax rates. Under the central asumption of 6 percent inflation the average marginal tax rate on income from equity was to be reduced by 11.6 percent – from 25.59 to 22.61 percent – and the corresponding average marginal tax rate on interest from corporate bonds was to be reduced by 16.1 percent – from 17.30 to 14.52 percent. Finally, the average marginal tax rate on labor income was to be reduced by 15.3 percent – from 29.67 to 25.12 percent. Given the constraint that the tax reform proposed by the Treasury was to be revenue neutral, reductions in average marginal tax rates were to be offset by broadening the definition of taxable income at both individual and corporate levels.

Broadening of the income tax base under the Treasury proposal would have been achieved by wholesale elimination of tax preferences for individuals and corporations. For example, the deduction for state and local income taxes would have been repealed and other state and local taxes would have been deductible only to the extent that they were incurred in income-generating activity. Property taxes on owner-occupied residential real estate would not have been deductible. Other proposed changes included the taxation of unemployment compensation, curtailment of the tax deduction for mortgage and other personal interest expenses, elimination of accelerated capital cost recovery, abolition of the investment tax credit, taxation of interest on private purpose municipal bonds, accrual basis taxation of earnings on life insurance policies, recovery of intangible drilling

Table 3.4 Investment tax credit and tax deduction of depreciation allowances

| | | 1 1986 Law | | | | 2 Treasury proposal | | | | 3 President's proposal | | | | 4 1986 Tax Act | | | |
| | | Corporate | | Noncorporate | | Corporate | | Noncorporate | | Corporate | | Noncorporate | | Corporate | | Noncorporate | |
	INF	Short	Long	Short	Long	Short	Long	Short	Long	Short	Long	Short	Long	Short	Long	Short	Long
Investment tax credit	0.00	0.0945	0.0423	0.0954	0.0056	0.0000	0.0000	0.0000	0.0000	0.0000	0.0000	0.0000	0.0000	0.0000	0.0000	0.0000	0.0000
	0.06	0.0944	0.0426	0.0953	0.0057	0.0000	0.0000	0.0000	0.0000	0.0000	0.0000	0.0000	0.0000	0.0000	0.0000	0.0000	0.0000
	0.10	0.0944	0.0427	0.0953	0.0057	0.0000	0.0000	0.0000	0.0000	0.0000	0.0000	0.0000	0.0000	0.0000	0.0000	0.0000	0.0000
Present value of capital consumption allowances	0.00	0.9223	0.6347	0.9204	0.5529	0.8926	0.4997	0.8981	0.3960	0.9471	0.6142	0.9490	0.4843	0.9472	0.5929	0.9515	0.4861
	0.06	0.8755	0.5569	0.8714	0.4609	0.9194	0.5479	0.9237	0.4441	1.0059	0.7320	1.0058	0.6487	0.8714	0.4626	0.8807	0.3407
	0.10	0.8469	0.5156	0.8416	0.4143	0.9275	0.5647	0.9313	0.4610	1.0452	0.8283	1.0437	0.7925	0.8281	0.4058	0.8397	0.2807

INF, annual rate of inflation.

costs in the production of petroleum and natural gas through amortization rather than immediate expensing, and many others.

The Treasury proposal included extensive provisions for indexing income and deductions from income for tax purposes for inflation. This proposal would have retained the indexing of tax brackets, personal exemptions and zero bracket amounts from the 1981 Tax Act to prevent the upward creep of tax brackets as a consequence of inflation. In addition, the proposal would have indexed capital gains, interest expenses, interest income, first-in–first-out (FIFO) inventory accounting and capital cost recovery.[14] Prior to the tax reform of 1986, a 60 percent exclusion of net capital gains was allowed as an adjustment of realized capital gains for inflation during the holding period of an asset. With the indexing of capital gains the 60 percent exclusion could no longer be justified as an adjustment for inflation and would have been eliminated under the Treasury proposal.

In order to provide relief from multiple taxation of divided income, the Treasury proposal would have allowed a 50 percent deduction of dividends from corporate income, as defined for tax purposes. In addition, the proposal would have completely eliminated multiple taxation for intercorporate dividends by excluding 50 percent of dividends received by corporations from taxable income. On average about 40–50 percent of after-tax corporate profits are distributed to the shareholders in the form of dividends, so that these provisions would have significantly reduced the tax burden on corporate equity. Column 2 of table 3.2 summarizes the key provisions of the Treasury proposal.

Utilization of the economic concept of income as the base for income taxation requires that capital cost recovery must coincide with economic depreciation. To achieve this objective the Treasury proposal would have classified producers' durable equipment into five-, eight-, 12-, 17- and 25-year property and structures into two categories with tax lives of 38 and 63 years. The corresponding annual rates of depreciation were 0.32, 0.24, 0.18, 0.12 and 0.8 for producers' durables and 0.05 and 0.03 for structures. In addition, the Treasury proposal would have indexed capital cost recovery for inflation. Table 3.4, columns 1 and 2 show that capital cost recovery under the Treasury proposal would have been more favorable than under the 1986 Tax Law for both short-lived and long-lived assets at a high rate of inflation; the reverse is true at a low rate of inflation.[15]

2.3 The President's proposal

The Treasury tax reform plan resulted in a great public outcry, especially among taxpayers who would have been adversely affected by the elimination of tax preferences. However, the rate reductions in the proposal attracted widespread approval and considerable public support. The Reagan Administration did not endorse the Treasury plan but set the Treasury staff to work on a revised proposal, duly delivered in May 1985.[16] The second Treasury tax reform was endorsed by the Administration and became known as the President's proposal. Not surprisingly, this proposal combined substantial reduction in tax rates at both individual and corporate levels with base broadening through the elimination of tax preferences.

The President's proposal would have followed the Treasury proposal by taxing individual income in only three tax brackets with statutory rates of 15, 25 and 35 percent. The President's proposal would also have raised personal exemptions and zero bracket amounts in order to compensate low income taxpayers for the loss in progressivity of the tax structure. The President's proposal would have maintained the favorable treatment of long-term capital gains under the 1986 Tax Law but would have reduced the proportion of capital gains excluded from income from 60 to 50 percent. In addition, beginning in 1991 taxpayers would have had the option of electing exclusion of 50 percent of capital gains from income for tax purposes or 100 percent inclusion of capital gains with complete indexing.

Under the President's proposal the corporate tax rate would have been graduated up to a top rate of 33 percent and corporate capital gains would have been taxed at a lower rate of 28 percent, as under the 1986 Tax Law. Table 3.1 shows the impact of the proposal on average marginal tax rates. These changes would have lowered the average marginal tax rates at the individual level by 19 percent and the average individual tax rate by 7 percent. We find that average marginal tax rates under the Treasury and President's proposals are similar, except that the tax rates on interest and labor income would have been slightly higher under the President's proposal.[17]

Like the Treasury proposal, the President's proposal was intended to produce the same tax revenue as the 1986 Tax Law. In order to offset the sharply lower statutory tax rates, the tax base would have been broadened by curtailing or eliminating tax preferences at both individual and corporate levels. In addition, many preferences favoring high income taxpayers would have been limited or abolished on grounds of fairness. Important changes in the list of tax preferences would have included the repeal of the investment tax credit, repeal of the deductibility of state and local income taxes and accrual-based taxation of earnings on life insurance policies.

Unlike the Treasury proposal, however, the President's proposal would not have indexed interest income and expenses. When combined with the option of indexing capital gains, this feature of the proposal would have reduced the cost of capital for projects with debt financing. Another implication of the deduction of nominal interest expenses is apparent in table 3.4, column 3, the present value of capital consumption allowances for short-lived assets is slightly greater than unity when inflation is 6 or 10 percent per year. Under our assumption that an increase in the rate of inflation would result in a point for point increase in the nominal rate of interest, the after-tax real interest rate becomes negative above a certain inflation rate.[18] The present value for long-lived assets in table 3.4, column 3, is smaller than unity only because our category of long-lived assets includes land and inventories as well as depreciable assets.

In order to alleviate multiple taxation of income from corporate equity, the President's proposal would have allowed a deduction of 10 percent of dividends paid from corporate income. Double taxation of intercorporate dividends would have been eliminated by excluding 90 percent of dividends received by corporations from taxable income. The President's proposal would have had the same effect as the Treasury proposal on the double taxation of intercorporate dividends, but it would have had less impact on double taxation at corporate and individual levels. Table 3.2, column 3, summarizes the specific provisions of the President's proposal pertaining to taxation of income capital.

The President's proposal would have replaced the Accelerated Cost Recovery System (ACRS) of the 1981 Tax Law with a new Capital Cost Recovery System (CCRS). An important difference from the Treasury proposal is that CCRS would have permitted accelerated capital cost recovery in order to provide systematic incentives for investments that are neutral across asset classes. Producers' durable equipment would have been classified into four-, five-, six-, seven- and ten-year capital cost recovery classes. Structures would have been assigned to a 28-year class. Furthermore, capital cost recovery under CCRS would have been indexed against inflation. This is one of the most important ideas carried over from the Treasury proposal.

2.4 The Tax Reform Act of 1986

The lengthy debate over tax reform was brought to a conclusion on October 22, 1986, by enactment of the Tax Reform Act of 1986. The main provisions of the new tax law took effect on January 1, 1987.[19] The Tax Reform Act preserved many features of the Treasury and President's proposals. The final legislation resulted in sharply lower tax rates for both individuals and corporations. The highest statutory tax rate for individuals was lowered from 50 to 28 percent.[20] The corresponding rate for corporations was lowered from 46 to 34 percent. The substantial reductions in tax rates were offset by sharp cutbacks in tax preferences for both individuals and corporations.

Table 3.1 shows that the tax reform reduced average marginal tax rates on various types of income in approximately the same proportion as the Treasury and President's proposals. For example, if the annual rate of inflation is assumed to be 6 percent, the average marginal tax rate on individual income from equity is reduced by 20.6 percent – from 25.59 to 20.33 – and the average marginal tax rate on interest income from corporate debt is reduced by 17.1 percent – from 17.30 to 14.34 percent. The reduction in the corporate income tax rate by 24.3 percent – from 50.84 to 38.47 percent – is even more dramatic. By contrast the average marginal tax rate on labor income is reduced by only 15.2 percent – from 29.67 to 25.17 percent.

The magnitude of the 1986 reductions in statutory tax rates for individuals and corporations is very large. It is not surprising that the base for income taxation at both individual and corporate levels had to be broadened very substantially in order to achieve revenue neutrality. Under the 1986 Tax Law individuals, estates and trusts were eligible for a 60 percent exclusion of realized net capital gains from taxable income. Corporations were taxed on capital gains at a rate of 28 percent, which was lower than the statutory corporate tax rate. Under the tax Reform Act of 1986, the 60 percent exclusion of capital gains from taxable income at the individual level was repealed and all corporate capital gains, whether long term or short term, were taxed at the statutory corporate tax rate.

In spite of the reduction in the individual income tax rates, the accrual-based average marginal tax rate on capital gains increased from 3.03 percent under the 1986 Tax Law to 5.62 percent under the Tax Reform Act 1986. The Tax Reform Act did not include a provision for excluding dividend payments from corporate income. In addition, the deductibility of dividends received by corporations was reduced from 85 to 80 percent. This change mainly affected the tax burden on corporate equity owned through life insurance and other insurance companies and had little impact on the overall tax burden on corporate equity.

The Tax Reform Act of 1986 also repealed the 10 percent investment tax credit for property placed in service after December 31, 1985. Since this tax credit was applicable mainly to investments in short-lived business assets, it had been a major source of non-neutralities in the taxation of income from different types of assets. Table 3.4 shows the differential impact of the investment tax credit on the cost of capital for short-lived and long-lived assets in the corporate and noncorporate sectors. Under the 1986 Tax Law the average rate of the investment tax credit in the corporate sector was 9.44 percent for short-lived assets and 4.26 percent for long-lived assets.[21] The repeal of the investment tax credit has substantially reduced differences in the tax treatment of assets of different types.

Compared with the 1986 Tax Law, the Tax Reform Act of 1986 spreads capital cost recovery over longer periods of time. The 1986 Act retains the three-year class, but automobiles, light duty trucks and property used in connection with research and experimentation have been moved to the five-year class. In addition, the 1986 Act provides for seven-, ten-, 15-, and 20-year capital cost recovery classes for equipment. Structures are classified into residential rental property and nonresidential property with tax lives of 27.5 years and 31.5 years, respectively.

Table 3.4 shows that the Tax Reform Act of 1986 increased the present value of capital consumption allowances for short-lived corporate assets at low or moderate rates of inflation and reduced the present value for high rates of inflation. This reflects the repeal of investment tax credit, since the basis of capital cost recovery was reduced by 50 percent of the investment tax credit under the 1986 Tax Law.[22] Capital cost recovery was made less rapid for producers' durable equipment, primarily through longer tax lifetimes. For structures the adoption of longer tax lives works in the same direction, reducing the present value of capital cost recovery.

3 Effective Tax Rates

The tax burden on capital income can be summarized by means of the effective marginal tax rates on income from each type of assets. Effective tax rates represent the complex provisions of tax law in terms of a single *ad valorem* tax rate. This tax rate is based on the social rate of return, defined as income per dollar of capital, adjusted for inflation and depreciation but not for taxes. This social rate of return can be compared with the corresponding private rate of return, which excludes all tax liabilities at both corporate and individual levels. The effective tax rate is defined as the difference between the social and private rates of return, divided by the social rate of return.[23]

To describe the Tax Reform Act of 1986, the pre-existing 1986 Tax Law and the alternative reform proposals presented by the Treasury and the President we present effective tax rates for assets held by three different legal forms of organization – corporate, noncorporate and household – and for short-lived and long-lived assets. We also present tax wedges among different types of assets, defined as differences between social rates of return on these assets. We give tax wedges for transfers between asset categories within a sector, between sectors and between the present and the future. We refer to these as interasset, intersectoral and intertemporal tax wedges.

In generating effective marginal tax rates and tax wedges we have employed parameters describing the alternative tax laws and tax reform proposals from tables 3.1–3.3. In addition, we have set the values of parameters describing the financial structure of each sector, the after-corporate-tax rate of return to corporate capital and the rate of interest at corresponding averages for the 1967–86 period. Property tax rates are set at 1986 values. Finally, we assume that an increase in the rate of inflation raises the nominal rate of interest point for point.

3.1 The 1986 Tax Law

We present effective tax rates under the 1986 Tax Law in table 3.5. With a 6 percent rate of inflation these rates are 2.4 percent for short-lived assets and 4.4 percent for long-lived assets in the corporate sector. The difference in the social rates of return between the two asset classes is 4.0 percent. This tax wedge represents the difference between the marginal productivities of long-lived assets and short-lived assets. Transferring one dollar's worth of capital from short-lived to long-lived assets would increase the national income in perpetuity by four cents per year with no additional investment. This is a very substantial tax wedge, comparable in magnitude with the social rate of return, suggesting that the potential gains from the tax reform are very large.

The provisions of tax law interact with the rate of inflation in determining the tax burden on capital income. First, a higher rate of inflation reduces the present value of capital cost recovery, since cost recovery is not indexed against the impact of inflation. Second, taxation of nominal interest income, coupled with tax deductibility of nominal interest expenses, tends to reduce the tax burden as the rate of inflation increases. For corporate and noncorporate assets the firm's marginal tax rate for the deduction of interest expenses is higher than the individual's marginal tax rate on interest income. On balance the tax burden on corporate and noncorporate assets increases with the rate of inflation.[24] As the rate of inflation rises, the tax burden on short-lived assets increases faster than that on long-lived assets. As a consequence the interasset tax wedge declines with the rate of inflation.

Under the 1986 Tax Law assets in the noncorporate sector have lower tax burdens than corresponding assets in the corporate sector.

Table 3.5 shows that the effective marginal tax rates for short-lived and long-lived assets are −15.2 and 31.2 percent respectively. These rates are substantially lower than the corresponding rates in the corporate sector. The interasset tax wedge between short-lived and long-lived assets is 3.0 percentage points. Although this tax wedge is smaller than that in the corporate sector, the interasset tax wedge in the noncorporate sector suggests substantial opportunities for gains from tax reform.

A striking feature of effective tax rates in the noncorporate sector is that the effective tax rate on short-lived assets is negative. The provisions for capital cost recovery and the investment tax credit are so favorable that the tax system, in effect, provides subsidies to noncorporate investment in short-lived assets. These subsidies take the form of "tax shelter" that can be used to reduce tax liabilities for other types of income. The effects of inflation on the tax burdens and the interasset tax wedge in the noncorporate sector are similar to that in the corporate sector. Inflation increases the tax burden on capital income and reduces the interasset tax wedge.

The value of capital services of household assets, such as the rental equivalent of owner-occupied housing or the services of consumers' durables, is not included in taxable income. However, effective tax rates on household assets are effected by provisions of the individual income tax, since payments for personal and mortgage interest are deductible and interest income from the debt claims on household assets is taxable. Like the assets in the corporate and noncorporate sectors, household assets are also subject to property taxes. Table 3.5 shows that, with 6 percent inflation, the effective tax rate on household assets is 12.7 percent. The rate increases slightly with inflation. Since the income from household assets is not taxable, there is no interasset tax wedge in the household sector.

Table 3.5 shows the intersectoral tax wedge under the 1986 Tax Law for short-lived and long-lived assets. When the rate of inflation is 6 percent per year, the intersectoral tax wedge between the corporate and noncorporate sectors is 0.9 percent for short-lived assets and 1.9 percent for long-lived assets. The wedges between the noncorporate and household sectors are −0.7 percent for short-lived assets and 2.3 percent for long-lived assets. The wedges between the corporate and household sectors are 0.2 percent for short-lived assets and 4.2 percent for long-lived assets. Unlike the interasset tax wedges, the intersectoral tax wedges tend to increase with the rate of inflation, since the tax burden of corporate assets increases faster than that of noncorporate assets, which in turn increases faster than that of household assets.

Table 3.5 Effective tax rates and the distortionary impacts of capital income taxation – 1986 Tax Law

	Corporate	Noncorporate	Household	Corporate–noncorporate	Corporate–household	Noncorporate–household
0% inflation						
Short-lived assets						
SROR	0.049	0.044	0.058			
GAP	−0.007	−0.011	0.007			
ETR	−0.133	−0.257	0.119			
Long-lived assets						
SROR	0.094	0.076	0.058			
GAP	0.039	0.021	0.007			
ETR	0.410	0.272	0.119			
All assets						
SROR	0.080	0.074	0.058			
GAP	0.025	0.018	0.007			
ETR	0.308	0.251	0.119			
Interasset tax wedge (short lived)	−0.045	−0.032				
Intersector tax wedge						
Short lived				0.005	−0.008	−0.014
Long lived				0.018	0.036	0.018

Table 3.5 (*cont.*)

	Corporate	Noncorporate	Household	Corporate–noncorporate	Corporate–household	Noncorporate–household
6% inflation						
Short-lived assets						
SROR	0.053	0.045	0.052			
GAP	0.001	−0.007	0.007			
ETR	0.024	−0.152	0.127			
Long-lived assets						
SROR	0.094	0.075	0.052			
GAP	0.042	0.023	0.007			
ETR	0.444	0.312	0.127			
All assets						
SROR	0.081	0.073	0.052			
GAP	0.029	0.021	0.007			
ETR	0.359	0.293	0.127			
Interasset tax wedge (short lived)	−0.040	−0.030				
Intersector tax wedge						
Short lived				0.009	0.002	−0.007
Long lived				0.019	0.042	0.023

Table 3.5 (*cont.*)

	Corporate	Noncorporate	Household	Corporate–noncorporate	Corporate–household	Noncorporate–household
10% inflation						
Short-lived assets						
SROR	0.056	0.045	0.048			
GAP	0.006	-0.004	0.006			
ETR	0.110	-0.085	0.133			
Long-lived assets						
SROR	0.093	0.074	0.048			
GAP	0.043	0.025	0.006			
ETR	0.461	0.337	0.133			
All assets						
SROR	0.082	0.072	0.048			
GAP	0.032	0.023	0.006			
ETR	0.387	0.319	0.133			
Interasset tax wedge (short lived)	-0.037	-0.029				
Intersector tax wedge						
Short lived				0.011	0.009	-0.002
Long lived				0.019	0.045	0.026

3.2 The Treasury proposal

Effective marginal tax rates on business assets given in table 3.6 are similar to those under the 1986 Tax Law. A comparison of tables 3.5 and 3.6 reveals that at 6 percent inflation the Treasury proposal would have slightly reduced the effective marginal tax rate from 35.9 to 35.1 percent for corporate assets and from 29.3 to 27.1 percent for noncorporate assets. Since the 1986 Tax Law does not index taxable income and tax deductions, the Treasury proposal would have increased the tax burden at a lower rate of inflation, but would have decreased it at a higher inflation rate.

The effective marginal tax rates under the Treasury proposal reflect the combined effects of the repeal of investment tax credit, the introduction of economic depreciation, lowering of statutory tax rates and indexing of interest income, interest expenses and capital gains. Of the many tax policy changes in the Treasury proposal, the repeal of investment tax credit would have had the greatest impact on effective tax rates on income from capital. Since short lived business assets received the most important benefits from the investment tax credit under the 1986 Tax Law, the increase in the tax burden on short-lived assets under the Treasury proposal would have been the most marked.

The objectives of the Treasury proposal were to reduce tax wedges among different forms of investment and to insulate the tax structure from the impact of inflation. We find that, first, the Treasury proposal would have reduced interasset tax wedges substantially. Under the 1986 Tax Law with 6 percent inflation, the tax wedges between short-lived and long-lived assets are 4.0 percent in the corporate sector and 3.0 percent in the noncorporate sector. They would have been reduced to only 1.2 percent and 0.6 percent, respectively, under the Treasury proposal. To the extent that the welfare cost of tax distortion increases with the tax wedge, reductions in the interasset tax wedge of this magnitude could have improved the efficiency of capital allocation within each sector significantly.

Second, the Treasury proposal would have substantially reduced the intersectoral tax wedges for long-lived assets, but would have had mixed effects for short-lived assets. The impact of the proposal on intersectoral tax wedges for short-lived assets would have depended on the rate of inflation. The Treasury proposal would have been relatively ineffective in eliminating the substantial intersectoral tax wedges for long-lived assets under the 1986 law, since long-lived assets would have borne a heavier tax burden than the short-lived assets under the proposal. In addition, corporate assets would have

Table 3.6 Effective tax rates and the distortionary impacts of capital income taxation – Treasury proposal

	Corporate	Noncorporate	Household	Corporate–noncorporate	Corporate–household	Noncorporate–household
0% inflation						
Short-lived assets						
SROR	0.080	0.071	0.060			
GAP	0.025	0.016	0.009			
ETR	0.310	0.224	0.156			
Long-lived assets						
SROR	0.091	0.077	0.060			
GAP	0.036	0.022	0.009			
ETR	0.397	0.284	0.156			
All assets						
SROR	0.088	0.076	0.060			
GAP	0.033	0.021	0.009			
ETR	0.373	0.280	0.156			
Interasset tax wedge (short lived)	−0.011	−0.006				
Intersector tax wedge						
Short lived				0.009	0.020	0.010
Long lived				0.015	0.031	0.016

Table 3.6 (*cont.*)

	Corporate	Noncorporate	Household	Corporate–noncorporate	Corporate–household	Noncorporate–household
6% inflation						
Short-lived assets						
SROR	0.076	0.065	0.060			
GAP	0.021	0.014	0.009			
ETR	0.280	0.207	0.157			
Long-lived assets						
SROR	0.088	0.075	0.060			
GAP	0.033	0.021	0.009			
ETR	0.379	0.275	0.157			
All assets						
SROR	0.085	0.075	0.060			
GAP	0.030	0.020	0.009			
ETR	0.351	0.271	0.157			
Interasset tax wedge (short lived)	−0.012	−0.006				
Intersector tax wedge						
Short lived				0.007	0.017	0.009
Long lived				0.013	0.029	0.016

Table 3.6 (cont.)

	Corporate	Noncorporate	Household	Corporate–noncorporate	Corporate–household	Noncorporate–household
10% inflation						
Short-lived assets						
SROR	0.075	0.068	0.059			
GAP	0.020	0.014	0.009			
ETR	0.271	0.203	0.158			
Long-lived assets						
SROR	0.087	0.075	0.059			
GAP	0.033	0.020	0.009			
ETR	0.373	0.272	0.158			
All assets						
SROR	0.084	0.074	0.059			
GAP	0.029	0.020	0.009			
ETR	0.345	0.268	0.158			
Interasset tax wedge (short lived)	−0.012	−0.007				
Intersector tax wedge						
Short lived				0.007	0.016	0.009
Long lived				0.013	0.028	0.016

been more heavily taxed than noncorporate assets which, in turn, would have been more heavily taxed than household assets.

Third, the repeal of investment tax credit would have increased the tax burden roughly as much as the reduction of the statutory tax rates would have decreased it at 6 percent rate of inflation. The average effective tax rate for the entire corporate sector would have changed only from 35.9 to 35.1 percent and the intertemporal tax wedge would have increased slightly from 2.9 to 3.0 percent. The effect of the repeal of investment tax credit is seen most clearly in the case of the short-lived business assets. At a 6 percent rate of inflation, the effective tax rate on short-lived corporate assets would have increased from 2.4 percent under the 1986 law to 28.0 percent under the Treasury proposal and the intertemporal tax wedge would have increased from 0.1 to 2.1 percent. The pattern is reversed for long-lived assets, since the intertemporal tax wedges would have been smaller under the Treasury proposal.

Finally, the Treasury proposal would have reduced the impact of inflation on the tax burden on capital income by defining taxable income to approximate economic income more closely. The tendency of the tax burden to decline with inflation under the Treasury proposal is due to incomplete indexing of interest payments.[25] To the extent that interest is not completely indexed, inflation tends to increase the after-tax real interest rate and reduce the present value of capital consumption allowances, even if the tax depreciation is completely indexed against inflation. However, incomplete indexing reduces the cost of debt financing. Table 3.6 indicates that the result of these two opposing effects would have been to reduce the marginal tax burden of capital with higher rates of inflation under the Treasury proposal.

3.3 The President's proposal

We summarize effective tax rates under the President's proposal in table 3.7. Overall, the effects of the President's proposal would have been similar to those of the Treasury proposal. The tax burden on income from capital would have increased at a low rate of inflation and decreased at a high rate. The interasset tax wedge in the corporate and noncorporate sectors would have been reduced; the intersectoral tax wedges of long-lived assets would also have been reduced, but effects on the tax wedges for the short-lived assets would have been mixed. However, a careful comparison of tables 3.6 and 3.7 reveals a number of subtle differences between the Treasury and the President's proposals, many of which are attributable to differences in the impact of inflation on the tax system.

Table 3.7 Effective tax rates and the distortionary impacts of capital income taxation – President's proposal

	Corporate	Noncorporate	Household	Corporate–noncorporate	Corporate–household	Noncorporate–household
0% inflation						
Short-lived assets						
SROR	0.077	0.069	0.061			
GAP	0.021	0.013	0.009			
ETR	0.271	0.187	0.154			
Long-lived assets						
SROR	0.091	0.077	0.061			
GAP	0.034	0.021	0.009			
ETR	0.381	0.273	0.154			
All assets						
SROR	0.086	0.076	0.061			
GAP	0.030	0.020	0.009			
ETR	0.351	0.268	0.154			
Interasset tax wedge (short lived)	−0.014	−0.008				
Intersector tax wedge						
Short lived				0.008	0.016	0.008
Long lived				0.014	0.029	0.016

Table 3.7 (*cont.*)

	Corporate	Noncorporate	Household	Corporate–noncorporate	Corporate–household	Noncorporate–household
6% inflation						
Short-lived assets						
SROR	0.066	0.061	0.056			
GAP	0.012	0.008	0.009			
ETR	0.182	0.134	0.162			
Long-lived assets						
SROR	0.080	0.070	0.056			
GAP	0.026	0.016	0.009			
ETR	0.330	0.235	0.162			
All assets						
SROR	0.076	0.069	0.056			
GAP	0.022	0.016	0.009			
ETR	0.290	0.229	0.162			
Interasset tax wedge (short lived)	−0.014	−0.008				
Intersector tax wedge						
Short lived				0.004	0.010	0.005
Long lived				0.011	0.024	0.013

Table 3.7 (*cont.*)

	Corporate	Noncorporate	Household	Corporate–noncorporate	Corporate–household	Noncorporate–household
10% inflation						
Short-lived assets						
SROR	0.058	0.057	0.053			
GAP	0.005	0.005	0.009			
ETR	0.091	0.089	0.167			
Long-lived assets						
SROR	0.073	0.065	0.053			
GAP	0.020	0.013	0.009			
ETR	0.271	0.196	0.167			
All assets						
SROR	0.068	0.064	0.053			
GAP	0.015	0.012	0.009			
ETR	0.224	0.190	0.167			
Interasset tax wedge (short lived)	−0.014	−0.008				
Intersector tax wedge						
Short lived				0.001	0.005	0.004
Long lived				0.008	0.019	0.011

With no inflation the President's proposal would have been more favorable to investment, since it would have imposed lower tax burdens on capital through the retention of accelerated schedules for capital cost recovery. At 6 or 10 percent inflation rates, the President's proposal would have been even more favorable to investment, since the indexing of capital consumption allowances would have been coupled with the deduction of nominal interest expenses. This would have increased the present value of capital consumption allowances at higher rates of inflation. In addition, inflation would have lowered the tax burden on capital as a consequence of the tax deductibility of nominal interest expenses. The value of the resulting deductions would have been greater than the additional tax liabilities resulting from the taxation of nominal interest income at the individual level. Similar reasoning can be applied to explain the decline of the intersectoral tax wedges with inflation.

Under the 1986 Tax Law and the Tax Reform Act 1986 capital cost recovery is not indexed for inflation, so that an increase in the inflation rate adds to the tax burden on income from capital. Under the Treasury proposal, the recovery of capital cost would have been indexed and interest would have been indexed incompletely. There would have been a slight tendency for the tax burden on capital income to decline with inflation. This tendency would have been strengthened under the President's proposal, since capital cost recovery would have been indexed while interest deductions would not. Tables 3.6 and 3.7 show that the President's proposal would have narrowed the intersectoral tax wedges relative to the Treasury proposal. By contrast the Treasury proposal would have had uniformly smaller interasset tax wedges.

3.4 The Tax Reform Act of 1986

Since the Tax Reform Act of 1986 embraced many of the ideas contained in the Treasury and President's proposals, the impact of the tax reform on effective tax rates and tax wedges is similar to that of the two proposals. Table 3.8 shows that the repeal of the investment tax credit more than offsets the reduction in the statutory tax rates, so that the overall tax burden on income from capital is increased. Despite the acceleration of capital cost recovery and lower marginal tax rates, the impact of the repeal of the investment tax credit is most evident in the increase of the tax burden on short-lived business assets. At 6 percent inflation, the Tax Reform Act of 1986 imposes an effective tax rate on short-lived assets of 38.2 percent in the corporate sector and 28.2 percent in the noncorporate sector,

Table 3.8 Effective tax rates and the distortionary impacts of capital income taxation – 1986 Tax Reform Act

	Corporate	Noncorporate	Household	Corporate–noncorporate	Corporate–household	Noncorporate–household
0% inflation						
Short-lived assets						
SROR	0.078	0.068	0.059			
GAP	0.022	0.012	0.007			
ETR	0.279	0.182	0.125			
Long-lived assets						
SROR	0.092	0.076	0.059			
GAP	0.036	0.020	0.007			
ETR	0.390	0.268	0.125			
All assets						
SROR	0.087	0.075	0.059			
GAP	0.031	0.020	0.007			
ETR	0.360	0.262	0.125			
Interasset tax wedge (short lived)	−0.014	−0.008				
Intersector tax wedge						
Short lived				0.009	0.019	0.009
Long lived				0.016	0.033	0.017

Table 3.8 (cont.)

	Corporate	Noncorporate	Household	Corporate–noncorporate	Corporate–household	Noncorporate–household
6% inflation						
Short-lived assets						
SROR	0.084	0.071	0.052			
GAP	0.032	0.020	0.007			
ETR	0.382	0.282	0.135			
Long-lived assets						
SROR	0.094	0.077	0.052			
GAP	0.042	0.026	0.007			
ETR	0.449	0.335	0.135			
All assets						
SROR	0.091	0.075	0.052			
GAP	0.039	0.025	0.007			
ETR	0.430	0.352	0.135			
Interasset tax wedge (short lived)	−0.010	−0.006				
Intersector tax wedge						
Short lived				0.012	0.031	0.019
Long lived				0.017	0.041	0.025

Table 3.8 (cont.)

	Corporate	Noncorporate	Household	Corporate–noncorporate	Corporate–household	Noncorporate–household
10% inflation						
Short-lived assets						
SROR	0.087	0.073	0.048			
GAP	0.038	0.025	0.007			
ETR	0.439	0.342	0.143			
Long-lived assets						
SROR	0.093	0.077	0.048			
GAP	0.045	0.029	0.007			
ETR	0.478	0.373	0.143			
All assets						
SROR	0.091	0.076	0.048			
GAP	0.043	0.028	0.007			
ETR	0.467	0.371	0.143			
Interasset tax wedge (short lived)	−0.006	−0.004				
Intersector tax wedge						
Short lived				0.014	0.039	0.025
Long lived				0.017	0.045	0.029

while the corresponding tax rates are 2.4 and −15.2 percent under the 1986 Tax Law.

For long-lived assets, effective tax rates are not much affected by tax reform. The effects of lower tax rates are approximately offset by the combined effect of longer cost recovery period and the repeal of the investment tax credit. At 6 percent inflation, the interasset tax wedges in the corporate and noncorporate sectors are only 1.0 and 0.6 percent while the corresponding figures are 4.0 and 3.0 percent, respectively, under the 1986 Tax Law. Table 3.8 shows that the effective tax rates on household assets are essentially unaffected by the reform, since the difference between the average marginal tax rates on equity and debt claims is nearly unchanged and property taxes remain the same.

Overall, the tax burden on the income from capital is increased by the 1986 tax reform. As a consequence, the intertemporal tax wedges are larger and the efficiency of intertemporal resource allocation is adversely affected. However, the interasset tax wedges are considerably reduced and the efficiency of interasset capital alloction is enhanced. At 6 percent inflation intersectoral wedges are increased for short-lived assets and decreased for long-lived assets.

Since the tax reform did not incorporate the indexing of capital income taxation, as provided in the Treasury proposal, the impact of inflation on effective tax rates and tax wedges under the Tax Reform Act of 1986 are similar to those under the 1986 Tax Law. The tax burden on income from capital increases with inflation. Since the tax burden on short-lived assets rises faster than that on long-lived assets, interasset tax wedges decline with the rate of inflation. The tax burden on corporate assets increases faster than that on noncorporate assets, which in true increases faster than that on household assets, so that intersectoral tax wedges increase with the rate of inflation

4 Tax Reform and Economic Growth

In this section we estimate the impact of alternative tax policies – the Treasury proposal, the President's proposal and the Tax Reform Act of 1986 – on US economic growth. We evaluate the effect of each of the alternative tax reform proposals by comparing the resulting level of welfare with that attainable under the "base case" given by the 1986 Tax Law. Since effective tax rates and tax wedges depend on the rate of inflation, we consider three alternative rates of inflation 0, 6 and 10 percent. In these comparisons we impose the requirement that the revenue and expenditure of the government sector are the same as in the base case.

We consider four alternative methods for adjusting tax revenues so as to keep the budgetary position of the government sector the same as in the base case. The first method is to increase or decrease government revenues by means of a "lump sum" tax or subsidy. We model a lump-sum tax by altering the budget constraint facing the representative consumer. A tax results in a contraction of the budget available to the consumer and a corresponding increase in government revenue. Similarly, a subsidy expands the budget available to the consumer and decreases government revenue. A lump-sum tax or subsidy does not distort decisions in the household or business sectors of the economy by altering the tax wedges facing the representative consumer or the representative producer.

We also consider three methods of adjusting government revenues that involve changes in tax-induced distortions. These include proportional adjustments to labor income taxes, sales taxes on investment and comsumption goods and taxes on income from both capital and labor. The labor income tax adjustment affects the tax rate of labor services, the sales tax adjustment affects the tax rates for consumption and investment goods and the income tax adjustment affects the rates for both capital and labor services. By considering all three methods we are able to assess the sensitivity of the welfare rankings of alternative tax policies to changes in the constraints imposed by the requirement of revenue neutrality.

4.1 The Tax Reform Act of 1986

We summarize the results of our simulations of US economic growth under alternative tax policies in table 3.9. An important conclusion that we can draw from table 3.9 is that the Treasury proposal, the President's proposal and the Tax Reform Act of 1986 all improve potential economic welfare substantially. In our central case with 6 persent inflation and a lump-sum tax adjustment, the President's proposal would have generated a welfare gain of $2452.2 billion, while the Treasury proposal would have generated a gain of $1907.6 billion. However, the welfare gain associated with the Tax Reform Act 1986 is only $448.4 billion.[26]

With no change in government expenditures the Tax Reform Act of 1986 results in more revenue than is necessary to keep the government in the same budgetary position as under the 1986 Tax Law. In order to leave government revenue the same under the two tax policies, tax revenues must be rebated to the household sector. Replacing the lump-sum tax adjustment with a distortionary tax adjustment lowers the rates of the distortionary taxes involved and improves the performance of the economy under the Tax Reform Act

Table 3.9 Welfare effects of tax reform (billions of 1987 US dollars)

Rate of inflation	Revenue adjustment	1986 Law	Treasury proposal	President's proposal	1986 Act
0%	Lump-sum tax	724.0	1489.6	1691.4	1561.8
	Labor income tax	478.2	1468.8	1642.4	1565.0
	Sales tax	400.3	1452.9	1614.6	1558.7
	Individual income tax	374.5	1456.1	1619.1	1563.1
6%	Lump-sum tax	0.0	1907.6	2452.2	448.4
	Labor income tax	0.0	1711.4	2170.4	746.9
	Sales tax	0.0	1600.1	2104.9	901.2
	Individual income tax	0.0	1595.8	2007.9	999.4
10%	Lump-sum tax	−477.1	2060.4	3015.6	− 200.8
	Labor income tax	−333.7	1791.6	2584.7	267.3
	Sales tax	−285.2	1623.5	2356.4	517.0
	Individual income tax	−221.9	1604.8	2353.1	748.6

In 1987, the national wealth (beginning of the year) and gross national product are projected to be $15,920.2 billion and $4,488.5 billion US dollars.

of 1986. By contrast, the Treasury and the President's proposals would have resulted in less revenue than the 1986 Tax Law. The welfare gains would have been smaller under the distortionary tax adjustments than under the lump-sum tax adjustment.

Another perspective on the economic impact of the alternative tax reform proposals is provided by a comparison of the welfare gains from tax reform with the private national wealth. The nominal value of the US private national wealth at the beginning of 1987 was $15,920.2 billion. Making use of this figure, we estimate that the welfare gains from the Treasury and the President's proposals would have been equivalent to increases of 12.0 and 15.4 percent, respectively, of US private national wealth in 1987.[27] The welfare gain from the Tax Reform Act of 1986 is equivalent to an increase of only 2.8 percent of the national wealth.

Under distortionary tax adjustments the welfare gains would have been somewhat smaller for the President's proposal and slightly smaller for the Treasury proposal. The gains are substantially larger for the 1986 Tax Reform Act. However, these gains are not sensitive to the differences among the distortionary tax adjustment.[28] If we consider a sales tax adjustment with a 6 percent inflation rate, the welfare gains would have been $1600.1 billion for the Treasury proposal and $2014.9 billion for the President's proposal. These gains would have totaled 10.1 and 12.3 percent of the US private national wealth in 1987. The corresponding welfare gain is $901.2 billion for the Tax Reform Act of 1986. This is equivalent to 5.7 percent of the national wealth.

It is worth recalling that inflation reduces the interasset tax wedges and increases the intertemporal and intersectoral tax wedges under the 1986 Tax Law and the Tax Reform Act of 1986.[29] Under the Treasury and President's proposals inflation has little effect on the interasset wedges but tends to reduce the intersectoral and intertemporal tax wedges. The results presented in table 3.9 show that inflation improves the performance of the economy under the Treasury and President's proposals and affects economic performance adversely under the 1986 Tax Law and the Tax Reform Act of 1986. We conclude that the positive impact of inflation on intertemporal and intersectoral resource allocation more than offsets its negative impact on interasset allocation.

Table 3.9 also shows how the welfare effects of alternative tax reforms would be affected by the rate of inflation. It is useful to focus on lump-sum tax adjustments since distortionary tax adjustments result in reallocations of resources due to substitutions as well as to changes in the rate of inflation. Economic welfare improves with higher inflation under the Treasury and President's proposals. However, welfare declines with inflation under the 1986 Tax Law and Tax Reform Act of 1986. This is due to the fact the tax burden on capital income is reduced with higher inflation under the two proposals, while inflation increases the tax burden on capital income under the 1986 Tax Law and the Tax Reform Act of 1986. An increase in the rate of inflation from 0 to 6 percent is sufficient to alter the welfare ranking between the Treasury proposal and the Tax Reform Act of 1986.

4.2 Alternative approaches to tax reform

We have measured the impact of the Tax Reform Act of 1986 on economic welfare, employing the 1986 Tax Law as a basis for comparison. We have also assessed the potential impact of the Treasury and President's tax reform proposals. We next consider alternative approaches to tax reform based on the elimination of tax wedges among different types of assets. As before, the growth path of the US economy under the 1986 Tax Law is taken as a basis for comparison. We measure the potential gains in economic welfare from changes in tax policy by comparing the resulting levels of welfare with those corresponding to the 1986 Tax Law.

For the purposes of this analysis we find it useful to distinguish between atemporal tax wedges and intertemporal tax wedges. The elimination of an atemporal tax wedge requires that the social rates of return on the corresponding assets are equalized within a given time period. We eliminate atemporal tax wedges among assets by equalizing the corresponding social rates of return at a weighted average of the social rates of return, where stocks of assets are used as weights. More precisely, we equalize social rates of return associated with balanced growth equilibrium under the 1986 Tax Law, using the balanced growth proportions of assets as weights.

To model the integration of the corporate and individual income taxes we set social rates of return on corporate assets equal to those on the corresponding noncorporate assets. This procedure does not affect the private rates in the two sectors, so that effective tax rates are not equalized between the sectors. The private rates of return of assets in different sectors differ for two reasons. The first is that debt–asset ratios differ across sectors. The second is that average marginal tax rates on individual income vary from sector to sector owing to the differences in the distribution of asset ownership among taxpayers in different income tax brackets.

We consider the elimination of five sets of tax wedges: (a) the interasset tax wedges within the corporate and noncorporate sectors; (b) intersectoral tax wedges between assets of the same type held in the corporate and noncorporate sectors; (c) intersectoral tax wedges among assets of the same type held in the business and household sectors, where the business sector includes both corporate and noncorporate business; (d) all the atemporal tax wedges in the business sector; and (e) all the atemporal tax wedges in the business and the household sectors. We also consider the integration of corporate and noncorporate taxes.

Elimination of an intertemporal tax wedge requires equalization of the social and private rates of return, so that the effective tax rate on the corresponding assets is reduced to zero. We consider two possible approaches to tax reform for eliminating intertemporal tax distortions. First, we consider the elimination of intertemporal tax wedges resulting from the income and property taxes. This leaves the sales tax on investment goods at its level in the base case, while reducing the effective tax rate on capital income to zero. Second, we eliminate the tax burden on capital altogether by removing the sales tax on investment goods as well as the taxes on income from capital and property taxes. These two approaches correspond to alternative implementations of consumption tax rules for the taxation of capital income.

We summarize the social rates of return, effective tax rates and the sum of the investment tax credit and the present value of tax deductions for capital cost recovery with the elimination of tax wedges among different classes of assets in table 3.10. Section A represents the base case corresponding to the 1986 Tax Law. Section B represents the elimination of interasset tax wedges within the corporate and noncorporate sectors. This can be achieved by setting the sums of the investment credit and the present value of tax deductions of capital cost recovery at the values specified in the table. The social rates of return and the effective tax rates must be the same for short-lived and long-lived assets within each sector, since the private rate of return is the same for all assets within the sector.

Table 3.10 Elimination of tax wedges: 1986 Tax Law

Class of assets	Capital stock[a]	Social rate of return	Effective tax rate	ITC + TZ
A 1986 Tax Law				
Corporate				
Short	0.0893	0.0518	0.0229	0.5395
Long	0.2563	0.0914	0.4460	0.3257
Noncorporate				
Short	0.0185	0.0433	−0.1544	0.3510
Long	0.2580	0.0731	0.3152	0.1409
Household				
Short	0.0909	0.0503	0.1301	0.0000
Long	0.2870	0.0503	0.1301	0.0000
B No within-sector interasset wedges				
Corporate				
Short		0.0812	0.3762	0.4652
Long		0.0812	0.3762	0.3942
Noncorporate				
Short		0.0711	0.2960	0.2552
Long		0.0711	0.2960	0.1641
Household				
Short		0.0503	0.1301	0.0000
Long		0.0503	0.1301	0.0000
C No intersector wedges: business assets				
Corporate				
Short		0.0504	−0.0052	0.5432
Long		0.0822	0.3840	0.3873
Noncorporate				
Short		0.0504	0.0068	0.3267
Long		0.0822	0.3913	0.0341
Household				
Short		0.0503	0.1301	0.0000
Long		0.0503	0.1301	0.0000

Table 3.10 (*cont.*)

Class of assets	Capital stock[a]	Social rate of return	Effective tax rate	ITC + TZ
D No intersector wedges: all sectors				
Corporate				
Short		0.0503	−0.0062	0.5433
Long		0.0708	0.2844	0.4639
Noncorporate				
Short		0.0503	0.0058	0.3268
Long		0.0708	0.2930	0.1677
Household				
Short		0.0503	0.1311	−0.0002
Long		0.0708	0.3821	−0.3766
E No tax wedges: all assets, business sector				
Corporate				
Short		0.0767	0.3397	0.4766
Long		0.0767	0.3397	0.4243
Noncorporate				
Short		0.0767	0.3476	0.2358
Long		0.0767	0.3476	0.0985
Household				
Short		0.0503	0.1301	0.0000
Long		0.0503	0.1301	0.0000
F No tax wedges: all assets, all sectors				
Corporate				
Short		0.0667	0.2408	0.5019
Long		0.0667	0.2408	0.4911
Noncorporate				
Short		0.0667	0.2499	0.2703
Long		0.0667	0.2499	0.2152
Household				
Short		0.0667	0.3444	−0.0666
Long		0.0667	0.3444	−0.3020
G Corporate tax integration: apply noncorporate social rates of return to corporate assets				
Corporate				
Short		0.0433	−0.1684	0.5610
Long		0.0731	0.3069	0.4486
Noncorporate				
Short		0.0433	−0.1544	0.3510
Long		0.0731	0.3152	0.1409
Household				
Short		0.0503	0.1301	0.0000
Long		0.0503	0.1301	0.0000

Table 3.10 (*cont.*)

Class of assets	Capital stock[a]	Social rate of return	Effective tax rate	ITC + TZ
H Zero effective tax rates (ETR = 0)				
Corporate				
Short		0.0506	0.0000	0.5425
Long		0.0506	0.0000	0.5986
Noncorporate				
Short		0.0500	0.0000	0.3279
Long		0.0500	0.0000	0.4100
Household				
Short		0.0437	0.0000	0.0265
Long		0.0437	0.0000	0.1202

[a]Capital stock in the steady state of the reference case (percent).
ITC, investment tax credit.
T, tax rate at the firm level.
Z, present value of capital consumption allowances.
Steady-state allocation of capital in the base case is used as the weights.
The annual rate of inflation is assumed to be 6 percent.

After interasset wedges are eliminated, the intersectoral and inter-temporal tax wedges remain.

In section C of table 3.10 we eliminate the intersectoral tax wedges between assets in the corporate and noncorporate sectors by equalizing social rates of return on short-lived assets in the two sectors. Similarly, we equalize social rates of return on long-lived assets. After the intersectoral tax wedges within the business sector are removed, the interasset tax wedges and intersectoral wedges between the business and household sectors still remain. In section D we also eliminate the intersectoral tax wedges between business and household sectors. This approach to tax reform eliminates all the intersectoral tax wedges, but creates an interasset tax wedge in the household sector where none existed before the change in tax policy. There are interasset tax wedges in the corporate and noncorporate sectors as well.

In section E of table 3.10 we eliminate both the interasset and intersectoral tax wedges in the business sector. Conceptually, the tax reforms represented in section E are a combination of the reforms represented in sections B and C. In section F all the atemporal tax wedges are eliminated, so that the only remaining sources of tax distortions are the intertemporal tax wedges. In section G, we eliminate the intersectoral tax wedges between corporate and non-corporate sectors by setting the social rates of return on corporate assets equal to the corresponding rates on noncorporate assets. The substantial reduction in tax revenue can be offset by a lump-sum tax or by proportional adjustments in the labor income tax, sales tax or individual income tax. Finally, in sector H all the intertemporal tax wedges are eliminated and the social and private rates of return are equalized for all assets.

4.3 Welfare impacts of tax reform

We summarize the welfare impact of the eight hypothetical tax reform proposals in table 3.11. Beginning with lump-sum tax adjustments, we find that the welfare gain from elimination of interasset tax wedges that exist under the 1986 Tax Law is $443.9 billion. The elimination of intersectoral tax wedges between assets in the corporate and noncorporate sectors yields welfare losses instead of gains. Given Harberger's (1966) analysis of the impact of the corporate income tax, this is a rather surprising result. The elimination of a tax wedge would usually be expected to increase the efficiency of resource allocation and improve the level of economic welfare. However, the demand for capital services is much more elastic in the noncorporate sector than in the corporate sector. Equalizing the social rates of return between the corporate and noncorporate assets reduces the total demand for the business capital services.

The third change in tax policy analyzed in table 3.11 is the elimination of intersectoral tax wedges between the household and business sectors. The results suggest that there is a very large potential welfare gain to be realized from this change in tax policy under the 1986 Tax Law. The estimated gain is $2262.6 billion at a 6 percent rate of inflation, which is much larger than the gain we have estimated for the Tax Reform Act of 1986. Given the substantial tax wedges between business and household assets under the 1986 Tax Law, this result is not surprising. For example, the intersectoral tax wedges for short-lived assets are 0.2 percent between the corporate and household sectors and −0.7 percent between the noncorporate and household sectors. The corresponding figures for long-lived assets are 4.2 percent and 2.3 percent, respectively.

The welfare gain from eliminating the interasset and intersectoral wedges among business assets is estimated to be only $326.4 billion under the 1986 Tax Law. The welfare gain from eliminating all atemporal tax wedges in the private sector of the US economy is estimated to be $2663.7 billion. The gain is much larger than the welfare gain resulting from elimination of interasset distortions within

Table 3.11 Welfare effects of tax distortions (billions of 1987 US dollars)

	1986 law
1 Within-sector interasset distortion	
Lump-sum tax adjustment	443.9
Labor income tax adjustment	248.1
Sales tax adjustment	168.7
Individual income tax adjustment	70.2
2 Intersector distortion: corporate and noncorporate sectors	
Lump-sum tax adjustment	−93.3
Labor income tax adjustment	−416.7
Sales tax adjustment	−523.8
Individual income tax adjustment	−715.5
3 Intersector distortion: all sectors	
Lump-sum tax adjustment	2262.6
Labor income tax adjustment	2156.9
Sales tax adjustment	2118.6
Individual income tax adjustment	2067.7
4 No tax distortion: corporate and noncorporate sectors, all assets	
Lump-sum tax adjustment	326.4
Labor income tax adjustment	69.2
Sales tax adjustment	−29.1
Individual income tax adjustment	−169.7
5 No tax distortion: all sectors, all assets	
Lump-sum tax adjustment	2663.7
Labor income tax adjustment	2603.9
Sales tax adjustment	2572.4
Individual income tax adjustment	2547.2
6 Corporate tax integration	
Lump-sum tax adjustment	1313.1
Labor income tax adjustment	493.4
Sales tax adjustment	238.1
Individual income tax adjustment	−274.5
7 Consumption tax rules (zero effective tax rates)	
Lump-sum tax adjustment	3853.9
Labor income tax adjustment	2045.4
Sales tax adjustment	1749.3
Individual income tax adjustment	2045.4
8 Consumption tax rules (zero effective tax rates) No sales tax on investment goods	
Lump-sum tax adjustment	4128.1
Labor income tax adjustment	1988.0
Sales tax adjustment	1722.1
Individual income tax adjustment	1988.0

Inflation is fixed at 6 percent per year.

wach sector and somewhat larger than that resulting from elimination of intersectoral tax distortions for all sectors. In view of the relative magnitude of these effects, we can attribute most of the welfare gain to elimination of intersectoral tax wedges between business and household assets.

The sixth change in tax policy we consider is the elimination of intersectoral tax wedges between assets in the corporate and non-corporate sectors. For this purpose we set social rates of return on corporate assets equal to the corresponding rates of return on noncorporate assets under the 1986 Tax Law. The effective tax burden on corporate assets is unambiguously reduced by this hypothetical change in tax policy. The estimated welfare gain from this change in tax policy is $1313.1 billion. The gain is about half of that attainable by eliminating all intersectoral tax wedges.

In the six changes in tax policy we have considered up to this point, we have focused attention on the distortionary impact of atemporal tax wedges. We next consider the elimination of inter-temporal tax wedges by setting effective tax rates on all types of income from capital equal to zero. We find that the elimination of intertemporal tax wedges generates huge welfare gains under lump-sum tax adjustment. When sales taxes on investment goods are also abolished, the welfare gain becomes even larger. Taking the 1986 Tax Law as the base case, the welfare gain from removing intertemporal tax wedges on all assets is $3853.9 billion. The elimination of the sales taxes on investment goods produces a gain of $4128.1 billion.

The magnitudes of welfare gains from elimination of the intertemporal tax wedges under distortionary tax adjustments presented in table 3.11 are substantially lower than those under lump-sum tax adjustment. The changes in marginal tax rates required to offset revenue losses can generate significant substitution effects. The welfare effects resulting from the elimination of intertemporal tax wedges, as given in table 3.11, are also sensitive to the choice among distortionary tax adjustments, since the required increase in tax revenue is large.

If a proposed tax reform is roughly revenue neutral, so that the magnitude of the required adjustment in tax revenue is small, the welfare ranking of alternative policy changes does not depend on the method for adjusting tax revenue. For a change in tax policy that involves substantial rate cuts with no compensating enhancement of tax revenues through base broadening, the welfare measures under lump-sum tax adjustment can be interpreted as upper bounds of the welfare gains that can be achieved. Any realistic tax reform involving revenue adjustment through changes in distortionary taxes would result in welfare gains well below those attainable under the hypothetical lump-sum adjustment.

The fact that the estimated welfare gains from the elimination of the intertemporal tax wedges is in the range of 4 trillion dollars suggests that the potential welfare gain from replacing the current system of income taxes with consumption-based taxes is very large indeed. However, the welfare gains are reduced by approximately half under the more realistic assumption that revenue losses are offset by distortionary tax adjustments. These welfare gains are still impressive. We conclude that improvements in the efficiency of intertemporal resources allocation must be carefully weighed against possible worsening of atemporal resource allocation as a consequence of distortions associated with taxes on consumption.

5 Conclusion

The Tax Reform Act 1986 increases the effective marginal tax burden on income from capital at any positive inflation rate. Nonetheless, the changes in economic welfare relative to the 1986 Tax Law is positive. The 1986 Tax Reform Act improves the efficiency of atemporal resource allocation sufficiently to offset the negative impact of greater effective tax rates on capital income. Higher rates of inflation result in a marked reduction in the sizable welfare gains from the 1986 tax reform at rates of inflation near zero. For example, we estimate that the welfare gain is $448.4 billion at a 6 percent rate of inflation, which amounts to 2.8 percent of US private national wealth in 1987. The 1986 Tax Reform Act substantially reduced interasset tax wedge within the business sector, so that potential welfare gains from further reductions are small.

An important feature of the Treasury and President's proposals is that the tax would have been largely indexed against inflation. By contrast the tax burden on income from capital under the Tax Reform Act of 1986 increases significantly with the rate of inflation. While the gains from the 1986 Tax Reform Act are comparable with those under the Treasury and President's proposals at inflation rates near zero, the gains under the two proposals are much greater at moderate or high rates of inflation. For example, the President's proposal would have resulted in a welfare gain of $2452.2 billion dollars at a 6 percent inflation rate, which dwarfs the corresponding gain from the Tax Reform Act of 1986. We conclude that insulating the tax system from the effects of inflation should remain a top priority for future tax reform.

However, the largest welfare gains from tax reform would have been obtained by transferring part of the tax burden on business capital to household capital. There are obviously important political obstacles to such a transfer. Limitations on the deductibility of mortgage interest and elimination of the tax deductibility of state and local property taxes were included in the Treasury proposal. However, only a very modest limitation of the deductibility of mortgage interest survived into the final 1986 tax reform legislation. The welfare gain from a tax policy that treats all forms of capital income symmetrically would have been $2663.7 billion dollars at a 6 percent inflation rate. This exceeds the gain from the 1986 Tax Act by $2215.3 billion dollars and outranks the gains from both the Treasury and President's proposals.

An alternative approach to equalizing the tax burdens between business and houshold assets would have been the 1986 Tax Law with a tax system based on consumption. At a 6 percent inflation rate the welfare gain from shifting to a consumption-based tax system from a system primarily based on income would have been much larger that the gain from the Tax Reform Act of 1986. This conclusion holds for any of the alternative methods we have considered for maintaining government revenue at the same level as under the 1986 Tax Law. The prospective revenue losses associated with elimination of capital income taxation would have required large increases in distortionary taxes. However, the resulting welfare losses would have been outweighed by gains in efficiency from eliminating capital income taxes.

Notes

1   The Tax Reform Act of 1986 was enacted into law on October 22, 1986, and took effect on January 1, 1987. The Treasury proposal was presented in November 1984 and the President's proposal May 1985. A detailed description of the Tax Reform Act of 1986 is given by the Joint Committee on Taxation (1986). The economic impact of the 1986 tax reform has been analyzed by the Office of Tax Analysis of the US Department of the Treasury (1987) and in the symposium edited by Henry Aaron (1987).

2   For example, in section 4 we find that the equalization of tax rates on corporate and noncorporate capital considered by Harberger (1966) actually reduced efficiency. However, we show that symmetrical tax treatment of income from business and household assets is a very promising avenue for tax reform.

3   Harberger's general equilibrium approach to the analysis of tax policy has been greatly developed by Ballard et al. (1985). The economic impact of the Tax Reform Act of 1986 has been analyzed, using an extension of this model, by Fullerton, Henderson and Mackie (1987). A recent survey of the literature on applied general equilibrium models for tax policy analysis is provided by Whalley (1988).

4 The literature on the effect of taxation on saving is reviewed by Sandmo (1985) and Summers (1984). The impact of the Tax Reform Act of 1986 on saving behavior is analyzed by Hausman and Poterba (1987).

5 Proposals for implementation of a consumption tax in the United States are discussed by the US Department of the Treasury (1977), Hall and Rabushka (1983) and Bradford (1986). Arguments against a consumption tax are presented by the US Department of the Treasury (1984), vol. 3.

6 The elasticity of labor supply and its implications for tax policy are discussed by Hausman (1981, 1985). The impact of the Tax Reform Act of 1986 on labor supply is analyzed by Hausman and Poterba (1987).

7 See Jorgenson and Yun (1986a) for a discussion of the model and Jorgenson and Yun (1986b) for an application to earlier changes in tax policy. The results presented in these papers are based on econometric models fitted to data covering the period 1955–80. An alternative approach to dynamic general equilibrium modeling of US tax policy is presented by Auerbach and Kotlikoff (1987).

8 Perfect foresight models of tax incidence have been presented by Hall (1971), Chamley (1981), Judd (1987) and many others.

9 We have analyzed the impact of the 1981 Tax Act on US economic growth in a previous paper. See Jorgenson and Yun (1986b), especially pp. 365–70.

10 The total tax cut was $0.1 + (0.1)(1.0 - 0.1) + (0.05)[1 - (0.1)(1 - 0.1)] = 0.23$.

11 These tax rates are based on detailed simulations of the Office of Tax Analysis individual income tax model presented by Cilke and Wyscarver (1987).

12 The statutory rates of the investment tax credit and the tax lifetimes are based on the estimates of Fullerton, Gillette and Mackie (1987).

13 See US Department of the Treasury (1984). The Treasury plan and its relationship of the Tax Reform Act of 1986 are discussed in detail by McLure and Zodrow (1987). McLure and Zodrow note that the definition of revenue neutrality did not take into account changes in the tax base. In the simulations of US economic growth presented below we consider the impact of these changes on government revenues.

14 Deduction of mortgage and other personal interest would not have been indexed under the Treasury proposal. Indexing of interest income and interest expenses would have been based on the assumptions that the real interest rate is constant at 6 percent per year and that inflation raises the rate of inflation point for point. To the extent that the actual real rate of interest deviates from 6 percent, the indexing would have been incomplete.

15 In this calculation, we have assumed that inflation rate increases the nominal interest rate point for point. Thus, the after-tax real interest rate would have declined with inflation and the present value of capital comsumption allowances would have increased with inflation under the Treasury proposal.

16 See US Department of the Treasury (1985). The provisions of the Treasury proposal, the President's proposal and the 1986 Tax Law are compared in chart 18, pp. 26–30.

17 In table 3.1 we assume that the taxpayers would elect to be taxed on real

capital gains when inflation is zero and 50 percent of nominal capital gains when inflation is 6 or 10 percent.

18 The after-tax real interest rate is $(1 - TQ)(i_0 + \pi) - \pi$, where i_0 is the real interest rate, π is the rate of inflation, and TQ is the corporate tax rate. The after-tax real interest rate is negative for an inflation rate above $(1 - TQ)i_0/TQ$.

19 The Tax Reform Act of 1986 is described by the Joint Committee on Taxation (1986). The economic impact of the 1986 tax reform is discussed in detail by Musgrave (1987) and Pechman (1987).

20 Owing to the phase-out of the 15 percent tax bracket and the personal and dependants' exemptions for high income taxpayers, the top marginal rate is as high as 33 percent for certain ranges of taxable inome. Statutory tax rates under the 1986 Tax Reform Act were higher for the transitional year 1987.

21 If capital cost recovery coincides with economic depreciation, equality of effective tax rates requires that the investment tax credit must be larger for long-lived assets than short-lived assets, since short-lived assets can take the credit more frequently than long-lived assets.

22 If we adjust the present value of capital consumption allowances by increasing the basis for capital cost recovery to 100 percent, we find that the tax reform reduced the present value of capital cost recovery for short-lived assets. In order to adjust capital consumption allowances under the 1986 Tax Law for the effect of the provision reducing the basis of capital cost recovery by 50 percent of the investment tax credit, we can multiply the present value of capital cost recovery in table 3.4 under the 1986 law by $1/(1 - 0.5ITC)$, where ITC is the rate of investment tax credit in the same table. For example, when the annual rate of inflation is zero, the adjusted present value of capital cost recovery for a short-lived corporate asset is $0.92223/1(1 - 0.5 \times 0.0944) = 0.9680$, which is larger than the corresponding value, 0.9472, under the Tax Reform Act of 1986.

23 The definition of effective tax rates is discussed in more detail in our earlier paper (Jorgenson and Yun, 1986b, 357-61). The effective tax rates presented below are based on the "traditional view" of corporate finance discussed by Poterba and Summers (1983). Effective tax rates at the corporate level have been compared for Germany, Sweden, the UK and the USA for the year 1980 by King and Fullerton (1984). These effective tax rates are based on the so-called "new view" of corporate finance. The literature on the new view is surveyed by Auerbach (1983). Auerbach (1987) presents effective tax rates based on the new view for different types of assets within the corporate sector under the Tax Reform Act of 1986. Fullerton, Gillette and Mackie (1987) give effective tax rates under the 1986 Tax Reform Act for both views of corporate finance.

24 Another mechanism, which we do not model, is that firms using the FIFO inventory accounting method overstate their profits and hence their taxable income when inflation is positive.

25 We assume that the real interest is 3.57 percent as opposed to the 6 percent used in the proposal. Under our assumptions interest income and expences would have been incompletely indexed and inflation would have had an impact on effective tax rates.

26 These welfare gains are measured in 1987 US dollars.

27 In interpreting these comparisons in terms of the US private national wealth, it is useful to bear in mind that the private national wealth includes only nonhuman wealth, while the welfare gains from tax reform accrue to the owners of nonhuman capital and also to recipients of labor income, which can be regarded as a return to human capital.
28 This does not imply that the distortionary effects of the taxes used for revenue adjustments are similar. Rather it reflects the fact that the size of the required revenue adjustments is not large enough to produce sizable differences.
29 To be more precise, inflation increases the intersectoral tax wedges under the 1986 Tax Law, but has mixed effects on the absolute size of the intersectoral tax wedges where the wedges have a negative sign.

References

Aaron, H. J. (1987) "Symposium on Tax Reform", *Journal of Economic Perspectives*, 1 (1) Summer, 7–10.
Auerbach, A. J. (1983) "Taxation, Corporate Financial Policy, and the Cost of Capital", *Journal of Economic Literature*, 21, (3) September, 905–40.
——, (1987) "The Tax Reform Act of 1986 and the Cost of Capital", *Journal of Economic Perspectives*, 1 (1), Summer 73–86.
——, and L. J. Kotlikoff (1987) *Dynamic Fiscal Policy*, Cambridge: Cambridge University Press.
Ballard, C. L., D. Fullerton, J. B. Shoven and J. Whalley (1985) *A General Equilibrium Model for Tax Policy Evaluation*, Chicago, IL: University of Chicago Press.
Bradford, D. F. (1986) *Untangling the Income Tax*, Cambridge, MA: Harvard University Press.
Chamley, C. (1981) "The Welfare Cost of Capital Income Taxation in a Growing Economy", *Journal of Political Economy*, 89 (3), June, 468–96.
Cilke, J. M. and R. A. Wyscarver (1987) "The Treasury Individual Income Tax Simulation Model", in US Department of the Treasury, *Compendium of Tax Research 1987*, Washington, DC: US Government Printing Office, pp. 43–77.
Fullerton, D., R. Gillette and J. Mackie (1987) "Investment Incentives under the Tax Reform Act of 1986", in US Department of the Treasury, *Compendium of Tax Research 1987*, Washngton, DC: US Government Printing Office, pp. 131–72.
——, Y. K. Henderson and J. Mackie (1987) "Investment Allocation and Growth under the Tax Reform Act of 1986", in US Department of the Treasury, *Compendium of Tax Research 1987*, Washington, DC: US Government Printing Office, pp. 173–202.
Hall, R. E. (1971) "The Dynamic Effects of Fiscal Policy in an Economy with Foresight", *Review of Economic Studies*, 38, (2), April, 229–44.
—— and A Rabushka (1983) *Low Tax, Simple Tax, Flat Tax*, New York: McGraw-Hill.

Harberger, A. C. (1962) "The Incidence of the Corporate Income Tax", *Journal of Political Economy*, 70, (3), June, 215–40.

—— (1966) "Efficiency Effect of Taxes on Income from Capital", in M. Krzyzaniak, (ed.), *Effects of the Corporation Income Tax*, Detroit, MI: Wayne State University Press, pp. 107–17.

Hausman, J. A. (1981) "Labor Supply", in H. J. Aaron and J. A. Pechman (eds), *How Taxes Affect Economic Behavior*, Washington, DC: Booking Institution, pp. 27–72.

—— (1985) "Taxes and Labor Supply", in A. J. Auerbach and M. S. Feldstein, (eds), *Handbook of Public Economics*, vol. 1, Amsterdam: North-Holland, pp. 213–63.

—— and J. M. Poterba (1987) "Household Behavior and the Tax Reform Act of 1986", *Journal of Economic Perspectives*, 1 (1), Summer, 101–19.

Joint Committee on Taxation (1981) *General Explanation of the Economic Recovery Tax Act of 1981*, Washington, DC: US Government Printing Office.

—— (1986) *Summary of Conference Agreement on H.R. 3838 (Tax Reform Act of 1986)*, Washington, DC: US Government Printing Office.

Jorgenson, D. W., and K.-Y. Yun (1986a) "The Efficiency of Capital Allocation", *Scandinavian Journal of Economics*, 88 (1), 85–107.

——, —— (1986b) "Tax Policy and Capital Allocation", *Scandinavian Journal of Economics*, 88, (2) 355–77.

Judd, K. L. (1987) "The Welfare Cost of Factor Taxation in a Perfect-foresight Model", *Journal of Political Economy*, 95 (4) August, 675–709.

King, M. and Don Fullerton (1984) *The Taxation of Income from Capital*, Chicago, IL: University of Chicago Press.

McLure C. E., Jr and George R. Zodrow (1987) "Treasury I and the Tax Reform Act of 1986: The Economics and Politics of Tax Reform", *Journal of Economic Perspectives*, 1 (1), Summer, 37–58.

Musgrave, R. A. (1987) "Short of Euphoria", *Journal of Economic Perspectives*, 1 (1) Summer, 59–71.

Pechman, J. A. (1987) "Tax Reform: Theory and Practice", *Journal of Economic Pespectives*, 1 (1), Summer, 11–29.

Poterba, J. M., and L. Summers (1983) "Dividend Taxes, Investment, and Q", *Journal of Public Economics*, 22 (2), November, 135–67.

Sandmo, A. (1985) "The Effects of Taxation on Saving and Risk Taking", in A. J. Auerbach and M. S. Feldstein (eds), *Handbook of Public Economics*, vol. 1, Amsterdam: North-Holland, pp. 265–311.

Summers, L. (1984) "The After-tax Rate of Return Affects Private Savings", *American Economic Review*, 74 (2), May, 249–53.

US Department of the Treasury (1977) *Blueprints for Basic Tax Reform*, Washington, DC: US Government Printing Office.

—— (1984) *Tax Reform for Simplicity, Fairness, and Economic Growth*, Washington, DC: US Government Printing Office, three volumes.

—— (1985) *The President's Tax Proposals to the Congress for Fairness, Growth, and Simplicity*, Washington, DC: US Government Printing Office.

—— (1987) *Compendium of Tax Research 1987*, Washington, DC: US Government Printing Office.

Whalley, J. (1988) "Lessons from General Equilibrium Models", in H. J. Aaron, H. Galper and J. A. Pechman (eds), *Uneasy Compromise: Problems of a Hybrid Income–Consumption Tax*, Washington, DC: Brookings Institution, pp. 15–50.

4

Indeterminacy in Applied Intertemporal General Equilibrium Models

Timothy J. Kehoe and David K. Levine

1 Introduction

In recent years large-scale applied general equilibrium models have increasingly gained acceptance as a tool for policy analysis. To study issues such as social security schemes, the national debt, monetary policy and international exchange rates it is essential that these models have an explicitly dynamic component. Roughly, the goal is to build more realistic descriptive models incorporating the features found in more stylized dynamic models, such as those in Diamond (1965), Lucas (1972) and Kareken and Wallace (1981).

The most ambitious effort in this direction is the work of Auerbach, Kotlikoff and Skinner (1983). To analyze public finance issues, they build an empirical overlapping generations model. To calculate equilibria the model is truncated to effectively have a long finite horizon. Since this procedure is rather artificial, an obvious question that arises is how sensitive the calculated equilibrium is to the way in which the model is truncated. As we point out here, there is a close connection between this question and the question of whether the underlying infinite horizon model is determinate. Unfortunately, and in contrast with models with a finite number of infinitely lived agents, overlapping generations models may not have determinate equilibria (Kehoe and Levine, 1985).

That an overlapping generations model might have a continuum of equilibria is well known. When counting the equations and unknowns in his equilibrium conditions, Samuelson (1958) himself has noted that "we never seem to get enough equations: lengthening our time period turns out always to add as many new unknowns as it supplies equations" (see also Samuelson, 1960). Gale (1973) has extensively studied the overlapping generations model with a single two-period-lived consumer in each generation and one good in each period. In such a model he finds that indeterminacy is always associated with equilibria that have nonzero amounts of nominal debt. Such indeterminacy is always one dimensional; in other words the equilibria can be indexed by a single number, e.g. the price of fiat money. Balasko and Shell (1981) have extended these results to a model in which there are many goods in each period but a single two-period-lived consumer in each generation, in fact, a consumer with a Cobb–Douglas utility function. Geanakoplos and Polemarchakis (1984) and Kehoe and Levine (1984a) have extended these results to a model with a single two-period-lived consumer with intertemporally separable preferences in each generation. Kehoe et al. (1986) have extended them to a model in which demand satisfies the assumption of gross substitutes. Calvo (1978) has constructed examples in which the indeterminacy is still one dimensional, indexed by the price of an asset such as land or capital.

In this paper we consider pure exchange overlapping generations models with n goods in each period. We argue that for a model with a nonzero stock of nominal debt there is potentially an n-dimensional indeterminacy, while for a model with no nominal debt there is potentially an $(n - 1)$-dimensional indeterminacy. Thus relative prices within a period can be indeterminate. Although our results agree with those previously known for the case where there is one good in every period, they indicate that indeterminacy does not depend on the existence of fiat money or other assets. Furthermore, even in pure exchange models with no aggregate debt or assets, our results indicate that equilibria may be indeterminate or not whether or not they are Pareto efficient.

How far do we have to go to construct examples in which there are indeterminate equilibria without fiat money or indeterminate equilibria that are Pareto efficient? We present an example in which the only departure from the simple model considered by Gale is that the single consumer in each generation lives three, rather than two, periods. Gale himself considers such models and conjectures that the results he obtains for the two-period-lived model carries over to them. Unfortunately, we provide a robust example that demonstrates that this is not the case. This stands in fundamental contrast with the static pure exchange model, where, although it is always possible to construct examples with continua of equilibria, such examples cannot be robust. As we shall see, our three-period-lived consumer model can also be viewed as a model with two-period-lived consumers in each generation and two goods in each period.

Indeterminacy of relative prices is possible for very plausible parameter values. In fact, the value of the crucial parameter in our example, the elasticity of substitution in consumption over time, has been chosen to agree with the empirical evidence. (See Auerbach,

Kotlikoff and Skinner (1983) and Mankiw, Rotemberg and Summers (1985) for summaries of this evidence.) Since the representative consumer in our example has a constant elasticity of substitution utility function, the value we have chosen, 0.2, allows some goods to be gross complements at some prices. In situations where goods are always gross substitutes we argue that indeterminacy of the type discussed in this paper is impossible. To guarantee gross substitutability, however, we need to set the elasticity of substitution greater than or equal to 1.0, which is an implausibly high value.

What does this mean for applied research such as that of Auerbach, Kotlikoff and Skinner (1983)? An obvious recommendation is to test the sensitivity of the model to terminal conditions. Our results indicate that this may be a substantial problem.

A second issue is empirical: indeterminacy is a property of overlapping generations models but not of models with finitely many infinitely lived dynasties (see Kehoe, Levine and Romer, forthcoming). Consequently the importance of the bequest motive, as discussed, for example, by Darby (1979) or Kotlikoff and Summers (1981), is crucial in whether or not sensitivity to endpoint conditions is likely to be important in practice. In addition, liquidity constraints, such as those of Bewley (1980, 1983), Scheinkman and Weiss (1986) or Levine (1989), tend to lead to overlapping-generations-type implications.

We begin by describing a simple stationary model and examining its steady state. We then study the behavior of equilibrium price paths around a steady state and characterize the dimensionality of paths that converge to the steady state. The second and third sections of this paper constitute a relatively nontechnical summary of the results of Gale (1973) and Kehoe and Levine (1984b, 1985). The fourth section presents a simple example of indeterminacy of relative prices. In the fifth section we argue that indeterminacy of equilibrium in the infinite model corresponding to acute sensitivity to terminal conditions in any truncated version of the model. In the sixth section we prove that indeterminacy is impossible if all goods are gross substitutes. In the seventh section we indicate how our results can be extended to models that have growing populations, models that are nonstationary for any finite number of periods and models that have equilibrium cycles. We conclude with a short discussion of some possible extensions of our results and their implications for applied work.

2 The Model and its Steady States

We begin by considering a model in which each generation lives two periods. As we shall explain, a model in which each generation lives more than two periods can be viewed as a special case of this model. Each generation $t \geq 1$ is identical and lives in periods t and $t + 1$. There are n goods in each period. The vector $p_t = (p_t^1, \ldots, p_t^n)$ denotes prices in t. The consumption and savings decisions of the (possibly many different types of) consumers in generation t are aggregated into excess demand functions $y(p_t, p_{t+1})$ when young and $z(p_t, p_{t+1})$ when old; y and z are of course, n-dimensional vectors. Excess demands are assumed to be homogeneous of degree zero,

$$y(\theta p_t, \theta p_{t+1}) \equiv y(p_t, p_{t+1})$$
$$z(\theta p_t, \theta p_{t+1}) \equiv z(p_t, p_{t+1})$$

(4.1)

for any $\theta > 0$, and to obey Walras's law

$$p_t' y(p_t, p_{t+1}) + p_{t+1}' z(p_t, p_{t+1}) \equiv 0 \tag{4.2}$$

Although the model is specified in terms of the excess demand functions y and z, it may be helpful to think of them as being derived from solutions to utility maximization problems of the form

$$\text{maximize } u_h(y^h + w_1^h z^h + w_2^h)$$
$$\text{subject to } p_t' y^h + p_{t+1}' z^h \leq 0 \tag{4.3}$$
$$y^h \geq -w_1^h \qquad z^h \geq -w_2^h$$

Here y^h is the vector of net trades made by consumer h in generation t when young, z^h is the vector of net trades when old, and w_1^h and w_2^h are endowment vectors. The aggregate excess demand functions are defined as

$$y(p_t, p_{t+1}) = \sum_h y^h(p_t, p_{t+1})$$
$$z(p_t, p_{t+1}) = \sum_h z^h(p_t, p_{t+1})$$

(4.4)

The form of the budget constraint in (4.3), and the assumptions of homogeneity and Walras's law that correspond to it, are implicitly equivalent to the assumption that consumers are allowed to trade goods with each other, even if the goods are consumed in different time periods. One institutional story to go with this assumption is that we allow creation of private debt, or inside money, i.e. consumer h can be thought of as having two budget constraints, $p_t' y^h + m_t^h \leq 0$ and $p_{t+1}' z^h - m_t^h \leq 0$, where m_t^h is the amount of money that he carries over from period t to period $t + 1$. We allow m_t^h to be negative, thus allowing borrowing. Adding these two budget constraints together eliminates m_t^h and yields the constraint in (4.3). The presence of public debt, or outside money, is a different matter, however, which, as we shall see, depends on initial conditions.

Viewing each consumer as facing a sequence of budget constraints provides us with an alternative way of viewing relative prices. The prices (p_t, p_{t+1}) considered above are the same prices that consumers face if there is a complete set of futures markets. Suppose instead that the consumer faces two budget constraints of the form

$$q'_t y^h + m^h_t \leq 0 \qquad (4.5)$$
$$q'_{t+1} z^h - m^h_t (1 + r_t) \leq 0$$

where q_t and q_{t+1} are vectors of spot prices and r_t is the interest rate on borrowing and lending between periods t and $t+1$. Again the budget constraints in (4.5) reduce to that in (4.3) if we set $p_t = q_t/(1 + r_1)(1 + r_2)\ldots(1 + r_{t-1})$.

We assume that excess demands are continuously differentiable for all strictly positive price pairs (p_t, p_{t+1}), which, as Debreu (1972) and Mas-Colell (1974) have shown, entails little loss of generality. We further assume that y and z are bounded from below and are such that some, but not all, prices approach zero, the sum of excess demand becomes unbounded; i.e. $e'[y(p_t, p_{t+1}) + z(p_t, p_{t+1})] \rightarrow \infty$ where e denotes the n vector whose every element is one. These assumptions are naturally satisfied when y and z are derived from utility maximization: if consumption of every good by every consumer must be non-negative, then an obvious lower bound for (y, z) is $(-w_1, -w_2)$ where w_1 and w_2 are the aggregate endowment vectors. If preferences are monotonically increasing in consumption, then when a single price goes to zero the excess demand for that good becomes infinite. Furthermore, if more than one price goes to zero, then excess demand for some, but perhaps not all, of the corresponding goods becomes infinite (see Arrow and Hahn, 1971, pp. 29–31).

Debreu (1974) has demonstrated that, for any y and z that satisfy the assumptions of homogeneity and Walras's law, there exists a generation of $2n$ utility maximizing consumers whose aggregate excess demand functions y^* and z^* agree with y and z on that set of positive relative prices uniformly bounded away from zero. There is a minor technical complication in that y^* and z^* may not agree with y and z as some relative prices approach zero. Utilizing a result due to Mas-Colell (1977), however, Kehoe and Levine (1984b) argue that we can ignore this qualification when studying the behavior of the excess demand functions near steady states. Consequently, for our purposes we are justified in viewing our assumptions as both necessary and sufficient for demand functions derived from utility maximization by heterogeneous consumers. As we shall see, however, the possibility of indeterminacy of relative prices in overlapping generations models does not depend on implausible aggregate excess demand functions or even on heterogeneity among consumers within a generation.

In addition to the consumers born in periods 1, 2, . . ., there is an initial old generation alive in period 1. Its excess demand function $z_0(p_1, m)$ depends on prices p_1 in the first period and the nominal savings m of the initial old generation. These savings can be thought of as outside or fiat money, at least if $m \geqslant 0$. Implicitly, as m changes, the distribution of savings between consumers in the initial old generation changes in a fixed way. We assume that z_0 is continuously differentiable, is homogeneous of degree zero,

$$z_0(\theta p_1, m) \equiv z_0(p_1, m) \tag{4.6}$$

for any $\theta > 0$, and obeys Walras's law,

$$p_1' z_0(p_1, m) \equiv m \tag{4.7}$$

An equilibrium for this economy is an initial level of nominal savings m and a price path $(p_1, p_2, . . .)$ for which excess demand vanishes in each period:

$$z_0(p_1, m) + y(p_1, p_2) = 0 \tag{4.8}$$

for $t = 1$ and

$$z(p_{t-1}, p_t) + y(p_t, p_{t+1}) = 0 \tag{4.9}$$

for $t > 1$. Repeated application of the equilibrium conditions and Walras's law implies that $-p_t' y(p_t, p_{t+1}) = p_{t+1}' z(p_t, p_{t+1}) = m$ at all times. Consequently, m is the fixed nominal net savings made by the young generation in each period. If m is non-negative it is easy to interpret it as fiat money. Even if it is negative, however, there are institutional stories to accompany it: think of an institution that makes loans to consumers when they are young and uses the repayment of these loans to make loans to consumers in the next generation.

A steady state of this economy is a relative price vector p and an inflation factor β such that $p_t = \beta^{t-1} p$ satisfies

$$z(\beta^{t-2} p, \beta^{t-1} p) + y(\beta^{t-1} p, \beta^t p) = z(p, \beta p) + y(p, \beta p) = 0 \tag{4.10}$$

Here $r = 1/\beta - 1$ is the steady state rate of interest. Notice that a steady state is not necessarily an equilibrium price path because it may not satisfy the equilibrium condition (4.8) in the first period. There are two types of steady states: real steady states in which $m = -p' y(p, \beta p) = 0$ and monetary, or nominal, steady states in which $m \neq 0$. On the one hand, Walras's law implies that $p'(y + \beta z) = 0$ and, consequently, that $\beta p' z = m$. On the other hand, the steady state condition (4.10) implies that $p'(y + z) = 0$ and, consequently, that $p' z = m$. Therefore $(\beta - 1)m = 0$, and any nominal steady state must have $\beta = 1$. Gale calls steady states in which $\beta = 1$ golden rule steady states because they maximize a weighted sum of individual utility functions subject to the constraint of stationary consumption over time. He calls real steady states balanced.

It is possible to construct examples in which a golden rule steady state is also balanced, i.e. in which $m = 0$ and $\beta = 1$ simultaneously. Such a steady state must satisfy $z(p, p) + y(p,p) = 0$ and $-p'y$ $(p, p) = 0$. Walras's law implies that this is a system of n independent equations; homogeneity implies that there are $n - 1$ independent unknowns. Consequently we would expect this system of equations to have a solution only by coincidence. In fact, Kehoe and Levine (1984b) prove that almost all economies do not have a steady state where both $m = 0$ and $\beta = 1$. They give the space of economies (y, z) that satisfy the assumptions of differentiability, homogeneity, Walras's law and the boundary condition a topological structure: two economies are close to each other if the values of demand functions and the values of their partial derivatives are close. The phrase "almost all" in this context means that the property holds for a subset that is open and dense: any sufficiently small perturbation of an economy that does not have a steady state where $m = 0$ and $\beta = 1$ results in an economy that still does not have such a steady state; for any economy that has such a steady state, however, there exist arbitrarily small perturbations that result in economies that do not have such steady states. A property that holds for almost all economies is called a generic property.

Gale proves that the model with a single two-period-lived consumer in each generation has a unique nominal steady state and, generically, a unique real steady state. The unique nominal steady state is where the price of the single good is constant over time. Walras's law implies that this situation does indeed satisfy the steady state condition (4.10). At this steady state the savings of the young person are not, in general, zero. Since there is only one consumer in each generation any trade that takes place must be between generations. Consequently, since there is only one good in each period, there can be trade only if there is a corresponding transfer of nominal debt from period to period. Any real steady state must therefore be given by a relative price ratio $\beta = p_{t+1}/p_t$ that makes the consumer prefer not to trade. Such a price ratio obviously exists; generically there is only one.

With many consumers in each generation but only one good in each period, nominal steady states are still unique but real steady states need not be: consider a static pure exchange economy with two consumers and two goods that has multiple, but determinate, equilibria. Robust examples of this sort are, of course, easy to construct (see, for example, Shapley and Shubik, 1977). Now construct an overlapping generations economy by assigning two such consumers to each generation and by letting one of the goods by available in the first period of their lives and the other in the second. Each of the different equilibria of the static ecomony now corresponds to a different real steady state of the overlapping generations economy in which the two consumers in each generation trade with each other but not with other generations. With many goods and many consumers neither real steady states nor nominal steady states need by unique. Kehoe and Levine (1984b) prove, however, that generically there exists an odd number of each type. Their arguments are similar to those used to prove that the number of equilibria of pure exchange economy is odd (see, for example, Varian, 1974). In similar vein, Kehoe et al. (1986) show that, if y and z satisfy the assumption of gross substitutes, then there is a unique steady state of each type.

Using a result due to Balasko and Shell (1980), we are able to examine the efficiency properties of steady states (see also Burke, 1987). Balasko and Shell consider models with a single consumer in each generation that satisfy a uniform curvature condition on indifference surfaces that is quite natural in a stationary setting such as ours. They demonstrate that a necessary and sufficient condition for an equilibrium price path of such a model to be Pareto efficient is that the infinite sum $\Sigma 1/\|p_t\|$ does not converge. (Here, of course, $\|\cdot\|$ is the ordinary Euclidean norm: $\|p_t\| = (p_t'p_t)^{1/2}$.) This result can easily be extended to models with many consumers in every generation. Consequently, a steady state of our model is Pareto efficient if and only if $\beta \leqslant 1$, in other words, if and only if the interest rate is non-negative. Price paths that converge to steady states where $\beta \leqslant 1$ are Pareto efficient; those that converge to steady states where $\beta > 1$ are not.

Every economy has a Pareto-efficient steady state since it always has a steady state where $\beta = 1$. In the model with one two-period-lived consumer with gross substitutes excess demands in each generation and one good in each period, Gale finds that the unique real state has $\beta < 1$ if and only if the unique nominal steady state has $m < 0$. Similarly, $\beta > 1$ at the real steady state if and only if $m > 0$ at the nominal steady state. In the more general model we cannot make such strong statements. We can, however, demonstrate that every economy has an odd number of steady states where $\beta \leqslant 1$ and $m \leqslant 0$. We sketch an argument below; details are given by Kehoe and Levine (1984b). This argument also makes it clear why every economy has an odd number of real steady states and an odd number of nominal steady states.

Consider the n functions

$$f_i(p, \beta) = y^i(p, \beta p) + z^i(p, \beta p) - \frac{p'[y(p, \beta p) + z(p, \beta p)]}{e'p} \quad (4.11)$$

Notice that, for any fixed $\beta > 0$, that the functions $f_i(p, \beta)$ have the formal properties of excess demand functions of a static pure exchange economy: they are homogeneous of degree zero in p and satisfy Walras's law, $p'f(p, \beta) \equiv 0$. Consequently, for any $\beta > 0$ there exists at least one value of p that solves the equations

$$f_i(p, \beta) = 0 \qquad i = 1, \ldots, n \quad (4.12)$$

Walras's law implies that this is a system of $n - 1$ independent equations; homogeneity implies that there are $n - 1$ independent unknowns. Consequently, it can easily be shown that solutions to this system of equations are generally smooth implicit functions of β. Our assumptions on the behavior of excess demand as some prices tend toward zero guarantee that there exists $\underline{\beta} > 0$ and $\overline{\beta} > \underline{\beta}$ such that any steady state value of β satisfies $\underline{\beta} < \beta < \overline{\beta}$.

There are two distinct ways for a pair (p, β) that satisfies (4.12) to be a steady state: if $-p'y(p, \beta) = 0$ or if $\beta = 1$. In either case Walras's law implies that $p'[y(p, \beta p) + \beta z(p, \beta p)] = 0$. Let

$$m(p, \beta) = -p'y(p, \beta p) \quad (4.13)$$

for any (p, β), and consider pairs m and β such that $m = m(p, \beta)$ and (p, β) satisfies (4.12). Unfortunately, m is not, in general, a well-defined function of β since for any β there may be more than one p such that (4.12) is satisfied. We are justified, however, in drawing diagrams like that in figure 4.1. There are a finite number of paths of pairs m and β that satisfy our conditions. Some of them are loops that do not intersect the boundary $\beta = \underline{\beta}$ or $\beta = \overline{\beta}$. It is possible, however, to demonstrate that generically there are an odd number of points of the form $(p, \underline{\beta})$ where (4.12) is satisfied and, similarly, an odd number of the form $(p, \overline{\beta})$. To make this plausible recall that the functions $f_i(p, \beta)$ have the properties of excess demand functions of a static pure exchange economy. It is well known that generically (in this case, for almost all β) there are an odd number of equilibria of such an economy. An even number, possibly zero, of pairs m and β are associated with paths that return to the same boundary $\beta = \underline{\beta}$. An odd number, at least one, therefore cannot return. Our boundary assumption implies that for $\underline{\beta} \leqslant \beta \leqslant \overline{\beta}$, the prices that satisfy (4.12) are uniformly bounded away from zero. Consequently, $m(p, \beta)$ remains bounded, and paths that start at $\beta = \underline{\beta}$ and do not return must eventually reach the boundary $\beta = \overline{\beta}$. Any path or loop may intersect itself, but it does not, in general, do so where $\beta = 1$ (or $\underline{\beta}$ or $\overline{\beta}$) or where $m = 0$.

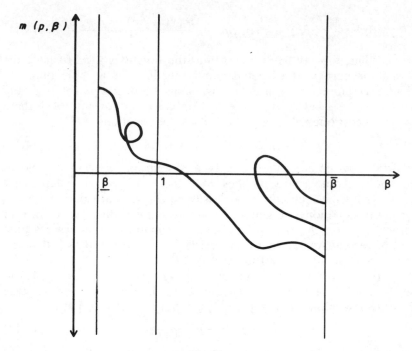

Figure 4.1

The boundary assumptions also imply that $m(p, \beta) > 0$ when $\beta = \underline{\beta}$ and $m(p, \beta) < 0$ when $\beta = \bar{\beta}$. Consequently, any path that starts at $\underline{\beta}$ and ends at $\bar{\beta}$ must intersect the line $m = 0$ an odd number of times. Similarly, any such path must intersect the line $\beta = 1$ an odd number of times. On the other hand, every loop or path that starts and ends at the same boundary intersects both $m = 0$ and $\beta = 1$ an even, possibly zero, number of times. Each of these intersections corresponds to a steady state. Generically, there is none where both $m = 0$ and $\beta = 1$. Experimenting with different possibilities, we can easily verify that any admissible graph must share with that in figure 4.1 the property that there are an odd number of steady states where $\beta \leqslant 1$ and $m \geqslant 0$ and an odd number where $\beta \geqslant 1$ and $m \leqslant 0$.

This theory has particularly strong implications when both types of steady states are unique. As we have remarked above, Kehoe et al. shows that this is always the case with gross substitutes. From the diagram we see that the situation is the same as Gale's one good case. The real steady state has $\beta < 1$ if and only if $m < 0$ at the nominal steady state, and $\beta > 1$ at the real steady state if and only if $m > 0$ at the nominal steady state.

3 Determinacy of Equilibrium Price Paths

We now focus our attention on the behavior of equilibrium price paths near a steady state. In addition to the requirement that markets clear in every period we require that prices converge to the steady state, i.e. that $(p_t, p_{t+1})/\|(p_t, p_{t+1})\| \to (p, \beta p)/\|(p, \beta p)\|$ at $t \to \infty$. We do this for two reasons. First, price paths that begin near and converge to a steady state are the most plausible perfect foresight equilibria. Agents can compute future prices using only local information. If prices are not converging to a steady state, however, then agents need global information and very large computers to compute future prices. Second, these price paths are the easiest to study: to determine the qualitative behavior of price paths near a steady state we can linearize the equilibrium conditions. Paths that do not converge may display very complex periodic, or even chaotic, behavior. It may be difficult to distinguish such paths from price sequences that satisfy the equilibrium conditions for a very long time but eventually lead to prices that are zero or negative, where excess demands explode, making a continuation of the sequence impossible.

Determinacy of equilibrium price paths that converge to a steady state may still leave room for indeterminacy. There may be paths that do not converge to a steady state but nevertheless always remain strictly positive and are therefore legitimate equilibria. Whether a model has a determinate path that converges to a steady state is a weak test. We shall establish, however, that there are robust examples of economies that fail even this test.

Consider again the conditions that an equilibrium price path must satisfy:

$$z_0(p_1, m) + y(p_1, p_2) = 0 \qquad (4.14)$$

for $t = 1$ and

$$z(p_{t-1}, p_t) + y(p_t, p_{t+1}) = 0 \qquad (4.15)$$

for $t > 1$. Once p_1 and p_2 are determined (4.15) acts as a nonlinear difference equation determining the rest of the price path. We begin by asking how many pairs (p_1, p_2) give rise to the price path that converges to a steady state $(p, \beta p)$. The stable manifold theorem from the theory of dynamic systems described, for example, by Irwin (1980) implies that, near $(p, \beta p)$, these questions can generically by answered by linearizing (4.15). We then ask how many pairs (p_1, p_2) are consistent with equilibrium in the first period. This question can be answered by linearizing (4.14). Pairs (p_1, p_2) that lie in the intersection of these two sets correspond to equilibrium price paths.

The dimension of this intersection can be deduced by a simple counting argument. If this dimension is greater than zero, there is a continuum of equilibrium price paths. If it is greater than unity, relative prices are indeterminate: not even by exogenously specifying the price level can we make price paths determinate. Details of the arguments presented below are given by Kehoe and Levine (1985).

Making use of the fact that derivatives of excess demand are homogeneous of degree minus one and that $(p, \beta p)$ is a steady state, we can write the linearized system as

$$z_0(p, m) + y(p, \beta p) + D_2 y(p_2 - \beta p) + (D_1 y + D_1 z_0)(p_1 - p) = 0$$
$$(4.16)$$

$$D_2 y(p_{t+1} - \beta^t p) + (D_1 y + \beta D_2 z)(p_t - \beta^{t-1} p)$$
$$+ \beta D_1 z(p_{t-1} - \beta^{t-2} p) = 0 \qquad (4.17)$$

where $D_1 y$ is, for example, the matrix of partial derivatives of y with respect to its first vector of arguments and where all derivatives are evaluated at $(p, \beta p)$. β shows up as a coefficient of $D_1 z$ and $D_2 z$ in (4.17) because homogenity implies that $D_1 z(\beta^{t-2} p, \beta^{t-1} p) = \beta^{2-t} D_1 z$ $(p, \beta p)$, for example, while $D_1 y(\beta^{t-1} p, \beta^t p) = \beta^{1-t} D_1 y$ $(p, \beta p)$. Differentiating the homogeneity assumption (4.1) with respect to θ and evaluating the result at $\theta = 1$ and $(p_t, p_{t+1}) = (p, \beta p)$ results in

$$D_1 yp + \beta D_2 yp = 0$$
$$D_1 zp + \beta D_2 zp = 0 \qquad (4.18)$$

Consequently, the linearized equilibrium conditions (4.16) and (4.17) can be rewritten as

$$D_2 yp_2 + (D_1 y + D_1 z_0)p_1 = D_1 z_0 p - z_0(p, m) - y(p, \beta p) \quad (4.19)$$
$$D_2 yp_{t+1} + (D_1 y + \beta D_2 z)p_t + \beta D_1 zp_{t-1} = 0 \qquad (4.20)$$

Kehoe and Levine (1984b) have shown that $D_2 y$ is generically nonsingular. Consequently, (4.20) can be solved for an explicit second-order difference equation. Using a standard trick, we can write this equation as the first-order system $q_t = Gq_{t-1}$ where $q_t = (p_t, p_{t+1})$ and

$$G = \begin{bmatrix} 0 & I \\ -\beta D_2 y^{-1} D_1 z & -D_2 y^{-1}(D_1 y + \beta D_2 z) \end{bmatrix} \qquad (4.21)$$

The stability properties of this difference equation are governed by the eigenvalues of G. The homogeneity assumption (4.18) implies that β is an eigenvalue of G since

$$G = \begin{bmatrix} p \\ \beta p \end{bmatrix} = \begin{bmatrix} \beta p \\ \beta^2 p \end{bmatrix} \qquad (4.22)$$

Differentiating Walras's law (4.2) and evaluating the result at $(p_t, p_{t+1}) = (p, \beta p)$ implies that

$$y(p, \beta p)' + p'D_1 y + \beta p'D_1 z = 0$$

$$z(p, \beta p)' + p'D_2 y + \beta p'D_2 z = 0 \qquad (4.23)$$

Consequently, unity is another eigenvalue since (4.23) and the steady state condition (4.10) imply that

$$p'[-\beta D_1 z \quad D_2 y]G = p'[-\beta D_1 z \quad D_2 y] \qquad (4.24)$$

In the case where $\beta = 1$ these are generically the same restriction, and we have information about only one eigenvalue.

It should now be clear why the case where $n = 1$ is so special: if homogeneity and Walras's law are the only restrictions that economic theory imposes on the dynamical system (4.15), then we can expect to be able to pin down at most two eigenvalues of (4.21). In the case where $n = 1$ this is all the eigenvalues, but in general there are $2n - 2$ left to be determined by the parameters of the model. In fact, Kehoe and Levine (1984b) prove that for any pattern of $2n$ eigenvalues, as long as (4.22) and (4.24) are satisfied and complex numbers come in conjugate pairs, there exists (y, z) that satisfies all our assumptions and gives rise to a matrix G with those eigenvalues.

We are interested in the set of initial conditions $q_1 = (p_1, p_2)$ for the linear difference equation $q_t = Gq_{t-1}$ for which $q_t/\|q_t\| \to q/\|q\|$ where $q = (p, \beta p)$. This set is a subspace of $\mathbb{R}^{2n}$ determined by the eigenvectors of G. Suppose that $(x_i, y_i) \in \mathbb{C}^{2n}$ is the eigenvector in complex $2n$-dimensional space associated with the eigenvalue λ_i:

$$\begin{bmatrix} 0 & I \\ -\beta D_2 y^{-1} d_1 z & -D_2 y^{-1}(D_1 y + \beta D_2 z) \end{bmatrix} \begin{bmatrix} x_i \\ y_i \end{bmatrix} = \lambda_i \begin{bmatrix} x_i \\ y_i \end{bmatrix} \qquad (4.25)$$

The first n equations state that $y_i = \lambda_i x_i$. If the eigenvalues of G are distinct, a condition that Kehoe and Levine (1984b) prove holds generically, then solutions to the difference equation $q_t = G(q_{t-1})$ take the form

$$\begin{bmatrix} p_t \\ p_{t+1} \end{bmatrix} = \sum_{i=1}^{2n} c_i \lambda_i^{t-1} \begin{bmatrix} x_i \\ \lambda_i x_i \end{bmatrix} \qquad (4.26)$$

where the complex constants $c_1, \ldots, c_{2n}$ are determined by the initial conditions

$$\begin{bmatrix} p_1 \\ p_2 \end{bmatrix} = \sum_{i=1}^{2n} c_i \begin{bmatrix} x_i \\ \lambda_i x_i \end{bmatrix} \qquad (4.27)$$

To ensure convergence to the steady state $(p, \beta p)$, we need to put a positive weight c_1 on the eigenvector $(x_1, \lambda_1 x_1) = (p, \beta p)$ and zero weights c_i on eigenvectors $(x_i, \lambda_i x_i)$ for which the modulus $|\lambda_i|$ is greater than β, i.e. we require that β is the dominant eigenvalue in (4.26).

Let n^s be the number of eigenvalues of G that are less than β in modulus. Reorder the eigenvalues so that $(x_2, \lambda_2 x_2)$, ..., $(x_{n^s+1}, \lambda_{n^s+1} x_{n^s+1})$ are the associated eigenvectors. Since eigenvectors associated with distinct eigenvalues are linearly independent and since complex eigenvectors show up in conjugate pairs, the n^s+1 eigenvectors $(p, \beta p), (x_2, \lambda_2 x_2), \ldots, (x_{n^s+1}, \lambda_{n^s+1} x_{n^s+1})$ span an $(n^s + 1)$-dimensional subspace of $\mathbb{R}^{2n}$. Initial values (p_1, p_2) that lead to convergence to the steady state have the form

$$\begin{bmatrix} p_1 \\ p_2 \end{bmatrix} = c_1 \begin{bmatrix} p \\ \beta p \end{bmatrix} + \sum_{i=2}^{n^s+1} c_i \begin{bmatrix} x_i \\ \lambda_i x_i \end{bmatrix} \tag{4.28}$$

Besides yielding a path that converges to the steady state ray, (p_1, p_2) must also satisfy the linearized equilibrium condition (4.19) in the first period. Let us first examine the situation where $m \neq 0$. In this case z_0 is not homogeneous of degree zero in p_1 alone, and, since $p_1' D_1 z_0(p_1, m) p_1 \equiv -p_1 z_0(p_1, m) \equiv -m \neq 0$, $D_1 z_0 p \neq 0$; fiat money, in fact, operates as numeraire. Consequently, (4.19) defines an n-dinemsional affine subset of prices (p_1, p_2) consistent with equilibrium in the first period. The intersection of this subset with the subspace of prices that yield a path that converges to the steady state generically has dimension $(n^s + 1) + n - 2n = n^s + 1 - n \ (\leq n)$. Roughly speaking, we say that $2n - n^s - 1$ of the $2n$ variables (p_1, p_2) are pinned down by the requirement of convergence to a steady state in (4.20) and n are pinned down by the equilibrium condition (4.19); this leaves $n^s + 1 - n$ variables free, which can be as many as n if $n^s = 2n - 1$.

These are several cases of interest. First, if $n^s < n - 1$, then generically there are no equilibrium paths that converge to this steady state. We call such a steady state unstable. Second, if $n^s = n - 1$, then stable equilibrium price paths are locally unique and, in a small enough neighborhood of the steady state, actually unique. We call such a steady state determinate. Third, if $n^s < n - 1$, then there is a continuum of locally stable paths. In fact, the (p_1, p_2) that generate these paths form a manifold of dimension $n^s + 1 - n$. We call such a steady state indeterminate. The $(n^s + 1 - n)$-dimensional affine subset of the corresponding linear system is, in fact, the tangent space to this manifold at $(p, \beta p)$, i.e. its best linear approximation.

Let us now consider the situation where $m = 0$. Since z_0 is now homogeneous of degree zero in p_1, $D_1 z_0 p = 0$. There are two considerations that reduce the dimension of the subspace of initial conditions that we are concerned with. First, since the equilibrium conditions (4.19) and (4.20) are now homogeneous of degree zero in p, p_1 and p_2, we can impose a price normalization and work in a $(2n - 1)$-dimensional affine subset of $\mathbb{R}^{2n}$, for example, by setting $p_1^1 = 1$. This allows us to fix the weight put on the eigenvector $(p, \beta p)$ in (4.27). Second, since $m = 0$, the initial price pair (p_1, p_2), and all subsequent pairs (p_t, p_{t+1}), must satisfy $p_1' y(p_1, p_2) = 0$. This implies that (p_1, p_2) cannot put any weight on the eigenvector (x_i, x_i) associated with the eigenvalue $\lambda_i = 1$ in (4.27).

To illustrate the latter point, let us linearize the restriction $-p_1' y(p_1, p_2) = m$ at $(p, \beta p)$:

$$-p'y - (y' + p'D_1 y)(p_1 - p) - p'D_2 y(p_2 - \beta p) = m \quad (4.29)$$

Homogeneity (4.18) and Walras's law (4.23) imply that we can simplify this to

$$\beta p'D_1 z p_1 \quad p'D_2 y p_2 = m \quad (4.30)$$

Suppose that $(x_i, \lambda_i x_i)$ is an eigenvector of G. Then (4.24) implies that

$$[\beta p'D_1 z \quad -p'D_2 y]\begin{bmatrix} x_i \\ \lambda_i x_i \end{bmatrix} = [\beta p'D_1 z \quad -p'D_2 y]G\begin{bmatrix} x_i \\ \lambda_i x_i \end{bmatrix}$$

$$= \lambda_i[\beta p'D_1 z \quad -p'D_2 y]\begin{bmatrix} x_i \\ \lambda_i x_i \end{bmatrix} \quad (4.31)$$

Consequently, for all $\lambda_i \neq 1$,

$$[\beta p'D_1 z \quad p'D_2 y]\begin{bmatrix} x_i \\ \lambda_i x_i \end{bmatrix} = 0 \quad (4.32)$$

Premultiplying (4.27) by $[\beta p'D_1 z \quad -p'D_2 y]$, we obtain

$$[\beta p'D_1 z \quad -p'D_2 y]\begin{bmatrix} p_1 \\ p_2 \end{bmatrix} - \sum_{i=1}^{2n} c_i[\beta_p'D_1 z \quad p'D_2 y]\begin{bmatrix} x_i \\ \lambda_i x_i \end{bmatrix}$$

$$m = c_j[\beta p'D_1 z \quad -p'D_2 y]\begin{bmatrix} x_j \\ x_j \end{bmatrix} \quad (4.33)$$

where (x_j, x_j) is the eigenvector associated with $\lambda_j = 1$. This implies that $c_j = 0$ if and only if $m = 0$. (Notice that in case where $m \neq 0$ and $\beta = 1$ it implies that $c_j = 1$ since $(x_j, x_j) = (p, p)$.)

Suppose that $m = 0$. Let $\bar{n}^s$ denote the number of eigenvalues of G that satisfy $|\lambda_i| < \beta$ excluding $\lambda_i = 1$ if $\beta > 1$. The set of prices $q_1 = (p_1, p_2)$ that satisfy $-p_1' y(p_1, p_2) = 0$ and the price normalization and give rise to a price path that converges to $q = (p_1, \beta p_2)$ forms an $\bar{n}^s$-dimensional set. The set of prices $q_1 = (p_1 \quad p_1)$ that satisfy $-p_1' y(p_1, p_2) = 0$ and the price normalization and are consistent with equilibrium in the first period forms an $(n - 1)$-dimensional set. Equilibrium price paths are associated with points in the intersection of these two sets, which generically has dimension $\bar{n}^s + (n - 1) - (2n - 2) = \bar{n}^s = 1 - n \ (< n - 1)$.

Although the eigenvalue $\lambda_i = 1$ is irrelevant for price paths in which $m = 0$, it is crucial for the behavior of paths where $m \neq 0$: if $m \neq 0$ initially, then the price path cannot converge to a steady state where $\beta < 1$, since $\lambda_i = 1$ must receive nonzero weight in (4.2) but λ_i is an unstable root. This makes good economic sense: there can be no equilibrium in which $m \neq 0$ that converges to a steady state with $\beta < 1$. The exponential deflation would cause the constant nominal money stock to become infinite in real terms. Although paths with $m \neq 0$ can converge to a steady state where $\beta > 1$, asymptotically the real money stock disappears because of inflation.

A warning should be given about the generic nature of our results. Although they hold for almost all economies, it is possible to think of examples that violate them: when there is a single two-period-lived consumer with an intertemporally separable utility function in each generation, for example, both D_2y and D_1z have rank one. Consequently, if there are two or more goods, we cannot invert D_2y. In this case, Kehoe and Levine (1984a) demonstrate that the situation is essentially the same as that in a model with only one good in each period: with nominal initial conditions there is at most a one-dimensional indeterminacy, and with real initial conditions no indeterminacy is possible. These results are, of course, closely related to those of Balasko and Shell (1981) and Geanakoplos and Polemarchakis (1984) cited earlier.

4 An Example with Three-period-lived Consumers

To construct an example of overlapping generations model with relative price indeterminacy, we cannot look at a model with one good per period and two-period-lived consumers, at a model with a single two-period-lived consumer with intertemporally separable utility in each generation, nor at a model with gross substitutes. In this section we consider an example with the simplest possible structure that allows relative price indeterminacy: there is a single good in each period and a single consumer with additively separable preferences in each generation who lives for three rather that two periods and who has constant elasticity of substitution (CES) preferences with an elasticity of substitution of 0.2. Balasko, Cass and Shell (1980) present a simple procedure for converting such a model into one in which consumers live two periods. Suppose that consumers live for k periods. Redefine generations $-k + 2, -k + 1 \ldots, 0$ to be generation 0, generations 1, 2,. . ., $k-1$ to be generation 1, and so on. Similarly, redefine periods. This procedure is illustrated in figure 4.2 for the case where $k = 3$. Notice that the number of goods in each period and the number of consumers in each generation both increase by a factor of $k - 1$.

In this transformation $k - 1$ period cycles become steady states. In fact, we can use this transformation to reduce the study of paths that converge to cycles of any finite length to the study of paths that converge to steady states. It is still the case in the transformed model that there are generically an odd number of steady states of each type, real and nominal. By performing the transformation one period at a time, we are able to demonstrate that the original model generically has an even number of cycles of each type of every length: we know that there are an odd number of steady states; performing the transformation for $k = 3$, we know that there are an

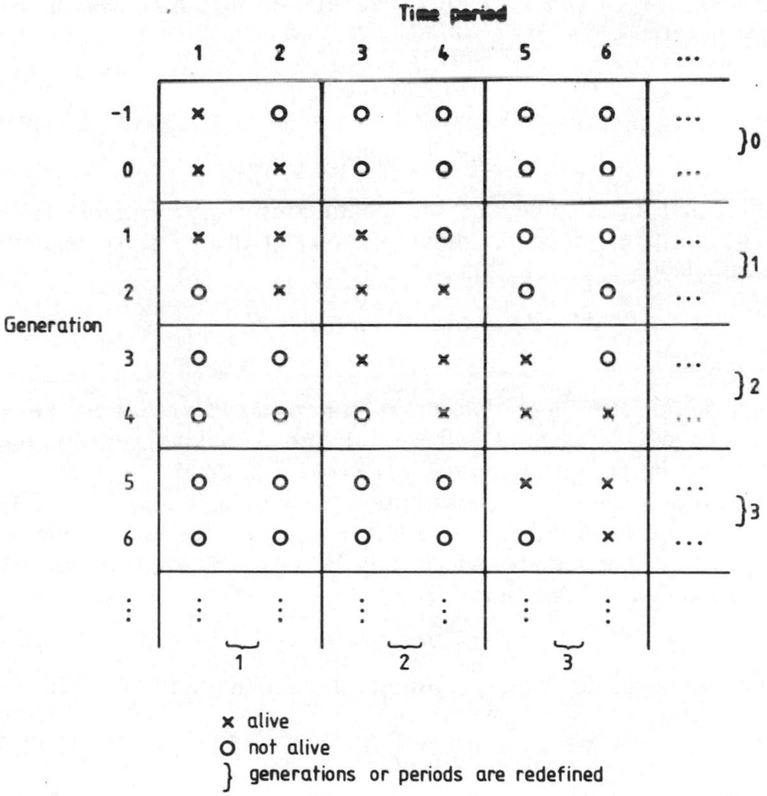

Figure 4.2

odd number of steady states and two cycles, and hence an even number, possibly zero, of two cycles; and so on. This result tells us nothing about the cycles of even length. If (p_1, p_2, p_1, p_2) is a nominal steady state, for example, then so is (p_2, p_1, p_2, p_1). It does, however, place restrictions on cycles of odd length.

Consider an economy in which the single consumer born in period t, where $t = 1, 2, \ldots$, lives for three periods and has the utility function

$$u(c_1, c_2, c_3) = \frac{1}{b}(a_1 c_1^b + a_2 c_2^b + a_2 c_3^b) \qquad (4.34)$$

where $a_1, a_2, a_3 > 0$ and $b < 1$. This is, of course, the constant elasticity of substitution utility function with elasticity of substitution $\eta = 1/(1 - b)$. If the consumer faces the budget constraint

$$p_t c_1 + p_{t+1} c_2 + p_{t+2} c_3 = p_t w_1 + p_{t+1} w_2 + p_{t+2} w_3 \qquad (4.35)$$

where (w_1, w_2, w_3) is his endowment stream, then his excess demand functions are

$$x_j(p_t, p_{t+1}, p_{t+2}) = \frac{a_j^\eta \sum_{i=1}^{3} p_{t+i-1} w_i}{p_{t+j-1}^\eta \sum_{i=1}^{3} a_i^\eta p_{t+i-1}^{1-\eta}} - w_j \qquad j = 1, 2, 3 \quad (4.36)$$

Notice that these functions are continuously differentiable for all strictly positive prices, are homogeneous of degree zero, and obey Walras's law:

$$p_t x_1(p_t, p_{t+1}, p_{t+2}) + p_{t+1} x_2(p_t, p_{t+1}, p_{t+2})$$
$$+ p_{t+2} x_3(p_t, p_{t+1} p_{t+2}) = 0 \qquad (4.37)$$

In addition to these consumers, there are two others, an old consumer who lives only in period 1 and a middle-aged consumer who lives in periods 1 and 2. The old consumer, consumer -1, derives utility only from consumption of the single good in the first period, so we need not specify a utility function. We endow him with m_{-1} units of fiat money, which may be positive, negative, or zero. His excess demand function is

$$x_3^{-1}(p_1, m_{-1}) = m_{-1}/p_1 \qquad (4.38)$$

The middle-aged consumer, consumer 0, has the utility function

$$u_0(c_2, c_3) = \frac{1}{b}(a_2 c_3^b + a_3 c_3^b) \qquad (4.39)$$

an endowment stream (w_2^0, w_3^0) of goods, and an endowment m_0 of fiat money. His excess demand functions are

$$x_j^0(p_1, p_2, m_0) = \frac{a_j^\eta\left(\sum_{i=1}^{2} p_i w_{i+1}^0 + m_0\right)}{p_{j-1}^\eta \sum_{i=1}^{2} a_{i+1}^\eta p_i^{1-\eta}} - w_j^0 \qquad j = 2, 3 \quad (4.40)$$

The equilibrium conditions for this economy are

$$x_3^{-1}(p_1, m_{-1}) = x_2^0(p_1, p_2, m_0) + x_1(p_1, p_2, p_3) = 0 \quad (4.41)$$

for $t = 1$,

$$x_3^0(p_1, p_2, m_0) + x_2(p_1, p_2, p_3) + x_1(p_2, p_3, p_4) = 0 \quad (4.42)$$

for $t = 2$ and

$$x_3(p_{t-2}, p_{t-1}, p_t) + x_2(p_{t-1}, p_t, p_{t+1}) + x_1(p_t, p_{t+1}, p_{t+2}) = 0$$
$$(4.43)$$

for $t > 1$.

By analogy with the two-period case, let $m = m_{-1} + m_0$. Multiplying the equilibrium conditions in the first two periods by the respective prices and adding yields an analog of (4.7):

$$m = -p_t x_1(p_1, p_2, p_3) - p_2 x_2(p_1, p_2, p_3) - p_2 x_1(p_2, p_3, p_4)$$
$$(4.44)$$

Repeated application of Walras's law (4.37) and the equilibrium condition (4.43) implies that

$$m = -p_t x_1(p_t, p_{t+1}, p_{t+2}) - p_{t+1} x_2(p_t, p_{t+1}, p_{t+2})$$
$$- p_{t+1} x_1(p_{t+1}, p_{t+2}, p_{t+3}) \qquad (4.45)$$

for all t: just as in the two-period-lived model, the amount of fiat money stays constant over time.

Steady states also have the same structure as in the two-period-lived model. There are two types, real steady states in which $\beta \neq 1$ and

$$m = -x_1(1, \beta, \beta^2) - \beta x_2(1, \beta, \beta^2) - \beta x_1(1, \beta, \beta^2) = 0 \quad (4.46)$$

and nominal steady states in which, $\beta = 1$ and $m \neq 0$.

In the three-period case, the linearized equilibrium conditions are

$$\beta^2 D_1 x_3 p_{t-2} + (\beta^2 D_2 x_3 + \beta D_1 x_2) p_{t-1} + (\beta^2 D_3 x_3 + D_1 x_1) p_t$$
$$+ (\beta D_3 x_2 + D_2 x_1) p_{t+1} + D_3 x_1 p_{t+2} = 0 \quad (4.47)$$

Here all derivatives are evaluated at $(1, \beta, \beta^2)$. The eigenvalues are the roots of the corresponding fourth-order polynominal. These come from a 4×4 matrix like that in (4.29).

Consider the following parameter values:

Period	1	2	3
a_i	2	2	1
w_i	3	15	2

where $b = -4$. Notice that the representative consumer discounts consumption over time, has a hump in his life cycle earnings profile and has an elasticity of substitution in consumption over time of $1/(1 + 4) = 0.2$. This economy has one nominal steady state and three real steady states. They can be found by tracing out the graph of the function $m(\beta)$ given by (4.46). Real steady states occur where $m(\beta) = 1$. This is illustrated in figure 4.3.

To determine the values of the roots of the forth-order polynominal that corresponds to (4.47) we start by evaluating the partial derivatives of the excess demand functions (4.40) at $(p_t, p_{t+1}, p_{t+2}) = (1, \beta, \beta^2)$. At $\beta = 1$, for example, these derivatives are

$$
\begin{bmatrix}
D_1 x_1 & D_2 x_1 & D_3 x_1 \\
D_1 x_2 & D_2 x_2 & D_3 x_2 \\
D_1 x_3 & D_2 x_3 & D_3 x_3
\end{bmatrix}
$$

$$
= \begin{bmatrix}
-2.29010 & 3.28375 & -0.99365 \\
-0.89664 & 1.89029 & -0.99365 \\
-0.78057 & 2.85867 & -2.07810
\end{bmatrix} \tag{4.48}
$$

(Notice that, since this matrix has some negative off-diagonal elements, (x_1, x_2, x_3) violates gross substitutability.) The polynomial that we are interested in is

$$-0.78057 + 1.96230\lambda - 2.47791\lambda^2 + 2.29010\lambda^3 - 0.99365\lambda^4 = 0$$

$$\tag{4.49}$$

One of the roots is, of course, $\lambda = 1$. The other three are 0.93286, $0.18594 + 0.89862i$ and $0.18594 - 0.89862i$, as can easily be verified.

The roots at all four steady states are listed in table 4.1. The modulus of the pair of complex conjugates at the steady state where $\beta = 0.93295$ is 0.84513; where $\beta = 1$ it is 0.91766.

Let us first focus our attention on the steady state where $\beta = 0.93295$. Let $m_{-i} = m_0 = 0$ and let $w_2^0 = 10.84636$ and $w_3^0 = 2$. It is straightforward but tedious to check that $(p_1, p_2, p_3, p_4) = (1, 0.93295, (0.93295)^2, (0.93295)^3)$ satisfies the conditions for equilibrium in the first two periods. Since $\beta = 0.93295$ is a steady state, this is a legitimate equilibrium price path. Our earlier arguments imply that this is only one continuum. Since $m_{-1} = m_0 = 0$, the excess demands of generations -1 and 0 are homogeneous of degree zero and we can normalize prices by setting $p_1 = 1$. We can then choose

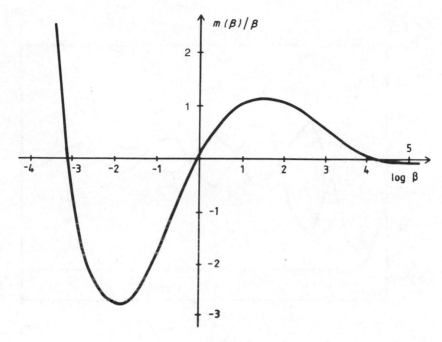

Figure 4.3

Table 4.1

	β		Other roots	
1	0.04239	1	0.47907	−0.01380
2	0.93295	1	0.17245 ± 0.82735i	
3	1	0.93286	0.18594 ± 0.89862i	
4	53.8056	1	2.04305	−121.45544

$p_2/p_1 = 0.93295 + \varepsilon$ for any small ε, positive or negative, and use the equilibrium conditions (4.41) and (4.42) to solve for p_3 and p_4. Using the equilibrium condition (4.43), we can then solve for an infinite price sequence. This price sequence must converge to unity where $p_{t+1}/p_t = 0.93295$ since the modulus of the root governing stability is less than 0.93295. The root $\lambda = 1$ is, as we have explained, irrelevant since $m = 0$ everywhere along this price path.

In fact, the value of ε need not be very small: every p_2/p_1 in the interval $0.26703 < p_2/p_1 \leq 16.67676$ determines a distinct equilibrium. Figure 4.4 illustrates some possibilities. Notice that

p_{t+1} / p_t

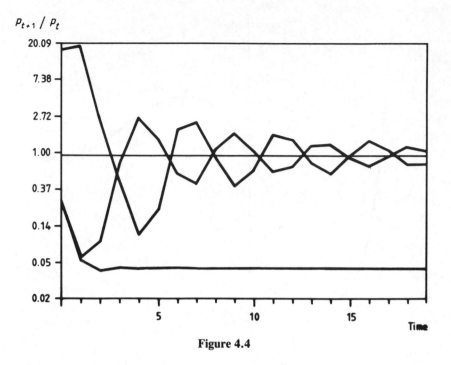

Figure 4.4

$p_2/p_1 = 0.26703$ determines an equilibrium that converges to the steady state where $\beta = 0.04239$. Otherwise, all values of p_2/p_1 outside this interval determine paths that eventually lead to a negative price.

Now consider the case where $m_{-1} = -0.08825$ and $m_0 = 0.18634$. Here it can be checked that $(p_1, p_2, p_3, p_4) = (1, 1, 1, 1)$ satisfies (4.41) and (4.42). In this case the excess demands of generations -1 and 0 are not homogeneous and we are not permitted a price normalization: money itself serves as numeraire. We can now choose $p_1 = 1 + \varepsilon_1$ and $p_2 = 1 + \varepsilon_2$ for any ε_1 and ε_2 small enough and use (4.41) and (4.42) to solve for p_3 and p_4. Again using (4.43), we can solve for an equilibrium price sequence that converges to unity where $p_{t+1}/p_t = 1$.

All these equilibria are Pareto efficient: those that converge to the steady state where $\beta = 0.93295$ all assign a finite value to the aggregate endowment, and so the standard proof of the first welfare theorem due to Debreu applies. Those that converge to the steady state where $\beta = 1$ satisfy the more general conditions for efficiency developed by Balasko and Shell (1980) and Burke (1987).

The relative price indeterminacy exhibited in this example does not need one of the consumers to come into the first year with negative fiat money. Suppose, for example, that $m_{-1} = 0$, that $m_0 = 0.09809$, and that $w_2^0 = 10.93461$ and $w_3^0 = 2$. Then $(p_1, p_2, p_3, p_4) = (1, 1, 1, 1)$ satisfies the equilibrium conditions in the first two periods. Again there is a two-dimensional indeterminacy. (Setting $m_{-1} = m_0 = 0$ does not, however, result in equilibrium conditions that are satisfied by $p_t = (0.93295)^{t-1}$.)

Notice that this example also has steady states of the more familiar sort: any equilibrium that converges to the steady state where $\beta = 0.04239$ is determinate. Any equilibrium that converges to $\beta = 53.80562$ and has no fiat money is also determinate. There is a one-dimensional manifold of paths that converge to the steady state if there is fiat money, however.

Choosing the parameters of this type of model suitably, we can illustrate other possibilities for behavior of equilibrium price paths near steady states. For example, the following parameter values correspond to an economy with four steady states with βs and other roots that are the reciprocals of those given above:

Period	1	2	3
a_i	1	2	2
w_i	2	15	3

where $b = -4$. Here the steady state where $\beta = 1$ is unstable: there are no paths that can approach it unless, by pure chance, $(1, 1, 1, 1)$ satisfies the equilibrium conditions in the first two periods. The steady state where $\beta = 1.07187 = (0.93295)^{-1}$ is also unstable for price paths with no nominal debt. There are, however, determinate price paths with nonzero nominal debt that converge to this steady state.

An essential feature of all the above examples is that they are robust: we can slightly perturb the parameters, and even the functional forms, of the demand functions of all the consumers, including the initial old consumers, and still have economy whose equilibria have the same qualitative features. We choose initial old consumers so that the steady state prices satisfy the equilibrium conditions in the first two periods only to make it easy to verify that there are prices that satisfy these equilibrium conditions and also converge to the steady state.

As we have explained, the examples of this section are special cases of a model with two two-period-lived consumers in each generation and two goods in each period. The main reason for using the three-period-lived model for examples is to keep the specifications as simple as possible. Suppose that consumer h, where $h = 1, 2$, in generation t solves the problem

$$\text{maximize} \frac{1}{\gamma_h} [\alpha_1^{1h}(c_t^1)^{\gamma_h} + \alpha_1^{2h}(c_t^2)^{\lambda_h} + \alpha_2^{1h}(c_{t+1}^1)^{\lambda_h} + \alpha_2^{2h}(c_{t+1}^2)^{\lambda_h}]$$

$$(4.50)$$

$$\text{subject to} \qquad \sum_{j=1}^{2} \sum_{k=1}^{2} p_{t=K-1}^j c_{t+k-1}^j \leq \sum_{j=1}^{2} \sum_{k=1}^{2} p_{t+k-1}^j w_k^{jh}$$

If we set $\gamma_1 = \gamma_2 = b$, $\alpha_1^{11} = \alpha_1^{22} = a_1$, $\alpha_1^{21} = \alpha_2^{12} = a_2$, $\alpha_2^{11}\alpha_2^{22} = a_3$

and $\alpha_2^{21} = \alpha_1^{12} = 0$, and similarly set w_k^{jh}, then this model is formally the same as the three-period-lived model. While this model needs 18 parameters to specify it, of which 15 are not subject to normalization, the simple three-period-lived model needs only seven, of which five are not subject to normalization. It is still the case, however, that any small perturbation in the parameters of the two-period-lived model results in an economy whose equilibria have the same qualitative features as do the examples that we have presented.

5 Implications for Finite Horizon Models

There is a close relationship between models with infinite time horizons and models with long, but finite, time horizons. On the one hand, models with infinite horizons are only interesting in so far as they provide insights into the properties of finite horizon models. On the other hand, to approximate the equilibria of an infinite horizon model on a computer we would have to truncate the model after a finite number of periods. In this section we explore the relationship between equilibria of the finite horizon model and equilibria of the truncated model.

One way to truncate the model at period T would be to fix the expectations of what prices would be in period $T + 1$. Suppose that (p, β) is a steady state. We could require that $p_{T+1} = \beta p_T$ in the terminal equilibrium condition

$$z(p_{T-1}, p_T) + y(p_T, p_{T+1}) = 0 \qquad (4.51)$$

or that $p_{T+1} = \|p_T\|\beta p$. (See Auerbach, Kotlikoff and Skinner (1983) for an example of this approach.) Another, sometimes equivalent, way to truncate the model would be to specify a terminal young generation y_T analogous to the initial old generation z_0.

This type of truncated model, which involves a finite number of variables in the same number of equilibrium conditions, generically has determinate equilibria. Furthermore, if the truncation date T is large enough, then an equilibrium of the truncated model serves as a reasonable approximation to an equilibrium of the actual model, at least in the early periods. In fact, the usual proof of the existence of equilibrium for the infinite horizon overlapping generations model depends on this property of the truncated model. We start by established the existence of equilibrium for the truncated model. We then construct a candidate for an equilibrium price path for the infinite horizon model by augmenting a vector of equilibrium prices $(p_1, p_2, \ldots, p_T)$ for the truncated model with prices $p_{T+1}, p_{T+2}, \ldots$ that are arbitrary. Letting the truncation date increase, we generate an infinite sequence of such price paths. Since we can use the boundary assumption on excess demand to prove that the space of possible price paths is compact in the product topology, this sequence has a convergent subsequence. Furthermore, since the equilibrium conditions are continuous in this topology, any limit point of the sequence is an equilibrium for the infinite horizon model (see, for example, Balasko, Cass and Shell 1980). There may, of course, be different limit points because of multiple equilibria, and that is why we need to consider subsequences converging.

Here convergence means convergence in the product topology: for any $\varepsilon > 0$ and any T there exists some $T' > T$ such that, if $(p_1, p_2, \ldots)$ is an infinite price path that satisfies the equilibrium conditions for the model truncated at T', then $(p_1, p_2 \ldots)$ is within ε of an equilibrium of the infinite horizon model for periods $1, 2, \ldots, T'$. Notice that we do not claim that this price path is within ε of an equilibrium of the infinite horizon model for periods $T + 1$, $T + 2, \ldots, T'$. Nor, unfortunately, can we make any strong statements about the relationship between T, T'. We do not know how long a truncation date is needed to approximate an equilibrium for ten periods, for example.

Two questions about this approximation naturally arise. How does indeterminacy in the infinite horizon model, where $\bar{n}^s > n - 1$, manifest itself in the truncated model? How does instability, where $\bar{n}^s < n - 1$, manifest itself? To answer the first question, let us consider an infinite horizon model with a continuum of equilibria that converge to the same steady state $(p, \beta p)$. Choose two different price paths in that continuum, $(\bar{p}_1, \bar{p}_2, \ldots)$ and $(\hat{p}_1, \hat{p}_2, \ldots)$. For large enough T both $\bar{p}_{T+1}$ and $\hat{p}_{T+1}$ are very close to the steady state price vector p and, consequently, very close to each other. (We can think of normalizing the price sequence not by requiring that $p_1^1 = 1$ but rather by requiring that $p_{T+1}^1 = 1$.) By truncating the model at period T using the terminal condition (4.51) with $p_{T+1} = \bar{p}_{T+1}$, we generate $(\bar{p}_1, \bar{p}_2, \ldots, \bar{p}_T)$ as an equilibrium; with $p_{T+1} = \hat{p}_{T+1}$, we generate $(\hat{p}_1, \hat{p}_2, \ldots, \hat{p}_T)$. No matter how large the difference between $\bar{p}_1$ and $\hat{p}_1$ there exists a T large enough so that $\bar{p}_{T+1}$ and $\hat{p}_{T+1}$ are arbitrarily close. Indeterminacy in the infinite horizon model can therefore be seen to manifest itself as sensitivity to terminal conditions in the truncated model, sensitivity that becomes more and more acute as the truncation date becomes larger and larger.

Another way to view this problem of indeterminacy credited by Calvo (1978) to Rolf Mantel is to consider the difference equation

$$z(p_{T-1-s}, p_{T-s}) + y(p_{T-s}, p_{T+1-s}) = 0 \qquad (4.52)$$

where $s = 1, 2, \ldots$, that runs backwards from the terminal conditions. It is trivial to show that the eigenvalues of the linearized versions of this difference equation are the reciprocals of the eigenvalues of the original system. If the original system has too many stable eigenvalues, the backwards system has too few and is therefore unstable: small changes in terminal conditions cause large changes in prices early in the price path.

Let us now turn our attention to the second question, the question of how instability manifests itself. Here we seem to be faced with a dilemma: We know that, if we truncate the model by requiring that $p_{T+1} = \|p_T\|\beta p$, we can compute an approximate equilibrium for the infinite horizon model. We also know, however, that it is extremely unlikely that for the infinite horizon model will have an equilibrium price path where p_{T+1} is close to these values. The solution to this dilemma lies in the nature of the approximation. We only know that the equilibria of the truncated model are close to the equilibria of the actual model in early periods; later they may diverge sharply. To approximate the equilibria of an infinite horizon model near an unstable steady state for any fixed number of periods we may have to choose a very large truncated date.

As we would expect, the problems of indeterminacy and instability represent two sides of the same coin. Indeterminacy manifests itself as sensitivity to terminal conditions. The larger the truncation date, the more sensitive prices early in the price path are to terminal conditions. Later prices, however, which all converge to the steady state, are relatively insensitive. Instability, in contrast, manifests itself as a need for a very large truncation date. The larger the truncation date is, the less sensitive prices early in the price path are to terminal conditions. Later prices, however, may diverge sharply from equilibrium prices for the actual model.

To see how indeterminacy manifests itself in a truncated model, let us consider again the simple three-period-lived model of the previous section. Figure 4.5 illustrates three equilibria that all converge to the steady state where $\beta = 0.93925$. The values of the price ratios p_{t+1}/p_t at these three equilibria are listed in table 4.2. Each of these three equilibria could be generated as an equilibrium of a truncated model with a suitable choice of a truncation date and terminal condition p_{T+1}/p_T. If, for example, we truncate the model at $T = 20$ and

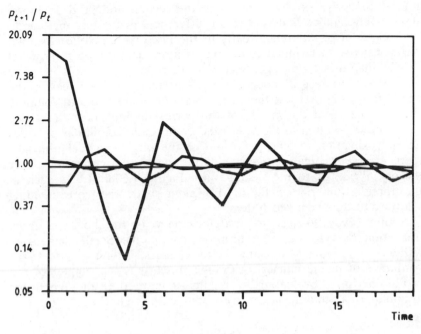

Figure 4.5

Table 4.2

		P_{t+1}/P_t	
1	0.60000	1.05000	15.00000
2	0.59283	1.01905	10.76314
3	1.6288	0.88803	1.59627
4	1.38525	0.83980	0.30447
5	0.91629	0.94206	0.10258
6	0.66010	1.01934	0.47445
7	0.81814	0.95572	2.58841
8	1.18550	0.87554	1.77892
9	1.11307	0.89228	0.64069
10	0.82698	0.96736	0.38120
15	0.82304	0.96522	0.60597
20	0.85527	0.95375	0.81664
25	0.89286	0.94270	0.94927
30	0.92050	0.93544	0.99605

impose the terminal conditions $p_{21} = 0.85527p_{20}$, then we generate
the first equilibrium. The terminal conditions $p_{21} = 0.95375p_{20}$ and

$p_{21} = 0.81664p_{20}$, however, result in the second and third equilibria respectively. Notice that very small differences in the terminal conditions cause large differences early in the price paths. Notice too that this sensitivity to terminal conditions is more acute if we truncate at $T = 30$ than it is if we truncate at $T = 20$.

One way to test a model for indeterminacy is to linearize the equilibrium conditions at the steady state of interest and to compute the eigenvalues of the matrix of the corresponding linear difference equation. A solution to the linearized equilibrium conditions provides an approximation to an equilibrium of the original model. Furthermore, this approximation becomes more and more accurate the closer the equilibrium is to the steady state. Figure 4.6 illustrates each of the three equilibria of figure 4.5 along with the corresponding solutions to the linearized system.

Another way to test for indeterminacy is to choose a large truncation date to vary the terminal conditions. Small changes in terminal conditions producing large changes in initial prices are symptoms of indeterminacy. Although this test is the simpler of the two to perform, evaluating its results is more difficult. What, for example, is a suitably larger truncated date? What works for one

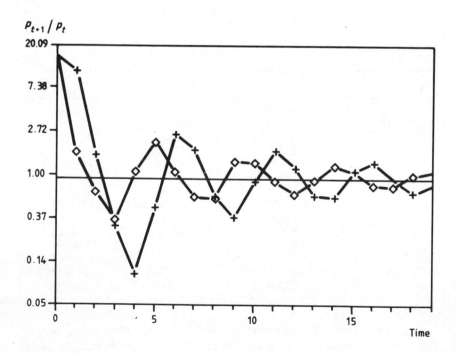

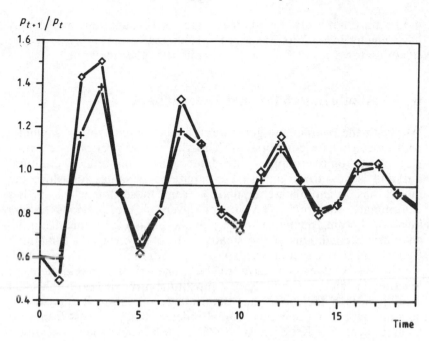

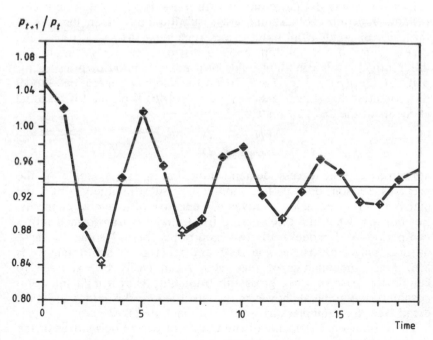

Figure 4.6

model may not work for another. This is because one model may have eigenvalues of its linearized system that are very close to the steady state values of β in modulus while the other may not.

6 Gross Substitutability and Determinacy

Although the overlapping generations model admits robust examples with indeterminate equilibria, such as that in the previous section, it also admits robust examples with determinate equilibria. The natural question is how to distinguish those parameter values for which the model has indeterminate equilibria from those for which it has determinate equilibria. The answer given in the previous section involves choosing numerical values for the parameters, linearizing the equilibrium conditions at the steady state of interest and computing eignvalues. In this section we explore one class of examples for which all this work does not have to be done: if the excess demand functions y and z exhibit gross substitutability, an easily checked condition, then the model has determinate equilibria if there is no nominal debt and a one-dimensional indeterminacy at most if there is nominal debt. See Kehoe et al. (1986) for a more detailed discussion.

In a static pure exchange model with n goods we say that an excess demand function $f(p)$ exhibits gross substitutability if an increase in the price of goods i, all other prices remaining the same, causes the excess demand for all but good i to rise. If f is continuously differentiable, this condition holds in a neighborhood of price vector p if $(\partial f_j/\partial p_i)(p) > 0$ for $j \neq i$. In an overlapping generations model this condition holds near a steady state $(p, \beta p)$ if all the off-diagonal elements of the $2n \times 2n$ matrix

$$\begin{bmatrix} D_1 y & D_2 y \\ D_1 z & D_2 z \end{bmatrix}$$

are positive. The excess demand function in the example in the previous section does not exhibit gross substitutability since the matrix (4.48) of partial derivatives has negative off-diagonal elements. Beware that when the three-period-lived model is transformed into a two-period-lived model with two goods per period some of these off-diagonal elements become zero and strict gross subtitutability is lost. Since the analysis of this section can easily by extended to handle this case of weak gross substitutability with a mild indecomposability requirement, however, we shall ignore this minor technical detail (see, for example, Arrow and Hurwicz 1960).

The off-diagonal elements of the matrix of partial derivatives of the demand functions (4.36) used in the previous section take the form

$$D_k x_j(p_t, p_{t+1}, p_{t+2})$$

$$= \frac{a_j^\eta p_{t+j-1}^\eta \left[w_k \sum_{i=1}^{3} a_i^\eta p_{t+i-1}^{1-\eta} + (\eta - 1) a_k^\eta p_{t+k-1}^{-\eta} \sum_{i=1}^{3} p_{t+i-1} w_i \right]}{\left(p_{t+j-1}^\eta \sum_{i=1}^{3} a_i^\eta p_{t+i-1}^{1-\eta} \right)^2} \tag{4.53}$$

Notice that, if $w_k > 0$, this expression is always positive when $\eta > 1$, when $\eta < 1$, however, it may become negative. This is a well known feature of demand functions derived from CES utility functions, including functions that nest CES utility functions for consumption within a single period (such as those used by Auerbach, Kotlikoff and Skinner, 1983): to guarantee gross substitutability, the elasticity of substitution between any two goods must be greater than or equal to one. Unfortunately, a large number of empirical studies indicate that the elasticity of substitution in consumption over time is substantially lower: somewhere between 0.07 and 0.51 centered around approximately 0.2 (see Auerbach, Kotlikoff and Skinner, 1983; Mankiw, Rotemberg and Summers, 1985). An excess demand function arising from a CES utility function with $\eta < 1$ may, in fact, exhibit gross substitutability near a steady state $(p, \beta p)$, but this must be checked for by evaluating all the off-diagonal partial derivatives of y and z.

To clarify the role that gross substitutability plays in guaranteeing determinacy of equilibria in overlapping generations models, let us recall why it guarantees that a static pure exchange model has a unique equilibrium (see, for example, Arrow and Hahn, 1971, pp 221–7). Suppose, to the contrary, that an excess demand function f exhibits gross substitutability and has two equilibria, two strictly positive vectors $\bar{p}$ and $\hat{p}$, not proportional to each other, such that $f(\bar{p}) - f(\hat{p}) = 0$. Consider the ratios $\bar{p}_i/\hat{p}_i$, where $i = 1, \ldots, n$; let v be the largest such ratio, and suppose it is achieved for good k. Homogeneity implies that $f_k(v\hat{p}) = 0$. Now raise every price $v\hat{p}_i$ for which $v\hat{p}_i < \hat{p}_i$ until it equals $\bar{p}_i$. Since $\hat{p}$ is not proportional to $\bar{p}$, there is at least one such price. Gross substitutability implies that, as each of these prices is raised, f_k increases, which implies that $f_k(\bar{p}) > 0$. This contradicts the assumption that both $\bar{p}$ and $\hat{p}$ are equilibria. Consequently, f cannot have multiple equilibria.

Let us now apply this argument to the overlapping generations model. We first establish that, in the case with no nominal debt, the equilibria that converge to a steady state $(p, \beta p)$ are determinate. We start by proving a slightly different result: if z_0, as well as y and z, exhibits gross substitutability, then there is at most one equilibrium that converges to $(p, \beta p)$. Suppose, to the contrary, that z_0, y and z

all exhibit gross substitutability and that there are two such equilibria, two sequences of price vectors $(\bar{p}_1, \bar{p}_2, \ldots)$ and $(\hat{p}_1, \hat{p}_2, \ldots)$, not proportional to each other, that satisfy the equilibrium conditions and converge to the same steady state. Again consider the ratios $\bar{p}_t^i/\hat{p}_t^i$, where $i = 1, \ldots, n$ and $t = 1, 2, \ldots$ Since $\bar{p}_t$ and $\hat{p}_t$ both converge to the same steady state, $\lim_{t \to \infty} \bar{p}_t^i/\hat{p}_t^i = \lim_{t \to \infty} \|\bar{p}_t\|/\|\hat{p}_t\|$, for $i = 1, \ldots, n$. This limit may be the maximum ratio, it may be the minimum ratio, or it may be neither. It cannot, however, be both the maximum and the minimum since the two sequences are not proportional. Consequently, either the maximum or the minimum must be achieved for some $v = \bar{p}_t^k/\hat{p}_t^k$. If $t > 1$, then we consider the equation

$$z^k(p_{t-1}, p_t) + y^k(p_t, p_{t+1}) = 0 \tag{4.54}$$

Homogeneity implies that $z^k(vp_{t-1}, vp_t) + y^k(vp_t) = 0$. If v is the maximum ratio, raises every price $vp_\tau^i < \bar{p}_\tau^i$ where $\tau = t - 1, t, t + 1$. If v is the maximum, then gross substitutability implies that $z^k(\bar{p}_{t-1}, \bar{p}_t) + y^k(\bar{p}_t, p_{t+1}) > 0$; if v is the minimum, then this expression is negative. Either situation contradicts the assumption that $(\bar{p}_1, \bar{p}_2, \ldots)$ is an equilibrium. If $t = 1$, then we apply the same argument to the equation

$$z_0^k(p_1, 0) + y^k(p_1, p_2) = 0 \tag{4.55}$$

Consequently, there cannot be multiple equilibria that converge to the same steady state.

This result implies that, if y and z exhibit gross substitutability, then equilibria that converge to the same steady state are determinate, regardless of z_0: our earlier discussion indicates that we can generically rule out the possibility of indeterminacy if we can generically rule out the possibility that the matrix G in the linearized equilibrium conditions satisfies $\bar{n}^s > n - 1$. Suppose, to the contrary, that y and z are such that G has $\bar{n}^s > n - 1$. Let us construct an excess demand function z_0 such that $z_0(p, 0) + y(p, \beta p) = 0$. Consider the Cobb–Douglas functions

$$z_0^j(p_1, 0) = a_j \frac{\sum_{i=1}^n p_1^i w^i}{p_1^i} - w^j \qquad j = 1, \ldots, n \tag{4.56}$$

Choose $\zeta > 0$ large enough so that $\zeta > -y^j(p, \beta p)$, for $j = 1, \ldots, n$. Set $a_j = p^j/\sum_{i=1}^n p^i$, where $(p^1, \ldots, p^n)$ is the steady state price vector, and set $w^j = \zeta + y^j(p, \beta p)$. It is now trivial to check that, for all p_1, $(\partial z_0^i/\partial p_1^i)(p_1) > 0$ for $i \neq j$ and that $(p, \beta p, \beta^2 p, \ldots)$ is an equilibrium for this economy. Since $\bar{n}^s > n - 1$, we know from our previous analysis that there is a continuum of equilibria. This is a contradiction, however, since we have already established that there can be at most one equilibrium.

Let us now argue that, in the case with nominal debt, there is at most a one-dimensional set of equilibria that converge to the same steady state. The argument is similar to the previous one. We start by proving that, if we fix the ratio between the price of that money and some index $\pi(p_1)$ of prices in the first period, $m = \pi(p_1)\mu$ where μ is a nonzero constant, then there is at most one equilibrium that converges to a given steady state. Let $\pi(p_1)$ be any price index, that is positive and homogeneous of degree one, e.g. $\pi(p_1) = p_1^1$. We now say that z_0 exhibits gross substitutability if there exsists such a price index such that an increase in p_1^i causes $z_0^j[p_1, \pi(p_1)m]$, $j \neq i$, to rise. An argument identical with that above establishes that, for any given m, there is at most one sequence $(p_1, p_2, \ldots)$ that converges to a given steady state and satisfies the equilibrium conditions. As we vary μ, however, we may allow additional equilibria. This implies that there is at most a one dimensional set of equilibria and, again arguing as above, that it must be the case that $n^s \leqslant n$. We now use the excess demand function

$$z_0^i(p_1, m) = a_j \frac{\sum\limits_{i=1}^{n} p_1^i w^i + m}{p_1^i} - w^j \qquad (4.57)$$

and again set $a_j = p^j/\Sigma p^i$ and $w^j = \zeta + y^j(p, \beta p)$.

7 Nonstationary Models

Thus far we have only considered stationary models and equilibrium price paths that converge to steady states of such models. In this section we indicate how our results can be extended to encompass models with some nonstationary structure and equilibrium price paths that converge to cycles of any finite length.

Let us first explain how our results can be extended to models with a constant rate of population growth. Suppose the demands of generations t are

$$y_t(p_t, p_{t+1}) = \alpha^{t-1} y(p_t, p_{t+1})$$

$$z_t(p_t, p_{t+1}) = \alpha^{t-1} z_1(p_t, p_{t+1})$$

$$(4.58)$$

Here $\alpha - 1$ is the rate of population growth. With a suitable redefinition of prices and excess demand functions, this model can be transformed into one we have been working with. Let $\hat{p}_t = \alpha^{t-1} p_t$, $\hat{y}(p_t, p_{t+1}) = \alpha y_1(p_t, \alpha p_{t+1})$ and $\hat{z}(p_t, p_{t+1}) = z(p_t, \alpha p_{t+1})$. Notice that $\hat{y}$ and $\hat{z}$ are homogeneous of degree zero if y_1 and z_1 are.

Notice too that if y_1 and z_1 satisfy Walras's law

$$p_t' y_1(p_t, p_{t+1}) + p_{t+1}' z_1(p_t, p_{t+1}) = 0 \qquad (4.59)$$

then so do $\hat{y}$ and $\hat{z}$:

$$0 = \alpha^{1-t} \hat{p}_t' y_1(\alpha^{1-t}\hat{p}_t, \alpha^{-t}\hat{p}_{t+1}) + \alpha^{-t}\hat{p}_{t+1}' z_1(\hat{p}_t, \alpha^{-t}\hat{p}_{t+1}) \quad (4.60)$$

$$= \hat{p}_t' \hat{y}(\hat{p}_t, \hat{p}_{t+1}) + \hat{p}_{t+1}' \hat{z}(\hat{p}_t, \hat{p}_{t+1})$$

Finally, notice that if p_t, $t = 1, 2, \ldots$ satisfies the equilibrium conditions

$$0 = z_{t-1}(p_{t-1}, p_t) + y_t(p_t, p_{t+1}) \qquad (4.61)$$

then $\hat{p}_t$, $t = 1, 2, \ldots$, satisfies the corresponding conditions

$$0 = \alpha^{t-2} z_1(\alpha^{2-t}\hat{p}_{t-1}, \alpha^{1-t}\hat{p}_t) + \alpha^{t-1} y_1(\alpha^{1-t}\hat{p}_t, \alpha^{-t}\hat{p}_{t+1}) \quad (4.62)$$

$$\hat{z}(\hat{p}_{t-1}, \hat{p}_t) + \hat{y}(\hat{p}_t, \hat{p}_{t+1})$$

This transformation is obviously invertible: if we know $\hat{p}_t$, $\hat{y}$ and $\hat{z}$, and the growth factor α, we can recover p_t, y_t and z_t. Nominal steady states are those where $\hat{p}_t = \hat{p}_{t+1}$, which is equivalent to $p_t = \alpha p_{t+1}$. This implies Samuelson's result that the rate of interest at such a steady state is, in fact, the growth rate of the population.

Arbitrary forms of nonstationarity can be incorporated into our framework as long as the model is stationary for all generations after some generation T. In this case the equilibrium conditions for the first $T + 1$ periods serve the same role that the equilibrium conditions for the first period do in the stationary model. Generically, they determine all but one of the price vectors $p_1, p_2, \ldots, p_{T+1}$. The remaining price vector may, or may not, be determined by the conditions that p_T and p_{T+1} give rise to a price path that converges to a steady state when viewed as initial values for the difference equation corresponding to the remaining equilibrium conditions. The analysis of relative price indeterminacy remains the same.

Geanakoplos and Brown (1985) and Santos and Bona (forthcoming) have extended our results to more general nonstationary models. They find that, just as in stationary models, there are potentilly n dimensions of indeterminacy if there is fiat money and $n - 1$ dimensions if there is not. While these results are of considerable theoretical interest, they have little relevance for applied models. If nothing else, even to store all the parameters of a truly nonstationary model would require a computer with an infinitely large memory.

A restrictive aspect of our analysis is that we have only analyzed price paths near steady states. In fact, however, our analysis immediately extends to price paths near any cycle of finite length. Recall that, when we redefine generations, time periods and goods to convert the three-period-lived model into a two-period-lived model, two-period cycles become steady states. In general, suppose that a model has a cycle of length k, i.e. that $(p_{t+1}, p_{t+2}, \ldots, p_{t+k}) = \beta(p_{t-k+1}, p_{t-k+2}, \ldots, p_t)$ satisfies the equilibrium conditions. Suppose we redefine generations, time periods and goods so that generations 1, 2,..., k are now generation 1 and so on. The cycle now corresponds to a steady state of the redefined model.

8 Concluding Remarks

Our results should be troubling to researchers interested in applications of the overlapping generations model. A model that does not give determinate results is not very useful for doing policy analysis. Unfortunately, the problem of indeterminacy of equilibria does not seem to be confined to pure exchange overlapping generations models. Muller and Woodford (1988) have extended the results presented here to stationary models that take into account production, including storage, infinitely lived assets and infinitely lived consumers. They find that, although the presence of infinitely lived assets, infinitely lived consumers or production may rule out nominal debt and inefficient equilibria, it does not rule out indeterminacy. They are able to identify a number of conditions that do rule our indeterminacy, however, just as we identify gross substitutability as such a condition in the pure exchange overlapping generations model. One obvious direction for future research is to find easily checked conditions that imply that a model has determinate equilibria. A warning should be given about the nature of our gross substitutability result. There is no presumption that gross substitutability implies determinacy of equilibrium in models with production. In static models with production, for example, gross substitutability in consumption does not imply uniqueness of equilibrium (see Kehoe, 1985).

It seems inevitable, however, that some very reasonable models have indeterminacy equilibria. Perhaps we are wrong to employ the hypothesis of perfect foresight. With adaptive expectations, for example, equilibrium price paths are generically determinate. Is there some general and economically meaningful way to choose a perfect foresight expectations mechanism that gives rise to determinate equilibria? If not, how far do we have to depart from the perfect foresight hypothesis to obtain determinacy?

That the overlapping generations model seems plagued by indeterminacy is not a satisfactory justification for completely abandoning it in favor of the model with a finite number of infinitely lived consumers. As Gale (1973) points out, "the reason for considering a population rather that a fixed set of agents is that the former is what in reality we have, the latter is what we have not". To build a useful intertemporal equilibrium model, however, it would be necessary to address the issues we have raised in this paper.

Note

The research persented in this paper was funded by Grants No. SES 82-09448 and No. SES 85-09484. Raees Hussain assisted with the figures, and Jon Burke constructed the numerical examples.

References

Arrow, K. J., and F. H. Hahn (1971) *General Competitive Analysis*, San Francisco, CA: Holden Day.

Auerbach, A. J., L. J. Kotlikoff and J. Skinner (1983) "The Efficiency Gains from Dynamic Tax Reform", *International Economic Review*, 24, 81–100.

Balasko, Y., D. Cass and K. Shell (1980) "Existence of Competitive Equilibrium in a General Overlapping Generations Model", *Journal of Economic Theory*, 23, 307–22.

——, and K. Shell (1980) "The Overlapping Generations Model, I: The Case of Pure Exchange without Money", *Journal of Economic Theory*, 23, 281–306.

—— and —— (1981) "The Overlapping Generations Model, III: The Case of Log-linear Utility Functions", *Journal of Economic Theory*, 24, 143–52.

Bewley, T. (1980) "The Optimum Quantity of Money", in J. H. Kareken and N. Wallace, (eds), *Models of Monetary Economies*, Minneapolis, MN: Federal Reserve Bank of Minneapolis.

—— (1983) "A Difficulty with the Optimum Quantity of Money", *Econometrica*, 51, 1485–504.

Burke, J. (1987) "Inactive Transfer Policies and Efficiency in General Overlapping Generations Economies", *Journal of Mathematical Economics*, 16, 201–22.

Calvo, G. (1978) "On the Indeterminacy of Interest Rates and Wages with Perfect Foresight", *Journal of Economic Theory*, 19, 321–37.

Darby, M. R. (1979) *Effects of Social Security on Income and the Capital Stock*, Washington, DC: American Enterprise Institute.

Debreu, G. (1972) "Smooth Preferences", *Econometrics*, 40, 603–12.

—— (1974) "Excess Demand Functions", *Journal of Mathematical Economics*, 1, 15–23.

Diamond, P. A. (1965) "National Debt in a Neoclassical Growth Model", *American Economic Review*, 55, 1126–50.

Gale, D. (1973) "Pure Exchanges Equilibrium of Dynamic Economic Models", *Journal of Economic Theory*, 6, 12–36.

Geanakoplos, J. D., and D. J. Brown (1985) "Comparative Statics and Local Indeterminacy of OLG Eeconomics: An Application of the Multiplicative Ergodic Theorem", Cowles Discussion Paper No. 773.
—— and H. M. Polemarchakis (1984) "Intertemporally Separable Overlapping Generations Economies", *Journal of Economic Theory*, 34, 207–15.
Irwin, M. C. (1980) *Smooth Dynamical Systems*, New York: Academic Press.
Kareken, J. H., and N. Wallace (1981) "On the Indeterminacy of Equilibrium Exchange Rates", *Quarterly Journal of Economics*, 96, 207–22.
Kehoe, T. J. (1985) "Multiplicity of Equilibria and Comparative Statics", *Quarterly Journal of Economics*, 100, 119–47.
—— and D. K. Levine (1984a) "Intertemporal Separability in Overlapping Generations Models", *Journal of Economic Theory*, 34, 216–26.
—— and —— (1984b) "Regularity in Overlapping Generations Exchange Economies", *Journal of Mathematical Economics*, 13, 69–93.
—— and —— (1985) "Comparative Statics and Perfect Foresight in Infinite Horizon Economics", *Econometrica*. 53, 433–53.
——, ——, A. Mas-Colell and M. Woodford (1986) "Gross Substitutes in Large Square Economies", Mathematical Sciences Research Institute Working Paper No. 07017-86.
——, —— and P. M. Romer (forthcoming) "Determinacy of Equilibria in Economies with Production and Finitely Many Infinitely Lived Consumers", *Journal of Economic Theory*.
Kotlikoff, L. J., and L. H. Summers (1981) "The Importance of Intergenerational Transfers in Aggregate Capital Accumulation", *Journal of Political Economy* 84, 706–32.
Levine, D. K. (1989) "Efficiency and the Value of Money", *Review of Economic Studies*, 56, 77–88.
Lucas, R. E. (1972) "Expectations and the Neutrality of Money", *Journal of Economic Theory*, 4, 103–24.
Mankiw, N. G., J. J. Rotemberg and L. H. Summers (1985) "Intertemporal Substitution in Macroeconomics" *Quarterly Journal of Economics*, 100, 223–51.
Mas-Colell, A. (1974) "Continuous and Smooth Consumers: Approximation Theorems", *Journal of Economic Theory*, 8, 305–36.
—— (1977) "On the Equilibrium Price Set of an Exchange Economy" *Journal of Mathematical Economics*, 4, 117–26.
Muller, W. J., and M. Woodford (1988) "Stationary Overlapping Generations Economies with Production and Infinite Lived Consumers" Part I: "Existence of Equilibrium" MIT discussion Paper No. 325; Part II: "Determinacy of Equilibrium", MIT Discussion Paper No. 326.
Samuelson, P. A. (1958) "An Exact Consumption-loan Model of Interest with or without the Social Contrivance of Money", *Journal of Political Economy*, 6, 467–82.
—— (1960) "Infinite, Unanimity, and Singularity: A Reply", *Journal of Political Economy*, 8, 76–83.
Santos, M. S., and J. L. Bona (forthcoming) "On the Structure of the Equilibrium Price Set of Overlapping-generations Economies", *Journal of Mathematical Economics*.
Scheinkman, J. A., and L. Weiss (1986) "Borrowing Constraints and Aggregate Economic Activity", *Econometrica*, 54, 23–46.

Shapley, L. S., and M. Shubik (1977) "An Example of a Trading Economy with Three Competitive Equilibria", *Journal of Political Economy*, 85, 873–5.

Varian, H. R. (1974) "A Third Remark on the Number of Equilibria of an Economy", *Econometrica*, 43, 985–6.

5

An Applied General Equilibrium Model of the Asset Markets in Sweden

Lars Werin

1 Introduction

In accordance with the Walras–Arrow–Debreu tradition, most work on applied general equilibrium (AGE) models has concerned markets for commodities, services and factors, or the "real" economy. But various attempts have been made to extend the work of financial markets. This has been done by adding a financial structure to the real model, or by formulating separate AGE models for the other half of the economy consisting of the markets for financial and real assets. A complete general equilibrium model should, of course, cover both real and financial markets and treat them alike. An accurate model of the market system should in fact include transaction costs and other forces which decide why a number of markets do not exist and why some markets attain equilibrium while others do not. However, as yet, the theoretical basis for the financial model is not as well developed as that for the real model. We could perhaps say that the financial general equilibrium model still waits for its Arrow and Debreu. The full market interdependence model with transaction costs has not even had its Walras.

If we take the AGE modeling to mean the construction of empirical models for disaggregated systems of markets along Walrasian lines, are attempts to build financial AGE models worthwhile and, even more, should we try to build full general equilibrium models comprising both real and financial markets? After all, financial markets are different from real markets, and they are not as well studied. Full real–financial models may become so complicated and unwieldy as to be practically useless. However, it is probably too early to determine the form that extensions of AGE modeling to the financial sphere should take. More experience has to be collected. A main purpose of the experiment reported here, which uses a specific AGE model of the Swedish asset market system, is to make a contribution in that direction.

A brief survey of the work done so far on financial general equilibrium models and the problems encountered provides useful background. The history of more formalized general equilibrium models covering financial markets does not begin in the Walrasian tradition but rather with the IS–LM model. In its original formulation that model contains only one real market, namely the market for the gross national product (GNP) aggregate of goods and services, assumed to be quantity adjusting, and two financial markets, namely the markets for money and bonds, both perfectly equilibrating. One of them can be excluded according to Walras's law. In practice – and somewhat unpedagogically – the bond market is nearly always chosen. The subsequent development has mainly followed two major, partly overlapping routes.

One route is to construct models for disaggregated systems of markets for financial assets (and usually real assets as well) along truly Walrasian lines. Most of these models are based on the theoretical framework of Tobin (1969). The major characteristic of that framework is the requirement that the analysis should concern holdings (stocks) of assets rather than flows of borrowing, lending and investment. Hence the empirical counterparts are balance sheets, or portfolios, rather than income and expenditure accounts.[1] One variant consists of fairly detailed econometric models of the complete system of asset markets, based rather loosely on the theory of portfolio choice, as for example a model by Tobin and associates (see Backus et al., 1980). Another variant comprises partial models for a small number of asset markets, derived strictly from the Markowitz–Tobin theory of portfolio choice (see for example Roley, 1979). Attempts have been made to integrate submodels of this kind in full, although greatly simplified, general equilibrium models, especially by Slemrod (1983, 1985). A full general equilibrium model, containing a somewhat richer financial structure but with weaker connections to portfolio theory, has been outlined by Feltenstein (1984).

The other major route is to extend macroeconometric models so as to comprise more elaborate financial systems than the IS–LM models from which most of them are ultimately derived. Much of the work along this route carried out during the last 10–15 years has also used the Tobin (1969) framework as the general theoretical basis. The two routes meet in models that lead to the IS–LM model by adding a simple IS structure to the asset system instead of adding a disaggregated asset structure to "real" models consisting of elaborated IS structures (see Tobin, 1982, for a basic analytical framework).

Neither the Walrasian nor the IS–LM based asset market model is without its problems. The standard method of formulating them numerically is of course econometric – or, to be more exact, stochastic – estimation, but it has turned out to be quite difficult to arrive at estimates conforming reasonably well to theoretical a priori requirements. Wrong signs, unrealistic magnitudes and difficulties in obtaining significant estimates abound. Intensive data and specification mining in search of plausible equations are legion. The study by Tobin and associates already referred to (Backus et al., 1980) gives an instructive and candid picture of the morass which this kind of work can get into even when it is in the best possible hands. It is understandable that more and more model builders resort to prior estimates (as did Tobin and associates in the study quoted) or to calibration methods.

Other problems, which do not arise or are less serious for real models, hamper attempts to build AGE type models for asset markets. One is that expectations play a much larger role in asset markets than in most markets for commodities and factors. Thus specific assumptions have to be made on the formation of expectations. As is well known, this is no easy matter. Another problem is that the preferences governing asset demand and supply concern mostly current values rather that quantities. Hence the amounts demanded and supplied change *directly* when their prices change, i.e. not via adjustment of behavior called forth by the price changes. This complication does not arise for ordinary commodities and services. Net wealth also changes directly for the same reason. The basic properties of such a system, e.g. conditions for the existence of an equilibrium have not been fully investigated.[?] An element of theoretical vagueness thus plagues these studies. In addition, some assets and debts that may be important are "implicit" only, as for instance public pension assets and liabilities and Ricardian (or Barro-type) tax debt – to the extent that it exists (see Barro, 1974). Thus if demanded and supplied amounts of assets are to be derived completely from portfolio choices, the implicit components ought to be included.[3] Quantity adjustment (or rationing) accompanied by spillover effects, which may be difficult to handle, also seems somewhat more common in financial markets than in markets for commodities and services. The inclusion of implicit public pensions and tax debt would in fact bring in additional quantity adjustment and spillover, since these components are imposed involuntarily on households. An even "deeper" problem with all disaggregated financial models concerns determinants of the scales of portfolios for financial intermediaries (i.e. the scale of their balance sheet totals). For most other sectors portfolios are ultimately constrained by net wealth. Intermediaries, however, typically have zero net wealth, and so some other portfolio component has to be assumed to play the role of scale factor or "pivot". The basic theory of the nature of financial firms gives few clues.[4]

Given the range of difficulties associated with building AGE models for asset markets, experiments are legitimate and fruitful. The project described here, still in its first exploratory stage, involves a rather detailed numerical model of the Swedish financial system (including some markets for real assets), constructed according to strict general equilibrium principles, although substantially simplified in various respects and very far from theoretical ideas on some important points. Hence it should perhaps modestly be called "simulation framework" rather than "model". No attempt is made to insert the framework in a full general equilibrium model covering real markets as well as asset markets.

The most important characteristic of the framework is that it depicts directly what happens in the asset markets and to the various portfolios after a disturbance. In other words, most components of the framework are straightforwardly "identified". Thus the framework lacks the black-box character that burdens so many econometric models. Much of the value it may have as a description of the actual financial structure or as an instrument for exploring reactions and effect channels derives *precisely* from this property. It means that various problems of specification which are solved in many econometric models by just adding variables that indirectly represent causal factors cannot be swept under the rug but *have to be* tackled openly. This might invite criticism which is equally relevant for other types of models which are better at hiding the underlying assumptions. The numerical formulation of the framework consists of a mixture of a "revealed preference" approach and guesswork, sometimes bordering on calibration.

A subsidiary purpose of the study, and the one that started it, is to analyze the effects of the very substantial budget deficits in Sweden in recent years. The first numerical application concerns budget deficit financing, a problem that clearly calls for some financial detail and thus a disaggregated model. It seems in fact generally useful to experiment with models that disaggregate over both assets and sectors, since this makes it possible to assess the role played by intermediation. Thinking along the lines of the Modigliani–Miller theorem leads us for instance to suspect that the effects of an exogenous change in the portfolio structure of an agent or a sector other than a household is dampened through arbitrage activities. Such arbitrage works to a large extent via intermediation.

Section 2 describes the analytical framework and its numerical formulation. In the framework, each sector chooses its portfolio by maximizing the expected combined rate of return, with risk considerations treated somewhat schematically. After a disturbance, as for instance a budget deficit, the system of asset markets adjusts in the ways that are essentially Walrasian, but with some elements of quantity adjustment or rationing. The numerical formulation includes 15 sectors of the Swedish economy and 30 assets. Section 3 presents the numerical application and adds further details on the adjustment process. Section 4 summarizes the results and provides some concluding comments on the methods of the study and the possibilities they may offer.

2 The Analytical Framework

The economy is divided into "exogenous" and "endogenous" sectors. The exogenous sectors comprise central and local government, the central bank and the rest of the world. Certain components of the central bank and rest of the world portfolios adjust passively to amounts chosen by the endogenous sectors. All other components of the portfolios of the exogenous sectors are given. Endogenous sectors comprise households, nonfinancial enterprises and various types of financial institutions. Every existing agent in the economy is included in some sector.

Each endogenous sector chooses a desired portfolio, represented by a vector of asset amounts. Holdings are positive and debts negative. All amounts are in current value, which implies what Tobin (1980) calls an assumption of "dollar-for-dollar fungibility between asset purchases and capital gains". While not fully realistic in the short run, such an assumption seems to be implicit in most models of portfolio choice and asset pricing. The choice of portfolio takes place by means of an unsophisticated optimization procedure. The sector chooses the portfolio in a set of "admissible" portfolios which maximizes the expected combined real return after tax. The admissible set is constrained, firstly, by the budget plane defined by the scale or "pivot" variable (usually net wealth) and the opportunities to buy and sell assets. Secondly, it contains mainly portfolio compositions observed to have been chosen by the sector over a series of years, and thus evidently found to be "safe". This makes it natural to speak of a revealed preference approach. Risk aversion is thus assumed to take the very simple form of permitting some portfolio compositions and forbidding others. The permitted, or admissible, compositions are equally good as far as risk is concerned, and maximization of expected rate of return has full play among them. The collection of admissible compositions also serves as a neat instrument for accommodating various institutional facts[5] and handling spillover effects caused by rationing.

After a disturbance, such as a budget deficit, which adds to certain components of the exogenous central government portfolio, excess supply or demand arises for various assets.[6] For a new equilibrium to be formed, either expected rates of return, or net wealth of various agents or both have to change in ways that make the agents choose portfolios compatible with an equilibrium. The experiments are in the realm of comparative statics, and thus the adjustment process in principle has no time dimension. The major properties of the process are the following.

An excess demand or supply in an asset market gives rise to some kind of adjustment, the character of which depends upon which adjustment regime is operating. For most assets the regime is ordinary price equilibration, which means that either the asset price or the interest rate is raised or lowered (or both asset price and interest rate change). With a change in an asset price, the amounts of the asset held change directly since they are measured in current value. The net wealth of each sector holding the asset also changes directly, which induces the sector to expand or contract all the components of its portfolio. However, an asset price change may also change the expected rate of return on the asset. It is assumed in the framework that a rise in an asset price, i.e. a capital gain, leads to a corresponding dampening of that part of the expected rate of return consisting of an expected capital gain, and vice versa for an asset price decrease. Thus a rise in the price of an asset stimulates demand for that asset via the net wealth effects but decreases demand via the substitution effect called forth by the induced fall in the expected rate of return. A change in an interest rate that is not accompanied by a change in the price of the asset is simpler since it does not affect net wealth directly but only the expected rate of return.

Another regime is quantity adjustment, which means that the amount held is determined involuntarily for the sectors on one side of the market, with asset price and rate of return given. This leads to spillover effects on the demand for and supply of the other assets.

Such a round of adjustments generates excess demand and supply for a number of assets leading to another round of adjustments. The process takes the form of an iterative procedure, which is simple in principle although somewhat complicated in practice. If the actual asset markets are actually stable, which is the normal situation, the interative process ought to converge toward a new equilibrium with new portfolios, net wealth, interest rates and asset prices since it is constructed to resemble actual market processes. Note, however, that the expansion of net wealth generated by increases in asset prices is to some extent destabilizing. Note also that even if stopping points, and hence equilibria, are found when a specific numerical model is applied, the theoretical vagueness concerning the existence in general of equilibria for these kinds of models is not dissolved.

The framework is described in more detail in the following sections. Section 2.1 gives a presentation of the general theoretical properties of the admissible sets and the principles of portfolio selection. Section 2.2 presents the assets and sectors distinguished in the empirical application and the numerical formulation of the admissible sets. Section 2.3 describes the formulation of the expected rates of return and introduces certain aspects of the adjustment process. Section 2.4 presents the adjustment regimes of the various markets. Section 2.5 is an overview of the full framework in formal mathematical terms.

2.1 General properties of admissible sets and portfolio selection

The principles of portfolio selection applied in the framework are illustrated in figure 5.1, although rather schematically since some major features require more than two dimensions to be presented adequately. Amounts of two assets are measured in current values along the axes. A portfolio composition is not admissible unless it is either a composition observed to have been chosen by the sector at a previous occasion or a convex combination of such observed compositions. The figure contains four observed ("basic") portfolio compositions for the sector studied, shown by the lines I–IV from the origin. (The empirical model contains eight basic compositions for each endogenous sector.) The collection of admissible compositions thus consists of the cone defined by these lines. In the simple case of figure 5.1, compositions II and III are in fact convex combinations of I and IV. When the number of assets exceeds the number of observed compositions, which is the case for the empirical model, it is unlikely that any observed composition is a combination of the others.

Evidently, the sector studied has always held positive amounts of asset 1 and negative amounts of asset 2, i.e. asset 2 is a debt for the sector. There is nothing to prevent a sector from sometimes holding an asset and sometimes supplying it to other sectors as a debt instrument. If this had been the case for asset 2, there would have been at least one line in the positive quadrant of the diagram. The cone of admissible compositions would then have been wider.

Portfolios also have to be attainable. First, at each occasion, the extent of the sector's portfolio is limited by its net wealth or, as hinted at in section 1, by some other scale variable for some of the financial intermediaries. Second, the attainable set is constrained by exchange opportunities. If the sector studied has net wealth as scale

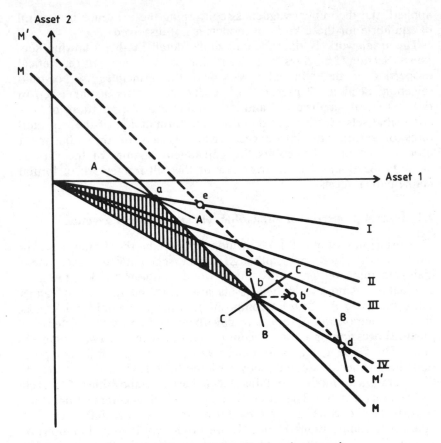

Figure 5.1 The portfolio selection framework

magnitude and both assets can be traded at prices given to the sector, the set of admissible portfolios is limited to the part of the cone inside the budget line MM, sloping at 45° since all points represent the same current value.

At each occasion, there is also a set of expected rates of return for the sector. The set defines a line (plane), as for example AA, BB or CC in the figure. If the expected rates of return are those given by AA, total return is maximized for portfolio a, which is thus chosen by the sector. With rates of return according to BB or CC, the sector chooses portfolio b. CC indicates that asset 1 gives a positive return as debt (and negative as asset held). This somewhat perverse situation can easily arise in an inflationary economy with nominal taxes.

If the boundary of the admissible set is a line segment as in figure 5.1, the choice of portfolio is extremely simple. With more than two assets, the boundary is an irregular multidimensional "hyperfacet", which makes the choice less trivial.

If, after a disturbance, the markets for assets 1 and 2 adjust by means of changes in current interest rates without accompanying asset price changes, the expected rates of return change in the same direction, since expected interest rates are assumed to follow current rates. The adjustment thus consists of switches from one portfolio to another within the given admissible set.

If the adjustment involves changes in asset prices, the process is more complex. Since asset amounts are measured in current values, a change in the price of an asset changes the amount of the asset, and thus displaces the initially held portfolio from one point in the figure to another.

Assume that the sector, at the given rates of return BB, holds portfolio b in figure 5.1 and that the price of asset 1 increases. The portfolio then contains more of asset 1, and is transformed into portfolio b'. Clearly the immediate effect of a change in an asset price is usually that the previously optimal portfolio becomes inoptimal; it may also become inadmissible. The price rise also alters net wealth, however, and hence shifts the boundary of the attainable set (to M'M' in figure 5.1).[7]

At the given expected rates of return BB, portfolio d becomes optimal, i.e. the sector issues more debt and increases its holding of asset 1 even further. But if, as assumed in the framework, the rise in the price of asset 1 dampens the expected capital gains from holding the asset, the rate of return line rotates counterclockwise. This introduces a substitution effect against asset 1, and may induce the sector to choose portfolio e.

The properties of such a process are illustrated further in figure 5.2. The amount Z_i in current values of a given asset i is measured along the horizontal axis and the expected rate of return $E(R_i)$ along the vertical axis; expectations are assumed to be the same for all agents. Assume for simplicity that the amount of the asset is given in physical terms in the short or medium-run period analyzed; we thus have a vertical supply curve which is S in the initial equilibrium. Demand concerns market values of the asset and is larger the higher the expected rate of return. The demand curve of the initial equilibrium is D, and expected rate of return is e. Now assume that there is an unexpected outward shift of the demand curve to D', called forth by an exogenous increase in net wealth or a decrease in the expected rate of return on a substitute asset. Clearly, a new equilibrium should require a lowering of $E(R_i)$. Assuming that the market

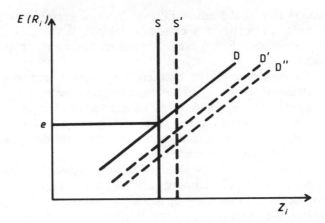

Figure 5.2 The market adjustment process

adjusts by means of asset price changes, excess demand drives up the price of asset i. This, firstly, increases the current value of the stock of the asset. S shifts outward to S', and net wealth increases for all holders of the asset, which shifts D' outward to D". But since the price of the asset has risen, some (or all) of the expected capital gain included in $E(R_i) = e$ has occurred; hence, secondly, $E(R_i)$ falls correspondingly. The new equilibrium is thus attained (if at all) by asset price changes which increase the current value of holdings, increase net wealth and decrease the expected rate of return.

2.2 Empirical formulation of the admissible sets

The empirical formulation for Sweden contains 15 sectors and 30 assets. They are listed in table 5.1, which presents the portfolios actually held at the end of 1980.

Each column in the table shows the portfolio for a sector. In addition there is a column showing the existing amounts of real capital. Of the 15 sectors the first 11 are endogenous, i.e. they choose portfolios in the way described, and the remaining four are exogenous. Of the 30 assets two are real, namely one-family houses and vacation houses (assets 29 and 30 in the table), which are the most important real assets held by Swedish households.[8] Other real assets are not included mainly because of a lack of good statistics.[9]

For the financial assets (numbers 1–28) there is a pairwise separation between assets denominated in Swedish currency ("SEK") and otherwise identical or similar assets denominated in foreign currencies

("FOR"). The coverage is not complete for these assets either. Thus loans between households and other "gray" loans are not included since there are no statistics whatsoever to indicate their importance. Household assets consisting of rights to various public pensions are omitted both for lack of data and because certain problems would arise if one tried to include them. Since the empirical application concerns budget deficits, however, an attempt has been made to bring in "Ricardian" (or Barro-type) implicit tax debt (number 28), in spite of the fact that it is extremely difficult to assess its size – and even to decide whether it exists at all. This component calls for further discussion. So do the components consisting of shares of various types (numbers 16–18), which are treated somewhat different-ly from the way they are treated in most other models.

The Ricardian doctrine, revived by Barro (1974), tells us that each addition to government debt leads to a corresponding tax liability for the current generation of individuals, since the new debt has to be serviced by additional taxes on the individuals themselves or their inheritors in the future. However, it appears that few economists believe in such a full offset. Nor is there any strong empirical evidence for it. Nevertheless most economists view the traditional assumption that taxpayers see no tax liability at all as too extreme. The majority opinion is probably that there may be *something*, but not very much, in the Ricardo–Barro idea.

An econometric study of Swedish saving behavior (Palmer, 1981) indicated that there was a perceived tax debt amounting to between 15 and 20 percent of the government debt. Although the study was done very carefully, there are many problems and pitfalls, and so the reliability of the estimate should be questioned. However, for lack of hard facts it was used as a general starting point for guessing the possible magnitude of the implicit tax debt in Sweden. Thus we assumed that the debt equals 20 percent of the "net" government debt, defined as the total central government debt *minus* half the value of the financial and real assets owned by the central government.[10] These assets were deducted since Ricardian logic seems to imply that, if taxpayers think of government debt as their own debt, they also see government assets as their own assets. However, the assets were counted at half value only, since many of them are probably considered less productive by taxpayers.

With these assumptions there was in fact no implicit tax debt in Sweden until 1978 but, in contrast, an "implicit asset" for the taxpayers (i.e. households). From 1978 the implicit debt has risen quite rapidly since government debt has expanded much faster than government assets. Thus the total central government debt was 25 percent of GNP in 1977, 65 percent in 1982 and about 70 percent in 1986.

Table 5.1 Portfolios of sectors of the Swedish economy on December 31, 1980 (millions of SEK)

	Households	Non financial enterprises (excluding real estate)	Real estate companies	Commercial banks	Savings banks	Agricultural cooperative banks	Insurance companies	Mortgage institutions	Finance companies	Investment companies	Social security funds	Local government	Central bank	Central government	Rest of the world	Real capital
1 Currency and coins. SEK	29896	3096	265	1876	642	118	–	–	–	–	–	134	–34372	65	–	–1720
2 Commercial banks' deposits in central bank. SEK	–	–	–	2804	–	–	–	–	–	–	–	–	–2804	–	–	–
3 Loans in central bank. SEK	–	–	–	–6225	–	–	–	–	–	–	–	–	6225	–	–	–
4 Deposits in Swedish banks, n.e.s.. SEK	184148	19239	1646	–127149	–75400	–18653	–	3	675	100	930	8151	–	5347	963	–
5 Deposits in Swedish banks. FOR	–	2119	181	–3355	–36	–	–	–	74	11	–	898	–	–	106	–
6 "Special" deposits in Swedish banks. SEK	–	28941	2476	–34019	–11076	–1205	–	4	1016	151	–	12262	–	1449	–	–
7 Bank and other certificates. SEK	–	5389	–	–8779	495	–	1884	–	42	1	–	868	–	–	–	–
8 Bank and other certificates. FOR	–	–	–	–890	–	–	–	–	–	–	–	–	–	–	892	–
9 Currency. deposits in foreign banks. FOR	–	652	–	29941	189	–	384	–	–	–	–	–	4232	–35186	–	–
10 Treasury discount notes. SEK	–	–	–	–	–	–	–	–	–	–	–	–	–	–	–	–
11 Treasury bills, SEK	40	2	–	10526	–	–	118	–	–	–	–	100	23200	–33986	–	–

Table 5.1 (cont.)

	Households	Non financial enterprises (excluding real estate)	Real estate companies	Commercial banks	Savings banks	Agricultural cooperative banks	Insurance companies	Mortgage institutions	Finance companies	Investment companies	Social security funds	Local government	Central bank	Central government	Rest of the world	Real capital
12 Savings bonds. public savings scheme. SEK	13282	–	–	–	–	–	–	–	–	–	–	–	–	-13282	–	–
13 Premium bonds. SEK	21125	–	–	–	–	–	–	–	–	–	–	–	–	-21225	–	–
14 Other bonds. debentures. SEK	8561	-20893	150	78109	18996	3545	57906	-160117	-847	-478	117126	-4282	8355	-112876	6745	–
15 Treasury bills. bonds, debentures, FOR	–	-8429	–	-1375	–	–	622	-2870	–	–	163	-1230	8278	-17573	22414	–
16 Shares, quoted on stock exchange. SEK	27320	-29849	-1375	-4997	–	–	6091	–	-373	-1903	1302	–	–	–	3787	–
17 Shares, other, SEK	24588	-35856	-4117	1358	577	11	236	79	322	814	–	2277	–	9911	–	–
18 Shares. FOR	-16925	13987	–	931	–	–	262	–	–	337	–	-949	–	–	-15517	–
19 Priority housing loans. SEK	–	–	15761	23058	7435	1143	–	–	–	–	–	–	–	–	–	–
20 Loans, other, SEK	248312	-132302	-87663	99728	56406	13281	38720	185493	3400	364	12775	-28854	662	82911	3391	–
21 Loans, FOR	–	-43214	–	-20566	-77	–	10	2439	-60	2	–	-260	-1299	-20303	83328	–
22 Trade credits, SEK	-2220	4558	-2338	–	–	–	–	–	–	–	–	–	–	–	–	–
23 Trade credits, FOR	11707	11707	–	–	–	–	–	–	–	–	–	–	–	–	-11707	–
24 Blocked accounts in central bank. SEK	–	5690	17	3	–	–	–	–	8	–	–	–	-5718	–	–	–

Table 5.1 (*cont.*)

	Households	Non financial enterprises (excluding real estate)	Real estate companies	Commercial banks	Savings banks	Agricultural cooperative banks	Insurance companies	Mortgage institutions	Finance companies	Investment companies	Social security funds	Local government	Central bank	Central government	Rest of the world	Real capital
25 Private insurance. SEK	34311	–	–	–	–	–	–34311	–	–	–	–	–	–	–	–	–
26 Loans between financial institutions (excluding CB). SEK	–	–	–	–26418	3333	2209	8260	–19312	–	–	30043	–	–	1921	–	–
27 Other financial assets and debts. SEK	32045	–77807	–6478	764	93	10	1065	1365	–1592	–109	5004	–4642	–50	50322	–	–
28 Implicit tax debt, SEK	–9400	–	–	–	–	–	–	–	–	–	–	–	–	9400	–	–
29 One-family houses	541000	–	–	–	–	–	–	–	–	–	–	–	–	–	–	–541000
30 Vacation houses	93000	–	–	–	–	–	–	–	–	–	–	–	–	–	–	–93000
Total	732559	–252970	–110997	15125	1575	459	81247	7084	2663	–710	167343	–15527	6709	–68768	60665	–635720

We now turn to the treatment of shares, of which there are three types in the framework: shares of Swedish companies quoted on the Swedish stock exchange; Swedish shares not quoted on the stock exchange; and shares of foreign companies (assets 16–18). All three types are entered both on the asset side for the sectors holding them and on the debt side for the issuing enterprise sectors. This is the treatment suggested, for example, in a basic work by Solomon (1963). The most common way of treating equity on the enterprise side in asset market models, however, is to enter the given stock of real capital owned by the enterprise and then to transform the stock to current equity values by means of Tobin's q.[11]

The method applied here has both advantages and disadvantages compared with the traditional approach, but the advantages appear to carry more weight. In particular, the market for shares is now treated exactly like the markets for all other assets, with explicit demand and supply sides. To enter shares indirectly as related by a valuation factor q to real capital is somewhat artificial, since neither theoretically nor empirically is there any simple relation between the equity of the firm and its real capital. In practice, the value of the equity represents the firm's full earning capacity. Even for manufacturing industry this nowadays derives largely from activities that have little to do with the firm's physical production apparatus, e.g. financial activities. And it is particularly true for financial enterprises, which may have large equity without any real capital at all.[12] Once again we run into problems in the theory of the nature of the firm. However, if Tobin's q is required, it is easily derived by relating the market value of shares generated in an application of the framework to available extraneous data on real capital.[13] Note also that by entering the supply of shares separately we do not distinguish between increases in supply caused by rising share prices and increases in supply due to new issues.

Our treatment means that debt in the form of equity rises when share prices rise. No firm would record a larger debt in its formal accounts. But there is a larger debt *implicitly*, since in the longer run the firm feels an obligation to provide share-owners with a return sufficient to encourage shareholding at the higher values. In practice, higher share prices are often a mirror image of an independent fall in investors' required rate of return.

Although this means that we anticipate the adjustment process, it is useful to examine first what happens to shares after disturbance. The dividend in kronor is given exogenously in a numerical application, since it is usually decided some time in advance. Many firms in fact strive to keep dividends rather stable in the medium run. Expressed as a rate of return, however, the dividend changes when share prices change. To the extent that, before the disturbance, share prices are expected to rise, and a rise takes place in the iterative adjustment process, expectations of further rises decline correspondingly, as already described. Another effect is that net wealth *increases* for sectors holding shares, and *decreases* for the enterprise sector that issued the shares.

Tables like table 5.1 have been compiled within the project for the end of each of the years 1977–84. The resulting eight portfolio compositions for each sector comprise the basic ingredients in the admissible sets of the endogenous sectors, as discussed in section 2.1.[14] Behind this is an assumption that we observe optimal portfolios only. In other words, agents are supposed to adjust very rapidly to changes in expected rates of return and net wealth.[15] The assumption is to some extent tested in section 3.

The admissible sets are constrained by net wealth for all sectors except the three bank sectors, mortgage institutions and investment companies (cf. column heading in table 5.1). These are pure inter- mediaries with net wealth approximately zero.[16] For the bank sector and mortgage institutions the amount of loans in SEK (asset 20) was chosen as scale or "pivot" variable mainly because it was found to be a large and stable component in their portfolios.[17] Furthermore, it has some character of instrument or "goal" magnitude for these sectors. For investment companies shares quoted on the stock ex- change (asset 15) were selected as pivot.

Spillover effects caused by quantity adjustment were treated by means of revising admissible sets to make them result in the required amount of the rationed component and correspondingly less or more of the other components, as described further in section 3. In the numerical application carried out in section 3, quantity adjustment was assumed for implicit tax debt only. Regulations such as changes in reserve requirements and obligatory bond holding could also be introduced through proper revisions of the admissible sets. In prin- ciple certain revisions of this kind seem to be called for in numerical applications concerning Sweden, at least up to the early 1980s, but for simplicity no revision was made in the application described in section 3.

2.3 Expected rates of return

When a portfolio is chosen, each agent (sector) formulates expected rates of return on each asset for the period during which the portfolio will be held. The rate of return on asset i, as expected by j, to be formulated in yearly terms in the numerically specified framework is

$$E^j(R_i^j) = [1 - E^j(t_{ri}^j)]E^j(r_i) + [1 - E^j(t_{gi}^j)]E^j(g_i) - E^j(\pi)$$
$$+ [1 - E^j(t_{si}^j)] E^j(s_i^j) + E^j(e) \qquad (5.1)$$

with the following components:

r_i is the rate of interest (dividend etc.) on asset i
t_{ri}^j is the rate on interest income from asset i for agent j
g_i is the rate of change in the market price of asset i (capital gain or loss)
t_{gi}^j is the tax rate on capital gain (or loss) on asset i for agent j
π is the rate of inflation
s_i^j is the value of direct services, expressed as a rate of interest, from j's holding of asset i (e.g. liquidity, direct return on house ownership after depreciation, gains from tax evasion through holding of cash etc.)
t_{si}^j is the tax rate on the value of direct services from j's holding of asset i
e is the rate of change in exchange rate (units of Swedish currency per unit of foreign currency, for assets denominated in foreign currency)

The rates of return are thus real returns after tax. The numerical formulation requires hypotheses on how expectations are formed and revised, as well as statistical information. The problems are formidable, but by no means unique to this study. We briefly examine the various components of the rates of return and assumptions about how expectations are formed, and discuss the empirical formulation. A general assumption is that expectations are the same for all agents; hence E^j can be replaced by E. The rates of return, however, may still differ between agents, since the tax rates and the value of direct services may be different.

Expected interest rates, expected dividends, are always assumed to equal current rates; thus $E(r_i) = r_i$ for all r_is which are not dividends. Hence, the rate in the initial situation equals the actual rate. The expected rate then changes successively along with the changes generated in the adjustment process. Dividends are expected to be unchanged in kronor, which means that they change as a rate of return when share prices change. For implicit tax debt a small given rate of interest is postulated.

The rate of change in the asset price, $g_i = \Delta p_i/p_i$, is a component of the rate of return for shares and houses (assets 16–18, 29–30).[18] Expectations of these changes are assumed to be formed in the following way. The initial expectation, held before the disturbance, is assumed to be that the price will rise by the expected rate of inflation $E(\pi)$ plus 5 percent. This corresponds approximately to the long-run increases in the prices of both shares and houses in Sweden and thus to "average" long-run expectations. If the price rises in the adjustment process, expectations are revised downward by the same amount until we reach $E(g_i) = 0$. If the price falls, $E(g_i)$ is revised upward. Complications arising if the disturbance is expected are discussed below. In formal terms, $E(g_i)$ can be written $E(\Delta p_i^0)/p_i^0$ where p_i^0 is the given price before the disturbance, and Δp_i^0 denotes the change from this price during the period when expectations are formed. If p_i is the price generated by the disturbance, we have

$$E(g_i) = \frac{E(\Delta p_i)}{p_i} = \frac{E(\Delta p_i^0)}{p_i^0} - \frac{p_i - p_i^0}{p_i^0} \qquad (5.2)$$

where the first term on the right-hand side is the exogenous initial expectation.

The rate of inflation is assumed to be perfectly foreseen by the agents; thus $E(\pi) = \pi$. There is some empirical support for such an assumption at least for the years around 1980 (see Jonung, 1981). For the exchange rate, the basic assumption is that agents expect it to be unchanged.[19] However, if adjustments lead to capital inflow or outflow, the assumption is that people expect the exchange rate to change somewhat upward or downward. We thus have a simple adjustment equation

$$E(e) = k_e \frac{\Sigma_i(\Delta z_i^f)}{\Sigma_i z_i^f} \qquad (5.3)$$

where z_i^f is the amount of asset i held by the rest of the world (f), and thus Σz_i^f is the net wealth of the rest of the world, and k_e is an adjustment coefficient, the value of which is set at 0.1. Thus the exchange rate is expected to change at one-tenth of the rate of capital inflow or outflow.[20] This seems approximately to accord with actual "feelings" and behavior in recent years.

The value of direct services (sometimes called "convenience value") consists of direct return from house ownership (net after depreciation), the value of liquidity derived from holding currency and deposits, and gains from tax evasion by holding currency. These are mainly "psychological" magnitudes and hence are difficult or impossible to observe empirically. In the application, the value of one-family house services was assumed to be 6 percent and that of vacation house services 4 percent of the current market value of these houses for households. The value of liquidity and tax evasion benefits was set at 5 percent for currency and 2 percent for deposits of households, and 3 and 1 percent respectively for other sectors. Moreover, premium bonds and insurance assets (assets 9 and 25) were assumed to have convenience values of 1 and 2 percent respectively for households. Foreign currency had a convenience value of 1 percent for banks.

The rate of return formula contains three collections of tax rates for each sector; t^j_{ri}, t^j_{qi} and t^j_{si} (one rate for each asset i). Most of them have to be rather crude representations of the true tax rates. For example, actual household tax rates differ between income and wealth groups, but this is disregarded since the framework contains only one household sector. Furthermore, some actual tax rates depend on deductions that may vary in size for many reasons. Capital gain taxes apply to realized gains only, and might depend on how long the asset has been held. In the application carried out in this study, all expected tax rates were assumed to equal their given initial levels and were expected to remain at these levels. For capital gains, the rates were crude estimates of the "present values" of the rates to be applied when the gains are realized in the future.

The assumption that tax rates are expected to stay at the initial level is particularly important for interpreting the results of the numerical application, which concerned a disturbance of the port- folios held at the end of 1980 corresponding to the actual budget deficit during 1981. Formally, applications are comparative statics experiments showing the situation that would have materialized at a given time if the exogenous variables had taken the values generated by the disturbance instead of the values they actually had. The adjustment process should, in principle, have no time dimension, although it is reasonable to imagine that it takes some time. For the experiment carried out an adjustment period of one year is reason- able, since the disturbance consisted of feeding the new government debt, issued throughout 1981, into the end-of-1980 portfolios. In other words, and as discussed further in section 2.4, we could express the problem as what the end-of-1981 asset market equilibrium would have looked like if the budget deficit had been the *only* disturbance in 1981. Now, it so happened that a tax reform involving major changes in capital taxation was announced suddenly in April 1981, to be carried out successively from 1982 onward. There is no doubt that the reform was mainly unforeseen. It naturally affected rate of return expectations from the day of the announcement and thus the port- folios actually chosen. Consequently, the results of the application reflect the effect of the 1981 deficits *if* a change in tax rates had not been announced. It is possible to insert expected rates of return that embody the new expected tax rates in the framework, but the problem is more clear-cut if we disregard the tax change.

Complications affecting all components of the expected rates of return arise when the disturbances analyzed are not unexpected one-shot changes. The large budget deficits in Sweden in the last decade were probably unforeseen during the first one or two (or even three) years, but after some time it became obvious that new large deficits were to follow. Thus if deficits are considered to bring about higher interest rates and asset prices, which is in fact the result of the numerical application of our framework and of various other studies, and if the agents have absorbed this knowledge and trust in it, then most of the rise of at least asset prices would take place in an early phase of the deficit development, i.e. as soon as the agents begin to realize that further large deficits will follow.[21] Somewhat imprecisely, we could say that the effects of second-stage deficits occurs *before* these deficits actually materialize.

When formulating the numerical estimates, various statistical sources were available, especially for interest rates, but data for interest rates seldom correspond exactly to the assets of the framework, most of which are aggregates of various, "elementary" assets.[22] For tax rates crude "average" rates were derived from the basic tax rules.

2.4 Adjustment regimes

As mentioned in the introduction to section 2 there are three major regimes of adjustment in asset markets; interest rate variation, asset price variation, and quantity variation at given interest rates and prices. The first two regimes are Walrasian in spirit and involve rules that decide how much the interest rate or asset price responds to an excess demand or supply. Quantity adjustment is a non-Walrasian disequilibrium regime, where rationing in one form or another takes place followed by spillover effects.

Interest rate regime is assumed for deposits, certificates, Treasury bills, bonds and various kinds of loans, all in Swedish currency.[23] For deposits it could be argued that there is "mixed" regime with quantity adjustment at given interest rates in the very short run, since banks have to accept all deposits, and interest rate adjustment in the somewhat longer run. However, if we applied quantity adjustment as a first adjustment step, accompanied by spillover into variations in banks' deposits in the central bank, and then introduced interest rate adjustment as a second step, the outcome would be the same as if the second step were introduced from the beginning. For bills and, in particular, bonds, interest rate variations generate corresponding changes in market prices. Thus the actual regime is "mixed". (It could just as well be considered as market price adjustment accompanied by changes in effective interest rates.) However, both bills and bonds have been short term in Sweden in recent years, with duration seldom exceeding five years. Until quite recently, there were hardly any true markets for existing bonds, which were usually held from issue until maturity.[24] So, for simplicity, market price changes for bills and bonds are disregarded. If all bills and bonds were similar it would be easy to include them, but aggregating bills and bonds with different nominal interest rates and times to maturity causes practical problems. Market price regime is assumed for shares in Swedish currency, one-family houses and vacation houses. For shares it might be argued that the true regime is mixed, since share price rises tend to be followed by increases in nominal dividends. However, as discussed in section 2.2, changes in dividends are usually made only at long intervals.

For assets denominated in foreign currency, price and interest rates are assumed to be given, which is the usual small country assumption. Thinking in terms of net supply curves, these curves are thus horizontal at given interest rates and prices. Hence, any excess demand or supply arising from the portfolio choices in Sweden is automatically accommodated by inflow or outflow of debt instruments. A similar assumption is made for Swedish currency and for banks' loans and deposits in the central bank. Thus changes in these components resulting from the portfolio choices of other sectors are assumed to be passively accommodated by the bank. For currency the price is unity and the interest rate zero. For central bank loans and deposits the price is again unity, while the interest rates consist of the discount rate, penalty rates etc. which are exogenous. In other words, the portfolio adjustment of the endogenous sector takes place with monetary policy unchanged.[25]

The fact that both capital flow and short-term components of the central bank adjust automatically implies that an inflow or outflow of capital should be thought of as accommodated by the central bank for the time being. Thus the balance on current account need not be affected. In the somewhat longer run there may be a connection between capital movements generated by portfolio behavior and the current account.

With regard to implicit tax debt, there is regular quantity adjustment with spillover, since the debt is imposed on households which have to invest it in one way or another. Much attention has been devoted to such spillover effects in recent theoretical literature (see for example Drèze, 1975, and Malinvaud, 1977), but as yet there is very little empirical information on the forms the effects take in practice. Barro (1974) made the extreme assumption that additions to implicit tax debt spill over only into extra demand for government bonds. If the implicit tax debt were 100 percent, there would be no effects on net wealth, interest rates and asset prices, and hence no portfolio effects via budget deficits. But it seems more realistic to assume that implicit tax debt spills over into extra demand for various kinds of long-term assets, like bonds, shares and houses. This is the assumption made in the application. The spillover demand is assumed to be distributed among these long-term assets according to their proportions in the household sector portfolio at the point of disturbance. Thus all vectors of admissible portfolio compositions for households were revised to express this redistribution of demand.

Quantity adjustment and spillover should perhaps be employed for some other assets as well, particularly savings bonds (asset 12), which each household can buy only in limited amounts. For simplicity this has not been done.

. The Walrasian price revision rules applied are

$$\frac{\Delta p_i}{p_i} = k_p \frac{\mathrm{ED}_i}{Q_i} \qquad (5.4a)$$

and

$$\frac{\Delta r_i}{r_i} = k_r \frac{\mathrm{ED}_i}{Q_i} \qquad (5.4b)$$

where p_i and r_i are the price index and interest rate of asset i, ED_i is the net sum of amounts of the asset over all portfolios (excess demand if positive, excess supply if negative) and Q_i is the numerically largest of the sum of positive amounts and the sum of negative amounts (gross total demand and supply respectively). The first rule is applied to markets with asset price regime, and the second to markets with interest rate regime. The reaction coefficients k_p and k_r are 0.5 and 1 respectively. Thus, for a relative excess demand of x percent, the interest rate was raised by x percent or the asset price was raised by $0.5x$ percent in the next iteration. The two coefficients are little more than guesswork. The general idea behind them is that the observed portfolio compositions for the years 1977–84 were similar, which indicates quite low own-price and own-interest-rate elasticities. Hence an elasticity of 0.5 for each supply and demand schedule seems reasonable except for the supply of houses, which is given in the short run and has zero elasticity. Furthermore, preliminary experiments suggested that larger coefficients would result in price and interest rate changes that seemed unrealistically high. Thus, in a sense, the guesses involve some "calibration". Even the chosen coefficients appear to give reactions that are somewhat too sharp. Altogether, the choice of reaction coefficients seems to be the weakest part of the framework.

2.5 An overview of the framework and the adjustment process

The ingredients of the framework and the various links in the adjustment process have been presented. In this section we survey the full framework in more formal terms and give an overview of the adjustment process.

The first component of the framework is the submodel describing the *portfolio selection* of the endogenous sectors. Each sector j chooses a portfolio $Z^j = (Z^j_1, \ldots, Z^j_n)$ of amounts in current values of the n assets by solving the following maximization problem:

$$\text{Maximize} \qquad [E(R^j)]'Z^j \qquad (5.5)$$

$$\text{subject to} \qquad Z^j = A^j X^j \qquad (5.6a)$$

$$X^j \geqslant 0 \qquad (5.6b)$$

$$(B^j)' = v^j \qquad (5.6c)$$

where a prime denotes a row vector and where

$E(R^j)$ is an n vector of expected rates of return, one for each asset
A^j is an $n \times g$ matrix with one column for each basic admissible portfolio composition, the elements defined so as to give unity for the pivot magnitude
X^j is a g vector giving the extent of use of each basic portfolio composition (each column of A^j) in the chosen portfolio Z^j
v^j is the pivot (a scalar), which for most sectors is net wealth (i.e. the sum of the elements of Z^j) and for some sectors is a particular portfolio component (i.e. a particular element of Z^j)
B^j is a summation vector of order g.

Clearly we have a linear programming problem, although it is extremely simple since there is just one major restriction (condition 5.6c). The solution requires the calculation of g vector problems only, namely $E(R^j)$ multiplied by each of the columns of A^j. The largest product indicates the optimum portfolio composition, to be used up to the limit given by the pivot. The vector $E(R^j)$ defines the rate of return line (plane) AA in figure 5.1, and the restrictions (5.6a), (5.6b) and (5.6c) define the configuration representing the admissible set.[26]

The expected rates of return, the pivot magnitude and the matrix of admissible portfolio compositions to the extent that it is affected by spillover effects are endogenous for each sector and are determined as follows.

For *expected rates of return* we have a function

$$E(R^j) = \psi^j(r, g, \text{CF}, \pi, t^j) \qquad (5.7)$$

where π and g are vectors of interest rates and capital gains with one element of each asset, CF represents the rate of capital flow defined by (5.3), governing exchange rate expectations, π is the rate of inflation and t^j is a vector of tax rates. Of these r, g and CF are endogenous. Variations in r affect the corresponding components of $E(R^j)$ directly in the way described in section 2.3, and variations in g and CF affect $E(R^j)$ as shown by expressions (5.2) and (5.3).

For the *pivot*, whether it is *net wealth* or a particular portfolio component, we have a simple relation

$$v^j = \psi(g) \tag{5.8}$$

describing the revaluation brought about by changes in asset prices.

The adjustment of *admissible portfolio compositions* because of spillover effects, generated by quantity adjustment, is schematically represented by the function

$$A^j = \lambda^j(d) \tag{5.9}$$

where d is a disequilibrium measure consisting of the transient excess demand ED_i for each quantity-adjustment market i (cf. the discussion in section 2.4).

For each *exogenous sector h* (including the "sector" consisting of given amounts of real capital; cf. the last column in table 5.1) we have

$$Z^h = \bar{Z}^h_I + Z^h_{II} \tag{5.10}$$

where Z^h is the portfolio of h, comprising an exogenous part $\bar{Z}^h_I$ and, for two of the sectors, an endogenous part Z^h_{II}. This contains amounts of currency and banks' loans and deposits if h is the central bank, and assets denominated in foreign currencies if h is the rest of the world.

The *equilibrium conditions* are

$$ED_i = \sum_j z^j_i + \sum_h Z^h_i = 0 \quad i = 1, \ldots, n \tag{5.11}$$

where ED_i is excess demand for asset i. In a sense the term "equilibrium condition" is less suitable for assets characterized by demand and supply equality achieved by quantity adjustment and spillover effects.

The full framework also contains the *price revision rules* (5.4a) and (5.4b).

We now turn to an overview of the full adjustment process. In the given initial situation a disturbance occurs. It may consist of changes in the portfolio of an exogenous sector (e.g. new central government borrowing). This directly gives rise to excess demand and supply of assets. (The application described below is of this kind.) Alternatively the disturbance may consist of exogenous changes in rate of return expectations or in admissible sets (e.g. because of regulation). Excess demand or supply is then generated for a number of assets by revisions of portfolios directly called forth by the disturbance.

Given the first-round excess demand and supply, the adjustment proceeds by iterations. Each iteration contains the following steps.

1 Interest rates are revised for assets with interest rate regime.
2 Asset prices are revised for assets with price regime. This leads to new net wealth for sectors holding the asset or having it as debt, new amounts held by exogenous sectors and revision of dividend rates for domestic shares.
3 Exchange rate expectations are revised in relation to the capital inflow or outflow of the preceding iteration.
4 Expected rates of return are revised to account for changes in interest rates, asset price changes and changes in exchange rate expectations.
5 Desired holdings of implicit tax debt resulting from the preceding iteration are adjusted so as to equal the given amount of such debt, with corresponding revisions of the admissible sets of households to account for spillover effects.[27]
6 New pivots are inserted, consisting of new net wealth according to (2) or the amount of loans or shares generated in the preceding iteration.
7 New optimal portfolios are derived for endogenous sectors.
8 New excess demands and supplies are calculated for various assets.

Other details of the adjustment process are presented along with the description of the numerical application in section 3.

Provided the process converges, the iterations can be continued until a new equilibrium is reached, i.e. excess demands and supplies become (approximately) zero. Since the project is still in an exploratory stage, no strict computer-adapted algorithm has been formulated. The application presented in section 3 was in fact not pursued until a stopping point of the adjustment process occurred. However, the three iterations carried out exhibited quite rapid convergence toward new levels of most, but not all, major variables. Since the analytical framework is very "coarse-grained" due to discontinuities of the attainable sets, it would in any case be impossible to attain a *perfect* equilibrium. The iteration process could be expected to "flicker" around an approximate equilibrium.

A further very important problem is whether an equilibrium obtained by the iteration is path dependent or not, i.e. whether it is sensitive to the choice of price revision rules and other ingredients of the adjustment process. No investigation of this kind has been made, but there seems to be some degree of path dependence. Behind this problem is the basic unsolved problem of the conditions necessary for an equilibrium in a model of this type.

3 A Numerical Application: Effects of Budget Deficits

A test of the reliability of the framework was made first. Expected rates of return for the various sectors as of December 31, 1980, were applied to the admissible sets. This caused eight of the 11 endogenous sectors to choose the end-of-1980 portfolio composition. For one sector the 1979 and 1980 compositions gave practically the same total rate of return. The tie between the two could be resolved only when a fourth decimal was included in the rate of return, and the choice then went in favor of 1979.[28] Two sectors chose more remote portfolios; one chose the 1977 portfolio and the other the 1983. Altogether, these results seem fairly encouraging. Furthermore, they suggest that adjustment to variations in rates of return are quite rapid.

As mentioned in section 1 only one empirical application has been made so far concerning the effects of Swedish budget deficits and, as just discussed, the application is in fact somewhat incomplete since the adjustment process has not been pursued all the way to the new equilibrium.

3.1 Layout of the experiment

In the situation described by the actual portfolios of December 31, 1980, a disturbance was assumed to occur consisting of an increase in central government debt of the same size and composition as the actual budget deficit during the year 1981. More precisely, the disturbance consisted of new central government domestic borrowing outside the central bank only, since borrowing in the central bank and in the rest of the world belongs to the exogeneous sphere.[29] This directly created excess supply in some asset markets. It also raised the wealth of the endogenous part of the economy, as described below. Thus the adjustment process was set into motion. If we take the outcome of the last iteration carried out as an approximation of the final stopping point, it describes the resulting changes in portfolios, net wealth, interest rates and asset prices. In other words, the outcome shows what would have occurred if the full budget deficit had appeared on the first day of the year, or perhaps better (and as already discussed) what would have occurred by the end of 1981 *if* the budget deficit was the only disturbance of the asset system during the year, *if* – in the spirit of partial equilibrium experiments – there were no repercussions back to asset markets via reactions in the "real" sphere (as for instance effects on the stocks of houses) and *if* the deficit of 1981 and its significance for the asset market were not anticipated by the agents in a previous year. In such a case some of the effects would have occurred already before December 31, 1980.

The partial equilibrium properties of the exercise are elucidated further by the treatment of wealth. The addition to central government gross indebtedness through domestic borrowing must give rise to a corresponding addition to domestic private (i.e. endogenous) gross wealth. (The addition to endogenous *net* wealth equals the gross increase minus the addition to implicit tax debt.) But then the course of events in the real markets outside the framework has to be compatible with such a development. One set of assumptions providing compatibility is the one made in the IS–LM model. In that model an excess of government expenditure over taxes gives rise to a multiplier process that expands income to the point where, given marginal propensity to save, new savings equal to the budget deficit are generated; new savings are of course the same as an addition to private wealth.[30]

The government domestic borrowing outside the central bank, and thus the disturbance, took the form shown in the first column of table 5.2. We find that the total change in this debt was 46.7 billion kronor or (see column 3) an addition of 39 percent to the stock of this kind of debt outstanding at the end of 1980.[31] Clearly, this was a substantial increase. We also find (column 1) that the composition of central government domestic debt outside the central bank changed along with the increase. For Treasury bills there was in fact a *decrease*. This shows that the distinction between government borrowing, debt management and open-market operations is blurred in practice. Column 2 gives the changes in central government domestic debt outside the central bank as a percentage of the *total* stock (including debt abroad or in the central bank) on December 31, 1980, of the various kinds of debt instruments. We find for example that government domestic borrowing outside the central bank using ordinary bonds as instrument added no less than 16.9 percent to the total amount of such bonds outstanding at the end of 1980. Column 3 relates changes in government domestic borrowing outside the central bank to the already existing government debt for the various debt instruments. New government borrowing using ordinary bonds as instrument meant that the amount of government bonds placed domestically outside the central bank increased by 44.9 percent.

Hence the total increase in gross private wealth was 46.7 billion kronor, and all of it was assumed to fall on the household sector. (In a full model comprising all real and financial markets the incidence of wealth increase would of course be determined endogenously.) Moreover, the increase was assumed to consist of bank deposits (asset 4).[32] There was also a rise in implicit tax debt, related to the

Table 5.2 Change in central government domestic debt outside the central bank, 1981

Debt instrument	1	2	3
	Change in million kronor	Change as percentage of total stock of debt instrument on Dec 31, 1980	Change as percentage of central government amount placed domestically outside the central bank on Dec 31, 1980
11 Treasury bills, SEK	−7938	−23.4	−23.4
12 Savings bonds, SEK	+300	+2.3	+2.3
13 Premium bonds, SEK	+3657	+17.2	+17.2
14 Other bonds, SEK	+50669	+16.9	+44.9
Total	+46668		+39.0

increase in *total* central government debt, as discussed in section 2.2. For 1981 the increase in implicit debt was 9.5 billion kronor when it was calculated in the way described in section 2.2. All of it, naturally, was assumed to burden the household sector. Consequently, the increase in household net wealth was 37.2 billion.

Thus altogether the initial shock consisted of

1 Additions to the central government portfolio of the amounts presented in table 5.2, with the accompanying excess supplies and demands,[33]
2 an increase in implicit tax debt for the household sector, accompanied by revision of all basic portfolio compositions of the admissible set of households so as to account for the spillover effect (cf. section 2.4),
3 an increase in net wealth of the household sector equal to new domestic government debt outside the central bank minus the increase in implicit tax debt, and
4 an increase in household deposits to the increase in gross wealth.

Hence in the first iteration the interest rates of the four assets with excess supply or demand changes according to the revision rule in expression (5.4). All endogenous sectors chose new optimal portfolios, the household sector within a larger net wealth. This resulted in excess demand or supply for practically all assets.

These excess demands and supplies set the adjustment process in motion as described in section 2.5.

3.2 Results

This section presents the major numerical results, while section 3.3 gives an analysis of the results with particular emphasis on the convergence properties of the adjustment process. While it seems as if the process converges steadily and the qualitative contents of the major results appear realistic, certain tendencies caused the interruption after the third interation. The factors behind these tendencies and the desirability to revise the framework so as to neutralize them are discussed. In section 3.4 the results of the application are compared with the actual development.

Table 5.3 presents interest rates (columns 1 and 2) and asset prices (columns 3 and 4) initially and after iteration 3, and thus the impact of the 1981 budget deficit on these variables. By defining asset quantities, all initial asset prices are unity. The excess demand or supply remaining after iteration 3 as a percentage of the numerically largest of total gross demand and total gross supply is shown in column 5. Figure 5.3 presents the development of the major interest

Table 5.3 Impact on interest rates and asset prices

	1 Interest rate	2	3 Asset price	4	5 Excess demand(+) or supply(−) after iteration[a]
	Initially	After iteration	Initially	After iteration	
1 Currency and coins, SEK	0	0	1	1	
2 Commercial banks' deposits in CB, SEK	0.060[b]	0.060[b]	1	1	
3 Loans in central bank, SEK	0.013[b]	0.013[b]	1	1	
4 Deposits in Swedish banks, n.e.s., SEK	0.105	0.083	1	1	+0.029
5 Deposits in Swedish banks, FOR	0.135[c]	0.135[c]	1	1	
6 "Special" deposits in Swedish banks, SEK	0.125	0.135	1	1	−0.193
7 Bank and other certificates, SEK	0.134	0.322	1	1	+0.279
8 Bank and other certificates, FOR	0.135[c]	0.135[c]	1	1	
9 Currency, deposits in foreign banks, FOR	0.135[c][d]	0.135[c]	1	1	
10 Treasury discount notes, SEK			1	1	
11 Treasury bills, SEK	0.129	0.096	1	1	+0.016
12 Savings bonds, public saving scheme, SEK	0.150	0.255	1	1	−0.083
13 Premium bonds, SEK	0.090	0.265	1	1	−0.305
14 Other bonds, debentures, SEK	0.140[e]	0.172[e]	1	1	−0.025
15 Treasury bills, bonds, debentures, FOR	0.125[f]	0.155[f]	1	1.186	−0.026
16 Shares, quoted on stock exchange, SEK	0.135[c]	0.135[c]	1	1.095	+0.019
17 Shares, other, SEK	0.040[g]	0.034[g]	1	1	
18 Shares, FOR	0.040[g]	0.035[g]	1	1	
19 Priority housing loans, SEK	0.050[c]	0.050[c]	1	1	
	0.127	0.158	1	1	−0.107

Table 5.3 (cont.)

	1	2	3	4	5
		Interest rate		Asset price	Excess demand(+) or supply(−) after iteration[a]
	Initially	After iteration	Initially	After iteration	
20 Loans, other, SEK	0.135	0.164	1	1	−0.035
21 Loans, FOR	0.140[c]	0.140[c]	1	1	
22 Trade credits, SEK	0.160	0.224	1	1	−0.060
23 Trade credits, FOR	0.150[c]	0.150[c]	1	1	
24 Blocked accounts in central bank, SEK	0.100[b]	0.100[b]	1	1	
25 Private insurance, SEK	0.120	0.098	1	1	−0.090
26 Loans between financial institutions (excluding central bank), SEK	0.135	0.101	1	1	+0.094
27 Other assets and debts, SEK	0.130	0.122	1	1	−0.105
28 Implicit tax debt, SEK	0.100[h]	0.100[h]	1	1	0
29 One-family houses	0	0	1	1.093	+0.064
30 Vacation houses	0	0	1	1.243	+0.102

[a] Relation to the largest of the two amounts total gross excess demand and total gross supply.
[b] Interest rate given by central bank policy.
[c] Interest rate given abroad.
[d] Not relevant 1981.
[e] Interest rate for sectors without compulsory holdings.
[f] Interest rate for sectors with compulsory holdings.
[g] Given nominal dividends related to current market value.
[h] Adjustment of quantities at given interest rate.

rates and asset prices up to iteration 3. Remaining excess demand or supply is also indicated.

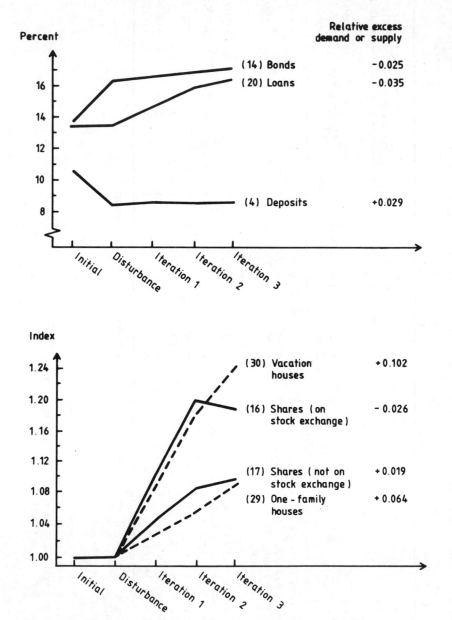

Figure 5.3 Simulation results for (a) major interest rates and (b) asset prices

We first look at the development of the major interest rates and asset prices. Figure 5.3 shows that interest rates for bonds and loans rise from around 14 percent to 16–17 percent after the third iteration. There seems to be a clear tendency for the rise to dampen; remaining excess demand or supply is only about 3 percent. However, a small excess demand or supply merely shows that the revision of the *own* rate of interest in the subsequent iteration would be very small. Cross-effects from other rates of return or the scale variable (net wealth etc.) may counteract, or quicken, the reduction in the excess demand or supply, a problem to which we will return. The rate of interest on ordinary deposits moves in the opposite direction. The entire decrease takes place as an immediate consequence of the disturbance and is obviously due to the assumption that the initial increase in household wealth consists of additions to such deposits. Clearly this assumption is one element of the analytical framework that should be reconsidered.

Prices of Swedish shares quoted on the stock exchange rise quite sharply, about 20 percent through the third iteration. Shares not quoted on the stock exchange rise about 10 percent. In both cases there is dampening – for the first category even a small decrease – in the third iteration. Remaining excess demand or supply is insignificant. Prices of both one-family and vacation houses also rise. For the latter category the rise is sharp. There is hardly any dampening, and remaining excess demand is large: around 6 percent for one-family and 10 percent for vacation houses.

The interest rate development is unusual for some minor assets, as is evident from table 5.3. The rate for bank certificates (asset 7) increases from 13 to at least 32 percent. Obviously the model does not work for these certificates, mainly because they were not introduced until 1980 and initially on a small scale only. Later they had to compete with Treasury discount notes (asset 10), which were introduced in 1982. Both these assets are similar in most respects to the existing "special" deposits (asset 6). Clearly, it is difficult or even impossible to take institutional changes of this kind into account in a model that has to rely on data for longer periods. The possibility of combining all these assets into one single asset may seem natural. However, it is not altogether tempting, since there has been a divergence of interest rates between them.

The results for savings and premium bonds (assets 12 and 13) are also somewhat curious. Since there is rationing for both of them, goods results could hardly be expected if we did not apply a quantity adjustment regime; for simplicity this was not done. However, it is suprising that there is excess supply instead of excess demand for both assets.[34] The development of interest rates on private insurance balances (asset 25) and for loans between financial institutions (asset 26) does not seem fully convincing either, but both these assets have special properties that may be difficult to catch.

3.3 Further analysis of the results

A general view of the convergence properties of the process is provided by table 5.4, which presents the sum of all excess demands and supplies (with positive sign) after the disturbance and each iteration. As an immediate consequence of the disturbance, the excess demand or supply rose for debt instruments used by the central government and for ordinary deposits. This led to revisions of expected rates of return and household net wealth, and hence to excess demand or supply for nearly all assets in the first iteration. This explains the upward jump in total excess demand and supply in iteration 1. The total then diminished "steadily" through iterations 2 and 3.

A major element in the adjustment of the full system of asset markets is the expansion of wealth and portfolios. Table 5.5 first repeats figures showing the increase in private recorded net wealth as a direct consequence of the issue of new government debt, which was 37.1 billion kronor (6 percent). Since asset prices were bidden up in the adjustment process, the total increase in net wealth after the third iteration was around 100 billion (16 percent). This is a very substantial increase, although probably somewhat exaggerated as we will find. The increase in net wealth enlarged all portfolios; thus the total gross sum of all financial components of the endogenous sectors rose by 315 billion (9 percent). In other words, government borrowing requires a sizable amount of new borrowing and lending *between* the endogenous sectors in order to be accommodated, i.e. a marked rise in intermediation. Although not surprising, this is perhaps one of the most interesting results of the application.

The effects on capital flows between Sweden and the rest of the world are also of interest. Table 5.6 shows that initially (at the end of 1980) there was a recorded net financial debt to foreign countries amounting to about 61 billion kronor. We find that there was a capital outflow in the first two iterations, but an inflow of similar size in the third iteration.[35] Thus no strong tendency toward either outflow or inflow seems to exist. This may seem natural since there are in fact two major counteracting forces affecting capital flows. First, the increase in domestic government debt should by itself lead to an outflow, since agents strive to diversify their portfolios away from such debt. Second, however, the increase in domestic debt raises domestic interest rates, creating a favorable substitution effect.

The outflow in the first two iterations led to certain expectations of devaluation (cf. expression 5.4).[36] In principle this should have intensified the outflow, but obviously the counteracting forces were strong enough. However, the switch between outflow and inflow is probably a consequence of the irregularities of the attainable sets, which tend to make the adjustments somewhat erratic.

We now look further at the results for individual interest rates and

Table 5.4 Total excess demand and supply (million kronor)

After disturbance	109.212
After iteration 1	234,052
After iteration 2	196,328
After iteration 3	168,411

Table 5.5 Wealth and intermediation

	Million kronor	Percentage of initial
Net private wealth[a] after disturbance	+37,143	+6
of which: central government domestic debt		
outside central bank	+46,668	
implicit tax debt	−9,525	
Net private wealth after iteration 3	ca. +100,000	ca. +16
Sum of financial portfolio components of endogenous sectors[b] (negative components with positive sign) after iteration 3 corresponds to "increase of intermediation"	1 315,000	+9

[a]Net wealth of endogenous sectors; included assets only.
[b]Implicit debt not included.

Table 5.6 Capital flows

	Net debt to the rest of the world (million kronor)	Capital inflow (+) or outflow (−) as percentage of net debt
Initially	60.665	
Iteration 1	68.314	−12.6
Iteration 2	71.295	−4.4
Iteration 3	60.504	+15.1

asset prices. The rise in interest rates for loans and bonds conforms to general theoretical expectations, e.g. those based on the IS–LM model, and with results of many other empirical studies. However, as already hinted at, the fall in the deposit rate is questionable and obviously results from the assumption that the private wealth increase corresponding to new government debt initially takes the form of increased deposits and thus of a quite substantial excess demand for this asset. The way out seems to be to stick to the assumption that the initial wealth increase takes the form of increased deposits but not to let this excess demand result in a lowered interest rate. Most of the excess demand was in fact eliminated in the first iteration.

The sustained rise in house prices raises more serious problems. The forces behind it can be explained as follows. There was an initial increase in household net wealth, and irrespective of which admissible portfolio compositions households choose, an excess demand for houses is generated. The excess demand is further stimulated by the spillover effects from the enlargement of implicit tax debt. The excess demand then raises the price of houses in the subsequent iteration, which raises net wealth still further but dampens the expected rate of return on house ownership somewhat. The former effect dominates and hence there is a further rise in demand for houses, and a further price increase. At the same time, some cross-effects from other rates of return stimulate, while others reduce, house demand.

As we see in figure 5.3 there was hardly any dampening of the house price inflation in the first three iterations. Eventually the price rise must taper off, however, since the coefficients for houses in all admissible vectors are less than unity (at most 0.739 for one-family houses and 0.149 for vacation houses).[37] But as long as house prices rise significantly, net wealth of households will increase and thus generate new excess demand or supply for the assets that carry weight in the household sector portfolio. So the fact that excess demand or supply has become very small for most assets after the third iteration is no guarantee that the markets for these assets are close to final equilibruim.

That house and share prices rise significantly is *qualitatively* a rather plausible consequence of the budget deficits, since these raise net wealth, and agents strive to diversify their portfolios to make them less loaded with government debt. To the extent that there is an offsetting increase in implicit tax debt, the rise in demand for houses and shares persists since these are long-term assets favored by spillover effects. However, the elements in the framework that determine the *strength* of the price rises are particularly weak. These elements are as follows.

1 The reaction coefficient k_p (see expression 5.4).

2 The assumption that the direct increase in gross wealth connected with the deficit goes only to households. Since households are the sole owners of houses, this may lead to an exaggeration of the increases in demand for houses.
3 True net wealth of the household sector is much larger than the net wealth defined in the framework, which does not include implicit pension assets etc. This means that the relative effect on household net wealth is exaggerated, which may lead to an exaggeration of the increases in demand for houses and shares.
4 Assumptions about the extent of implicit tax debt and spillover effects of such new debt. If the extent of the debt is underestimated, and/or spillover effects on shares and houses are overestimated, the increase in demand for shares and houses is overrated.

The problem raised by (2) would be solved automatically if the framework was inserted in a full real–financial model. The model in its entirety would then decide how new income and wealth created by budget deficits is distributed among sectors. To include implicit pension assets and other wealth components omitted in the framework would by itself solve problem (3), but new problems probably would arise.

The strength of the asset price effect can be illustrated further by the following calculation. We found that the 1981 deficit raised prices of shares quoted on the stock exchange by around 20 percent and prices of one-family and vacation houses by *at least* 8 and 24 percent respectively, which were the rises attained in iteration 3. For the whole "deficit period" 1977–86 the increase in central government domestic debt outside the central bank was around 450 billion kronor compared with 47 billion for 1981 alone. Thus the total rise in government domestic debt should by itself have led to a rise in share prices of around 200 percent, of one-family houses of *at least* 80 percent and of vacation houses of *at least* 240 percent. However, the calculation does not take into account a rise in net wealth, and thus in "portfolio capacity", for many other reasons. And there is nothing in the framework that decides *when* these rises should have taken place. Most of the rise in shares, for which markets are at least nearly efficient, would probably have occurred in the early phase of the process when agents began to realize what was happening.

3.4 A comparison with the actual development

Since the deficits constituted only one force, although probably one of the strongest, among many others that affected the asset markets, judging the validity of the results by comparing them with the actual development is difficult. However, an attempt to compare leads to the following.

The relevant interest rates for portfolio behavior are the real rates after tax. The analysis of the application was confined to nominal rates only, because expectation on inflation and taxes were assumed unchanged. If we look at the real interest rates (before tax) in Sweden during the "deficit period" starting in 1977, there was a rise from roughly −1 percent in 1976–7 to roughly +6 or +7 percent in 1986, although subject to fluctuations. The rates were above average foreign rates for the whole period. Thus the actual development cannot be considered as inconsistent with the results of the application.

For share prices there has been an unprecedented increase, amounting to about 700 percent from 1976 to 1986, much larger than in most other countries. However, special factors obviously contributed substantially to the increase. A series of devaluations has boosted the profitability of Swedish enterprises, and taxation of shares has been mitigated by various schemes. Clearly, however, the actual development of share prices supports the results of the application. It could hardly be explained fully without including the deficits as a driving force.

House prices rose sharply during the first part of the period, and then fell or stagnated. Thus prices of both one-family and vacation houses rose in nominal terms by about 55 percent from 1976 to 1980. From 1980 the prices of one-family houses fluctuated sharply but ended up in 1984 on about the same level as in 1980, while prices of vacation houses increased by between 10 and 15 percent. The prices of both kinds of houses seem to have increased not insignificantly in 1985 and 1986.[38] The tax reform announced in the spring of 1981 was a major factor behind the abrupt break in development (cf. section 2.3). Again, the actual development can hardly be viewed as inconsistent with the qualitative results of the application.

Nominal net wealth of households as defined in the framework actually rose by exactly 100 percent from 1977 to 1984, while inflation was about 85 percent. Nearly all the rise was due to increased nominal holdings of shares and houses. The sum of financial portfolio components of the endogenous sectors, providing a measure of the extent of intermediation, rose by 142 percent. These figures also seem to agree with the results derived from applying the framework.

4 Concluding Comments

The study has two purposes: to explore the possibilities for extending AGE modeling to the financial sphere, and to add to our understanding of the channels, directions and size of the effects of budget deficits. The first purpose is served by constructing a numerical model of a system of asset markets along lines which, although strictly Walrasian, differ from those usually followed. The second purpose is served by applying the model – or, more modestly, "framework" – to an analysis of the effects of recent substantial budget deficits in Sweden.

A first major result is that budget deficits, financed domestically outside the central bank, lead to increases in major interest rates (nominal as well as expected real). This is a traditional standard result. The increases are called forth as follows. New interest-bearing debt must be accommodated in private portfolios. Apart from regulatory devices this requires rates of return on such debt to increase relative to the return on competing assets. However, the rise in wealth that accompanies the expansion of government debt diminishes the upward pressure somewhat. The rise in interest rates creates a gap between domestic and foreign rates, which counteracts the tendencies toward an outflow of capital generated by the rise in wealth combined with the desire to diversify portfolios.

A second major result is a rise in the prices of domestic shares and houses. The strength of the rise is probably much exaggerated, at least for houses, but qualitatively the result seems well founded. Studies from other countries have led to similar conclusions, but the result is by no means intuititively obvious. The force behind it is mainly the expansion of nominal wealth for the household sector in particular. This expansion is, in fact, reinforced by the rise in shares and house prices itself. Taken together with the result for interest rates, we find that the crowding out caused by the rise in real interest rates is counteracted by crowding *in* caused by higher values of Tobin's q for both houses and real capital in production, although the extent of the two forces is outside the scope of this study. The possibility of such a situation has been analyzed in general terms, for example, by Tobin (1963, 1969) and Friedman (1978).

A third result of some interest is the role played by the expansion of wealth and intermediation as important channels of adjustment. The role of implicit tax debt as a factor that dampens the growth of wealth but stimulates demand for long-term assets through the backdoor of spillover effects is also illuminated. The numerical estimates of these forces connected with implicit tax debt are little more than guesswork, however.

It is too early to determine conclusively the value of the methods applied and the possibilities they offer. The major advantage of the framework in this study is the directness of its approach, or, in other words, the absence of most of the black-box properties that burden many other types of analysis. In addition, the framework simplifies numerical formulation and can accommodate substantial disaggregation of both sectors and assets, if that is desirable. A major weakness is that calibrating the strength of the various forces in the framework accurately is difficult.

To test strictly whether the framework can satisfactorily represent actual asset markets, one would have to carry out an application that includes *all* the exogenous disturbances that have taken place in a particular year, but this is quite difficult in practice. However, the rather loose general comparison described in section 3.4 between the results of the application and the actual development provided some support for it.

Notes

Financial support has been provided by the Bank of Sweden Tercentenary Fund. Helpful comments from Michael Cheung, Peter Dixon, Christopher Hall, Kari Lantto and Christopher Sardelis are gratefully acknowledged.

1 Such a position had been taken before, e.g. in important – although somewhat overlooked – articles by Fisher (1933), Hicks (1935) and McKean (1949). Keynes took the same position, although it is hardly visible in the simple IS–LM model since only one asset is treated explicitly.

2 The problem is touched upon by Hahn (1965, pp. 131–2), who analyzes the existence of equilibrium in Patinkin's (1956, 1965) general equilibrium model. The real balance effect of Patinkin's model is in principle of the same kind as the effects just discussed.

3 Other potentially important assets that are hard to define and measure are immaterial rights (such as patent rights) and human capital.

4 See for instance Fama (1980). The Modigliani–Miller theorem (Modigliani and Miller, 1958) and the Ricardo–Barro hypothesis in fact tells us that *all* units of the economy except households have zero net worth.

5 For example, that banks do not sell insurance or that insurance companies do not accept deposits, as well as the existence of so-called "preferred habitats".

6 Other disturbances that could be analyzed are open-market operations, variations in reserve requirements, or exogenous changes in expected rates of return (e.g. changes called forth by variations in the discount rate or world market interest rates).

7 Similar shifts take place when pivots other that net wealth are revalued.

8 Coins in circulation are also a real asset, treated together with currency (asset 1).

9 The same applies to condominium rights, which are of growing importance for Swedish households.

10 Local government, which is very important in Sweden, is in principle allowed to incur debt only to acquire assets capable of yielding a monetary return.

11 Some models use this procedure for one-family and vacation houses as well; see for instance Agell (1986).

12 For foreign shares it is also rather difficult to include the corresponding real capital explicitly.

13 In principle the framework could include *both* shares *and* real capital as portfolio components for the enterprise sectors. To the extent that there are true markets for enterprise real capital, this would be quite a natural step.

14 Most of the figures are taken from the financial statistics of the Swedish Central Bureau of Statistics. Some adjustments (partly based on "informed guesses") have been necessary, *inter alia* to achieve the division into amounts in SEK and amounts in FOR. Data for real assets are based on various statistical sources. The "estimation" of implicit tax debt (28) was discussed in section 2.2.

15 An assumption of this type is implicit in various other methods, e.g. calibration methods used in applied general equilibrium models.

16 Net wealth is defined as the net value of the components included in the tables. For households, true net wealth is of course much larger.

17 Tobin (1969) uses deposits as scale magnitude.

18 Note that most studies combine capital gains and interest rates (including dividends etc.) into one single rate of return, consisting of change in market value. This procedure makes it difficult to apply different tax rates to different types of return. It also hides the distinction between interest rate adjustment and asset price adjustment.

19 Sweden (between devaluations) has a fixed exchange rate against a given basket of currencies. Thus the assumption is that this weighted exchange rate is unchanged.

20 Expectations seem to be such that, if there is a devaluation, it will be by 10 percent. Thus an expected rise in the exchange rate of 1 percent means that people think the probability of devaluation is around 10 percent.

21 This is true in particular for the share prices, since the markets for shares are approximately efficient.

22 The interest rates as of December 31, 1980, are presented in table 5.3, column 1.

23 Treasury discount notes (asset 10) did not appear until 1982 in Sweden. (The small components for 1982–4 were added to certificates in formulating the vectors for the three years in the admissible sets.) Interest rate adjustment was also applied for insurance (asset 25).

24 The habit of sticking to acquired bonds means that "locking-in" effects are small. It is of some interest to note that while such effects were widely discussed in the United States in the 1950s when the bond rate rose from $2\frac{1}{2}$ to $3\frac{1}{4}$ percent, little attention was paid to them in the late 1970s when bond rates rose more sharply (cf. Wojnilower, 1980).

25 Thus "unchanged monetary policy" is defined as unchanged interest rates for deposits in and loans from the central bank, unchanged reserve requirements and given holdings of bonds, Treasury bills and loans to other agents than banks (i.e. absence of open-market operations). Another way of defining "unchanged monetary policy", common in the literature, is to stipulate unchanged supply of assets having the character of "money" attained by suitable measures taken by the central bank. This definition seems less fruitful, however, since to keep the stock of "money" constant would require variations in the central bank interest rates or in reserve requirements, which would call forth adjustment of endogenous

portfolios. Note that the treatment of monetary policy as given means that changes in that policy would constitute an exogenous disturbance and hence a potential object of experiments using the framework.

26 If two (or more) compositions are equally profitable, AA coincides with a facet of the attainable set instead of the vertex. There is then nothing in the submodel to decide which portfolio is chosen.

27 Households can of course desire more implicit tax debt than the amount implied by the central government portfolio, since it is one way for households to borrow. The excess demand or supply of implicit tax debt generated in the iterations turned out to be very small, however.

28 We thus have a case when the rate of return hyperplane has (practically) the same slope as one of the multidimensional facets of the admissible set.

29 Borrowing abroad affects endogenous implicit tax debt, however.

30 As we shall see, the process generates further wealth increases through capital gains.

31 *Total* central government net borrowing (including borrowing abroad and in the central bank) during 1981 was 54.4 billion kronor, an increase of 31 percent. The current value of the debt also increased somewhat in 1981 because a devaluation of the krona raised the value of the foreign debt.

32 Practically the whole addition to deposits was eliminated in the first iteration. Still, the assumption gave rise to certain problems to be discussed below.

33 The new implicit tax debt is an additional asset in the central government portfolio as well.

34 Note that realistic tax rates were applied to both these kinds of bond in calculating their expected rates of return.

35 The disturbance was defined so as not to include the new government borrowing abroad. Thus the disturbance had no direct effect on the net foreign debt.

36 The assumed reaction implies that the first iteration led to an expected devaluation of the krona by 1.26 percent, and second by another 0.44 percent.

37 In the calculations coefficients had six decimals.

38 But note that the data on house prices are rather poor.

References

Agell, J. (1986) *The Effects of Capital Taxation. An Equilibrium Asset Market Approach*, Uppsala: Almqvist & Wiksell International.

Backus, D., C. Brainard, G. Smith and J. Tobin (1980) "A Model of U.S. Financial and Nonfinancial Behavior", *Journal of Money, Credit and Banking*, 12 (2), 259–93.

Barro, R. J. (1974) "Are Government Bonds Net Wealth?", *Journal of Political Economy*, 82 (6), 1095–116.

Drèze, J. (1975) "Existence of an Exchange Equilibrium under Price Rigidities", *International Economic Review*, 16 (2), 301–20.

Fama, E. F. (1980) "Banking in the Theory of Finance", *Journal of Monetary Economics*, 6 (1), 39–58.

Feltenstein, A. (1984) "Money and Bonds in a Disaggregated Open Economy", in E. Scarf and J. B. Shoven (eds), *Applied General Equilibrium Analysis*, Cambridge: Cambridge University Press.

Fisher, I. (1933) "The Debt-Deflation Theory of Great Depressions", *Econometrica*, 1 (4), 337–57.

Friedman, B. M. (1978) "Crowding Out or Crowding In? Economic Consequences of Financing Budget Deficits", *Brookings Papers on Economic Activity*, 3, 593–641.

Hahn, F. H. (1965) "On Some Problems of Proving the Existence of an Equilibrium in a Monetary Economy", in F. H. Hahn and F. P. R. Brechling (eds), *The Theory of Interest Rates*, London: Macmillan.

Hicks, J. R. (1935) "A Suggestion for Simplifying the Theory of Money", *Economica, New Series*, 2 (1), 1–19.

Jonung, L. (1981) "Perceived and Expected Rates of Inflation in Sweden", *American Economic Review*, 71 (5), 961–5.

McKean, R. N. (1949) "Liquidity and a National Balance Sheet", *Journal of Political Economy*, 57 (6), 506–22.

Malinvaud, E. (1977) *The Theory of Unemployment Reconsidered*, Oxford: Blackwell.

Modigliania, F. and M. H. Miller (1985) "The Cost of Capital, Corporation Finance, and the Theory of Investment", *American Economic Review*, 48 (3), 261–97.

Palmer, E. E. (1981) *Determination of Personal Consumption. Theoretical Foundation and Empirical Evidence from Sweden*, Stockholm: Konjunkturinstitutet.

Patinkin, D. (1956, 1965) *Money, Interest, and Prices*, 1st edn, 1956, 2nd edn 1965, New York: Harper and Row.

Roley, V. V. (1979) "A Theory of Federal Debt Management", *American Economic Review*, 69 (5), 915–26.

Slemrod, J. (1983) "A General Equilibrium Model of Taxation with Endogenous Financial Behavior", in M. Feldstein (ed.) *Behavioral Simulation Methods in Tax Policy Analysis*, Chicago, IL: University of Chicago Press.

—— (1985) "A General Equilibrium Model of Taxation that Uses Micro-Unit Data: With an Application to the Impact of Instituting a Flat-Rate Income Tax", in J. Piggott and J. Whalley (eds) *New Developments in Applied General Equilibrium Analysis*, Cambridge: Cambridge University Press.

Solomon, E. (1963) *The Theory of Financial Management*, New York: Columbia University Press.

Tobin, J. (1963) "An Essay on the Principles of Debt Management", in *Commission on Money and Credit: Fiscal and Debt Management Policies*, Englewood Cliffs, NJ: Irwin.

—— (1969) "A General Equilibrium Approach to Monetary Theory", *Journal of Money, Credit, and Banking*, 1 (1), 15–30.

—— (1980) *Asset Accumulation and Economic Activity*, Oxford: Blackwell.

—— (1982) "Money and Finance in the Macroeconomic Process", *Journal of Money, Credit, and Banking* 14 (2), 171–204.

Wojnilower, Albert M. (1980) "The Central Role of Credit Crunches in Recent Financial History", *Brookings Papers on Economic Activity*, 2, 277–326.

PART III

International Trade

6

The Common Agricultural Policy of the European Community and the World Economy: A General Equilibrium Analysis

Jean Marc Burniaux and Jean Waelbroeck

1 Introduction

The Common Agricultural Policy (CAP) has been at the centre of attention for many years. For more than a decade it was a prized achievement of European integration, as the only economic policy other than trade policy that was completely integrated. Subsequently, the CAP became a source of apparently insoluble problems, as Finance Ministers sought in vain to contain the generosity of their agricultural colleagues. Britain fought stubbornly to get back part of a contribution to the Community budget which, it felt, served mainly to pay for agricultural spending that brought it limited benefits and, finally, the Community's mounting exports caused anger in Australasia, developing countries and, most importantly perhaps, in the powerful United States.

Some years ago, we devoted a short non-technical paper to this topic which focused on the CAP's impact on the developing world (Burniaux and Waelbroeck, 1985). Since then, the importance of the subject has not lessened. We have substantially improved the model used in the earlier paper. It seems appropriate to return to the topic with a broadened focus that covers the world as a whole and a theoretical analysis of the mechanisms through which the agricultural policies of the Community influence the world economy.

The discussion is organized as follows. After a description of the model and the design of the runs, the discussion turns to the impact of agricultural protection on major European macroeconomic aggregates. The following section estimates the impact of alternative agricultural policies on the budget of the European Community (EC). In a third section the mechanisms by which the CAP influences the rest of the world are sketched out in theoretical terms and the model's results are discussed from this point of view. The last section is devoted to the impact of European agricultural protection on other regions in the world.

2 The Model

The model used is "RUNS", built by Burniaux as part of the modelling programme constructed for the World Bank in the Université Libre de Bruxelles, in a programme of research support for the World Development Reports (see Burniaux, 1987). It differs from the "Varuna" version of the model by trading off a smaller amount of regional disaggregation against a more elaborate description of agriculture.

The goal was to study the implication for the developing world of developed country policies and such major economic events as changes in oil prices. This emphasis on developing countries is reflected both in the regional disaggregation of the model and in the choice of products. The regions are as follows: developing oil exporting countries; Mediterranean countries (a nondescript group of countries bordering the Mediterranean, including the Maghreb, Lebanon, Cyprus and Malta, plus Yemen); Africa south of the Sahara; low income Asia, i.e. the Indian peninsula plus Burma; east Asia; other non-oil-exporting countries of Asia; Latin America and the Caribbean; northern Europe; southern Europe; resource-rich developed countries, including South Africa; and the rest of the world, i.e. the Council for Mutual Economic Aid (CMEA) countries, mainland China and Japan.

RUNS, as originally constructed, did not contain an EC region. Work is in progress to recalibrate the model fully to identify such a region. For this paper, we have carried out a provisional recalibration that uses data for the former "northern Europe" aggregate to construct an EC region with the proper size and protection rates. It is our belief that, given the large overlap between the Community and the former "northern Europe" aggregate, full recalibration, although desirable, will not affect the results meaningfully: we are far more interested in discovering the effect of the theoretical innovations that will be experimented with on this occasion.

Reflecting the emphasis on agriculture, the model includes 13 agricultural products: wheat, rice, coarse grains, coffee, cocoa, tea, cotton, wool, tobacco, vegetable oils, sugar, meat and other foods. For non-agricultural products, RUNS is slightly more detailed than Varuna, adding fertilizers to the capital goods, other manufactures, energy and services identified in that model.[1]

Construction of these models was greatly facilitated by the availability of two data bases. One is the world social accounting matrix constructed by the Economic Projections Department of the World Bank under the direction of P. Miovic. The other is the aggregation of the Food and Agriculture Organization (FAO) trade and utilization data tape, undertaken at the International Institute for Applied Systems Analysis (IIASA), principally by U. Sichra. We are grateful to the FAO and the IIASA Food and Agriculture Program (FAP) group for permission to use these data.

It was not feasible to estimate all the coefficients of a world agricultural model including its large non-agricultural component. Where possible, we followed the established procedure of "picking up coefficients from the literature". There are gaps in the literature, however, and we had to undertake a substantial amount of estimation. For the agricultural production function, the literature that we used to pick the coefficients was produced as part of the research project.[2] A substantial effort was also undertaken, however, to estimate extended linear expenditures system demand functions. This largely confirmed the indications provided by such studies as those of Lluch, Powell and Williams (1977). Another critical source for a model that emphasizes agriculture was Mundlak's (1979) study of the determinants of rural urban migration. The estimation of policy equations that reflect the agricultural price policies pursued in the various countries is described in greater detail below.

A crucial feature of the model is that the rural and urban sectors are entirely separate: in fact, these sectors are treated as separate countries, whose trade flows could if needed be calculated explicitly. This sharp separation is warranted by the crucial importance of agriculture in the development process. It makes it possible to take account of such major characteristics of those sectors as the role of wage rigidity in the non-agricultural sector and differences in consumption patterns between rural and urban areas.

Price determination is competitive. For urban goods, the familiar Armington (1969) assumption is made that the goods exported by different groups of countries are imperfect substitutes. In contrast, agricultural goods are perfectly substitutable, i.e. each of the 13 categories identified has one world price. The world price of energy is determined exogenously in terms of the numeraire, the average export price of manufactures by the Organization for Economic Cooperation and Development (OECD) countries, reflecting the assumption that the Organization of Petroleum Exporting Countries (OPEC) is able to index oil prices to the export prices of manufactures produced by the main developed trading nations.[3]

We use wedges between supply and demand prices to represent most market imperfections. The market power of OPEC is represented by a variable export levy, which absorbs the difference between the cost of production of oil and the target price of oil that it sets. Protection is represented by fixed *ad valorem* duties, which are taken to describe both import tariffs and the tariff equivalent of non-tariff barriers. For agriculture, a more sophisticated representation of the prevailing systems of protection is used.[4] This recognizes that governments seek to moderate fluctuations in the parity between agricultural and non-agricultural prices but are not entirely successful in achieving this goal. Domestic prices, therefore, move in response to both the prices of non-agricultural value added and the prices on world markets. These policies may be represented by appropriate econometric equations, using estimates for the main countries in each of the model's regions. These define the prices of the various products as weighted averages of their world prices and of the price index of urban value added. Variable import levies and export subsidies implement these policies.[5]

Fix-price general equilibrium theory is used to take account of the fact that urban labour markets do not clear.[6] The real wage is not fully rigid, however. It is assumed to lie three-quarters of the way from an exogenous target to the wage rate that would clear the labour market in each region, subject to the wage behaviour of the rest of the world. In studies of developed countries, it is usual to account for wage rigidities in terms of trade union power. In developing countries unions are often weak, but experience shows that a considerable rigidity does result from inchoate but powerful resistances that find expression in sudden political explosions, which developing country governments have learned to fear ever since the days when bread price riots by the Roman plebes led to the introduction of state trading for food grains and to the free distribution of wheat to parts of the Imperial City's population.[7]

The interplay between two market imperfections, wage rigidity and agricultural price policies, accounts for powerful feedbacks that are important to an understanding of the impact of modifying European agricultural protection. Reducing this protection will tend to raise world agricultural prices. In what in the model's jargon are called "adjusting countries", i.e. those countries where governments allow agricultural prices to move in step with world prices, this will increase the price of food and raise the urban cost of living, exerting pressure on real wages and thus causing a drop in employment and output.[8]

In each region, both rural and urban consumers choose their consumptions by maximizing an extended linear expenditures system utility function subject to their budget constraint. This demand is allocated to the production sectors by an input–output scheme. The production functions of the two subsectors are entirely separate. In the urban sector, constant elasticity of substitution (CES) production functions define the energy and non-energy values added as functions of the labour force and available capital stock. Labour flows freely between urban industries. The energy and non-energy capital stocks are specific; the allocation of investment between these industries is a policy variable. Agricultural production is described by a multi-input–multi-output production function.[9] The input components of these are CES production functions, which combine physical capital inputs (such as bullocks, tractors and irrigation), labour and such intermediate inputs as fertilizers into notional "vegetal" and "animal" productive resources. The output component transforms these resources into commodities. This involves transformation functions that reflect the decreasing returns in production of each good. The functions are calibrated to match the agricultural supply elasticities that are found in the econometric literature.

The flow of capital between the rural and urban sectors is a crucial aspect of the development process. Lack of data made it impossible to estimate appropriate equations. It was decided to assume that rural saving finances agricultural investment while urban saving finances investment in the rest of the economy. As for foreign aid, its allocation between the two sectors is a policy variable.[10]

The allocations of urban investible funds to the energy and non-energy sectors and of agricultural investible funds to the various forms of physical capital are exogenous. The growth of the available labour force in urban and rural areas depends on the natural growth of population (United Nations projections) and on migration from country to town, influenced by the relevant population levels and per capita income differentials.[11]

It is useful to say something about the main parameter values used. In the countryside, the short-run elasticities of supply of the various agricultural commodities are in the range 3–8. Total agricultural output in each region does respond to higher prices in the short run, which induce farmers to use more intensively inputs from the non-farm sector; the short-run elasticity of aggregate supply is quite low, however. The long-run elasticity is significantly larger. It incorporates the gradual response of the supply of labour and capital to price changes. Higher agricultural prices slow down labour migration to the cities and increase the rural capital stock by raising the savings of farmers.

3 Design of the Runs

Calibrating a model to reproduce the data of a base year is a widely used, albeit often criticized, procedure in equilibrium modelling. The calibration of the models built in Brussels was even more extensive. They were designed for use in the preparation of the World Development Reports of the World Bank. The staff of that institution has a wide knowledge of the prospects of developing countries, and it seemed desirable to tap this expertise in drawing up the Reports' forecasts. For this reason, it was decided that the models should be used only to assess the sensitivity of the world economy to shocks. The models were therefore calibrated not only to the base year situation but also to the World Bank's forecasts.

We have followed this procedure here. The reference run that was calibrated reproduces the general pattern of the World Development Reports forecasts. There are some differences, however. The projections of growth in the European economy are more pessimistic than the World Bank's. The same is true for agricultural prices.

As explained above, RUNS contains equations that reflect how governments set agricultural prices. The sample used in the estimates ended in 1978. These data cover in the main a period of continuing prosperity, when the budgetary pressures confronted by the EC were less acute than they are now. These equations tend to overpredict the evolution of domestic agricultural prices in recent years. Clearly budgetary pressure, and perhaps also aggressive US trade policy, has led the Council of Agricultural Ministers to become less generous to farmers.

It is difficult to say how the CAP will evolve. In modelling work, it is normal practice to describe as the "base run" the projection that seems to be most realistic. As we do not feel that we know what the future holds in store, we have avoided describing a run as the "base case". The forecast obtained by calibration of the model is denoted the "historical policies case".

We shall discuss three other runs.

1 The first is the orthodox "free trade run" that every trade modeller is expected to calculate. In this run, the variable levies and export subsidies that characterize the CAP are set equal to zero. The so-called "structural aids" to agriculture, however, are allowed to continue to increase as in the past. The assumptions that underlie this run are thus less extreme than the "complete abolition of subsidies to agriculture" which the US government has been demanding in the Uruguay Round negotiations on agriculture. This demand, we believe, is electoral talk.

2 The second reflects an even more moderate view of future trade liberalization. It is assumed that tariffs are halved and that prices move parallel to world prices thereafter; in the terminal year, protection is less than half the 1986 level.

3 The third assumes a quite modest touching up of historical policies. It modifies the latter to take account of the December 1986 decisions of the EC Agricultural Council (a 10 per cent cut in the beef price and the milk production quota). It seemed interesting to

assess the impact of a decision that was widely described at the time as a "fundamental turnaround of the CAP".

4 The Results

4.1 The impact of agricultural protection on the European Community economy

4.1.1 The historical record and the impact of alternative policies on European Community agriculture

We shall start with a discussion of the historical record and the implications of the alternative policy assumptions for EC agriculture. The figures are to be found in table 6.1.

Europe's agricultural lobbyists could only feel proud of themselves as the first 15 years of economic integration came to an end. The income parity between their members and the urban population had risen steadily. Farmers have fared less well since then. It is hard to assess the basic trend of agricultural incomes, because it depends to a substantial extent on weather. It does seem, however, that farmers have lost many of the gains they had made in comparison with the urban population.

This is the result of less generous price policies, not of reduced dynamism. The rate of growth of productivity in agriculture has hardly changed, at a time when it fell by half in the rest of the economy. Output has continued to grow as in the past. Since the sharp deceleration of European economic growth has affected consumption of agricultural products, the rural economy's remarkable dynamism has swollen the surpluses that have plagued the Commission's policy making.

4.1.2 The implications of a return to the historical policy pattern

Europe's farmers continue to muster considerable political power, however. Events move swiftly in politics. Agricultural protection may be irrational, but politicians do not mind irrational policies if they bring votes. It is not inconceivable that the farm lobby could again be strong enough to force a return to the policies of yesteryear, especially if a failure of the Uruguay Round negotiations causes a period of disillusionment with the market-oriented policies that are in fashion today. The "historical policy patterns" simulation evaluates how Europe's economy would develop in such a context. As table 6.1 shows, the result would be a resumption of the slow improvement in the relative position of the farm population, whose per capita income

Table 6.1 The Common Agricultural Policy: past and projected trends

	Rural VA	Rural price VA	Rural income	Rural pop.	Rural inc/cap	Urban VA	Urban price VA	Urban income	Urban pop.	Urban inc/cap	Parity[a] (end period)	Parity ratio (end period)
1960–71	1.70	2.80	4.60	−4.50	9.50	4.90	4.70	9.80	1.10	8.60	0.90	na
1971–8	1.90	7.70	9.70	−3.00	13.20	3.10	9.40	12.80	0.40	12.30	0.90	0.65
1978–83	1.80	4.20	6.00	−2.70	8.90	1.20	9.00	10.80	0.20	10.50	−1.60	0.61
Historical policies												
1978–86	1.38	−2.23	−0.88	−2.86	2.04	1.79	0.34	2.14	0.37	1.76	0.28	0.66
1986–95	0.76	1.21	1.97	−3.11	5.24	2.22	2.18	4.45	0.33	4.10	1.14	0.74
Free trade												
Free trade	−0.82	−9.07	−9.82	−5.16	−4.92	2.97	1.30	4.31	0.41	3.88	−8.20	0.30
50% protection cut	0.29	−3.90	−3.62	−3.85	0.24	2.55	1.80	4.40	0.36	4.02	3.78	0.48
Dec 86 Council decisions	0.60	0.98	1.59	−3.19	4.93	2.24	2.15	4.44	0.34	4.09	0.84	0.72

VA, value added at constant market prices; price VA for the past, current market prices; price VA for simulations, ratio of the price of value added to export prices of developed countries, the model numeraire; pop., population; inc/cap, income per capita; na, not available. The runs are defined as follows: historical policies, agricultural prices set according to the historical pattern of Council decisions, as reflected by regression data up to 1978; free trade, nominal protection abolished in 1986, after which domestic prices follow world prices; 50% protection cut, protection cut by half in 1986, after which agricultural domestic prices follow world prices; Dec 86 Council decisions, a less generous protection policy, reflecting the decisions taken by the Agricultural Council in December 1986 (a 10 per cent reduction in the milk quota and a 10 per cent cut in beef prices).

[a]Parity, rural income per capita minus urban income per capita.

Source: Eurostat, *National Accounts by Sectors*

would rise to three-quarters of the income level in the cities. How should such a situation be appraised?[12]

We must first note that these ratios should not be taken at face value. Farmers are a much larger fraction of the population in the poor than in the wealthy EC countries, and so low income farmers have larger weights in calculations of average rural incomes than their urban compatriots have in the urban income averages. It is thus quite possible for average farm incomes in the Community to be sharply lower than average urban incomes, although in each country farmers are as well off as their urban neighbours. Another bias is that the figures do not reflect the quite large earnings which the rural population draws from non-agricultural activities.

"Average figures" are misleading from another point of view. The distribution of incomes among farmers is very uneven. According to the European Commission's estimates, a quarter of farmers accounts for three-quarters of output. Sector-wide averages are not very meaningful as sources of information on poverty in this part of the economy.

4.1.3 Free trade in agricultural products?

With due allowance for these cautionary remarks, there is no doubt that the free trade run describes a bad situation for farmers. The parity ratio falls to half its 1960 level. The model does contain equations that take account of out-migration as the result of a drop in the parity ratio.[13] The result is thus not due to forgetting that income disparities induce a movement of labour to industries where earnings are good. Some readers may feel that the model underestimates the sensitivity of migration to income differences. It should be remembered, however, that half of Europe's farmers are over 50 years old, an age at which it is quite difficult to get another job; they would find it very difficult to move to the cities if agricultural incomes were reduced.

The "no protection" run therefore describes a textbook situation. We ran it to allow comparisons with other studies, not because free trade is a likely event. There are excellent reasons to call for reduced protection of agriculture, but there would be little political support in Europe for policies that reduce so sharply the welfare of a respected group of the population.

4.1.4 The December 1986 decisions of the European Community Agricultural Council

The next run suggests that the December 1986 decisions of the Community's Agricultural Council, widely hailed at the time as a revolutionary turnaround in policy making, were not extremely significant. The Council decided to reduce the milk quota and the beef price by 10 per cent. Table 6.1 shows that the impact of the measures, although not negligible, was not as large as might be thought in view of the large proportion of beef and dairy products in the net output of agriculture. The reason is that, as a general equilibrium system, the model takes into account the ability of farmers to produce a different good if price or quota reductions make production of one good less profitable.

Our calculations therefore show that these widely heralded measures were "not enough" (they were, in addition, not properly implemented.[14]) December 1986 was a politically important date, however, since the lack of the usual vigorous reaction of the farm lobby signalled to politicians that scaling down protection had become politically feasible. The system of "stabilizers" agreed on at the beginning of 1988 is much more far reaching in its implications. How politicians will use it is not yet clear.

4.1.5 A reduction by half of agricultural protection

We finally describe briefly an option that may be more attainable than an immediate shift to free trade. This involves cutting by half in 1986 the difference between domestic and world prices of agricultural products and shifting thereafter to an "adjusting" price setting pattern. Although the run is denoted in the tables as "cutting protection by half", the reduction is larger in practice, since it makes prices fall after 1986 instead of rising.

Table 6.1 shows that this price policy also imposes a considerable sacrifice on the agricultural sector. The parity ratio falls to a level that is a fifth below that of 1960. It seems clear that such a measure would have to be combined with efforts to create alternative employment opportunities in rural areas and to offer early pensions to older farmers so as to syphon income to farm households and to promote the consolidation of farms. It is indeed on structural policies of this sort that the European Commission as on other occasions in the past, has been focusing its thinking.[15] The rural and urban sectors are so closely meshed together in Europe that there is real scope for measures of this type.

4.2 Agricultural liberalization and the European Community budget

The growing cost of the CAP has been the main cause of the shift of the EC to less protectionist agricultural policies. How much would trade liberalization help the EC budget? In this section, we present the results of very simple calculations based on a side model of RUNS. Using our simulations, we calculate the export subsidies that would have to be paid and subtract the variable levies on imports of goods which the EC still imports. Storage costs, it is assumed, are proportional to net export subsidies. Rough adjustments allow for quirks of the system, such as the exemption from import levies of agreed amounts of sugar imported from African, Caribbean and Pacific states. It is assumed that the other agricultural and non-agricultural expenditures grow in real terms at the same rate as in the past. Import duties are proportional to imports of manufactures.[16] Other resources (a small item) also grow as in the past in real terms.

These calculations, we think, overestimate the budget saving that would result from lower agricultural support prices. The preceding section has emphasized how large the resulting drop in agricultural incomes would be. It is not very realistic to assume, as is done here, that "other subsidies" to farmers have identical values in all the simulations. It is highly probable that part of the budget saving generated by a reduction in export subsidies would flow back to farmers as adjustment assistance.

A more refined calculation is of course possible, but we think that it would not produce more accurate results. Budget receipts and expenditures of the Community may respond in dozens of ways to freer trade, according to how the liberalization is carried out. It seems best to stick to a simple calculation that captures the basic forces that shape the budget.

Tables 6.2 and 6.3 show that cutting agricultural protection, although it produces substantial budget savings, does not provide a definitive cure of the Community's budget difficulties. Leaving aside the unrealistic free trade solution, halving subsidies would bring at best a respite. The reason is that behind the highly visible increase in agricultural spending other expenditures have risen swiftly, in part because of the enlargement of the Community. It is hard to imagine that this situation will change, given the responsibilities that will accrue to the Commission with the unification of the internal market.

4.3 The impact of trade liberalization in the European Community on the rest of the world

4.3.1 The basic transmission mechanisms

It is useful to trace the main chains of impacts of reduced protection on the rest of the world economy.[17] We shall compare the historical policies and free trade runs. The reader should keep in mind that the first implies domestic prices that exceed those which result from the

Table 6.2 Past and projected trends of the European Community budget (historical policies run) billion European Currency Units)

	1979	1980	1983	1986	1995
Resources	14602	16066	24766	39211	95314
Custom duties	5189	5906	6989	8005	11291
VAT[a]	4738	7259	13699	27300	79456
Agricultural import levies	2143	2002	2295	1885	1907
Other	2532	899	1783	2021	2660
Expenditures	14373	16296	24877	39211	95314
Export refunds	4888	5472	5033	7860	23338
Storage	1658	1617	2893	5780	15027
Other agricultural expenditures	4298	4827	8681	13095	29165
Other non-agricultural expenditures	3529	4380	8270	12475	27784
Equilibrium VAT share	0.79	0.73	1	1.76	3.89

[a]We use the term value-added tax (VAT) to describe this source of income both for the past and the future although, formally, the system of burden sharing is now on a GNP rather than a value-added tax basis *Source*: 1879–83. Bureau of Agricultural Economics 1985.

Table 6.3 Effects on the European Community budget of changing the Common Agricultural Policy (per cent)

	Eq. VAT share, 1986	Eq. VAT share, 1995
Historical policies	1.76	3.89
Free trade	0.89	2.03
50% protection cut	1.48	2.79
Dec 86 Council decisions	1.64	3.75

Eq. VAT share, share of value-added tax that balances the Community budget.

Community's present pattern of policies and that full elimination of protection by 1995 is an unlikely event. The impact of the cuts in protection that might actually take place would be some fraction of those that are discussed here.

1 In a fixed-real wage model such as RUNS, it has been explained that supply shocks have a powerful impact on non-agricultural employment and output.[18] Non-agricultural value added in the Community rises by 2.8 per cent in the free trade run compared with the historical policies run. This raises the Community's import demand, which stimulates growth elsewhere.
2 Farmers everywhere have more to spend, raising domestic demand for urban goods. This effect is larger in regions that have relatively closed economies, where little of the increased farm incomes spills out abroad as increased imports.
3 To pay for increased agricultural imports, the Community has to export more services and manufactured goods. This reduces world prices of manufactures.[19]
4 The 10.1 per cent reduction in EC production which lower support prices cause lifts prices both on world markets and on domestic markets in the other regions. This has two consequences.
   (a) Outside the Community the rise in food prices relative to non-food prices exerts an upward pressure on real wages and reduces the profitability of urban output. The impact is particularly large in "adjusting" countries that allow their domestic agricultural prices to follow changes in world prices.
   (b) There is an improvement in the terms of trade of regions like Latin America that specialize in the export of agricultural products. These regions need to export fewer non-agricultural products to balance their foreign payments than would otherwise be necessary. This mitigates the pressure of world markets on the prices of manufactures in those regions. As a result, the profitability of urban production decreases less than in regions

that specialize in the export of manufactures. The negative impact of a liberalized CAP on urban output may in fact be positive.

4.3.2 Mechanism through which protection affects world prices of agricultural products

How much would agricultural prices rise if the EC moved to free trade? The answers to important policy questions depend on this.

1 It is often asserted that world prices are so distorted by protectionist measures that they have lost any significance as guides to economic policy.[20] There is no doubt that Europe is so large that its policies affect world prices. This causes a kind of optical illusion because, since world prices would rise if protection was removed, subtracting world from domestic prices overstates the gain that protection brings to producers. Economists agree that the proper way to measure protection is to subtract from domestic prices not the "tariff-ridden" prices, but those that would obtain if protection were removed.

2 The Community is a large net exporter of temperate agricultural products, and a large net importer of tropical ones. It is often thought that, for that reason, its agricultural policy harms only developed food exporters. This disregards the complex web of substitutions that links together the supply and demand of all products. It is interesting to see how the model evaluates such interactions.

3 Finally, it is often argued in the Community that, because it lowers world agricultural prices, protection unwittingly contributes to the war to curb hunger by making food cheaper outside Europe. Is it true that safeguarding the incomes of Bavarian farmers helps to feed the starving peasants of the Sahel and outlying districts of Ethiopia?

4.3.3 The impact of agricultural trade liberalization on world prices

Tables 6.4 and 6.5 evaluate the impact on world prices of the removal of protection and compare the results derived from RUNS with those obtained by other general equilibrium agricultural models. It turns out that this impact is indeed substantial, although the increase in world prices is only a fraction of the initial protection level.

Table 6.4 presents, in addition to historical data, our estimates of the change in world prices that would result from the removal of protection measured as the difference between the historical policy pattern and free trade runs.

Table 6.4 Agricultural world market prices: past and projected trends and effects of agricultural liberalization in the European Community

	Past, 1951–78[a]	Past, 1978–83[a]	Base run, 1978–95[b]	CAPI, 1986[c]	CAPI, 1995[c]
Wheat	−2.1	−1.6	−2.4	11.7	18.2
Rice	−1.3	−6.4	−1.9	2.9	4.3
Coarse grain	−2.9	0.5	−1.1	7.5	8.4
Sugar	−0.9	−6.4	−1.9	34.8	34.9
Meats	−0.1	−1.5	−1.7	12.8	13.7
Oils	−2.1	−5.1	0	6.7	15.2
Tropical tree crops	na	na	1.5	2	4.6
Other foods	na	na	−2.8	7.7	16.2
Non-foods	na	na	0.2	6	9.1

na not available.
[a]Yearly growth rates in constant dollars, deflated by the average index of OECD prices, the model numeraire.
[b]Historical policies run, yearly growth rates of world prices expressed relative to the OECD numeraire.
[c]Percentage differences between the prices predicted by the free trade and historical policy patterns runs.
Source: World Bank, *Commodity Trade and Price Trends:* wheat, rice, maize, sugar, beef, soya.

Table 6.5 Agricultural world market price reactions: comparisons with other studies (elasticities of world prices with respect to the protection rates)

	RUNS, 1986	RUNS, 1995	Parikh,[a] 2000	Anderson and Tyers[b]	Anderson and Tyers[c]
Wheat	0.21	0.13	0.08	0.12	0.40
Rice	na	0.19	0.02	0.11	0.03
Coarse grain	0.19	0.25	1.1	0.19	0.08
Sugar	0.12	0.09	na	na	0.06
Meats	0.15	0.14	0.58	0.18	0.11
Oils	0.09	na	na	na	na

na, not available.
[a]Parikh et al. (1987).
[b]Anderson and Tyers (1984)
[c]Anderson and Tyers, quoted in World Bank, 1986, pp. 112 and 129.

The largest price effects are on sugar, meats and other foods, a category that is heavily weighted by dairy products. These products have narrow world markets and high initial protection levels. It is interesting to note that the long-term impact is significantly larger than the short-term one for other foods, but not for meats or sugar. This suggests that the long-term elasticity of supply outside the

Community is higher for the second than for the first category of goods. This appears reasonable, given that New Zealand is the only large exporter of dairy products apart from the Community.

The wheat price rises more than that of coarse grains, which reflects the higher initial protection of the first product. This is of significance to developing countries that are large net importers of wheat but could with appropriate policies export significant amounts of maize.

The lowest impacts are on the prices of the warm climate products, tropical beverages and rice, and of agricultural raw materials (cotton, wool, rubber, etc.). This again is reasonable. It is interesting, however, that although the Community does not produce coffee, tea and cocoa, and produces very little rice, the change in prices of these goods is not negligible.

How do these results compare with those obtained by other modellers? Table 6.5 answers the question. The elasticities drawn from RUNS are somewhat higher than those which other models imply. Those which the World Development Report version of the Anderson and Tyers model imply are surprisingly low (and surprisingly different from their other results). It may be guessed that they used high supply and demand elasticities in that work.

4.4 The impact of reduced agricultural protection on global production and on nutrition levels in the rest of the world

4.4.1 The impact on production and purchasing power

How would agricultural trade liberalization in the EC affect economic growth elsewhere? Table 6.6 suggests that these effects are on the whole not very large. With only one exception, the effects on rural and urban values added have the expected positive and negative signs respectively. Latin America, the exception, is an interesting case that illustrates well the complexity of general equilibrium interactions. That region has the strongest terms of trade gains of all, a result that reflects both the composition of its agricultural exports and imports and its favourable balance of trade for these goods. As in other regions, the increased agricultural prices raise the cost of living and negatively affect the profitability of urban production. In contrast (again as in other regions), the income of farmers increases, raising their demand for services and manufactures. The supply elasticity of aggregate agricultural output is particularly high in Latin America, however, which enhances the income gains of the rural population. Also, because import propensities are low, most of the increased purchasing power of farmers is spent on domestic goods. All this

Table 6.6 Impact of full liberalization of agricultural trade in the European Community on macroeconomic aggregates in other regions of the world (percentage changes in comparison with the reference scenario)

	Real income	GDP	Rural VA	Urban VA	Terms of trade	Rural/urban parity
Low income countries						
Asia (excluding China)	−0.1	−0.3	0.1	−0.5	2.1	3.1
Africa	−0.5	−0.8	0.1	−1.3	1.0	4.9
Middle–Upper Income Countries						
Latin America	1.2	0.2	0.7	0.1	6.0	5.2
South-east Asia	0.5	−0.1	0.1	−0.2	0.6	4.8
Oil producers	0.2	0.0	0.0	0.0	0.6	0.6
US and other developed food exporters						
	0.3	0.0	1.5	−0.1	3.4	12.4

GDP, gross domestic product.
VA, value added at constant market prices.
Real income, gross domestic product at market prices deflated by the domestic consumption price index.
Rural/urban parity, the ratio between rural and urban value-added prices.

explains why domestic demand for manufactures and services in Latin America grows enough to overcompensate the negative impact of expensive food on the profitability of urban production.

In contrast, Africa also has a favourable balance of trade for agricultural commodities but is to a greater degree specialized in the export of tropical commodities. Also, the African economies are more open than those of Latin America, so that a larger proportion of the increased demand which higher agricultural incomes generate spills out to the rest of the world. The results for the other regions may be understood with the same kind of reasoning. In the developed food-exporting countries, rural output rises significantly and urban output drops slightly. As farm output is a small fraction of gross national product (GNP) in that region, the impact on aggregate production is nil.

For agricultural output, the pattern of results described by table 6.6 is predictable. Throughout the developing world, rural output increases as world agricultural prices rise in response to the cut in protection. Rural food consumption increases substantially more in percentage terms; it reflects the combined impact on farm demand of higher output and an improved parity ratio, moderated by the impact of prices on rural food demand.

Oil producers tend to insulate their agricultural producers from fluctuations in world markets almost completely. For this reason, the change in the world prices of agricultural and non-agricultural commodities has no impact on the level or composition of their output.[21]

The terms of trade changes are by and large as big as the production effects. They are favourable for all other regions.[22] "Real income" is GNP deflated by the consumer price index. It too improves appreciably.

4.4.2 European agricultural protection and food consumption in the rest of the world

Finally, it is interesting to examine the impact of lower protection on food demand in the developing world. Does the CAP, by restraining food consumption and stimulating food production in Europe, enable the poor in the developing world to be better fed, thus contributing to the satisfaction of a fundamental "basic need"?

As shown by table 6.7, the model simulations do not disprove the idea that European agricultural protection causes the rest of the world to be better fed. In all regions except Latin America, removing Europe's agricultural protection reduces food consumption. The drop

Table 6.7 Impact of abolishing European Community agricultural protection on food production and demand in developing countries

	Food production	Food demand	Rural Food/cap	Urban Food/cap	Food price
Low income countries					
Asia (excluding China)	0.2	−0.5	1.2	−1.7	1.4
Africa	0.2	−0.6	1.5	−2.4	2.0
Middle–Upper Income Countries	0.6	−0.2	1.0	−0.9	2.5
Latin America	1.3	0.0	2.0	−1.6	4.9
South-east Asia	0.3	−1.0	1.8	−1.7	3.1
Oil producers	0.1	0.0	0.3	−0.1	0.5
US and other developed food exporters	4.8	−1.7	3.1	−3.0	6.6

Food/cap, food per capita.
Food demand includes feed uses.
The food price is expressed as a ratio to the consumption price index.

is an urban problem, however: food consumption in rural areas rises everywhere. The explanation is of course that the income gain which farmers derive from higher prices dominates the impact on demand of higher prices. Farmers eat more because they earn more: it is in the cities that demand is curtailed. To the extent that World Bank data suggests that seven-eighths of the absolute poor are rural dwellers, the impact of the CAP on the fulfilment of the basic needs of the poorest consumers cannot be regarded as favourable.

This is of course a rough calculation. It would indeed be desirable to build a more elaborate model that distinguishes several rural social groups. In seminars to which these results were presented, an argument was brought up so regularly that it is useful to answer it here. This is that – if rural wages are sticky in nominal terms – it is possible for higher prices to enrich land-owning peasants while landless workers suffer. Such a pattern of events is indeed theoretically possible, but we feel that it would be a strange world where rural wages fail to rise in step with other rural incomes.[23]

5 Conclusions

The main contribution that models can make to policy thinking is to outline more clearly the principal mechanisms and magnitudes that are at stake. Our results confirm that the agricultural policy of the Community has shifted toward a reduced willingness to shield farmers from fluctuations in world prices. The gaps between domestic and world prices have on average continued to increase in recent years, but this is mainly because world prices have plunged in response to a more aggressive export policy of the United States. It has ceased to be true that, as in the years covered by the historical policies regressions, world prices are largely disregarded in the Agricultural Council's annual price setting exercises.

This evolution corresponds to a broad shift to more market-oriented policies in Europe that has a counterpart in other highly protected industries like steel and shipbuilding. The shift does not merely reflect faith in the market. Of equal importance has been a better understanding by governments of the very large budget cost of bucking market trends and that keeping prices artificially high is a Sisyphean task that has no end.

The simulations of the simple EC budget submodel have illustrated how expensive it would have been to continue the CAP of the past. They also suggest, however, that even the implementation of free trade in agricultural products would not provide a permanent cure for the Community's periodic budget crises. The Commission's growing responsibilities will entail rising costs. From a political point of view, it is of course desirable that scaling down agricultural spending convinces the Community's critics that the funds which governments provide to the Community serve other purposes than the provision of a comfortable old age to a sunset industry.

The simulation results do confirm the idea that the CAP has impeded the recovery of the EC from its prolonged recession – and that the more rigorous policies of recent years have contributed to the better performance of Europe's economy. The model's estimates of this effect are not reliable enough, however, to make it worthwhile to highlight the precise number of jobs that would be created as a result of reduced agricultural protection. The model's results are essentially the idea that reducing very high protection makes food cheaper, which moderates wage demands and makes Europe's industries more competitive. This is common sense. The effect is very hard to measure, however. The magnitude could be twice as large, or half as small, as that which RUNS has produced.

The calculations show that the cost to farmers of removing protection is extremely high. This is easily understood, in view of how high protection has become and given that modern farming requires costly non-agricultural inputs so that price cuts lead to proportionally larger cuts in incomes. The mobility of farm workers is low, so that less generous pricing of farm products will impose incomparably harder adjustment problems than those which the decline of other industries pose.

The Commission has been airing yet again old, obvious, but sensible ideas about how to facilitate this adjustment by early pensions and by creating jobs in rural areas. We think that success in the Uruguay Round negotiations on agriculture would also help a great deal. Our calculations show that a unilateral move to free trade by the Community raises world prices appreciably. Perhaps the Commission should become bolder in its approach to the current General Agreement on Tariffs and Trade (GATT) negotiations on agricultural protection that offer a unique chance of achieving a reduction of protection by all agricultural exporters. Extrapolating from our result about the impact on world prices of a unilateral reduction in protection, it is clear that a multilateral one would increase world agricultural prices substantially. This would mitigate the sacrifices that freer trade would impose on protected farmers.[24]

According to RUNS, the impact of agricultural trade liberalization in the Community on gross domestic product and real income in other regions is positive. This is the result of a balance between gains in agriculture and losses in the urban economy. The analysis of the interplay between the economic forces through which the impact of agricultural liberalization affects other countries is also a useful result.

Finally, the simulation results kill the widespread idea that agricultural protection, because it makes Europe produce more and consume less, helps to feed the poor in developing countries. Is it a disappointment to discover that helping Franz-Josef Strauss gain rural votes in Bavaria by keeping the Community's grain prices high did not put more food in the mouths of the poorest of our fellow human beings? As so often in modelling, an apparently paradoxical result has a very straightforward explanation: seven out of eight of those whom the World Bank designates as the "absolute poor" are farmers, whose livelihood depends on selling what they produce at decent prices.

Notes

1 Dairy products will be identified separately in the recalibrated model, instead of being included in "other foods".
2 See Mundlak and Hellinghausen (1982) for the basis of the model coefficients.
3 It would have been straightforward to endogenize the world price of oil by defining supply functions indicating how OPEC responds to changes in demand, and with hindsight it is clear that this would have been desirable. The estimation of supply functions for oil was not possible, however. OPEC took control of oil prices only in 1973, and thus the number of data points available at the time the model was built was far too small to make it possible to estimate such functions.
4 This idea is borrowed from the model of international relations in agriculture (MOIRA). See Linneman et al (1979)
5 These behaviour functions were estimated on the basis of data on domestic and world prices of agricultural products, drawn from the IIASA aggregation of the FAO supply and utilization tape.
6 Implicitly, unemployment in the model is, in the jargon of fix-price equilibrium theory, of the "classical" type. It is not feasible in a model without money to represent the "Keynesian" unemployment which is caused by an inadequate level of aggregate demand.
7 It would have been desirable to differentiate wage behaviour by region to recognize the fact that resistance to real income changes is much stronger in some regions than in others. This was not done, because data on urban labour incomes in the developing world are very poor, with available information limited by and large to the wages of narrow groups of privileged workers in the urban formal sector.
8 Other mechanisms intervene in addition, working through the terms of trade and their impact on the balances of payments of the various regions and the impact of world prices on agricultural output.
9 This is described in greater detail by Burniaux (1987).
10 It is used in the urban sector in the simulations of the paper.

11 The principal source used was Mundlak (1979). This author used time-series and cross-section data for various countries, drawn from the World Banks' World Tables.

12 In the simulations presented in the original version of the paper, the per capita incomes of farmers exceeded those of the urban population in 1995. The projected per capita incomes of farmers are now lower, because the model takes account of the gradual reduction in the ratio of value added to output that is brought about by the evolution of agricultural technology.

13 The equations also take account of the impact of urban unemployment in discouraging rural workers from moving to the cities.

14 In particular, farmers who overproduced were given the quotas of underproducing farmers, undermining the discipline that is necessary to make a quota system effective. Of course, as always, there was cheating. Full implementation of the measures was, however, assumed.

15 These ideas are not new, but their implementation has become more urgent as agricultural incomes have come under pressure. For a recent expression of this kind of thinking, see for example the *Le Monde Rural* document which the Commission has circulated (Commission of the European Communities, 1987).

16 No adjustment is made for the possible impact of the tariff reductions that could result from the Uruguay Round. This does not affect the results strongly, as the Community's tariff receipts are not a large source of revenue.

17 In this section, we use the textbook free trade case to illustrate the argument. Using the results from the halved protection would lead to similar conclusions.

18 In RUNS, wages are not fully rigid. They are assumed to move three-quarters of the way to the market clearing level. Even with this limited rigidity, the disequilibrium real wage multiplier is quite powerful.

19 The Community, although it has come to be a net exporter of temperate agricultural commodities, remains a net importer of agricultural products. Its terms of trade would deteriorate.

20 We remember a staff member of the Agricultural Directorate of the Commission, speaking in the University of Brussels six years ago, who asserted that world prices would rise so much if Community protection was removed that EC consumers would have to pay more for food than if it was maintained. The Commission now speaks with a different tongue.

21 The improvement in the terms of trade of the oil producers is an artefact that depends on the assumptions that are made about oil prices. These are assumed to move in proportion to the export prices of manufacturers of the OECD area, an arbitrary assumption. Other, equally reasonable assumptions would lead to different results.

22 They are of course quite negative for the EC.

23 That food demand in the countryside and in the cities increases and decreases respectively when EC agricultural trade is liberalized is a robust result of the model. That consumption per capita of the whole population drops is not. Average consumption of the whole population tended to increase in runs undertaken with an earlier version of the RUNS model (Burniaux and Waelbroeck, 1985).

24 OECD calculations of "producer subsidy equivalents" (PSEs), as yet unpublished, show that almost all developed country exporters, including most of the self-styled "fair trading countries" of the Cairns Group, heavily support their agricultural exporters. Everyone is dumping, and prices would clearly rise substantially if this stopped.

References

Anderson, K., and R. Tyers (1984) "European Community Grain and Meat Policies: Effects on International Prices, Trade and Welfare", *European Review of Agricultural Economics*, 11 (4), 367–94.

Armington, P. (1969) "A Theory of Demand for Products Distinguished by Place of Production", *IMF Staff Papers*, 16, 159–78.

Bureau of Agricultural Economics (1985) "Agricultural Policies in the European Community", Canberra: Australian Government Publishing Service, Policy Monograph No. 2.

Burniaux, J. M. (1987) *Le Radeau de la Méduse: analyse des dilemmes alimentaires*, Paris: Economica.

—— and J. Waelbroeck (1985) "The Impact of the CAP on Developing Countries: a General Equilibrium Analysis", in C. Stevens and J. Verloren van Themaat (eds), *Pressure Groups, Policies and Development, the Private Sector and EEC–Third World Policy*, London: Hodder and Stoughton, pp. 122–40.

Commission of the European Communities (1987) *Le Monde Rural*, Brussels: Commission of the European Communities.

Eurostat, *National Accounts by Sectors*, Luxembourg: Statistical Office of the European Communities.

Linneman, H., J. De Hoogh, M. A. Keyzer and H. D. J. Van Heemst (1979) *Moira: Model of International Relations in Agriculture*, Amsterdam: North-Holland.

Lluch, C., A. A. Powell and R. A. Williams (1977) *Patterns in Household Demand and Savings*, New York: Oxford University Press.

Mundlak, Y. (1979) "Intersectoral Factor Mobility and Agricultural Growth", Washington, DC: International Food Policy Research Institute, Research Report No. 6, ch. 2.

—— and R. Hellinghausen (1982) "The Inter-country Production Function: Another View", *American Journal of Agricultural Economics*, 64, November, 664–72.

Parikh, K. S., G. Fischer, K. Frohberg and O. Gulbrandsen (1987) *Toward Free Trade in Agriculture*, Food and Agriculture Program, Dordrecht: Martinus Nijhoff.

World Bank (1986) *World Development Report 1986*, Washington, DC: World Bank.

World Bank, *Commodity Trade and Price Trends*, Washington, DC: World Bank.

7

Foreign Exchange Retention and Trade Incentives: A General Equilibrium Evaluation for Yugoslavia

Mathias Dewatripont, Wafik Grais and Gilles Michel

1 Introduction

When faced with a current account disequilibrium, countries are often reluctant, for political reasons, to depreciate their currencies. As a result, import licensing, quotas, administrative allocation of foreign currency and other forms of quantitative restrictions on imports are often necessary. Such policies create a bias against exports, as foreign exchange is valued below its implicit equilibrium level. To overcome the implications of this undesired side effect, a frequent corrective measure is to make the right to import dependent on export performance. This combination of measures and countermeasures has been put in place at various times in countries such as India, Pakistan, the Republic of Korea and Colombia (see Bhagwati, 1978) among others.

When these policy packages are in place they result in a complex set of incentives that is difficult to disentangle. On the one hand, import rationing, the result of the overvaluation of the domestic currency, discourages exports. On the other hand, the rents induced by this rationing of imports are partially channeled into export earnings. Exporting firms are thus able to relax their own import constraint, a situation that induces agents to export simply in order to get access to limited imports.

Following persistent balance-of-payments problems since the late 1970s and several attempts to ration imports, between 1983 and 1985 Yugoslavia instituted a rigid but sophisticated system of foreign exchange allocation through administrative means. Exporters were allowed to retain only part of their foreign exchange earnings, with the remaining amounts channeled partly to the central bank to finance final imports and other essential foreign exchange payments and partly to firms with low exports but high import needs to finance their intermediate imports. The country thus managed to cope with the threat of external illiquidity and was able to keep its balance of payments in check. However, the overall effect of the regime on productive efficiency, export orientation, import substitution and income distribution was strongly questioned.

This paper investigates the incentives implied in a foreign trade regime combining import rationing and foreign exchange retention in the context of a general equilibrium model applied to Yugoslavia. While Bhagwati and Srinivasan (1975) have provided a detailed analysis of a similar type of policy package for India in a partial equilibrium set-up, to our knowledge this is the first time a full general equilibrium framework has been used. This approach is particularly useful because it allows, through the use of counterfactual experiments, an assessment of the complex structure of relative incentives in the economy and a determination of the extent to which the link between import rights and export performance compensates for the overvaluation of the currency and whether the system discriminates in favor of or against exports.

As shown by Bhagwati and Srinivasan (1975), because parts of the rents resulting from import rationing are channeled into exports, both importers and exporters react to "implicit" price signals that are different from observable market price. Shocks that affect the system (e.g. changes in world trade or policy) alter these implicit prices by altering the severity of import rationing; they also induce changes in export behavior that cannot be analyzed on the basis of market prices alone. In addition, such a system is clearly "self-limiting", to use Bhagwati and Srinivasan's terminology. A rise in exports, by improving the external payments situation, lowers import rationing and thus ultimately reduces the incentive to export (since exports are partly motivated by the need to relax the import constraint). In this paper, we investigate the effect of changes in the intensity of the import–export link on overall export performance.

The focus of the paper is on trade incentives and export performance, not on overall growth performance.[1] It does not address macroeconomic stabilization issues. The analysis assumes an invariant macroeconomic policy environment.

The applied general equilibrium approach also permits an empirical investigation of the trade and distributive effects of partial trade liberalization. Partial liberalization has attracted much attention in recent years (see, for example, the survey of Edwards, 1984) because many governments throughout the world have become convinced that they need to liberalize their economies but have felt it politically difficult to do so all at once. In Yugoslavia, the policy issue is whether liberalization schemes should apply to all agents or first be limited to some categories of importers. Because the choice of approach may have strong distributive implications, it is important to be able to assess the effects of the various foreign trade regimes on final users and on different categories of intermediate importers. Up to 1985 and at present, importers are treated differently, depending on their ability or inability to export. In particular, final importers face rigid import constraints, in contrast with some intermediate importers that, by varying their exports, can alter the constraints they face.

The model we use for these investigations is derived from an applied general equilibrium model of the Yugoslav economy (Robinson and Tyson, 1985). The Robinson–Tyson (RT) model accounts for the most important specific structural features of the Yugoslav economy, notably the labor market and the distribution of income inside firms. Its treatment of external trade, however, is quite similar to that of other models for small semi-industrial economies (see, for instance, Dervis, de Melo and Robinson, 1982). We therefore had to modify it to represent the foreign exchange rationing mechanism and the resulting flows of foreign exchange prevailing in Yugoslavia.

The formal treatment of import rationing is based on the approach of Neary and Roberts (1980), which permits the computation of the implicit or virtual import premia for rationed goods.[2] It is particularly suited for this study, where the link between import rights and export performance needs to be captured. Implicit import premia are used to derive the implicit export premia that such a link implies.

The organization of the paper is as follows. Section 2 briefly reviews Yugoslavia's balance-of-payments problems from the late 1970s up to 1985. It also describes the institutional framework of the 1983–5 foreign exchange allocation system. The modeling framework used and the way it captures import rationing, foreign exchange retention and the link between exports and imports are described in section 3. The calibration of the model and the solution approach are presented in section 4. Finally, section 5 describes the counterfactual experiments carried out to assess the effects of a change in the ratio of foreign exchange earnings surrendered to the central bank and the changes in the degrees of liberalization.

2 External Disequilibria and Foreign Exchange Regime in Yugoslavia: 1979–1985

During most of the 1970s, import rationing was not a significant instrument of balance-of-payment managements in Yugoslavia. Instead, the Federal authorities offered tax incentives to promote exports and avoid a significant depletion of international reserves at the official exchange rate. Firms were allowed to use their export earnings freely, i.e. without compulsory surrender to the central bank. The only discretionary policy concerned the allocation of import rights to firms that did not have direct access to foreign exchange through exports.

The second oil shock put this foreign exchange policy to a severe test. In the presence of a significant overvaluation of the currency, the current account deficit soared to 5 percent of gross domestic product in 1979. Subsequently, the deficits were gradually reduced – mainly through import reduction – while foreign lenders became increasingly reluctant to raise the level of their exposure. By 1982, foreign exchange reserves represented only 35 percent of their 1978 level. The height of the crisis came in 1982, when internal circulation of foreign exchange almost disappeared. This situation led to major disruptions in export and import flows, which both fell by more than 10 percent. Yugoslavia was becoming illiquid and entering a serious foreign exchange crisis. In order to restore foreign exchange circulation in the economy and make possible an orderly servicing of external debt, around the middle of 1982 the authorities introduced a system of administrative allocation of foreign exchange. A formal surrender requirement was imposed immediately, and shortly thereafter a link between import rights and export performance was introduced.

The system operated between 1983 and the end of 1985. Basically, it involved the creation of two pools of foreign exchange. The first, managed directly by the central bank, came essentially from a fixed portion (54 percent) of all foreign earnings of the producing sector, which had to be surrendered to the central bank.[3] This pool was used to (a) discharge official obligations, including the replenishment of the reserves of the central bank and the servicing of the foreign debt it had contracted, (b) finance priority imports of consumer goods and energy, and (c) cover selected other transfer payments. Allocation among these uses was essentially a budgeting operation with a certain degree of flexibility.

The second foreign exchange pool was financed essentially by the 46 percent of foreign exchange earnings not surrendered to the central bank.[4] This pool was used to service the debts of enterprises and to pay for intermediate imports. It was allocated according to import rights as follows. Each enterprise received an entitlement of foreign exchange.[5] That for a firm without foreign exchange earnings was equal to past average imports plus anticipated debt obligations, while that for foreign exchange earners was defined as a percentage of their foreign exchange receipts, determined on the basis of historical export–import behavior and anticipated debt obligations.

The entitlements were adjusted so that overall they equaled the projected amount of resources in the second pool, with periodic adjustments to correct for differences between actual developments and projections. Thus transactions in the second pool were, in effect, limited to the (positive or negative) difference between each firm's entitlement and 46 percent of its export earnings. If a firm had an entitlement larger than 46 percent of its outlays, it had the right to purchase the difference from this pool; otherwise, it had to sell it to the pool. Transactions on the second pool were supposed to be made at the official exchange rate.

This foreign exchange allocation system, together with debt relief arrangements and a substantial real depreciation of the currency (35 percent between October 1982 and July 1984), allowed for an orderly servicing of foreign debt obligations and some reserve accumulation. The current account showed a surplus in 1983 and thereafter. As noted, however, the adjustment was taking place mainly on the import side, where the extent of rationing was quite severe. Furthermore, because of the individualized import rights, the system led to a high degree of market segmentation and created specific incentives for individual firms to export in numerous instances where doing so was not competitive. These ultimate effects of the system on the productive structure, efficiency in production and signaling to agents became major issues.

3 A General Equilibrium Model for Analyzing the Foreign Exchange Allocation System

Our aim is to assess quantitatively the incentives implied by the Yugoslav foreign exchange allocation system in place from 1983 to 1985. We use a model that is uncluttered by unnecessary institutional or behavioral refinements but that, at the same time, accommodates a detailed representation of the foreign exchange allocation system. The framework of the model is described in the first subsection below, while the following subsections look specifically at the aspects of trade and foreign exchange.

3.1 The general equilibrium framework

The model used, called DGM (for Dewatripont–Grais–Michel), is a modified version of the RT model.[6] The DGM model simplifies many of the features of the RT model but expands the treatment of foreign trade in order to capture the foreign exchange allocation system prevailing between 1983 and 1985. The RT model, while standard in its treatment of foreign trade, technology and household behavior, incorporates two specific features of the Yugoslav labor market. First, it captures the observed stability of employment in Yugoslavia by assuming that a fraction of the labor force is guaranteed employment in each sector. Only the remaining portion of the work force is allocated in order to equalize marginal value products across sectors. Value added is thus distributed among three factors of production in each sector: capital, immobile labor and mobile labor. Second, income distribution does not coincide with marginal value products as a set of transfers captures the need to distribute profits in a way that is consistent with the social ownership of firms.

Other behavioral assumptions of the RT model are as follows: a Cobb–Douglas utility function is used to allocate household consumption; fixed proportions are used to allocate investment by destination and origin; Leontief technologies are used for intermediate inputs; and constant elasticity of substitution (CES) production functions are used for value added. Composite goods are assumed to be a CES mix of domestic and imported goods (following the Armington, 1969, assumption), a reflection of the imperfect substitution between such goods. Finally, the small country assumption is made concerning imports while the volume of exports is kept exogenous. The model does not distinguish between "convertible" and "nonconvertible" trade, as two-thirds of total trade are realized in convertible currency and the issue of foreign exchange rationing concerned only this part of external trade.

The RT model is simplified in several respects. First, its level of disaggregation is reduced from 18 sectors to seven and from two household categories to one. Second, exports and imports are treated symmetrically by assuming a constant elasticity of transformation (CET) between supplies to the domestic and foreign markets respectively.[7] A final simplification concerns the macroeconomic savings investment equilibrium: for comparative statics experiments, the model is run with an exogenous real investment target. The adjustment of savings to investment is realized through endogenous household savings rates (while foreign savings are kept exogenous in foreign currency, and government and firms save according to exogenous rates).

3.2 Foreign exchange flows captured in the model

Figure 7.1 indicates how the 1983–5 foreign exchange allocation system is captured in the DGM model.[8] This representation follows closely the actual flows associated with external transactions of goods and services.[9] Foreign exchange flows are organized around two

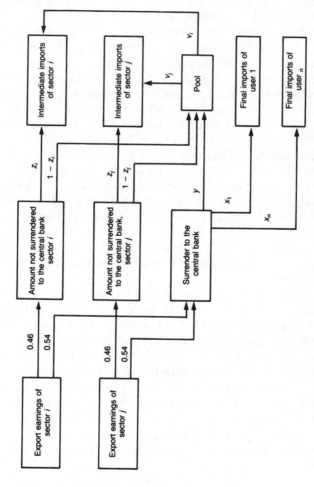

Figure 7.1 Foreign exchange flows captured in the model

pools. The first (called "surrender to the central bank" in the figure) is financed by the portion of foreign exchange earnings that each exporter has to surrender to the central bank (54 percent). Part of these resources are allocated for various final imports, in fixed proportions x_i for each use $i = 1, 2, \ldots, n$; a share y of the total surrendered foreign exchange $(y + \Sigma_{i=1}^{n} x_i = 1)$ is channeled to the second foreign exchange pool (hereafter Pool). The Pool also receives sector-specific fixed shares of sector export earnings that are not surrendered to the central bank (z_j for sector j). Total resources in the Pool are allocated in fixed proportions to finance intermediate imports (v_i for section i with $\Sigma_{i=1}^{7} v_i = 1$).

Two types of sector could thus be distinguished: "net exporters", which have entitlements smaller than 46 percent of their exports so that $z_i \leq 1$ and $v_i = 0$; and "net importers", which have entitlements larger than 46 percent of their export earnings so that $z_i = 0$ and $v_i > 0$.[10]

3.3 Import demands and export supplies: virtual prices

3.3.1 Notional and effective import demands

The foreign exchange allocation system described above results in a complex set of agent-specific foreign exchange quotas. To account for this effect, we introduce agent-specific rationing schemes into the model and replace notional demand by effective demand for rationed agents.[11] The existence of a black market in foreign exchange is assumed away so that agents effectively trade at the official rate as the system was supposed to operate.

Following Neary and Roberts (1980), we use the concept of virtual prices to compute agents' demand in the presence of rationing. Virtual prices are defined as those that would induce an unrationed agent to behave in the same manner as when faced with a given vector of ration constraints. Assume the following maximization problem for a given agent:

$$\max_{a_i, b_j} U(a_1, \ldots, a_m, b_1, \ldots, b_n)$$

such that

$$\sum_{i=1}^{m} p_{a_i} a_i + \sum_{j=2}^{n} p_{b_j} b_j \leq E \qquad (7.1)$$

$$b_j \leq \bar{b}_j \qquad j = 1, \ldots, n$$

where each a_i accounts for an unconstrained good, each b_j for a constrained good (with quota $\bar{b}_j$), p_{a_i} and p_{b_j} for their respective prices (which the agent takes as given) and E for total expenditures (also taken as given). The method consists of finding virtual prices, $p_{b_j}^v = p_{b_j}(1 + \varepsilon_j)$, for $j = 1, \ldots, n$, such that the following unconstrained program yields $b_j = \bar{b}_j$ for $j = 1, \ldots, n$:

$$\max_{a_i, b_j} U(a_1, \ldots, a_m, b_1, \ldots, b_n)$$

such that

$$\sum_{i=1}^m p_{a_i} a_i + \sum_{j=2}^n p_{b_j}^v b_j \leqslant E' \tag{7.2}$$

where E', defined as $E + \Sigma_{j=1}^n \varepsilon_j b_j$, is taken as a fixed amount by the agent.

Neary and Roberts show that the solutions to (7.1) and (7.2) are identical, so that the virtual price approach takes into account spillover effects in a rigorous way. In essence, the ε_j are tax rates for rationed goods, although the taxes are not actually paid: the "tax" is channeled back into the income of the agent, who trades at the official price.

The Yugoslav foreign exchange allocation system may, however, result either in a constraint on the value of a specific good that can be imported, as in (7.1), or in a constraint on the amount of foreign exchange available to a given agent to import whatever goods he wishes. Private consumption for which the Government sets quotas for each good corresponds to the former category. Government consumption, investment and intermediate inputs make up the latter category, which requires an optimization program that is slightly different from (7.1). The optimizing program of each agent in the model is described below.

Private consumption   The representative household faces one import quota for each good, and its rationing rates ε_j are product-specific. Given the assumptions of a Cobb–Douglas utility function and CES trade aggregation functions, the unconstrained program of the household is

$$\max_{D_i, M_i} \prod_i \{[\alpha_i D_i^{-\rho_i} + (1 - \alpha_i) M_i^{-\rho_i}]^{-1/\rho_i}\}^{\beta_i}$$

such that

$$\sum_i p_{D_i} D_i + \sum_i p_{M_i}(1 + \varepsilon_i) M_i \leqslant E' = E + \sum_n \varepsilon_i M_i \tag{7.3}$$

where D_i and M_i are the domestic and imported varieties of good i, α_i and ρ_i are the share and substitution parameters of the trade aggregation function for good i, and β_i is the share parameter of the utility function for the composite good i. The virtual prices

$p_i^v = p_{M_i}(1 + \varepsilon_i)$ are determined in order to have $M_i = \bar{M}_i$ (import quotas) at the optimum (note that p_{M_i} includes tariffs). A quota for the import of good i thus has a spillover effect on the demand for the domestic good i and on the demand for all other goods. Spillovers toward savings are ruled out, since savings are determined to match the exogenously set investment.

Government consumption The Government faces a global foreign exchange constraint and an identical rationing rate ε_g for all its imports. Given the Armington assumption as well as the Cobb–Douglas utility specification, the unconstrained program of the Government is

$$\max_{D_i, M_i} \prod_i \{[\alpha_i D_i^{-\rho_i} + (1 - \alpha_i)M_i^{-\rho_i}]^{-1/\rho_i}\}^{\beta_i}$$

such that

$$\sum p_{D_i} D_i + \sum \mu_{M_i}(1 + \varepsilon_g)M_i \leqslant E' = E + \varepsilon_g \sum M_i \qquad (7.4)$$

In this case, the virtual prices $p_i^v = p_{M_i}(1 + \varepsilon_g)$ are determined so as to equate $\sum p_{M_i} M_i$ with the foreign exchange quota. The quota affects the allocation of the exogenous amount of public consumption by changing the proportions of domestic and imported varieties of each good, and the proportions of each composite good, in total public consumption.

Fixed investment Total investment is first allocated in fixed proportions by sector of destination. Each sector then allocates its investment by sector of origin, taking into account its own foreign exchange quota. Since the model assumes that investment by origin is determined by fixed proportions in real terms, each investing sector faces a program of the form

$$\max_{D_i, M_i} \{\min_i [\frac{1}{\gamma_i} \alpha_i D_i^{-\rho_i} + (1 - \alpha_i)M_i^{-\rho_i}]^{-1/\rho_i}\}$$

such that

$$\sum_i p_{D_i} D_i + \sum_i p_{M_i}(1 + \varepsilon_1)M_i \leqslant E' = E + \varepsilon_1 \sum_i M_i \qquad (7.5)$$

where i represents a sector producing investment goods for the sector under consideration, and γ_i is the amount of good i bought by the investing sector for each unit of investment. The virtual prices $p_i^v = p_{M_i}(1 + \varepsilon_1)$ are determined so as to equate $\sum_i p_{M_i} M_i$ to the foreign exchange quota faced by the investing sector (who thus faces a rationing rate ε_1). Such a quota affects the proportion of domestic and imported varieties of each good bought by the investing sector.

Intermediate inputs Each producing sector faces a foreign exchange quota. Its objective is to minimize intermediate cost for a given level of production.[12] Given the assumption of a Leontief technology for intermediate inputs, the program of the producing firms in a given sector is

$$\min_{D_i, M_i} \left\{ \sum_i p_{D_i} D_i + \sum_i p_{M_i} (1 + \varepsilon_Q) M_i \right\}$$

such that

$$\min_i \left\{ \frac{1}{\gamma_i} \left[\alpha_i D_i^{-\rho_i} + (1 - \alpha_i) M_i^{-\rho_i} \right] \right\} \geqslant Q \qquad (7.6)$$

where γ_i is the amount of good i necessary for the producing sector under consideration to produce one unit of its own good. As indicated, Q is a negative function of unit intermediate costs exclusive of $\Sigma_i \varepsilon_Q M_i$, which is fed back into value added.

At the optimum, ε_Q is determined so as to equate $\Sigma_i p_{M_i} M_i$, the total amount of intermediate imports purchased, with the foreign exchange quota. A drop in the quota requires a rise in ε_Q at the new optimum. Such a rise lowers $\Sigma_i p_{M_i} M_i$ to the new quota through two effects: a substitution effect toward domestic inputs for an unchanged Q (since a rise in ε_Q implies a rise in the virtual price of imports), and a scale effect, since Q is a negatively affected by the rise of intermediate unit costs (*exclusive* of $\Sigma_i \varepsilon_Q M_i$) because the agent is forced away from its desired M_i / D_is.

3.3.2 Exports

Import rationing is combined with an export incentive in the form of a link between access to foreign exchange for intermediate imports and export performance. The essence of such a system is to channel part of the rents generated by import rationing into export earnings.[13] The virtual price approach to import rationing provides a natural way of modeling this import–export link, since the export incentive is a function of the import premium rate computed in this approach.

In the absence of a link between import rights and export performance, and with a CET function between exports and domestic production, a sector j allocates its supply between the domestic and export markets according to the following rule:

$$\frac{X_j}{D_j} = \kappa_j \left(\frac{p_{D_i}}{p_{X_i}} \right)^{\alpha_j} \qquad (7.7)$$

where X_j and D_j are the export and domestic supplies of sector j, κ_j is a sector-specific constant and α_j is the elasticity of transformation for sector j. The export price p_{X_j} is the dollar price of exports, including subsidies, multiplied by the official exchange rate ER.

In figure 7.1, export earnings are divided into three components: (a) the 54 percent surrendered to the central bank, at a rate $ER_1 = ER$; (b) the 46 percent of $1 - z_j$ sold on the foreign exchange pool, at a rate $ER_2 = ER$; and (c) the remainder, 46 percent of z_j, not converted into domestic currency but used directly for imports. A rationed firm j will obviously use its retained foreign exchange rather than sell it at the official rate. In fact, given an intermediate import rationing rate ε_{Q_j}, the opportunity cost of foreign exchange for the rationed firm is $ER(1 + \varepsilon_{Q_j})$. Therefore, a firm will not sell its foreign exchange below this rate.

The virtual price of exports is thus

$$p_j^v = p_{X_j}[1 + (1 - z_i) \times 0.46\varepsilon_{Q_i}] \tag{7.8}$$

and firms optimize according to (7.7), where p_{X_j} is replaced by p_j^v. Consequently, other things being equal, exports depend positively on ε_{Q_j}, the premium rate for intermediate imports (a reflection of the incentive to export simply to get access to imports), and on the retention rate of foreign currency, $(1 - z_j) \times 0.46$.

4 Model Calibration and Solution

The experiments are performed using a data set for 1982. Tables 7.1 and 7.2 provide selected information about the structure of the economy and key elasticities. Note that the elasticities of substitution between imported and domestic goods are assumed to be identical across users for each sector.[14]

Table 7.3 shows that three sectors (agriculture, energy and construction) are net importers, i.e. do not cover their import needs using solely 46 percent of their export earnings. These sectors are thus buyers of foreign exchange from the Pool. The three other sectors (heavy and light industries and productive services)[15] are net exporters and retain less than 46 percent of their export earnings (respectively 44 percent, 36 percent and 29 percent). The total net contribution of producing sectors to the Pool is slightly negative, and the residual is provided by the central bank. It represents the difference between the 54 percent of export earnings surrendered to the bank and the use of foreign exchange for final imports and debt repayments.

Table 7.4 shows the import rationing assumptions. As rationing rates are neither published nor easily measurable, the base estimates are based on circumstantial evidence. All rationing rates (the ε of the

Table 7.1 Structure of the economy by sector (percent)

Sector	Share of the sector in total			Exports/ domestic supply	Imports/ domestic supply
	Output	Private consumption	Investment (by origin)		
Agriculture	16.3	13.5	3.1	1.6	6.0
Energy	3.7	3.9	0.0	1.1	39.6
Construction	8.6	0.3	43.0	1.5	0.1
Heavy industry	15.4	5.5	38.5	15.4	27.5
Light industry	15.7	33.4	7.9	14.5	18.3
Productive services	28.0	37.6	7.5	10.1	3.3
Nonproductive services	12.3	5.8	0.0	–	–
Total	100.0	100.0	100.0		

Table 7.2 Production, import and export elasticities

Sector	Elasticities of substitution		Elasticities of transformation for exports
	Production	Imports	
Agriculture	3.0	2.0	1.5
Energy	0.0	0.6	1.5
Construction	1.25	0.6	0.5
Heavy industry	1.5	0.6	1.5
Light industry	1.5	0.8	1.5
Productive services	1.75	0.6	1.5
Nonproductive services	1.75	–	–

Table 7.3 Net foreign exchange contribution per sector (millions of 1982 US dollars)

Sector	Exports	Intermediate imports	Contribution to Pool
Agriculture	278.3	338.0	−218.7
Energy	139.2	675.9	−616.3
Construction	238.6	357.8	−258.3
Heavy industry	3,876.6	1,689.8	99.4
Light industry	4,174.8	1,491.0	417.5
Productive services	3,001.9	874.7	497.0
Total	11,709.4	5,427.2	−79.5

Table 7.4 Premium rates for imports and exports (percent)

Sector	Good-specific quotas on imports for private consumption	User-specific quotas[a]		
		Investment imports	Intermediate imports	Exports
Agriculture	68	72	88	40
Energy	65	67	99	46
Construction	–	75	89	41
Heavy industry	72	65	70	31
Light industry	67	66	57	21
Productive services	64	61	49	14

[a]Premium rate for government consumption is 77 percent.

previous subsection) are roughly between 50 and 100 percent with those for final users between 60 and 77 percent. On the intermediate imports side, rationing is assumed to be more intensive for sectors with higher import–export ratios, a reflection of the advantage given by direct access to foreign exchange through own exports. The premium rates for exports are computed as described in section 3.3.2, using intermediate import rationing rates and retention rates for foreign exchange. The export incentive embodied in the system is lower for net exporters, whose import rationing is less severe and whose retention rates are lower.

The model is implemented using the TV software, which allows for an easy representation of the Neary–Roberts approach to rationing. The software is based on a Social Accounting Matrix (SAM) description of the economy and solves the model using a Newton-type algorithm. For a description of the approach and solution procedure, see Drud, Grais and Pyatt (1983).

5 Retention Rates, Foreign Exchange Liberalization and Trade Performance

5.1 Foreign exchange retention: a self-limiting export incentive

The first two experiments illustrate the self-limiting nature of foreign exchange retention as an export incentive. In a system without any import–export link, an increase in firms' access to imports can only help exports. This pattern is not necessarily true here, since the incentive to export depends positively on the intensity of import rationing.

Both experiments involve lowering the surrender rate to the central bank from 54 to 49 percent, a measure that shifts import rights away from final demand and toward intermediate users. In scenario 1, the "freed" amount of foreign exchange is sold to the Pool, so that the change benefits only net importers.[16] In scenario 2, firms are allowed to keep the extra foreign exchange for their own imports, and the change benefits mainly net exporters.[17]

In the first scenario the rationing rates for imports of intermediates decrease relatively more for the first three sectors, which are net importers, while the opposite occurs under scenario 2 (table 7.5). In a similar fashion, the rationing rates for final imports rise in both scenarios. The changes are particularly significant for investment goods, since for them substitution possibilities between composite goods are ruled out (see section 3.3.1).

In both scenarios, total exports decrease in comparison with the base scenario (table 7.6). In effect, helping the exporting sectors by improving their access to imports affects exports negatively. This result quantifies the "self-limiting" nature of foreign exchange retention as an export incentive. Three effects are at play in determining export behavior.

1 Better access to imports of intermediates means, *ceteris paribus*, an improved composite mix of domestic and imported inputs for firms and therefore lower unit intermediate costs, higher output and higher exports.
2 Better access to imports of intermediates also reduces the intensity of their rationing, which lowers the virtual price of exports and discourages exports.
3 In scenario 2, the relaxation of the import constraints is realized through higher foreign exchange retention rates, a measure that, for a given level of import rationing, raises the virtual price of exports for the net importers.

In scenario 1, the third effect is not present, and effect (2) dominates effect (1). Exports decrease significantly for those sectors whose import constraints are relaxed, i.e. the net importers. In scenario 2, effect (2) dominates the other two for net exporters. The value of price elasticities of import demand is crucial here. The lower the elasticities in absolute value, the larger the drop in rationing rates for a given increase in import rights.[18] Note that, in scenario 2, exports rise for net importers. The reason is that the drop in exports for net exporters lowers their contribution to the Pool and decreases the availability of imports for net importers, a situation that raises their virtual export prices.

The foregoing results demonstrate the lack of transparency of such

Table 7.5 Premium rates for imports (percent)[a]

	Private consumption			Investment			Intermediate		
Sector	Base	Sc 1	Sc 2	Base	Sc 1	Sc 2	Base	Sc 1	Sc 2
Agriculture	68	82	85	72	180	193	88	22	69
Energy	65	128	123	67	183	198	99	7	92
Construction	–	–	–	75	200	217	89	11	83
Heavy industry	72	121	128	65	183	199	70	56	39
Light industry	67	106	110	66	180	195	57	41	26
Productive services	64	117	124	61	180	194	49	39	15

Sc, scenario.
[a]Premium rate for government consumption is 77 percent in the base scenario, 142 percent in scenario 1 and 151 percent in scenario 2.

Table 7.6 Premium rates for exports and export performance

	Premium for exports			Base case exports	Increase in export volumes (%)	
Sector	Base	Sc 1	Sc 2		Sc 1	Sc 2
Agriculture	40	11	35	279	−11.2	5.1
Energy	46	4	46	146	−14.1	−0.3
Construction	41	6	43	236	−8.4	3.8
Heavy industry	31	25	20	3,883	−0.2	−0.9
Light industry	21	15	11	4,174	−1.0	3.1
Productive services	14	11	6	3,022	−2.2	−6.0
Total				11,740	−1.6	−2.7

Sc, scenario.

a foreign allocation system as an incentive to exports. While retention schemes act as an export incentive in the presence of import rationing, exports are not behaving monotonically with respect to retention rates. Moreover, predictions about the sign of the export response to a variation in these retention rates are very difficult to make, since the answer depends on the value of unobserved sector-specific rationing rates.

5.2 Liberalization of foreign exchange allocation

The other set of experiments concerns liberalization of the foreign exchange regime. All flows described in figure 7.1 are valued at the same exchange rate, reflecting the prevailing regulatory framework.

However, foreign currency can possibly be sold at different prices at different stages of the allocation process. Partial liberalization, for example, can be limited to the Pool. The central bank would buy and sell its currency at an administered rate ER_1 and firms would be allowed to buy and sell freely on the Pool at a flexible market-determined rate ER_2. Full liberalization would mean that all agents would be allowed to buy and sell freely on a unified market at a flexible rate.

The experiment is scenario 3 simulates a liberalization limited to exports and intermediate imports, with the regime for final importers unchanged. Such a partial liberalization scheme may be attractive if the authorities want to liberalize the foreign exchange allocation for firms without letting the prices of consumer imports rise. In scenario 4, full liberalization is assumed, with a unified foreign exchange market and a unique flexible exchange rate. The results are summarized in tables 7.7 and 7.8.

Specifically, the exchange rate for transactions involving the central bank is maintained unchanged in scenario 3. However, the share of export earnings (46 percent) not surrendered to the central bank can be sold or bought freely by firms on the Pool at a flexible exchange rate. As such, the value of foreign exchange for all intermediate imports is now equalized among sectors (it is ER_2, the equilibrium exchange rate of the Pool). The same is also true for all exports, but at a different exchange rate $0.54ER_1 + 0.46ER_2$ (where ER_1 is the official exchange rate for central bank transactions). The average rate reflects the situation that part of export earnings are surrendered to the central bank at ER_1 and part are sold on the free Pool at ER_2. This liberalization scheme removes intermediate import rationing and implies that the virtual prices for exports and intermediate imports coincide with the market prices.

The effect of partial liberalization on export volumes is difficult to predict a priori. While exporters receive a higher dinar price for their goods (since ER_1 is smaller than $0.54ER_1 + 0.46ER_2$), the elimination of import rationing removes the incentive to export simply in order to get better access to imports. Furthermore, virtual export prices (which, after liberalization, coincide with market prices) can go either way. In effect, and as shown in Table 7.8, although the exchange rate for the Pool rises by 53 percent in comparison with the official rate, the increase is not enough to prevent virtual export prices from decreasing in four sectors.[19] Exports in these four sectors are reduced. In the other two sectors (light industry and productive services), lower initial premium rationing rates for intermediate imports mean that virtual export prices rise. Thus, exports rise in these two sectors (which are large net exporters) and allow aggregate

Table 7.7 Premium rates for imports (percent)[a]

Sector	Private consumption			Investment			Intermediates		
	Base	Sc 3	Sc 4	Base	Sc 3	Sc 4	Base	Sc 3	Sc 4
Agriculture	68	62	0	72	46	0	88	0	0
Energy	65	61	0	67	48	0	99	0	0
Construction	–	–	–	75	55	0	89	0	0
Heavy industry	72	63	0	65	43	0	70	0	0
Light industry	65	58	0	66	42	0	57	0	0
Productive services	64	47	0	61	40	0	49	0	0

Sc, scenario.
[a]Premium rate for government consumption is 77 percent in the base scenario, 65 percent in scenario 3 and 0 in scenario 4.

Table 7.8 Changes in virtual export prices and in export performance[a]

Sector	Virtual export price		Base case exports	Increase in export volume (%)	
	Sc 3	Sc 4		Sc 3	Sc 4
Agriculture	−10.9	−2.9	279	−12.3	−4.3
Energy	−14.5	−6.8	146	−35.7	−31.5
Construction	−11.5	−3.5	236	−6.2	−5.6
Heavy industry	−4.7	3.8	3,883	−0.5	8.1
Light industry	3.1	12.4	4,174	8.9	19.5
Productive services	9.5	19.3	3,022	6.6	9.4
Total			11,740	3.8	11.4

Sc, scenario
[a]In scenario 3, the Pool exchange rate depreciates by 53 percent, implying a depreciation of the average exchange rate facing exporters by $(0.0 \times 0.54) + (0.53 \times 0.46)$, i.e. 24 percent, in comparison with the base scenario. In scenario 4, the fully flexible exchange rate depreciates by 36 percent in comparison with the exchange rate in the base scenario.

real exports to rise by 3.8 percent, despite the drop in export volumes in the other four sectors.

This overall increase in exports allows total imports to rise and their virtual price to decrease. The premium rates for final imports are lower and, for intermediate imports, the 53 percent rise in the exchange rate at which they are bought is smaller than the initial levels of premium rates (except for productive services, which had the lowest premium rate of all intermediates).

If partial liberalization allows for moderate gains in export earnings, full liberalization improves export volumes much more strongly. In scenario 4, aggregate export volumes rise by 11.4 percent in comparison with the base case. The difference between the two scenarios is quite intuitive. Both systems cut the link between import rights and export performance, but scenario 4 also leads to a rise in export prices by liberalizing the exchange rate at which final importers buy their goods. In this system, all virtual prices coincide with market prices, and foreign exchange is valued at the same rate for all transactions. Contrary to scenario 3, firms get the same exchange rate for intermediate imports and for exports. Their imports are thus cheaper than in scenario 3 (they pay 36 percent above the initial rate instead of 53 percent), and their exports are more highly valued (they get 36 percent above the initial rate for the full amount of export earnings, instead of 53 percent above the initial rate for 46 percent of export earnings plus the initial rate for the remaining 54 percent of export earnings).[20]

The main lesson is that liberalization schemes limited to intermediate imports produce small gains in exports in comparison with full liberalization. In our context, it appears that the main deterrent to exports is the subsidization of final imports by exporters, while the retention scheme limits the negative effect of intermediate import rationing on export performance.

A final issue is that of the overall effect of the foreign exchange allocation scheme on incentives to export. The overall export gain in scenario 4 in comparison with the base case shows that, in the aggregate, the administrative allocation system discriminates against exports. That conclusion does not, however, apply to net importers, whose virtual export prices decrease in scenario 4. For these sectors, it appears that the foreign exchange allocation scheme through the import–export link, did discriminate in favor of exports and create an overincentive to export. For net exporters, the import–export link instead compensates only partially for the overvaluation of the currency. In fact there is an overall reallocation of the export effort in favor of large exporting sectors.

5.3 Alternative import substitution elasticities

The robustness of the foregoing results is assessed through changes in the key behavioral parameters of the model. Specifically, the four scenarios are now run with sharply increased import substitution elasticities, raised to 1.5 for heavy industry and productive services and to 2.5 for the other sectors. While these figures certainly overestimate the degree of import substitution in the economy, they are far enough from the initial value to provide a good assessment of the robustness of the foregoing results.

The conclusion from these experiments are as follows.

1 All the results from the liberalization scenarios remain valid under the new import substitution elasticities. The flexible exchange rate rises by 58 percent in scenario 3 and by 45 percent in scenario 4 (compared with 53 percent and 36 percent previously), and aggregate export volumes rise by 5.1 percent in scenario 3 and 20.2 percent in scenario 4 (compared with 3.8 percent and 11.4 percent previously). In effect, these liberalization schemes involve cuts in the prices of virtual intermediate import prices. With higher trade substitution elasticities, the import response is therefore stronger, and the result is higher equilibrium exchange rates and export volumes.

2 In the first two scenarios, higher elasticities entail that increased intermediate import availability leads to less significant declines in import rationing rates and thus less disincentive against exports. Aggregate export volumes decrease by only 0.8 percent in scenario 1 (compared with a decrease of 1.6 percent in section 4.1) and even increase by 0.6 percent in scenario 2 (compared with a decrease of 2.7 percent in section 4.2).

6 Conclusion

Three conclusions emerge from the above analysis. The first is the usefulness of the notion of virtual prices (Neary and Roberts, 1980) in modeling rationing in a general equilibrium framework which captures linkages between exports and imports. Virtual prices and implicit premia provide a natural way to identify the scarcity value of a rationed commodity, i.e. the actual signal to which operators respond. The second conclusion is a general equilibrium confirmation of the Bhagwati and Srinivasan (1975) partial equilibrium observation of the self-limiting nature of foreign exchange retention as an export incentive. Increased foreign exchange retention without a dual free market provides an incentive to export for net importers and may even be a disincentive to net exporters. Finally, the third conclusion is the expected dominance of a market allocation of foreign exchange with a free exchange rate over an administered allocation with an administered exchange rate in terms of promoting exports. The larger the portion of foreign exchange allocated at a market-determined exchange rate, the stronger is the export response.

Notes

The views expressed in this paper are those of the authors and should not be interpreted as those of the World Bank.

1 Several authors have investigated the link between foreign trade regimes and growth in detail. See in particular Bhagwati (1978), Krueger (1978) and Balassa (1985).

2 This approach was first implemented in a general equilibrium context by Ahmed *et al.* (1985) and Grais, de Melo and Urata (1986).

3 In addition to a portion of workers' remittances and tourism earnings.

4 In addition to a share of workers' remittances and selected credits.

5 Called its socially verifiable reproduction need.

6 For a detailed presentation and policy experiments, see Robinson and Tyson (1985) and Robinson, Tyson and Dewatripont (1986).

7 As first suggested by Powell and Gruen (1968).

8 In a general equilibrium model without money, foreign exchange flows are simply flows of claims toward foreign goods, while the exchange rate is the relative price between a prespecified domestic good and a prespecified foreign good (taking as given the relative price structure of foreign goods and the relative price structure of domestic goods).

9 The model abstracts from debt flows. Since debt repayments are exogenous across comparative statics experiments, nothing would be gained by taking them into account.

10 Note that, in this system, a proportional increase in exports across all sectors leads to the same proportional increase in import rights for each user since, at all stages, foreign exchange is allocated through fixed proportions. If there is a rise of exports in a single sector i all final importers benefit through the share of export earnings surrendered to the central bank. The same is true for net importers, since the central bank allocates part of its resources to the Pool. In addition, net importers benefit if sector i is a net exporter and thus has to channel part of its export earnings directly into the Pool. Finally, net exporters do not benefit from a rise in exports in sector i, since their import rights come solely from their own export earnings.

11 As constrained optimization with rationing leads agents to change their demand in all unrationed markets; see, for instance, Benassy (1982).

12 That level is determined so as to equalize the marginal value product of mobile labor across sectors. Target output Q is thus a negative function of unit intermediate cost (since the marginal product of mobile labor is valued after deducting the intermediate costs).

13 This system is similar to a "tariff drawback" scheme, where firms are partially exempted from tariffs when they export; in this case, however, firms are exempted at user-specific and variable rates that depend on the intensity of import rationing.

14 Except when the amount imported is too small, in which case (in order to avoid convergence problems) fixed proportions are used.

15 "Non-productive services", which are mainly public services, are not traded.

16 If the new surrender rate is s, the z_i are lowered to $\tilde{z}_i$ in order to have

0.46z_i = $(1 - s)\tilde{z}_i$ for all i; in this way the foreign exchange entitlement as a percentage of foreign exchange earnings remains unchanged.

17 In this second case, again with the new surrender rate s the $1 - z_i$ are lowered to $1 - \tilde{z}_i$ in order to have 0.46 $(1 - z_i) = (1 - s)(1 - \tilde{z}_i)$ for all i.

18 See section 5.3 for the sensitivity analysis.

19 Those sectors with the most severe import rationing and the highest retention rates, and thus with the highest initial premium rationing rates.

20 In scenario 3, ER = 0.54(1.0) + 0.46(1.53) = 1.2438, against ER = 1.36 in scenario 4.

References

Ahmed, S. A., A. Bhattacharya, W. Grais and B. Pleskovic (1985) "Macroeconomic Effects of Efficiency Pricing in the Public Sector in Egypt", Washington, DC: World Bank Staff Working Paper No. 726.

Armington, P. (1969) "A Theory of Demand for Products Distinguished by Place of Production", *IMF Staff Papers*, 16, 159–76.

Balassa, B. (1985) "Exports, Policy Choices and Economic Growth in Developing Countries after the 1973 Oil Shock", *Journal of Development Economics*, 18, 23–36.

Benassy, J. P. (1982) *The Economics of Market Disequilibrium*, New York: Academic Press.

Bhagwati, J. (1978) *Foreign Trade Regimes and Economic Development: Anatomy and Consequences of Exchange Control Regimes*, New York: National Bureau for Economic Research.

—— and T. N. Srinivasan (1975) *Foreign Trade Regimes and Economic Development: India*, New York: National Bureau for Economic Research.

Dervis, K., J. de Melo and S. Robinson (1982) *General Equilibrium Models for Development Policy*, Cambridge: Cambridge University Press.

Drud, A., W. Grais and G. Pyatt (1983) "The TV-approach: A Systematic Method of Defining Economywide Models Based on Social Accounting Matrices", in T. Basar and L. F. Pau (eds), *Dynamic Modeling and Control of National Economies*, New York: Pergamon.

Edwards, S. (1984) "The Order of Liberalization of the Balance of Payments: Should the Current Account be Opened Up First?" Washington, DC: World Bank Staff Working Paper No. 710.

Grais, W., J. de Melo and S. Urata (1986) "A General Equilibrium Estimation of the Effects of Reductions in Tariffs and Quantitative Restrictions in Turkey in 1978", in T. N. Srinivasan and J. Whalley (eds), *General Equilibrium Trade Policy Modeling*, Cambridge, MA: MIT Press.

Krueger, A. (1978) *Foreign Trade Regimes and Economic Development: Liberalization Attempts and Consequences*, New York: National Bureau for Economic Research.

Neary, J. P., and K. Roberts (1980) "The Theory of Household Behavior under Rationing", *European Economic Review*, 13, 25–42.

Powell, A., and F. Gruen (1968) "The Constant Elasticity of Transformation Production Frontier and the Linear Supply System", *International Economic Review*, 9, 315–28.

Robinson, S., and L. Tyson (1985) "Foreign Trade, Resource Allocation, and Structural Adjustment in Yugoslavia: 1976–1980", *Journal of Comparative Economics*, 9, 46–70.

——, —— and M. Dewatripont (1986) "Yugoslavia Economic Performance in the 1980s: Alternative Scenarios", in Joint Economic Committee, US Congress, *East European Economies: Slow Growth in the 1980s*, vol. 2, *Country Studies*, Washington, DC: US Government Printing Office.

8

A Decade of Applied General Equilibrium Modelling for Policy Work

Alan A. Powell and Tony Lawson

1 Introduction

This paper is mainly retrospective. Dale Jorgenson asked David Vincent and ourselves to cooperate in producing an account of the experience in applied general modelling of the Impact Project and its main sponsor, the (Australian) Industries Assistance Commission (IAC). Vincent's contribution to this meeting of the Task Force (chapter 9) gives a view from within the largest public sector user of the ORANI model (whose standard form is described by Dixon et al., 1982). He tells us how general equilibrium policy simulations affected the advice given by the Commission in a number of recent enquiries into tariffs and other industry assistance arrangements, and reports the light that the ORANI model has shed on Australia's most pressing macroeconomic problem of the mid-1980s, namely, the almost unprecedented collapse during 1985–6 in Australia's terms of trade.

In this paper we seek to complement his account with a discussion of the following issues.

1 What are the distinctive elements in Impact's experience which account for the Project's success in having CGE modelling used routinely in the policy-advising process?
2 What were the strategic design choices that affected the outcome?
3 What is the ideal composition of a team for carrying out CGE research with a policy focus?
4 How do institutional arrangements impinge on the above questions?

(Above, we use the convenient CGE abbreviation for "computable general equilibrium", which we do not distinguish in this paper from applied general equilibrium.) Before offering our thoughts on the above issues, we give a brief survey of the uses to which Impact's CGE models (ORANI, SNAPSHOT, and ORANI–MACRO) have been put, not only by Australian governments, Federal and State, but also by academic researchers. This survey is meant (a) to substantiate our claim that Impact's CGE models, especially ORANI, have received wide acceptance in Australia as the preferred method for policy analysis of intersectoral issues and (b) to illustrate the very wide range of issues amenable to such analysis. We hope that this descriptive material will whet the appetite for the nostrums which we then offer in answer to questions (1)–(4) above.

The balance of this paper is organized as follows. Our brief survey of applications appears next. Then follows a short section on the historical and institutional imperatives out of which the Project grew. The fourth section deals with strategic issues in model design (some of this material repeats earlier views put by one of us – see Powell, 1981). Aspects of project management are discussed in the fifth section, while in the sixth and final section we sum up, and prognosticate on what the future of policy modelling may hold.

2 A Synoptic Review of a Decade of Use of Impact Project Models

This section[1] updates earlier surveys by Dixon et al. (1982, section 50), Parmenter and Meagher (1985) and Powell (1985a).

Apart from the applications discussed in the sections below, the ORANI modelling project has generated a substantial stream of literature on the reliability of estimated CGE responses (Pagan and Shannon, 1985, 1987) and on the appropriate values of parameters (Cronin, 1985; IAC, 1984b; Powell, 1985b). A review of the entire project was made halfway through its first decade by Freebairn (1980).

Because of the Impact Project's policy of open access to its models, we cannot be aware of all the applications which have been developed, particularly in the government sector. Our coverage therefore has a bias towards model simulations that have been publicly reported. It includes not only the Impact models but the nine other applications of CGE models of Australia that are known to us.

The publicly documented policy studies are listed in table 8.1, while table 8.2 identifies unpublished applications of which we are aware. Not listed in either table are several recent (1986 and later) *forecasting* (as distinct from policy analytic) studies made with the ORANI model; e.g. Dixon (1986), Dixon, Johnson and Parmenter (1988),

Dixon and Parmenter (1986, 1987b) and Dixon, Parmenter and Horridge (1987).

One of the unusual features of the Impact Project has been its cross-institutional affiliations and the conscious decision to encourage as wide a use of the models as possible. To give more indication of this, in the discussion that follows, applications are considered in terms of six broad categories of users.

2.1 Applications by the impact team

The wide range of applications to which the ORANI model is amenable has been illustrated in numerous papers produced by the Impact team over the last decade. Three strands of activities can be identified:

1 analyses of the effects of particular economic shocks, with varying emphasis on industries, occupations and the macroeconomy;
2 examination of the robustness of these analyses to changes in the parameters, data and/or closure of the model;
3 the identification of policy options which, according to the model, would achieve important macroeconomic objectives (e.g. policies to increase employment without running into further trade balance or inflation problems).

The applications chosen by the modellers also identify some of the key economic issues perceived to have influenced the direction of the Australian economy over the last ten years; an idea of the scope of these issues is given by the subject headings of table 8.1.

The emphasis on protection reflects not only the strong institutional links between Impact and the IAC but also the importance that has been attached to this topic generally by applied economists in Australia. It should be noted that although these studies indicate the extent to which different groups win or lose from industry assistance, important efficiency gains from trade reform (e.g. via scale effects) are not captured except in recent exploratory work by Cory and Horridge (1985) and by Horridge (1987a, b).

2.2 Applications by the industries assistance commission

The use of CGE models by the IAC is covered in some depth in the review paper by David Vincent (chapter 9). In these remarks an attempt is made to give some idea of the breadth of applications of the ORANI model.

Table 8.1 Selective bibliography of Australian computable general equilibrium policy applications

Application	Policy simulations conducted by					
	Impact	IAC	Other federal agencies	State governments and regional modellers	Academics / graduate students	Private sector
A Effects of protection	Powell (1977, 1982)	IAC (1977)	Crowley and Martin (1982	Dixon, Parmenter and Sutton (1978b)	Evans (1972)[a]	Chai and Dixon (1985)
	Dixon et al. (1977)	IAC (1982b)	Crowley, O'Mara and Campbell (1983)	IAC (1981c)	Klijn (1974)[a]	Dixon, Parmenter and Rimmer (1985, 1986)
	Dixon, Parmenter and Sutton	IAC (1987a)	ABARE (1988)	Higgs, et al. (1981)	Meltzer (1980)	Higgs (1986b)
	Powell and Parmenter (1979)	IAC (1981c) (1977)		Madden, Challen and Hagger (1981)	Aislabie (1981, 1983, 1985)	
	Parmenter. Sams and Vincent (1981)	IAC (1987e)		Liew (1982)	Warr and Parmenter (1984)	
	Dixon et al. (1982)	Wright and Cowan (1980)		Dixon et al. (1982)	Parmenter and Meagher (1985)	
	Cooper (1983)			Parmenter (1983a)	Siriwardana (1985)[a]	
	Higgs, Parmenter and Powell (1984)			Higgs, Parmenter and Rimmer (1983)	Horridge, Parmenter and Warr (1987)	
	Dixon, Parmenter and Powell (1984)			Fraser and Salerian (1986)	Hepburn (1987)	
	Bruce (1895)			Brown and Camilleri (1986)		
	Cooper, McLaren and Powell (1985)					
	Horridge (1985, 1987a, b)					
	Higgs (1988b)					

Table 8.1 (cont.)

	Policy simulations conducted by					
Application	Impact	IAC	Other federal agencies	State government and regional modellers	Academics/graduate students	Private sector
B Exchange rates	Powell (1977) Dixon, Parmenter and Sutton (1977) Dixon, Parmenter and Powell (1982, 1983) Higgs (1987)	Fallon and Thompson (1987)		Hagger, Challen and Madden (1983)	Horne (1985)	Business Council of Australia (1985) Higgs (1986b)
C International trade (other)	Vincent (1980b)	IAC (1979)	Bateman (1984)		Warr and Lloyd (1983) Dixon and Johnson (1986)	Stoeckel and Cuthbertson (1987)
D Terms of trade	Dixon, Harrower and Powell (1977) Dixon, Parmenter and Sutton (1978a) Agrawal and Meagher (1987)	Vincent (chapter 9) Fallon and Thompson (1987) IAC (1981e)			Dixon and Parmenter (1987a)	Higgs (1986b) Higgs and Stoeckel (1987)

Table 8.1 (*cont.*)

	Policy simulations conducted by					
Application	Impact	IAC	Other federal agencies	State governments and regional modellers	Academics / graduate students	Private sector
E Supply shocks Oil	Vincent et al. (1979, 1980) Vincent (1980a)				Higgs (1981)	Cook and Porter (1984) Higgs (1986a, b)
Mining (resources boom)	Dixon, Harrower and Powell (1977) Dixon, Parmenter and Sutton (1978a) Powell and Parmenter (1979) Higgs, Parmenter and Powell (1984)		Stoeckel (1978, 1979)[a]	IAC (1981c) Madden, Challen and Hagger (1982) Fraser (1984, 1986a, b)		
Technical change	Dixon and Vincent (1980)[a] Rimmer (1984)		BIE (1981a)[a]	Madden and Challen (1983)		
Drought		Vincent (1983)	Campbell, Crowley and Demura (1983)			

Table 8.1 (*cont.*)

	Policy simulations conducted by					
Application	Impact	IAC	Other federal agencies	State governments and regional modellers	Academics/graduate students	Private sector
F Macroeconomic policy, especially expanding activity without inflation or trade balance problems	Dixon, Powell and Parmenter (1979) Parmenter (1983b) Dixon and Powell (1984)	IAC (1982c) Dee (1987a, 1989)		Bonnell, Parmenter and Rimmer (1985)	Norman (1981) Parmenter and Meagher (1985) Dixon, McDonald and Meagher (1984) Feltenstin (1986a, b)[a] Meagher and Parmenter (1987)	Higgs (1896b)
G Other employment and wage issues	Dixon, Parmenter and Sutton (1978a) Higgs, Parham and Parmenter (1981) Powell (1985c) Agrawal (1986)			Challen, Hagger and Madden (1983, 1984)	Corden and Dixon (1980) Bonnell, Chew and Dixon (1984) Bonnell et al. (1985) Piggott and Whalley (1986)[a] Bonnell (1987)	Dixon (1987b)
H Immigration			Norman and Meikle (1985)		Cook and Dixon (1982) Bonnell and Dixon (1982, 1983)	

Table 8.1 (*cont.*)

	Policy simulations conducted by						
Application	*Impact*	*IAC*	*Other federal agencies*	*State governments and regional modellers*	*Academics/ graduate students*	*Private sector*
I Government taxes, charges, expenditure and regulations	Cooper and McLaren (1983) Meagher and Agrawal (1986) Horridge (1987c) Agrawal and Meagher (1987) Agrawal, Meagher and Parsell (1987)	IAC (1986a, d) Dee (1987b)	BAE (1985)	Ministry of Economic Development, Vic. (1982) Madden, Challen and Hagger (1983) Burke (1983, 1984) Meagher et al. (1985) Meagher and Parmenter (1986) Parsell (1987) Fraser (1986b)	Castle and Guest (1980) Meagher (1983, 1986) Piggott (1983)[a] Parmenter and Meagher (1985) Chapman and Vincent (1985, 1986, 1987) Liew (1985) Meagher and Parmenter (1985) Blampied (1986) Sugden (1987)	Higgs (1986b)
J Industry studies Long-run prospects	Dixon, Harrower and Powell (1977)		BIE (1981b)[a] Fitzpatrick and McKeon (1982)[a]	Dixon (1987a) Johnson and Kee (1987)		

Table 8.1 (cont.)

Policy simulations conducted by:

Application	Impact	IAC	Other federal agencies	State governments and regional modellers	Academics/graduate students	Private sector
Agriculture	Vincent and Ryland (1981) Dixon, Parmenter and Powell (1982, 1983) Dixon et al. (1983) Higgs (1988a)	IAC (1983c, d) Vincent (1985) IAC (1988)	Crowley and Martin (1982) Quiggan and Stoeckel (1982) Campbell, Crowley and Demura (1983)	Fraser and Salerian (1987)	Dixon (1985a, b)	Parmenter (1985) Higgs (1986b)
Glass, glassware		IAC (1987d)				
Construction					Dixon (1987b)	
Fertilizers		IAC (1982a) IAC (1985a, b)	BAE (1984)			
Forestry, timber		IAC (1981b)		Madden and Hagger (1985)		Johnson (1985)
Mining				Fraser (1984, 1986a, b)		Higgs (1986a)
Food			PJT (1979)			
Textiles, clothing		IAC (1986b)				

Table 8.1 (*cont.*)

	Policy simulations conducted by					
Application	Impact	IAC	Other federal agencies	State governments and regional modellers	Academics/ graduate students	Private sector
Chemicals, plastics		IAC (1986c) Vincent (1986)				
Petroleum products		IAC (1986a, d) Mannion, Tillack and Vincent (1987)			Truong (1986) Hall, Truong and Nguyen (1987)	
Iron and steel	Rimmer (1984)					
Motor vehicles		IAC (1978) IAC (1981a) IAC (1984a)				
Transport			Lawson (1979)			
Tourism				Hagger, Madden and Challen (1984)		
Pulp, paper, printing		IAC (1987b)				
Defence			Bateman (1984) Liew (1985)			

[a]These citations do not refer to applictions of ORANI.

Nowadays the model is used for most major IAC inquiries in which interindustry or economy-wide effects may be important, e.g. chemicals and plastics (IAC, 1986c), glass and glassware (IAC, 1987d), iron and steel (IAC, 1983a, b), motor vehicles (IAC, 1978, 1981a), pulp, paper, paper products and printing (IAC, 1987b), textiles, clothing and footwear (IAC, 1986b), wheat (IAC, 1983c, 1988) and wood products (IAC, 1981b). In some instances partial equilibrium models with similar behavioural assumptions to the ORANI model are used; the results of these smaller models may in turn be used as an input to the ORANI model. An example of this is provided by the inquiry into heavy commercial vehicles (IAC, 1984a).

Acceptance of ORANI within the IAC was gradual. Initially there was scepticism, both about the model's ability to capture the likely effects of changes in assistance to an industry on the rest of the economy and about its ability to deal realistically with important specific features of the industry under review. The latter problem was largely overcome by the development of procedures to model such industries in greater detail while remaining within the ORANI framework (see chapter 9).

The model's treatment of interindustry and economy-wide effects was accepted more readily for agricultural-sector inquiries such as that into fertilizers (IAC, 1982a, 1985a, b). This readier acceptance reflects, in part, a consensus on the applicability of competitive theory to behaviour in agriculture, as well as the relatively strong detail on multiproduct agricultural industries built into the standard version of ORANI (Dixon et al., 1983).

The inquiry into the taxation of petroleum products (IAC, 1986a, d) represented an interesting development of the use of ORANI in the IAC. Taxes on petroleum products are a significant source of revenue to the Australian Government and are levied on intermediate usage and final consumption. The model was used to analyse the effects of these taxes on international competitiveness and resource allocation, taking into account the implications for the Government's net budgetary position, as well as the effects of tax exemptions on intermediate usage. These simulations required the addition of a large amount of fiscal detail to the ORANI mainframe. Recent developments in computer packages (Pearson, 1986, and numerous computer documents by Pearson and Codsi – see Powell, 1988, appendix 2) mean that such major modifications can now be handled on a routine basis.

ORANI has also been used for more general studies of the effects of protection and other economic factors on the Australian economy (IAC, 1977, 1979, 1982b, c, 1987e).

Table 8.2 Summary of unpublished applications carried out for Australian government agencies

Application	Client/date
Production of aircraft in Australia	Australian Government Aircraft Study Group, 1979; Hawker-Siddeley, 1983
Distortions inhibiting food processing	Bureau of Agricultural Economics (BAE), 1986
Costs to farmers of assistance to manufacturing	BAE, 1985; IAC submission to Technical Group on Farm Costs, Treasury, 1985
Expansion of mineral exports	BAE, 1981
Changes in world demands for meats	BAE, 1979, 1980
Deterioration in the balance of trade	BAE, 1986
Various shocks on the Australian economy	IAESR for the Bureau of Labour Market Research, 1985
Reductions in the cost of coastal shipping	Business Regulation Review Unit (BRRU), 1986
Costs of tighter safety regulations on manual handling	BRRU, 1987
Changes in the price of sugar	Department of Business and Consumer Affairs, 1979
Protection of textiles, clothing and footwear	Department of Industry, Technology and Commerce, 1986
Some costs of quarantine regulations	Quarantine Review Committee, 1988
Departmental review of policies	Department of Primary Industries and Energy (DOPIE), 1987
Effects of changes in funding of wool promotion	DOPIE, 1987
Oil price rises	Department of National Developmnet, 1978, 1979; Treasury (national wage case), 1980)
Disruption of oil supplies	Department of Resources and Energy, 1985
Assistance to agricultural industries	Submission by W. A. McKinnon, Chairman of the IAC, to the (Balderstone) Working Group on Agricultural Policy, 1982
Effects of assistance on migrants	Submission by W. B. Carmichael, Chairman of the IAC, to the Migrant and Multicultural Programs and Services, 1986
Payroll tax exemptions	Ministerial Task Force on Long Term Economic Growth, 1985
Increased road and rail freight charges	National Road Freight Industry Inquiry, 1984

Table 8.2 (*cont.*)

Application	Client/date
Price increases resulting from the devaluation of the Australian dollar	Treasury, 1985
Analysis of the effects of changes in industry assistance for the May 1988 Economic Statement	Treasury, 1988

2.3 Applications by other commonwealth agencies

Much of the use of Impact models by other federal agencies is unpublished or undocumented. Some agencies have used Impact training courses to develop the in-house expertise necessary to carry out their own applications. Most rely on the IAC (which has a formal responsibility to assist other federal agencies in this matter) to do the analysis for them. On occasions the Impact Research Centre or the Institute of Applied Economic and Social Research (IAESR) at the University of Melbourne are commissioned. The Canberra-based Centre for International Economics also extended the market for this kind of work in 1987. Several of the unpublished studies of which we know are listed in table 8.2.

These applications again demonstrate the diversity of uses to which the ORANI model has been put; but, more importantly, a glance at their dates indicates that this usage is growing. This reflects increased acceptance of the general equilibrium approach to policy analysis as well as the steady diffusion of staff with training in this field (gained in most cases at the IAC and/or Impact).

The major public sector user (other than the IAC) has been the Bureau of Agricultural Economics (BAE), which has a long-standing record in applied economic research and which at one time had a Director who built a CGE model for his doctoral thesis (Stoeckel, 1978). In 1987 the scope of the BAE was expanded to include resource economics, the new institution being known as the Australian Bureau of Agricultural and Resource Economics (ABARE). Several papers published by the Bureau's officers are listed in table 8.1. They have used ORANI to analyse the effects on agriculture of protection for manufacturers (Crowley and Martin, 1982; Crowley, O'Mara and Campbell, 1983; Quiggan and Stoeckel, 1982) as well as the general economic effects of a major continent-wide drought (Campbell, Crowley and Demura, 1983). They have also used results from ORANI in submissions to IAC inquiries (e.g. BAE, 1984) and to the Economic Planning Advisory Council (BAE, 1985). In 1987, ABARE undertook a major study designed to examine priorities for policies falling within the ambit of the Department of Primary Industries and Energy (ABARE, 1988). The ORANI model was used as a basis for analysing the intersectoral effects of changes in assistance to a wide range of industries. Other studies are in progress.

The Bureau of Transport Economics used ORANI to analyse the economy-wide effects of increased road and rail charges (Lawson, 1979), while the Bureau of Industry Economics (BIE) used Impact's SNAPSHOT model to explore the long-run implications for Australian industries of foreseen technical changes (BIE, 1981a, b; Fitzpatrick and McKeon, 1982).

In association with the Committee for Economic Development of Australia (CEDA), the Department of Immigration and Ethnic Affairs used the ORANI and BACHUROO models in a major study of the economics of immigration. The study included long-run simulations of the effects of immigration on industries (Norman and Meikle, 1985). The ORANI model has even been used to consider the strategic defence implications of disruptions to Australia's overseas trade (Bateman, 1984).

2.4 Applications by state governments and by regional modellers

The ORANI Regional Equations System (ORES) was developed by the Impact team (Dixon, Parmenter and Sutton, 1978b). This approach to regional disaggregation followed the "tops-down" procedure (as developed initially by Leontief et al., 1965). There was widespread interest in this development, presumably because nothing (other than unconstrained input–output) had previously been available to analyse the effects of national policies on the Australian states. Work for the Treasury of the New South Wales Government (Dixon, 1987a) used ORES to disaggregate, to the state level, medium-run forecasts for the Australian economy.

With state and Federal support, the Centre for Regional Economic Analysis (CREA) was set up at the University of Tasmania in 1980. It has used the ORANI–ORES model for much of its analysis. Topics analysed by Challen, Hagger and Madden of CREA include the impact on the Tasmanian economy of reductions in protection (Madden, Challen and Hagger, 1981), the devaluation of the Australian dollar (Hagger, Challen and Madden, 1983), the mining boom (Madden, Challen and Hagger, 1982) and a decline in tourism

(Hagger, Madden and Challen, 1984).

Regional modelling was enhanced by allowing explicitly for regional industries in the national ORANI model. These industries were located entirely in one region. The (consequential) improvement in the analyses is demonstrated in papers by Higgs et al. (1981) and Higgs, Parmenter and Rimmer (1983), who re-examined the regional effects of protection using this new method. The latter may be seen as a compromise between the "tops-down" approach of ORES and the extremely data-hungry "bottoms-up" approach (Liew, 1982, 1984). In Tasmania, CREA took up this new methodology with applications to the effects on the state economy of subsidizing employment (Challen, Hagger and Madden, 1983), of technological change (Madden and Challen, 1983) and of the export of woodchips (Madden and Hagger, 1985). This hybrid approach was also followed in IAC (1983d, 1987b). Current work in progress by Madden (1985, 1987) disaggregates the national economy into two major parts: the region of focus (Tasmania) and the rest of Australia. This extension of ORANI treats the two tiers of government, federal and state, in a fairly detailed way.

Regional modelling was taken up at the University of Western Australia in the mid-1980s; examples include papers by Fraser (1984, 1986a, b) on the effects on the state economy of the expansion of mining, and studies by Fraser and Salerian (1986, 1987) of the regional effects of protection and of the importance of agricultural exports to the state of Western Australia.

In association with the North Australia Research Unit of the Australian National University, the IAESR is currently modelling the economy of the Northern Territory (Bonnell, Parmenter and Rimmer, 1985; Parmenter and Meagher, 1987).

The Victorian State Government has used ORANI to study the effects on Victoria of changes in electricity pricing (Ministry of Economic Development, Victoria, 1982) and of changes to indirect taxes and to workers' compensation charges (Burke, 1983, 1984; Meagher and Parmenter, 1986), while the South Australian Government sponsored a study (Meagher et al., 1985) of proposed changes to taxation of the wine industry, which is an important activity in that state.

2.5 Applications by academics, including graduate students

Since its inception, the Impact Project has encouraged the involvement of Australian academic economists. Undergraduates, graduates and teaching staff have all made contributions to the theoretical framework, to parameterizing the models and to applying them to a large range of issues.

There are about 20 universities in Australia. Economists from at least 12 of them have contributed to or made use of the ORANI model. Although in part this reflects the mobility of academics associated with the original development of the model, it also reflects a wide recognition of its usefulness as a tool for applied economics, as well as the Project's policy of open access.

The first applications emanated from universities in Melbourne, where the Impact Project was being developed. Relative to the traditional effective rate concept, Meltzer (1980) demonstrated the superiority of a practical general equilibrium approach for explaining the resource allocative effects of protection, while Norman (1981) was able to use ORANI to attach some numbers to the famous Swan (1963) diagram of internal and external balance.

In the late 1970s and early 1980s, Peter Dixon led a strong team of applied general equilibrium modellers at La Trobe University, whose work was focused on the effects of structural change on different labour market groups (Bonnell and Dixon, 1982, 1983; Cook and Dixon, 1982) and on the effects of fiscal policies on industries (Meagher, 1983). This interest in fiscal issues had precedent in the work of Corden and Dixon (1980), who used ORANI to see whether a cut in hourly labour costs made possible by lower direct taxes could improve employment without creating budgetary problems for the Australian economy. More recently, Chapman and Vincent (1985, 1986, 1987) used the model to see whether the removal of payroll taxes could be beneficial.

Several undergraduates including Hepburn (1987), Higgs (1981) and Sugden (1987), have used ORANI for honours work. Respectively they studied the effect of variable tariff heights oil pricing policy, and the implications of moving to a broadly based consumption tax. Their respective universities were Melbourne, La Trobe and Macquarie. At the Australian National University another honours candidate (Hooi, 1983) evaluated the Impact Project's estimates (Alaouze, 1977; Alaouze, Marsden and Zeitsch, 1977) of the Armington (1969, 1970) elasticities used by ORANI.

The final strand of academic research which we shall mention examines various protective devices. Warr and Parmenter (1984) analysed government procurement policies, while Warr and Lloyd (1983) estimated the impact of Australia's trade policies upon less developed countries. A study of the effects of a 'Buy Australian' policy has been published recently (Horridge, Parmenter and Warr, 1987).

The IAESR is directed by Peter B. Dixon, who was Associate Director of the Impact Project until 1984. The Deputy Director of the IAESR is Brian R. Parmenter, a former Acting Director of Impact. Work at the IAESR over recent years has focused on the use of ORANI for short-run (Dixon, McDonald and Meagher, 1984) and long-run (Dixon, 1986, 1987a; Dixon and Parmenter, 1986, 1987b) forecasts and the analysis of taxation (Dixon, 1985a; Meagher and Parmenter, 1985). Currently work in association with the Impact team is extending the use of ORANI to analyse income distribution issues (Agrawal, 1986; Agrawal and Meagher, 1987; Agrawal, Meagher and Parsell, 1987; Meagher and Agrawal, 1986). A steady stream of papers analysing Australia's protection policy, international trade possibilities and the agricultural sector has also been produced (Dixon, 1985a, b; Dixon and Johnson, 1986). The focus of recent applied work has been strongly on the adjustment of the national economy to Australia's terms of trade (e.g. Dixon and Parmenter, 1987a). Because the IAESR, although an academic institution, is highly dependent on corporate sponsorship of research, its work also features prominently in the next section.

2.6 Private sector applications

The first users of the ORANI model in the private sector were various business organizations such as the National Farmers' Federation (NFF), the Confederation of Australian Industry and the Business Council of Australia (BCA). Use tended to be confined to the reporting of other applications rather than initiating new work. A recent example is the work by BCA (1985) which looked at estimates of the price effects of the devaluation of the Australian dollar generated by different models, including ORANI. A simplified version of ORANI was used by the Monash University Centre for Policy Studies for a report (sponsored by the Australian Mining Industry Council (AMIC)) on the quantitative impact of the minerals sector on the Australian economy (Cook and Porter, 1984).

In 1985 the NFF asked the IAESR at the University of Melbourne to carry out a study of the costs to farmers of protection of manufactures (Parmenter, 1985). ORANI-based analysis of the same issue was also undertaken by the IAC and the BAE, and the three studies were submitted to a Technical Group on Farm Costs established by the Australian Government (thankfully no large divergence of opinion emerged from the three studies!). The estimated magnitudes of the effect on farm costs were significantly lower than estimates based on the approach of Clements and Sjaastad (1983), which had provided the stimulus for the establishment of the Technical Group.

This is probably a portent of things to come. Increasingly we can expect a number of ORANI-based analyses of the same subject to be undertaken by different interest groups and submitted to government. If, owing to different closures, parameters or shocks, the results differ widely, CGE policy analysis will have come of age.

To date, the major work undertaken with a significant element of private sector sponsorship at the Impact Research Centre is the comprehensive study by Higgs (1986b) of adjustment pressures on the agricultural sector. This was supported, in part, by the Australian Wool Corporation. Subsequently Higgs (1986a) undertook a similar, but much briefer, analysis of the mining sector for the AMIC. Other sponsored work at Impact includes an analysis of the sensitivity of the results of tariff simulations to assumptions about Australia's export responsiveness (Dixon, Parmenter and Rimmer, 1985). However, the greatest impetus for future use of the ORANI model by the private sector is likely to come via the IAESR.

The IAESR's first CGE-based study to be sponsored by a company was an analysis of the short-term economic effects of environmental constraints on forest industries (Johnson, 1985). Work on the macroeconomic and sectoral consequences of shorter standard working hours in the construction and related industries was commissioned by the Master Builders' Federation of Australia (Dixon, 1987b). The major extensions of the ORANI model into medium-term forecasting (mentioned above) were sponsored by the Royal Bank of Canada (Dixon, 1986) and by AMIC (Dixon and Parmenter, 1987a, b). Most recently, the IAESR's forecasting facility has been put to use in a study of the prospects for industries to 1991–2 in the light of Australia's current trading difficulties – this work was commissioned by ESANDA Ltd (Dixon, Johnson and Parmenter, 1988). Developments at the IAESR and Impact on the use of CGE modelling in portfolio selection (e.g. Higgs, 1988b) seem likely to attract further private sector interest.

2.7 Evidence of successful transfer

One criterion for judging the success of an open-access policy information system is the extent to which the system has been used by professionals who were not intimately involved in its construction. On this basis, the ORANI suite of models has been exceptionally successful. Of the 177 distinct citations listed in table 8.1 and the 26 undocumented applications listed in table 8.3, all but nine were applications of Impact models, mostly of ORANI. In fact, of the 203 items listed in these two tables, 190 were applications of ORANI. If we define as the "model builders" the authors of the definitive

ORANI volume (Dixon et al., 1982), plus Powell (as director) and Dr R. Rimmer (who was heavily involved in producing ORANI code), then of these 190 applications of ORANI, 129 did not involve any model builder as an author. The user-friendliness of the GEM-PACK code with which ORANI is now implemented, moreover, will improve future accessibility.

3 Historical and Institutional Background

This record of intellectual enquiry into the general equilibrium effects of policies may be more than coincidentally related to the fact that Australia is (was?)[2] among the most highly protectionist countries in the world when it comes to manufacturing. Gough Whitlam, Australian Prime Minister in 1974, forcefully reminded Australian manufacturers of this fact (Rattigan, 1986, p. 216). This assertion is not just polemics – it can be verified objectively by asking (a) what Western country (other than New Zealand) has, for 30 years, completely failed to expand the share of international trade in its GDP and (b) in which other country of comparably small economic mass does international trade account for such a small share of economic activity. Table 8.3 offers some pertinent statistics.

Australian economists, and New Zealand and other economists resident in Australia, have contributed disproportionately to the theory of international trade. (Names springing readily to mind are Max Corden, Bob Gregory, Bharat Hazari, Murray Kemp, Peter Lloyd, Richard Manning, Ian McDougall, Albert Schweinberger, Pasquale Sgro, Richard Snape, Peter Warr and Alan Woodland.)

In other countries the IAC is being cited as an institutional model for informing government opinion, and the public, "of the consequences of government actions for specific industries" (e.g. Rivlin, 1984, cited by Gruen in the foreword to Rattigan, 1986). Finally, the success of the ORANI team led by Peter B. Dixon has given Australian work on the use of CGE models for the analysis of international trade a standing second to none. This work itself built on Evans's (1972) CGE model of protection in Australia, which was seen internationally as a major pioneering effort.

Have Australian economists become fascinated with international trade (a) because of or (b) in spite of the fact that Australia has so little of it?

We lack the expertise necessary to answer this riddle. What we can point to is the fact that Australia had *applied* the Stolper–Samuelson theorem (1941) to policy more than 30 years before it was *invented*! Almost from the earliest days of federation it was taken as an article

Alan A. Powell and Tony Lawson

Table 8.3 Comparative openness of the Australian economy to intenational trade

		Exports as a percentage of GDP		
Country	GDP[a] (1984)	Base year (1955)	Final year (1984)	Rate of growth (% per year)
Australia	173.8	16.6	13.7	−0.7
Austria	64.3	17.0	24.5	1.3
Belgium	78.1	30.8	66.2	2.7
Canada	336.7	15.5	26.8	1.9
France	489.9	10.1	19.9	2.4
Germany	613.2	14.2	28.0	2.4
Greece	33.5	7.6	14.4	2.2
Italy	348.4	7.7	21.1	3.5
Japan	1,157.5[b]	8.4	12.7[b]	1.5
Netherlands	122.5	34.3	53.6	1.6
New Zealand	23.3[b]	26.2	23.2[b]	−0.4
Norway	54.7	18.7	34.5	2.1
Spain	161.3	7.0[c]	14.6	3.1
Sweden	94.8	17.6	31.0	2.0
United Kingdom	425.5	15.6	22.1	1.2
United States	3,619.2	3.9	6.0	1.5

[a]Gross domestic product expressed in billions (i.e. 10^9) of US dollars.
[b]Data are for 1983.
[c]Data are for 1960.
Source: International Monetary Fund, *International Financial Statistics Yearbook*, 1985

of faith by an impressive majority of Australia's elected legislators that tariffs were friendly to labour (for more details, see Powell, 1982). No CGE analysis of which we are aware – including a cliometric study of the Colony of Victoria as it was in 1880 (Siriwardana, 1985) – supports this viewpoint. Living in this topsy-turvy world, Australian economists perhaps have felt the need to do battle on the tariff front to reassure themselves that they have not lost their grip on reality (which is exactly what they are accused of by the protectionists).

The circumstances of the reform of the Tariff Board in 1967 and the creation in 1973 of its successor, the IAC, followed by the Impact Project in 1975, have been documented by the Commission's exceptionally far-sighted and courageous first Chairman (Rattigan, 1986). That so distinguished a gathering as this Task Force would be interested in what we have to say, we see as fitting testimony to the service rendered to the theory and practice of economic policy by Alf Rattigan.

Rattigan and his chief of staff Bill Carmichael (subsequently Chairman of the IAC from 1985 to 1988) perceived that the fragmented approach to industry policy which had prevailed prior to 1967 had left a gaping hole in the principle of public accountability for government action. To a first approximation, sectoral policies in the short run are zero-sum games. Unfortunately, tariffs and other protective measures tend to be games with payoff matrices having many dimly perceived elements – especially those applicable to the losers. It is necessary for open, informed and honest government to make explicit the full payoff matrix, not just the gains to the principal winners. This much was clear to the leadership of the IAC when CGE modelling was in its infancy. Rattigan and Carmichael were aware that the economy had to be seen as a system – obviously decisions taken in one area (manpower or immigration) could make nonsense of those taken in another (tariffs) if the interconnectedness of the economy was ignored. In 1973 Rattigan asked one of us (Powell) to set up a policy information system which would allow sensible advice to be given on industry assistance in an economy-wide framework. At the same time he was taking steps to mobilize an integrated data base (Rattigan, 1986, pp. 192–3) and to recruit the necessary professional expertise in-house to make best use of the new facility.

4 Design Aspects

It will be clear that we, and the Impact Project, came into CGE analysis from the "muddy boots" arena, not the cloisters of Arrow–Debreu theory. Data and policy relevance have always been the imperative driving the work of the Project. This, and the use of a team approach, marked Impact apart from most comparable efforts other than Norway's multisectoral growth (MSG) modelling project pioneered by the late Leif Johansen (1960) (see Førsund et al., 1985, for an account of recent developments). Whilst not exactly a design feature, these emphases on (a) an integrated data base spanning the areas of interest to the IAC and the other participating government agencies in areas such as labour, immigration and housing, and (b) policy relevance *as seen by policy makers* had important consequences for the way in which we went about our work. So too did the attention we gave to (c) human capital formation – more than 100 participants passed through intensive "hands-on" residential training courses on the use of Impact models run by Impact over the period 1981–4 (Powell, 1985a, pp. 62–5), while many more have benefited from on-the-job training at the IAC and/or Impact, or from courses in the use of the ORANI model run by the IAC. Unlike Norway's MSG team, from the start it was our goal that the ORANI model be usable by as many policy analysts as possible. The recent initiation by Pearson (1986) of a research programme to develop flexible, portable, computer code for CGE analysts has already enabled researchers at several sites other than the Impact Centre to install and run ORANI on their own mainframes.

4.1 Strategic choices

A simplified flowchart tracing important design decisions taken early in the life of the Project is given in figure 8.1. We have already pointed out that the IAC's management believed that a comprehensive economy-wide analytical framework was essential to the proper function of the Commission. Economy-wide models then in use were later classified by Challen and Hagger (1979) as follows:

1 Keynes–Klein (KK) models, of which the work of Wharton Econometric Forecasting Associates (e.g. 1981) is a leading example;
2 Phillips–Bergstrom (PB) models, of which the continuous-time disequilibrium model of Bergstrom and Wymer (1976) is a leading example;
3 Walras–Johansen (WJ) models, which include all applied general equilibrium work – although Challen and Hagger made finer distinctions in a later version of their taxonomy (1983). Below we simply use the CGE label to describe this class.

The KK class was ruled out because the *ad hoc* approach to disaggregation usually employed within it was judged to be unsuitable for the analysis of intersectoral interactions. Even where formal input–output methods are used within a KK model, the smorgasbord approach towards the definition of other variables and towards the specification of other relationships tends to produce a model which is poorly integrated; moreover, the price behaviour generated by the simple input–output extension may lack credibility. The kinds of simulations required for analysis of compositional changes in the economy would clearly go beyond the purpose (macroeconomic policy analysis and forecasting) for which the KK class was constructed. The inability of these models to handle major compositional events was devastatingly revealed in the wake of the Organization of Petroleum Exporting Countries (OPEC) oil shocks of the 1970s.

　　The PB class of models is formulated in continuous time. Typically, such a model consists of a set of differential equations specifying the

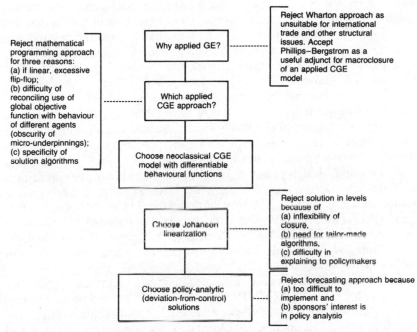

Figure 8.1 Simplified account of strategic choices in model design adopted by the Impact Project, 1975–1985

rates of adjustment of endogenous variables as functions of the gap between the current value of the variable and some equilibrium or target value; the latter are specified in auxiliary equations to be functions of exogenous variables (see Bergstrom and Wymer, 1976). Such an ambitious approach to dynamics seemed clearly to go beyond the data base which we could hope to mobilize; also, it had only been feasible with relatively small systems. (We did, nevertheless, find a way of capitalizing on the strengths of the PB approach (of which more later).)

The above discussion makes it seem that we adopted the CGE approach because that was all that was left. In fact we were attracted to CGE analysis by positive factors, especially by its very strict insistence on an exhaustive treatment of the interactions among industries, both on the demand and on the cost sides.

4.2 Which computable general equilibrium approach?

As of mid-1974 it is fair to characterize the state of applied general equilibrium analysis as follows: two schools were well established, and a third was in its infancy. The first of the established schools was Johansen's Norwegian group, whose adherents, except for Taylor and Black (1974), seemed to be confined to that group; the second was the mathematical programming/development planning school, which had many adherents (for typical work see Bruno, 1966; Evans, 1972; Goreux and Manne, 1973 and Sandee, 1960). The third, fledgling, school was differentiated from Johansen's group by a somewhat narrower interpretation of the notion of equilibrium, and by the habit of solving its models in the levels rather than in log differential form. Shoven and Whalley (1972, 1973, 1974), provide early examples of the work of this third (by now dominant) school.

In the initial design phase of 1975–6, the recruitment to the project of Peter B. Dixon was the decisive element. Dixon had built a prototype CGE model of Korea while at the International Monetary Fund (IMF); he joined Impact with the express purpose of continuing this type of modelling. It was clear that the major model which he had in mind would not deal with (a) monetary or financial markets or (b) labour supply.

To handle the latter it was decided to build an economic–demographic model BACHUROO, which was reported on at the first meeting of this Task Force (Powell, 1983).[3] Dixon recommended that we build two CGE models: SNAPSHOT for long-term analysis and ORANI for shorter-term work. The first of these belonged to the mathematical programming class, and the second to the Johansen class. SNAPSHOT was used as a consistency framework for checking the implications of foreseen technological changes (BIE, 1981a, b; Dixon and Vincent, 1980); for the same reasons as applied to Evans' earlier (1972) work, it did not lend itself to the analysis of international trade. In SNAPSHOT a perfectly substitutable import was available for each local product; this led to excessive "flip-flop".

ORANI's development proceeded in parallel with SNAPSHOT. The use of the Armington (1969, 1970) specification gave ORANI a much better chance of endogenizing imports realistically; moreover, we began to perceive that the latter model also could be used to produce "snapshots" of the economy in a relatively distant future year (ten or more years away, say); in due course this led to the abandonment of SNAPSHOT. An additional reason for not going on with SNAPSHOT was the realization that the solution algorithm would have to be redeveloped with every non-trivial extension of the model.

The account so far is at about the level of the second box from the top in figure 8.1. Basically, we resiled from the use of the mathematical programming approach for reasons (a) and (c) listed in the figure. A third reason for caution, which Peter Dixon emphasized from the beginning of the Project, is listed as (b) in figure 8.1: used incautiously, the programming approach can result in an economy-wide objective function being specified in a way which, whatever its merits from a normative economics standpoint, is not satisfactory from the viewpoint of positive economics. The problem is that the maximization of such a global function may not be consistent with plausible micro behaviour on the part of all agents. Thus SNAP-SHOT was *not* initially formulated as a mathematical program with a global objective function. Rather, each agent's behaviour was specified and this information was used to define an equilibrium for the system; to develop an efficient algorithm for the solution of the model we *then* made use of mathematical programming. While this is no more than following standard practice in general equilibrium analysis, such practice was not always followed by members of the development planning school.

4.3 Why Johansen?

The attractions of differentiable technological and behavioural functions caused us to arrive at the third box in figure 8.1. While discontinuities are undoubtedly present in the real world behaviour of individual agents, they are much less common in the observed behaviour of aggregates at the level at which we were working (about 100 industries and about ten occupations). We chose Johansen-style solutions for the three reasons listed in figure 8.1: (a) given the non-linear structural form of a typical neoclassical CGE model, moving between closures could become a major exercise, but for the policy work planned with ORANI, however, flexibility of closure was essential; (b) neoclassical CGE models solved in the levels, like their forerunners in the mathematical programming school, require tailor-made algorithms, and these would have to be redeveloped with each change of specification and/or closure of the model; and most importantly (c) Johansen-style solutions are *much* easier to explain to policy makers than are solutions in the levels; moreover, Johansen-style solutions decompose additively into effects which are specific to the individual component shocks.

To grasp point (c) it is not necessary to go beyond a comparison of the Johansen and the levels form of factor demand equations based on constant elasticity of substitution (CES) technology.

Johansen form

$$\begin{array}{l} \text{\% ch. in} \\ \text{lab dem} \end{array} = \begin{array}{l} \text{\% ch. in} \\ \text{output} \end{array} - \sigma \times \begin{array}{l} \text{(\% ch. in wage rate relative to cost of} \\ \text{primary factors in general)} \end{array}$$

$$(8.1)$$

Levels form

$$L = \frac{Y}{A}\left(\frac{\delta}{W}\right)^{\sigma} (\delta^{\sigma} W^{1-\sigma} + (1-\delta)^{\sigma} R^{1-\sigma})^{\sigma/(1-\sigma)} \qquad (8.2)$$

where Y and L are the amounts of output and labour, W and R respectively are the wage rate and the rental price of capital and A, δ and σ are parameters. To see the advantages of the additive decomposition of a Johansen solution, one need do no more than peruse the tables in chapter 9.

4.4 What sort of solution?

The final issue concerned the type of solution. The meaning of an "equilibrium" – which for the most part seems to be used as a synonym for "a solution to a CGE model" – has effectively been defined by what CGE modellers actually do. Some modellers have regarded only certain types of solution as valid objectives of CGE analysis – in particular, solutions in which supply and demand are equal for all commodities and all factors. Both Malinvaud (1973, pp. 5–8) and Hahn (1985, p. 3) regard this focus as too narrow. At Impact we have often utilized closures in which a price is exogenized and the corresponding excess demand endogenized. The leading case in point is the labour market, where (at least until the mid-1980s) extremely rigid real wages were an undisputed short-run feature of the actual Australian economy. The standard ORANI closure (Dixon et al., 1982, p. 143) involves an exogenously set real wage and the endogenization of employment.

There is another aspect of solution choice. Comparative statics can be intertemporal or contemporaneous. In each case, two solution points for the simulated economy are compared. In the intertemporal case, the points correspond to calendar dates – 1988 and 1990, say. The difference between the values of an endogenous variable at these two dates is then interpreted to be the result of different settings of the exogenous variables in 1988 and 1990. In the contemporaneous approach, however, we consider the difference between two 1990 solutions for the endogenous variable in question; this difference is attributed to a "shock" introduced into the values of the exogenous variables generating the initial 1990 solution. Elsewhere (Cooper, McLaren and Powell, 1985, p. 417) we have referred to such differences as contemporaneous differential comparative statics (CDCS) solutions. These are the analogues of "deviation-from-control" solutions in macrodynamics; they answer questions such as the following: relative to the values which they would otherwise have taken, by how much would output, employment and profitability in industries a, b, c, ... differ in about two years' time as a consequence of a planned increase of z per cent in the tariff on product x? Differentials of the sort defined by questions framed in this way define the field of policy analysis. Forecasting is much more ambitious; it requires estimation not only of deviations from control but also of a control path which depicts the future course of events as accurately as possible. The reasons for eschewing forecasting (as listed in figure 4.1) were (a) the sheer difficulty of assembling believable scenarios on the very large number of exogenous variables driving ORANI (see Powell, 1981, pp. 231–2) and (b) the desirability of keeping the questions, and answers, focused sharply on the policy shock. To these we would add (c): it is better to attempt to crawl before entering an Olympic marathon. (In fact, contemporary developments with the ORANI model include its extension to forecasting; the first such application is reported by Dixon (1986); see sections 2.5 and 2.6.)

4.5 Macroeconomic closure

The account so far has abstracted from two important aspects: (a) macroeconomic closure and (b) long-run versus short-run closure. It has been clear at least since the work of Patinkin (1965) that it is not valid to visualize the economy as being dichotomized into two blocks, in the first of which are determined all real magnitudes and all relative prices and in the second of which are endogenized only money demand and the price level. The problem is that the determination of all real magnitudes (at levels where excess demands are zero) by relative prices alone is sufficient to ensure equilibrium in the money market (the excess demand for money is just the excess supply of goods (by Walras's law), while the supply of money is exogenous). Thus no scope exists for a separate role for a purely monetary market; in particular, such a market in isolation could not determine the absolute price level (for a fuller discussion, see Adams, 1988). The Impact paradigm as originally formulated (Powell and Lawson, 1975) did postulate the separability of the economy into a "macro" block and a "micro" block; while no monetary or financial variables appeared in the latter, real variables (in particular, aggregate consumption and investment) did appear in the former. This formulation was developed because ORANI, as originally conceived by Peter Dixon, lacked equations sufficient to endogenize aggregate consumption C, aggregate investment I and the price level P in most policy-relevant closures of the model. For short-run analysis, a model based on macroeconomic ideas could be used to endogenize C and I and thus to drive the microeconomy. Hence this approach made provisions for the possible non-neutrality of money in the short run, while insisting that the *disaggregation* of the real economy was faithful to Walrasian ideas.

ORANI's lack of macroclosure meant that policy analysts routinely would have to set exogenously:

(i)   one of the price level or the exchange rate (as numeraire),

(ii) one of the real wage or the aggregate level of employment,

(iii) one of real absorption $(C + I + G)$ or the balance of trade surplus $(X - M)$. (Cooper, McLaren and Powell, 1985, p. 415)

This selection is referred to as the analyst's choice of a "macroeconomic environment" under which to conduct his policy simulations.

Contemporaneous with our work was the development by Peter Jonson and co-workers at the Reserve Bank of Australia of a small PB model concentrating heavily on monetary and financial variables, endogenizing about a dozen of these, plus C, I and P, and not much else. We borrowed the Bank's model (Jonson and Trevor, 1981), modified it slightly, and dubbed the resulting model MACRO (Cooper, 1983, p. 28). The aim was to use MACRO to provide ORANI with a short-run macroeconomic closure. As far as we are aware, nobody had previously attempted to interface a macrodynamic model with a comparative static one. This presented a major theoretical challenge which was solved in a series of papers by Cooper and McLaren which are summarized by Cooper, McLaren and Powell (1985).

The problem was attacked as follows. ORANI contains aggregate variables which appear in MACRO.

> These variables are measured quarterly and track the observed real world data with reasonable precision (using this term in the context of macrodynamic modelling). The behaviour of these variables in MACRO . . . sets the standard for empirical validation. A method for interfacing ORANI and MACRO is then devised which is conditional on the (as yet) unknown length of the ORANI short run. It is required that those variables which are endogenous to both models should have values, in the interfaced system, which are in agreement at the unknown lag equal to the ORANI short run. The latter is then found as the period of time elapsing between the injection of a shock in government spending and the achievement of such consistency in the double endogeneities (*i.e.*, variables endogenous to both models; namely, output, the domestic price level, employment

and imports). The period so estimated is 7.9 quarters (Cooper, 1983). (Powell, 1985b, p. 50)

Basically, this method allows equations from a dynamic continuous-time model to be transformed so as to permit them to be added to a comparative static model such as ORANI; the augmented model can be solved in the usual Johansen form.

Empirical results with the interfaced ORANI–MACRO system confirmed that ignoring possible macroeconomic feedbacks from tariff shocks introduced only second-order errors; i.e. solving ORANI in stand-alone mode with an exogenous macroeconomic environment would give a good approximation to the results obtained from ORANI–MACRO. Thus for most policy work involving sectoral shocks, macroeconomic closure is not a major issue. Nevertheless, given the macroeconomic difficulties facing the Australian Government, fiscal issues are now so prominent that a further approach to macroeconomic closure has been developed at the Melbourne IAESR. Although its use is much wider than just trade-related issues, this approach takes explicit account of the differences in tax revenues caused by a sectoral shock such as a change in one or more tariffs (Meagher and Parmenter, 1985). A standard closure of ORANI with this extension (known as the NAGA module) allows exogenization of the public sector borrowing requirement (rather than absorption).

4.6 Long-run versus short-run closure

The most frequently used closure of ORANI is described in full as "the neoclassical short-run with slack labour markets" (or more briefly just as the "standard short-run closure"). The term "slack labour markets" indicates the assumption, alluded to in section 4.4, that real wages are rigid, labour of all types is in excess supply, and as a consequence that employment is demand determined. Industry-specific capital stocks are taken as exogenous; the adjustment period must be short enough that any new capacity coming on stream as a result of the shock can be ignored but long enough to allow firms to attain new cost-minimizing compositions of variable inputs. Investment demand responds to the shock, but the new capital created is assumed not to come into production until the period following the solution period.

With industry-specific capital stocks set exogenously, their rental prices, and rates of return, are endogenized in ORANI's short-run closure; in long-run closures, these roles are reversed. Thus Australia is seen as a "small country" in the world capital market.

Politics being what it is (especially in a country where the electoral cycle never exceeds three years), the short-run closure was clearly the one relating most closely to the policy clients' self-perceived needs. This is why the short-run closure was developed first (in 1975). However, as explained in section 4.2, there was also an interest from the beginning in the long-run consequences of tariff and other policies.

Dixon (1978) had demonstrated early in the life of the Project that the existing class of CGE models, including ORANI, was not suitable for estimating the long-term costs of protection. In particular, however convenient from the viewpoint of generating an easily interpretable economic story, the assumption of globally constant returns to scale inevitably meant that some of the most costly consequences of protectionism would be overlooked. Logically prior to our attempting to develop a CGE model allowing for scale effects was the tidying-up of some aspects of ORANI's long-run macroeconomic closure. In particular, if a simulated shock injected in (say) 1980 resulted in a much larger aggregate capital stock in 1990, it would be necessary to know how this was achieved before we could understand the implications for the domestic economy. At one extreme, the growth in capacity might have been financed entirely by domestic savings; at the other, all this growth might have been financed by foreign capital inflow. The latter would have implications for payments to service rentals on capital – gross national product could well diverge substantially from gross domestic product.

To handle this problem within the CDCS framework requires that at least some primitive dynamics be specified to link the base period (e.g. 1980) with the year (e.g. 1990) for which CDCS solutions are computed – this much is required to allow the necessary stock–flow accounting to be done. A consistent procedure was developed on a prototype by Dixon, Parmenter and Rimmer (1984) and further explored by Horridge and Powell (1984), resulting in an operational method for use on the full ORANI model (Horridge, 1985). This long-run closure is now a part of the standard ORANI tool kit. It does not cope with scale economies, however. We shall return to this issue in section 6.

5 Management Aspects

We believe that Impact would have had much less chance of success if it had been attempted to run the Project

1 entirely within a university,

2 entirely within a government agency,
3 without full public documentation of data, methods and results,
4 entirely in the federal capital, Canberra,
5 without detailed involvement of the policy-making clientele in the design stages, or
6 at anything less than a full arm's length from executive government.

The Project (however financed) would not have prospered in a purely academic environment for two reasons. Firstly, academic proclivities in the choice (and approach to the solution) of problems are biased towards what is intellectually novel, irrespective of the scope for application. This bias is not irrational in terms of career strategy – papers showing an original turn of mind are much more likely to lead to academic promotion than papers whose immediate usefulness is obvious but which lack creative novelty. This emphasis on "pure research" may be socially justified since, if universities do not take the long view, it is unlikely that any other institutions will. Nevertheless we believe that current practices in the academic economics profession discourage many talented researchers from the painstaking kind of empirical research that is needed for policy modelling. This makes it harder to do credible CGE policy work in a purely academic setting.

Secondly, academics in the social sciences do not like to be directed. A researcher whose creative urges take him off at some interesting tangent does not respond well when it is pointed out to him that he is being paid to solve the original, not the tangential, problem. Again, there are good and bad aspects to this. On the plus side, he may have discovered something of major importance, such as a new line of attack on a difficult problem. On the negative side, a whole team may be seriously delayed while waiting for some crucial input from him.

At the other extreme, trying to run a major research effort within the strictures of a bureaucracy has problems. The first is how to ensure that the creative spark of young researchers is not killed when the many quality reports which they prepare never get beyond some official's desk. The second is bureaucrat's obsession with secrecy. This not only prevents the best young professional talent from striving for an excellence which, if achieved, would remain forever anonymous; it also prevents the work of an agency from receiving the kind of outside professional criticism and feedback which keeps its researchers on their toes. But against these drawbacks there are two enormous advantages: (a) civil servants, by and large, are willing to accept direction; and (b) the quality of data and relevance of empirical work *are* taken seriously.

To make the best of both worlds Impact had to create an environment in which public servants could work at their creative best. It was necessary, not only to ensure that the work of the Project was public, but to establish the custom of civil servants' publishing under their own names. There was some bureaucratic resistance to this at first; at least in the case of the IAC, however, a workable publications policy was established which resulted in many of the public servant members of the Project team making contributions which became widely quoted. (The most celebrated case is the 1982 ORANI volume, three of the co-authors of which were public servants at the time of the final draft.)

The academic connection was important for the following reasons.

1 The shortage of skilled manpower precluded the assembly in-house of a complete team.
2 It is doubtful whether career-line civil servants would have been able to insist that the quality of ideas should determine how the Project developed rather than the bureaucratic rank of the adherents to the ideas; involving academics in a leadership role gave this a much better chance of success.
3 Keeping a "shop front" open in the university sector gave immediate access to a new ideas under development in economic theory and econometrics; moreover, it made it easier to identify consultants (e.g. Russel J. Cooper, Keith R. McLaren) with the skills to solve analytically challenging problems.
4 A university affiliation enabled the Project to provide opportunities for, and to benefit from, graduate research training (the Project produced Ph.D. graduates and Masters graduates at the rate of about one in each category per year over the decade ending in 1985, as well as providing many less formal opportunities for research internships (for details see Powell, 1985a, pp. 42–8)).
5 The academic connection insisted on peer group assessment of the quality of the Project's work through attempts at refereed publication.

Quite apart from quality control through peer group assessment, full public documentation of data and methods was a precondition for acceptance (or for informed rejection!) of the Impact policy information system. Given the desire of many influential people, both inside and outside Government, that such work should not continue, it would otherwise have been relatively easy to discredit the Project by commissioning secret assessments claiming that the quality of the work was inferior. (In the early days of the Project, one of us (Powell) was shown (but not allowed to copy) such a secret report which was commissioned by a very senior bureaucrat with the express aim of terminating Impact on the grounds of incompetence. Fortunately, this move had been foreseen, and the Committee of Officials investigating the Project (see Rattigan, 1986, p. 270) also had in front of it the opinions of some world leaders in economic modelling.)

Canberra is a city in which the concerns seen by the Government as most pressing on a day-to-day basis dominate the ambience of the civil service. It is not a good environment for basic research by public servants on policy issues. This is well illustrated by the mistake we initially made of holding ORANI training courses in Canberra. Most of the (predominantly civil service) student participants would check their desks at 8:00 am before turning up for lectures at 9:00 am. If anything of significance had come up, their span of attention for economic analysis was reduced almost to zero; if they turned up at all at lectures, they would hurry back to the office at lunch time. In the evenings, when they were supposed to be doing homework, they would instead be burning the midnight oil in an attempt to complete office work. The location of the basic research and development group outside Canberra involved some logistic difficulties; however, such location away from day-to-day pressures in policy advising did allow a research ambience to develop.

The detailed involvement of clients in the design stage of model building is no more than common sense. It ensured that the models when completed could, and would, be used for policy analysis.

Keeping basic research and development at arm's length from executive government is another common-sense requirement. When political imperatives are allowed to override longer-term professional judgements on questions such as when a model is ready to produce credible policy simulations, the whole operation is put irreversibly at risk. Impact had two levels of insulation from the executive: firstly, the convening agency, the IAC, is an independent advisory body and not part of the executive; secondly, the Project was set up to provide tools and human capital development for policy advisers and not to provide the advice itself.

6 Conclusion and Perspective for Future Policy Modelling

At the beginning of this paper we posed four questions. We are now in a position to provide an answer to them in summary form. Briefly, then, to what do we attribute Impact's success in establishing CGE modelling in Australia as a practical policy tool?

First, both the sponsors and the researchers took data and empirical relevance to be of signal importance. Second, quality control was assured by very full documentation and an open style of management which invited critical feedback, not only from clients and protagonists in the policy debate but from other modellers. Third, a productive team was assembled by exploiting favourable complementarities between the academic and the civil service approaches to research. Fourth, the emphasis on Johansen solutions of the contemporaneous differential comparative statics type paid good dividends for three reasons: (a) because it focused discussion quite strongly on the policy shock under review; (b) because it allowed great flexibility in moving between closures of the model; (c) because it allowed computation of solutions on a routine basis; these were relatively inexpensive, from the viewpoints both of code development and of central processor time. Fifth, keeping the basic research group of the Project at a full arm's length from executive government was an essential ingredient; it is doubtful whether this could have been achieved without university involvement. Sixth, the clients were fully involved at the design stage. Seventh, Impact writers have put much effort into explaining, as non-technically as possible, the principal mechanisms responsible for the results obtained in particular policy simulations. In 1985, the Australian Prime Minister issued this challenge to economists:

> Effective communication is not merely informing people of the outcome of your analysis. It involves communicating an intuitive understanding of the reasons why such judgments should be supported. Success in this regard will ensure that modelling efforts, and the associated commitment of resources, are adequately rewarded in terms of their influence on policy development. (Address of welcome by the Rt. Hon. R. J. Hawke to the visiting Chinese members of the Bilateral Australia–China Working Party on the Role of Economic Modelling in National Economic Management, December 2, 1985)

Eighth, acceptance of the ORANI model was aided enormously by formal and informal training courses that enabled policy analysts to make independent hands-on use of the model. Finally, the Project was fortunate in the extreme to attract Peter B. Dixon to design and supervise the building of the ORANI model.

What do we expect the next decade of CGE modelling in Australia to hold? First, let us state that we are optimistic that the ORANI model and its derivatives will survive as a policy instrument, however uncomfortable that may be for some influential Australian figures of the political Left and of the Right. This is because the CGE approach is the only plausible calculus available for determining the consequences for different agents in the economy of the myriad of policy decisions which governments routinely take. As for methodological developments and the extension of Australian CGE work into new applications, we foresee[4]

1 a much more detailed disaggregation of taxes and of the fiscal system (along lines in ORANI pioneered by Meagher, 1986; Meagher and Parmenter, 1985; and Dee, 1987a, 1989),
2 the creation of many more special-purpose models, at the IAC and elsewhere, around the core of the ORANI model,
3 the development (mainly at the Melbourne IAESR) of a CGE model for forecasting (see Dixon, Johnson and Parmenter, 1988),
4 the development of a monetized CGE model (probably mainly at the Impact Research Centre) drawing on the work of Feltenstein (1986) and others (e.g. Dee, 1986; Vincent, 1985);
5 following Harris (1983, 1984), the development of a CGE model allowing for oligopolistic pricing and scale economies in some import-competing industries, perhaps along the lines of the Australian prototypes developed by Cory and Horridge (1985) and Horridge (1987a),
6 the progressive relaxation of many of the technological assumptions of standard ORANI to incorporate accumulating econometric knowledge on matters such as materials–materials substitution (see, for example, Truong, 1986),
7 the extension (mainly at the IAESR and the Impact Research Centre) of the ORANI framework in order to map from the functional to the personal distribution of income, and to allow a start to be made on the welfare analysis of a wide variety of policies (see Agrawal, Meagher and Parsell, 1987, for an early application),
8 increasing attention to the labour supply side of CGE modelling, with emphasis on incentives affecting labour market attachment (see Piggott and Whalley's, 1986, novel development, within a CGE model, of the consumption and labour/leisure decisions of a household with two working partners),
9 the development (at the IAESR, with New Zealand cooperation) of an Australia–New Zealand CGE model, which focuses on trade relations between the two countries,
10 the diffusion of flexible and portable computer code, currently under development at the Impact Research Centre (Pearson, 1986), for the solution of CGE models, and finally[5]
11 the incorporation of explicit intertemporal optimization by agents into Australian CGE models, particularly in the treatment of consumption and investment. This work might build on papers by Adams (forthcoming) (household consumption and portfolio be-

haviour), Cooper and McLaren (1986) (household consumption and labour supply) and Wilcoxen (1985a, b, 1987) (investment).

The institutional environment in which these developments take place will alter, partly as a consequence of (10) above, which will make it much easier for new applied CGE analysts to enter the field. This may not, in the beginning, be very advantageous, as relatively few Australian economists have an adequate training in CGE analysis. To the extent that they can do so within an educational system which is badly equipped to supply a high level of professionalism in economics, we would hope to see Australian universities attempting to rectify this.

Notes

1 This section has been updated since the Laxenburg Task Force meeting in August 1986; it now covers applications published before the end of 1987 and some work in progress at that time. Where the latter has subsequently been published, we cite the 1988 published version.
2 In May 1988 the Australian Government announced a program for the progressive reduction of most tariffs, by 1992, to 10 or 15 per cent *ad valorem*. The most highly protected sectors – namely motor vehicles, and textiles, clothing and footwear – were set respective goals, for 1992 and 1995 respectively, of 35 per cent and 45–55 per cent. Even though these two sectors account for a large part of the trade-destroying potential of the Australian tariff (see Dixon, Parmenter and Powell, 1984), the tariff reductions in the case of motor vehicles do consistute a considerable lowering of the overall level of protection.
3 For a description of the state of this model's development at the time when shrinking research resources caused planned refinements to be abandoned, see Sams and Williams (1983).
4 Since this paper was presented in August 1986, many of these forecasts have come to fruition.
5 Item (11) was added, with some benefit from hindsight, in July 1988.

References

Papers issued by the Impact Project may be obtained by writing to the Impact Project Information Officer, Mr Mike Kenderes, Industries Assistance Commission, PO Box 80, Belconnen, ACT 2616, Australia, who will supply a catalogue on request.

ABARE (Australian Bureau of Agricultural and Resource Economics) (1988) "Primary Industry Assistance in an Economy-wide Context", Canberra: ABARE, Discussion Paper No. 88.1.
Adams, P. D. (forthcoming) "The Extended Linear Expenditure System with Assets", *Economic Record*.

—— (1988) "Incorporating Financial Assets into ORANI – the Extended Walrasian Paradigm", Ph.D. Thesis, University of Melbourne, December, ch. 2.

Agrawal, N. (1986) "ORANI Income Distribution Model: Labour Market Issues", Impact Project Preliminary Working Paper No. IP-29, December.

—— and G. A. Meagher (1987) "Distributional Effects of Alternative Policy Responses to Australia's Terms of Trade Deterioration", Impact Project Preliminary Working Paper No. IP-31, August.

——, —— and B. F. Parsell (1987) "Analysing Options for Fiscal Reform in the Presence of Involuntary Unemployment", Impact Project General Paper No. G-81, December.

Aislabie, C. J. (1981) "The Sectoral Impact on Employment of Some Economic Policies: An Australian Case Study", *Metroeconomica*, 33, 175–91.

—— (1983) "The Australian Tariff as a Selective Employment Policy Instrument: An Empirical Study", *Australian Economic Papers*, 22 (40), June, 119–31.

—— (1985) "Subsidies as an Alternative to the Australian Tariff", *Applied Economics*, 17 (4), August, 589–601.

Alaouze, C. M. (1977) "Estimates of the Elasticity of Substitution between Imported and Domestically Produced Goods Classified at the Input–Output Level of Aggregation", Impact Project Working Paper No. 0–13, October.

——, J. S. Marsden and J. Zeitsch (1977) "Estimates of the Elasticity of Substitution between Imported and Domestically Produced Commodities at the Four-digit ASIC Level", Impact Project Working Paper No. 0–11, July.

Armington, Paul, S. (1969) "The Geographic Pattern of Trade and the Effects of Price Changes", *IMF Staff Papers*, 16, July, 176–99.

—— (1970) "Adjustment of Trade Balances: Some Experiments with a Model of Trade Among Many Countries", *IMF Staff Papers*, 17, November, 488–523.

BAE (Bureau of Agricultural Economics) (1984) *Assistance for the Consumption and Production of Fertilisers*, Submission to the Industries Assistance Commission, Canberra: Australian Government Publishing Service.

—— (1985) *The Implications of Taxation Reform for the Rural Sector*, Submission to the Economic Planning Advisory Council, Canberra: Australian Government Publishing Service, May.

Bateman, W. S. G. (1984) *Australia's Overseas Trade: Strategic Considerations*, Canberra: Strategic and Defence Studies Centre.

Bergstrom, A. R., and C. R. Wymer (1976) "A Model of Disequilibrium Neoclassical Growth and its Application to the United Kingdom", in A. R. Bergstrom (ed.), *Statistical Inference in Continuous Time Econometric Models*, Amsterdam: North-Holland.

BIE (Bureau of Industry Economics) (1981a) "The Long Run Impact of Technological Changes on the Structure of Australian Industry to 1990–91", Canberra: Australian Government Publishing Service, Research Report No. 7.

—— (1981b) "The Structure of Australian Industry – Past Developments and Future Trends", Canberra: Australian Government Publishing Service, Research Report No. 8.

Blampied, C. W. (1986) "Telecom Australia: Cross-subsidies and Taxes", Impact Project General Paper No. G-64, January.

Bonnell, S. M. (1987) "The Effect of Equal Pay for Females on the Composition of Employment in Australia", *Economic Record*, 63 (183), December, 340–51.

——, T. C. Chew and P. B. Dixon (1984) "Measuring the Impact of Structural Change on Groups in the Australian Labour Market", in G. Steinmann (ed.), *Economic Consequences of Population Change in Industrialized Countries*, Berlin: Springer-Verlag, pp. 343–59.

—— and P. B. Dixon (1982) "The Impact of Structural Change on the Employment of Migrants in Australia during the Seventies", in D. Dixon (ed.), *The Economics of Australian Immigration*, Sydney: Sydney University, pp. 13–20.

—— and —— (1983) "A Measure of the Incidence of the Costs of Structural Change: the Experience of Birthplace Groups in the Australian Labour Force during the Seventies", *Economic Record*, 59 (167), December, 398–406.

——, B. R. Parmenter and R. J. Rimmer (1985) "Macroeconomic Policy and Employment in the Northern Territory", in D. Wade-Marshall and P. Loveday (eds), *Employment and Unemployment*, Darwin: Northern Australia Research Unit.

——, ——, —— and M. E. Scorgie (1985) "Modelling the Effects of Changes in Junior Wage Rates on Teenage Unemployment: How Far Can We Go with Available Data?", in P. A. Volker (ed.), *The Structure and Duration of Unemployment*, Canberra: Australian Government Publishing Service, pp. 91–103.

Brown, N., and A. Camilleri (1986) "Regional Impact of Industry Assistance", Canberra: Australian Government Publishing Service, Economic Planning Advisory Council, Council Paper No. 20, June.

Bruce, Ian A. (1985) "The Sensitivity of ORANI 78 Projections to the Database Used", Impact Project Preliminary Working Paper No. OP-53, July.

Bruno, Michael (1966) "A Programming Model for Israel", in I. Adelman and E. Thorbecke (eds), *The Theory and Design of Economic Development*, Baltimore, MD: Johns Hopkins University Press, ch. 12, pp. 327–52.

Burke, R. H. (1983) "The Short-run Economic Impact of Changes in Levels of Indirect Taxes for Victoria", mimeo, Melbourne, Department of Industry, Commerce and Technology, Victoria.

—— (1984) "The Short-run Economic Impact of Workers' Compensation in Victoria – An Application of the ORANI 78 Model", supporting paper No. 1 (revised) to Department of Industry, Commerce and Technology, Victoria, Submission to the Committee of Enquiry into the Victorian Workers' Compensation System 1983–84, Melbourne.

Business Council of Australia (1985) "Devaluation, Inflation and Wages", *Business Council Bulletin* 17, September, 14–24.

Campbell, R., P. Crowley and P. Demura (1983) "Impact of Drought on National Income and Employment", *Quarterly Review of the Rural Economy*, 5 (3), August, 254–7.

Castle, R. G., and J. F. Guest (1980) "The Effects of Reductions in Government Expenditure on the Private Sector: Input–Output Analysis for

Australia", paper presented at the 50th ANZAAS Congress, Adelaide.

Chai, S. S., and P. B. Dixon (1985) "Protection in Australia – A Description", University of Melbourne, Institute of Applied Economic and Social Research, Working Paper No. 8/1985, September.

Challen, D. W., and A. J. Hagger (1979) "Economy-wide Modelling with Special Reference to Australia", paper presented to the Eighth Conference of Economists, La Trobe University, August; available from Department of Economics, University of Tasmania, Hobart, Tasmania 7000, Australia.

—— and —— (1983) "Macroeconometric Models: A Taxonomy", *Australian Economic Review*, Third Quarter, 26–33.

——, —— and J. R. Madden (1983) "Cost Subsidisation and Unemployment in Tasmania", University of Tasmania, Centre for Regional Economic Analysis, Paper No. RS-05, October.

——, —— and —— (1984) "Unemployment Policy – Packages for Tasmania", University of Tasmania, Centre for Regional Economic Analysis, Paper No. RS-06, January.

Chapman, R., and D. P. Vincent (1985) "Payroll Taxes: An Investigation of the Macroeconomic and Industry-Level Effects of Their Removal", Kensington, NSW: University of New South Wales, School of Economics, Working Paper No. 75.

—— and —— (1986) "Payroll Taxes in Australia, Part I: Background and Theoretical Analysis", *Economic Analysis and Policy*, 16 (2), September, 121–35.

—— and —— (1987) "Payroll Taxes in Australia, Part II: An Economy-wide Approach to Estimating the Effects of Their Removal", *Economic Analysis and Policy*, 17 (2), September, 149–77.

Clements, K. W., and L. A. Sjaastad (1983) "How Protection Taxes Exporters", mimeo, Department of Economics, University of Western Australia.

Cook, L. H., and P. B. Dixon (1982) "Prospects for Migrants in the Australian Workforce", *Australian Economic Papers*, 21 (38), June, 69–84.

—— and M. G. Porter (eds) (1984) *The Mineral Sector and the Australian Economy*, Sydney: George Allen and Unwin.

Cooper, R. J. (1983) "A Tariff Experiment on the Interfaced ORANI–MACRO System", Impact Project Preliminary Working Paper No. IP-18, April.

—— and K. R. McLaren (1983) "The ORANI–MACRO Interface: An Illustrative Exposition", *Economic Record*, 59 (165), June, 166–79.

—— and —— (1986) "A Generalized Intertemporal Model of Commodity Demands and Labour Supply", Impact Project Preliminary Working Paper No. IP-26, February.

——, —— and A. A. Powell (1985) "Short-run Macroeconomic Closure in Applied General Equilibrium Modelling: Experience from ORANI and Agenda for Further Research", in J. Piggott and J. Whalley (eds), *New Developments in Applied General Equilibrium Analysis*, New York: Cambridge University Press, pp. 411–40.

Corden, W. M., and P. B. Dixon (1980) "A Tax-Wage Bargain in Australia: Is a Free Lunch Possible?", *Economic Record*, 56 (154), September, 209–21.

Cory, P., and M. Horridge (1985) "A Harris-style Miniature Version of

ORANI", Impact Project Preliminary Working Paper No. OP-54, June.

Cronin, M. R. (1985) "The ORANI Model in Short Run Mode: Theory Versus Observation", *Australian Economic Papers*, 24 (44), June, 24–36.

Crowley, P. T., and G. Martin (1982) "Manufacturing Industry Assistance and the Rural Sector", *Quarterly Review of the Rural Economy*, 4 (4), November, 288–94.

——, L. P. O'Mara and R. Campbell (1983) "Import Quotas, Resource Development and Intersectoral Adjustment", *Australian Economic Papers*, 22 (41), December, 384–410.

Dee, P. S. (1986) *Financial Markets and Economic Development*, Tübingen; J. C. B. Mohr (Paul Siebeck), Kieler Studien 198.

—— (1987a) "The Theoretical Structure of Fiscal ORANI", Research Memorandum, Industries Assistance Commission, Canberra. First issued May 1986; revised April.

—— (1987b) "The Effects of Government Size on Economic Performance: A Quantitative Assessment of the Balanced Budget Multiplier", paper presented to the 16th Conference of Economists, Surfers' Paradise, Queensland, August 23–7.

—— (1989) "FH–ORANI: A Fiscal ORANI With Horridge Extension", Impact Project Preliminary Working Paper No. OP-66, March.

Dixon, P. B. (1978) "Economies of Scale, Commodity Disaggregation and the Costs of Protection", *Australian Economic Papers*, 17 (30), June, 63–80.

—— (1985a) "Taxation and Farm Costs: Indirect Taxes and the Farmer", in *Proceedings – Agricultural Costs Conference*, Perth: Rural and Allied Industries Council, April, pp. 53–65.

—— (1985b) "Agriculture in the Australian Economy, Unlocking Farm Potential", University of Melbourne, Institute of Applied Economic and Social Research, Working Paper No. 3/1985, May.

—— (1986) "Prospects for Australian Industries and Occupations, 1985 to 1990", *Australian Economic Review*, First Quarter, 3–28.

—— (1987a) "Medium-run Forecasts for the State Economies Using the ORANI Model", University of Melbourne, Institute of Applied Economic and Social Research, Working Paper No. 5/1987, July.

—— (1987b) "The Effects on the Australian Economy of Shorter Standard Working Hours in Construction and Related Industries", *Australian Bulletin of Labour*, 13 (4), September, 264–89.

——, J. D. Harrower and A. A. Powell (1977) "Long Term Structural Pressures on Industries and the Labour Market", *Australian Bulletin of Labour*, 3 (3), June, 5–44.

—— and D. Johnson (1986) "Competitiveness Indices and Trade Performance", *Australian Bulletin of Labour*, 12 (3), June, 154–72.

——, —— and B. R. Parmenter (1988) "Medium-run Forecasts for the Australian Economy using a Computable General Equilibrium Model". University of Melbourne, Institute of Applied Economic and Social Research Working Paper No. 4/1988, March.

——, D. McDonald and G. A. Meagher (1984) "Prospects for the Australian Economy, 1983–84 and 1984–85", *Australian Economic Review*, Second Quarter, 3–25.

—— and B. R. Parmenter (1986) "Medium-run Forecasts for the Australian

Economy Using the ORANI Model", mimeo, paper presented at the Third IIASA Task Force Meeting on Applied General Equilibrium Modelling, Laxenburg, Austria, August 25–9; available from the author at the Institute for Applied Economic and Social Research, University of Melbourne, Parkville, Victoria 3052, Australia.

—— and —— (1987a) "Foreign Debt Stabilization and the Terms of Trade: Implications for Australia, end-1984 to end-1990", in R. Fraser (ed.), *Paying the Banker: Facing Australia's Foreign Debt Problem*, Canberra: Australian Mining Industry Council, appendix 1, pp. 79–138, September.

—— and —— (1987b) "Recent Developments in Forecasting with the ORANI Model", University of Melbourne, Institute of Applied Economic and Social Research, Working Paper No. 8/1987, September.

——, —— and M. Horridge (1987) "Forecasting Versus Policy Analysis with the ORANI Model", in H. Motamen (ed.), *Economic Modelling in the OECD Countries*, London: Chapman and Hall, ch. 28, pp. 653–66.

——, —— and A. A. Powell (1982) "Farm Incomes in Australia and the Real Exchange Rate: ORANI Simulations with a Back-of-the-Envelope Explanation", Impact Project General Paper No. G-38, September.

——, —— and —— (1983) "Farm Incomes and the Real Exchange Rate in Australia: Evidence from the ORANI Model", *Journal of the Australian Institute of Agricultural Science*, 49 (4), 203–6.

——, —— and —— (1984) "Trade Liberalization and Labour Market Disruption", *Journal of Policy Modeling*, 6 (4), November, 431–54.

——, ——, —— and D. P. Vincent (1983) "The Agricultural Sector of ORANI 78: Theory, Data and Application", in A. C. Kelley, W. G. Sanderson and J. G. Williamson (eds), *Modeling Growing Economies in Equilibrium and Disequilibrium*, Proceedings of an IIASA Meeting, November 1980, Durham, NC: Duke Press Policy Studies, pp. 237–74.

——, —— and R. J. Rimmer (1984) "Extending the ORANI Model of the Australian Economy: Adding Foreign Investment to a Miniature Version", in H. E. Scarf and J. B. Shoven (eds), *Applied General Equilibrium Analysis*, New York: Cambridge University Press, ch. 12, pp. 485–533

——, —— and —— (1985) "The Sensitivity of ORANI Projections of the Short Run Effects of Increases in Protection to Variations in the Values Adopted for Export Demand Elasticities", in K Ingenfelt and D. Hague (eds), *Structural Adjustment in Developed Open Economies*, London: Macmillan, pp. 411–7.

——, —— and —— (1986) "ORANI Projections of the Short-run Effects of a 50 Per Cent Across-the-board Cut in Protection Using Alternative Data Bases", in T. N. Srinivasan and J. Whalley (eds), *General Equilibrium Trade Policy Modeling*, Cambridge, MA: MIT Press, pp. 33–60.

——, ——, G. J. Ryland and J. Sutton (1977) *ORANI, A General Equilibrium Model of the Australian Economy: Current Specification and Illustrations of Use for Policy Analysis*, Canberra: Australian Government Publishing Service (out of print).

——, —— and J. Sutton (1977) "Industry Implications of International Trade Policy: Experiments with the ORANI Model", Impact Project General Paper No. G-06, September.

——, —— and —— (1978a) "Some Causes of Structural Maladjustment in the Australian Economy", *Economic Papers*, 57, January, 10–26.

——, —— and —— (1978b) "Spatial Disaggregation of ORANI Results: A Preliminary Analysis of the Impact of Protection at the State Level", *Economic Analysis and Policy*, 8 (1), March, 35–86.

——, ——, —— and D. P. Vincent (1982) *ORANI: A Multisectoral Model of the Australian Economy*, Amsterdam: North-Holland.

—— and A. A. Powell (1984) "Researching a Non-experimental System: the Impact Models of the Australian Economy", *Australian Quarterly*, 56 (4), Summer, 374–86.

——, —— and B. R. Parmenter (1979) *Structural Adaptation in an Ailing Macroeconomy*, Melbourne: Melbourne University Press.

—— and D. P. Vincent (1980) "Some Economic Implications of Technical Change in Australia to 1990–91: An Illustrative Application of the SNAPSHOT Model", *Economic Record*, 56 (155), December, 347–61.

Evans, H. D. (1972) *A General Equilibrium Analysis of Protection: the Effects of Protection in Australia*, Amsterdam: North-Holland.

Fallon, J., and L. Thompson (1987) "An Analysis of the Effects of Recent Changes in the Exchange Rate and the Terms of Trade on the Level and Composition of Economic Activity", *Australian Economic Review*, Second Quarter, 24–36.

Feltenstein, A. (1986a) "Financial Crowding Out: Theory with an Application to Australia", *IMF Staff Papers*, 33 (1), March, 60–89.

—— (1986b) "An Intertemporal General Equilibrium Analysis of Financial Crowding Out: A Policy Model and an Application to Australia", *Journal of Public Economics*, 31, 79–104.

Fitzpatrick, M. D., and R. McKeon (1982) "Patterns of Production in the 1980s", mimeo, paper presented to 52nd ANZAAS Congress, Brisbane, May.

Førsund, F. M., M. Hoel and S. Longva (eds) (1985) *Production, Multisectoral Growth and Planning*, Amsterdam: North-Holland.

Fraser, R. W. (1984) "Individual Industry Developments in Mining and Mining-Related Areas and Their Impact on the W. A. Economy", *Economic Acitivity* 27 (1), January, 1–11.

—— (1986a) "Three Views of the Contribution of the Extractive Industries to the Western Australian Economy", *Resources Policy*, 12 (1), March, 47–61.

—— (1986b) "The Effects of Taxing Gold on the Western Australian Economy", Perth: Western Australian Gold Mining Policy Committee, Submission to the Federal Inquiry into the Taxation of Gold Mining, ch. 7, May.

—— and S. Salerian (1986) "Tariff Protection and the Western Australian Economy: An ORANI-ABS View", *Economic Activity*, 29 (3), July, 1–9.

—— and —— (1987) "Agricultural Exports and the Western Australian Economy", *Australian Journal of Agricultural Economics*, 31 (1), April, 74–82.

Freebairn, J. W. (1980) "The IMPACT Project: A Review", *Economic Record*, 56 (152), March, 17–35.

Goreux, L. M., and A. S. Manne (eds) (1973) *Multi-level Planning: Case Studies in Mexico*, Amsterdam: North-Holland.

Hagger, A. J., D. W. Challen and J. R. Madden (1983) "The 1983 Devaluation and the Australian Economy" (revised), University of Tasmania, Centre for Regional Economic Analysis, Paper No. RS-04, May.

——, J. R. Madden and D. W. Challen (1984) "Analysis of the Impact of a Recession in Tourism on the Tasmanian Economy", University of Tasmania, Centre for Regional Economic Analysis, Paper No. RS-07, April.

Hahn, F. (1984) *Equilibrium and Economics*, Oxford: Blackwell.

Hall, V. B., T. P. Truong and V. A. Nguyen (1987) "A Fuel Substitution Tax Model: ORANI–LFT", School of Economics, University of New South Wales and Department of Econometrics, University of Sydney, draft paper prepared for the Australasian Econometric Society Meeting, Christchurch, July.

Harris, R. (1983) (with D. Cox) *Trade, Industrial Policy and Canadian Manufacturing*, Toronto: Ontario Economic Council.

—— (1984) "Applied General Equilibrium Analysis of Small Open Economies with Scale Economies and Imperfect Competition", *American Economic Review*, 74 (5), December, 1016–31.

Hepburn, G. (1987) "Reducing Variability in Protection: A Simulation with the ORANI Model", essay submitted for assessment as part of the requirements of the B. Com. Honours year in the Department of Economics at the University of Melbourne.

Higgs, P. J. (1981) "The Short-run Effects on the Australian Economy of Alternative Oil-pricing Policies", Impact Project General Paper No. G-36, November.

—— (1986a) "Australian Mining and the Economy: A General Equilibrium Analysis", *Resources Policy*, 12 (2), June, 117–32.

—— (1986b) *Adaptation and Survival in Australian Agriculture – A Computable General Equilibrium Analysis of Economic Shocks Originating Outside the Domestic Agricultural Sector*, Melbourne: Oxford University Press.

—— (1987) "How Domestic Economic Conditions Influence the Real Exchange Rate", University of Melbourne, Impact Project General Paper No. G-79, September; also in *Review of Marketing and Agricultural Economics*, 56 (1), April 1988, 82–8.

—— (1988a) "Domestic Trade Distortions and Australian Agriculture", Impact Project General Paper No. G-83, April.

—— (1988b) "A Forward-looking Approach to Portfolio Analysis Using a Computable General Equilibrium Model", Impact Project Preliminary Working Paper No. IP-37, June.

——, D. Parham and B. R. Parmenter (1981) "Occupational Wage Relativities and Labour–Labour Substitution in the Australian Economy: Application of the ORANI Model", Impact Project Preliminary Working Paper No. OP-30, August.

——, B. R. Parmenter and A. A. Powell (1984) "The Scope for Tariff Reform Created by a Resources Boom: Simulations with the ORANI Model", *Australian Economic Papers*, 23 (42), June, 1–26.

——, —— and R. J. Rimmer (1983) "Modelling the Effects of Economy-wide Shocks on a State Economy in a Federal System", Impact Project Preliminary Working Paper No. OP-37, January.

——, ——, —— and L. Liew (1981) "Incorporating Regional Dimensions in Economy-wide Models: A Preliminary Report on a Tasmanian Version of ORANI", in R. E. Glass and K. B. O'Connor (eds), *Papers of the Australian and New Zealand Section of the Regional Science Association, 6th Meeting, August 1981*, Melbourne: Australian and New Zealand

Section of the Regional Science Association, pp. 217–40.

—— and A. Stoeckel (1987) "The Impact of a Range of Economic Policies on Australia's Balance of Trade", Impact Project General Paper No. G-80, September.

Hooi, N. O. (1983) "The Elasticity of Substitution between Imported and Domestically Produced Commodities: An Evaluation", Economics IV Honours sub-thesis, Australian National University.

Horne, J. (1985) "Sectoral and Macroeconomic Effects of Movements in Real Exchange Rates: The Case of Australia", mimeo, International Monetary Fund, Washington, DC.

Horridge, J. M. (1985) "Long-run Closure of ORANI: First Implementation", Impact Project Preliminary Working Paper No. OP-50, February.

—— (1987a) "The Longterm Costs of Protection: An Australian Computable General Equilibrium Model", Ph.D. Thesis, Department of Economics, University of Melbourne, April.

—— (1987b) "Increasing Returns to Scale and the Long Run Effects of a Tariff Reform", Impact Project Preliminary Working Paper No. OP-62, August.

—— (1987c) "The Long-run Costs of Tighter Safety Regulations", Impact Project Preliminary Working Paper No. OP-64, November.

——, B. R. Parmenter and P. G. Warr (1987) "Buying Australian", Economic Record, 63 (182), 231–46.

—— and A. A. Powell (1984) "Long-run Closure of ORANI: A Proposal", Impact Project Preliminary Working Paper No. OP-46, April.

IAC (Industries Assistance Commission) (1977) Structural Change and Economic Interdependence, Canberra: Australian Government Publishing Service, July.

—— (1978) Light Commercial and Four-wheel Drive Vehicles and Heavier Commercial Vehicles and Components, Canberra: Australian Government Publishing Service, Report No. 169, May.

—— (1979) Annual Report 1978–79, Canberra: Australian Government Publishing Service.

—— (1981a) Passenger Motor Vehicles and Components – Post 1984 Assistance Arrangements, Canberra: Australian Government Publishing Service, Report No. 267, June.

—— (1981b) Wood and Articles of Wood, Canberra: Australian Government Publishing Service, Report No. 275, August.

—— (1981c) The Regional Implications of Economic Change, Approaches to General Reductions in Protection, Discussion Paper No. 3, Canberra: Australian Government Publishing Service.

—— (1982a) Phosphatic and Nitrogenous Fertilisers, Canberra: Australian Government Publishing Service, Report No. 229, February.

—— (1982b) Approaches to General Reductions in Protection, Canberra: Australian Government Publishing Service, Report No. 301, March.

—— (1982c) Annual Report 1981–82, Canberra: Australian Government Publishing Service.

—— (1983a) Certain Iron and Steel Products (Interim Report), Canberra: Australian Government Publishing Service, Report No. 312, January.

—— (1983b) Certain Iron and Steel Products and Certain Alloy–Steel Products, Canberra: Australian Government Publishing Service, Report No. 321, May.

—— (1983c) *The Wheat Industry*, Canberra: Australian Government Publishing Service, Report No. 329, September.

—— (1983d) *The Dairy Industry*, Canberra: Australian Government Publishing Service, Report No. 333, November.

—— (1984a) *Heavy Commercial Vehicles, Parts and Accessories*, Canberra: Australian Government Publishing Service, Report No. 343, February.

—— (1984b) "The ORANI Trade Parameters: Papers and Proceedings of a Workshop, 14 April 1983", Impact Project General Paper No. G-58, September.

—— (1985a) *Interim Report on Fertilisers – Assistance for the Consumption of Fertilisers and Short Term Arrangements for the Production of Phosphatic Fertilisers*, Canberra: Australian Government Publishing Service, Report No. 360, March.

—— (1985b) *Fertilisers*, Canberra: Australian Government Publishing Service, Report No. 372, October.

—— (1986a) "Certain Petroleum Products", Draft Report, IAC, Canberra, March.

—— (1986b) *The Textiles, Clothing and Footwear Industries*, Canberra: Australian Government Publishing Service, Report No. 386, May.

—— (1986c) *The Chemicals and Plastics Industries*, Canberra: Australian Government Publishing Service, Report No. 390, May.

—— (1986d) *Certain Petroleum Products – Taxation Measures*, Canberra: Australian Government Publishing Service, Report No. 397, November.

—— (1987a) *Export Concessions*, Canberra: Australian Government Publishing Service, Report No. 399, January.

—— (1987b) *Pulp, Paper, Paper Products and Printing Industries*, Canberra: Australian Government Publishing Service, Report No. 401, February.

—— (1987c) *Assistance to Agricultural and Manufacturing Industries*, Canberra: Australian Government Publishing Service, June.

—— (1987d) *Glass and Glassware*, Canberra: Australian Government Publishing Service, Report No. 404, June.

—— (1987e) *Annual Report 1986–87*, Canberra: Australian Government Publishing Service.

—— (1988) *The Wheat Industry*, Canberra: Australian Government Publishing Service, Report No. 411, February.

Johansen, L. (1960) *A Multi-sectoral Study of Economic Growth*, Amsterdam: North-Holland.

Johnson, D. (1985) "The Short Term Economic Effects of Environmental Constraints on Forest Industries", *Review of Marketing and Agricultural Economics*, 53 (3), 149–56.

—— and P. K. Kee (1987) "Socio-demographic and Economic Profile of the Goulburn Valley with Forecasts to 1991", University of Melbourne, Institute of Applied Economic and Social Research, Working Paper No. 12/1987, November.

Jonson, P. D. and R. G. Trevor (1981) "Monetary Rules: A Preliminary Analysis", *Economic Record*, 53 (157), 150–67 (see especially the appendix).

Klijn, N. (1974) "Revaluation and Changes in Tariff Protection – The Short-term Effects with Special Reference to Agriculture", paper presented to the 18th Conference of the Australian Agricultural Economics Society, Perth.

Lawson, A. (1979) "The Effects of Increases in Transport Costs on Consumer Prices", in Bureau of Transport Economics, *The Long Distance Road Haulage Industry*, Canberra: Australian Government Publishing Service.

Leontief, W. W., A. Morgan, K. Polenske, D. Simpson and E. Tower (1965) "The Economic Impact – Industrial and Regional – of an Arms Cut", *Review of Economics and Statistics*, 47, August, 217–41.

Liew, L. H. (182) "Regional Disaggregation of a National Economic Model: The 'Bottoms-up' Approach", Impact Project Preliminary Working Paper No. OP-34, August.

—— (1984) "A Johansen Model for Regional Analysis", *Regional Science and Urban Economics*, 14 (1), February, 129–46.

—— (1985) "The Impact of Defence Spending on the Australian Economy", *Australian Economic Papers*, 24 (45), December, 326–36.

Madden, J. R. (1985) "A Proposal for Extending CREA's Regional General Equilibrium Model Capabilities", paper prepared for the Macro-Econometric Models Workshops, 14th Conference of Economists, University of New South Wales, May.

—— (1987) "The Structure of the Tasmain Model", University of Melbourne, Institute of Applied Economic and Social Research, Working Paper No. 11/1987, October.

—— and D. W. Challen (1983) "Technology and the Tasmanian Economy", in K. Nichols (ed.), *Science, Technology and Employment*, Hobart: Tasmanian Division of the Australian and New Zealand Association for the Advancement of Science, pp. 26–37.

——, —— and A. J. Hagger (1981) "The Effects on the Australian Economy of Some Alternative Trade Liberalisation Policies", University of Tasmania, Centre for Regional Economic Analysis, Paper No. RS-01, December.

——, —— and —— (1982) "The Effects on the Tasmanian Economy of the Resources Boom", University of Tasmania, Centre for Regional Economic Analysis, Paper No. RS-02, March.

——, —— and —— (1983) "The Grants Commission's Relativities Proposals: Effects on the State Economies", *Australian Economic Papers*, 22 (41) December, 302–21.

—— and A. J. Hagger (1985) "Tightening of Woodchips Export Licensing: Short-run Effects on the Tasmanian Economy", University of Tasmania, Centre for Regional Economic Analysis, Paper No. RS-09, December.

Malinvaud, E. (1977) *The Theory of Unemployment Reconsidered*, Oxford: Blackwell.

Manne, A. S. (1963) "Key Sectors of the Mexican Economy 1960–70", in A. S. Manne and H. M. Markowitz (eds), *Studies in Process Analysis*, New York: Wiley, ch. 16, pp. 379–400.

Mannion, G. R., R. L. Tillack and D. P. Vincent (1987) "The Effects of Higher Petroleum Product Excises and Alternative Policy Responses to Lower Crude Oil Prices", paper presented to the 31st Conference of the Australian Agricultural Economics Society, University of Adelaide.

Meagher, G. A. (1983) "Fiscal Policy and Australian Industry: the Effects of a Change in the Mix of Direct and Indirect Taxation", La Trobe University Economics Discussion Paper No. 7/83, May.

—— (1986) "An Empirical Analysis of the Effects of a Change in the Mix of

Direct and Indirect Taxation on the Australian Economy", *Australian Economic Papers*, 25 (46), 47–56.

—— and Nisha Agrawal (1986) "Taxation Reform and Income Distribution in Australia", *Australian Economic Review*, Third Quarter, 33–56.

—— and B. R. Parmenter (1985) "Some Short Run Effects of Shifts from Direct to Indirect Taxcation", University of Melbourne, Institute of Applied Economic and Social Research, Working Paper No. 10/1985, September.

—— and —— (1986) "The Economic Effects of Reductions in Industries' Costs Associated with Reforms to the Workers' Compensation System", University of Melbourne, Institute of Applied Economic and Social Research, Working Paper No. 3/1986, April.

—— and —— (1987) "The Short-run Macroeconomic Effects of Tax-mix Changes", University of Melbourne, Institute of Applied Economic and Social Research, Working Paper No. 1/1987, April.

——, ——, R. J. Rimmer and K. W. Clements (1985) "Special Purpose Versions of a General Purpose Multisectoral Model: Tax Issues and the Australian Wine Industry", in J. Piggott and J. Whalley (eds), *New Developments in Applied General Equilibrium Analysis*, New York: Cambridge University Press, pp. 283–92.

Meltzer, B. D. (1980) "A Comparison of Some Effective Rate of Protection Calculations with the Results of a General Equilibrium Model", Impact Project General Paper No. G-26, May.

Ministry of Economic Development, Victoria (1982) *A Submission to the Committee of Enquiry into the State Electricity Commission of Victoria*, April.

Norman, N. R. (1981) "The Impact Macrofix: An Exposition", *Australian Economic Papers*, 20 (36), June, 183–5.

—— and K. F. Meikle (1985) *The Economic Effects of Immigration on Australia*, vol. II, Melbourne: Committee for the Economic Development of Australia Study, P Series, No. 27, April.

Pagan, A. R. and J. H. Shannon (1985) "Sensitivity Analysis for Linearized Computable General Equilibrium Models", in J. Piggott and J. Whalley (eds), *New Developments in Applied General Equilibrium Analysis*, New York: Cambridge University Press, pp. 411–40.

—— and —— (1987) "How Reliable are ORANI Conclusions?", *Economic Record*, 63 (180), March, 33–45.

Parmenter, B. R. (1983a) "Multiregional Modelling of the Australian Economy: Experience from the IMPACT Project", Impact Project General Paper No. G-50, August.

—— (1983b) "The IMPACT Macro Package and Export Demand Elasticities", *Australian Economic Papers*, 22 (11), December, 411–17.

—— (1985) "What Does Manufacturing Protection Cost Farmers? A Review of Some Recent Australian Contributions", University of Melbourne, Institute of Applied Economic and Social Research, Working Paper No. 7/1985, July; reprinted in *Australian Journal of Agricultural Economics*, 30 (2–3), August–December 1986, 118–27.

—— and G. A. Meagher (1985) "Policy Analysis Using a Computable General Equilibrium Model: A Review of Experience at the IMPACT Project", *Australian Economic Review*, First Quarter, 3–15.

—— and —— (1987) "ORANI–NT: An Economic Model of the Northern Territory", mimeo, University of Melbourne, Institute of Applied Economic and Social Research, March.

——, D. Sams and D. P. Vincent (1981) "Who Pays for Home Consumption Pricing Schemes?", *Economic Record*, 57 (157), June, 168–79.

Parsell, B. F. (1987) "Reductions in Government Spending in the ORANI–NAGA Framework", University of Melbourne, Institute of Applied Economic and Social Research, Working Paper No. 10/1987, October.

Patinkin, D. (1965) *Money, Interest and Prices*, 2nd edn, New York: Harper and Row.

Pearson, K. R. (1986) "Automating the Computation of Solutions of Large Economic Models", Impact Project Preliminary Working Paper No. IP-27, March; reprinted in *Economic Modelling*, October 1988.

Piggott, J. (1983) "The Microeconomic Effects of Tax–Inflation Interactions: General Equilibrium Estimates for Australia", in A. R. Pagan and P. K. Trivedi (eds), *The Effects of Inflation – Theoretical Issues and Australian Evidence*, Canberra: Australian National University, Centre for Economic Policy Research, Conference Papers, pp. 137–77.

—— and J. Whalley (1986) "The Tax Unit and Household Production: A General Equilibrium Approach", mimeo, Department of Economics, University of Sydney.

Powell, A. A. (1977) *The IMPACT Project: An Overview, March 1977*, Canberra: Australian Government Publishing Service.

—— (1981) "The Major Streams of Economy-wide Modeling: Is Rapprochement Possible?", in J. Kmenta and J. B. Ramsey (eds), *Large-Scale Macro-Econometric Models: Theory and Practice* Amsterdam: North-Holland, ch. 9, pp. 219–64.

—— (1982) "Resources and Resource Allocation Policy", 20th Shann Memorial Lecture of the University of Western Australia, September 1981, *Australian Bulletin of Labour*, Supplement No. 3, March.

—— (1983) "Aspects of the Design of BACHUROO, an Economic-Demographic Model of Labor Supply", in A. C. Kelley, W. C. Sanderson and J. G. Williamson (eds), *Modeling Growing Economies in Equilibrium and Disequilibrium*, Durham, NC: Duke Press Policy Studies, pp. 277–300.

—— (1985a) "IMPACT Project Report – A Brief Account of Activities over the Period 1st February 1982 to 28th February 1985 with a Prospectus for Further Developments", University of Melbourne, Impact Project Report No. R-05, April.

—— (1985b) "Short-run Applications of ORANI: An Impact Project Perspective", *Australian Economic Papers*, 24 (44), June, 37–53.

—— (1985c) "Real Wages and Employment – An Econometric View", in J. Hyde and J. Nurick (eds), *Wages Wasteland: The Australian Wage Fixing System*, Sydney: Hale and Iremonger, pp. 19–28.

—— (1988) "IMPACT Project Report – A Brief Account of Activities over the Period 1st March 1985 to 31st December 1987 with a Prospectus for Further Developments", University of Melbourne, Impact Project Report No. R-07, February.

—— and A. Lawson (1975) "IMPACT: An Economic–Demographic Model of Australian Industry Structure – Preliminary Outline", Impact Project Working Paper No. I-01, September.

—— and B. R. Parmenter (1979) "The IMPACT Project as a Tool for Policy Analysis: Brief Overview", *Australian Quarterly*, 51 (1), March, 62–74.

Prices Justification Tribunal (1979), *Processed Food Industry*, Melbourne: Australian Government Publishing Service, August.

Quiggan, J. D., and A. B. Stoeckel (1982) "Protection, Income Distribution and the Rural Sector", *Economic Papers*, 1 (2), September, 56–71.

Rattigan, A. (1986) *Industry Assistance – The Inside Story*, Melbourne: Melbourne University Press.

Rimmer, R. J. (1984) "The Long Term Effects of Improved Labour Productivity in the Australian Basic Iron and Steel Industry", Impact Project Preliminary Working Paper No. OP-47, May.

Rivlin, A. M. (ed.) (1984) *Economic Choices 1984*, Washington, DC: Brookings Institution.

Sams, D. and P. Williams (1983) "An Economic–Demographic Model of Australian Population, Labour Force and Households", Impact Project Working Paper No. B-18, August.

Sandee, J. (1960) *A Long Term Planning Model for India*, New York: Asia Publishing House; Calcutta: Statistical Publishing Company.

Shoven, J. B., and J. Whalley (1972) "A General Equilibrium Calculation of the Effects of Differential Taxation of Income from Capital in the U.S.", *Journal of Public Economics*, 1, 281–321.

—— and —— (1973) "General Equilibrium with Taxes: A Computational Procedure and an Existence Proof", *Review of Economic Studies*, 40, October, 475–89.

—— and —— (1974) "On the Computation of Competitive General Equilibrium on International Markets with Tariffs", *Journal of International Economics*, 4, November, 341–54.

Siriwardana, M. (1985) "A Multi-sectoral General Equilibrium Model of Tariff Protection in the Colony of Victoria in 1880", Ph.D. Dissertation, School of Economics, La Trobe University.

Stoeckel, A. B. (1978) "A General Equilibrium Study of Mining and Agriculture in the Australian Economy", Doctoral Dissertation, Department of Economics, Duke University, Durham, NC.

—— (1979) "Some General Equilibrium Effects of Mining Growth on the Economy", *Australian Journal of Agricultural Economics*, 23 (1), April, 1–22.

—— and S. Cuthbertson (1987) *The Game Plan – Successful Strategies for Australian Trade*, Canberra: Centre for International Economics.

Stolper, W. F., and P. A. Samuelson (1941) "Protection and Real Wages", *Review of Economic Studies*, 9 (1), November, 58–73.

Sugden, C. (1987) "The Effect on Economic Activity of a Change in the Tax Mix", thesis submitted in partial fulfilment of the requirements for the degree of Bachelor of Economics with Honours in Economics, Macquarie University, November.

Swan, T. W. (1963) "Long-run Problems of the Balance of Payments", in H. W. Arndt and W. M. Corden (eds), *The Australian Economy*, Melbourne: Cheshire.

Taylor, L., and S. L. Black (1974) "Practical General Equilibrium Estimation of Resource Pulls under Trade Liberalization", *Journal of International Economics*, 4, April, 35–58.

Truong, T. P. (1986) "ORANI FUEL: Incorporating Interfuel Substitution into the Standard ORANI Framework", Impact Project Preliminary Working Paper No. OP-58, October.

Vincent, D. P. (1980a) "Some Effects of Changing Oil Prices on the Australian Economy", in *Energy: Crisis or Opportunity?* Seminar Proceedings, Geelong: Marcus Oldham Farm Management College, pp. 83–92.

—— (1980b) "Some Implications for the Australian Economy of Trade Growth with Newly Industrialising Asia: The Use and Limitations of the ORANI Framework", in K. Anderson and A. George (eds), *Australian Agriculture and Newly Industrialising Asia: Issues for Research*, Canberra: Australia–Japan Research Centre, pp. 360–95.

—— (1983) "Drought, World Recession and the Growth in Real Labour Costs: A Comparative Analysis of Their Effects on Domestic Activity", mimeo, paper presented to the Victorian Branch of the Australian Agricultural Economics Society.

—— (1985) "Exchange Rate Devaluation, Monetary Policy and Wages: A General Equilibrium Analysis for Chile", *Economic Modelling*, 2 (1), January, 17–32.

——, P. B. Dixon, B. R. Parmenter and D. C. Sams (1979) "The Short Term Effect of Oil Price Increases on the Australian Economy with Special Reference to the Agricultural Sector", *Australian Journal of Agricultural Economics*, 23 (2), August, 79–101.

——, ——, —— and —— (1980) "Implications of World Energy Price Increases on the Rural and Other Sectors of the Australian Economy", in K. M. W. Howes and R. A. Rummery (eds), *Energy and Agriculture*, Perth: CSIRO, pp. 29–39.

—— and G. J. Ryland (1981) "Adjustment Pressures on the Agricultural Sector of an Open Economy: the Australian Situation", in M. A. Bellamy and B. L. Greenshields (eds), *The Rural Challenge*, International Association of Agricultural Economists Occasional Paper No. 2, Aldershot: Gower (for the International Association of Agricultural Economists), pp. 132–6.

Warr, P. G., and P. J. Lloyd (1983) "Do Australian Trade Policies Discriminate Against Less Developed Countries?", *Economic Record*, 59 (167), December, pp. 351–64.

—— and B. R. Parmenter (1984) "Protection through Government Procurement", Discussion Paper No. 91, Centre for Economic Policy Research, Australian National University, March.

Wharton Econometric Forecasting Associates (1981) *The Wharton Annual Model Post-meeting Forecast*, vol. 1, June.

Wilcoxen, P. J. (1985a) "Numerical Methods for Investment Models with Foresight", Impact Project Preliminary Working Paper No. IP-23, July.

—— (1985b) "Computable Models of Investment with Foresight", Impact Project Preliminary Working Paper No. IP-25, October.

—— (1987) "Investment with Foresight in General Equilibrium", Impact Project Preliminary Working Paper No. IP-35, November.

9

Applied General Equilibrium Modelling in the Australian Industries Assistance Commission: Perspectives of a Policy Analyst

David P. Vincent

1 Introduction

The Industries Assistance Commission (hereafter the Commission) is an independent statutory authority of the Australian Government. Its main function is to advise the Government on industry assistance matters.

Over the past eight years the Commission has made regular use of applied general equilibrium modelling techniques, based around the ORANI model framework,[1] to support its analysis of industry economic policy issues. Staff of the Commission over this period have also on numerous occasions used the ORANI framework to assist the economic analysis process in other agencies of the Australian Government. These include the Treasury (in the context of the analysis of macroeconomic policy issues), the Bureau of Agricultural Economics (analysis of agricultural economic policy issues), the Department of Energy and Resources (analysis of resource policy issues) and the Department of Employment and Industrial Relations (analysis of employment issues).[2]

Although the Commission, in seeking to enhance the quality of its economic analysis, is a prominent user of applied general equilibrium techniques, it has relied largely on the Impact Research Centre,[3] an institution located 700 km from the centre of government administration and quite detached from the policy advisory process, for the initial development of the ORANI model and subsequent theoretical improvements to enhance its policy relevance. The Commission lacks both the skills and the research environment necessary to undertake such developments. Commission staff maintain regular contact with Australian industry through the Commission's inquiry programme and with staff in other agencies of the Australian Government engaged in the economic policy advisory process. They are well placed to communicate to model builders the real world relevance of the theoretical assumptions which form the building blocks of an applied general equilibrium model and to suggest the directions more policy-relevant research should take.

There is a close and continuous interaction between on the one hand the model builder, located in a university environment and in pursuit of academic goals, and on the other hand the policy analyst, a permanent employee of the Australian Government. This interaction, which is conducted at both the formal level through meetings to discuss the direction and progress of model-building research and informally by staff to staff contacts, is mutually beneficial in a number of respects. Firstly, it ensures that model builders are kept closely informed of the direction of the economic policy debate within the government sector and of the research priorities likely to contribute to this debate. Secondly, it serves to highlight areas where existing model specification needs to be modified to approximate reality better. Thirdly, it considerably shortens the lag between the enhancement of a model and its application to the analysis of a contemporary policy problem within the Government. Fourthly, it increases the profile and exposure of model builders by ensuring that the results of analyses of economic issues of immediate concern to the Government are published in Commission reports which are widely circulated and subject to extensive public scrutiny and debate, both by the economics profession and by the public generally.

The Commission has now accumulated considerable experience in the use of applied general equilibrium techniques to analyse a wide variety of narrowly specific industry policy and general economic policy issues. Amongst other things this experience has served to highlight the strengths and limitations of the applied general equilibrium framework in these uses and the problems encountered in ensuring that the economic insights derived from the models are reflected in the eventual policy outcomes. This paper provides an account of the role played by applied general equilibrium modelling, as depicted by the ORANI framework, within the Commission in the course of its framing of advice to the Government on commercial policy issues and in its consultations with other government agencies engaged in advising on other aspects of economic policy.

The paper is structured as follows. Section 2 outlines the institutional setting within which the Commission operates, its interpretation of its statutory responsibilities and the potential usefulness of applied general equilibrium analysis in fulfilling these responsibilities. Section 3 presents in some detail four recent applications of applied general equilibrium analysis by Commission staff. The applications chosen provide a convenient set of case studies with which to illustrate the type of policy question addressed, the way in which general equilibrium techniques have been used to address the question, the results obtained and the effectiveness of the analysis in contributing to an understanding of the policy question under study. Section 4 discusses the major problems encountered in the Commission's use of ORANI to analyse industry assistance issues. Section 5 considers the issue of the communication of model results. Concluding remarks are contained in section 6.

2 The Institutional Setting

The Commission is an independent statutory authority created by an Act of Parliment in 1974. Its main functions are to advise the Government on the nature and extent of assistance which should be given to Australian industries and to report annually on the structure of industry assistance in Australia and its effects on the economy. Assistance is defined broadly to include, in addition to traditional border protection measures such as tariffs, quantitative import restrictions and export subsidies, any other form of tax, subsidy or institutional arrangement which confers a benefit on one sector of the economy at the expense of another. The Commissions's focus therefore extends to all sectors of the economy and to the industrial structure of economic activity as a whole. Because of its independence, the Commission is in a position to provide disinterested policy advice in an area inevitably subject to conflicting pressures from special interest groups.

The Commission comprises no fewer than five and no more than nine Commissioners. Each is appointed by the Government for a fixed term. In addition, Associate Commissioners are sometimes appointed for particular inquiries. Commissioners and Associate Commissioners are drawn from a broad spectrum of Australian society[4] including private industry, the government sector, labour unions and the academic community: consequently, their collective expertise is wide ranging. While their role is primarily to offer advice to the Government on economic issues, there is no requirement that Commissioners have a background in, or any particular level of understanding of, economic thought.

Commissioners are assisted by a staff of permanent public servants. Most staff are trained in at least one area of economics, with microeconomics, econometrics and agricultural economics being well represented.

2.1 The Commission's inquiry role

The Commission is required to inquire into and report on specific issues of industry assistance referred to it by the Government. Generally, the Government must seek the Commission's advice before it changes the structure of assistance afforded to industries. There is, of course, no statutory or constitutional requirement for the Government to follow the Commissions's advice, and in practice the Government in many cases does not do so.

The Commission must complete its report, including all supporting economic analysis, within a specified time period which is dependent on the nature, size and complexity of the inquiry.[5] Typically, two of three Commissioners or Associate Commissioners are appointed to a particular inquiry.

Since its creation, the Commission has completed about 400 specific inquiries. These have encompassed a wide range of economic issues which impinge on industry performance and resource allocation. They include border protection instruments, domestic industry incentives, budgetary and taxation policy issues, natural resource management and issues concerning public choice and property rights.

2.1.1 The public inquiry process

A unique and extremely important aspect of the Commission's operations is its active attempts to encourage public participation in its policy advisory procedures and public scrutiny of its recommendations and the reasons underlying them. Public understanding of both the costs of adjustment to a more efficient industry structure and the benefits likely to accrue to the community as a whole is seen by the Commission as being crucial to overcoming the resistance of directly affected groups to a change in assistance.

After receiving a reference from the Government the Commission seeks written submissions from all interested parties – industry organizations, trade unions, domestic producers, importers and consumer groups. A draft report is prepared which generally includes an account of the activities under reference and their importance in the economy, an evaluation of the relevant economic issues, an analysis of major proposals advanced by interested parties and a discussion and analysis of options. The draft report, which is distributed to inquiry participants and to the press as well as being available to the public on request, provides interested parties with an opportunity to examine the Commission's analysis and proposals and to comment on them either through written submissions or at a subsequent public hearing.

Any person may submit evidence at a public hearing at which participants are asked to present their submission and to respond to Commissioners' questions. In their submissions, participants frequently comment, both favourably and unfavourably, on aspects of the Commission's applied modelling work. Participants may also comment on the submissions of other participants.

After taking into account the views of participants at the public hearings, the Commission issues a final report for consideration by the Government. This report is published by the Government generally before a government decision is taken on its recommendations.

The Commission as an institution plays no further part in the policy formation process once its report is sent to Government. However, staff are sometimes requested to undertake additional model simulations concerning possible policy options by the departments responsible for translating the Commission's policy recommendations into actual policy.

2.2 The Commission's policy guidelines

In examining the issues referred to it by the Government, the Commission is required to have regard to a number of policy guidelines expressed in fairly general terms. They require that an economy-wide perspective be adopted which considers, in addition to the problems facing directly affected sectors, the welfare of the community as a whole. Specifically, the guidelines reflect the Government's stipulated desire to

1 encourage the development and growth of efficient Australian industries which are internationally competitive, export oriented and capable over the longer term of operating with minimum levels of assistance;
2 facilitate the adjustment of industries to stuctural change and that of persons affected by these changes, having regard to the need to minimize any social and economic hardship that may be involved; and
3 have regard to the activities of other industries and consumers likely to be affected by assistance changes.

2.3 The Commission's annual reporting role

The Commission's annual report documents the changes in assistance arrangements afforded to various activities in the Australian economy over the previous year. In addition, summary measures of the level of assistance accruing to each industry, expressed in terms of nominal and effective rates of assistance, and how assistance levels to various activities and for the economy as a whole have changed over time are reported. This information is subsequently used both inside and outside the Commission as input into applied general equilibrium modelling and other studies that measure the effects of such assistance changes on resource allocation in the economy.

2.4 Other Commission activities

In addition to its inquiry programme and annual reporting role, the Commission is active in two other areas. The first concerns research into interrelationships within and between industries and the incentives environment in which each industry operates. The broad aim of this research is to increase public understanding of the extent and nature of various interventions and restrictions in the Australian economy and their effects on resource allocation and community living standards. The results of this reseach are disseminated to the Australian public through reports on specific inquiries, the annual report, Commission discussion papers and papers presented by staff at professional conferences and in published journals.

The second involves the responsibility of the Commission to maintain the economic models of the Impact Project, particularly the ORANI model, and to ensure that all agencies of the Australian Government have access to these models. In the case of the ORANI model, this requires a significant resource commitment from Commission staff. The model's input–output data base, parameter file and computer code are continually updated to incorporate newly released information on the input–output structure of Australian industries and occupations, improved estimates of parameters, model modifications and extensions, and improved computational procedures.

Within the Australian Government bureaucracy, the expertise required to apply the ORANI model to economic policy issues is concentrated heavily in the Commission.[6] Consequently, the Commission's responsibility to ensure access to the model for all other Australian Government agencies places staff in a policy-analytic consulting role to these agencies. Typically, Commission staff are briefed by staff of other agencies on the nature of the policy problem confronting them. Commission staff then determine how the model is to be used to address the problem, the appropriate choice and settings of exogenous variables, and parameter settings. Simulations are undertaken and assistance is provided with the interpretation of results. The users of the results must be sufficiently briefed on the important assumptions underlying the structure of the model to ensure that an appropriate perspective is placed on any policy conclusions drawn from them.

2.5 The role of applied general equilibrium modelling in the Commission

The foregoing discussion of the Commission's responsibilities and the guidelines it must consider highlights the potential relevance to the Commission of an economy-wide analytical framework of industry and work force composition. The guidelines explicitly recognize that assistance given to one sector will affect production, investment and employment in other sectors and hence overall economic performance and community living standards. They require that the Commission balance the longer-term gains from an improved allocation of re-sources against the capacity of affected industries and occupations to accommodate, in the short term, the required adjustments.

Ideally, to fulfil its statutory responsibilities, the Commission requires an analytical framework possessing the following capabilities.

1 It must trace the interactions between producing and consuming activities in considerable detail. Existing and proposed assistance arrangements reviewed by the Commission often discriminte con-siderably between quite specific and closely related activities. In order to determine the impact of such arrangements and the effects of moving towards a less discriminatory assistance regime, such activities and their interdependences must be explicitly modelled.[7]

2 It must incorporate, at the individual activity and commodity level, the full range of assistance instruments commonly applied in the Australian situation. These include tariffs and quantitative restric-tions on imports, taxes and subsidies on exports, taxes and sub-sidies on production and sales, and set combinations of these such as those embodied in home consumption pricing arrangements for agricultural products.

3 It must permit both a short-term analysis of the adjustment pressures likely to confront industries and occupations following a change in assistance and a longer-term analysis of the eventual effects on resource allocation and aggregate economic efficiency when resources have responded fully to the adjustment pressures imposed upon them.

In recent years a number of references sent to the Commission have involved substantial parts of Australian manufacturing industry.[8] This is likely to continue in the future.[9] In such cases it is necessary to analyse in considerable detail interactions within activities under reference as well as between these activities and the rest of the economy.

Political pressures from vested interests in Australia are such that assistance reform is generally not undertaken unless the Government can be convinced that the short-term employment disruption in directly affected sectors is manageable. The Commission's model-based analyses of the short-term employment effects, which are closely scrutinized by both Government and industry, make a vital contribution to the information base in this area. The interests of labour and capital in protected sectors often put forward what the Commission considers to be exaggerated estimates of the adverse consequences for their industry of proposed assistance reductions. Such estimates are invariably derived from a partial framework. If the Commission did not possess the capacity to undertake an economy-wide analysis of adjustment pressures, the claims advanced by industry groups would go largely uncontested.

In considering the magnitude of the adjustments involved, the Commission has chosen to abstract from short-term trade cycle influences and other transient shocks to the economic environment; i.e. its focus has been on the short- and longer-term[10] implications of implementing a proposed policy recommendation assuming that all aspects of the economic environment shaping industry growth prospects, apart from those inherent in the policy change, will remain constant. This avoids taking a view about how growth prospects for the activities under reference are likely to evolve over time. Adjustment pressures as calculated therefore do not purport to measure how many jobs *will* be lost or gained in a particular industry but only those likely to be lost or gained as a result of the Commission's recommendations.

2.5.1 *The ORANI framework*

For many industry inquiries undertaken by the Commission, the value of goods under reference is small compared with gross domestic product (GDP) and the activities producing these goods have only minor forward and backward linkages with other sectors of the domestic economy and international trade. In such instances the economy-wide implications of changes in assistance to the activities can safely be ignored and a partial equilibrium treatment of the economic issues is considered adequate.[11]

For inquiries where activities under reference represent a significant component of industrial production and have important linkages with other sectors, the ORANI framework, a conventional general equilibrium framework of the Johansen type, is used on a routine basis. This framework has proved sufficiently flexible to incorporate the major categories of assistance arrangements identified by the Commission. The ORANI framework, being comparative static, provides projections of the effects of a given policy change at only one point in time. These projections are identified as being either short term or longer term depending on (a) the model closure adopted and hence the degree of resource mobility envisaged to take place, (b) values assigned to elasticity parameters and (c) the nature of the change under consideration.

The typical form of use of ORANI is to provide projections of the short- and longer-term effects of a specified economic change while abstracting from all other influences that operate to shape the development of industries and the economy as a whole.[12] This form of use corresponds closely to the Commission's interpretation of the way in which it should consider assistance changes. The absence of a treatment of short-term dynamics in ORANI has not to date been of particular concern to the Commission.

2.5.2 Special purpose industry models constructed within ORANI

Although the standard ORANI model distinguishes 112 producing activities, 114 commodity categories facing various degrees of competition with imported commodities, ten types of labour occupations and seven types of agricultural land, this disaggregation is generally insufficient for the type of industry analysis undertaken by the Commission. However, standard ORANI provides a convenient starting point around which so-called special purpose versions can be constructed. The Commission now has considerable expertise in constructing special purpose versions of ORANI.[13]

These models are in effect detailed industry models which elaborate linkages among component parts of the activities under reference, as well as between these parts, other sectors and international trade. Because such models recognize that the economy is subject to overall constraints such as those imposed over the longer term by factor supplies and the foreign account, indirect linkages between the performance of industries resulting from these constraints are automatically in place.

Typically for a one-year inquiry a modelling team of two or three persons has about three months to construct and implement a special purpose version of ORANI. In addition to the timing constraint, a computer budget constraint and constraints on the availability of data and parameters temper the modelling ambitions of the team. Before modelling work can commence the team must develop a thorough appreciation of the activities under reference, their interrelationships, the incentive environment in which the activities operate and hence the range of policy issues likely to confront the Commission. On the basis of this information decisions are made as to which of the activities under reference and which assistance instruments require explicit modelling.

Given the time constraint under which staff operate, the initial model specification stage is a crucial one. Considerable judgement is required in deciding, at this early stage in the inquiry process, the factors relevant to the policy problem being analysed while abstracting from others considered to be of lesser importance. The time constraint is such that only minor modifications to the structure of the basic model can be implemented as the inquiry progresses.

After determining the set of intersectoral interdependences and assistance instruments which require explicit modelling, the next stage involves modifying ORANI's standard input–output data base to capture these interdependences, modifying the theoretical structure where required to incorporate economic responses not allowed for in the basic model, and assigning values to the set of parameters accompanying the model modifications.

In undertaking the modifications the team interacts closely with staff employed within the industries under reference. Industry staff may be asked to respond to a detailed questionnaire seeking (a) data on interdependences between activities, (b) estimates of key substitution parameters (particularly substitution elasticities between domestic and imported sources) and (c) information upon which the Commission can conduct an econometric analysis of price responsiveness. In some industry modelling exercises close cooperation is achieved between Commission and industry staff. The benefits are mutual. The realism, quality and potential acceptance of the modelling work is enhanced through the incorporation of detailed information at the industry level. Industry staff, as well as experiencing at first hand the procedure to be followed in making an economy-wide as opposed to a partial assessment of the effects of an economic change, gain access to the modelling framework.

3 Selected Examples of the Use of Applied General Equilibrium Modelling by the Commission

In this section four recent examples of applied general equilibrium modelling conducted within the Commission are discussed in some detail. The examples have been chosen to provide a balanced representation of the type of policy issues analysed, the way in which the standard ORANI model is modified to accommodate them, and the problems encountered.

The first example refers to the analysis of marketing arrangements for the dairy industry. While the Australian agricultural sector[14] as a whole is export oriented with major parts such as wool, beef and cereal grains operating with minimal levels of assistance, the sector contains significant pockets of highly assisted activities such as dairying. The Commission frequently receives references from the Government to advise on assistance arrangements for these activities. Assistance arrangements in agricultural activities are generally complex, involving a package of domestic instruments supported by traditional border protection measures such as tariffs and quantitative restrictions on imports.

A further complication with agriculture is that the domestic price discrimination component of the assistance package commonly requires, in addition to Australian Government legislative support, complementary legislation from each of the states in which the commodity is produced. There is a natural tendency for the producer lobby in each state to pursue its own interests irrespective of the implications for the industry in other states. In Australia, climatic conditions, and hence dairy production technologies, differ from state to state as well as between regions in each state. An essential prerequisite to achieving a policy package which is acceptable to each state industry is an analysis of the effects of any proposed assistance changes on the performance of the industry in each state as well as its performance in aggregate.

The second example refers to a study of assistance arrangements in the chemicals and plastics industries. These activities represent about 10 per cent of the value added of the Australian manufacturing sector. This study is representative of many undertaken in various areas of manufacturing. Typically, the industries involved are domestic oriented, obtaining market share against competing imports with the assistance of tariffs. In the case of chemicals and plastics, the existing structure of assistance reflects the selective imposition of tariffs to encourage local production at the expense of imports in the trading environment which existed nearly two decades earlier.

The third example is taken from a recent study into assistance for the consumption of phosphatic and nitrogeneous fertilizers. In that study the analysis was broadly based, referring to assistance to agriculture relative to that for manufacturing and the relative impact on agricultural competitiveness of a range of influences including assistance measures.

The final example concerns the use of the model to address an adjustment issue of considerable importance in the contemporary Australian economic debate – that of accommodating a severe decline in the foreign terms of trade. While the Commission does not have a responsibility to advise the Government in this area, it needs to be aware of the differential pressures imposed on sectors by terms of trade changes and the appropriate macroeconomic policy responses. Analyses such as this of general macroeconomic issues are conducted periodically by Commission staff and made available to the relevant policy departments and the Australian economics profession.

3.1 Analysis of assistance arrangements for the Australian dairy industry

A full report of the analysis of assistance arrangements for the Australian dairy industry is contained in IAC (1983). The terms of reference for the inquiry required the Commission to report on the nature and extent of assistance that should be provided for the industry. The effects of past government regulatory arrangements have been to facilitate in each state two types of activity: (a) the production of market milk (with a regulated supply and price); and (b) the production of manufactured milk, purchased by dairy factories for processing into a range of products consumed locally and/or exported. Some such products including butter, certain varieties of cheese, skim milk powder, casein and whole milk powder (termed leviable products) are protected by differential rates of tax on domestic sales, the proceeds of which are used to subsidize exports, again at differential rates. The result is large disparities in assistance between products. The Commission's recommendations, which sought to simplify the assistance structure while modestly reducing its overall level, involved the replacement of these arrangements with a uniform domestic levy on all milk to fund a uniform rate of export subsidy of 20 per cent on all exported dairy products.

To analyse the adjustment pressures involved, ORANI-MILK, a detailed model of milk production, processing and final sales, was created within the ORANI framework. Modifications to the standard model to achieve this involved (a) the disaggregation of the single milk cattle and milk product activities into the detailed product by industry matrices of tables 9.1 and 9.2,(b) the specification of household demand behaviour to allow for direct substitution between different types of dairy products,[15] and (c) the incorporation of joint production features in the milk manufacturing process.[16]

As shown in table 9.1, six farm milk cattle activities are distinguished, one for each state. Each produces two products, its respective state milk and meat cattle (representing the sale of dairy cattle for slaughter). There is one manufactured milk activity producing seven products. Three of these (butter, skim milk powder and casein) are modelled as being produced in fixed proportions in a single manufacturing process. This process competes with four other processes (leviable cheese, non-leviable cheese, whole milk powder and other milk products) in the output mix of the activity. Production in the remainder of the economy is accounted for by a further 29 industries, eight of which are farm based, producing agricultural commodities other than farm milk and dairy cattle. Some of these industries, such as chemical fertilizers and glass products, are important suppliers to the farm milk cattle and manufactured milk activities.

Table 9.2 indicates that each state's farm milk is sold to the corresponding state market milk industry as well as to the manufactured dairy products industry. The products of the state milk industries (the respective bottled milk commodities) are consumed by households. Manufactured dairy products are used for higher stage processing, consumed by households and exported.

Tables 9.1 and 9.2 represent only a small part of the input–output data base of ORANI-MILK. On the input side a further 30 commodity categories (with both domestic and imported components) and land, ten types of labour occupations, and capital are distinguished. Sales of domestic and imported commodities to the 13 dairying activities and a further 29 industry categories representing the rest of the economy are modelled. All these flows are expressed in basic values. In addition there are commodity by industry matrices capturing the margins, taxes and subsidies on these flows. Since the main assistance mechanism of the dairy industry involves taxing sales to domestic consumers to subsidize exports, it is essential that the wedge between producer and consumer prices be captured.

To illustrate the underlying economic mechanisms the effects of (a) removing current assistance arrangements and (b) adding the new assistance arrangements were simulated separately. Under current arrangements the producer receives an equalized return from domestic and export sales with domestic sales taxed to support export subsidies. The shock in (a) was derived by calculating the extent to which the set of existing domestic taxes raised the prices of each dairy product to consumers and the extent to which export subsidies on each product increased the prices received by producers. The Commission's recommendations of a uniform tax on all milk to finance a uniform 20 per cent subsidy on all dairy products were simulated by increasing the farm gate milk prices in each state by the extent of the required levy and by manipulating the model's export subsidy variables to increase the prices received by exporters of dairy products by 20 per cent.

Some results for the short term[17] are shown in table 9.3. They indicate negligible macroeconomic effects, only a slight, although differential, impact across states on dairy farm incomes, and significant compositional changes in the production, household consumption

Table 9.1 Production linkages within the dairy sector of ORANI-MILK[a]

Commodity/industry	Farm milk sector[b]						Market milk sector[b]						Manufactured milk[c]
	NSW	VIC	QLD	SA	WA	TAS	NSW	VIC	QLD	SA	WA	TAS	
Farm milk (NSW)	79												
Farm milk (VIC)		82											
Farm milk (QLD)			81										
Farm milk (SA)				84									
Farm milk (WA)					76								
Farm milk (TAS)						70							
Bottled milk (NSW)							100						
Bottled milk (VIC)								100					
Bottled milk (QLD)									100				
Bottled milk (SA)										100			
Bottled milk (WA)											100		
Bottled milk (TAS)												100	
Butter													17(A)
Cheese (non-leviable)													9(B)
Cheese (leviable)													19(C)
Skim milk powder													4(A)
Casein													2(A)
Whole milk powder													7(D)
Other milk products													42(E)
Meat cattle	21	18	19	16	24	30							

[a]Figures in the table denote the commodity composition of each industry's production expressed in percentages and sum to 100 down each column. For example, 17 per cent of the output by value of the manufactured milk industry is butter and 7 per cent is whole milk powder.

[b]Australian States are denoted as follows: NSW, New South Wales; VIC, Victoria; QLD, Queensland; SA, South Australia; WA, Western Australia; TAS, Tasmania.

[c]The letters A, B, C, D and E denote the five production processes allowed for in the manufactured milk industry. Producers in that industry are assumed to adjust their output mix between these processes in response to changes in the relative prices received from the processes. The commodities butter, skim milk powder and casein are assumed to be produced in fixed proportions in the one manufacturing process.

Source: IAC, 1983, p. 201

Table 9.2 Demand linkages within the dairy sector of ORANI-MILK[a]

Commodity/ industry[b]	Farm milk sector[b]						Market milk sector[b]						Manufactured milk	29 other industries	Household consumption	Exports
	NSW	VIC	QLD	SA	WA	TAS	NSW	VIC	QLD	SA	WA	TAS				
Farm milk (NSW)							64						32		4	
Farm milk (VIC)								20					74		6	
Farm milk (QLD)									68				25		7	
Farm milk (SA)										68			25		7	
Farm milk (WA)											83		13		4	
Farm milk (TAS)												24	67		9	
Bottled milk (NSW)													2		98	
Bottled milk (VIC)													3		95	2[c]
Bottled milk (QLD)													2		98	
Bottled milk (SA)													3		97	
Bottled milk (WA)													2		98	
Bottled milk (TAS)													5		95	
Butter													13	4	50	33
Cheese (non-leviable)														1	99	
Cheese (leviable)													41	5	27	27
Skim milk powder													9	11	33	47
Casein													11	23		66
Whole milk powder													3	6	23	68
Other milk products													51	8	36	5

[a]Figures in the table denote sales percentages of domestically produced commodities and sum to 100 across each row. For example, row 1 indicates that 64 per cent of the total sales of Farm milk (NSW) is absorbed by the NSW bottled milk industry and 32 per cent is used for manufacturing.

[b]Australian States are denoted as follows: NSW. New South Wales; VIC Victoria; QLD. Queensland; SA. South Australia; WA. Western Australia; TAS. Tasmania.

[c]Australian Bureau of Statistics data indicate a small amount of exports of bottled milk. These exports have been allocated to Victoria.

Source: IAC, 1983. p. 202

Table 9.3 Some short-term adjustment implications of the Commission's assistance recommendations for the dairy industry[a]

Variable	Removal of current assistance			Addition of recommended assistance		
	Removal of export subsidies[f]	Removal of domestic tax	Total effect[b]	Addition of export subsidies	Levy on all milk	Net effect[c]
Macroeconomic variables						
Real GDP	0.1	0.05	0.15	-0.12	-0.01	0.02
Aggregate employment	0.14	0.06	0.20	-0.17	-0.01	0.03
Index of consumer prices	-0.82	-0.21	-1.03	0.95	0.00	-0.07
Aggregate imports	-0.41	-0.07	-0.48	0.47	-0.00	-0.01
Aggregate exports	0.34	0.20	0.54	-0.33	-0.04	0.16
Balance of trade	107	37	144	-114	-6	24
Economy-wide real wage	0.00	0.00	0.00	0.00	0.00	0.00
Industry output[d]						
Manufactured dairy products	-7.6	1.2	-6.4	8.1	-0.9	0.8
Industry employment						
Milk cattle (NSW)	-17	-5	-22	21	-3	-3
Milk cattle (VIC)	-43	4	-39	47	-5	2
Milk cattle (QLD)	-13	-6	-19	18	-3	-4
Milk cattle (SA)	-13	-5	-18	17	-3	-4
Milk cattle (WA)	-7	-7	-14	11	-2	-5
Milk cattle (TAS)	-35	2	-33	39	-5	1
Manufactured milk	-10	2	-8	10	-1	1

Table 9.3 (cont.)

Variable	Removal of current assistance			Addition of recommended assistance		
	Removal of export subsidies	Removal of domestic tax	Total effect[b]	Addition of export subsidies	Levy on all milk	Net effect[c]
Net farm income[c]						
Milk cattle (NSW)	−32	−10	−42	41	−6	−6
Milk cattle (VIC)	−81	7	−74	89	−10	5
Milk cattle (QLD)	−26	−11	−36	34	−5	−7
Milk cattle (SA)	−25	−10	−36	34	−6	−8
Milk cattle (WA)	−14	−13	−27	22	−4	−9
Milk cattle (TAS)	−67	4	−63	74	−9	3
Milk cattle (AUS)	−55	−1	−57	64	−8	−1
Commodity outputs						
Butter	−21	3	−18	8	−1	−11
Cheese (non-leviable)	−13	−13	−25	5	−1	−21
Cheese (leviable)	−22	4	−18	8	−1	−11
Skim milk powder	−21	3	−18	8	−1	−11
Whole milk powder	3	5	8	8	−1	15
Casein	−21	3	−18	8	−1	−11
Other milk products	6	1	7	8	−1	15
Farm milk (NSW)	1.9	−0.6	−2.4	2.4	−0.3	−0.4
Farm milk (VIC)	−4.9	0.4	−4.5	5.4	−0.6	0.3
Farm milk (QLD)	−1.5	−0.6	−2.1	2.0	−0.3	−0.4
Farm milk (SA)	−1.5	−0.6	−2.1	2.0	−0.4	−0.5
Farm milk (WA)	−0.8	−0.7	−1.5	1.3	−0.2	−0.5
Farm milk (TAS)	−3.9	0.3	−3.7	4.4	−0.5	0.2

Table 9.3 (cont.)

Variable	Removal of current assistance			Addition of recommended assistance		
	Removal of export subsidies	Removal of domestic tax	Total effect[b]	Addition of export subsidies	Levy on all milk	Net effect[c]
Exports						
Butter	-67	8	-59	26	-3	-36
Cheese (leviable)	-94	-2	-96	32	-3	-66
Skim milk powder	-74	-17	-91	33	-3	-61
Whole milk powder	10	-12	-2	16	-2	12
Casein	-31	5	-26	12	-1	-16
Other milk products	189	27	216	131	-5	342
Household consumption of domestic products[a]						
Butter	3	1	4	-2	-0	2
Cheese (non-leviable)	-13	-13	-26	5	-1	-21
Cheese (leviable)	21	15	36	-11	0	25
Skim milk powder	41	34	75	-22	1	53
Whole milk powder	-17	56	39	-10	1	31
Other milk products	-1	-3	-4	-6	-0	-10
Bottled milk (Australia)	1	-2	-0	-1	-0	-1
Imports[g]						
Butter	-51	0	-51	38	-0	-13
Cheese (non-leviable)	-39	-24	-62	30	-0	-32
Cheese (leviable)	-47	1	-45	40	-0	-5
Skim milk powder	-34	2	-31	39	-0	7

Table 9.3 (cont.)

Variable	Removal of current assistance			Addition of recommended assistance		
	Removal of export subsidies	Removal of domestic tax	Total effect[b]	Addition of export subsidies	Levy on all milk	Net effect[c]
Whole milk powder	−29	19	−9	21	1	13
Casein	−8	0	−8	37	−0	29
Other milk products	−20	2	−22	34	−0	11

[a] All results are expressed as percentage changes except for the balance of trade which has the units millions of 1 Australian dollars at the 1977–8 exchange rate with the US dollar.

[b] Column sum results are subject to apparent errors due to rounding of results for individual components.

[c] Net effect is the total effect plus addition of export subsidies plus levy on all milk.

[d] Note that the output projection for each state milk cattle industry is the same as the output projection for the corresponding farm milk commodity. Each milk cattle industry produces milk and dairy cattle for slaughter in proportions.

[e] Calculated as an appropriately weighted sum of the returns to labour, capital and land employed in the industry. The result for Australia as a whole is a weighted sum of the state results.

[f] Casein is not consumed directly by households.

[g] Note that base period imports for butter, skim milk powder, whole milk powder and casein are less than $2 million (1977–8).

Source: IAC. 1983. p. 209

and exports of dairy products. Under existing arrangements, exports of the "other milk products" category are heavily penalized by export subsidies to butter, leviable cheeses and skim milk powder especially, while household consumption of skim milk powder and whole milk powder is penalized relative to bottled milk. Farm incomes and labour demands in the Victorian and Tasmanian milk cattle industries increase moderately at the expense of those in other states. The output boost to manufactured dairy products from the removal of the domestic taxes on these products exceeds their output reductions resulting from the uniform levy on all milk. Victoria and Tasmania sell a greater share of their production to manufacturing milk than is the case with the other states.

3.2 Analysis of tariff options for chemicals and plastics

A detailed account of the Commission's applied general equilibrium modelling work for the analysis of tariff options for chemicals and plastics is contained in IAC (1986b). In the inquiry the Commission was asked to advise on options available to the Government to improve the competitiveness and efficiency of the chemicals and plastics industries in ways which would enhance their contribution to the economy. The Commission considered that growth and development of these industries should be determined by market-based incentives. Its emphasis was therefore on the reform of existing government interventions, the main one being the tariff. Current *ad valorem* tariff rates range from zero to 45 per cent, with wide disparities in rates between similar goods. The Commission considered reductions in high levels of protection and a narrowing in assistance disparities to be prerequisites to increasing the competitiveness and efficiency of the chemicals and plastics sector.

ORANI-CHEM, a detailed model of chemicals and plastics production and sales, was constructed in order to evaluate the short- and longer-term implications for component parts of chemicals and plastics, and for the economy as a whole, of reform of the tariff structure for these activities. This model divides production in the economy into 55 industry groups producing 57 commodity categories. Thirty of these industry groups and 32 commodity categories refer to chemicals and plastics. The disaggregation was chosen to capture the effects of the existing disparate tariff rates within chemicals and plastics. Products with widely different tariff rates were identified separately. In addition, different product processes, different production streams (e.g. inorganic and petrochemical–organic) and different stages in the production chain were explicitly modelled.

The commodity and industry sectors distinguished in ORANI-

CHEM are listed in table 9.4. Each commodity category is classified according to its position in the production chain. The classification A denotes petrochemical feedstocks and other raw materials (petroleum and coal products, natural gas etc). Classification B denotes basic intermediates (olefines, aromatics and various organic and inorganic chemicals). Classification C denotes derivative intermediates (resins, polymers and various organic and inorganic chemicals) more advanced in the production chain. Classification D denotes plastic and rubber products while E denotes chemical products. Eight of the industries are modelled as producing either multiple products in fixed proportions or products also produced by other industries. For example the petrochemical complex represented by industry 3 (Botany olefines) produces petroleum products, olefines and aromatics, polyethene and polypropylene. All these products are also produced by a second petrochemical complex (Altona).[20]

The input–output data base for ORANI-CHEM was constructed by updating the Australian 1978–9 input–output tables[21] to 1983–4 using data from the manufacturing census and other sources and then incorporting information on the input cost structure and sales disposition for each of the categories distinguished in table 9.4. This information was supplied by firms and industry associations in response to a specially designed questionnaire. Firms also assisted in the specification of model parameters, particularly import substitution elasticities.[20]

The model was used to analyse the effects of four tariff options. These are as follows: (a) ceiling 15, the Commission's preferred option, which is a tops-down tariff reform in which all general rates which exceed 15 per cent are reduced to 15 per cent; (b) ceiling 20 in which all general rates exceeding 20 per cent are reduced to 20 per cent; (c) broad-banding around three tiers with 2 per cent for petrochemical feedstocks and other raw materials, 15 per cent for plastic and rubber products, chemical products, synthetic resins and other final derivative basic chemicals and 5 per cent for all other products under reference; and (d) uniform 15, a uniform general rate of 15 per cent on all products.

In deriving the tariff changes, consideration had to be given to the operation of current tariff preferences to imports sourced from developing countries (DCs). In some instances, the preference tariff from DCs was considered to be the operative tariff rather than the specified general tariff. A further complication concerned the Government's stated intention to replace the existing DC scheme in July 1986 with a scheme which provides a uniform preference margin of 5 percentage points. The effects of this change were modelled separately.

Table 9.5 contains model projections of the short-term effects of each option and the announced changes to DC preferences on profitability (measured by real net value of production) and employment demand. While substantial adjustment pressures are projected on parts of basic industrial chemicals, especially at the top end of the production chain, the effects for chemicals and plastics as a whole are projected to be minor under all options.

Under the Commission's preferred option the Victorian PVC industry is projected to suffer the largest profitability squeeze. PVC is particularly sensitive to import competition and would receive a large reduction in its tariff. Unlike many chemicals and plastics which receive a cost benefit owing to reduced tariffs on their inputs, Victorian PVC uses imported VCM, the tariff on which will remain constant under the Commission's recommendations. The petrochemical complexes are projected to suffer considerably. While their immediate products (ethylene, propylene and butadiene) are not subject to import competition, their profitability is heavily dependent on demands for the final products which experience a reduction in their protection against imports.

The model was also used to place a perspective on the projected adjustment pressures from tariff reform by comparing them with the effects of other changes in the economic environment, in particular the very large nominal and real devaluation of the Australian dollar which occurred during the inquiry. Projections of the devaluation required to offset the effect on the profitability of basic industrial chemicals, the hardest hit sector, of the ceiling 15 tariff option indicated that a nominal devaluation of about 30 per cent (zero money wage indexation) to about 50 per cent (50 per cent money wage indexation) would be required. These results suggested that the real devaluation which occurred between January 1985 and May 1986 would have provided a boost to the profitability of this part of chemicals and plastics almost equal to the adverse effects projected to follow from the implementation of the Commission's preferred tariff option.

Longer-term projections were also derived from the model. The Commission considered that output volumes and capital employed in basic industrial chemicals activities, which are extremely capital intensive, would probably remain constant for a considerable period despite the increased competition from imports. Model projections indicated the extent to which unit production costs would need to be reduced to allow basic industrial chemicals activities to maintain their output in the reduced assistance environment. Additional information on firm structure and performance was then used to assess the scope for achieving cost reductions of the order indicated.

Table 9.4 Commodities and industries distinguished in the ORANI-CHEM model

Relationship to ABS input–output sector[a]	Commodity/ industry	Commodity number	Industry number	Industry value added as a percentage of total value added of chemical and plastics activities[b]	Position in the production chain	Import substitution elasticities	
						Short term	Longer term
27.08	Rural	1	1			1.7	2.6
	Petroleum and coal products	2	2		A	0.4	0.6
27.02	Olefines and aromatics[c]	3			B	10	10
27.02	Polyethylene[d]	4			C	25	25
27.02	Polypropene	5			C	25	25
27.02	Ethylene oxide derivatives	6			C	25	25
27.02	Caustic soda	7			B	15	15
27.02	Polyvinyl chloride	8			C	25	25
27.02	Botany olefines		3				
27.02	Botany other[c]		4				
27.02	Altona		5				
27.02	Polyvinyl chloride (Victoria)		6				
27.02	Other organic (current tariff > 15)[f]	9	7	3.8	B,C	15	15

Table 9.4 (cont.)

Relationship to ABS input–output sector[a]	Commodity/industry	Commodity number	Industry number	Industry value added as a percentage of total value added of chemical and plastics activities[b]	Position in the production chain	Import substitution elasticities	
						Short term	Longer term
27.02	Other organic (current tariff < 15)	10	8	0.9	B,C	1	1
27.02	Other inorganic (current tariff > 15)[g]	11	9	2.9	B,C	10	10
27.02	Other inorganic (current tariff < 15)[h]	12	10	5.5	B,C	0.5	0.5
27.02	Styrene monomer	13	11		B	25	25
27.02	Synthetic rubber	14	12		C	25	25
27.02	Styrene resins[i]	15	13		C	25	25
27.02	Other resins (current tariff > 15)[j]	16	14	4.2	C	25	25
27.02	Other resins (current tariff < 15)	17	15	0.5	C	1	1
27.02	CSR chemicals[k]	18	16		B,C	25	25
27.02	Soda ash	19	17		B	15	15
27.04	Pharmaceuticals and veterinary products[l]	20	18			2	2
27.04	Pesticides	21	19	2.2	E	1	2
27.05	Detergents	22	20	4.3	E	3	5

Table 9.4 (cont.)

Relationship to ABS input–output sector[a]	Commodity/ industry	Commodity number	Industry number	Industry value added as a percentage of total value added of chemical and plastics activities[b]	Position in the production chain	Import substitution elasticities	
						Short term	Longer term
27.05	Soaps and toothpaste etc.	23	21	2.5	E	2	3
34.03	Pipes and fittings, conduits	24	22	2.5	D	2	2
34.03	Blow moulding	25	23	4.6	D	1	1
34.03	Other moulding	26	24	11.3	D	4	4
34.03	Extruded profiles and hose	27	25	1.0	D	5	5
34.03	Extruded films and bags	28	26	4.8	D	7	7
34.03	Extruded sheet and floor tiles	29	27	2.7	D	7	7
34.03	Vinyl calendered and coated film/sheet	30	28	1.3	D	7	7
34.03	Cellular plastics[m]	31	29	2.5	D	0.5	0.5
34.03	Reinforced and other plastics[n]	32	30	4.9		3	3
27.03	Paints	33	31	6.3	E	2	3
27.06	Cosmetics and toilet preparations	34	32	5.1	E	2	3
27.07	Other chemical products[p]	35	33	9.1	E	2	3

Table 9.4 (cont.)

Relationship to ABS input-output sector[a]	Commodity/industry	Commodity number	Industry number	Industry value added as a percentage of total value added of chemical and plastics activities[b]	Position in the production chain	Import substitution elasticities	
						Short term	Longer term
27.01	Chemical fertilizers	36	34		B	1.7	2.5
	Metallic ores and coal	37	35			0.5	0.7
	Oil and gas	38	36		A	0.5	0.7
	Other minerals	39	37		A	2	3
	Export food products[q]	40	38			0.5	0.7
	Non-export food products	41	39			2.2	3.3
	Textiles, clothing and footwear	42	40			3.1	4.6
	Wood and wood products	43	41			2	2.9
	Bags and containers	44	42			1.1	1.7
	Paper, paper products and printing	45	43			1.3	2.0
	Glass, clay and concrete	46	44			1	1.5
	Basic metals[r]	47	45			0.8	1.3
	Metal products	48	46			1.8	2.7
	Motor vehicles	49	47			5.2	7.8
	Machinery equipment and other manufacturing	50	48			0.9	1.4

Table 9.4 (cont.)

Relationship to ABS input-ouput sector[a]	Commodity/industry	Commodity number	Industry number	Industry value added as a percentage of total value added of chemical and plastics activities[b]	Position in the production chain	Import substitution elasticities	
						Short term	Longer term
34.02	Rubber products	51	49		D	1.5	2.3
	Utilities	52	50			0	0
	Housing, building and construction	53	51			0	0
	Wholesale and retail trade and repairs	54	52			0	0
	Transport	55	53			1.3	2
	Business and private services	56	54			0	0
	Government services	57	55			0	0

CSR, Colonial Sugar Refining.

[a]The ORANI-CHEM chemical and plastics industries are derived from the following ABS input-output industries: 27.02 (other basic chemicals); 27.03 (paints); 27.04 (pharmaceuticals, veterinary products and pesticides); 27.05 (soap and other detergents); 27.06 (cosmetics and toilet preparations); 27.07 (other chemical products); 34.03 (plastic and related products). See ABS (1984).

[b]Entries for some industries are not given for reasons of confidentiality.

[c]Olefines and aromatics include ethylene, propylene, butadiene, benzene, toluene and xylene.

[d]Includes high density, low density and linear low density polyethylenes.

[e]Includes chloroalkali, vinyl chloride monomer, polyvinyl chloride, ethylene and derivatives, polyethylene oxide derivatives, carbon tetrachloride and perchloroethylene.

[f] Includes organic pigments, alkyl benzene, organic surfactants, hydrocarbon solvents, carbon tetrachloride, perchloroethylene, propylene oxide derivatives, acetone, phenol, formaldehyde and other items.

[g] Includes phosphoric acid, sodium tripolyphosphate and other phosphates, titanium dioxide pigments, inorganic pigments and other items.

[h] Includes sulphuric and other inorganic acids, industrial gases and other items.

[i] Includes polystyrene, acrylonitrile butadiene styrene, expanded polystyrene and styrene butadiene latex.

[j] Includes alkyl, amino, phenolic and unsaturated polyester resins and acrylic emulsions.

[k] Products produced by CSR, including oxo-alcohols, phthalic anhydride, phthalate plasticizers, acetic acid and vinyl acid.

[l] Only a small proportion is under reference.

[m] Includes flexible foam and rigid cellular plastics.

[n] Includes fibreglass reinforced plastics, plastic tape, non-vinyl calendered and coated goods, and other plastic and related goods not elsewhere classified. Many items in this category are treated as textiles for the purposes of the tariff. The proportion of activity in this category which is under reference is uncertain.

[p] Includes explosives, inks, adhesives, waxes, polishes and creams, gelatin and many other items.

[q] Includes all sales, both export and domestic, of meat products and sugar.

[r] Includes alumina.

Source: IAC, 1986b, vol. 2, p. 360

Table 9.5 Effects in the short term of each option on net value of production (value added) and labour demand[a] in chemicals and plastics sectors (per cent)

Industry	DC Value added,[b] 1983–84 (million dollars)	DC Labour demand	Ceiling 15 Value added	Ceiling 15 Labour demand	Ceiling 20 Value added	Ceiling 20 Labour demand	Broad-banding Value added	Broad-banding Labour demand	Uniform 15 Value added	Uniform 15 Labour demand
Botany olefines, polyproplene, and polyethylene	-4	-3	-19	-15	-13	-11	-19	-15	-14	-12
Botany other	-5	-4	-25	-19	-19	-15	-27	-21	-27	-21
Altona	-6	-4	-23	-15	-17	-11	-23	-15	-24	-15
Polyvinyl chloride (Victoria)	-11	-9	-43	-36	-32	-27	-43	-36	-44	-37
Other organic (current tariff > 15)	0	0	-13	-11	-8	-6	-17	-14	-6	-4
Other organic (current tariff < 15)	0	0	-2	-1	-1	-1	-2	-1	11	8
Other inorganic (current tariff > 15)	0	0	-7	-5	-3	-2	-14	-10	-2	-1
Other inorganic (current tariff < 15)	0	0	-1	-1	0	0	-2	-1	3	3
Styrene monomer	0	0	-26	-20	-17	-13	-31	-23	-35	-27
Synthetic rubber	-8	-7	-15	-13	-7	-6	-15	-13	-27	-23
Styrene resins	-1	0	-19	-15	-11	-9	-17	-14	-23	-19
Other resins (current tariff > 15)	1	1	-17	-14	-15	-12	-17	-14	-22	-18

Table 9.5 (cont.)

Industry	Value added, 1983–84 (million dollars)	DC		Ceiling 15		Ceiling 20		Broad-banding		Uniform 15	
		Value added	Labour demand	Value added	Labour demand	Value added	Labour demand	Value added	Labour demand	Value added	Labour demand
Other resins (current tariff < 15)		1	0	-2	-2	0	0	-2	-2	1	1
CSR Chemicals		-10	-8	-5	-4	7	6	-4	-4	-10	-8
Soda ash		0	0	-4	-4	0	0	-13	-11	-4	-3
Basic industrial chemicals	887	-2.2	-1.6	-15.0	-11.1	-10.2	-7.5	-16.5	-12.2	-13.9	-10.3
Pesticides	57	0	0	0	0	0	0	0	0	0	0
Detergents	110	-1	0	1	1	1	1	1	1	1	1
Soaps, toothpaste etc	63	0	0	0	0	1	1	0	0	2	1
Paints	159	0	0	0	0	1	1	1	0	1	1
Cosmetics, toiletries etc	130	0	0	0	0	0	0	0	0	-1	-1
Other chemical products	230	0	0	0	0	0	0	2	2	2	1
Chemical products	749	0.1	0.1	0.3	0.3	0.4	0.4	1.0	0.8	0.8	0.7
Pipes, fittings and conduits	64	0	0	0	0	0	0	0	0	0	0
Blow mouldings	117	0	0	0	0	0	0	0	0	0	0
Other mouldings	286	0	0	-3	-2	0	0	-3	-2	-4	-3
Extruded profiles and hose	25	-1	-1	-3	-3	-2	-2	-3	-3	-4	-5
Extruded films and bags	123	-3	-3	-6	-6	-2	-2	-6	-6	-6	-6

Table 9.5 (cont.)

Industry	Value added,[b] DC 1983–84 (million dollars)	DC Value added	DC Labour demand	Ceiling 15 Value added	Ceiling 15 Labour demand	Ceiling 20 Value added	Ceiling 20 Labour demand	Broad-banding Value added	Broad-banding Labour demand	Uniform 15 Value added	Uniform 15 Labour demand
Extruded sheet and floor tiles	69	-4	-3	-6	-5	-2	-2	-6	-5	-7	-6
Calendered and coated film/sheet	32	-4	-3	-7	-6	-2	-2	-7	-6	-7	-6
Cellular plastics	64	0	0	0	0	0	0	0	0	0	0
Reinforced and other plastics	125	0	0	-2	-2	1	1	-2	-2	-3	-3
Plastics products	905	-0.7	-0.5	-2.7	-2.2	-0.5	-0.4	-2.7	-2.2	-3.4	-2.7
Total chemicals and plastics	2,541	-1.1	-0.5	-6.2	-2.9	-3.7	-1.5	-6.5	-3.0	-5.9	-2.9
Selected other sectors											
Rural	12,300	0.1	0.1	0.4	0.3	0.2	0.1	0.4	0.3	0.3	0.2
Metallic ores and coal	5,300	0.2	0.1	0.8	0.5	0.5	0.3	0.8	0.6	0.6	0.4
Oil and gas	740	-0.7	-0.5	-2.8	-2.0	-2.1	-1.5	-3.0	-2.1	-2.9	-2.1
Export food	2,300	0.1	0.1	0.4	0.4	0.2	0.2	0.4	0.4	0.2	0.2
Motor vehicles	2,200	0.1	0.1	0.6	0.5	0.3	0.3	0.6	0.5	0.3	0.3
Basic metals	4,000	0.1	0.1	0.9	0.5	0.6	0.3	1.1	0.6	0.7	0.4
Rubber products	390	0.1	0.1	0.3	0.3	0.2	0.2	0.3	0.3	-0.1	-0.1

Table 9.5 (*cont.*)

Industry	Value added,[b] 1983–84 (million dollars)	DC		Ceiling 15		Ceiling 20		Broad-banding		Uniform 15	
		Value added	Labour demand	Value added	Labour demand	Value added	Labour demand	Value added	Labour demand	Value added	Labour demand
Economy-wide measures											
Real GDP (%)	178,000	0.00		0.02		0.02		−0.02		−0.04	
Aggregate employment (persons)	6,000,000		−400		2,400		1,800		2,500		−3,300

CSR. Colonial Sugar Refining.

[a]All projections are in percentage changes from the levels they would have reached in the absence of changes in the assistance arrangements for chemicals and plastics.

[b]Value added, or net value of production, is not provided for the basic industrial chemicals industries because many of the data are confidential.

Source: IAC, 1986b, vol. 2, p. 379

3.3 Effects of assistance and other factors on agricultural competitiveness

In an inquiry into whether assistance should be provided for the consumption and production of fertilizers in Australia (see IAC, 1985), the Commission was asked to comment on current levels of assistance to the rural sector relative to that of other sectors together with other factors affecting agricultural competitiveness.[21] The standard ORANI model was used to address these issues. Because of its quite detailed treatment of agriculture and the broad nature of the instruments under investigation, the standard model was adequate for this exercise.

Table 9.6 contains short-term[22] projections for industry output and income of the removal of measured assistance to agricultural and manufacturing industries. Nominal assistance rates for manufacturing industries refer to 1982–3. They include tariffs and the tariff equivalents of import restrictions. Measured agricultural assistance includes that provided by home consumption price schemes, export inspection services, tariffs, adjustment assistance, research funding, concessional credit, income tax concessions and fertilizer subsidies. Effects of removing assistance to the rural sector are simulated for both 1981–2 and 1982–3. The 1981–2 rate is more representative of the rate for the last decade.[23] The effects of removing assistance to manufacturing and to agriculture are shown separately. This allows an assessment of the extent to which assistance provided for agriculture offsets the effect on agricultural performance of assistance provided for manufacturing.

The removal of assistance to manufacturing while assistance to agriculture is maintained is projected to increase real output of the agricultural sector as a whole by 5 per cent and the real net value of agricultural production by 13 per cent. Rural industries most dependent on exports (the mixed farming industries of the pastoral, wheat–sheep and high rainfall zones producing wool, grains and beef cattle, the northern beef industry and the sugar-cane-dominated other farming export sector) benefit most. Industries with greater reliance on the domestic market for their sales benefit less. The cost burden on agriculture of assistance to manufacturing appears, in the short term, to be roughly twice the magnitude of the boost to agriculture provided by agricultural assistance at 1981–2 levels. Assistance to agriculture for 1982–3 nearly offsets the effects on agriculture of assistance to the manufacturing sector.

The international competitiveness of Australian agriculture is affected by many factors in addition to assistance provided for manufacturing industries. These include management of the macroeconomy with respect to wages, government expenditure and exchange rate policy, and world commodity prices. As part of the analysis for the fertilizer report, the model was used to assess the relative contribution of each of the above factors to agricultural competitiveness. For comparison, an assessment of the effects of changing the price of fertilizers was also included. The results shown in table 9.7 were derived from a short-run version of ORANI in which changes in the international competitiveness of the economy as a whole arising from the above factors are assumed to be reflected in changes in the balance of trade. To facilitate the comparison of effects, the size of each change has been standardized to cause the same effect on the real net value of production of agriculture. They indicate that an improvement in agricultural competitiveness sufficient to raise the real net value of agricultural production by 1 per cent could be achieved by a uniform 6.1 per cent cut in assistance to manufacturing (column 1), a 0.2 per cent reduction in real wages throughout the economy (column 2), a 5.1 per cent reduction in real government expenditure (column 3) or a 3.1 per cent increase in international prices of all Australian agricultural export commodities (column 4). It could also be achieved by a 0.6 per cent devaluation of the exchange rate (assuming zero wage indexation) (column 5), a 0.7 per cent devaluation (assuming 30 per cent wage indexation) (column 6), an 11 per cent devaluation (assuming 70 per cent wage indexation) (column 7) and an 18.1 per cent reduction in the price of all fertlizers (column 8).

These results were useful in demonstrating that the fertilizer subsidy (which at the time represented only 6 per cent of the average user price) is a relatively unimportant determinant of agricultural competitiveness.

3.4 Macroeconomic adjustment to a decline in the foreign terms of trade

The relevant paper describing macroeconomic adjustment to a decline in the foreign terms of trade is by Fallon and Thompson (1986). The work grew out of a request to the Commission by the Australian Treasury to estimate, using the ORANI model, the effect of the recent (calender year 1985) devaluation of the Australian dollar on the general price level under alternative assumptions concerning the degree of wage indexation.[24] Amongst other things, the results pointed to a significant improvement in the trade balance in the short term from the devaluation should less than full indexation of money wages be achieved. This improvement has not materialized despite a

Table 9.6 Projections of the short-term effects on agriculture of the removal of industry assistance[a]

Variable	Removal of assistance of manufacturing	Removal of assistance to agriculture		Removal of assistance to manufacturing and agriculture	
		1981–2 assistance	1982–3 assistance	1981–2 assistance to agriculture	1982–3 assistance to agriculture
Output					
Pastoral zone	4.4	−2.5	−2.8	1.9	1.6
Wheat – sheep zone	3.9	−2.2	−2.9	1.7	1.0
High rainfall zone	5.5	−2.7	−3.3	2.8	2.2
Northern beef	9.0	−3.4	−5.2	5.6	3.8
Milk cattle and pigs	3.1	−2.1	−2.9	1.0	0.2
Other farming export (sugar cane, fruit)	9.1	−2.6	−6.8	6.5	2.3
Other farming (vegetables, cotton, oilseeds, tobacco)	2.4	−6.3	−6.4	−3.9	−4.0
Poultry	4.5	−2.2	−2.9	2.3	1.6
All agriculture[b]	5.0	−2.8	−4.0	2.2	1.0

Table 9.6 (*cont.*)

Variable	Removal of assistance of manufacturing	Removal of assistance to agriculture		Removal of assistance to manufacturing and agriculture	
		1981–2 assistance	1982–3 assistance	1981–2 assistance to agriculture	1982–3 assistance to agriculture
Real net value of production					
Pastoral zone	12.3	−5.9	−7.8	5.4	4.5
Wheat – sheep zone	13.7	−8.0	−10.0	5.7	3.7
High rainfall zone	15.0	−7.4	−9.1	7.6	5.9
Northern beef	28.2	−10.8	−16.6	17.5	11.6
Milk cattle and pigs	7.3	−5.0	−6.8	2.3	0.5
Other farming export (sugar cane, fruit)	17.6	−5.1	−13.1	12.4	4.5
Other farming (vegetables, cotton, oilseeds, tobacco)	3.8	−9.9	−10.1	−6.2	−6.3
Poultry	10.6	−5.0	−6.7	5.5	3.9
All agriculture	13.0	−7.2	−9.9	5.8	3.1

[a] All projections are percentage deviations from the value the variable would have taken in the absence of any change in assistance after an adjustment period of about two years.
[b] Represents a weighted average of results for the eight agricultural industries.
[c] Represents real returns to land, capital and labour (both hired and that of the owner-operator).
Source: IAC, 1985

Table 9.7 Size and effects of selected changes required to increase the real net value of agricultural production by 1 per cent in the short term[a]

	1	2	3	4	5	6	7	8
	6.13 per cent across the board decrease in tariffs on manufacturing industries	0.21 per cent real reduction in real wages	5.12 per cent reduction in government expenditure	3.09 per cent increase in all world agricultural commodity prices	0.59 per cent devaluation of the exchange rate with zero wage indexation	0.68 per cent devaluation of the exchange rate with 30 per cent wage indexation	1.08 per cent devaluation of the exchange rate with 70 per cent wage indexation	18.05 per cent reduction in the price of all fertilizers
Real output								
Pastoral zone	0.33	0.36	0.36	1.17	0.36	0.36	0.36	0.23
Wheat – sheep zone	0.31	0.29	0.30	1.09	0.29	0.29	0.29	0.37
High rainfall zone	0.44	0.18	0.44	0.73	0.18	0.18	0.18	0.40
Northern beef	0.71	0.65	0.72	0.39	0.65	0.65	0.65	0.58
Milk cattle and pigs	0.24	0.23	0.22	0.00	0.23	0.23	0.23	0.15
Other farming export (sugar cane, fruit)	0.71	0.63	0.66	-0.13	0.63	0.63	0.63	0.62
Other farming (vegetables, cotton, oil-seeds, tobacco)	0.18	0.23	0.08	-0.25	0.23	0.23	0.23	0.30
Poultry	0.35	0.32	0.35	0.05	0.32	0.32	0.32	0.24
All agriculture[b]	0.39	0.33	0.37	0.53	0.33	0.33	0.33	0.37
Index of agricultural costs[c]	-0.48	-0.44	-0.48	0.19	0.15	0.24	0.59	-1.15

Table 9.7 (cont.)

	1 6.13 per cent across the board decrease in tariffs on manufacturing industries	2 0.21 per cent reduction in real wages	3 5.12 per cent reduction in government expenditure	4 3.09 per cent increase in all world agricultural commodity prices	5 0.59 per cent devaluation of the exchange rate with zero wage indexation	6 0.68 per cent devaluation of the exchange rate with 30 per cent wage indexation	7 1.08 per cent devaluation of the exchange rate with 70 per cent wage indexation	8 18.05 per cent reduction in the price of all fertilizers
Real net value of production[d]								
Pastoral zone	0.99	0.99	0.99	0.61	0.99	0.99	0.99	0.64
Wheat – sheep zone	1.99	1.03	1.08	1.64	1.00	1.00	1.00	1.31
High rainfall zone	1.09	1.15	1.23	1.99	1.15	1.15	1.15	1.07
Northern beef	2.23	2.02	2.23	1.20	2.02	2.02	2.02	1.80
Milk cattle and pigs	0.57	0.53	0.53	0.0	0.58	0.58	0.58	0.35
Other farming export (sugar cane, fruit)	1.28	1.32	1.29	0.0	1.32	1.32	1.32	1.19
Other farming (vegetables, cotton, oil-seeds, tobacco)	0.28	0.43	0.14	-0.30	0.48	0.48	0.48	0.47
Poultry	0.84	0.81	0.85	0.12	0.81	0.81	0.81	0.55
All agriculture[b]	1.00	1.00	1.00	1.00	1.00	1.00	1.00	1.00

[a]All projections are percentage deviations from the value the variable would have taken in the absence of the change specified at the top of the respective column.
[b]Represents a weighted average of results for the eight agricultural industries.
[c]Includes all material inputs (domestic and imported) and the price of labour.
[d]Represents real returns to land, capital and labour (both hired and that of the owner-operator).

substantial decline in average real unit labour costs. The major reason is considered to be the severe decline in the foreign terms of trade which has occured since mid-1985. Over the 18 months to the end of June 1986, this decline is assessed by Commission staff to be about 21 per cent.

The standard ORANI model was used to assess the impact of this terms of trade decline (expressed in foreign import and export price movements at the 114 sector level) on economic activity, employment demand and the balance of trade in the short term. The size of the real wage and real expenditure adjustments to accommodate the projected declines in aggregate employment demand and the balance of trade were then calculated. Some results are shown in table 9.8.

They inidicate that, assuming fixed real wages and real expenditure, the decline in the foreign terms of trade is projected (column 1) to reduce real GDP by 4.1 per cent, reduce aggregate employment demand by 1.3 per cent and add 7.5 billion 1984–5 Australian dollars to the balance of trade deficit. The balance of trade decline could be arrested by a 5.5 per cent cut in real domestic expenditure, but with no real wage adjustment aggregate employment demand would fall by a further 1.6 per cent (columns 2 and 3). However, the balance of trade decline could be arrested with no adjustment to real expenditure by a very large (7.6 per cent) cut in real wages (column 4). As column 5 shows, this would significantly overcompensate for the reduction in employment demand associated with the terms of trade decline. Columns 6 and 7 indicate that reductions in real domestic expenditure of 3.4 per cent and in real wages of 2.9 per cent would be required to compensate for the effects of the terms of trade decline on both the balance of trade and aggregate employment demand.

Comparing these results with the real wage reduction achieved to date by partial wage discounting of the price effects of the devaluation suggests that a further cut in real wages may be necessary to correct for both the initial imbalance of the trade account existing at the start of 1985 and the deterioration caused by the recent sharp decline in the foreign terms of trade. Given the size of the foreign terms of trade decline it is therefore not surprising that a turnaround on the balance of trade has not to date been observed following the devaluation.

4 Problems Encountered in Analysing Economic Policy Issues with ORANI

Each of the applications of the ORANI model to policy issues within the government sector suffers in some degree from the following:

1 deficiencies in the data base and parameter file;
2 conflict between the basic theory and the real world situation;
3 specifying the problem statement; and
4 inability to measure resource use efficiency.

A number of these problems are accentuated by the Commission's need for considerable sectoral detail in its industry assistance work. The problems are considered in turn.

4.1 Data base and parameters

The standard ORANI model data base is derived from the official Australian input–output tables (see Australian Bureau of Statistics (ABS), 1984) and model coefficients in the form of cost and sales shares are derived from this data base. Commission staff update the data base biennially as new input–output tables are released. These tables are generally about seven years out of date, current tables being for 1982–3. In applications which refer to general policy issues such as that undertaken for the fertilizer inquiry, the absence of a more recent data base is not of major concern. However, in detailed industry policy work, the data base becomes more critical. Key aspects, particularly those relating to import shares of the domestic market,[25] are often found to differ substantially from those in the 10 tables. As far as possible, staff attempt to incorporate more recent information on import shares and other aspects of the data base. Because a complete update can never be undertaken the *ad hoc* procedure adopted is not particularly satisfactory.[26]

A second problem with the data base which invariably arises with industry modelling studies concerns the level of aggregation. Aggregation problems are often pointed out to the Commission by industry participants who find it difficult to reconcile their detailed understanding of the structure of one small part of an industry category with the information incorporated in the model on the structure of the category as a whole. Although as indicated by ORANI-MILK and ORANI-CHEM considerable interindustry detail is often captured in industry studies, significant aggregation problems remain. In ORANI-CHEM, for example, some sectors contained activities protected by disparate tariff rates leading to aggregation bias in determining the effects of tariff changes. Despite its treatment of regional production at the state level and a detailed treatment of manufactured dairy products far in excess of that captured in other modelling studies of the Australian dairy industry, ORANI-MILK was criticized for its failure to distinguish different supply prospects in regions within states and its lack of a treatment of wet products with short shelf lives.

Table 9.8 Projections of the short-term effects of the decline in the foreign terms of trade and the real wage and real expenditure adjustments needed to accommodate the decline[a]

	1	2	3	4	5	6	7
	Terms of trade decline	Expenditure adjustment to offset balance of trade effect	Total	Real wage adjustment to offset balance of trade effect	Total	Real wage and real expenditure adjustments to offset balance of trade and employment effects	Total
Real GDP	−4.1	−1.4	−5.5	4.1	0.0	0.7	−3.4
Aggregate employment	−1.3	−1.6	−2.9	6.1	4.8	1.3	0.0
Balance of trade	−7.5[b]	7.5	0.0	7.5	0.0	7.5	0.0
Real domestic expenditure	0.0[b]	−5.5	−5.5	0.0[b]	0.0	−3.4	−3.4
Real wage	0.0[b]	0.0[b]	0.0[b]	−7.6	−7.5	2.9	−2.9

Column 3 = column 1 + column 2.
Column 5 = column 1 + column 4.
Column 7 = column 1 + column 6.
[a]All projections are in percentage changes except the balance of trade which is in billion of 1984–5 Australian dollars.
[b]This value was set exogenously at zero.
Source: Fallon and Thompson, 1986

The great amount of sectoral detail incorporated in industry models such as ORANI-CHEM places onerous demands on parameter values as well as data. Because input–output data are required at only one point in time, the data base to support the level of disaggregation can usually be found. It is too much to expect that econometrically based estimates of all the accompanying parameters will be available or could be estimated from the available data. In several recent inquiries, the Commission has supplemented the available parameter file with information provided by firms concerning how a particular part of their industry might respond if confronted with a particular set of relative price changes. The experience has indicated that firms can confidently indicate the extent of substitution likely to follow in both the short term and longer term from a shift in relative prices.

4.2 The applicability of the basic theory

The aspect of the ORANI model's theoretical structure which is most frequently refuted by real world evidence concerns its treatment of prices. Key assumptions are that basic (i.e. ex-factory) prices are uniform across users and producers and that competitive conditions exist in all economic activities – producing, importing, exporting, transporting (margins) etc. Contradictions of these assumptions are often observed. In some cases it is possible to adjust the model to capture an alternative form of behaviour.[27] In others it is not.

On occasions, projections derived from the model under the assumption of competitive behaviour, although incorrect, play the valuable role of drawing attention to the deviation from competitive conditions existing in a particular part of the economy. Consider for example the results in table 9.5 from the ORANI-CHEM model. They indicate that the PVC activity is projected to suffer the largest decline in short-term profitability from the Commission's preferred tariff option (ceiling 15). Locally produced PVC, which competes strongly with imported PVC, faces a large reduction in its tariff (from 30 to 15 per cent). Furthermore, unlike other basic chemical activities it would not receive a direct cost benefit from reduced tariffs on inputs. Its main input, VCM (which accounts for over 50 per cent of the value of production of PVC and is used solely for this purpose), has a tariff of only 2 per cent. Implicit in the ORANI-CHEM story is the assumption of competitive conditions in importing. However, evidence gathered by the Commission suggested that, in response to a reduction in the tariff on its product, the PVC activity would be able to negotiate a cheaper price for imported VCM, the supplier of which was an overseas parent company. The model therefore was considered to overestimate the adjustment pressures likely to be experienced by the local PVC industry.

4.3 The problem statement

The Commission uses the ORANI framework for "what if" policy analysis. Results are interpreted as showing by how much the economy would deviate from its control position in a future year as a result of the implementation in the base year of the recommended changes in assistance. The control position represents the *ceteris paribus* position of the economy in the projection year. In short-run model applications it is assumed[28] that the model's base period data base (sometimes updated to include later information on import shares etc) provides an adequate description of the production and sales structure of the *ceteris paribus* economy in the solution year about two years hence.

In some instances, however, the Commission is asked to advise on assistance arrangements to be implemented at a future date in a situation where the arrangements already in place are likely to change significantly and thereby change the structure of the affected industries between the present and the time at which the recommendations are envisaged to take effect. This sequence of events occurred in two recent inquiries in which the ORANI framework was used, namely the inquiry into chemicals and plastics (IAC, 1986b) and the inquiry into textiles, clothing and footwear (IAC, 1986a). In the case of chemicals the problem was a minor one, involving a government decision to replace the existing system of diverse (in terms of rate and country or origin) DC preferences with a uniform preference rate of 5 percentage points on all DC imports. Hence the effects of the Commission's recommendations needed to be assessed using a benchmark assistance environment that take into account the effects of the new DC preference arrangements on operative tariffs.

In the case of textiles, clothing and footwear, the problem was considerably more important. Currently, import quotas are in place, the tariff equivalent of which changes over time according to changes in the real exchange rate and the rate at which quota volumes are increased relative to total domestic demand for the products concerned.

To obtain model projections of the effects of changing assistance arrangements at a future date requires that the tariff equivalent of the present protection regime be known at this future date. This necessitates taking a view about how factors such as the international competitiveness of the economy will evolve between the present and the solution year. In the Commission's analysis the problem was side-stepped by defining the problem statement to assume a tariff equivalent of current arrangements in the solution year equal to that in the base year. It seems likely that the only way this type of problem will be satisfactorily overcome is by generating forecasts of the underlying growth path of sectors of the economy under existing and planned assistance arrangements.

4.4 Resource use efficiency

The Commission has interpreted the term efficiency in its guidelines to involve encouraging a sectoral allocation of a fixed resource base such that the real national income earned by this resource base is enhanced. In pursuing a more efficient allocation of the economy's resources, the Commission is guided by the principles of international trade theory. Its approach would be a good deal more convincing,[29] however, if it could demonstrate analytically that, once resources had responded fully to the adjustment pressures imposed on activities in the short term from its recommended assistance changes, the real income earned by the economy from the "improved" allocation of resources exceeded that earned from the existing allocation.

Significant improvements in long-run modelling with ORANI have been achieved by the IMPACT research team in recent times.[30] These have centred around endogenizing both the gross national product (GNP) (income accruing to Australians being taken as an appropriate measure of national welfare) and the GDP by modelling the extent of foreign ownership.[31] Despite these improvements, ORANI remains an unsuitable framework for assessing the longer-term efficiency implications of economic changes.

Its unsuitability stems from deficiencies in two areas. Firstly, at the detailed industry level with which the Commission works the standard model does not allow a general treatment of substitution prospects between commodities in production and consumption.[32] Reducing or eliminating existing distortions in production and consumption is always a key aim of the Commission's recommendations on changes in assistance arrangements. Secondly, standard ORANI, being constructed around the traditional framework of international trade theory, does not incorporate key features of industrial organization such as imperfect competition and economies of scale[33] and scope thought to be important in determining the efficiency costs of protection.[34]

Work is proceeding at the Impact Centre to correct both deficiencies. The creation of more flexible computer programs should allow the ready incorportion into detailed industry versions of ORANI of a treatment of substitution prospects in production which is constrained only by the information base (see Pearson, 1986).

Cory and Horridge (1985) have shown how scale economies and

imperfect competition can be incorporated into a Harris-style miniature version of ORANI. Preliminary results suggest that the key
factor determining the size of the welfare gains to the economy from
a cut in protection is the degree of imperfect competition in the home
market which in turn governs the extent to which firms reduce
product prices in response to a decrease in the price of the imported
equivalent. Considerably more research is required before this and
other features of the industrial organization approach can be incorporated into a detailed industry version of ORANI of the type used in
specific inquiries.

5 Communication of Model Results

Because the applied general equilibrium models used by the Commission are large, and therefore appear complex to non-modellers, an
important challenge facing the modeller is that of communicating the
insights from the models to others involved in the policy advisory
process. The communication challenge exists at three levels:

1 between the modeller and other staff involved in the inquiry
  process;
2 between the modeller and Commissioners responsible for the policy
  recommendations of the inquiry; and
3 between the Commission and outside participants in the economic
  debate.

5.1 Communication at the staff level

At the staff level the ability to analyse economic issues using applied
general equilibrium models is concentrated in the Economic Studies
and Information Division.[35] Staff from this and other Divisions assist
Commissioners in inquiries. There is invariably a difference in opinion between modellers and other staff concerning the role that
modelling should play in particular inquiries. A present Commission-
er has observed "the natural tendency of modellers to promote their
models and ignore those characteristics of industries and markets
which cannot be readily handled, and the equally natural tendency
for those who deal with the details of particular firms and markets to
carp about the needs for assumptions to be more realistic" (Mauldon,
Duncan and Cronin, 1980, p. 8). While it is always easy to identify
what has been left out of a model it is a good deal more difficult to

assess the extent to which the omitted factors, if included, would modify the initial conclusions.

The main way the staff to staff communications problem has been tackled has been through the organization within the Commission of detailed training courses on the use and limitations of applied general equilibrium modelling for economic policy analysis. As a result of such courses, some progress has been made in broadening the understanding within the Commission of applied general equilibrium modelling techniques in analysing industry assistance issues. Nevertheless, when considering industry assistance issues, most Commission staff still feel more comfortable with partial equilibrium models, such as that provided for the effective rate of protection concept, than with the applied general equilibrium approach.

5.2 Communication at the Commissioner level

As part of the inquiry process Commissioners hold on-site discussions with major interest groups. This enables them to obtain a first-hand assessment of the way that the activities under reference operate and the issues of relevance to the inquiry. As a result Commissioners often develop firm opinions concerning the appropriate set of policy recommendations and their likely effects. There is a natural tendency to seek from model analyses analytical support for these opinions. In some instances this is forthcoming and the assurances provided by the model enhance the convictions with which the recommendations are made. In others, model results contradict firmly held opinions. In the process of reconciling model results with opinions both the reasons underlying the opinions and the assumptions underlying the model are brought sharply into focus. Both may be subsequently changed. Sensitivity analysis is sometimes called for to establish the robustness of model conclusions. The outcome is invariably a more structured and internally consistent set of arguments than if the model had not been used.

An example of the importance of a model in checking an assessment gained from discussions with industry representatives was provided in the enquiry into chemicals and plastics. A view was formed from these discussions that reduced tariffs on resin would enhance the growth prospects of plastic product industries. This view was unable to take into account the full package of tariff changes recommended at the conclusion of the inquiry. The ORANI-CHEM model, by decomposing the effects on plastic products of various components of the package of tariff changes (table 9.9), was able to show the extent to which tariff reductions on the product would negate and in some instances reverse the favourable effects of reduced tariffs on resins.

Table 9.9 Decomposition of the longer-term effects on plastic product outputs of the commission's preferred tariff option for chemicals and plastics (per cent)[a]

| Plastic product | Effects on plastic product output of tariff changes for | | | |
	Resin inputs	Own tariff	Other inputs	Total
Pipes, fittings and conduits	0.5	−0.3	0.0	0.2
Blow mouldings	0.1	0.0	0.0	0.1
Other mouldings	1.6	−3.6	0.1	−1.9
Extruded profiles and hose	2.3	−4.8	0.3	−2.2
Extruded films and bags	7.2	−11.2	0.2	−3.8
Extruded sheet and floor tiles	4.2	−8.3	0.1	−4.0
Vinyl calendered and coated film/sheet	2.6	−7.6	0.2	−4.8
Cellular plastics	0.1	0.0	0.0	0.1
Reinforced and other plastics	1.2	−2.6	0.3	−1.1
Total plastic products	2.2	−4.1	0.1	−1.8

[a]The additional effects of the 5 percentage point preference margin for DCs are included in these results.
Source: IAC, 1986b

5.3 Communication of model results to the wider community

Model projections of the effects of changes in assistance arrangements are communicated to the wider community through published reports on each inquiry. In this way the Commission responds directly to the challenge issued by the supporters of industry protection of "tell us where the additional jobs will come from to compensate for jobs lost in protected activities". Model projections are often widely reported and assessed in the media. The analytical framework underlying them has also been subject to close scrutiny in the newspaper columns of economic feature writers as well as in the academic community.

While the Commission's economy-wide analytical approach has

now found general acceptance amongst the academic community and most government agencies with economic policy responsibilities, its acceptance level in the wider community is considerably lower.[36] A major reason concerns the difficulty non-economists have in comprehending the "what if" of *ceteris paribus* framework in which the model is used when analysing proposed changes in assistance. For example, while there is a strong economic logic underlying the mechanisms whereby a reduction in assistance to say basic chemicals would, *ceteris paribus*, result in improved job prospects in export-oriented agricultural and mining activities, it is difficult to sell this message to a community well informed by the media of the severe adjustment problems currently being experienced by these activities because of depressed world prices for their products.

The importance of gaining a measure of acceptance in the general community that the benefits of reduced assistance to industries will outweigh the costs should not be underestimated. Unless this can be achieved the rate of progress in lowering assistance is likely to be slow. To increase acceptance of the need for change requires that the community be thoroughly informed of the benefits and costs. Projections from the Commission's economy-wide modelling framework have over the years provided valuable insights into the means whereby policies which discriminate in favour of one sector of the economy are paid for by others. However, because these projections have abstracted completely from all other factors which influence the growth prospects of industry, they have been judged on occasions by important sections of the community to be not particularly relevant. Broadening the projections to include a treatment of how other influencing factors are likely to evolve may help increase the plausibility and hence level of community acceptance of model-based projections of the effects of moving towards a less interventionist industry policy stance.

6 Concluding Remarks

The Commission has a statutory responsibility to consider the effects of its industry assistance recommendations on all other sectors of the economy in addition to directly affected sectors and on community living standards. The applied general equilibrium framework is at present the most suitable analytical framework for undertaking this task. Applied general equilibrium modelling therefore forms an integral part of the Commission's evelution of changes in industry assistance arrangements. Such modelling provides a means of tracing in detail, in an internally consistent economy-wide framework, the mechanisms whereby assistance changes in one part of the economy impact on the overall level and distribution across all sectors of economic activity and employment. In addition, it provides projections of the orders of magnitude involved. Such modelling also permits a thorough exploration of the implications of alternative assumptions concerning the macroeconomic and microeconomic environments in which the changes are envisaged to take place. In this way, the robustness of policy insights can be checked.

Continued support for the Impact Project has enabled the Commission's modelling work to remain state of the art. This has enhanced the Commission's reputation in the Australian economic community and the professionalism of its applied economic staff.

The degree to which the Commission's applied general equilibrium modelling work has enhanced the quality of its analysis of economic policy issues and influenced its subsequent policy advice to the Government has varied considerably from application to application. In some situations it has been possible to incorporate into the model sufficient detail to capture convincingly the essence of the problem under study. In others, the abstraction from reality provided by the model has been judged to provide an unrealistic or inadequate treatment of factors thought likely to be of importance in shaping the outcome. Nevertheless, in such situations the model, by providing a framework around which a line of argument can be developed, has imposed some intellectual rigour on the structure of the economic discussion. In addition, it has made explicit what might otherwise remain implicit while helping to sharpen perspectives about what the important and less important factors are likely to be.

Experience at the Commission has shown that it is unrealistic to expect any one applied economic model, no matter how comprehensive, to satisfy all its needs when considering industry assistance arrangements. The Commission's approach has been to exploit the flexibility of the standard ORANI model by incorporating within it highly detailed industry models. This approach, despite its heavy demands on data and parameters, has proved reasonably successful. Projections from such models have been instrumental in providing a balanced assessment of the macroeconomic and sectoral output, income and employment implications of current assistance arrangements and proposed changes to them. These projections are weighed against the projections of interest groups, particularly those representing directly affected sectors, in the ensuing public debate concerning the desirability of the Commission's recommendations.

The application of applied general equilibrium modelling to quite specific areas of economic activity has frequently revealed a conflict between the model's view of how the economy operates and real world evidence. In some instances appropriate modifications to model structure can be undertaken. In others where this is not possible, the experience provides a salutory reminder of the extent to which models of economic systems abstract from reality. They cannot hope to include all the relevant factors. From the Commission's viewpoint, the most unsatisfactory aspect of its implied general equilibrium modelling framework is its inability to determine, with any degree of confidence, the longer-term effects of its recommendations and alternative proposals on the efficiency with which resources are used in the economy and the overall level of economic welfare likely to result. For these reasons, applied general equilibrium modelling is viewed by the Commission principally as providing some economic rigour about the way judgements are made concerning the appropriate policy recommendations. The formulation of a quantitative model, no matter how impressive, does not remove the need for judgement.

The Commission has always been willing to expose its economic modelling to public scrutiny. Details of model structure, data base (where confidentiality requirements can be met) and parameters are either published as a matter of course or readily available. In addition, the Commission allows interested parties to use its models, sometimes with a model closure and parameter assignment which reflects a view of how the economy operates quite contrary to its own. This serves to increase the respect of such parties for the professionalism of the Commission's applied economic analysis and its recommendations.

While the ready public exposure of its modelling work and underlying assumptions has increased the vulnerability of the Commission to unscrupulous critics, it has also significantly enriched the quality of Australian applied economic analysis, particularly in the industry policy area.

Notes

The views expressed are my own and do not necessarily reflect those of the Industries Assistance Commission. I am indebted to Tony Lawson, Roger Mauldon, Alan Powell and John Sutton for helpful comments and to colleagues in the Economic Studies and Information Division of the Industries Assistance Commission for undertaking the analyses upon which I have drawn freely in writing the paper:

1 The standard ORANI model is described by Dixon et al. (1982). The model was developed as part of the Impact Project, a cooperative venture researching the structure of the Australian economy. The Project is

supported by a number of Australian Government agencies, the most prominent being the Industries Assistance Commission, and three Australian universities. As is discussed later, most applications of the ORANI framework undertaken to assist the Commission in its analysis of industry policy issues involve significant modifications to the standard ORANI model.

2 A survey of applications of the ORANI framework to industry and other policy issues is contained in Chapter 7. This survey illustrates the great flexibility of ORANI with respect to the range and types of policy issues it can analyse.

3 The Impact Research Centre is located on the campus of the University of Melbourne. The Centre, directed by Professor A. A. Powell, provides the Impact Project's basic research and development unit. See Powell (1985) for a recent account of the activities of the Centre.

4 It is important, so as not to compromise the value of the Commission as a source of disinterested policy advice, that its membership appear balanced, i.e. contain persons drawn from each of the important interest groups in the community.

5 The usual time period specified for a reasonably substantial reference is 12 months. The Commission also receives short-term or interim inquiries in which the government seeks advice on whether any immediate action or assistance is necessary for an industry. The duration for such inquiries is, for example, 60–90 days. In these situations there is generally insufficient time to undertake any significant applied economic analysis.

6 This is despite the attendance, at very detailed training courses on the structure and use of the ORANI model, of employees of most Australian Government agencies with a potential interest in using the model for policy analysis. The experience suggests that, by and large, while the training course programme has successfully conveyed to government employees outside the Commission the potential role of the model in assisting their analysis of certain types of economic policy issues, it has not left them with sufficient confidence and expertise to conduct that analysis without assistance from the Commission.

7 As an example, consider the case revealed in the Commission's recent inquiry into the chemicals and plastics industries (Industries Assistance Commission (IAC), 1986b) of vinyl chloride monomer (VCM) activity. The product of this activity is consumed as a feedstock input by the polyvinyl chloride (PVC) activity which is subsequently used to make various types of plastic products. Under current arrangements, domestic production of VCM is protected against imported VCM by an *ad valorem* tariff of 2 per cent. Domestic PVC is protected by a 30 per cent tariff while nominal rates of protection for using plastic product industries are 20–5 per cent. Clearly, each component of the production chain must be modelled separately to assess the effects of rationalizing the tariff structure in this part of manufacturing industry.

8 Two examples are (a) a just-completed inquiry into the chemicals and plastics industries (IAC, 1986b), which involved analysing in detail the relationship between petrochemical feedstocks, various stages in the production of basic chemicals, formulated chemical products and fabricated plastic products, and (b) a current inquiry into pulp, paper, paper products and printing which encompasses the interactions between the

production of pulp from waste paper or raw wood, the use of this production in a range of industries including newsprint, paper, paperboard and tissues, and paperboard containers.

9 The shift in emphasis away from specific industry references towards those encompassing wider parts of the production chain followed from a recommendation to the Government in a recent public review of the functions and performance of the Commission (Uhrig, 1984). Other recommendations in this review which have elevated the importance of applied general equilibrium modelling to the Commission's work programme are a requirement that the Commission present and evaluate a range of options in addition to its preferred option and a requirement that the Commission focus less on border protection and more on other industry assistance instruments.

10 The short and longer term are often defined rather arbitrarily. While on occasions the Commission recommends the phased introduction of a proposed assistance change with the timing of each phase made explicit, the degree of phasing chosen reflects essentially a judgement, which is unsupported by numerical analysis, concerning the capacity of an industry to adjust.

11 Partial equilibrium models constructed by the Commission are sometimes quite sophisticated. An example is the Commission's model of dried vine fruits production and sales (IAC, 1984). This incorporated a treatment of production relationships differentiated by region, sales relationships differentiated by end use (processing, household demands and export demands), competition from imports in each of the domestic uses for the products, and relationships equating supplies with demands for dried vine fruits commodities and primary factors and prices with costs in domestic production, exporting and importing.

12 In several recent industry references the government has requested that the Commission advise on longer-term growth prospects for the industries concerned. To address this issue requires a consideration of how the full range of factors determining industry growth prospects, including assistance arrangements, will evolve over time. Recent work by Dixon and others (Dixon, 1986) suggests that a version of ORANI modified to provide forecasts as distinct from "what if" type projections has the potential to play an important role in forecasting industry growth prospects and identifying the key factors contributing to these prospects.

13 Some recent examples are ORANI-MILK, a model of dairy production and processing (IAC, 1983), ORANI-CHEM, a model of chemical and plastics production and sales (IAC, 1986b), and ORANI-TCF, a model of textiles, clothing and footwear activities (IAC, 1986a).

14 An unusually large proportion of policy applications of the ORANI model have been oriented towards the analysis of issues of concern to the agricultural sector. These include changes which impinge directly on agriculture, e.g. changes in various types of agricultural assistance instruments, and changes whose initial effects are elsewhere but which nevertheless are important determinants of agricultural prosperity, e.g. changes in manufacturing industry tariffs and changes in government spending. The key factor determining the adjustment pressures on agriculture of an economic change is the extent to which that change affects the farm cost structure (closely dependent on the general level of costs in the economy)

relative to the product price (determined in world markets). It is the ability of the applied general equilibrium framework to endogenize this cost–price ratio within an economy-wide framework incorporating the region-specific multiproduct nature of Australian agriculture that makes it a particularly useful tool for agricultural policy analysis.

15 The specification of household demand behaviour in standard ORANI is based on preference independence in an additive utility function. This implies that the marginal utility that consumers derive from each commodity is independent of their consumption of any other commodity. While this assumption is tenable for broadly based consumption aggregates, it is not realistic at the level of dairy product disaggregation in ORANI-MILK. Using the method of Clements and Smith (1983) the 13 consumer products derived from farm milk production were allowed to interact fully in the utility function while the additive preference assumption was preserved for the other broadly defined groups.

16 Standard ORANI allows industries to produce a range of competing products only in the agricultural sector. This treatment was extended to milk manufacturing.

17 Key macroeconomic assumptions underlying the short term (considered to represent an adjustment period of about two years) are (a) fixed capital and land in each industry with the farm owner-operator considered part of the capital stock in farm-based industries, (b) a demand-determined hired labour market with a constant real wage for all occupations, (c) a fixed level of real domestic absorption with changes in real GDP reflected in changes in the balance of trade, and (d) a fixed nominal exchange rate with changes in international competitiveness reflected in changes in the domestic price level relative to world prices.

18 The two petrochemical complexes use different feedstocks and hence produce different proportions of those products.

19 This is the latest year for which input–output tables are available in Australia.

20 Firms were asked to assess the changes in quantities of imports and domestic commodities in response to specified changes in relative prices. Values for the import substitution elasticities were deduced from these estimates and are shown in table 9.4.

21 For a detailed general equilibrium-based study of the effects on agriculture of a range of economic shocks originating outside the sector see Higgs (1986).

22 The short-term environment in table 9.6 assumes that capital and land used in each industry remain constant. It also assumes that wages in the economy are fully indexed to the consumer price index (i.e. are constant in real terms) and that real absorption in the economy adjusts to maintain the balance of trade at its level before the removal of assistance.

23 Disaster relief from the 1982 drought and lower export prices for some products resulted in a much higher rate of assistance to agricultural activities for 1982–3.

24 Australia has a centralized wage fixing system under the control of the Arbitration Commission. Information on the consumer price effects of exchange rate changes is used as input into the wage deliberations of the Arbitration Commission.

25 In ORANI, the import share of the domestic market is an important

determinant of the effects of a given reduction in assistance on an industry's activity level and employment demand.

26 A further problem concerns transient influences in the data base which are not "typical" of the structure of the economy in a "normal" year. Where these are known to be large, an attempt is made to typicalize that part of the data base.

27 In a reference currently before the Commission, the model is being used to simulate industry assistance provided via export concessions. These allow for a rebate of the duty on imported inputs when used in production for exports. The imported content of domestic sales of the same good is not subject to rebate. Hence the basic cost of the good sold domestically exceeds that of the good exported, which contradicts ORANI theory. The deviation in basic prices, however, can be incorporated by disaggregating the activity into two components, one solely exported and one solely for the domestic market with each component using the same production technology and capital stock. A duty rebate on the imported inputs to the export part can then be applied without affecting directly the cost of production of the domestic part.

28 This assumption is in most instances a reasonable one.

29 With the government now requiring the Commission to specify a range of assistance options together with its preferred option, the need to demonstrate the efficiency implications of particular patterns of resource use has been brought more sharply into focus.

30 See Horridge (1985) for a complete description of the improved long-run closure of ORANI.

31 Early long-run closures with the model (e.g. Vincent, 1980) lacked a satisfactory measure of national welfare. With land and labour assumed to be fixed in aggregate and the absolute real rate of return in the economy assumed to be given by the world rate in this closure, an increase in GDP resulted mainly from an increase in the aggregate capital stock. To the extent to which this was achieved by an inflow of foreign capital, the increase in GDP, by failing to take into account that rentals on foreign-owned capital would accrue to foreigners, would overstate the benefits accruing to Australians from the reform under study.

32 Implementing direct substitution effects in consumption via the nested utility approach of Clements and Smith (1983) has not always proved satisfactory.

33 Evidence collected during the inquiry into chemicals and plastics identified some heavily protected components of the sector in which production was concentrated in a few firms each unable to exhaust economics of scale. This evidence sits uncomfortably with the ORANI-CHEM model assumptions of perfect competition and constant returns to scale.

34 Harris (1984) has shown that the inclusion of industrial organization concepts such as imperfect competition and scale economies into the traditional applied general equilibrium framework can lead to significantly increased estimates of the welfare costs of protection.

35 The Commission also has two Inquiry Divisions with responsibility for the preparation of inquiry reports and a Policy Co-ordination and Development Division responsible for determining the approach of the Commission to assistance issues, preparing the annual report and documenting assistance levels in each sector. Staff in these Divisions are generally not

346   *David P. Vincent*

oriented towards quantitative economic modelling.
36 For example, in presenting his views on how to revitalize Australian
industry, a prominent trade union leader recently asserted that "One
urgent and essential condition for rejuvenating Australia's manufacturing
industry is for the disbanding of the IAC, in its present form, and the
destruction of the ORANI model" (Halfpenny, 1986, p. 89).

References

ABS (Australian Bureau of Statistics) (1984) *Australian National Accounts:
Input–Output Tables, 1978–79*, Canberra: Australian Government Pub-
lishing Service.
Clements, K. W., and M. D. Smith (1983) "Extending the Consumption Side
of the ORANI Model", Canberra: Industries Assistance Commission,
Impact Preliminary Working Paper No. OP-38.
Cory, P., and M. Horridge (1985) "A Harris-style Miniature Version of
ORANI", Canberra: Industries Assistance Commission, Impact Project
Preliminary Working Paper No. OP-54.
Dixon, P. B. (1986) "Prospects for Australian Industries and Occupations,
1985 to 1990", *Australian Economic Review*, 73, First Quarter, 3–28.
——, B. R. Parmenter, J. Sutton and D. P. Vincent (1982) *ORANI: A Multi-
sectoral Model of the Australian Economy*, Amsterdam: North-Holland.
Fallon, J., and L. Thompson, (1986) "An Analysis of the Effects of Recent
Changes in the Exchange Rate and the Terms of Trade on the Level and
Composition of Economic Activity", paper presented to 15th Conference
of Economics, Monash University, Australia, August 25–9.
Halfpenny, J. (1986) "Union view", in Bureau of Industry Economics,
*Revitalising Australian Industry – the Paths and Prospects for Long Term
Growth: Conference Paper and Proceedings*, Canberra: Australian
Government Publishing Service, pp. 87–99.
Harris, R. G. (1984) *Trade, Industrial Policy and Canadian Manufacturing*,
Toronto: Ontario Economic Council.
Higgs, P. J. (1986) *Adaption and Survival in Australian Agriculture*, Mel-
bourne: Oxford University Press.
Horridge, M. (1985) "Long-run Closure of ORANI: First Implementation",
Canberra: Industries Assistance Commission, Impact Project Preliminary
Working Paper No. 0P-50.
IAC (Industries Assistance Commission) (1983) *The Dairy Industry*, Can-
berra: Australian Government Publishing Service, Report No. 333.
—— (1984) *The Dried Vine Fruit Industry*, Canberra: Australian Government
Publishing Service, Report No 351.
—— (1985) *Fertilisers*, Canberra: Australian Government Publishing Service,
Report No. 372
—— (1986a) *The Textile, Clothing and Footwear Industries*, Canberra:
Australian Government Publishing Service, Report No. 386.
—— (1986b) *The Chemicals and Plastics Industries*, Canberra: Australian
Government Publishing Service, Report No. 390.
Mauldon, R. G., R. C. Duncan, and M. R. Cronin, (1980) "Use of Economic
Models Within a Policy-oriented Organisation: The Industries Assistance

Commission", mimeo. Available from Industries Assistance Commission, Canberra.

Pearson, K. R. (1986) "Automating the Computation of Solutions of Large Economic Models", Canberra: Industries Assistance Commission, Impact Project Preliminary Working Paper No. IP-27.

Powell, A. A. (1985) Impact Project Report No. R-05, mimeo, 67 pp. Available from Industries Assistance Commission, Canberra.

Uhrig, J. (Chairman) (1984) *Review of the Industries Assistance Commission: Report*, Canberra: Australian Government Publishing Service.

Vincent, D. P. (1980) "Some Implications for the Australian Economy of Trade Growth with Newly Industrialising Asia: The Use and Limitations of the ORANI Framework", in K. Anderson and A. George (eds), *Australian Agriculture and Newly Industrialising Asia: Issues for Research*, Canberra: Australia–Japan Research Centre, pp. 360–95.

PART IV
Economic Planning

10

General Equilibrium Approaches to Energy Policy Analysis in Sweden

Lars Bergman and Stefan Lundgren

1 Introduction

1.1 The major issues

As in many other countries there was a major shift in public concern about energy policy issues in Sweden at the beginning of the 1970s. To some extent this was due to a generally increasing concern about natural resource scarcity and environmental quality as well as about the safety aspects of the large-scale nuclear power program Sweden then had recently embarked upon. However, it was the dramatic oil price increase of 1973–4 that brought energy policy issues to the focus of public debate and the top of the political agenda. Since then energy policy has continued to be one of the major political issues in Sweden.

Over the years several specific energy policy issues have attracted public attention for a more or less extended period. However, three major, interrelated issues have been present throughout. The first is related to the level, composition and growth of energy consumption. The development of these variables became a political issue in connection with a government proposal to Parliament in 1975. According to this proposal, Sweden's energy policy should aim at reducing domestic energy consumption growth from a post-war average of 5 percent per annum to 2 percent per annum between 1973 and 1985, and to zero growth from 1990.[1] Later, the zero energy growth goal was replaced by relatively detailed targets for the composition and level of energy supply and demand for the coming decades.

The second major issue is the choice of appropriate energy policies in view of Sweden's high dependence on imported oil. This issue had two different aspects. One was related to the adjustment to the real oil price increase that occurred during the 1970s. The other was related to the observed volatility of world oil prices and the commonly held view that both short-term and long-term oil price predictions were inherently uncertain.

On the first point the general policy conclusion was pretty clear: Sweden's consumption of oil should be reduced, presumably a lot more than the consumption of other forms of energy. The issue was rather by how much, and to what extent, the consumption reduction should be brought about by government intervention rather than by normal market forces. On the second point the opinions tend to be a lot more mixed, and no explicit policy strategy has so far been formulated. Thus it is not at all clear how the recent fall in oil prices will affect energy policies in Sweden.

The third, and politically most significant, energy policy issue is related to the future role of nuclear power in Sweden's energy system. At the beginning the key issue was *whether* Sweden's nuclear energy program should be discontinued. However, it rather soon became an issue about *when* nuclear energy should be phased out: before 1990 or at the end of the economic lifetime of the 12 reactors in operation or under construction.

The outcome of the 1980 referendum was a victory for the second alternative, and as a result the Parliment decided that all nuclear power plants should be taken out of operation before the year 2010. In recent years the nuclear power issue has increasingly become an issue about which technologies on the supply side, and which adjustments on the demand side, could secure the nuclear power discontinuation at minimum social cost. A closely related issue, again, is the role of government intervention, and the use of specific policy instruments, in this transition of Sweden's energy system.

1.2 Hypotheses about energy–economy interactions

The public concern about energy-related issues has induced a quite profound reorientation of Swedish energy policy; the degree of government intervention in domestic energy markets has increased significantly, and for the first time in the post-war period energy policy goals are stated in terms of target energy supply and demand patterns. The specific measures which have added up to these changes explicitly or implicitly reflect hypotheses about how the cost and availability of energy affect the economy as a whole. In fact, much of the controversy about energy policy issues reflects different views on how the energy sector affects the rest of the economy and vice versa.

Of course Sweden is not unique in this respect, but two specific features of the Swedish economy suggest that the issue of energy–economy interactions is particularly relevant and important in the Swedish case. One is that the energy consumption, per capita and per unit of gross domestic product (GDP), is higher in Sweden than in most other countries. Thus, energy price increases in Sweden would lead to relatively large direct real income losses. To some extent the relatively high energy intensity is a function of climatic factors and a relatively high per capita income, but the energy-intensive consumption and industrial specialization patterns also reflect the fact that Sweden, owing to her endowment with hydro power resources, has had comparatively low electricity prices during the entire post-war period.

The second is that Sweden is a "small open economy", i.e. a country facing approximately parametric world market prices on tradeables and having a relatively large foreign trade sector. In addition to the fact that Swedish exports on average are rather energy intensive, this means that domestic energy taxation, or domestically induced energy cost increases, might produce significant shifts in the industrial structure. Thus, domestic energy policies significantly differing from the energy policies in other countries could induce a sectoral and regional reallocation of resources, which in the short and medium term might lead to increased unemployment.

1.3 Models of energy–economy interactions

Altogether this suggests that the economic aspects of national energy policies should be analyzed within an economy-wide framework. Moreover, that framework should allow for a realistic representation of the major mechanisms by which a national economy can adjust to higher energy prices and various energy policy measures. In short, some kind of computable general equilibrium (CGE) model in which the energy sector is emphasized is called for.

These rather general considerations induced a research program on economy-wide models of resource allocation in an open economy which was aimed at elucidating the interaction between the energy sector and the rest of the economy.[2] The research activities have led to the development and application of a number of different models. To some extent these reflect different modeling approaches (see Ysander, 1986). Yet it is fair to say that most of the models that have been developed and applied in order to shed light on the economy-wide implications of energy policies in Sweden are computable general equilibrium (CGE) models in the tradition established by Johansen's (1960) so-called multisectoral growth (MSG) model. This means that all the major energy policy issues referred to above have been analyzed within the framework of numerical models with strong links to Walrasian general equilibrium theory and the neoclassical theory of economic growth.

1.4 Purpose of the paper

The purpose of this paper is to review briefly and discuss three Swedish CGE models designed for energy policy analysis. These models all represent the end result of a major part of the above-mentioned research program. They were all developed at the Stockholm School of Economics and the International Institute for Applied Systems Analysis (IIASA) but they are aimed at elucidating rather different problems. The basic idea behind this paper is to show how the specific set of problems that the model was designed to highlight has affected its design. In addition to the specification of the models some of the applications and main simulation results are briefly discussed. Issues related to the empirical estimation of the models' parameters, as well as issues related to solution techniques, will only briefly be touched upon.

The first model, which is dealt with in section 2, was initially intended for analysis of some economic aspects of the proposed zero energy growth policy in Sweden. In particular it was designed to shed light on how domestic energy policies aimed at reducing energy consumption or energy consumption growth are likely to affect the equilibrium aggregate real income and the sectoral allocation of resources.

The second model, which is dealt with in section 3, was intended for analysis of the economy's adjustment to unanticipated oil price increases. In particular it was intended to reflect the rigidities imposed by the initial allocation of real capital and the initial technological coefficients in the energy-consuming sectors. Moreover, the model was designed for analysis of energy policy strategies aimed at reducing the economy's vulnerability to unanticipated world market oil price changes.

The third model, which is dealt with in section 4, was particularly designed for analysis of policies aimed at controlling the use of nuclear power. Thus it was intended to elucidate the impact of nuclear power discontinuation policies on the supply and demand for electricity, as well as on real income and sectoral allocation of resources in the economy as a whole.

2 Modeling the Impact of "Zero Energy Growth"

The idea that Sweden's energy policy should aim at reducing energy consumption growth was initially presented in the middle of the 1970s. Zero energy growth was considered a desirable target, but its attainment was conditional upon the overall economic impact of the proposed policies.

However, at that time no study of the economic consequences of zero energy growth, or any other target energy consumption growth rate, had been carried out. Moreover, such a study would not have been a very straightforward task, given the lack of suitable economy-wide models and data. Thus, the exact policy implications of the declaration of the zero energy growth goal were not at all clear, but the declaration certainly induced a lot of interest in how, and to what extent, the implementation of such a goal would affect the economy.

2.1 A static model of energy–economy interactions

The first Swedish model aimed at incorporating the essential mechanisms by which the economy adjusts to increasing scarcity of energy was presented by Bergman (1980). In terms of solution procedure and general modeling approach it was a direct extension of Johansen's MSG model. However, it also differed significantly from it in the sense that it allowed endogenous substitution of other inputs for energy, as well as endogenous determination of foreign trade.

The model was later somewhat elaborated and a tailor-made computer code, developed by Andras Por, made it possible to solve the models in the equilibrium levels rather than the relative rates of change of the endogenous variables. In addition to the practical advantages, the tailor-made computer code also made it possible to relax some *ad hoc* assumptions necessitated by the original solution method.

Various versions of the model are presented by Bergman (1981, 1982), Bergman and Mäler (1981, 1983) and Bergman and Ohlsson (1983). The final version of the model is described in sections 2.2–2.4.

2.2 General characteristics

The model is intended to simulate long-run equilibrium resource allocation patterns in a small open economy at a certain point in time. The endowment with capital and labor is exogenously given. By exogenously adjusting capital and labor endowments and solving the model for at least two points in time, a process of economic growth can be simulated.

There are no sector-specific resources, and capital and labor are fully mobile across sectors. The technology is assumed to exhibit constant returns to scale, and in each sector capital, labor, fuels and electricity are substitutable factors of production. The use of manufactured nonenergy inputs, however, is proportional to the output level of the sector in which the inputs are used.

Producers maximize profits, and the single "representative" household maximizes utility subject to a budget constraint. All product and factor markets are treated as if they were competitive, and relative product and factor prices are assumed to be flexible enough to clear all markets.

The agents of the economy face parametric world market prices on traded goods. Contrary to the standard Heckscher–Ohlin model, however, the goods produced in the "home" country are not perfect substitutes for goods produced in other countries. Accordingly the model has relative-price-dependent import and export demand functions, reflecting the trade-offs by agents at home and abroad between goods produced in the home country and goods produced in other countries. In other words, the model incorporates the so-called Armington assumption.[3,4]

Although the Armington assumption is incorporated in most CGE models of open economies, it is hard to justify within the framework of conventional microeconomic theory. This is particularly the case in a long-run model with mobile and homogeneous capital and labor. However, in a model dealing with large aggregates of goods rather than individual products, the Armington assumption can be defended as a shorthand representation of the availability of a number of unique factors of production which, owing to the high level of aggregation, cannot be given an explicit treatment.

The consumption of energy in the model economy can be controlled by means of a set of exogenously determined energy tax parameters. If the energy taxes are increased, energy consumption is reduced through the operation of several adjustment mechanisms. One is that increased energy prices might reduce aggregate output in the economy as a whole. The second is that the sectoral composition of production and the commodity composition of consumption is adjusted in an energy-saving direction. The third is that capital and labor are substituted for energy in the production sectors. Thus, in terms of the adjustment mechanisms incorporated, the model exhibits quite a lot of "realism".

2.3 Formal statement of the model

With this review of the general features of the model as a background, we can turn to the equations. The model describes an economy with $n + 3$ production sectors producing $n + 3$ goods of which n are tradeables. There is no joint production, and each good is produced in one sector only. Thus there is no real distinction between domestically produced goods and domestic production sectors.

In the following exposition, goods and sectors will be denoted interchangeably by i and j. The production sectors are numbered form 0 to $n + 3$, 0 being the sector producing fuels and 1 the electricity-generating sector, while $n + 1$ is a private sector producing nontradeable goods, and $n + 2$ is the public sector. There is also a "book-keeping" sector $n + 3$ in which different goods are aggregated into one single capital good. On the demand side all households are represented by an aggregated household sector.

As a consequence of the assumptions about the technology, the unit cost function can be divided into two parts. The first represents the minimum cost of fuels, electricity, capital, and labor per unit of output, while the second represents the corresponding cost of nonsubstitutable inputs. In the following, the first part is called "the net unit cost function". The producer's equilibrium condition can now be written as

$$P_j = \kappa_j^*(W_j, R_j, P_0^D, P_1^D, t) + \sum_{i=2}^{n} P_i^D a_{ij} + P_j^C b_j$$

$$j = 0, 1, \ldots, n + 2 \qquad (10.1)$$

where $\kappa_j^*(.)$ is the net unit cost function, P_j the price of output, P_i^D the price of composite good i, P_j^C the price of complementary imports used as inputs in sector j, W_j the wage rate in sector j, R_j the user cost of capital in sector j and t an exogenous shift parameter. The constants a_{ij} represent the input of composite good i per unit of output in sector j and b_j is the corresponding parameter for input of complementary imports in sector j.

The heterogeneity of labor is roughly accounted for by an exogenous wage structure, i.e.

$$W_j = \omega_j W \qquad j = 0, 1, \ldots, n + 2 \qquad (10.2)$$

where W is a general wage index and the ω_js are constants. The user cost of capital is defined by

$$R_j = P_{n+3}(\delta_j + R) \qquad j = 0, 1, \ldots, n + 2 \qquad (10.3)$$

where P_{n+3} is the price of the aggregated capital good, δ_j the rate of depreciation in sector j and R the real rate of interest. The price index of capital goods is defined by

$$P_{n+3} = \sum_{i=1}^{n} P_i^D a_{i,n+3} \tag{10.4}$$

where the coefficients $a_{i,n+3}$ sum to unity. The equilibrium prices of composite goods are given by the unit cost functions of the composites, i.e. by

$$P_i^D = \begin{cases} (1 + \tau_i)\Phi_i(P_i, P_i^W) & \text{when } i = 0, 1 \\ \\ \Phi_i(P_i, P_i^W) & \text{when } j = 2, 3, \ldots, n \end{cases} \tag{10.5}$$

where $\Phi_i(.)$ is the unit cost function corresponding to the linearly homogeneous "production" function defining composite good i and P_i^W is the exogenously given world market price, in domestic currency, of goods with classification i. The parameter τ_i is an exogenously determined tax rate on the use of fuels and electricity, respectively. This is the main instrument by which aggregate energy consumption can be controlled in the model economy.

Having now defined all prices and unit cost functions, the derivation of the complete model is quite straightforward. As the technology exhibits constant returns to scale, the sectoral production levels are determined from the demand side, where three types of demand should be distinguished: two types of demand for composite goods (intermediate demand and final demand by the household sector) and export demand for the production sector outputs.

By Shephard's lemma and the assumptions about technology, the intermediate demand is given by

$$X_{ij} = \begin{cases} \dfrac{\partial \kappa_j^*(.)}{\partial P_i^D} X_j & \text{when } i = 0, 1 \\ & \quad\quad\quad\quad j = 0, 1, \ldots, n + 2 \quad (10.6) \\ a_{ij}X_j & \text{when } i = 2, 3, \ldots, n \end{cases}$$

where X_{ij} is the use of composite good i in sector j and X_j is the gross output in sector j. Household demand is given by a function of the following type:

$$C_i = C_i(P_0^D, \ldots, P_i^D, \ldots, P_n^D, P_{n+1}, E) \qquad i = 0, 1, \ldots, n + 1 \tag{10.7}$$

where C_i is household demand for good i, E is total household consumption expenditure, and the functions $C_i(.)$ are derived from the assumption that the household sector maximizes utility subject to a budget constraint.

By Shephard's lemma, the demand for competitive imports is given by

$$M_i = \frac{\partial \Phi_i(.)}{\partial P_i^W} \left(\sum_{j=0}^{n+3} X_{ij} + C_i \right) \qquad i = 0, 1, \ldots, n \qquad (10.8)$$

i.e. import demand is a function of the prices P_i and P_i^W and the domestic demand for composite goods. Applying the same assumptions for "the rest of the world" thus means that export demand is given by functions of the type

$$Z_i = Z_i(P_i, P_i^W, t) \qquad i = 1, 2, \ldots, n \qquad (10.9)$$

where Z_i is export demand for domestically produced goods with the classification i. As the home economy is assumed to be small, the use of composite goods in the rest of the world is approximately equal to the production in the rest of the world. Thus the size of the world market can be represented by the exogenous shift parameter t.

Given the different demand equations, the equilibrium conditions for the markets for domestically produced goods are given by

$$X_i = \frac{\partial \Phi_i(.)}{\partial P_i} \left(\sum_{j=0}^{n+3} X_{ij} + C_i \right) + Z_i \qquad i = 0, 1, \ldots, n$$

$$(10.10)$$

$$X_i = C_i \qquad i = n + 1, n + 2 \qquad (10.11)$$

$$X_{n+3} = I + \sum_{j=0}^{n+2} \delta_j \frac{\partial \kappa_j^*(.)}{\partial R_j} X_j \qquad (10.12)$$

where C_{n+2} is the exogenously given public consumption and I is total net investments which also are exogenous.

At the equilibrium, household consumption expenditures E must be equal to the factor incomes of the household sector less net taxes and household savings. Instead of specifying such an equality explicitly, it is determined implicitly by a current account constraint. Thus, it holds that

$$\sum_{i=1}^{n} P_i Z_i = \sum_{i=0}^{n} P_i^W M_i + \sum_{j=0}^{1} P_j^C \bar{M}_j + D \qquad (10.13)$$

where $\bar{M}_j$ is the demand for complementary imports and D is an exogenous variable representing net foreign transfers and net interest payments on foreign debt, expressed in domestic currency units.

Finally, as capital and labor are inelastically supplied, the equilibrium conditions for the factor markets become

$$K = \sum_{j=0}^{n+2} \frac{\kappa \partial_j^*(.)}{\partial R_j} X_j \tag{10.14}$$

and

$$L = \sum_{j=0}^{n+2} \frac{\partial \kappa_j^*(.)}{\partial W_j} X_j \tag{10.15}$$

where K is total capital supply and L is total labor supply. Altogether these expressions, after appropriate substitutions, yield $6n + 15$ equations in the $6n + 15$ unknowns: $X_0, \ldots, X_{n+3}, C_0, \ldots, C_{n+1}; Z_1, \ldots, Z_n; M_0, \ldots, M_n; P_0, \ldots, P_{n+3}; P_0^D, \ldots, P_n^D; E; W;$ and R.

2.4 Sectors, functional forms and parameter values

The computer code used to solve the model permits the user to decide the number of sectors. The model has been implemented in a 36-sector version, but in most applications the number of production sectors has been seven (see table 10.1). This reflects a desire to keep the number of sectors at the smallest possible level which is compatible with a meaningful analysis of the issues the model is intended to elucidate.

In order to implement the model, it is necessary to specify the functions $\kappa_j^*(.)$, $\Phi_i(.)$, $C_i(.)$ and $Z_i(.)$. Moreover a large number of parameters have to be estimated. When the model was developed, it was not possible to carry out the econometric work that would have been desirable. Instead the construction of data bases and parameter estimation had to be based on literature surveys and collaboration with other researchers. In view of this it seemed reasonable to choose functional forms with a small number of parameters, preferably with a simple economic interpretation.

On the basis of these considerations, the following nested constant elasticity of substitution (CES) Cobb–Douglas structure was chosen for the representation of the technology:

$$X_j = A_j(a_j F_j^{\rho_j} + b_j H_j^{\rho_j})^{1/\rho_j} e^{\lambda} j^t \qquad \text{for all } j$$

$$F_j = K_j^{\alpha_j} L_j^{1-\alpha_j} \qquad \text{for all } j$$

$$H_j = (c_j X_{1j}^{\gamma_j} + d_j X_{2j}^{\gamma_j})^{1/\gamma_j} \qquad \text{for all } j$$

where K_j is capital input, L_j labor input, X_{ij} input of produced intermediate goods and X_j output.[5]

Except for the substitution parameters ρ_j and γ_j and the technological change parameters γ_j, all the production function parameters were estimated on the basis of input–output data for 1979. The substitution parameters were "guesstimated" on the basis of literature

Table 10.1 Adopted values of some key parameters

Sector	$(1 - \rho_j)^{-1}$ [a]	$(1 - \gamma_j)^{-1}$ [b]	ξ_j [c]	μ_j [d]
0 Fossil fuels	0.25	0.25	–	0.5
1 Electricity	0.25	0.25	1.0	0.5
2 Mainly import-competing industries	0.75	0.75	2.0	4.0
3 Mainly exporting energy-intensive industries	0.75	0.75	5.0	0.5
4 Other mainly exporting industries	0.75	0.75	4.0	2.0
5 Sheltered industries and service production	0.75	0.75	2.0	
6 Public services	0.75	0.75	–	–
7 Capital goods (book-keeping sector)	–	–	–	–

[a] Elasticity of substitution between capital–labor and fuels–electricity.
[b] Elasticity of substitution between fuels and electricity.
[c] Elasticity of substitution between Swedish and foreign goods abroad.
[d] Elasticity of substitution between Swedish and foreign goods in Sweden.

surveys, while the technological change projections were taken from the long-term economic surveys made by the Ministry of Finance.

Household demand, the $C_i(.)$ functions, is represented by a linear expenditure system. This choice was essentially motivated by the fact that such systems had been estimated on Swedish data. However, as the estimated systems implied a set of demand functions for ten consumer commodity groups, a transformation matrix defining the consumer goods as linear combinations of the composite goods had to be estimated.

The aggregation functions defining the composite goods consumed in the home country and the composite goods consumed in the rest of the world were all specified as CES functions. The CES specification is convenient since it leads to import and export functions which are relatively easy to estimate. The actual values of the parameters of the import and export demand functions were determined on the basis of literature surveys. Table 10.1 summarizes the values for some of the key parameters which were adopted in the final version of the model. In some of the earlier versions slightly different values were used.

2.5 Applications and simulation results

As has already been mentioned, several variants of the model have been implemented and applied in analyses of different energy policy issues (see Bergman, 1978, 1981 and Bergman and Mäler, 1981). Although the general structure of the model is the same in all cases, there are some differences. Thus, Bergman's (1978) paper that was especially aimed at analyzing the impact of zero energy growth had only one aggregated energy sector. Moreover, the total consumption of energy was in effect treated as an exogenous variable, while the energy tax rate was treated as an endogenous variable.

However, Bergman (1981) later treated the domestic supply of electricity as an exogenous variable, while the electricity tax rate was treated as an endogenous variable. Moreover, part of the base year capital stock in the electricity sector, corresponding to the nuclear power capacity in place, was treated as a policy variable.

In order to indicate what kind of simulation results the model has generated, we will briefly review the major results of the analysis of the economic impact of an energy policy strategy aimed at zero energy growth in the long run. The exposition is entirely based on Bergman's earlier work (Bergman, 1978).[6]

The study was designed in the following way. First, two projections of the development of the Swedish economy between 1980 and 2000 were made. The first, "base case", projection was based on recent forecasts on the model's exogenous variables and an assumption that world market oil prices would increase by 2 percent per annum in real terms between 1980 and 1990 and by 5 percent per annum between 1990 and 2000. On the whole the base case reflected a slowdown of the growth of the Swedish economy. The other projection, the "rapid growth" case, was based on the assumption that technological change and capital accumulation would continue in accordance with post-war trends. With respect to all other exogenous variables, however, the rapid growth case was identical with the base case.

The declared target energy consumption growth rates were 2 percent per annum between 1973 and 1985 and zero growth thereafter. Both projections implied higher rates of energy consumption growth. Thus the projected level of energy consumption was considerably higher than the target level in both cases (see table 10.2). In other words the proposed constraints on energy consumption were likely to be binding.

Table 10.2 Calculated values of selected macroeconomic variables in the year 2000 under various assumptions about productivity growth and energy policy (1980 = 100)

	The base case		The rapid growth case	
	No constraint on energy consumption	Constraint on energy consumption	No constraint on energy consumption	Constraint on energy consumption
GNP	148	147	202	196
Real household consumption	174	174	243	238
Energy consumption	163	110	231	110
Industrial employment	60	58	77	58

GNP, gross national product.

The next step was to impose an additional tax on energy consumption and to adjust the tax rate so that the target energy consumption path was attained. A summary of the resuts can be found in table 10.2.

If the level of aggregate real household consumption is taken as a rough measure of welfare, the results suggest that the cost of implementing the zero energy growth strategy would be negligible under base case conditions.[7] Under rapid growth conditions the cost would be considerably higher, but still low enough to be compatible with a relatively fast growth of narrowly defined economic welfare.

The model results also suggested that the sectoral reallocation of labor resulting from the proposed energy strategy would be rather modest. Instead there would be a considerable sectoral reallocation of capital, especially from the energy sector to the rest of the economy. In other words, under zero energy growth conditions a significant share of gross capital formation would be used for energy conservation rather than for energy production purposes.

In order to highlight the operation of the different adjustment mechanism, the total energy consumption reduction in the base case was decomposed into four components. Moreover, that exercise was carried out under three alternative assumptions about the elasticity of substitution between energy and the capital–labor composite. The results are summarized in table 10.3.

Table 10.3 Decomposition of the base case energy consumption reduction[a]

Elasticity of substitution	VOL	COMP	INP	DIR	TOT
0.10	24	6	32	39	100
0.25	13	6	57	23	100
0.50	2	5	79	13	100

TOT, the total change in energy consumption; VOL, the change in energy consumption due to change in aggregate production, provided aggregate production is composed in the same way as at the initial point in time; COMP, the change in energy consumption due to changed composition of aggregate production; INP, the change in energy consumption due to changed energy input coefficients; DIR, the change in energy consumption due to changed direct consumption of energy in the household sector.
[a]Percentage shares of the reduction in energy consumption by the year 2000, resulting from a constraint on energy consumption, that can be assigned to various components under various assumptions about the substitutability of energy and composite capital–labor.

The results in table 10.3 clearly indicate that the relative importance of the different adjustment mechanisms operating within a general equilibrium system critically depends on the elasticity of substitution between energy and other factors of production. Thus the model turned out to be a tool for identification of important topics for research on the interaction between the energy sector and the rest of the economy.

3 Modeling the Adjustment to Oil Price Changes

One of the exogenous variables of the model discussed in the preceding section is the world market price of oil. Thus the model can be used for analyses of the impact of exogenously determined oil price variations. However, since the model is designed to simulate long-run equilibrium resource allocation patterns, it can only elucidate the impact of an oil price change after all agents have completely adjusted to the new relative price of oil. Even if such results are interesting, much of the concern about the impact of oil price increases is related to problems in connection with the process of adjustment to unanticipated changes in world market oil prices.

This was the prime motivation for the development of a "dynamic" version of the model presented in the preceding section. The new model was intended to depict the economy's adjustment, over a period of ten to 15 years, to unanticipated changes in the price of oil and other exogenous conditions. The major application of the model was to measure the Swedish economy's vulnerability to unexpected oil price increases and, in particular, the extent by which domestic energy policies could reduce that vulnerability.

The research initiated by these general considerations resulted in a model called ELIAS (energy, labor and investment allocation and substitution), presented by Bergman (1982, 1986) and Bergman and Mäler (1983a, b). Its distinguishing features are that it is a multiperiod model and that it explicitly accounts for the rigidities imposed by the initial allocation of capital as well as the initial technological coefficients. More precisely, a distinction is made between the *ex ante* and the *ex post* technological constraints.

3.1 Technology and producer behavior

The "dynamic" model is based on the static model described in section 2. In particular the unit cost function on the right-hand side of equation (10.1) is taken to represent the technological constraints *ex ante*. Thus, in the planning stage, when a new production unit is designed, the relation between expected unit production cost κ_j and expected input prices is given by

$$\kappa_j = \kappa_j^*(P_0^D, P_1^D, W_j, R_j; v) + \sum_{i=2}^{n} P_i^D a_{ij} + P_j^C b_j$$

$$j = 0, 1, \ldots, n + 2 \qquad (10.16)$$

where v is a time index and the other variables have the same interpretation as in equation (10.1). The specification above implies that the *expected* values of P_0^D, P_1^D and W_l are functions of the current values of these variables. In the simplest case the expected values coincide with the current values. This means that producers are assumed to have static expectations, i.e. that they expect current prices to prevail in the future as well. However, by means of a set of parameters other assumptions about expectation formation can be simulated.

The *ex ante* unit cost function is crucial in at least two ways. First it is the basis for the technological design and investment decisions. Second, once the technological design and investment decisions are made, it defines the *ex post* profit functions, i.e. the technological constraints on production decisions. More precisely the relation between the *ex ante* unit cost functions and *ex post* profit functions are as follows.

At a given point in time, say t producers know the *ex ante* production function, and they hold certain expectations about the future development of goods and factor prices. By evaluating the *ex ante* unit cost function at these prices and applying Shepherd's lemma, the cost-minimizing input coefficients in the new vintage of production units can be determined. Thus the energy input coefficients $a_{t+1.ij}$ in the production units, which are designed in period t and taken into operation in period $t + 1$, become

$$\frac{\partial \kappa_i^*(.)}{\partial P_i^D} = a_{t+1.ij} \qquad \begin{array}{l} i = 0, 1 \\ j = 0, 1, \ldots, n + 2 \end{array} \tag{10.17}$$

and the corresponding capital and labor input coefficients become

$$\frac{\partial \kappa_j^*(.)}{\partial R_j} = k_{t+1.j} \qquad j = 0, 1, \ldots, n + 2 \tag{10.18}$$

$$\frac{\partial \kappa_j^*(.)}{\partial W_j} = l_{t+1.j} \qquad j = 0, 1, \ldots, n + 2 \tag{10.19}$$

On the basis of the *ex ante* unit cost functions and the current prices of output, it is possible to define a measure of the expected rates of return on investments in each of the sectors at time $v = t$, $\widetilde{R}_j(t)$ for $j = 0, 1, \ldots, n + 2$. More precisely $\widetilde{R}_j$ is defined by

$$\widetilde{R}_j(t) = \frac{P_j(t) - \kappa_j(t)}{P_{n+3}(t)k_{t+1.j}} j = 0, 1, \ldots, n + 2 \tag{10.20}$$

On the basis of the variables $\widetilde{R}_j(t)$, sectoral gross investments are determined by means of investment functions defined later in the exposition.[8] It is assumed that, once an investment is made in a given sector, the capital goods in question are tied to that sector. It is also assumed that energy input coefficients cannot be varied *ex post*; i.e. all the $a_{t+1.ij}$ are variables in period t and constants from period $t + 1$ and so on. These added restrictions together with the *ex ante* production functions define the *ex post* production functions of vintage t. By definition the *ex post* functions can be written as functions of the input of labor only, and they exhibit decreasing returns to scale in that factor.

The *ex post* production functions differ across vintages for two reasons. First, these functions reflect the technological progress only up to the period in which the vintage in question was designed. Second, the fixed energy input coefficients are most likely to differ across different vintages of production units in a given sector.

Moreover, the *ex post* production functions shift over time owing to exogenously determined depreciation of the fixed capital stock.

On the basis of the *ex post* production functions and profit maximization, a set of profit functions $\pi_{vj}(.)$, one for each vintage of production units in each sector, can be derived:

$$\pi_{vj} = \pi_{vj}(P^*_{vj}, W_j; t) \quad v = 0, 1, \ldots, t \quad (10.21)$$
$$j = 0, 1, \ldots, n + 2$$

where π_{vj} is the gross profit in production units of vintage v in sector j and

$$P^*_{vj} = P_j - \sum_{i=0}^{1} P^D_i a_{vij} - \sum_{i=2}^{n} P^D_i a_{ij} - P^C_j b_j \quad j = 0, 1, \ldots, n + 2$$

$$(10.22)$$

Having defined the profit functions, the derivation of the output supply and input demand functions is quite straightforward. Thus by Hotelling's lemma the supply of output $X_{vj}(t)$ from production units of vintage v in sector j in period t becomes

$$\frac{\partial \pi_{vj}(.)}{\partial P^*_{vj}} = X_{vj}(t) \qquad v = 0, 1, \ldots, t \quad (10.23)$$
$$j = 0, 1, \ldots, n + 2$$

and by adding over vintages the total supply of output $X_j(t)$ from sector j in that period is determined:

$$\sum_{v=0}^{t} X_{vj}(t) = X_j(t) \qquad j = 0, 1, \ldots, n + 2 \quad (10.24)$$

$$\frac{\partial \pi_{vj}(.)}{\partial W_j} = -L_{vj}(t) \qquad v = 0, 1, \ldots, t \quad j = 0, 1, \ldots, n + 2$$

$$(10.25)$$

$$\sum_{v=0}^{t} L_{vj}(t) = L_j(t) \qquad j = 0, 1, \ldots, n + 2 \quad (10.26)$$

$$X_{ij}(t) = \begin{cases} \displaystyle\sum_{v=0}^{t} a_{vij} X_{vj}(t) & \text{when } i = 0, 1 \\[2mm] & \hspace{2cm} j = 0, 1, \ldots, n + 2 \\[2mm] a_{ij} X_j(t) & \text{when } i = 2, 3, \ldots, n + 2 \quad (10.27) \end{cases}$$

$$\bar{M}_j(t) = b_j X_j(t) \qquad j = 0, 1 \quad (10.28)$$

which completes the derivation of the model's output supply and input demand functions.

3.2 The determination of exports

The specification of export and import demand functions in the static model discussed in section 2 reflects a consistent application of the so-called Armington assumption. In the first versions of the "dynamic" model this property was retained. However, later the export demand functions were dropped, and in the final version of the model exports are determined in the following way.

The supply of output from each traded sector is assumed to be a composite made up of goods for domestic use and goods for export. The prices of exports are exogenously determined by world market conditions, while the prices of domestically consumed goods are endogenously determined by the interplay of supply and demand factors on domestic markets. It is assumed that the demand for inputs is independent of the composition of output and that there is a constant scale-independent elasticity of transformation between the two types of output. Under these conditions it holds that

$$P_i = \chi_i(P_i^N, P_i^W) \qquad i = 0, 1, \ldots, n \qquad (10.29)$$

where P_i is the producer unit revenue of composite output i, P_i^N is the price of the goods with the classification i sold on the domestic market and $\chi_i(.)$ is the unit revenue function. Note that there are several types of goods with the classification i. As before P_i^W is a world market price.

On the basis of equation (10.29) and Shephard's lemma, the supply $N_i(t)$ of domestically produced goods on domestic markets in period t is given by

$$N_i(t) = \frac{\partial \chi_i(.)}{\partial P_i^N} X_i(t) \qquad i = 0, 1, \ldots, n \qquad (10.30)$$

$$N_{n+1}(t) = X_{n+1}(t) \qquad (10.31)$$

while the supply of exports is given by

$$Z_i(t) = \frac{\partial \chi_i(.)}{\partial P_i^W} X_i(t) \qquad i = 0, 1, \ldots, n \qquad (10.32)$$

3.3 Final demand and prices

The demand for goods in the model economy can be subdivided into two categories, intermediate and final demand. As the determination of intermediate demand was discussed above, it remains to specify the final demand functions.

Domestic agents are assumed to demand a composite of imported and domestically produced nonexported goods with the classification

i, and the composite is defined by means of a "production" function aggregating goods from the two sources of supply.

As in the static model this function is assumed to be linearly homogeneous and to apply to all domestic users of the goods in question. Thus the price P_i^D of the composite good can be defined by the unit cost function of that good, i.e.

$$P_i^D = \Phi_i(P_i^W, P_i^N) \qquad i = 0, 1, \ldots, n$$

where $\Phi_i(.)$ is the unit cost function of the composite good demanded by domestic agents. By Shephard's lemma, the demands for imports and domestically produced goods are given by the partial derivatives of the function $\Phi_i(.)$.

There are three types of demand for the composite good used by domestic users, namely household demand, public sector demand and investment demand. The last two categories are both exogenously determined, while household demand is determined in the same way as in the static model. Moreover, the level of household consumption expenditures is implicitly determined by a current account constraint. This constraint can be written

$$\sum_{i=0}^{n} P_i^W(t) \frac{\partial \chi_i(.)}{\partial P_i^W} X_i(t) - \sum_{i=0}^{n} P_i^W(t) M_i(t) - \sum_{j=0}^{1} P_j^C(t) \bar{M}_j(t) = D(t)$$

$$(10.33)$$

where $D(t)$ is the exogenously determined net flow of foreign transfer and interest payments.

3.4 Equilibrium conditions

Within the model economy there are three groups of goods markets: the markets for domestically produced goods, the markets for imports (other than complementary imports) and the markets for complementary imports. The equilibrium conditions for the first group of markets become

$$\frac{\partial \chi_i(.)}{\partial P_i^N} X_i(t) = \frac{\partial \psi_i(.)}{\partial P_i^N} \left[\sum_{j=0}^{n+3} X_{ij}(t) + C_i(t) \right] \qquad i = 0, 1, \ldots, n$$

$$(10.34)$$

$$X_i(t) = C_i(t) \qquad i = n + 1, n + 2 \tag{10.35}$$

$$X_{n+3}(t) = I(t) \tag{10.36}$$

where $C_{n+2}(t)$ is the exogenously determined consumption of public services, and $P_{n+3}(t)I(t)$, gross investment expenditure, is a constant fraction of the endogenously determined gross national income.

In the same way, and noting that the supply of imports is assumed to be completely elastic, the equilibrium conditions for the imported goods become

$$M_i(t) = \frac{\partial \psi_i(.)}{\partial P_i^{\text{W}}} \left[\sum_{j=0}^{n+2} X_{ij}(t) + C_i(t) \right] \qquad i = 0, 1, \ldots, n$$

(10.37)

$$\bar{M}_j(t) = b_j X_j(t)$$

(10.38)

On the basis of equations (10.25) and (10.26) and the assumption about exogenously determined labor supply $L(t)$ the labor market equilibrium condition becomes

$$L(t) = \sum_{j=0}^{n+2} L_j(t)$$

(10.39)

Thus, given the values for $L(t)$, $C_{n+2}(t)$, $D(t)$, $P_i^{\text{M}}(t)$, $P_i^{\text{Z}}(t)$ and $P_j^{\text{C}}(t)$, the model endogenously determines the equilibrium pattern of resource allocation and relative prices of nontraded goods as well as the real wage rate at time t.

3.5 Applications and simulation results

The "dynamic" model was developed primarily for a study of the energy policy implications of oil price uncertainty (Bergman and Mäler, 1983a). This study was to a large extent inspired by the public debate on this policy issue initiated by the quite dramatic oil price increases in 1973–4 and 1979. It was also inspired by the more general observation that the lack of suitable future markets, in conjunction with price-inelastic supply and demand for oil, is likely to produce a rather unstable development of world oil prices. Thus unpredictible short-run oil price increases and decreases, rather than the Hotelling type of long-run gradual increases, might be the major problem in this field for an oil importing country like Sweden.

This line of reasoning raised two major issues. The first was essentially an empirical one, concerning the possible economic impact of unexpected oil price increases. The second was a policy issue, essentially related to the possibilities of identifying a set of policy measures capable of reducing the Swedish economy's vulnerability to unexpected oil price increases. On the latter issue several commentators argued that consumers of oil should be induced to adjust their oil consumption to a level consistent with a high future price of oil. Such a policy, it was claimed, would reduce the real income losses caused by unexpected oil price increases and thus be beneficial for the society as a whole.

Leaving aside the questions about which future oil price level agents should be induced to adjust to and which policy measures should be used to accomplish such an adjustment, we will briefly summarize some results from a model-based analysis of this particular proposal. This analysis was carried out by means of a variant of the "dynamic" model in which the demand for Sweden's exports was assumed to be relatively price inelastic in the Armington fashion. The policy experiment was designed in the following way.

The initial point in time was 1979 and the results of various policy measures were evaluated by means of conditional forecasts for 1991. It was assumed that the long-run trend of oil price development implied an annual rate of increase by 2 percent per annum between 1979 and 1991. Moreover, the assumed development of capital formation, technical change etc. led to an annual GDP growth by 2.3 percent and an annual oil consumption growth by 0.9 percent.

For the oil price realization in 1991 two outcomes were considered. The first was that the actual price in 1991 would coincide with the price implied by the long-run trend. The second was that the price of oil would turn out to be 60 percent above the trend value. Nothing was assumed about the probability of these two outcomes.

Two energy policy strategies were considered. The first, strategy 0, was a "passive" strategy in the sense that no attempt was made to influence the agents' expectations about future oil prices. Together with other assumptions this implied a case with static expectations, i.e. the choice of technology in new production units was assumed to be made on the basis of the relative prices prevailing at the point in time when investment decisions were made. Strategy 1 implied that agents were induced to choose technological coefficients on the basis of the long-run trend of future oil prices. However, the policy measures only concerned the expectations about oil prices. Thus investment decisions were based on a mixture of static and forward-looking expectations.

To sum up, the experiment was based on two oil price realizations in 1991 and two policy strategies for the period 1979–91. In order to compare the outcomes Hicksian equivalent variations were computed on the basis of the model simulation results. The resulting estimates are summarized in tables 10.4 and 10.5. For convenience they are expressed in terms of deviations from the outcome under strategy 0 and the oil price realization "trend".

On the basis of the results presented a few rather interesting observations can be made. The first is that the real income loss resulting from an unexpected 60 percent oil price increase seems to be quite significant. This of course reflects the fact that, under the assumed conditions, Sweden's oil import bill is around 6 percent of

Table 10.4 Estimated equivalent variations 1991 (million SEK at the 1979 price level)

		Oil price realization	
Energy policy strategy	Trend	Trend + 60%	Real income loss[a]
Strategy 0	0	23,470	23,470
Strategy 1	−520	−20,480	19,960

[a]Real income loss = Trend − (Trend + 60%).

Table 10.5 Estimated equivalent variations 1991 (percent of estimated gross national income in 1981, under strategy 1 and trend conditions)

	Oil price realization	
Energy policy strategy	Trend	Trend + 60%
Strategy 0	0	−3.8
Strategy 1	−0.1	−2.4

gross national income, but it also reflects two properties of the model: the low short-run elasticity of oil demand and the relative-price-dependent export demand implied by the Armington assumption.

The low short-run price elasticity of oil demand observed in the model simulations to a large extent reflects the assumptions about sector-specific capital and fixed *ex post* energy input coefficients. However, the long-run price elasticity of oil demand is considerably higher. This is because the *ex ante* production functions allow substitution of other factors for oil, and investments in new production units can be concentrated on less oil-intensive sectors. Thus, a permanent oil price increase will induce a gradual downward adjustment of oil consumption. In the present discussion, however, we are only concerned with the short-run properties of the model.

The above-mentioned difference between short-run and long-run price elasticities reflects an important aspect of reality. A somewhat more dubious effect originates in the specification of the export demand functions: as the oil import expenditures increase and the current account deficit is exogenously given, export revenues have to increase. However, owing to the relative-price-dependent export demand functions, the increase of export revenues is accomplished through a combination of quantity increase and price decrease. In other words there is an additional terms of trade loss resulting from the oil price increase. It turned out that the magnitude of this additional real income loss was critically dependent on the values of the highly uncertain estimates of the price elasticity of export demand. Once this was realized the model was redesigned along the lines indicated in section 3.4.

The second point to note in the results presented in table 10.4 is that the absolute magnitude of the estimated real income loss to a large extent depends on the energy policy strategy adopted. These results clearly suggest that Sweden's "oil price vulnerability" is reduced if new production units are designed to be "oil efficient". However, the reduced vulnerability is not a free lunch; there is a cost associated with strategy 1.

It is particularly interesting to note that strategy 1 leads to a loss even when the oil price realization coincides with the expected oil price level, i.e. when the oil price attains the trend value. This shows that what really matters is the expectations about the entire system of relative prices, and not the expectations about a single, and relatively unimportant, price.

4 The Impact of Nuclear Power Discontinuation

The third version of a CGE model of the Swedish economy was inspired by policy issues related to the large build-up of nuclear power capacity in Sweden.[9] In particular, the decision of Parliament following a referendum in 1980, to ban nuclear power investments and to announce that nuclear power would not be allowed after 2010 was the prime motivation to develop a version of the CGE model which could adequately elucidate the economic consequences of such a policy.

4.1 The discontinuation policy

During the 1970s the power industry's nuclear power expansion plans came under increasingly fierce attacks from groups concerned about the safety and environmental hazards of nuclear power. Their arguments had a notable influence on public opinion and the debate culminated in the 1980 referendum on the future use of nuclear power. The outcome of the referendum, manifested in the present nuclear power policy, was that the 12 nuclear power reactors will be used during their remaining lifetime, but that no new investments in nuclear power capacity will be allowed. Since the conventional estimate of the lifetime of a nuclear power reactor is 25 years, this means that after 2010 nuclear power will not be used in Sweden.

The nuclear power discontinuation policy is likely to lead to a social cost for two reasons. First, the nuclear power capacity will be scrapped prematurely if the technological lifetime of the reactors should turn out to be longer than 25 years. Second, the ban on new nuclear power investments involves a cost if alternative power technologies remain, as at present, more costly than nuclear power.

4.2 Model formulation requirements

To study the effects of restrictions on the use of nuclear power the CGE model must be sufficiently detailed to explicitly allow such restrictions. This is not the case for the two model versions discussed above. In those versions the electricity sector, as well as the other production sectors, is represented by aggregated neoclassical production functions. The production functions cannot be related to specific production technologies. They are estimated relations between, on the one hand, the gross output and, on the other, inputs of capital, labor, energy and nonenergy intermediate inputs. The production function is defined relative to a set of feasible production technologies. It gives the maximal gross output which can be obtained from given amounts of inputs when the production technology, or a combination of production technologies, is chosen optimally toward this end. Restrictions on the use of certain production technologies mean that the feasible set of production technologies changes. As a result the production function will in general also be different. Consequently an analysis of the general equilibrium impact of such restrictions would require the use of a different production function for each type of restriction studied.

This would clearly be very inconvenient. A better approach is to directly introduce a representation of the technology set into the CGE model. The most tractable way of doing this is to employ an activity analysis model of the technology. It is a simple way of summarizing technological information, and the linear activity analysis production model is well suited to numerical manipulations. Another advantage is that many existing models of single sectors are of this type.

The latter point was a strong agrument when the present model version was developed. To properly analyze different policies toward the use of nuclear power we needed a more detailed representation of the electricity production technology than was provided by the neoclassical production functions of the earlier model versions. Such a more detailed production model was also available in the form of an existing sector model of electricity and heat production, which formed a part of a partial equilibrium model of the electricity and heat markets. By integrating the electricity production model with a general equilibrium structure, the richer information of the former could be exploited in applications of the latter. In particular it made it possible to study the effects of restrictions on the use of nuclear power in a general equilibrium framework.

There are no conceptual difficulties involved in the integration of an activity analysis production model in the CGE model. In fact much general equilibrium theory has been concerned with linear production models. Instead the potential problems are practical. The model versions discussed in the previous two sections are essentially equation systems which are solved for the equilibrium prices. The numerical methods which are used to solve them, however, are not applicable in the context of an activity analysis model. In order to discuss this it is first convenient to express the CGE models in a more compact form.

Let $Z^T(p) = [z_1(p), z_2(p), \ldots, z_n(p)]$ be a vector of excess demands at the prices $p^T = (p_1, p_2, \ldots, p_n)$ and let $v^T = (v_1, v_2, \ldots, v_n)$ be a vector of the total initial endowments of the economy, where n is the number of commodities in the model. The previously discussed model versions can formally be summarized as equation systems

$$z(p) - v = 0 \qquad (10.40)$$

which are solved for the equilibrium prices p.

Suppose now that the general equilibrium model is such that it is possible to single out a subset of producers which produce and supply to the rest of the economy – a limited number, say m, of the n commodities in the economy. These producers are the only ones who can produce these m commodities and they cannot produce any of the remaining $n - m$ commodities. Then this group of producers can unambiguously be treated as a distinct sector of the economy, where the sector is defined by its m outputs. Suppose also that the production technology of this sector can be represented by an activity analysis model. Let the excess demand functions $z(p)$ in (10.40) now summarize the demand and supply behavior of the rest of the producers and the household sector.

To make this structure more apparent let p^m denote the prices of the m sector outputs and p^n denote the prices of the remaining commodities. In a similar way the excess demand functions can be partitioned into the two sets $z^m(p)$ and $z^n(p)$ for the two groups of commodities and the initial endowments in the two sets v^m and v^n. The activity technology matrix can be partitioned into A^m and A^n, where A^m is the $m \times k$ matrix containing the rows of the sector commodities, A^n is the $(n - m) \times k$ matrix containing the rest of the rows and k is the number of activities in the activity analysis model. The equilibrium conditions in (10.40) can now be rewritten as

$$z^m(p^m, p^n) - A^m y = v^m$$

$$z^n(p^m, p^n) - A^n y = v^n$$

$$p^{mT}[z^m(p^m, p^n) - A^m y - v^m] = 0$$

$$p^{nT}[z^n(p^m, p^n) - A^n y - v^n] = 0$$

$$\left[A^{mT}, A^{nT}\right]\begin{bmatrix} p^m \\ p^n \end{bmatrix} \leq 0 \qquad y^T\left[A^{mT}, A^{nT}\right]\begin{bmatrix} p^m \\ p^n \end{bmatrix} = 0$$

$$y \geq 0 \qquad p^m \geq 0 \qquad p^n \geq 0 \qquad (10.41)$$

In this framework z^m is the total demand in the economy for the m sector outputs, $A^m y$ is the supply and $A^n y$ is the sector's input demand for commodities from the rest of the economy.

The general equilibrium model depicted above must be solved by numerical methods which can handle weak inequalities and complementary slackness. This is not the case for the numerical methods which are used for the first two model versions. Thus an alternative solution method must be devised. Another practical problem arises when the sector production model and the CGE model have different commodity classifications. Typically, the sector model has a more disaggregated commodity list since it is especially designed for a more detailed analysis of a single sector in the economy. In order to incorporate the sector model in the general equilibrium model it is then necessary to introduce a commodity aggregation interface between the two models.

One suitable computational approach for the model in (10.41) which also has a long tradition in connection with activity analysis models is the optimization approach. It rests on the equivalence between efficient and competitive equilibrium allocations. Numerical optimization algorithms are applied in order to identify efficient allocations in the general equilibrium model.[10] According to the fundamental equivalence theorems of competitive analysis the equilibrium allocation can be found among these.

However, this equivalence can break down for several reasons, e.g. if the model contains nonconvex production technologies or preferences. Another and more importance case is when the model contains commodity taxes (and also distortions which could be expressed equivalently as commodity taxes). The fundamental equivalence theorems of competitive analysis are then in general not valid. This is a serious limitation of the optimization approach. It is important to be able to account for taxes and similar parameters in applied general equilibrium models even when they are not designed especially for tax studies. The model data bases are often calibrated so that the models can replicate a base year allocation based on actual national accounts, which contain taxes, trade margins, sectoral wage differences etc. To do this it is necessary to use tax parameters in the model.

Lundgren (1985) showed that with unit taxes (and/or distortions which could formally be expressed as unit taxes) it is possible to compute the equilibrium at given taxes by a slight modification of the optimization approach. In its original form the optimization approach means that a standard Pareto problem is solved, i.e. a maximum of a welfare function is computed subject to a number of market equilibrium and production technology constraints. The modification which is required to handle commodity taxes is that an expression for total tax receipts should be subtracted from the objective function of the Pareto problem.[11]

This result extends the usefulness of the optimization approach and it was adopted for the third CGE model version. The optimization approach also has the advantage that it makes it possible to solve the model by standard nonlinear programming algorithms. It means, for instance, that it is fairly easy to change various details of the model. In this respect the third model version is more flexible than its two predecessors.

4.3 The integrated model

The integrated model was constructed by incorporating an electricity production model with the dynamic model which was described in section 3. For this purpose the dynamic model was first reformulated as a Pareto-type optimization problem following the approach suggested by Lundgren (1985). The neoclassical production function for the electricity sector in the dynamic model was then replaced with an activity analysis electricity production model taken from a partial equilibrium model of the electricity and heat markets. The resulting integrated model is solved by a nonlinear optimization algorithm.[12]

The integrated model, like the dynamic model, is a medium-term model of resource allocation, characterized by sector-specific capital stocks and a vintage structure for the existing capital. Given the distribution of the capital stock over the different sectors and vintages, the integrated model determines the sectoral allocation of production and factor use, the flow of intermediate deliveries and the composition of the final demand (private and public consumption, gross investments and foreign trade) as well as a set of market clearing commodity and factor prices. For the electricity sector it determines the utilization of different electricity production technologies. Since the integrated model contains a detailed representation of the electricity production technology it is possible to capture the effects on the rest of the economy of restrictions on the use of, for instance, nuclear power and, since the electricity sector model is embedded in a general equilibrium structure, the production of electricity is determined simultaneously with the allocation of resources in the rest of the economy. Thus, the integrated model makes it possible to assess the mutual interconnections between the electricity sector and the rest of the economy.

The integrated model can be used to simulate a development over time for the model economy by solving it for a sequence of consecutive time periods. The only intertemporal linkage between the periods is the amount of total gross investments. They are exogenous and their sectoral allocation is determined recursively once the one-period equilibrium has been computed, exactly in the same way as for the dynamic model. The electricity sector, however, is treated differently. The investments in different electricity production technologies are not determined recursively, but simultaneously with the one-period equilibrium. In this way the joint determination of production, prices and investments in the electricity sector, which is a very attractive feature of the original sector model, is also preserved in the integrated model.

This is not a very satisfactory treatment of the sectoral allocation of investments. It was only adopted temporarily in order to retain the investment allocation model of the dynamic model, while still allowing for the simultaneous determination of production and investment decisions in the electricity sector. A more satisfactory treatment would be to let production and investment decisions be simultaneously determined also in the nonelectricity sectors. The increased flexibility which the optimization approach allows makes it in principle straightforward to introduce such a change in the model. However, it also increases the nonlinearity of the model. Any such change must therefore be implemented with care so that the model remains numerically tractable.

4.4 Applications and conclusions

The integrated model has been used to assess the economic consequences of the present nuclear power discontinuation policy and for an evaluation of the nuclear power investment program (see Lundgren, 1985, chs 4 and 5).

The main lesson from the nuclear power discontinuation exercise is that in spite of rather dramatic effects on the electricity price and the electricity demand the impact on the rest of the economy is quite limited. Without nuclear power the long-run marginal cost of electricity can be expected to increase by approximately 60 percent. The corresponding decline in the electricity demand is in the long run around 15–20 percent. However, the effects on the overall economy are limited. GDP is 0.7 percent lower if nuclear power is discontinued than it would be have been if nuclear power had been kept in operation. There are only small effects on the structural composition of production and foreign trade and on relative prices (except the electricity price). The most noticeable effects are, not surprisingly, a lower production and lower exports from the energy-intensive export industries.

A similar result emerges from the second application. Although the analysis indicates that the massive and in time concentrated nuclear power investments have led to a temporary excess capacity in electricity production, the efficiency loss inflicted on the economy seems to be limited. According to the simulations GDP would have been approximately 0.5 percent higher if the nuclear power investments had been sufficiently low to avoid the excess capacity.

The general lesson to be learned from these applications of the integrated model seems to be that large and dramatic changes within the electricity sector still have a rather limited impact on the rest of the economy. The main explanation is of course that the cost share of electricity in most sectors of the economy after all is rather low, around 2–5 percent. Although it is important to have the option of evaluating sector–specific changes in a general equilibrium framework, the effects on the rest of the economy are often not strong enough to warrant that this is done with a very elaborate sector model. Instead it is better to perform the general equilibrium analysis with a rather aggregated sector model to economize on the computational effort. The more detailed analysis of the consequences for the single sector can instead be done within a partial equilibrium context.

5 Concluding Remarks

The models discussed in the preceding sections have been developed within an ongoing research program at the Stockholm School of Economics. One aim of the program is to provide models and quantitative analyses that can elucidate the relevant economic aspects of energy policy problems which are a major concern for both the general public and decision makers within firms, organizations and government. This means that the models discussed here will be redesigned, and new models will be developed, as the focus of the Swedish energy policy debate changes.

Although it is difficult to predict the issues that will be the most important in the future, one very broad topic is a major candidate for systematic analyses: the choice of the general structure of the Swedish energy supply system. In view of the decision to phase out nuclear power, the likely development of a north European natural gas market, the research and development efforts to develop domestic energy sources, such as biomass and peat, and the increasing awareness of the so-called acid rain problem, this choice is likely to have significant economic and environmental effects. It is thus a very reasonable task to try to identify and quantify the consequences of various alternatives.

Future model development, however, is not only a matter of what economic issues to focus on. To a very large extent it is also a matter of improving the quality of the models, in terms of both general specification and empirical relevance.

Notes

1 It should be noted that the actual growth of Sweden's energy consumption between 1973 and 1985 turned out to be 0 percent per annum, a fact that at least to some extent can be ascribed to the policies that were implemented.

2 The research was partly conducted as a joint research project, "Energy and Economic Structure", involving scholars from the Stockholm School of Economics, the Industrial Institute for Economic and Social Research and the University of Stockholm. Most of the funding was provided by the Energy Research and Development Commission. (A significant part of the research has been carried out at, and in collaboration with, the International Institute for Applied Systems Analysis, Laxenburg, Austria.)

3 The terminology is due to Armington (1969), who treated goods with the same statistical classification but different country of origin as less than perfect substitutes. Moreover domestic users of a good with a given statistical classification were taken to use a mixture (composite) of imported and domestically produced goods with that classification.

4 It is well known that the incorporation of the Armington assumption affects the qualitative properties of a CGE model with more tradeable goods than (homogeneous and mobile) factors. Thus, solutions with positive production of all tradeables are feasible, and in fact typical,

outcomes. Moreover, a variant of the optimum tariff argument applies: by taxing its own exports the home country can secure welfare gains at the expense of the rest of the world.

5 Note that $X_{ij} = a_{ij}X_j$ for $i = 2, 3, \ldots, n$ for all j.

6 Compared with table 10.1, the sectoral disaggregation as well as the adopted parameter values were slightly different in this version of the model. Thus the "base case" value for the elasticity of substitution between the single aggregated energy commodity and the capital–labor composite factor was taken to be 0.25 in all six production sectors. Moreover, the price elasticity of export demand was assumed to range between 1.0 and 3.0, with the highest value for the most energy-intensive sector.

7 Whether the possible benefits of such a strategy exceed the cost is another question, not dealt with in the study.

8 Total gross investments are determined by total savings which, in turn, are determined by a fixed rate of saving out of national income.

9 The first commercial nuclear power reactor began to operate in 1972 and the last of the planned 12 reactors was put on line in 1985. Currently the energy capacity of the nuclear power system is around 60 TWh per annum which amounts to almost 50 percent of the annual electricity production.

10 Since the three model versions discussed in this paper only have one household sector, the set of efficient allocations usually contains only one element. This of course facilitates the application of the optimization approach.

11 The approach is discussed in detail by Lundgren (1985, ch. 2). The intuition can perhaps be seen from the fact that for a one-consumer economy the budget constraint can be expressed as

$$e(q, u) - T = Y(p, v) \tag{1}$$

where $e(q, u)$ is the consumer's expenditure function, T is total tax revenues, $Y(p, v)$ is the national income function and q is the vector of consumer prices which differ from the producer prices p due to commodity and factor taxes.

At given prices and taxes the expenditure function is a monotone transformation of the utility function and can thus itself be used as a utility indicator of the underlying preferences. Total tax revenues are also a function of the physical allocation in the economy. Consequently the left-hand side of the budget constraint is a function of the physical allocation in the economy. Since a competitive equilibrium implies that profits are maximized, the budget constraint can be used to prove that a competitive equilibrium with taxes yields a maximum of the left-hand side in (1). This fact can be used to actually compute the competitive equilibrium provided that the particular transformation of the utility function which the left-hand side in (1) constitutes can be identified. It is possible to do this and it can in fact be done fairly quickly for certain types of commonly used utility functions like the Cobb–Douglas.

12 We have used the MINOS nonlinear programming system. See Murtagh and Saunders (1981).

References

Armington, P. S. (1969) "A Theory of Demand for Products Distinguished by Place of Production", *IMF Staff Papers*, 16, 159–78.

Bergman, L (1980) "Energy Policy in a Small Open Economy: The Case of Sweden", *IIASA Reports*, 1(1), 1–48.

—— (1981) "The Impact of Nuclear Power Discontinuation in Sweden", *Regional Science and Urban Economics*, 11, 269–86.

—— (1982) "A System of Computable General Equilibrium Models for a Small Open Economy", *Mathematical Modelling*, 3, 421–35.

—— (1986) "ELIAS – A Model of Multisectoral Economic Growth", in B. C. Ysander (ed.), *Two Models of an Open Economy*, Stockholm: Industriens Utredningsinstitut.

—— and K.-G. Mäler (1981) "The Efficiency–Flexibility Trade-off and the Cost of Unexpected Oil Price Increases", *Scandinavian Journal of Economics*, 83, 243–68.

—— and —— (1983a) "Oil Price Uncertainty and National Energy Strategies", in L. Bergman, K. G. Mäler, T. Nordström and B. C. Ysander (eds), *Energy and Economic Structure*, Stockholm: Industriens Utredningsinstitut.

—— and —— (1983b) *Kärnkraftsavveckling och energi-politiska strategier. En samhällsekonomisk analys* (Nuclear Power Discontinuation and Energy Policy Strategies. An Economic Analysis), Stockholm: Ministry of Industry, DsI Report 19.

—— and L. Ohlsson (1983) "Changes in Comparative Advantage and Paths of Structural Adjustment and Growth in Sweden, 1975–2000" *IIASA Reports*, 3(2), 375–405.

Johansen, L. (1960) *A Multi-sectoral Study of Economic Growth* (second enlarged edn, 1974) Amsterdam: North-Holland.

Lundgren, S. (1985) *Model Integration and the Economics of Nuclear Power*, Stockholm: Ekonomiska Foskningsinstitutet.

Murtagh, B., and M. Saunders (1981) "A Projected Lagrangian Algorithm and its Implementation for Sparse Nonlinear Constraints", Stanford, CA: Department of Operations Research, Stanford University, Technical Report SOL 80-IR.

Ysander, B. C. (ed.) (1986) *Two Models of an Open Economy*, Stockholm: Industriens Utredningsinstitut.

11

Two Alternative Disequilibrium Models for a Planned Economy

Wojciech Charemza and Vladimir Dlouhý

In this paper two disequilibrium macroeconomic models of a centrally planned economy (CPE) are presented. Both of them are founded on the basis of the Barro–Grossman theory with explicitly formulated notional and effective demand and supply functions and emphasized role of planners' behaviour. The first model, the quantity rationing model (QRM), is a fixed-price fixed-wage type, with a supply multiplier on the household side. The planners' decisions result from constrained export demand, supply and import demand functions.

The second model, the plan adjustment model (PAM), differs from the QRM mainly in its approach to the formation of plans. Plans are assumed to be the result of a compromise between planners' and enterprises' expectations which eventually lead to a plan adjustment mechanism. Also, in the PAM wages are endogenized by a "wage illusion" mechanism and the consumption supply function is of the residual type.

The models are compared, their flaws and advantages are discussed and possibilities for empirical implementations are surveyed.

1 Introduction

Many economists of various orientations find the general idea of disequilibrium very attractive for understanding the performance of a CPE. This reflects a conventional wisdom about the functioning of the socialist economies; it has been believed for a long time that CPEs suffer from chronic excess demand, that demand does not equal supply either on separate markets or in aggregate. At the same time, this assertion has been supported by anecdotal evidence, e.g. by unsystematic observation of the CPE's economic reality (the existence of shortages, queues, informal or even formal rationing etc.).

Only recently, in the last decade, have more systematic attempts appeared with the aim of putting the conventional wisdom about CPEs' economic performance on more solid ground. Hence two extremely important directions of research should be distinguished: (1) models with quantity rationing (disequilibrium models), where demand and supply are treated symmetrically and disequilibria of either sign are allowed but not assumed; (2) models based on the assumption that the permanent existence of shortages is typical in a CPE.

The theoretical sources of disequilibria macromodels are well known. The whole theory is basically of a neo-Keynesian nature and stems first of all from Barro and Grossman (1971, 1974, 1976) and Malinvaud (1977) (with many antecedents, see Portes, 1986, p.3). The present CPE models are, in many aspects, based on the theoretical specifications of Muellbauer and Portes (1978). Portes himself has been a leading figure in the process of forming the disequilibrium macrotheory of CPEs. In a series of papers he not only arrived at the theoretical specifications of the model (Portes, 1979, 1981), but also laid the foundation for its basic assumptions (Portes, 1974, 1977, 1978). Now, after almost a decade, one can conclude that we have at our disposal a relatively general theoretical model of a CPE; this model reflects many important institutional characteristics and at the same time forms a basis for some kind of empirical verification.

It is obvious that a general and aggregate type of macromodel must be based on rather simplifying but rigorous assumptions. Consequently, the model has to stimulate discussion and criticism, ranging from partial objections concerning the specification to the entire refutation, not only of the model itself, but of all macroeconomics in CPEs as such.

Disequilibrium macromodelling of CPEs was originally motivated by an attempt to evaluate the evidence for repressed inflation in these economies. Neoclassical elements of the model called primarily for elucidation of the notion of macroeconomic equilibrium in a CPE as a state of rest, where markets do not clear (Dlouhý, 1984), and in this sense these models are essentially general equilibrium models, representing "an interrelated system of markets in which actions are made consistent within the unit period" (Muellbauer and Portes 1978, p.790); but this is still the common ground for most models of CPEs including Kornai's macroeconomic generalization of the concept of shortage (Kornai, 1080, 1982). However, a distinctive feature of "standard" disequilibrium macromodels is scepticism toward sustained repressed inflation as an inherent characteristic of CPE performance. From the very beginning it was claimed that the permanent existence of repressed inflation must be formulated as a hypothesis and only appropriate empirical tests can reject or confirm the same. This kind of strategy asked for a specification of the model with a "reasonable" alternative to repressed inflation. Clearly, disequilibrium macro-models à la Barro–Grossman and Malinvaud were initially used.

In this paper two generally specified models of these common roots are discussed. The first, originated by Portes and continued by Dlouhý (1984) is a fixed-price–fixed-wage (quantity rationing) model. The second one differs from the former mainly in the consumption formation mechanism, endogenized wages and plan formation algorithm. The models are compared, their advantages and shortcomings are pointed out and the problem of application in an operational, directly estimated form is especially emphasized.

2 A Quantity Rationing Model

On a very aggregate level, macroeconomic institutional characteristics of CPEs are rather simple. There are no complex monetary flows and institutions, the basic role is played by the central plan and the planning hierarchy. Prices and wages are fixed by the centre, the resources are distributed in physical units and money plays only a passive role. Foreign trade flows are virtually separated from the internal economy, as the foreign trade prices are not linked with the internal prices. The basic equilibrating mechanism consists of short-term adjustments to the consumption goods market and, mainly, of the planners' reactions and adjustments in pursuing the main economic targets (steady growth rate, full employment, internal and external balance etc.). The whole idea of modelling in CPEs is heavily based on the assumption that both behavioural and techno-logical regularities exsist in these economies; this assumption we consider as already proved. However, we must admit that many of the existing characteristics of the functioning of CPEs create new, system-specific problems: prices fixed by the centre obviously do not clear the market but, moreover, bring distorted information about the scarce resources, the cost structure etc.

In dynamics, theoretical problems of growth in CPEs were clearly set up, e.g. by Kalecki (1972); the main growth barriers consist of consumption, labour force and foreign trade. These barriers together with the assumption of full employment, determine the model; problems of full capacity utilization, however, require its adequate solution.

There are several important blocks which have their place in more or less all macroeconomic models of both CPEs and market economies: production functions, determining the level of gross or net output, an aggregate consumption function, an investment function, export and import functions, the chain from investment outlay to gross capital formation, an increase in capacities and an increase in output, inflationary feedback etc. Following the taxonomy of Welfe (1985), one can specify a closed loop bottleneck multiplier describing the spread of scarcities of supplies in certain industries to the whole economy; the existence of shortages and disequilibrium calls for the construction of disequilibrium indicators, usually expressing certain adjustment mechanisms.

However, the general structure of macroeconomic models, as has been described above, does not contain any endogenous, explicitly built-in, equilibrating mechanism. At the same time, all existing models tend to stress that the dominance of the supply side and growth is driven essentially by a (sometimes modified) supply accelerator. Several years ago, this led Portes to the conclusion that "a better basis for a structural model will be the more symmetrical quantity rationing framework, appropriately adapted to the CPE context" (Portes, 1977). Since then, the macroeconomic models with quantity rationing of CPEs have been developed.

In this framework, it is more likely that an explicit specification of the equilibrating mechanism exists in the model: the feedback excess demand or supply to planners' behaviour and endogenous quantity adjustment. The theoretical model is much more simple: it has only two markets (for consumption goods and labour) and two agents (households and planners). Both subjects maximize their utility function; preferences of the households are defined on consumption and leisure, and intertemporal maximization of the appropriate utility functions gives the constrained and unconstrained demand for goods and supply of labour. The preferences of planners are defined on consumption and government expenditures. During the period of plan construction they maximize their utility function subject to several contraints determined by technology, expectations about the behaviour of households, desired end-period inventories and foreign trade conditions. In the current period, planners realize possible errors in expectations about the technology and households' behaviour and adjust the magnitude of relevant variables, namely supply of consumption goods and supply of exports.

This approach allows for explicit treatment of spillovers between the two markets and the whole specification of the model leads to the standard classification of the short-run outcomes: Keynesian unemployment, repressed inflation, classical unemployment and under-consumption.

In the description of a QRM based on these positions, we follow the notation of Portes (1979, 1981):

y, gross national product;
c, consumption;
g, government expenditure;
in, investments;
gs $= g -$ in;
s, stock of inventories;
e, volume of exports;
i, volume of imports;
l, employment;
w, wages;
m, stock of money;
pe, foreign price of one unit of domestic output (in foreign currency);
pi, foreign price of one unit of imported goods (in foreign currency);
p, term of trade ($p =$ pe/pi);
B, balance of trade in foreign currency;
pw, US dollar index of unit values of imports of industrial countries (world price);
wa, volume of imports of industrial countries in US dollars.

Flow variables for the current period are written without time subscript, flows for the previous period have the subscript -1 (or more generally L). For stock variables, 0 denotes the value at the beginning of the current period; the end-period value is written without subscript. Superscripts e and p denote expetations and planned values, and superscripts d and s stand for demand and supply. When dealing with disequilibrium situations, constrained functions are marked by bars, i.e. $\bar{c}^d(.)$.

The behaviour of households has been formalized by Muellhauer and Portes (1978) and by Portes (1981). We have the following demand for goods and supply of labour:

$$c^d = \begin{cases} c^d(w, m_0) & l = l^s \leqslant l^d \\ \bar{c}^d(w, m_0, l) & l = l^d < l^s \end{cases}$$

$$l^s = \begin{cases} l^s(w, m_0) & c = c^d \leqslant c^s \\ \bar{l}^s(w, m_0, c) & c = c^s < c^d \end{cases} \tag{11.1}$$

Effective demand and spillovers correspond to definition number 1 in Portes (1977), e.g. agents on the short side of one market present their notional demand as their effective demand in the other market, and the effective demand of the agents on the long side is their notional demand less spillover proportional to the difference between their realized transaction and their notional demand in the constrained market. We will not discuss the equation (11.1) further and the reader is referred to Muellbauer and Portes (1978) and Portes (1981).

As far as the planners are concerned, their preferences are defined on consumption and government expenditure. During the period of the plan construction, they maximize their utility function $U = U(c, g)$ subject to several constraints, which will be discussed below. We define a vector of planners' expectations (m_0^e, s_0^e, B_L^e, pi^e, pe^e), and we suppose that the centre also has certain expectations about the technology and the behaviour of the households. We consider only a balanced plan, where an aggregate balance between output and end use is required:

$$y = c + g + s - s_0 + e - i \qquad (11.2)$$

Technology is represented by a production function. For the sake of simplicity we assume that, in the short run, the capital is fixed and does not enter into the production function; we then have only two inputs, namely labour and imported goods (consumption goods are not imported):

$$y = F(l, i) = lf\left(\frac{i}{l}\right) \qquad (11.3)$$

where the second equality is based on linear homogeneity of function F.

A balanced plan further requires consumption goods supply to equal household demand and planners' demand for labour to equal household supply. In the process of plan formation this can be formalized by the following constraints:

$$c = c^d(w, m_0^e) \qquad (11.4)$$

$$l = l^s(w, m_0^e) \qquad (11.5)$$

Following Portes (1979) we suppose that end-period desired inventories are proportional to the output

$$s = \beta y \qquad (11.6)$$

In constructing the plan, the centre is also constrained by a balance of trade target; this target is determined by the previous balances, e.g.

$$B = \delta(B_L^e) \qquad (11.7)$$

Imports depend on the conditions in the foreign trade sector; regarding the shape of the production function (11.3), we specify the demand for imports in the form

$$\frac{i}{l} = i(pi^e, pe^e, B_L^e) \qquad (11.8)$$

Supply of exports is then given by the trade balance target and imports

$$e^s = \frac{1}{pe^c} B + \frac{1}{p^c} i \tag{11.9}$$

and hence exports are considered as a necessary cost to pay the imports.

Equations (11.2) and (11.9) represent the constraints in the planners' maximizing problem max $U = U(c, g)$. Let $\phi(c, g) = 0$ be the implicitly defined boundary of the feasible region. The equilibrium, condition

$$-\left(\frac{dg}{dc}\right)_{\phi=0} = \frac{\partial U/\partial c}{\partial U/\partial g}$$

can be written as

$$U_1 c_1^d + U_2\{[(1 - \beta)H(.) + 1 - \frac{1}{p^c}i(.)]l_1^s - c_1^d\} = 0 \tag{11.10}$$

where $H(.) = f[i(pi^c, pe^c, B)]$.

The solution of the system (11.2)–(11.10) is a vector of planned values $(y^p, c^p, g^p, s^p, e^p, i^p, l^p, w^p, B^p)'$; each of these planned values depends on the expectations $(m_0^c, s_0^c, B_L^c, pi^c, pe^c)$.

During the period of plan implementation, the planners know the real magnitude of variables m_0, s_0, B_L, pi and pe, and they realize possible errors in expectations about technology and household behaviour. Again, for details we refer to the articles mentioned above, and here we only summarize the main facts. The wage and the government expenditures are to be kept on planned levels $w = w^p$ and $g = g^p$; the main variables, which the planners adjust during the current period, are the supply of consumption goods and the supply of exports. In this general skeleton of a CPE, these two supply functions are specified in the simplest form:

$$c^s = c^s(y, m_0, s_0) \tag{11.11}$$

$$e^c = e^c(y, pi, pe, B^p) \tag{11.12}$$

One refinement is now in order. For the imports, we accept the "small country assumption" and consider the import price as given. On the other hand this does not have to be exact for the exports. During the period of plan construction, it can still be realistic to suppose that planners expect export prices to be as given; however, as has been argued elsewhere (see Burkett, Portes and Winter, 1981), this is too unrealistic for the period of plan implementation. Hence the demand for CPE exports must be specified; we do this in a simple form with world economic activity, export price and world price as arguments:

$$e^d = e^d(a, \text{pe}, \text{pw}) \tag{11.13}$$

Equilibrium conditions $e = s^s = e^d$ determines the level of transaction and the price.

The complete QRM can be written as follows:[1]

$$
\begin{aligned}
y &= c + \text{gs}^p + \text{in} + s - s_0 + e - i \qquad (11.14)\\
y &= lf(\mathbf{\cdot})\\
c^d &= c^d(w^p, m_0)l = l^s \leqslant l^d\\
&\quad \bar{c}^d(w^p, m_0, l)l = l^d \leqslant l^s\\
c^s &= c^s(y, m_0, s_0)\\
c &= \min(c^d, c^s)\\
l^d &= l^p\\
l^s &= l^s(w^p, m_0)c = c^d \leqslant c^s\\
&\quad \bar{l}^s(w^p, m_0, c)c = c^s < c^d\\
l &= \min(l^d, l^s)\\
s &= \beta y\\
\frac{i}{l} &= i(\text{pi}, \text{pe}, B^p)\\
e &= e^s(y, \text{pi}, \text{pe}, B^p)\\
e &= e^d(\text{wa}, \text{pe}, \text{pw})
\end{aligned}
$$

The preceding specification of the model leads to the standard classification of the short-run outcome; the well-known possibilities are Keynesian unemployment (K:$l^d < l^s$, $c^d < c^s$), repressed inflation (R:$l^d > l^s$, $c^d > c^s$), classical unemployment (C:$l^d < l^s$, $c^d > c^s$) and underconsumption (U:$l^d > l^s$, $c^d < c^s$).

It is not difficult to do some comparative statics exercises. If we start from R and substitute the basic identity for y, we have the following system:

$$(1 - \beta)F[l, i(\text{pi}, \text{pe}, B^p)] = c^s\{F[l(\text{pi}, \text{pe}, B^p)], m_0, s_0\} + \text{gs}^p$$

$$+ \text{in} - s_0 + e - i(\text{pi}, \text{pe}, B^p) \qquad (11.15)$$

$$l = l^s(w^p, m_0, c^s\{F[l, i(\text{pi}, \text{pe}, B^p)], m_0, s_0\})$$

$$e = e^s\{F[l, i(\text{pi}, \text{pe}, B^p)], \text{pi}, \text{pe}, B^p\}$$

$$e = e(\text{wa}, \text{pe}, \text{pw})$$

System (11.15) directly determines equilibrium values l^+, e^+, pe^+ and in^+, which are the functions of the vector of exogenous variables of this model (this vector we label x)

$$l^+ = \lambda(x) \qquad e^+ = \zeta(x) \qquad \text{pe}^+ = \eta(x) \qquad \text{in}^+ = \mu(x)$$

We denote partial derivatives of equilibrium values with respect to x_i by λ_i, ζ_i, η_i and μ_i. Differentiating (11.15) we obtained the following system:

$$(1 - \beta - c_1^s)F_1\lambda_i - \zeta_i + [1 + (1 - \beta - c_1^s)F_2]i_2\eta_i - \mu_i = z_1$$
$$(1 - c_1^s\bar{l}_3^s F_1)\lambda_i \qquad\qquad -c_1^s\bar{l}_3^s F_2 i_2\eta_i \qquad\qquad\qquad = z_2 \quad (11.16)$$
$$-e_1^s F_1\lambda_i + \zeta_i \qquad\qquad - F_2 i_2 e_3^s\eta_i \qquad\qquad\qquad = z_3$$
$$\zeta_i \qquad\qquad - e_2^d\eta_i \qquad\qquad\qquad\qquad = z_4$$

where $z_1, \ldots, z_4$ are the appropriate right-hand sides. The determinant of (11.16) can be written as

$$(1 - c_1^s\bar{l}_3^s F_1)(e_3^s - e_2^d) + F_2 i_2 e_1^s > 0 \qquad (11.17)$$

If we compare (11.17) with the result of Portes (see Portes, 1981, p. 575), we observe a similarity: we obtained a supply multiplier (in the Barro–Grossman sense) which takes into account foreign trade; the expression $1 - c_1^s\bar{l}_3^s F_1$ is a usual multiplier of the sequence $y \rightarrow c \rightarrow l$, $e_3^s - e_2^d$ considers the relation between exports and price and $e_1^s F_2 i_2$ considers the sequence $i \rightarrow y \rightarrow e$.

The above model can also be used for investigating the relations between internal and external balance in CPEs. Portes (1979) discussed this problem and introduced a simple diagrammatic apparatus to explore the relations between internal and external balance simultaneously. Government expenditures were fixed at the planned level and it was supposed that the main planners' policy instruments are direct controls over wages w and exports e. Holzman (1980) and Ames (1980) in comments on Portes's paper pointed out that imports rather than exports could be used as policy instruments. Below we present the results of this modification.

Taking i as a policy instrument reflects the changes in foreign trade conditions at the beginning of the 1980s. Nowadays, exports are often not regarded as "a necessary evil to pay for imports" but, given the fall of world economic activity, the centre has problems with its allocation etc. In this situation, it is easier for the planners to cut the imports to achieve a given balance of trade target B^p. Formally, supply of exports depends on the output and foreign trade conditions

$$e = e^s(y, pe, pi, B^p) \qquad (11.18)$$

and import is determined by

$$i = \frac{1}{pi}B + pe \qquad (11.19)$$

To simplify our exposition, assume in this section a small country assumption for exports as well, i.e. the export price pe is given.

External balance is achieved when the balance of trade policy target is satisfied. Internal balance is achieved when aggregate sources equal uses (Portes, 1979). We substitute into (11.19) and obtain

$$i = \frac{1}{\text{pi}}B + pe^s\{F[l^s(w), i], \text{pi}, \text{pe}, B^p\} \qquad (11.20)$$

which implicitly defines the trade-off between the imports and wages under external balance. A similar trade-off can be defined when the internal balance is continuously attained

$$(1 - \beta)F[l^s(w), i]$$

$$= c^d(w) + g - s_0 + e^s\{F[l^s(w), i], \text{pi}, \text{pe}, B^p\} - i \qquad (11.21)$$

The positive effects of this approach are straightforward: apart from the above-mentioned specification of equilibrating mechanism, disequilibrium models significantly clarified our understanding of households' and planners' behaviour and their interaction on the very aggregated level. At least in the theoretical framework, we have a general equilibrium non-Walrasian model for a CPE with, in Kornai's words, "real" and "control" spheres, built-in adjustment towards equilibrium and a representation of plan construction that assumes that the planners are rational in their behaviour.

There are many problems with this approach as well. The often cited empirical problems, where the lack of appropriate methods for estimation of the multimarket model with quantity rationing is stressed, do not have to be the most crucial problems. They certainly prevent us from using this model more actively and from measuring such relevant and highly important magnitudes as the parameters of supply multiplier, excess demand on both markets etc. However, there are more important objections from the theoretical point of view; they come primarily from Kornai (1980, 1982) but also from the experienced builders of large econometric models (for more detailed discussion see Portes, 1986 and Dlouhý, 1985). Kornai explicitly refuses to accept the short side rule, claiming that when dealing with the data on the macrolevel, shortage and slack are usually presented simultaneously. This, obviously, is of microeconomic origin and the whole problem is one of aggregation. In the disequilibrium literature this has already been recognized by Muellbauer (1978) and worked out e.g. by Gourieroux and Laroque (1985) and Martin (1985) and especially by Burkett (1988), who had the interesting idea of bridging the gap between the Kornai and Portes approaches by simultaneously considering shortages and slacks in an econometric model.

There are, naturally, other objections from econometricians. Welfe (1985) finds the classifications of the economic regimes of CPEs developed by these models (see above) inferior when compared with the typology based on the constraints in material input. This is a legitimate point, especially for the practising economists – it is not easy to imagine today's CPEs to be in a demand-constrained regime of Keynesian unemployment with demand-driven growth. It should be stressed, however, that there are widespread doubts about the strict prevalence of repressed inflation – see several empirical confirmations of the global equilibrium on the consumption goods market in at least some CPEs (Klaus and Rudlovcak, 1982; Portes and Winter, 1980; and others). However, there is no other way to test the hypothesis of repressed inflation or that of Keynesian unemployment than to specify the model that allows for disequilibrium of either sign.

Numerical interactability of the whole model and the obvious interest in measuring the disequilibria on the particular markets caused the increased interest in specifying quantity-rationed models for the consumption goods market. For instance, Charemza and Quandt (1982) supplemented the classical "one-market" model with the fourth equation for the planned value of transaction, which in turn enters demand and supply equations. The plan formation is made endogenous and, given the specification of equations, the model has a built-in adjustment towards market clearing which can be compared with that of price adjustment in other disequilibrium models (for further discussion of this and similar approaches in empirical modelling see Charemza, forthcoming).

3 A Plan Adjustment Model

The PAM described in this section is also of a Barro–Grossman type. It is developed from a less general model of Charemza and Gromicki (1988). For the sake of comparability with the QRM we have shortened the model by dropping the investment sector; also the model's symbolic representation has been changed to be at least in some respects consistent with that of the QRM.

The PAM has much in common with the QRM, especially since the functions representing the households' behaviour are derived in a similar way. The difference is in the way the models explicitly involve the households' expectations in their utility function. This gives an additional threshold in consumption demand and labour supply functions, which switch not only between their effective and notional values but also according to future expected price and quantity restrictions.

We have to change the notation slightly. An asterisk as a superscript denotes the expression connected with household behaviour; superscript r denotes state firm (enterprise) behaviour and the absence of (additional) superscripts corresponds to planners' behaviour. These superscripts are omitted where there is no room for confusion, for instance we are using c^d rather than the more rigorous c^{*d}. Superscripts p still stands for a planned variable, but now it is not a planners' wish but a value agreed between planners and enterprises. Households create a non-planning sector. To avoid using too many superscripts we have moved e, the notation for expectations, down – it is now a subscript. More precisely, it stands for a value of a variable expected *in the past* for the *present* time. The expectations made *at present* concerning *future* values of a variable are denoted by the subscript F. For instance, c_F^{*d} expresses the amount of consumption demand expected by households where the expectations are made at the current time for the future; c_e^{*d} stands for similar expectations, but made in the past for the present.

While consumption might be constrained either by labour or by a future consumption market, or by both, the consumer demand equation is given as (with expected signs of particular first derivatives in brackets, below the variables)

$$c^d = c_{kc}^d \{ \underset{(+)}{w}, \underset{(+)}{m_0}, \underset{(+)}{c_F^*} \max[0, \text{sgn}(c_F^{*d} - c_F^*)], \underset{(-)}{l} \max[0, \text{sgn}(l^s - l^d)] \}$$

(11.22)

where $kc = 1, \ldots, 4$ and corresponds to four possible sets of constraints namely

$$kc = 1 \text{ if sgn}(c_F^{*d} - c_F^*) = -1 \text{ and sgn}(l^s - l^d) = -1;$$
$$kc = 2 \text{ if sgn}(c_F^{*d} - c_F^*) = 1 \text{ and sgn}(l^s - l^d) = -1;$$
$$kc = 3 \text{ if sgn}(c_F^{*d} - c_F^*) = -1 \text{ and sgn}(l^s - l^d) = 1;$$
$$kc = 4 \text{ if sgn}(c_F^{*d} - c_F^*) = 1 \text{ and sgn}(l^s - l^d) = 1.$$

Thus it is clear that the notional and effective consumption demand functions of the QRM correspond to a special case of (11.22), in particular $c^d(.)$ of the QRM is $c_1^d(.)$ of the PAM and $\bar{c}^d(.)$ of QRM is $c_3^d(.)$.

The practical applications function (11.22) can be written in a simpler form, without the explicit thresholds. For instance, if the utility function is of the Cobb–Douglas type, function (11.22) is linear and consequently the subscript kc can be omitted since the total derivative is then identical for all kcs.

The labour supply equation can be derived in a similar manner. The difference is that we are considering future inflation as affecting labour instead of future quantity restraints

$$l^s = l_{kc}^s \{ \underset{(+)}{w}, \underset{(+)}{m_0}, \underset{(+)}{\dot{p}c}_F \max[0, \text{sgn}(\dot{p}c_F)], \underset{(-)}{c} \max[0, \text{sgn}(c^d - c^s)] \}$$

(11.23)

where pc stands for the consumer price and a dot over a variable denotes its first derivative (in continuous time) or first difference (in a discrete time) with respect to time. Again, the index kc orders the constraints, from kc = 1 (no constraints) to kc = 4 (quantity constraints from the present consumption market and a future shadow price effect).

So far the model is a straightforward generalization of the QRM. On the state side, the differences between these models are more substantial. One of the most important consists of using a residual-type consumption function

$$\frac{c^s}{pc} = y - g - \text{in} - s + s_0 - e + i \qquad (11.24)$$

where all the variables on the right-hand side are in real terms. With this equation, strongly supported by some (e.g. Green and Higgins, 1977; Libura, 1979) but dismissed by others (Portes and Winter, 1977), a production function should be directly included in the model. In turn, labour demand is a result of a compromise between planners and enterprises. An enterprise tends to maximize its "importance", mainly through increases in its employment and investment, not necessarily in direct connection with profit or output maximization. Nevertheless, in its activity an enterprise is constrained in its expectations of production targets, namely[3]

$$l_c^{rd} = l_{c}^{rd}(y_c^r)$$
$$\phantom{l_c^{rd} = l}(+)$$

At the same time planners are forming their expectations concerning labour demand, equal to l_c^d. If one considers the expectations variables as rational in the Muth (1969) sense (e.g. as unbiased predictions conditional on all the relevant information generated by the system in the past), i.e.

$$l_c^{rd} = E(l|H_L^r)$$
$$l^{rd} = E(l|H_L)$$

(where H_L^r and H_L stand for the information sets from the past as available for enterprises and planners, respectively), it is clear that their expectations might be equal to each other only if the information sets are identical. If, alternatively, the expectations are understood in a wider sense, i.e. also taking into account future extraneous constraints, which might be limits for the Muth rational expectations, then

$$l_c^{rd} = \max[E(l|H_L^r), \bar{l}_c^r]$$
$$l_c^d = \max[E(l|H_L), \bar{l}_c]$$

where the extraneous future constraints on labour are denoted $\bar{l}^r_c$ and $\bar{l}_c$. These might be identified with population limits, cultural, health and ecological constraints, etc. Again these are not necessarily identical for planners and enterprises. In a general vision of a "moderate" CPE, plans are not commanded from the planners "down" to enterprises, but result from some kind of bargain (compromise) between the two sides. Let us define this compromise function for labour l^B as

$$l^B = l^B(l^{rd}_c, l^d_c)$$

where $l^B \in [\min(l^{rd}_c, l^d_c); \max(l^{rd}_c, l^d_c)]$. The result of this compromise is the labour demand function

$$l^d = l^B(l^{rd}_c, l^d_c) \tag{11.25}$$

It is important to note that l^d is an amount of labour demanded from the state side as a whole (planners and enterprises together) from the households. We deliberately refrain from identifying the result of labour bargaining with a "plan" for labour. It is assumed that planners might not be as powerful when confronting households. The officially announced labour plans might, or might not, be equal to l^d; they are equal if the process of plan formation is identical with that described above. The household–state part of the model is completed by the minimum conditions

$$c = \min(c^d, c^s) \tag{11.26}$$

$$l = \min(l^d, l^s) \tag{11.27}$$

A formulation of the production function in PAM is close to the original proposition of Barro and Grossman (1976, p. 11), i.e. output is a function of labour demand and government expenditure (public services). A threshold is assumed for labour rationing, which leads to

$$y^s = y^s_{ky}\{\underset{(+)}{l}, \underset{(+)}{g}, l^d \underset{(+)}{\max}[0, \operatorname{sgn}(l^d - l^s)]\} \tag{11.28}$$

where ky = 1 if $\operatorname{sgn}(l^d - l^s) \neq 1$, and ky = 2 otherwise. Evidently in certain cases, e.g. where (11.28) is linear (or linear in logarithms), the subscript can be dropped since the value of the function is identical for both signs of labour excess demand. For instance, if one believes in the Cobb–Douglas-type specification of the production function, the suggested form of (11.28) is

$$y^s = l^\alpha g^\beta \exp\{\gamma(l^d - l)\max[0, \operatorname{sgn}(l^d - l^s)]\}$$

The central role in the model is played by two adjustment equations, which endogenize wages and plans for output. The wage equation is derived from the so-called "wage illusion" effect, according to which workers are paid better for all the disutilities connected with rationing. Maximizing the workers' disutility function with respect to wages gives (see Charemza and Gronicki, 1988)

$$w = w_{kw}\left\{ \underset{(-)}{w}_L, \underset{(+)}{\frac{y}{l}}, \underset{(-)}{c^s} \max[0, \text{sgn}(c^d - c^s)] \right\} \qquad (11.29)$$

where kw changes according to the restrictions imposed by consumption excess demand. The "wage illusion" effect is revealed for positive consumption excess demand. Its destructive character is evident where the function is expanded in a Taylor series around c^d:

$$w \approx w_1\left(w_L, \frac{y}{l}\right) + (c^d - c^s)\frac{\partial w}{\partial c^1}\left(w_L, \frac{y}{l}\right) \qquad \text{if } c^d > c^s$$

The positive consumption excess demand in a given period stimulates an increase of wages, which in turn leads to an increase of excess demand without affecting consumption supply and prices. This inevitably leads to instability of the system and is a source of unstable (explosive) consumption excess demand. In other words, dynamics of the model generate only a one-way switch in (11.29) – from w_L to w – without the possibility of switching the "disequilibrium disaster" off Obviously the PAM cannot be identified either with a fixed-price equilibrium or a "normal shortage" model.

The next equation of the model is the plan adjustment equation; it describes the way of plan formulation and its adjustment towards disequilibrium. The postulated process of plan formation is analogous to some extent to that used for deriving the labour demand function Nevertheless, since the process is "closed" in the sense that it is not directed towards the unplanned household sector, the revealed result is a plan for outcome rather than demand (this has essential consequences for empirical verification of the model since the plan is observed, while demand might not be observed). We start from expectations of firms and planners. The essential difference lies in firms' and planners' ways of forming expectations. While firms are forming their expectations either in the rational Muth sense, e.g.

$$y_c^r = E(y|H_L^r)$$

or as the constraint expectations

$$y_c^r = \max[E(y|H_L^r, \bar{y}_c^r]$$

where $\bar{y}_c^r$ stands for the constraints concerning output and expected by firms, the planners come up with *incomplete expectations*, which might again be formulated as unbiased predictions or as constraint expectations that are, nevertheless, conditional on the incomplete set of information from the past. Some information concerning the hard constraints, which cannot be a subject of eventual compromise because of their nature are excluded. The planners' incomplete expectations $y_c^\sim$ are given by

$$y_c^\sim = E(y|\overline{H}_L)$$

or

$$y_c^\sim = \max[E(y|\overline{H}_L), \tilde{y}_e]$$

where $\overline{H}_L$ is a set of information from the past excluding that of the hard constraints $\overline{\overline{y}}_e$, i.e. $\overline{H}_L = H_L \backslash \overline{\overline{y}}_e(H_L)$. Consequently $\tilde{y}_e$ now stands for a set of soft constraints, which might be relaxed as a result of compromise between planners and firms.

The postulated plan is a result of a compromise (bargain) between planners and firms; it is also affected by the hard constraints leading to the equation

$$y^P = y^P[y^B(y_c^\sim, y_c^r), \overline{\overline{y}}_e] \tag{11.30}$$

where $y^B(.)$ is a compromise function formulated analogously to that used for deriving labour demand, e.g. with its values being between $y_c^\sim$ and y_e^r. The notation of hard constraints needs some explanation. This might be either an upper (or lower) limit for production, in which case (11.30) takes the form

$$y^P = \max[y^B(y_c^\sim, y_c^r), \overline{\overline{y}}_e]$$

or a limit of a production factor (e.g. $y_e = \overline{\overline{y}}_e(l_e)$ in the case of expected labour shortages, or $\overline{\overline{y}}_e = \overline{\overline{y}}_e(i_e)$ in the case of expected import bottlenecks, or both).

The entire PAM planning procedure can be summarized in the following steps.

1 Planners and enterprises formulate their expectations; enterprises use all their relevant information from the previous periods while planners exclude information which generates signals about prospective hard constraints.
2 Confrontation of the planners' and enterprises' expectations results in compromise (there is room for some iterative planning schemes – see for example Weitzmann, 1979; Cave and Hare, 1981; and Bennett, 1985).
3 The compromise is subject to correction by the expected hard constraints.
4 An initial, officially published, plan is a result of (1) and (3). Subsequently it can be a subject of revisions during the period of plan implementation (assuming that planning is flexible enough) with respect to changes in hard constraints – from expectations to realizations.

To evaluate the adjustment nature of the plan function let us assume that limitations of labour create a hard constraint and (11.30) takes the form

$$y^{\mathrm{p}} = y^{\mathrm{p}}[y^{\mathrm{B}}(.), l_e] \qquad \text{if } l_e < l_e^{\mathrm{d}}$$

Evidently, if $l_e^{\mathrm{d}} \geq l_c$ there is no labour constraint in the planning process. Expanding the plan function into a Taylor series around l^{d} and taking its first two components gives

$$y^{\mathrm{p}} \approx y^{\mathrm{p}}[y^{\mathrm{B}}(.), l^{\mathrm{d}}] + (l_e - l^{\mathrm{d}})\frac{\partial y^{\mathrm{p}}}{\partial l_e}[y^{\mathrm{B}}(.), l^{\mathrm{d}}]$$

where the *ex ante* adjustment process is evident. This becomes a quantity adjustment process if planners possess perfect knowledge about future labour constraints, i.e. $l_e = l$ if $l^{\mathrm{s}} < l^{\mathrm{d}}$.

The model is completed by import demand and export supply functions. Imports and exports are primarily a function of planned and expected output. While export is caused by a plan for a given year, import is a function of the planners' expectations about the future planned outcome y_{F}^- formed in a sequence

$$y_{\mathrm{F}}^{\sim} = \max[E(y_{\mathrm{F}}|y_{\mathrm{F}-1}^{\mathrm{p}}, H_0), \tilde{y}_{\mathrm{F}}]$$

and also

$$y_{\mathrm{F}}^{\mathrm{p}} = y_{\mathrm{F}}^{\mathrm{p}}(y_{\mathrm{F}}^{\sim}, \overline{\overline{y}}_{\mathrm{F}})$$

The way of forming planners' expectations on future plans is therefore similar to the formula derived for the one-year-ahead planning (resulting in y_e^{p}) but with the assumed superior position of planners over the enterprises. The import demand and supply equations take the form

$$i - i_{\mathrm{ki}}^{\mathrm{d}}\{\underset{(+)}{y}{}^{\mathrm{p}}_{\mathrm{F}}, \underset{(+)}{\mathrm{bp}}, \; c_{\Gamma}\underset{(+)}{\max}[0, \; \mathrm{sgn}(c_{\Gamma}^{\mathrm{d}} - c_{\mathrm{F}}^{\mathrm{s}})]\} \tag{11.31}$$

$$e = e_{\mathrm{ke}}\{\underset{(+)}{y}{}^{\mathrm{p}}, \underset{(-)}{c}_{\mathrm{L}}\max[0, \; \mathrm{sgn}(c_{\mathrm{L}}^{\mathrm{d}} - c_{\mathrm{L}}^{\mathrm{s}})]\} \tag{11.32}$$

where ki and ke correspond to particular disequilibrium situations on future (expected) and previous consumption markets and bp is the balance of payments. The foreign trade equations are virtually non-price equations, reflecting only external payments and internal consumption constraints.

4 Comparison and Final Remarks

Both the QRM and the PAM describe essentially the same system, which consists of one household and a state. In the PAM the state side is divided into a central planner and an enterprise; their encounters result in a compromise (bidding), which gives demand for labour and a plan for output. As in the QRM, in the PAM labour is exchanged for money (through wages) and goods. Instead of using domestic prices as a means of exchange, there is a barter with some kind of quantity and monetary pressure on the market. The quantity pressure in the QRM is revealed through a production function (with an explicit multiplier) and the monetary pressure is revealed through a consumption supply function. In the PAM households' quantity pressure goes through a production function and through constraints in plan adjustment and labour demand functions; there is no explicit monetary pressure, apart from that which is indirect and apparently of a rather weak strength generated via planners' and enterprises' expectations.

As far as the models are to be a form of some approximation of an existing CPE, their shortcomings are evident. The most severe in consequences seems to be a lack of a "second economy" (a parallel market).[4] This affects the disequilibrium character of the market, mainly because of the more salient nature of demand and supply in the case of the existence of a parallel, official or unofficial market with a freely negotiated price. As is pointed out by Nuti (1986), this eventually leads to confusion in the definition of demand and supply and consequently in that of a shortage or disequilibrium phenomenon, since the price on the parallel market often clears the aggregate. Knowing the reality of CPEs, the indirect assumption about the absence (or ideal isolation) of a parallel market seems particularly tight.

Other limitations of the QRM and the PAM result mainly from the a priori admitted supply multiplier, of which the existence is often questioned in light of the full employment principle (see Holzman, 1980; Kemme and Winiecki, 1984; Winiecki, 1985; and especially Ames, 1980, who came up with an interesting alternative to the labour supply function). Also the residual-type consumption supply function of the QRM seems to be a significant simplification of reality.

Nevertheless, the clear advantage of the two models is that they are both empirically operational, i.e. their estimated representation can be consitently and fully derived from the general form. The model of Charemza and Gronicki (1987), sensibly (in a statistical sense) estimated using data for Poland, 1960–80, is entirely nested within the QRM. It has been derived under rather strong assumptions about the permanent existence of repressed inflation and with the deterministic specification of the wage and plan adjustment functions. Nevertheless, these restrictions have been practically inevitable for the estimation of a relatively large latent variable disequilibrium model (see Charemza, forthcoming).

Up to now the QRM has not been estimated in its full form. Because of its virtually non-adjustment character, its estimation, which services empirical applications to single-market analyses, is relatively cumbersome. For the consumption market the empirical papers as derived from the QRM are those of Portes and Winter (1980), Klaus and Rudlovak (1982) and, for a microeconomic market, Viktorinova (1986). For foreign trade the papers of Burkett, Portes and Winter (1981) and Dlouhý and Dýba (1982, 1985, 1986), should be mentioned. It is worth noting some papers of a mixed nature: see, for example, Charemza amd Gronicki (1982), who implement the QRM ideas in a PAM approach for the foreign trade model and vice versa (i.e. the estimation problem for a quantity-rationing type of model with a plan adjustment function, which is discussed by Charemza and Quandt, 1982, followed by extensions and empirical applications by Portes et al., 1984, 1985).

Notes

W. Charemza gratefully acknowledges the financial support of Economic and Social Science Council Research Grants Nos B00230025 and B00232171.

1 We divide government expenditures into the social consumption gs and investment in; gs can be fixed at the planned level gs^p and investment is a residual variable in our model.
2 We expect the following signs of the derivatives: F_1, $F_3 > 0$, $0 < F_2 < 1$; c_1, $l_3 > 0$, l_1, l_1 unknown; i_1, $i_3 < 0$, $i_2 > 0$; e_1, e_2, e_3, $e_1 > 0$; e_1^d, $e_1^d > 0$, $e_2^d < 0$.
3 For comparison, investment equations of PAM are not presented here and all variables connected with investments apart from the investments variable in (11.24) are omitted. Note that the model does not explain government expenditures and stocks: nevertheless, investments are no longer residual.
4 For a disequilibrium model explicitly involving a second economy see Charemza (1989).

References

Ames, E. (1980) "Contractual Methods in the Study of Planned Economies: A Reconciliation of Tyson and Portes", in E. Neuberger and L. A. Tyson (eds), *The Impact of International Economic Disturbances on the Soviet Union and Eastern Europe*, New York: Pergamon.
Barro, R. J., and H. J. Grossman (1971) "A General Disequilibrium Model of Income and Employment", *American Economic Review*, 61, 82–93.
—— and —— (1974) "Suppressed Inflation and the Supply Multiplier", *Review*

of Economic Studies, 41, 97–104.

—— and —— (1976) *Money, Employment and Inflation*, Cambridge, Cambridge University Press.

Bennett, J. (1985) "Planning Under Market Socialism when Iteration is Incomplete", *Journal of Comparative Studies*, 9, 252–66.

Burkett, J. P. (1988) "Slack, Shortage and Discouraged Consumers in Eastern Europe: Estimates Based on Something by Aggregation", *Review of Economic Studies*, 55, 493–506.

Burkett, J. P., R. Portes and D. Winter (1981) "Macroeconomic Adjustment and Foreign Trade of Centrally Planned Economies", Cambridge, MA: National Bureau for Economic Research Working Paper No. 736.

Cave, M., and P. Hare (1981) *Alternative Approaches to Economic Planning*, London: Macmillan.

Charemza, W (1989) "Disequilibrium Modelling of Consumption in the Centrally Planned Economy", in C. M. Davis and W. Charemza (eds), *Models of Disequilibrium and Shortage in Centrally Planned Economies*, London: Chapman and Hall.

—— (forthcoming) "Computational Controversies in Disequilibrium and Shortage Modelling of Centrally Planned Economies", *Journal of Economic Surveys*.

—— and M. Gronicki (1982) "Rational Expectations and Disequilibrium in a Model of Foreign Trade Behaviour: The Case of Poland", *Economics of Planning*, 18, 53–64.

—— and —— (1988) *Plans and Disequilibria in Centrally Planned Economies*, Warsaw: PWN; Amsterdam: North-Holland.

—— and R. E. Quandt (1982) "Models and Estimation of Disequilibrium for Centrally Planned Economies", *Review of Economic Studies*, 49, 109–16.

Dlouhý, V. (1984) "Macroeconomic Disequilibrium Model of Centrally Planned Economy", *Ekonomicko-Matematicky Obzor*, 20, 347–87.

—— (1985) "On the Problem of Macroeconomic Modelling in Centrally Planned Economies", paper presented at the Econometric Society World Congress, Boston, MA.

—— and K. Dýba (1982) "Modelling Czechoslovak Foreign Trade Flows with Non-socialist Countries", paper presented at the Conference of the Association for Applied Econometrics, Budapest.

—— and —— (1985) *Ekonometricky Model Ceskoslovenske Obchodni Bilance*, Prague: Academia.

—— and —— (1986) "The Impact of External Disturbances on the Czechoslovak Trade Balance with Non-socialist Countries", in W. Milo and M. Miszczyński (eds), *Macromodels and Forecasts of National Economy*, Warsaw: Polish Scientific Publishers.

Gouriéroux, C., and G. Laroque (1985) "The Aggreagation of Commodities in Quantity Rationing Models", *International Economic Review*, 26 681–700.

Green, D. W., and C. I. Higgins (1977) *SOVMOD I: A Macroeconometric Model of the Soviet Union*, New York: Academic Press.

Holzman, F. O. (1980) "A Comment to the R. Portes Paper 'Internal and External Balance in a Centrally Planned Economy'", in E. Nueberger and L. . Tyson (eds), *The Impact of International Economic Disturbances on the Soviet Union and Eastern Europe*, New York: Pergamon.

Kalecki, M. (1972) *Selected Essays on the Economic Growth of the Socialist and the Mixed Economy*, Cambridge: Cambridge University Press.

Kemme, D., and J. Winiecki (1984) "Disequilibrium in Centrally Planned Economies", mimeo, University of North Carolina, Greensboro, NC.

Klaus, V., and V. Rudlovcak (1982) "Savings Function as an Inverse Problem of Disequilibrium Consumption Modelling: A Case Study of Czechoslovakia", paper presented at the Conference of the Association for Applied Econometrics, Budapest.

Kornai, J. (1980) *Economics of Shortage*, vols 1 and 2 Amsterdam: North-Holland.

—— (1982) *Growth, Shortage and Efficiency*, Oxford: Blackwell.

Libura, U. (1979) *Konsumpcja a wkorzystanie mozliwosci produkcyjnych w gospodarce socjalistycznej*, Warsaw: PWN.

Malinvaud, E. (1977) *The Theory of Unemployment Reconsidered*, Oxford: Blackwell.

Martin, C. (1985) "A General Framework for Disequilibrium Modelling", London: Birkbeck College, Discussion Paper No. 181.

Muellbauer, J. (1978) "Linear Aggregation in Neoclassical Labour Supply", London: Birkbeck College, Discussion Paper No. 54.

—— and R. Portes (1978) "Macroeconomic Models with Quantity Rationing", *Economic Journal*, 88, 788–821.

Muth, J. F. (1969) "Rational Expectations and the Theory of Price Movements", *Econometrica*, 29, 315–35

Nuti, D. M. (1986) "Hidden and Repressed Inflation in Soviet-type Economics: Definitions, Measurements and Stabilization", *Contributions to Political Economy*, 5, 37–82.

Portes, R. (1974) "Macroeconomic Equilibrium under Central Planning" Stockholm: International Institute for Economic Studies, University of Stockholm, Seminar Paper No. 40.

—— (1977) "Effective Demand and Spillovers in Empirical Two-market Disequilibrium Models", Cambridge, MA: Harvard Institute of Economic Research, Research Paper No. 595.

—— (1978) "Macroeconomic Modelling of Centrally Planned Economies: Thoughts on SOVMOD I", Cambridge, MA: Harvard Institute of Economic Research, Research Paper No. 621.

—— (1979) "Internal and External Balance in a Centrally Planned Economy", *Journal of Comparative Economics*, 3, 325–45.

—— (1981) "Macroeconomic Equilibrium and Disequilibrium in Centrally Planned Economies", *Economic Inquiry*, 19, 325–45.

—— (1986) "The Theory and Measurement of Macroeconomic Disequilibrium in Centrally Planned Economies", London: Centre for Economic Policy Research, Discussion Paper No. 91.

——, R. E. Quandt, D. Winter and S. Yeo (1984) "Planning the Consumption Goods Market: Preliminary Estimates for Poland, 1955–1980", in P. Malgrange and P.-A. Muet (eds), *Contemporary Macroeconomic Modelling*, Oxford: Blackwell.

——, ——, —— and —— (1985) "Estimating the Size of Plan Errors", Princeton, NJ: Financial Research Center, Princeton University, Research Memo No. 48.

—— and D. Winter (1977) "The Supply of Consumption Goods in Centrally

Planned Economies", *Journal of Comparative Economics*, 1, 351–65.

—— and —— (1980) "Disequilibrium Estimates for Consumption Goods in Centrally Planned Economies", *Review of Economic Studies*, 46, 137–59.

Viktorinova, B. (1986) "Specifkacia a odhad parametra funkci dopytu a ponuky v nerovnovaznom modeli", *Ekonomicko-Matematicky Obzor*, 22 144–59.

Weitzman, M. (1970) "Iterative Multilevel Planning with Production Targets", *Econometrica*, 38, 50–65.

Welfe. W. (1985) "Econometric Macromodels of Unbalanced Growth", paper presented at the conference Models and Forecasts 85, Bratislava.

Winiecki, J. (1985) "Portes ante Portas: A Critique of the Revisionist Interpretation of inflation under Central Planning". *Comparative Economic Studies*, 27, 25–52.

12

Computable General Equilibrium Models for Socialist Economies

Péter Kis, Sherman Robinson and Laura D. Tyson

1 Introduction

There is a long tradition in socialist countries of using multisectoral models to provide the analytic basis for economic planning. Input output models have long been used in various forms to solve the "material balances" problem in quantitative planning. Dynamic input–output models, some quite elaborate, have also been used both for medium-term five-year plans and for long-run prospective planning.[1] There has also been a great deal of research and experimentation with linear programming models, although they have never been widely used in actual planning exercises.[2] This work flourished in an environment where direct quantitative controls were the major policy instruments and where the price system was not viewed as important. Since the late 1960s, however, there have been major reform movements in some socialist countries which have sought to improve economic performance by instituting a new economic system incorporating increased use of market mechanisms and price incentives. Hungary and Yugoslavia were leaders in this movement.

During the past decade, multisectoral computable general equilibrium (CGE) models have been widely used in developing countries to analyze issues such as income distribution and structural adjustment.[3] These models simulate the workings of a market economy in which suppliers and demanders interact across markets in response to price signals. In its purest form, a CGE model provides an empirical implementation of the Walrasian model of production and exchange under perfect competition. However, in most applications – especially in developing countries – modelers have moved far from the Walrasian ideal and have incorporated a variety of "structuralist" features that explicitly recognize the existence of rigidities and imperfections in actual economies. A CGE model thus need not assume that decisions of producers and consumers reflect profit and utility maximization in a system of competitive markets, but can incorporate a wide variety of institutional and behavioral specifications. What is assumed is that economic performance is at least in part the outcome of decentralized decisions made by producers and consumers in response to market signals. Thus, suitably adapted, a CGE model should provide a good framework for policy analysis in a post-reform socialist economy.

CGE models have been developed for two Eastern European countries: Hungary and Yugoslavia. Both models were developed under the auspices of the World Bank to analyze issues of structural adjustment in the medium term. They focus on the impact of changes in foreign capital inflows and international trade on the structure and performance of the economy. The Yugoslav model was developed at the World Bank, while the Hungary model is based at the National Planning Office (NPO) of Hungary. Various applications of the Yugoslav model are described by World Bank (1983), Robinson and Tyson (1985) and Robinson, Tyson and Dewatripont (1986). The Hungary model has been used to support analysis within the World Bank.[4]

In this paper, we describe the basic features of the Hungarian and Yugoslav CGE models, identifying the important similarities and differences between them. Since descriptions of the Yugoslav model are already published, we focus the discussion more on the Hungarian model. We also present some results of simulations of the Hungarian model over the 1981–5 period. A comparison of model results under alternative assumptions allows identification of how economic performance would have been affected by different economic conditions. In this paper, the simulations are designed to determine the relative importance of external shocks and internal policy responses to economic performance in Hungary during the 1981–5 adjustment period. The focus is on the genesis of the foreign exchange shortage and the nature of policy reaction to it during the period. Simulations with a similar focus for Yugoslavia have already been published.[5]

2 Computable General Equilibrium Models

The models operate by simulating the operation of markets for factors, products and foreign exchange. They are highly nonlinear, with equations specifying supply and demand behavior across all markets. A solution for a given year generates market clearing prices and quantities for sectoral output, employment and foreign trade, producing all the elements of the circular flow in the economy. The Hungary model has 12 production sectors, three labor categories and two household types. The Yugoslav model has 18 sectors, four labor categories and two household types. Both models include institutions comprising government, the "rest of the world" and an aggregate capital account which serves the function of a financial sector that collects savings and allocates investment funds to sectors. Depending on the method of counting, the models have around 1,000–1,500 equations that are solved for each period in a dynamic simulation.

2.1 Production and employment

In CGE models, the usual practice is to specify that sectors maximize profits, given neoclassical production functions and competitive output and factor markets. In the Yugoslav model, the assumption of profit maximization is replaced by a more complex set of relationships that attempt to capture the operation of self-managed firms. The specification is discussed by Robinson and Tyson (1985). The net effect is to make enterprises less responsive to price signals and to generate personal incomes of workers that do not equal their marginal revenue products (or efficiency wage). In the Hungary model, the specification is closer to the neoclassical version, although we have experimented with alternative specifications. In one, firms are assumed to set a target output, which they then modify only partly in response to market signals. Their actual supply in this case is a weighted average of the target and profit-maximizing output, with targets being updated over time according to a lagged adjustment process. In the historical period, the two alternatives yielded very similar results, so we decided to stay with the neoclassical specification since it was simpler. In other applications, the differences might well be important.

For two sectors, mining and electricity, the Hungary model deviates from the neoclassical assumptions. In these sectors, domestic prices are assumed to be fixed and a different mechanism from price adjustment is assumed to work to clear the market. For electricity, supply is assumed to adjust through variations in capacity utilization so that supply always equals demand. In the mining sector, which includes oil, imports are assumed to adjust so as to equate supply and demand.

In both models, aggregate employment for each labor category is fixed exogenously and the models solve for equilibrium wages and the sectoral allocation of labor. Within each period, sectoral capital stocks are assumed to be fixed, so the models solve for sectorally differentiated "profit" rates, or marginal revenue products for capital.

Since the models incorporate sectoral taxes and subsidies, it is possible to compute profits both before and after taxes and so use the models to explore the size of the distortions induced by the tax and subsidy systems.

2.2 Foreign trade

These models are designed to focus on issues of trade policy, especially the ways in which an economy can adjust to shortages of foreign exchange. In one variant, the models treat all the sources of foreign exchange – exports, foreign capital inflows, net factor income, remittance income and reserve changes – as exogenous. In a second variant, sectoral exports are determined endogenously and are assumed to be a function of the relative price to domestic producers of domestic versus export sales.[6] In both models, exports were specified exogenously for the base historical run, while endogenous export functions were specified for some counterfactual experiments.

Both models assume that domestically produced tradeable goods and imports are imperfect substitutes. For each tradeable sector, consumers demand a composite good which is a constant elasticity of substitution (CES) aggregation of domestic and imported goods. Trade substitution elasticities vary by sector. Given this approach, the demand for imports depends on the relative price of domestically produced and imported goods. The world prices of imports and exports are fixed, but the domestic prices depend on trade policy instruments such as the exchange rate, tariffs and subsidies. This specification makes the domestic price system relatively autonomous compared with earlier multisector models in which domestic and foreign goods were assumed to be perfect substitutes. This treatment assumes a continuum of tradeability by sector, where the responsiveness of domestic prices depends on the relative shares of imports and exports in total domestic supply, as well as on the trade substitution elasticity and the export supply elasticity.

Both Hungary and Yugoslavia carry out a substantial fraction of their trade with other socialist countries. For example, in 1979–81, trade with socialist economies accounted for 57 percent of Hungary's exports and 52 percent of Hungary's imports. The comparable figures for Yugoslavia were 45 percent and 29 percent respectively (Balassa and Tyson, 1985). Hungary is a member of the Council for Mutual Economic Aid (CMEA) and trade with these countries is carried out on the basis of long-term contracts and at prices that often differ significantly from world market prices. Most of this trade is denominated in rubles, although a significant and increasing share is denominated in convertible currencies.[7] Yugoslavia, unlike Hungary, is not a member of CMEA, and most of its trade with the Eastern bloc is based on world market prices and denominated in convertible currencies.[8] In addition, Yugoslavia's trade with the East is not based on long-term contracts and hence tends to be more variable than Hungary's trade with the East. As an illustration, there are often substantial short-run deficits in the direction of Yugoslav exports from West to East in response to changing market opportunities.

Because of the significant share of CMEA trade in total Hungarian trade, and the special features of this trade, the CGE model for Hungary distinguishes between ruble and nonruble trade flows.[9] CMEA exports and imports denominated in rubles are set exogenously, reflecting the type of relatively long-term contracts characterizing this trade. Western trade, or trade denominated in dollars, is determined endogenously to achieve equilibrium in the foreign exchange market.[10] The model has two exchange rates, one for rubles and one for dollars. Historically, the ruble exchange rate has been fixed and unchanging, although implicit tariffs and subsidies have been imposed which serve to keep the effective ruble and dollar exchange rates roughly in line. In the Hungary model, when we do experiments which vary the exchange rate, we move the two rates together in order to keep the calculation simple.

The total demand for foreign exchange in both the Yugoslav and Hungarian models is determined by summing desired imports across all sectors. The total is compared with the supply of foreign exchange arising from exports and all other exogenous sources (including net foreign capital inflows, reserve decumulation and factor income from abroad). When both dollar and ruble exports are specified exogenously, in effect the balance of trade is exogenous in the models. An adjustment mechanism is specified to equate the supply and demand for foreign exchange. One variant is to specify a flexible exchange rate which adjusts endogenously to clear the foreign exchange market. Another variant is to fix the exchange rate and specify an endogenous rationing mechanism to achieve the equilibrium level of imports.

In the Yugoslav model, a complicated rationing scheme is specified which contains elements of both fix-price and flex-price rationing. The model seeks to capture in a stylized way the elaborate and complex system by which foreign exchange is rationed in Yugoslavia. In the Hungary model, there is a much less complex quantity rationing scheme where demanders of sectoral imports are forced to accept only a fraction of their desired imports, given the diseqilibrium price arising from the fixed exchange rate.[11] This quantity rationing rate is assumed to vary sectorally, with some sectors such as agriculture being more severely rationed. The effect of quantity rationing is that demanders of imports receive less than they wish at the existing price, but are subsidized in that they pay less for the imports they receive than they would if a free market prevailed.

Note that, in the Hungary model, oil imports are not rationed. As noted above, the domestic price of the mining sector, which includes oil, is fixed and imports are assumed to clear the market. While there was apparently no direct rationing of oil during the 1981–5 period, this treatment is probably an oversimplification. In fact, the model tends to generate oil imports somewhat above those actually observed in the historical base run. In Yugoslavia, there was severe direct rationing of oil and gasoline during the period, and the model is specified to reflect it.

Import rationing generates a "scarcity premium" or rent on imports that strongly encourages import substitution but generates a wedge in incentives against exports. In addition, the allocation of scarce imports to enterprises at a price reflecting only the official exchange rate represents a major subsidy to the recipients. The effect is to provide major hidden subsidies to heavy users of imported intermediate and capital goods and to distort their efficient allocation among competing uses, leading to losses of output.

The difference between the actual cost of rationed imports and their value to demanders is unobservable in an actual economy. However, in the CGE model, we can compute this difference since we specify the underlying behavioral functions. The resulting value of quantity rationing (VQR) measures the amount demanders would be willing to pay for imports (valued at the margin) minus the amount they actually pay. The VQR can be seen as a measure of the "chaseable rents" generated in the system by import rationing. The existence of such rents undoubtedly elicits "rent seeking" behavior on the part of various actors in the system.[12] Even with tight controls and goodwill, any significant level of VQR must generate a major strain on the economic system. We capture this phenomenon in both models by assuming that there are sectoral efficiency losses which are a function of each sector's demand for imports of intermediate and capital goods. Thus, sectors which are more import dependent are subsidized by import rationing because they receive rationed imports at a lower price, but they are hurt because they must bear efficiency costs arising from the rationing. The aggregate value of this efficiency loss is assumed to be a function of the aggregate VQR.

2.3 Demand, prices and macroclosure

The demand side of the model works by tracing through the circular flow the incomes generated in the productive sectors and modeling the various demands they induce. Consumers are assumed to have price-sensitive expenditure functions: linear expenditure systems for two consumers in the case of the Hungary model; simple fixed sectoral expenditure shares in the case of the Yugoslav model. Government demand is modeled with fixed expenditure shares. In both models, aggregate government consumption is exogenous, government revenue is endogenous (given a variety of tax parameters) and government savings are determined residually. Enterprises and households also have savings functions, so the model will complete the circular flow, generating total savings and hence a demand for investment goods.

Given supply and demand for each sector, the CGE model solves endogenously for a set of equilibrium wages, prices and an exchange rate or import rationing rate to clear the markets for labor, products and foreign exchange. The model is Walrasian in spirit in that the equilibrating mechanisms work through changes in relative prices. The absolute price level is set through the choice of a wholesale price index as numeraire whose value is projected exogenously over time. All price changes should be viewed relative to this exogenous index. In particular, variations in the exchange rate affect the balance of trade through their impact on the relative price of tradeables to nontradeables – the real exchange rate. A devaluation raises the price in domestic currency of imports and exports relative to domestic goods sold on the domestic market. The effects are (a) to induce producers to produce import substitutes and to export and (b) to induce demanders to increase their demand for domestic goods over imports. Given that all capital flows and the aggregate price level are exogenous, there is no place in the model for endogenous macroeconomic linkages between the exchange rate, domestic inflation, interest rates and international capital flows. The model seeks a flow equilibrium in the balance of trade, not an asset equilibrium in the money and bond markets. While there are clearly interesting relationships among these exogenous variables that provide the subject of much macroeconomic theory, such relationships are all exogenous to the CGE model.

Changes in the model's exchange rate required to achieve equilibrium in the balance of trade can be viewed as measuring required changes in the economy's nominal exchange rate, given the choice of numeraire. In trade theory models, it is often convenient to choose the nominal exchange rate as numeraire in order to focus on the relative price changes that drive the model. In the CGE model, the equilibrating mechanism works through changes in the real exchange rate, but it is much more convenient to choose a numeraire such that the exchange rate is recognizable. As long as it is remembered that any calculation is conditional on the assumptions about foreign capital inflows and the aggregate price level, there is no theoretical problem with this approach.

The problem of achieving macroeconomic balance between aggregate savings and investment is a separate issue involving what has been called the "macroclosure" of the model. Many ways are discussed in the literature for achieving savings–investment equilibrium in CGE models, corresponding to various theoretical views about how the macrosystem works.[13] In the Yugoslav model, a number of different closure rules were specified, depending on the particular application of the model. For some experiments, the model was savings driven, with aggregate investment set equal to endogenously determined savings (known as neoclassical closure). Sometimes aggregate real investment was set exogenously, with institutional savings rates assumed to adjust to achieve macrobalance (known as Johansen closure). Finally, in some forward runs described by Robinson, Tyson and Dewatripont (1986), a special Yugoslav closure was specified in which inflation is endogenous and nominal personal incomes are exogenous. All these closures were developed to capture the stylized facts of the Yugoslav system under various policy regimes.

The macroclosure problem is much easier to handle in the Hungary model applied to the 1981–5 period. During this period, Hungarian policy makers set aggregate investment targets in quantitative terms and enforced them through direct control of investment projects. The savings required to finance the aggregate investment target were generated by appropriating most of the investible surplus generated by enterprises and by maintaining relatively tight control over the course of real income paid in the state sector of the economy. This is the mechanism employed in the Hungary CGE model and it represents a direct forced-savings closure.

In Yugoslavia, although closure is in fact achieved via forced savings, inflation which erodes the purchasing power of nominal incomes is a critical component of the process. The process is difficult to model within the CGE framework, since the model does not contain any asset markets. In Hungary, where there are direct controls over enterprise saving and real incomes, which are critical to the adjustment process, it is much easier to incorporate the process within the CGE model.

3 Hungary: 1981–1985

In the past, when faced with a balance of payments problem, Hungarian policy makers have responded by imposing quantitative rationing of imports and, to a lesser extent, by increasing exports through the imposition of export targets. Little use was made of exchange rate policy. When faced with foreign exchange shortages after the second oil crisis, Hungary again resorted to a system of quantity controls.

There are several explanations for the continued use of quantity controls, rather than an active exchange rate policy, during the 1981–5 adjustment period in Hungary. First, the prevailing price regulations linked domestic and world prices, which meant that a devaluation would automatically tend to increase the prices of both tradeables and nontradeables, with inflationary consequences for the aggregate price level. The Hungarian authorities were generally concerned about aggravating price pressures, since the gradual reduction of consumer subsidies was by itself already pushing the aggregate price level upward. Second, given the softness of enterprise budget constraints, the responsiveness of enterprises to changes in the exchange rate could not be relied upon to produce the adjustment required by external constraints.[14] Third, quantity controls give state and party authorities direct control over the distribution of critical resources among competing claimants.

The incentive effects of the quantity controls chosen were antithetical to the thrust of the economic reforms that were introduced in 1979. Those reforms call for a major shift toward greater reliance on market mechanisms and a concomitant change in the nature of the policy instruments that the government uses to guide the economy. What we observe in the 1981–5 period is an uneasy mix of policies, some of which are aimed at increasing the role of the market while others involve direct rationing of imports, especially through control over investment, and direct pressure on enterprises to export. The experiments with the CGE model show the impact of some of these contradictions.

Starting in the late 1970s, the Hungarian economy faced a steady deterioration in its ability to borrow abroad. After 1980, export earnings also stagnated, and the economy faced increasingly severe shortages of foreign exchange after 1981.[15] Figures 12.1 and 12.2 indicate the trends. After 1980, Hungary had to generate surpluses in its balance of trade in order to meet its obligations in the capital account. The worst year was 1982, with the current and capital accounts moving into surplus in 1983. However, figure 12.2 shows a steady fall in the dollar value of imports after 1980. The foreign exchange shortages required real as well as financial adjustments.

3.1 The base run

The model takes up the story in 1981, with the base run covering the period 1981–5. Table 12.1 presents selected macrovariables from the base run. In general, the base solution values are very close to

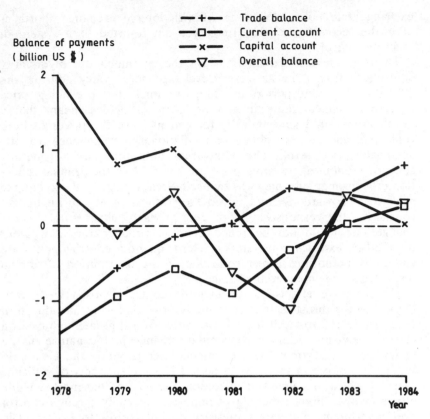

Figure 12.1 Balance of payments in Hungary.

historical data – within a percent or so for almost all macro aggregates.[16] Table 12.1 shows the impact of the foreign exchange shortages on economic performance. Growth rates are well under historical trends, and 1983 was an especially hard year. The model solution for 1985 reflects estimates of exogenous variables as of the summer of 1985. However, the basic results from the counterfactual experiments are not sensitive to changes in the terminal year.

Given the foreign exchange shortages, the stagnation of export earnings during this period was especially worrisome. Did export earnings stagnate because of a decline in demand in Western markets, or were there problems with export supply in Hungary? The question is important. If exports were hurt because of domestic policy choices, then it is necessary to make policy changes in order to generate exports in the future.

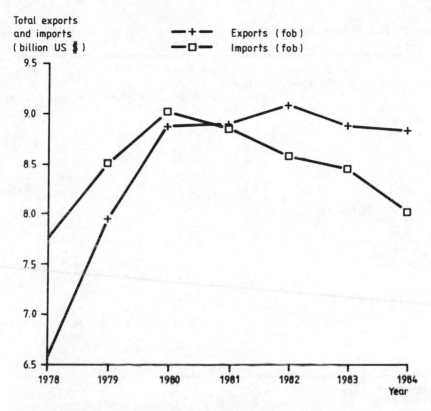

Figure 12.2 Total exports and imports in Hungary.

The growth of real exports, shown in table 12.1, was quite good. In 1981–2, the growth rate was about the same as that of gross domestic product (GDP), but it was significantly faster thereafter. The stagnation of export earnings was due to a decline in dollar prices, which was partly due to the revaluation of the dollar relative to Hungary's major trading partners during this period. The detailed price trends will be considered below.

Table 12.1 also indicates that the ruble–dollar composition of exports changed very little during the period. The convertible currency share of exports remained around 55 percent, with only a very slight drop to 54 percent in 1983. Thus, neither the dollar volume nor the structure of exports changed during this period. While there was undoubtedly some decline in Western demand for Hungarian exports, Hungary was able to maintain the value share of its Western exports.

Table 12.1 Macroeconomic variables for Hungary: base run, 1981–1985 (percent)

	Private consumption	*Government consumption*	*Fixed investments*	*Exports*	*Imports*	*GDP*
Real growth rates						
1981–2	1.70	−0.76	−3.35	2.65	−3.80	2.75
1982–3	−2.55	4.14	−4.29	7.14	−0.35	1.10
1983–4	3.52	−6.65	−7.57	7.41	0.33	2.95
1984–5	4.02	−1.31	2.51	5.02	2.83	4.12
1981–5	1.64	−1.22	−3.24	5.54	−0.27	2.73
Ratios to current GDP						
1981	58.1	9.6	25.1	42.7	38.5	
1982	57.2	9.7	24.8	41.3	36.0	
1983	58.3	10.1	25.1	42.8	38.6	
1984	57.1	9.3	21.6	45.7	36.9	
1985	57.4	9.0	20.9	45.4	35.7	
Nonruble trade shares						
1981				55.9	53.4	
1982				55.2	48.9	
1983				54.0	48.0	
1984				55.4	49.5	
1985				55.6	50.8	

Real GDP accounts are defined in 1981 prices.
GDP shares: exports are valued in domestic prices; imports are valued in world prices multiplied by the official exchange rate.
Nonruble trade shares (nonruble trade divided by total trade): exports and imports are valued in trading prices multiplied by the official exchange rate.

However, the convertible currency share of imports dropped significantly, indicating that the import rationing was much more severe on imports from the West.

While real exports increased, the data and model results indicate that there were major changes in domestic incentives against exporting. Figure 12.3 presents data on exchange rate and price movements in the 1981–5 period. Hungary did devalue the forint against the dollar, and the devaluations were larger than the changes in the domestic price level. However, Hungary's major trading partners during this period experienced a revaluation of their currencies against the dollar, so the dollar import and export prices facing Hungary fell. The result is that the real effective exchange rate actually revalued slightly during this period. Thus in a period of foreign exchange shortage, which would normally call for a real

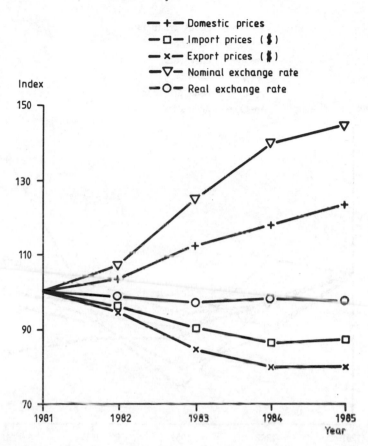

Figure 12.3 Prices and exchange rates in Hungary, 1981–1985.

devaluation, there was no such policy response. Note also that there was a small shift in the international terms of trade against Hungary – dollar export prices fell more than dollar import prices – which exacerbated the foreign exchange problem and would normally call for a larger real devaluation.

The real exchange rate is interesting only as an indicator of incentives for exporting and import substitution. We also have direct evidence of the shift in incentives. Figure 12.4 presents data on the ratio of the price that a sector receives for an export sale to the price that it receives for a sale on the domestic market. These prices are in

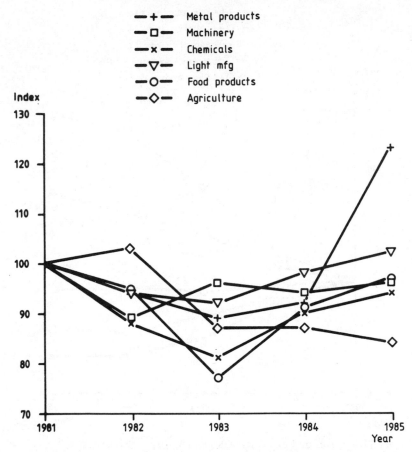

Figure 12.4(a) Ratio of export to domestic prices in Hungary, 1981–1985, for dollar trade.

forints, including all indirect taxes and subsidies, and so measure the incentive facing a producer to sell on the world market versus the domestic market. The data are presented separately for six sectors, which together comprise 96 percent of merchandise exports in 1981, for ruble and nonruble exports. When the index falls below 100, it indicates a deterioration in export incentives relative to the base year 1981.

Figure 12.4 shows that there was a major deterioration in export incentives during this period, especially for nonruble trade. The interesting question that arises from these data is how Hungary managed to increase real exports, in spite of the decline in export incentives. Given the foreign exchange shortages, policy makers

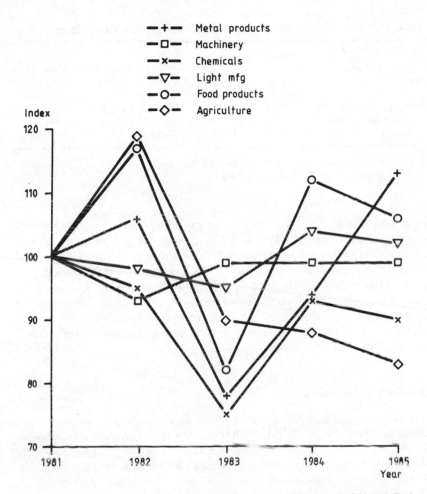

Figure 12.4(b) Ratio of export to domestic prices in Hungary, 1981 1985, for ruble trade.

apparently resorted to quantity controls, setting export targets for enterprises.[17] Quantity targeting of exports represented a significant step away from the reforms in the economic system that were stated as goals around 1980.

Table 12.2 presents data from the base run on the extent of quantitative rationing of imports. The ratio of actual to desired imports, assumed to be equal to 100 percent in 1981, fell to 91.2

Table 12.2 Import rationing indicators for Hungary: base run (percent)

Ratio	Year				
	1981	1982	1983	1984	1985
Import rationing rate	100.0	94.1	92.0	91.2	92.3
VQR/value added	0.0	7.9	10.6	11.2	9.0
Capacity utilization	100.0	97.0	96.1	95.8	96.4

Import rationing rate, ratio of actual to desired imports.
VQR, aggregate value of quantity rationing rents.

percent in 1984. While this degree of rationing seems moderate when compared with, say, Turkey in 1978, it still has a significant impact on the economy because the overall trade share is so high.[18] The total value of the chaseable rents, or VQR, represents 8–11 percent of total value added. Distortions of this magnitude generated significant windfall gains and losses across sectors and must have led to misallocation of resources. In the model, capacity utilization is specified as a function of these rents, and generates losses of 3–4 percent of real value added.

3.2 Foreign capital inflows

To measure the impact of foreign exchange shortages, we performed an experiment in which the exchange rate was specified exogenously at the same values as in the base run and foreign capital inflows were determined endogenously to achieve an equilibrium balance of trade. Exports were also maintained at their base run values. The results of this experiment are shown in figure 12.5. Instead of moving to a trade surplus in 1982, the economy maintains a deficit throughout the period. The cumulative difference is 4.14 billion US dollars, or about a billion dollars a year from 1982.

The billion dollars a year represents the additional foreign capital inflows that would have been required to support the policy of maintaining a roughly constant real exchange rate without resorting to quantity rationing. The failure of export growth was clearly important to this result. Note, however, that the common International Monetary Fund (IMF) advice of devaluing to maintain a constant price-level-deflated exchange rate would have been badly off the mark for Hungary in this period. Hungary did maintain a roughly constant real effective exchange rate during this period, relative to

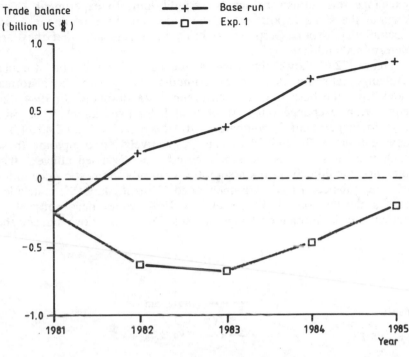

Figure 12.5 Trade balance in Hungary, 1981–1985.

the 1981 equilibrium exchange rate. However, model results indicate that this rate was not an equilibrium real exchange rate, given the significant degree of import rationing during the period.

The elimination of quantity rationing, which is part of experiment 1, leads to a significant improvement in growth. In the base run, the growth rate of real GDP in the 1981–5 period is 2.7 percent a year. In experiment 1, it rises to 3.9 percent. This increase in output, of course, also increases the demand for imports and thus contributes to the increased capital inflows implied in the experiment.

3.3 Equilibrium exchange rates

Assuming a fixed exchange rate and allowing the balance of trade to be determined endogenously is a very unrealistic assumption for Hungary during this period. In the next two experiments, we instead assume that foreign capital inflows are fixed exogenously and that the exchange rate adjusts to achieve equilibrium. In experiment 2, we assume the same exports as in the base run. In experiment 3, we assume that exports respond to price incentives and that they are determined endogenously.

Figure 12.6 shows the time sequence of equilibrium nominal exchange rates for the two experiments, along with the historical rates from the base run. The differences are dramatic. In 1984, the equilibrium exchange rates are 66.9 Ft/\$ for experiment 2 and 56.6 Ft/\$ for experiment 3, compared with the actual value of 48 Ft/\$ – devaluations of 39 and 18 percent respectively. In comparing these exchange rates, it must be remembered – as discussed above – that they are conditional on the assumptions that the domestic price index and the balance of trade are unchanged. Thus it cannot be concluded that a devaluation of 39 percent in 1984 would have sufficed to equilibrate the foreign exchange market. The model does indicate the

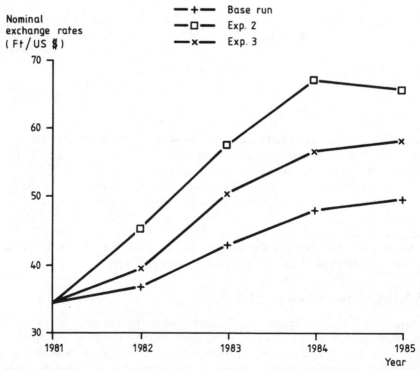

Figure 12.6 Nominal exchange rates in Hungary, 1981–1985.

incentive problems that arise when the real exchange rate is out of equilibrium and the effect on the structure of incentives, production and trade of achieving the correct rate, even though it ignores the macroeconomic problems policy makers face in trying to achieve the correct rate.

In experiment 3, the economy is assumed to adjust exports according to price incentives. Table 12.3 shows the sectoral changes in real exports in experiment 3 compared with the base run. Overall, aggregate real exports are modestly higher, ranging from 1.5 to 4.8 percent over the base run. The reason for only a moderate increase in exports is that exports in the base run were higher than they should have been, given the underlying price incentives, because of quantitative targets. The changes in the exchange rate in experiment 3 essentially correct the incentive bias against exports evident in the base run, effectively making the actual exports "incentive compatible". The somewhat greater increase in the dollar value of exports is due to compositional changes, with increased exports in sectors where dollar prices are higher.

The changes in the structure of exports are dramatic. Metal products and machinery increase their shares, while chemicals and food products decline. These changes arise in an assumed international environment in which Hungary is able to sell all it exports at the exogeneously specified world prices. Since ruble exports are fixed exogenously, all these structural changes are assumed to occur through shifts in trade with the West. While it is feasible to model exports with international demand functions as well as domestic

Table 12.3 Changes in export structure in experiment 3: flexible exchange rate with export response (percent)

Sector	Deviation from base run			
	1982	*1983*	*1984*	*1985*
Metal products	16.9	7.4	7.3	34.4
Machinery	6.0	18.4	17.7	12.2
Chemicals	3.7	−18.0	−11.1	−15.6
Light manufacturing	3.4	2.9	4.3	2.0
Food products	4.4	−11.2	−8.1	−8.8
Agriculture	8.0	−2.7	8.3	4.9
Productive services	−9.7	8.5	−7.1	−11.0
Total real exports	4.8	2.0	3.0	1.5
Total US dollar exports	5.1	3.0	4.2	3.0

supply functions, such a treatment requires empirical work on Hungarian export markets that is not currently available. The CGE model indicates the importance of changes in export structure. Testing the reasonableness of the model's results requires further analysis, preferably at a more microeconomic level.

3.4 Investment

As part of its program of macroeconomic adjustment, Hungary cut back on investment dramatically in 1984. The share of fixed investment in GDP dropped by 3.5 percentage points (from 25.1 percent in 1983 to 21.6 percent in 1984). In most semi-industrial countries, such a cutback in investment would also decrease import demand since a large share of capital goods is imported. To see whether Hungary would display a similar effect, we did an experiment which was identical with experiment 1 except that we kept the investment share of GDP at its 1981 value in every year. From table 12.1, the implication is that the investment share is 3.5 percentage points higher in 1984 than in the base run.

The results indicate that the effect on import demand is minor. Total imports fall very slightly, by 0.5 percent in 1984, but there are some significant changes in composition. Imports of investment goods rise, while those of food and agriculture fall. The shift in the composition of demand also affects the agricultural terms of trade, with agricultural prices about 4 percentage points lower in the high investment experiment. Higher investment implies less consumption, and consumption is more food intensive, so the shift in structure leads to a fall in food demand.

Restraining investment thus does not have a significant effect on aggregate import demand in an environment with no rationing. However, it is clearly easier to impose import rationing in the investment goods sectors, where the government has more direct controls over investment plans. Investment restraint is a logical part of an import rationing regime. Indeed, evidence from the Hungarian case indicates that investment restraint was a critical ingredient in overall import rationing for two reasons. First, by imposing the major share of import cutbacks on capital goods, available foreign exchange would be used to keep up the flow of imported intermediate inputs required to maintain production and exports. Consumer imports were severely rationed, but such rationing is much less disruptive of production than severe rationing of intermediate inputs would have been. Second, investment cutbacks were consistent with the objective of maintaining real consumption levels, despite macroeconomic austerity. The link between investment restraint and consumption is suggested by the simulation results, which produce an aggregate consumption level in 1984 that is about 5 percent lower in the high investment experiment.

3.5 Summary

The simulation experiments indicate that a number of countervailing forces were at work in Hungary during the 1981–5 period. It would have required about a billion dollars a year in additional funds to avoid the need for any adjustment, which represents an increase in annual imports of over 10 percent. The adjustment mechanism chosen was to ration imports, without attempting any real devaluation of the exchange rate. The exchange rate policy led to further quantity controls designed to maintain export levels in the face of deteriorating incentives.

All these quantity controls led to a variety of distortions in both import and export markets. On the import side, the difference between the cost of rationed imports at the official exchange rate and their value to demanders amounted to about 5–7 percent of GDP, or about a quarter of the import bill. In the model, these distortions imply decreases in capacity utilization of around 4 percent, significantly lowering growth.

The experiments indicate that an active exchange rate policy, including aggressive devaluation to maintain price incentives in an environment of free markets, would have improved performance. There are a number of qualifications to this result, however. The model assumes that such a policy could have been implemented while still maintaining macroeconomic balance and controlling inflation. Under the prevailing economic mechanism, it is also not clear that an active exchange rate policy would have been as effective as the model predicts. As discussed earlier, the price mechanism is less effective in a regime of soft budget constraints, and the CGE model overstates the responsiveness of the economy to changes in incentives.

Finally, one should note that Hungary also introduced a major reform in the price system during this period designed to bring domestic prices of tradeables in line with world prices. During this transition phase, they were apparently reluctant to introduce additional shocks to relative prices, as well as the inflationary shock that would have resulted from aggressive devaluation. Hungary chose to emphasize macrocontrol and to postpone adjustment in the structure of production and trade. While understandable during this period, such an approach is at odds with the stated goal of introducing further reforms in the economic mechanism in the coming years.

4 Conclusion

In terms of methodology, the development and use of CGE models for Yugoslavia and Hungary demonstrate the feasibility of adapting the CGE framework to incorporate the important institutional features of socialist economies. In this adaptation, the models have evolved a long way from their neoclassical Walrasian antecedents. Variants of both models specify rules of enterprise behavior that attempt to capture the stylized facts characterizing behavior in the two economies. The models also allow neoclassical disequilibria in both import and export markets and specify rationing rules – which differ in the two models – in the presence of disequilibrium prices. The Hungary model separates ruble and nonruble trade, incorporating two exchange rates. The Hungary model also allows fix-price sectors, with quantities adjusting rather than prices. Both models also permit a variety of macroeconomic specifications to achieve savings–investment and balance of trade equilibria.

There are a number of areas where there is need for further methodological work in applying CGE models to socialist countries. Some of these areas reflect the lack of accepted theoretical explanations rather than any computational problems. For example, the treatment of the labor market is inadequate. The models tend to overstate the ease of adjusting sectoral employment and clearing the aggregate labor markets. In both economies, enterprises appear to see trade-offs between changes in employment and capacity utilization that are not captured in these models. The difficulty is that we do not yet have a theoretical description of enterprise behavior that is exact enough to permit incorporation into an empirical model.

While the models are far from Walrasian, they still reflect their Walrasian roots. In particular, they do not capture macroeconomic interactions among variables such as the price level, the exchange rate, interest rates and monetary aggregates. These models do not incorporate asset markets and can only capture macro interactions through what are essentially *ad hoc* macroclosure specifications. The problems of incorporating macrofeatures such as asset markets into CGE models is an area of active research, but the current state of the art is still quite crude.[19] The models are best applied to problems in which relative prices, incentives and economic structure provide the focus of the analysis.

While neat, applying a Walrasian neoclassical model in a situation where its assumptions are not satisfied cannot yield valid welfare analysis or sensible empirical results. Realism requires a more structuralist approach that attempts to incorporate non-neoclassical behavioral relations and institutional structures characteristic of these countries. The conflict is real, but we tend to view this situation as a challenge to theorists rather than as a criticism of applied modelers. At present, the lag between a new theoretical specification and our ability to implement it in an empirical model is probably shorter than at any previous time in the history of economics. The challenge is to provide theoretical models of socialist practice that capture the stylized facts and that are complete enough to permit empirical estimation and inclusion in an economy-wide model.

Notes

1 See, for example, Augusztinovics (1984), who describes a variety of such models applied to Hungary.
2 For a discussion of the development of linear programming models in Hungary, see Kornai (1974).
3 For a discussion of CGE models applied to developing countries, see Dervis, de Melo and Robinson (1982) and Robinson (1989). Manne (1985) provides an updated survey of country applications and Shoven and Whalley (1984) survey work on CGE models of developed countries focusing on issues of public finance and international trade.
4 The NPO–Bank model of Hungary builds on important earlier work by Zalai (1983), who built the first CGE model applied to Hungary. The model of Yugoslavia was built with the assistance of two Yugoslav researchers, Joze Mencinger and Lovro Pfajfar, who have used it for policy analysis in Yugoslavia. See Pfajfar and Mencinger (1984).
5 Robinson and Tyson (1985) analyze the 1976–80 period, while Robinson, Tyson and Dewatripont (1986) look at the 1981–4 period and also discuss forward runs for 1985–90.
6 The specific form of the export function is that the ratio of export sales to domestic production is a logistic function of the ratio of the export price to the domestic sales price. See Dervis, de Melo and Robinson (1982, ch. 7) for a detailed discussion. An alternative functional form we have tried in the Hungary model is a constant elasticity of transformation (CET) function, which gives similar results. This approach is described by Condon, Robinson and Urata (1985). In both variants, econometric work is sorely needed to estimate the parameters. We have had to rely on "guesstimates" in the applications discussed here.
7 The share of Hungary's imports from socialist countries in convertible currencies is around 12 percent. The share of exports to socialist countries in convertible currencies has risen from 14 percent in 1970 to over 24 percent in 1981. See World Bank (1984).
8 Yugoslavia only recently began to publish trade statistics on a clearing and nonclearing basis. The figures show that on average about 80 percent of Yugoslavia's trade with socialist countries was on a clearing basis between 1980 and 1982. This implies that a substantial portion of Yugoslavia's convertible currency earnings on Eastern bloc markets was not available

to cover its convertible currency deficit with the West during this period.

9 At the time the CGE model for Yugoslavia was constructed, data breaking down imports and exports between Eastern and Western sources were not available at the sectoral detail required for the model.

10 As noted earlier, Western trade and trade denominated in dollars are not exactly the same, since some Eastern trade is carried out on the basis of convertible currencies. The model only distinguishes between trade denominated in rubles and trade denominated in convertible currencies (measured in dollars).

11 The details of the specification are discussed by Dervis, de Melo and Robinson (1982, ch. 9) and, for the Yugoslav model, by World Bank (1983).

12 For a theoretical discussion of this phenomenon, see the classic article by Krueger (1974). Dervis and Robinson first incorporated rent seeking into the CGE framework in their model of Turkey. Since then, it has been used in a number of models. For a description of the approach, see Dervis, de Melo and Robinson (1982).

13 For a survey of various macroclosure rules, see Rattso (1982) and Robinson (1989). Robinson and Tyson (1984) discuss different conceptual frameworks for considering macro issues in CGE models.

14 For a discussion of soft budget constraints, see Kornai (1980). Even through Hungary shares the features of soft budget constaints with its East European neighbours, it is an oversimplification to characterize it as a pure shortage economy in which enterprises struggle to produce as much as possible with little regard to costs or salability of output. The real issue in Hungary is not the existence of sensitivity of enterprises to price signals, including the exchange rate, but the degree of such sensitivity. What seems certain is that such sensitivity is weaker than in market economies based on private ownership, profit maximization and hard budget constraints.

15 For a comparison of the Yugoslav and Hungarian experience during this period, see Balassa and Tyson (1985). Tyson, Robinson and Woods (1988) also compare the experience of the two countries, concentrating on the role of the International Monetary Fund (IMF).

16 For the gross domestic product (GDP) accounts we have adhered to United Nations system of national accounts (SNA) definitions, which differ somewhat from standard Hungarian accounting conventions. There are differences in the valuation of exports and imports, as well as the standard problems in moving from the material product system (MPS) of accounts to the SNA. There are also minor differences in trade statistics arising from the fact that we use input–output data. Exports and imports of services are defined slightly differently in the input–output and foreign trade statistics, and there may also be differences in the sectoral definitions.

17 The mechanisms by which these targets were set and compliance encouraged is complex, involving political entities as well as economic institutions. Some explicit subsidies were also used. See Tyson (1985) for a discussion.

18 See Dervis and Robinson (1982) and Lewis and Urata (1983) for similar calculations for Turkey.

19 See Robinson and Tyson (1984) and Robinson (1989) for a methodological discussion of the issues involved. Lewis (1985) has built a CGE model of Turkey that incorporates a simple set of asset markets and endogenizes interest rates and inflation.

References

Augusztinovics, M. (ed.) (1984) *Long-term Models at Work*, Budapest: Akademiai Kiado.

Balassa, B., and L. D. Tyson (1985) "Policy Responses to External Shocks in Hungary and Yugoslavia: 1974–76 and 1979–81", in Joint Economic Committee, US Congress, *East European Economies: Slow Growth in the 1980's*, vol. 1: *Economic Performance and Policy*, Washington, DC: US Government Printing Office.

Condon, T., S. Robinson and S. Urata (1985) "Coping with a Foreign Exchange Crisis: A General Equilibrium Model of Alternative Adjustment Mechanisms", in A. S. Manne (ed.), *Economic Equilibrium: Model Formulation and Solution*, Amsterdam: North-Holland, Mathematical Programming Study No. 23.

Dervis, K., and S. Robinson (1982) "A General Equilibrium Analysis of the Causes of a Foreign Exchange Crisis: The Case of Turkey", *Weltwirtschaftliches Archiv*, 118 (2), 259–80.

——, J. de Melo and S. Robinson (1982) *General Equilibrium Models for Development Policy*, Cambridge: Cambridge University Press.

Kornai, J. (1974) *Mathematical Planning of Structural Decisions*, 2nd edn, Amsterdam: North-Holland.

—— (1980) *The Economics of Shortage*, Amsterdam: North-Holland.

Krueger, A. O. (1974) "The Political Economy of the Rent-seeking Society", *American Economic Review*, 64 (3), 293–303.

Lewis, J. D. (1985) "Macroeconomic Adjustment with Alternative Market Structures", Harvard Institute for International Development, Harvard University, Discussion paper.

—— and S Urata (1983) "Turkey: Recent Economic Performance and Medium-term Prospects, 1978–1990", Washington, DC: World Bank Staff Working Paper No. 602.

Manne, A. S. (ed.) (1985) *Economic Equilibrium: Model Formulation and Solution*, Amsterdam: North-Holland, Mathematical Programming Study No. 23.

Pfajfar, L., and J. Mencinger (1984) "Zamrzavanje cena i Cenovna Ravnoteza", *Privredna Kretanja Jugoslavije*, March.

Rattso, J. (1982) "Different Macroclosures of the Original Johansen Model and Their Impact on Policy Evaluation", *Journal of Policy Modelling*, 4 (1), 85–97.

Robinson, S. (1989) "Multisectoral Models", in H. Chenery and T. N. Srinivasan (eds), *Handbook of Development Economics*, Amsterdam: North-Holland, ch. 18.

—— and L. D. Tyson (1984) "Modelling Structural Adjustment: Micro and Macro Elements in a General Equilibrium Framework", in H. Scarf and

J. B. Shoven (eds), *Applied General Equilibrium Analysis*, Cambridge: Cambridge University Press.

—— and —— (1985) "Foreign Trade, Resource Allocation, and Structural Adjustment in Yugoslavia: 1976–1980", *Journal of Comparative Economics*, 9, 46–70.

——, —— and M. Dewatripont (1986) "Yugoslav Economic Performance in the 1980's: Alternative Scenarios", in Joint Economic Committee, US Congress, *East European Economies: Slow Growth in the 1980's*, vol. 2: *Country Studies*, Washington, DC: US Government Printing Office.

Shoven, J. B., and J. Whalley (1984) "Applied General-equilibrium Models of Taxation and International Trade", *Journal of Economic Literature*, 22 (3), September, 1007–51.

Tyson, L. D. (1985) "The New Hungarian Economic Reforms and Their Likely Effects on Enterprise Behavior", mimeo, Department of Economics, University of California, Berkeley, CA, August.

——, S. Robinson and L. Woods (1988) "Conditionality and Adjustment in Hungary and Yugoslavia", in J. C. Brada, E. A. Hewett and T. A. Wolf (eds), *Economic Adjustment and Reform in Eastern Europe and the Soviet Union*, Durham, NC: Duke University Press.

World Bank (1983) *Yugoslavia: Adjustment Policies and Development Perspectives*, Washington, DC: World Bank.

World Bank (1984) *Hungary: Economic Development and Reforms*, Washington, DC: World Bank.

Zalai, E. (1983) "A Nonlinear Multisectoral Model for Hungary: General Equilibrium versus Optimal Planning Approaches", in A. C. Kelley, W. C. Sanderson and J. G. Williamson (eds), *Modeling Growing Economies in Equilibrium and Disequilbrium*, Durham, NC: Duke University Press.

13

Modelling and its Environment in Hungarian Medium-term Planning

Zsolt Ámon and István Ligeti

Models have been used in national economic planning in Hungary for several decades. During that period significant changes have taken place in the nature of economic processes and the economic development of the country as well as in the problems to be solved by economic management. Consequently, economic management itself, including the system of planning, has gone through equally significant changes. The application and progress of planning models have more or less closely followed the high priority economic policy issues and the changes in planning.

Focusing on the tasks of medium-term planning and partly related to the scope of annual planning tasks, this paper gives an account of the changing conditions of planning and the models applied. Our efforts are, of course, not intended to present a fully comprehensive picture. We only aim to describe the typical economic problems of the various periods and the models developed to solve them while we concentrate on the tasks. Out of the set of models we highlight those which we think have been, on the one hand, characteristic of a given period and, on the other, of decisive importance for future development.

The first part of the paper will give a brief overview of the major events up to the 1980s. The second part is devoted to the present planning models, introducing the reader to the environment – the major economic events, the process of planning and the subjective conditions of modelling – under which modelling is implemented. It is followed by a summary of the major features of currently used models which have been developed to analyse the individual comprehensive sets of planning problems, while supplementary as well as basic efforts are touched upon. Firstly, some development trends that derive from existing conditions are outlined.

1 Modelling in the Planning Practice up to the 1980s

The actual pattern of the system of national economic planning in Hungary is the outcome of an evolutionary process of four decades. During this period both the theory and the practice of national economic planning made considerable progress.

At the beginning of the 1950s the Hungarian economy still reflected the burden of war damage in several aspects. Although Hungary possessed restricted resources, the urgent need to promote industrial activity arose. At the same time, however, there was a lack of wide experience of planning work. Thus, necessarily, strong centralization prevailed in the planning activity.

In these years of national economic planning, consistent changes of branch structures, certain equilibrium problems of the national economy and the principles of price adjustment were first outlined in an exact way. The input–output table proved to be an adequate exact tool for expressing these problems. The possibilities offered by input–output tables and related analytical methods were more and more widely applied in statistics and practical planning. Since 1958 the application of input–output balances has become regular and general. In the course of elaborating the third Five Year Plan (from 1966 to 1970) the input–output table was organically built into the arsenal of plan coordination.

The input–output tables expressing the main interrelations of planning continue to play an important role now. The models which were later developed are either based on or closely connected with the input–output tables, which investigate the interrelations at a given point in time. This static version of the model is still used in the actual planning system.

In the course of the third Five Year Plan (from 1966 to 1970), prior to the reform of economic management, a comprehensive analysis of national economic planning and the drawing up of prospective development trends took place. The most important characteristic of this activity was that the tasks of national economic planning were investigated in a wider framework of economic management where the realization of economic policy goals was primarily assured by economic regulation.

The aim was to increase the influence of national economic planning on the development of the national economy as a whole and to give more room to initiatives based on enterprise and individual interest. Another important endeavour in the further development of planning was to modernize its scientific bases and system of instruments.

When formulating the problems of planning two questions arose which gave a further impulse to developing mathematical methods. One question was the formulation of general allocation problems and the other (partly connected with the first) the coordination of activities of central management organs with those at enterprise level while giving priority to objectives of the national economy as a whole. Increasing allocation problems gave an impetus to the investigation of linear and non-linear programming models in national economic planning. The first results of the investigations were partly related to the first question and partly to the second.

On the basis of the well-known Dantzig–Wolfe decomposition procedure, Kornai and Lipták elaborated a special algorithm for so-called two-level planning (Kornai, 1988), with the help of which calculations of an experimental character were carried out.

The elements and interrelations of the model were mainly expressed in physical terms. The model contained plan suggestions for investments, technological development and foreign trade for about 500 selected products of 46 branches.

It should be mentioned that experimental calculations and investigations were carried out to connect individual material balances (drawn up in physical terms) that played an especially significant role in the planning practice of this period in order to formulate a *synthetic material balance* to establish their comparability in terms of value and to solve the problem of their common programming.

By the period of the fourth Five Year Plan (from 1971 to 1975) the economic management reform already perceptibly contributed to scientifically and economically well-based planning work. Because the earlier planning activity was mainly oriented towards physical terms, the linking of planning in physical and value terms and the analysis of financial processes became an urgent task.

The linear programming model of the fourth Five Year Plan (Ganczer, 1976) met the new requirements of planning. The model was a tool of coordination both in physical and value terms. In Hungarian planning practice it was the first plan model which represented the system of economic interrelations in a differentiated structure: it comprehensively contained the main physical elements of production and turnover, programming production, investment, foreign trade and financial relations of 207 product balances in 63 industrial sectors and 13 coordinating branches.

The model comprised all sectors of the national economy and contained all elements of the reproduction process: production, distribution and utilization and also the main elements of economic regulators.

The major features of the regulator system were also taken into consideration when constructing the model. The fixed elements were included as parameters of various constraints, while the alterable flexible parts were the variables to be determined by the model.

The model was static: it set a programme for the final year of the Five Year Plan period. From the point of view of modelling approach it was crucial that the model was not considered as a tool indispensable for determining the "optimal national economic plan" but as a facility for formulating plan variants.

In the course of calculations with the large linear programming model constructed for the purposes of the fourth Five Year Plan the question of further development had already been raised. The direction of further development was motivated first by two problems of the planning work.

1 The problem of coordinating the medium- and long-term plans arose in connection with elaborating the long-term plan.
2 Decisions differing in their nature have to be taken at different stages of continuous planning activity. It is evident that the questions arising might be included in different models.

On the basis of these two orientations the following requirements were emphasized when elaborating the models (Báger, 1974) for the fifth Five Year Plan.

1 The justified requirement that more and more complex interrelations should be considered in the course of planning cannot be met by further developing a unique model. Therefore several problem-oriented models have to be built.
2 In compliance with the different stages of planning, special models have to be constructed.
3 It is necessary to step forward from a static approach toward a dynamic model approach.
4 Links must be created between models.

In 1973 as a result of previous research work the models of the fifth Five Year Plan were adopted as a part of the actual planning methodology (see figure 13.1).

In the first stage of planning, in the stage of *formulating* economic policy concepts, three models were applied in parallel: the main task of a macroeconomic aggregated three-sector dynamic model (Ligeti, 1973; Ligeti and Sivak, 1978) was the continuous investigation of the allocation of investments and its relation to consumption. The growth path was controlled by the allocation of investments among the sectors of the economy. Thus the results of the model largely

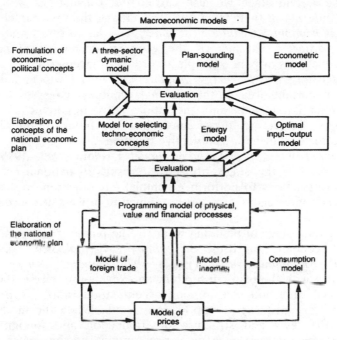

Figure 13.1 The model system of the fifth Five Year Plan

contributed to the dynamic investigation of one of the basic problems of economic growth, i.e. that of the ratio of accumulation to consumption.

The other macroeconomic model was a *dynamic simulation* Dániel et al. (1972) (plan-sounding) model in which, tracing the consequences of some hypothetical decisions, several growth scenarios were drawn up, thus offering a favourable possibility for a many-sided analysis of some macroeconomic indicators.

With the elaboration of the third macroeconomic model a new approach was adopted in the planning practice. It was the first time that an *econometric model* was built into the system of plan models. Although it was quite simple, only concentrating on the major interrelations of production, consumption and accumulation, it opened the way to further econometric applications and enriched the instruments of planning methods.

The economic policy concepts and the results of the above three models provided an appropriate starting point for the model calculations at the second stage of planning work, i.e. in the period of elaborating the national economic plan conceptions.

At the second stage we also carried out calculations with three models differing in their functions. The task of the first model – that of *sorting economic–technological concepts* – was to select and evaluate the different variants of the economic–technological concept forming the basis of plan concepts according to given criteria.

The second was the *energy programming model* which, enlarging on this important area of the national economy, covered the individual energy balances and the utilization alternatives of major consumers. Subject to these constraints the model optimized the energy structure for various objective functions.

The *input–output programming model* (Ámon, 1973, 1975), the third element of this stage, utilized the results of national economic balance calculations to perform a complex investigation and analysis of the main interrelations of the reproduction process at coordination branch level.

At the third stage of planning work, in the phase of elaborating the national economic plan itself, the *comprehensive, physical, value and financial programming model* (Báger, 1974; Ganczer, 1976) used, in accordance with the plan conception, an exogenously given consumption growth rate and consumption–accumulation ratio, given prices and predetermined export–import constraints. When the model was solved, the level and structure of production and foreign trade turnover, the required investment programme and the values of the various financial variables were determined.

The elements of the model system prescribed by the methodology were elaborated with two exceptions and, during the period of the fifth Five Year Plan (from 1976 to 1980), contributed at each stage of planning to formulating plan conceptions and plan computations.

In connection with the model system of the fifth Five Year Plan, however, it must be mentioned that – as well as the positive results – there were also negative experiences.

In the course of both the fourth and the fifth Five Year Plans, the results of calculations carried out with the physical–value–finanacial model lagged behind the deadlines for planning. Thus the results could not be taken into consideration during finalization of the plan and the model could not be built directly into the tense schedule of planning work. The results could only be utilized subsequently for analytical purposes. In the course of further research the problems of handling large-scale models had to be taken into account much more seriously.

During the second half of the 1970s new tendencies emerging in the world economy set new and more urgent tasks for the Hungarian economy. Consequently in planning work attention was focused on new aspects.

1 The role of foreign trade and investigations of the prerequisities of economic equilibrium were given greater importance.
2 A greater claim arose towards elaborating forecasts for a longer period and analysing the impacts and consequences of long-term decisions.
3 Attention was focused on improving the regulator system so that it would be more responsive to changes in economic processes.

In the earlier years the Five Year Plan models simulated the process of plan coordination. One particular feature during the elaboration of the sixth Five Year Plan was that even in the final period of planning work a number of open questions remained, and for their analyses several macroeconomic variants had to be drawn up. The tasks and nature of model computations had therefore to be determined in a different way.

Accordingly the role of the large central model and its adjoining satellites in working out the fourth and fifth Five Year Plans was taken over by three models equal in rank.

With regard to economic contents, the central volume model can mostly be characterized as a *dynamic national economic balance* at sectoral level which, by a special handling of imports and exports, enables a comprehensive investigation of foreign trade. As to its composition, it was a linear programming model containing about 1300 variables and 1200 constraints. The model followed up the time path of the most important macroeconomic real processes in the interval 1980–90. The years 1980, 1981, 1982, 1985 and 1990 were analysed in detail, while the years 1983–4 and 1986–9 were treated in a more aggregated way.

The second element was the price model. Its task was to work out new price variants for a given year starting from the given price system as a basic price and taking into account the most important factors influencing price movements (such as price regulating systems, costs and world markets price forecasts). Aggregated values rather than individual products were used in the model (in a breakdown of 19 coordinating branches), and thus price variants appeared not as factual prices but in the form of price indices compared with the basic price level.

In compliance with the price system introduced from January 1, 1980 (but obviously with strong abstractions), the model includes four price forms in the domestic production market: prices following exports, prices following imports, cost-based (cost plus) prices and fixed (maximized) prices. The output of each branch towards individual users was distributed according to these four price forms; the average price indices of producers and users were given by the weighted average of price forms.

For the price model the volumes (production, inputs, final utilization and factual or estimated figures of exports and imports) were treated exogenously. Regarding its structure, the model was a linear equation system of 600 variables.

The *regulation model* was made up of two blocks. As to its economic contents, it described the most important stages of income redistribution. The volume plan and the price system were given; its only task was to adjust the redistribution process within a given price system to given production and utilization proportions. Therefore it did not deal with the forms of redistribution prior to obtaining the enterprise profits (social security contributions, subsidies and taxes built into costs) since the latter influence prices.

The first block contained a non-linear non-simultaneous-equation system of a few thousand variables; the other was a linear programming model with 500 variables and 300 constraints. Thus the first block of the model could also be called a simulation model which follows the greater part of the redistribution process, from the beginning to the end, up to the threshold of the second block. It is simpler, however, to call it a calculation procedure which, with various assumptions, produces the input data for the second block.

In the second block, only the most important income holders and the most important income flows were represented. The income holders were the enterprises, development funds, the state budget, households and the credit sphere.

A great part of income flows among income holders specified here takes place already in the first block. In the second block only the redistribution channels are included. The variables of the second block represent these channels or, more precisely, the income quantity that flows through them annually.

2 Planning Models in the 1980s

2.1 The modelling environment

The highest priority of the Five Year Plans of the 1960s and 1970s was a perceivable increase in the standard of living, which was accompanied by a relatively high planned growth rate. The factors of production posed no significant obstacle to rapid growth; although the structural labour shortage in the 1980s caused problems, the expansion of fixed assets was guaranteed by a high investment rate. The imports necessary for dynamic production prior to 1973 could be secured without liquidity problems, while the flow of commodities and the terms of trade were properly balanced. As a result of the price explosion in 1973–4 and later in 1979, Hungary suffered from adverse and sustained changes in the terms of trade which meant that the accumulated debts swelled to a critical size while growth was still dynamic up to 1979. Although with a delay, the economic policy took a new path in 1979 and assigned – quite understandably – top priority to restoring and improving the external equilibrium.

The only way of improving the external balance of payments was to eliminate the balance of trade deficit and to achieve surplus. This could be realized in two ways:

1 by an *offensive* approach, i.e. by stepping up efficient exports and substituting imports;
2 by a *defensive* approach, i.e. by curtailing imports and substituting them with domestic commodities.

The first approach meant active response to changes in the international market, structural adjustment and maintenance of dynamic economic growth, while the second implied slowing down economic growth, internal equilibrium problems and losses due to the shortage economy as well as restrictions.

In practice, the two types of response appear in combination, and yet the nature of economic development is determined by the factors which become predominant. Hungary has not yet been able to implement the offensive active approach. Efficiency gain has lagged behind the intended rate, and the country's export capacities have shown only moderate improvement; in addition to the unfavourable turn in internal conditions, development has also been hampered by deteriorating external conditions, and therefore the development resources necessary for acceleration could not be generated. In the 1980s the Hungarian economic management was compelled to implement the defensive approach. This clearly led to restricted domestic absorption, import rationing, depressed growth rates, stagnating living standards and temporary decline.

As a result, economic management was left with limited room for manoeuvring. In preparing the seventh Five Year Plan, it was necessary to outline development alternatives which seek the conditions of economic dynamism under varying circumstances. The key tasks of the seventh Five Year Plan are the following: reducing the disadvantages stemming from the structure of the Hungarian economy, focusing on efficiency and quality in production and preparing the economy for changes in external conditions, i.e. increasing the ability to adjust. A comprehensive improvement of the economic management system and the continuing reform process are meant to create an economic environment which will force significant changes to take place.

The change in the nature of planning obviously has had an impact on planning methods. The tasks which have become more complex and allow for less tolerance contributed to the application of more sophisticated instruments. In the field of planning models some earlier efforts have grown more intensive, compared with earlier stages of Hungarian planning practice, while new approaches have evolved simultaneously.

2.1.1 Decision making mechanism in economy-wide planning

Similarly to any complex and target-oriented activity, the system of national economic planning (Balassa, 1979) is in fact a chain of several hierarchical decisions. The evolution and the development of the planning system over time were accompanied by a set of planning decisions which were linked with the technology of planning. The set of decisions varies depending on the period covered by planning. The various planning models had to be fitted into the system of decision making so that they would not disturb the established order of decisions. This is a rather difficult task, since in the process of planning – which is usually iterative and includes several feedbacks – one has to find the points where the results of modeling can be incorporated with the greatest possible efficiency. Improper timing may cause the bulk of the work to be lost.

In the following we shall give a brief account of the process of five-year planning (see figure 13.2). (The case is basically different from long-term planning and less significantly different from annual planning.) When describing the various stages of work, we shall also indicate the possible points for incorporating models as well as the nature of such models.

Elaboration of economic policy ideas This stage involves the elaboration – more recently, in various scenarios – of the most important elements of economic policy, the system of priorities for the plan and the major indices and rates for economic development. This work is performed almost exclusively at the macroeconomic level and is intended to highlight only the most significant elements and to avoid if possible the risk of certain projections becoming too rigid at an early stage, thus imposing constraints on further work and reducing the ability of planning to adjust to changing circumstances. (In part the scenarios are designed for this purpose.) The elaboration of economic policy ideas can be divided into the following phases.

1 Analysis of recent economic processes gives an opportunity for comprehensive economic analysis as well as for applying models based primarily on time-series analysis, for basically *ex post* investigations and for exploring the causalities and cycles inherent in the economy.

2 Prognoses and forecasts closely linked with the phase of analysis are to be prepared to investigate economic processes and the major development trends; such investigations are not active but are based on historic trends and deal with the evolution of economic events. Naturally, econometric models could be widely applied here.

3 Apart from automatically projecting historic trends into the future, it is necessary to forecast expected external conditions with a high degree of probability, which is out of the scope of planning and economic management. This work currently focuses on the assessment of the expected available physical and financial resources and attaches particular importance to the external and international economic conditions which have been and are expected to be decisive for Hungary. Until now, modelling has not played a major role here. In future, greater importance should be assigned to forecasting international economic processes and to adopting the results of international modelling work by establishing links and contacts.

4 The previous preparatory phases can provide a basis for outlining a range of measures to accommodate sociopolitical objectives as determined by prevailing economic trends as well as internal and external conditions limiting the scope of movement. It is in this phase that the social, political and economic priorities for the oncoming plan are laid down. This process primarily calls for political considerations and decisions and – together with external constraints – basically influences the economic policy ideas and major scenarios on which planning is based.

5 The next phase is focused on quantifying the economic policy ideas and elaborating various growth trends. While basically concentrating on real growth trends, this phase will determine alternative growth trends. Of course the various scenarios do not rely solely on forecasts and priorities but also use assumptions concerning economic policy measures, ideas to improve the economy's efficiency and their expected results. By combining the various assumptions, various scenarios for growth, equilibrium and distribution are described at the level of the major categories of the national accounts. It is here that modelling is used most actively and in widest scope, for which a variety of model types is required. In the phase of preparing the seventh Five Year Plan we successfully applied a one-sector growth model.

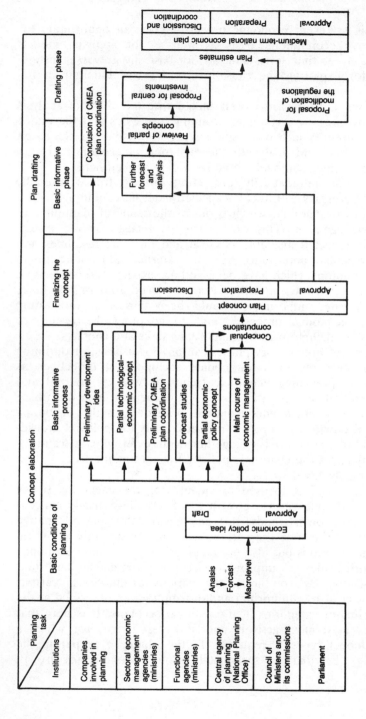

Figure 13.2 Schematic chart of the division of labour and process of national economic planning using the example of medium-term planning: *, sectoral agencies are responsible for a branch of the economy (e.g. industry, agriculture etc.) and functional agencies are responsible for some comprehensive function (e.g. finances, employment, prices, banking etc.).

6 The first stage of planning is concluded by the approval of the economic policy ideas. The documents describing the multi scenario ideas, their evaluation and justification, the advantages or disadvantages of the various scenarios and the probability of their occurrence are submitted for consideration to leading political, government and social organizations which will in turn determine the directions of further work by selecting the scenarios for continued analysis.

Elaborating the plan concept   Government approval of the economic policy ideas gives the go-ahead for elaborating the plan concept. On the basis of the approved ideas, economic policy objectives are coordinated with the instruments for implementing them – usually more than one scenario and not only at the macroeconomic level. While the economic policy ideas focus only on the major aspects (growth and major indices) within the scope of real economic processes and describe the major trend, efforts and scope of economic policy, the concept also covers the consistency between real processes and financial and income processes, giving a detailed disaggregated description of production and distribution and the set of instruments for plan implementation.

As a first step, the economic policy as reflected in the economic policy ideas is concretized at a macrolevel (growth, consumption, accumulation, external equilibrium, real wages, real income etc.). This is followed by determination of the final demand and the sectoral estimates for foreign trade, usually in more than one scenario.

At this point the work is expanded and involves all functional as well as sectoral (industrial and branch) planning units within the Planning Office. It is in this phase that scenarios for sectoral production and distribution including sectoral income generation estimates are prepared on the basis of the final demand including foreign trade estimates, as well as the information and forecasts concerning the factors of production already established. Model calculations are also made in this phase to support plan coordination in a disaggregated form directly.

These "rough" computations are coordinated from two aspects. Coordination is directed at the following:

1 on the one hand, production and distribution processes based on the system of national accounts and input–output relations;
2 on the other, ensuring consistency in terms of value and structure between the generated income and final expenditure (financial and income balances, input–output methods).

Both coordination phases, which run parallel in practice, result in several feedbacks that may in some cases even modify the major relations of the conceptual plan. A large number of internal relations are examined within the two coordination aspects including, of course, proper linkages with the elements of the regulation system, with prices, production factors etc. Once again the consistency analysing models become prominent in this phase and equilibrium models can also be applied with great efficiency. The latter can effectively be used to analyse internal relations of the plan concept, such as the relations between production and foreign trade and between internal and external price levels and the exchange rate, as well as the substitution of production factors, the impact of external equilibrium on internal economic processes etc.

After the iterative process of coordination has been concluded, the conceptual scenarios are formed with appropriate subjective probability. These scenarios are yet to be discussed widely in society; following coordination with all the interest-representing social and scientific bodies concerned, the documents describing the concept are reviewed and considered by the government, indicating another phase of coordination. Subsequently, the course for elaborating the concrete draft plan is selected together with the scenario on which the draft will be based.

Elaborating the final draft plan   The same logical pattern is used for elaborating the final draft plan as for the plan concept. The only marked difference is that while the plan concept may include several scenarios which vary significantly in terms of the economic policy and management behaviour to be followed, the draft plan comprises only one proposal. (It should be noted, however, that the plan includes a whole set of measures and ideas with respect to the attitude that the central economic management must adopt should any unexpected external condition, which was not considered in the preparation phases of the plan, present itself; this fact assumes further implicit scenarios.)

Another important difference from the plan concept is that the draft plan also incorporates the set of instruments for plan implementation based on the full scope of concrete measures and decisions. (The plan concept only contains the principles and the course for the set of instruments.) In addition to the decisions on living standards, development, production, foreign trade, pricing, monetary and credit policies, it comprises the decisions on the basic principles as well as the actual scope of the regulation system.

Although this phase is generally focused on elaborating one scenario, that single scenario may be subject to significant changes in the iterative process of coordination, and it is also possible that the final outcome of the detailed preparation will be different from any scenario included in the plan concept.

Although the major outlines of the plan have been determined, there is still ample room for using the models. The most practical models are primarily those which analyse either the consistency of the plan or the impact of some factors and decisions and the changes in the economic environment. These models are the coordination models already in use as well as the multisector econometric and equilibrium models.

2.1.2 Changes in human factors and the institutional framework

The Council for Mutual Economic Aid (CMEA) countries began to use planning models under relatively special circumstances. These countries, including Hungary, introduced the system of central planning a few years after the war; the apparatus and institutional system of central planning evolved in parallel. The institutional system was basically linked to the system of central planning, i.e. to plan directives; the inherent hierarchical relations and decision-making structures therefore showed the same linkages. This fact itself could have created a favourable environment for modelling, since it could well have been institutionalized.

In the late 1950s and early 1960s when modelling was started in planning in Hungary, the pathfinders were a few mathematicians and economists who taught themselves the necessary knowledge of economics and planning for lack of formal professional training. A landmark in creating the personal conditions for modelling in Hungary was the introduction of formal education for economic mathematicians at the Karl Marx University of Economics in 1960 after the evolving needs had been recognized; this meant that properly qualified specialists were produced every year – first for government agencies and later for enterprises.

A peculiar situation presented itself at the Planning Office during the first organized modelling experiments. The work was generally performed under the direction of one of the renowned economists who had been pioneering modelling in Hungary and who was joined by a group of ambitious young specialists. Modelling was done in isolation – especially at first – and consequently planning economists also split into two groups: traditional planners and modellers. This made modelling and the integration of its results into the planning process considerably more difficult.

The preparation of the 1968 reform and its introduction provided a more favourable situation for modelling experiments. This was primarily reflected in a change in the way of thinking that accompanied the reform, a change that involved the application of mathematical methods, the use of developing computer techniques and a rethinking of earlier ideas about planning and economic management. The institutional system and planning practice, however, did not keep pace with the changes in the way of thinking. The planning apparatus and the organization of national economic planning institutions could not immediately adjust to the new requirements and therefore conflicts and contradictions arose between the new functions and the existing institutions and they detracted from the efficiency of the models, although several institutional changes were effected and the predecessors of the currently functioning new organizations were formed. Most planning specialists – even some renowned experts – looked on the new methods with suspicion. This phenonomeon, which was characteristic mainly of the late 1960s and early 1970s, in large part prevented national economic planning from utilizing the results of related sciences, primarily mathematics.

The separation has considerably eased recently, although we still cannot claim that mathematical methods have fully and naturally been incorporated in national economic planning.

In general, it can be stated that Hungary already has a sufficient number of properly qualified specialists to deal with economic and mathematical models, including planning models. In this sense the supply of specialists cannot be considered a bottleneck in increasing the efficiency of modelling.

2.2 Major issues of modelling in planning

In 1979, parallel to the shift in economic policy, the attitude and approach of national economic planning to problems underwent considerable changes. The economic policy urgently called for the development of planning and planning methods as the Hungarian economy entered the intensive phase of development. Planning models are natural elements in this development.

As the attitude of planning changed, requiring increasingly differentiated and multifaceted approaches, modelling followed suit. We abandoned the use of large systems since some of their elements were not prepared in time and the models could not be operated as partial systems in a real sense either in time or in substance; therefore they failed to add up to one real system for lack of the appropriate integral linkages. The early period was even marked by computer difficulties as there were no efficient facilities available for solving the large-scale linear programming problems; thus the results were delayed and their use aborted.

It should be noted here that from time to time there were

occasions in Hungarian modelling practice (and, it is assumed, elsewhere too) when we tried to find possible applications of a fashionable modelling trend. Problems encountered in real life thus remained in the background for lack of methods while model calculations only appeared as illustrations of a given method.

Beyond the concrete needs of planning, this experience also justifies the adoption of a problem-oriented, differentiated and flexible approach in modelling since it is this approach that we generally try to take in planning as well.

Planning of the national economy has undergone significant changes in the past few years.

1 The problem-oriented nature of planning has increased. This means that certain issues of great importance for economic development (e.g. external equilibrium, increase of export capacities, structural adjustment etc.) should be given special treatment. This in turn requires appropriate model types to be developed and used and calls for a special information base.

2 Uncertainty has increased, particularly in view of dependence on the world economy, and at the same time there has been a growing need for "open planning". This has made it a very difficult and delicate task to inform professional and social circles since the plan scenarios under preparation contain both the favourable and the relatively unfavourable trends of economic development.

3 Partly related to the above-mentioned uncertainty, the demand for elaborating different plan scenarios has increased. Recently these scenarios have not been active and competing alternatives that would facilitate the selection of the optimum growth trend; instead they have been adjustment alternatives depending on the different trends of changes in external conditions. Modelling has an important role to play in elaborating such scenarios and evaluating the expected consequences in a consistent manner.

Thus, we think that modelling used in economy-wide planning at present and in the near future should concentrate on the following major issues.

Detailed analysis of economic equilibrium, including primarily the external balance position Modelling should cover the reasons that caused the equilibrium to be upset and the internal economic processes and trends that cumulated in the balance problems irrespective of international economic trends. At the same time efforts have to be made to find ways of recovery.

Identifying and analysing the selective growth structure With slow economic growth and the scarcity of resources it is especially important to allocate resources efficiently and selectively. This has burdened planning and economic policy with grave problems since tension has already arisen in several fields as a result of low resource generation and reduced allocation for investment purposes. It is vital to identify and develop modelling instruments which are suitable for investigating problems in sufficient detail.

Planning "blocks" of the economy The planning practice of the 1970s treated economic processes mainly at the sectoral level, basically because of the information base and to a lesser extent the institutional structure. The need to consider functionally homogeneous major economic units (e.g. manufacturing industries, primary industries etc.) has strengthened. Conditions have to be created for collecting the necessary information and certain related principles have to be created. Several steps have already been taken in this direction, e.g. the structure of the pricing system basically reflects this approach. A number of modelling approaches follow this breakdown.

Coordination between the regulation system and planning This is one of the most controversial fields of planning since there is a parallel need for stability of the regulation system and for its adjustment to the planned economic process. The greatest problem is caused by the difficulty of assessing the relative impacts of the various regulators and the response of the participants of the economy, and this very fact may from time to time trigger conflicts between the planned processes and the affected interests. This field requires extensive work in order to analyse and forecast the behavioural patterns of economic units – and this should not be done only with the instruments of modelling.

Hence in the development of planning methodology, the models to be elaborated and those already functioning as well as their combined application should provide effective support for solving the above problems on the basis of versatile and problem-oriented information and methodology.

2.2.1 Consistency of growth trends

In current modelling practice the possibilities of medium-term economic growth are considered from several angles. The description of the processes was basically limited to the real sphere in the first stage.

In the early stage of preparing the seventh Five Year Plan, a one-sector growth model was successfully adopted and used to produce several hundred macroscenarios. This was necessary because the forecasts available and the assumptions made in an early stage of planning may vary over a wide range. After selecting and appropriately classifying the quantified scenarios – which were systematically elaborated – a few typical scenarios were obtained. Different possible values of the following factors[1] were taken into consideration for elaborating the scenarios: the change in the non-ruble export capacity, the required size of balance of trade (in line with the equilibrium requirements and the forecasts of the international money market), the change in import efficiency and the internal distribution of the gross domestic product.

The model solutions provided consistent scenarios for GDP and domestic final demand, including consumption and accumulation. Certain scenario groups can be omitted because of the low probability of occurrence, while the remaining ones can be classified into three groups. The first group comprises those scenarios under which the low level of internal efficiency is coupled with an unfavourable turn in the external conditions. We included in the second group the solutions which were favourable either from external or from internal aspects. The third group only comprises explicitly favourable scenarios. Later in planning, the highest subjective probability was assigned to the scenarios of the second group on which further detailed planning was also based.

In the subsequent stages of planning, we used models disaggregated according to the sectoral breakdown of planning. Thus the framework of the PRONOSIS model system takes shape on the basis of earlier developed models. The model system relies on three models which are different in their approach and the tasks to which they are oriented.

The DINAMO model (Augusztinovics, 1981) is intended to analyse the consistency of the volume trends of the real sphere planned in sectoral detail and the relation of the trends to desirable long-term development ideas. It is an organic continuation of the central volume model used in the sixth Five Year Plan, more appropriately adjusted in its structure to the planning categories and thus creating the possibility of "standby" modelling. This model compares the investment requirements estimated from the capital intensity of individual sectors with the investment possibilities which result from the projected changes in material consumption and import requirements at the planned level of exports and consumption. The model adopts the basic plan ideas for the items of final demand.

Major elements of the model are the sectoral input–output tables, lagged investment equations, import balances and the net amount of debts. It is a linear programming model in this mathematical form, using combined objective functions and maximizing the value of the sum of cumulative, discounted consumption and the sum of fixed assets at the end of the period.

The tensions of the economic structure as mentioned formerly lend particular importance to the tasks of radical structural changes. Therefore we have developed problem-oriented information bases in order to facilitate economic analyses at subsectoral and even enterprise level. In addition to traditional analyses, enterprises were classified on the basis of efficiency criteria with the help of factor analysis and a mutlidimensional ordering procedure. The first phase of the studies concentrated on three subsectors which are important for the Hungarian economy but have to be heavily subsidized from the state budget (these are coal mining, ferrous metallurgy and the meat processing industry). This was followed by selection of the opposite pole, i.e. subsectors which possess advantageous features for selective development.

It seemed justified to elaborate a prognosticating model using a different approach to check the planned changes in volume trends. The econometric model known as forecasting final demand (FFD) which is used for projecting the items of final demand describes the major decisive trends of the economy on the basis of the past year's statistics. The FFD is an econometric model which includes some input–output relations in addition to stochastic relations.

Besides traditional planning in real terms and focusing on volume trends, price and income distributions have gained importance in recent years. The projection of price and income processes is supported by the price and income model (PRIN) which describes the domestic price and income trends under the planned system of economic regulations and at forecast external prices, assuming given volume trends. The model can therefore be used to indicate the aggregate impacts of the changes in any one element of the regulating system and also facilitates consideration and quantification of the various alternatives of the exchange rate policy and the tax system.

The combination of the above two models (PROGPLAN) (Hunyadi, Kovács and Neményi, 1987) gives a simultaneous forecast of the real trends, prices and incomes. The relation between the two models is indicated in figure 13.3. International prices and export demand are given as exogenous factors. Planning is to determine the projected producer and consumer prices as well as the real income which, if considered exogenous, can be used to calculate the path of real trends. Then, with the help of the PRIN model, prices and incomes can be determined on the basis of the real growth trend as forecast by the FFD model and the expected changes in regulations during the period in question. The discrepancies between prices and income given exogenously and those calculated can supply useful information for creating consistency in the plan.

The analysis of the macroeffects of changes in regulation is complemented by the models which describe at a microeconomic level, i.c. for the enterprises operating under different conditions, the impacts of changes in regulation on restructuring and the expected response of enterprises. Such model computations have been made in the case of the wage regulations system and export promotion as well as to assess the expected impacts of the personal income tax and the value-added tax introduced from January 1, 1988, and to coordinate them with the 1987 system of accounting.

Calculations have regularly been made using the models for both the annual plans and the seventh Five Year Plan, in the various phases of planning. The analyses have been directed at forecasting economic processes under changing conditions and at drawing up plan alternatives while evaluating their consistency. The analysis for testing the impacts of changes in regulations and for providing a sound basis for structural changes has evolved over the past two years. This multifaceted approach is useful In establishing the consistency of the volume trends, in indicating the tension points in the plan by comparing the statistical causal relationships inherent in the projected trends, in analysing the relation between volume, price and income trends and in assessing whether the planned changes in regulation would work towards implementing the national economic plan.

2.2.2 Study of economic equilibrium and disequilibrium

The economic changes of recent years have set the study of economic equilibrium as perhaps the most important task in planning work. The issue of equilibrium has evolved in planning in its full complexity. It was the issue of external equilibrium that was raised most sharply. However, the tensions it implies are of course also felt in the internal balance situation and may exert their impact to the detriment of both equilibria.

Model studies use a threefold approach: the objective we have set is to carry out a multifaceted (static) study of economic equilibrium by setting up a general equilibrium-type model group and by making maximum use of the experience and information sources of formerly applied input–output models and models aimed at optimum allocation.

The models include the most important primal and dual macroeconomic relations and analyse the balance positions as a function of

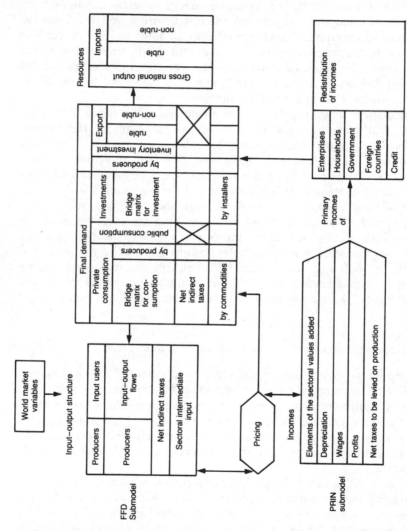

Figure 13.3 Framework of the PROGPLAN model

some key parameters. Physical relations within the models are based on equations that can be obtained from sectoral balances. Production relations consider three primary resources, i.e. non-substitutable imports, fixed assets and labour. In contrast with traditional planning practice, we permit certain resources (fixed assets, labour, domestic and imported products) to substitute for one another. The structure of costs and pricing regulations form the dual part of the model. Selection from among the various scenarios is made with the help of key parameters. Such parameters primarily facilitate the selection of the various types of production functions and various ways of handling foreign trade relations (demand or supply functions, exchange rate and import substitution). A major benefit of the model lies in its variability and close link to the categories of planning work.

Analyses have been prepared for 1981–5 by further developing the established model framework and by utilizing its two concrete specifications (Kis, 1985; Kis, Robinson and Tyson, 1986; Zalai, 1982, 1983, Cseko and Zalai, 1984). The studies are centred around exchange rate policy, inflation and the balance of payments. In analysing these relations, special attention had to be given to the specificity that there are no established behaviour patterns for the changes in the price mechanism and that price changes are less efficient under soft budget constraints.

A dynamic version of the model covering a time span of five years has been elaborated at the National Planning Office with the assistance of the World Bank; computations are currently being performed.

An asymmetric Neumann-type quasi-dynamic model (Belsö et al., 1984; Csernátony, Ligeti and Medvegyev, 1984) was used for the related analysis of growth and balance problems. Research prior to applications proved the existence of equilibrium for a wide category of asymmetric models. The applied specification was motivated by two factors: the approach to planning attitude and planning tasks, and the possibility of solutions using relatively uncomplicated instruments. The model embraces two plan periods and uses the traditional planning nomenclature in analysing the potential of economic growth. On the basis of primal and dual relations, it determines the production and price structures and the related growth rate as well as the average profit rate characteristic of the economy; also, it investigates the sectoral differentiation of the same. The model can effectively be used to analyse to what extent the external equilibrium and budget balance are affected by different growth rates, and what budgetary subsidies are included in the prices of the individual sectors. The model was used to prepare the computations necessary to lay the foundations for the economic policy alternatives of the annual plan as well.

Issues related to equilibrium naturally imply the analysis of dise-quilibrium in the economy. The multimarket disequilibrium model (Hulyák, 1986) of the Hungarian economy was prepared by using disequilbrium theory. This model identifies the major tension points of the economy, based on the 1965–81 time series. As a major line of the analysis, it describes how the external and internal disequilibria in the lagged structure of the economic processes can be resolved at the expense of one another; it also demonstrates that the restrictive internal economic policy also has a negative impact on the external balance position with some delay. The results of the model have been a useful contribution to the *cycle analysis* of Hungarian economic processes. The model is basically of analytical character. However, it can also be used for forecasting for a shorter time span if it can be assumed that there will be no significant interruptions in economic policy and management. In its present form it is used to compare the period since 1981 with *ex post* forecasts.

The correlation between external and internal equilibria has been analysed with an aggregated regulation model (Ligeti, 1985) also. Compared with studies aimed at achieving a required level of the trade balance, this model has raised the issue of the retractive influence that is exerted on the economic processes by changing the balance. The model calculations confirmed the earlier analyses which indicated that for a long period of time the external and internal equilibria work against each other and that this is also reflected in the cyclical changes of the macroprocesses. The model also showed that forced growth in any one period has a cycle-inducing effect.

The models used in the practice of planning for analysing the growth trends and balance positions of the national economy at the macrolevel are complemented by model developments which are aimed at identifying long-term growth trends with the instruments of *dynamic factor analysis* (Bánkövi, Veliczky and Ziermann, 1982) and at highlighting the major factors of growth. Such models are sup-plemented by the results of applied research which are geared to expanding the general equilibrium model system dynamically and to indicating the inertia and tolerance towards regulation in economic processes.

2.2.3 Planning intersectoral complexes

Planning work has acquired a specific feature in recent years whereby in certain cases the practice of sector-oriented planning was discon-tinued and endeavours were made to create a planning methodology for comprehensive blocks. This change is also reflected in model building. It has resulted in models that indicate the specific features of the individual blocks such as the agroindustries and the energy economy.

The agroindustries model Related to the work of the International Institute of Applied Systems Analysis (IIASA), a simulation model has been elaborated for the Hungarian agroindustries (Kelemen et al., 1985) and has been linked with the IIASA's world-wide agroindustries model.

This model describes the processes of production, sales, consumption and foreign trade in agroindustry. The model analyses are aimed at simulating the consequences of various economic policy alternatives.

Agroindustries are described within the overall macroeconomic processes by considering the changes in real trends within the constraints established in planning and by including the correlations in price, income and volume trends. The model contains the possibilities of demand, supply and price adjustment, describes income generation and the system of income redistribution as well as the changes in the position of income earners, and links economic development with the actual generation of resources.

The starting year for the model is 1982. From that year on, 10–15-year trends have been simulated. The economy has been divided into three sectors: agriculture (large-scale and small-scale farms separately), agroindustries and the aggregate of the national economy. The model gives special attention to 46 agricultural and processed commodities.

For the preparation of the seventh Five Year Plan, the calculations were focused on the following economic policy dilemmas:

1 substitutability of grain for export or livestock-feeding purposes,
2 substitutability of live animal exports and meat exports and
3 relations of consumer price subsidies and consumer price changes in the scope of agroindustrial commodities.

Energy model The prolonged energy crisis which started in the mid-1970s gravely affected Hungary and largely contributed to external balance problems. Ever since then, how to ensure efficient energy supply has been a central issue in national economic planning. Although energy modelling began parallel to the first application of planning models, this trend received additional impetus and its use spread in the mid-1970s, while the scope of applied models widened.

In addition to energy modelling at various institutions, yet not fully independent of its results and experience, the National Planning

Office also prepared an energy model which fitted into the system of planning models, with the aim of supporting planning decisions for energetics. The model was originally used in three steps:

1 A slightly modified version of the DINAMO model was used to quantify the general economic environment of the energy sector.
2 On that basis, a linear energy sector model provided the development and import implications of energy supply for a time span up to the year 2000.
3 This solution furnished additional inputs for the DINAMO model, giving the starting point for a new iteration.

This approach, however, did not prove to be appropriate; since both models are linear, the results obtained were extreme and rigid. Further development efforts were aimed at elaborating an independent energy model which would cover the whole economy at macro-level but would enlarge and detail the elements of the energy sector. This model already makes use of the dynamic approach and non-linear techniques of general equilibrium models.

3 Directions of Future Progress

The next step to be taken in utilizing and improving the efficiency of models in planning should invariably be directed towards narrowing the special gap between modelling and traditional planning. To this end, the incorporation of models in planning work should be improved and the recipient environment of modelling should be made more favourable. These two efforts are favourably affected if the analysis of the relevant economic and planning issues to be answered, rather than the technique of model building, is put in the centre. Cooperation between the specialists active in various fields of planning is essential for producing properly detailed models. With the application of planning models, the question of which special fields the long-term development activities should be concentrated on arises. The following factors give orientation for setting long-term development trends.

1 The experience accumulated in the application of models must be taken into account.
2 Main international trends and the results of basic research can be outlined and are decisive.
3 The processes are favourably influenced by the widening use of personal computers in the near future, which is expected to increase the scope of direct applications significantly.

4 The approach in national economic planning is undergoing changes which will lay emphasis on the recognition of dynamic properties of the economy and the treatment of quality factors.

From the viewpoint of developing the methodology, the first three factors are obvious. The consistent use of the dynamic approach partly means a shift of emphasis in the planning approach and partly requires improvement of applied instruments in modelling. The directions of development should therefore be linked with the stages of the decision-making process.

Improving the information supply The major tasks of development are to supply the computerized information systems of the government administration with coordinated actual data, to improve the methods of expected and preliminary estimates in planning, continuously to assess changing needs as a result of developing planning and to establish integrated computer systems.

Developing the methods of analysis and forecasting This development implies two directions: it makes use of the possibilities presented by traditional econometric instruments and it is intended to use the results of mathematical systems theory. Major areas of development are analysis of macrotrends, analysis of the plan and planning with models and investigation of disequilibria.

Study of the regulation possibilities of economic processes The modification of the regulation system as a whole or of its individual elements affects the macroprocesses; consequently, they come closer to the targets set by the plan. The effect of changes in regulation evidently goes through a long chain. The developments are directed at three stages which can be distinguished relatively clearly. The first stage is to indicate the impact that the changes in regulation will have on the economic entities. The typical behaviour patterns that evolve are to be analysed in the next step and, finally, their macroeffects should be assessed.

Developing the methodology to support decision making in a strict sense The majority of formerly used models belong to this category. On the basis of experience, three tasks have been focused on particularly. The consistency to be created between the activities performed at various levels calls for the further development of hierarchical models. The issue of multiobjective optimization is naturally incorporated in the specific ideas of planning. Finally, the flexible use of the models requires the development of an interactive decision-support system.

Note

1 This means a deviation from the established practice since neither labour nor tied-up assets were considered among the factors for elaborating scenarios. The reason is that these factors have not put a constraint on growth recently, from the quantitative side at least. The real restriction is imposed by imports and production efficiency.

References

Ámon, Zs. (1973) "Népgazdasági mérlegmodell az V. ötéves terv kialakításához" (A model balance for working out the fifth Five Year Plan), *Statisztikai Szemle*, LI, 12, pp. 1220–36.
—— (1975) "Aggregate, Input–Output-based Linear Programming in Drawing up the 5th Five Year Plan for the Hungarian Economy", paper presented to Winter Symposium of the Econometry Society, Geneva.
Augusztinovics, M. (ed.) (1981) *Népgazdasági modellszámítások a VI. ötéves terv kidolgozásához* (National economic model computations for the sixth Five Year Plan), Budapest: National Planning Office of Hungary, p. 115.
Báger, G. (1974) "Az V. ötéves terv modellrendszere" (The model system of the fifth Five Year Plan), *Közgazdasági Szemle*, XXI, 521–36.
Balassa, Á. (1979) *A magyar népgazdaság tervezésének alapjai* (Foundations of planning the Hungarian economy), Budapest: *Közgazdasági és Jogi Könyvkiadó*.
Bánkövi, Gy, J. Veliczky and M. Ziermann (1982) "Multivariate Time Series Analysis and Forecast", in W. Grossmann (ed.) *Probability and Statistical Inference*, Dordrecht: D. Reidel, pp. 29–34.
Belso, L., Cs. Csernátony, I. Ligeti, P. Medvegyev and A. Tihanyi (1984) *A makrogazdasági egyensúly egy nem-lineáris modellje* (A non-linear model of macroeconomic equilibrium), Budapest: Tervgazdasági Intézet.
Cseko, J., and E. Zalai (1984) *Egy többszektoros, általános egyensúlyi típusú modellcsalád (HUMUS) matematikai leírása és számítógépes algoritmusának vázlata* (Mathematical description of a multisector general equilibrium model family (HUMUS) and an outline of its computer algorithm), Budapest: National Planning Office of Hungary.
Csernátony, Cs., I. Ligeti and P. Medvegyev (1984) "A Non-linear Open von Neumann Model and its Application", International Institute of Applied Systems Analysis Collaborative Paper, Laxenburg.
Dániel, Zs., A. Jónás, J. Kornai and B. Martos (1972) "Tervszondázás" (Plan-sounding), *Közgazdasági Szemle*, September.
Ganczer, S. (ed.) (1976) *Népgazdasági tervezés és programozás* (National economic planning and programming), Budapest: Közgazdasági és Jogi Könyvkiadó.
Hulyák, K. (1986) "An Econometric Disequilibrium Macromodel for Hungary", paper presented at the World Congress of the Econometric Society, Cambridge, MA.
Hunyadi, L., Á. Kovács and J. Neményi (1987) *An Econometric Input–*

Output Type Model of the Hungarian Economy, Informacne Systemy, 15, 5, pp. 445–56.

Kelemen, K., S. Povilaitis, T. Tétényi and J. Vincze (1985) *A magyar élelmiszergazdaság modellje* (Model of the Hungarian food economy), Budapest: National Planning Office of Hungary.

Kis, P. (1985) "A Computable General Equilibrium Model in the Macro Planning Process" (Manuscript) Budapest: National Planning Office of Hungary.

—— S. Robinson and L. D. Tyson (1986) "Computable General Equilibrium Models for Socialist Economies", paper presented at the 5th IFAC/IFORS Conference on Dynamic Modelling and Control of National Economies, Budapest.

Kornai, J. (1968) "A többszintü népgazdasági programozás modellje" (The model of multilevel economy-wide programming), *Közgazdasági Szemle*, January, XV, 1, pp. 54–68 and 2, pp. 173–90.

Ligeti, I. (1973) "An Optimal Growth Model for the Hungarian National Economy", 5th Conference on Optimization Techniques, Rome, in *Lecture Notes in Computer Science*, 4, pp. 324–34, Berlin, Heidelberg, New York: Springer Verlag.

——(1985) "A makrostruktúra és a konvertibilis külkereskedelmi mérleg" (The macrostructure and the balance of trade against convertible currencies), *Közgazdasági Szemle*, XXXII, 10, pp. 1210–24.

—— and J. Sivák (1978) *Növekedés, szabályozás és stabilitás a gazdasági folyamatokban* (Growth, regulation and stability in economic processes), Budapest: Közgazdasági és Jogi Könyvkiadó.

Zalai, E. (1982) "Computable General Equilibrium Models: An Optimal Planning Perspective", *Mathematical Modelling*, 3, pp. 437–59.

—— (1983) "A Non-linear Multisectoral Model for Hungary: General Equilibrium versus Optimal Planning Approaches", in A. C. Kelleq, W. C. Sanderson and J. G. Williamson (eds), *Modelling Growing Economies in Equilibrium and Disequilibrium*, Durham, NC: Duke University Press.

Index

Aaron, H. J. 105
Accelerated Cost Recovery System (ACRS) 73
activity analysis general equilibrium (AGE)
    models 23, 24
Adams, P. D. 267, 275
Adelman, I. and Robinson, S. 12
Adelman–Robinson model 12–14
adjustment process, overview of 170–3
adjustment regimes 168–70
admissible sets 155–8
    empirical formulation of 158–64
Africa 211
Agell, J. 25, 33, 37, 44, 55, 188
    and Edin, P.-A. 53
Agrawal, N. 257
    and Meagher, G. A. 245, 247, 248, 257
    et al. 248, 257, 275
agriculture 300–1, 324–5
    free trade 203
    liberalization 204–5, 207–10
    protection 201–4; and food consumption 212–
        13; effects on world prices 208; impact of
        abolishing 212; impact of reduced 210–13;
        reduction by half 204
agroindustries model 455
Ahmed, S. A. et al. 238
Aislabie, C. J. 244
Alaouze, C. M. 256
    et al. 256
Ames, E. 391, 400
Ámon, Z. and Ligeti, I. 431
Ámon, Zs. 436
    and Ligeti, I. 26
Anderson, K. and Tyers, R. 209
applied general equilibrium (AGE) models
    analytical framework 153–73
    asset markets 149–91
Armington, P. 27, 197, 227
Armington, P. S. 256, 264, 356, 380
Armington assumption 12, 27, 356, 380
Arrow, K. J.
    and Hahn, F. H. 115, 141
    and Hurwicz, 140

asset demand functions 35
asset market model 37–44, 149–91
    behavioural functions 38
    heterogeneous expectations 38
    heterogeneous stocks of physical capital 37
    institutional setting and level of aggregation
        37
    numerical application 44–7
    small open economy 39–44
    stochastic modeling 38
    treatment of housing assets 37
assets markets
    excess demand or supply in 154
    tax capitalization effects in 33–57
asset prices 181, 184, 185
asset risk 36
Atkinson, A. and Stiglitz, J. 54
Auerbach, A. 55
Auerbach, A. J. 107
    and Kotlikoff, L. J. 106
    et al. 25, 111, 112, 113, 134, 141
Augusztinovics, M. 427, 449
Australia
    applications by academics 255–7
    applications by state governments and
        regional modelers 254–5
    applications carried out for government
        agencies 252
    computable general equilibrium (CGE) policy
        applications 244–50
    factors influencing economy 251
    and international trade 259–60
    see also Industries Assistance Commission
        (IAC)
Australian Bureau of Agricultural and
    Resource Economics (ABARE) 244, 253,
    254
Australian Bureau of Statistics (ABS) 331
Australian Mining Industry Council (AMIC)
    257–8

Backus, D. et al. 150, 151
BAE see Bureau of Agricultural Economics

Báger, G. 434, 436
Bailey, M. J. 39
balance-of-payments problems 220–4, 412, 439
Balasko, Y.
  and Shell, K. 112, 118, 126, 132
  et al. 126, 135
Balassa, Á. 440
Balassa, B. 238
  and Tyson, L. D. 428
Ballard, C. L. et al. 105
Bánkovi, Gy. et al. 454
Barro, R. 35
Barro, R. J. 151, 159
  and Grossman, H. J. 384, 396
Bateman, W. S. G. 245, 250, 254
Bavaria 215
Belso, L. 453
Benassy, J. P. 238
Bennett, J. 398
Bergman, L. 3, 27, 355, 362, 365, 368
  and Lundgren, S. 26, 351
  and Mäler, K.-G. 355, 362, 365, 370
  and Ohlsson, L. 355
Bergstrom, A. R. and Wymer, C. R. 262, 263
Bergström, V. and Södersten, J. 55
Bewley, T. 113
Bhagwati, J. 218, 238
  and Srinivasan, T. N. 218, 237
Blampied, C. W. 248
Bonnell, S. M. 247
  and Dixon, P. B. 247, 256
  et al. 247, 255
Bradford, D. F. 106
Drainard, W. and Tobin, J. 33, 35, 53
Brennan, M. 33
Brook, A. et al. 25
Brown, N. and Camilleri, A. 244
Bruce, I. A. 244
Bruno, M. 264
budget constraints 114, 115, 128
budget deficits 174–86
Dulow, J. and Summers, L. 36
Bureau of Agricultural Economics (BAE) 206, 248, 249, 253, 254
Bureau of Industry Economics (BIE) 246, 248, 255, 264
Burke, J. 118, 132
Burke, R. H. 248, 255
Burkett, J. P. 392
  et al. 389, 401
Burniaux, J. M. 196, 215
  and Waelbroeck, J. 195, 216
Business Council of Australia (BCA) 245, 257

calibration method 19
Calvo, G. 112, 136
Campbell, R. et al. 246, 253
capital accounting framework 34–5
Capital Cost Recovery System (CCRS) 73
Carmichael, W. 261
Castle, R. G. and Guest, J. F. 248
Cave, M. and Hare, P. 398
centrally planned economy (CPE) models 383–404

Centre for Regional Economic Analysis (CREA) 254
Chai, S. S. and Dixon, P. B. 244
Challen, D. W.
  and Hagger, A. J. 262
  et al. 247, 255
Chapman, R. and Vincent, D. P. 248, 256
Charemza, W. 393, 401
  and Dlouhý, V. 26, 383
  and Gronicki, M. 393, 397, 400, 401
  and Quandt, R. E. 393, 401
Charmley, C. 106
chemicals industry 301, 311–13, 342
Cilke, J. M. and Wyscarver, R. A. 106
Clements, K. W.
  and Sjaastad, L. A. 257
  and Smith, M. D. 344, 345
clothing 334, 343
Cobb–Douglas functions 7, 19, 20, 22, 142, 223, 226, 227, 360, 394, 396
Commission of the European Communities 216
Common Agricultural Policy (CAP) 195–217
Commonwealth Agencies 253, 4
computable general equilibrium (CGE) models 241, 259, 261, 262, 270, 274–6, 353, 4, 356
  activity analysis approaches 23–5
  approaches 263–5
  and Armington assumption 380
  developing countries 12–14
  development of 3, 6
  econometric approaches 19–23
  Harberger–Scarf–Shoven–Whalley approach 14–19
  level of aggregation 5
  main characteristics and uses of 3–6
  multicountry 4
  nuclear power discontinuation 373–9
  one-country 4
  operation of 406–12
  policy applications 244
  recent developments 25–6
  socialist economics 405–30
  solution 266
Condon, T. et al. 427
Confederation of Australian Industry 257
constant elasticity of substitution (CES) functions 16, 19, 20, 198–9, 223, 226, 265, 360, 361
constant elasticity of transformation (CET) 223, 228
contemporaneous differential comparative statics (CDCS) 266
convenience value 166
Cook, L. H.
  and Dixon, P. B. 247, 256
  and Porter, M. G. 246, 257
Cooper, R. J. 244, 269, 272
  and McLaren, K. R. 248, 268, 276
  et al. 244, 266, 268
Corden, W. M. and Dixon, P. B. 247, 256
Cory, P. and Horridge, M. 243, 275, 335
Council for Mutual Economic Aid (CMEA) 196, 408–9, 445
Cox, J. et al. 53

Cronin. M. R. 242
Crowley, and Demura, 249
Crowley. P. T. and Martin. G. 244, 249, 253
  et al. 244, 253
Csernátony, Cs. et al. 453
Cycle analysis 454

dairy industry 302–11, 331
Dantzig–Wolfe decomposition procedure 433
Darby, M. R. 113
Debreu, G. 115
decision-making
  mechanism of 440
  process of 457
  support methodology 457
Dee. P. S. 247, 248, 275
demand modeling 410–12
Dervis, K.
  and Robinson, S. 428
  et al. 26, 220, 427, 428
Devarajan, S. et al. 13
developing countries 12–14, 312
Dewatripont, M. et al. 26, 218
DGM (Dewatripont–Grais–Michel model) 222–3
Diamond, P. A. 111
differential tax incidence 39
DINAMO model 449, 456
disequilibrium models 383–404
Dixon, P. B. 23, 242, 247–9, 254, 256–9, 264,
    267, 270, 274, 343
  and Johnson, D. 245, 257
  and Parmenter, B. R. 243, 245, 257, 258
  and Powell, A. A. 247
  and Vincent, D. P. 246, 264
  et al. 241–9, 251, 254, 257–9, 266, 270, 275,
    276, 341
Dlouhý, V. 384, 385, 392
  see also Charemza, W. and Dlouhý, V.
Domar, E. and Musgrave, R. 36
Drèze, J. 169
Drud, A.
  and Kendrick, D. 25
  et al. 231
dynamic factor analysis 454
dynamic simulation 435

Ebrill, L. P. and Possen, U. M. 34, 47, 53
econometrics 19–23, 435
economic equilibrium and disequilibrium 447,
    451–4
economic growth 58–110
economic planning
  Hungary 405–30
  Yugoslavia 405–30
Economic Recovery Tax Act (ERTA) 62
Edwards, S. 219
electricity production model 377
ELIAS model 365
employment 407
endogenous sectors 153, 171
energy consumption 364

energy-economy interactions
  hypotheses 352–3
  models of 353–4
  static model 355
energy modeling 455–6
energy policy, Sweden 351–82
energy programming model 436
equilibrium conditions 172, 369–70, 376
equilibrium exchange rates 421–4
equilibrium price paths, determinacy of 121–6
European Community 195, 201–5, 207–10
  December 1986 decisions 203–4
Eurostat 202
Evans, H. D. 244, 259, 264
exchange rates, equilibrium nominal 422
exogenous sectors 153, 172
expected interest rates 165
expected rates of return 164–8, 171
export functions 361
export incentives 228, 231–3
export supplies 225–9
exports, determination of 368
external balance 447
external disequilibria 220–2

Fallon, J. and Thompson, L. 245, 325, 327, 332
Fama, E. F. 188
Feldstein, M. 33, 34, 47, 51
  and Summers, L. 36
Feltenstein, A. 5, 150, 247, 275
fertilizers 301
financial programming model 436
financial sector general equilibrium model 40
finite horizon models 134–40
first in–first out (FIFO) inventory accounting
    71
Fisher, I. 188
Fitzpatrick, M. D. and McKeon, R. 248, 254
Food and Agriculture Organisation (FAO) 197
Food and Agriculture Program (FAP) 197
footwear 334, 343
forecasting final demand (FFD) model 450
forecasting methods 457
foreign capital inflows 420–1
foreign exchange 218–40, 413, 414, 420
  allocation liberalization 233–6
  allocation system 222–9
  flows captured in model 223–5
  liberalization 231–7
  retention rates 231–3
foreign trade 301, 325–30, 391, 408–10, 437
Førsund, F. M. et al. 261
Fraser, R. W. 246, 248, 249, 255
  and Salerian, S. 244, 249, 255
Freebairn, J. W. 242
Friedman, B. and Roley, V. 54
Friedman, B. M. 187
Friend, I.
  and Blume, M. 54
  and Hasbrouck, J. 45, 55
Fullerton, D. et al. 18, 106, 107

Gale, D. 111, 113, 117, 118, 145
GAMS 25

Ganczer, S. 433, 436
Geankoplos, J. D.
  and Brown, D. J. 144
  and Polemarchakis, H. M. 112, 126
GEM-PACK code 259
General Agreement on Tariffs and Trade
  (GATT) 214
general equilibrium models x–xi, 4, 59
  applied intertemporal 111–48
  communication of model results 336–9
  financial sector 40
  foreign exchange allocation 222–9
  policy work 241–90
Ginsburgh, V. A. and Wealbroeck, J. L. 6, 23,
  24
Gordon, R. H. and Bradford, D. 55
Goreux, L. M. and Manne, A. S. 264
Goulder, L. and Summers, L. 53
Gouriéroux, C. and Laroque, G. 392
government risk sharing 39
Grais, W.
  et al. 238
  see also Dewatripont, M. et al.
Green, D. W. and Higgins, C. I. 395
gross domestic product (GDP) 15, 298, 330,
  344, 353, 371, 379, 415, 449
gross national product (GNP) 150, 211–12, 335
gross substitutability 140–3, 145
Grossman, S. and Shiller, R. 54
growth models 449
growth trends consistency 448–51

Hagger, A. J. et al. 245, 250, 254, 255
Hahn, F. 266
Hahn, F. H. 188
Halfpenny, J. 346
Hall, R. E. 106
  and Rabushka, A. 106
Hall, V. B. et al. 250
Harberger, A. C. 6, 14, 58, 101, 105
Harberger–Scarf–Shoven–Whalley models 12–
  19
Harris, R. 25, 275
Harris, R. G. 345
Hausman, J. A. 106
  and Poterba, J. M. 106
Hawke, R. J. 274
Hayashi, F. 33, 54
Heckscher–Ohlin model 356
Hendershott, P. and Hu, C. 34
Hepburn, G. 244, 256
HERCULES 25
Hicks, J. 53
Hicks, J. R. 188
Higgs, P. J. 244–9, 256, 258, 344
  and Stoeckel, A. 245
  et al. 244, 246, 247, 255
Holzman, F. O. 391, 400
Hooi, N. O. 256
Horne, J. 245
Horridge, J. M. 243, 244, 248, 270, 275
  and Powell, A. A. 270
  et al. 244, 256
Horridge, M. 345

Hudson, E. A. and Jorgenson, D. W. 20
Hudson–Jorgenson model 21
Hulyák, K. 454
Hungary 406
  economic planning 405–30
  energy crisis 455
  energy model 455
  Five Year Plans: third 432; fourth 433–4;
    fifth 434, 436; sixth 437, 449; seventh 439,
    441, 448, 451, 455
  medium-term planning 431–59
  planning models: up to 1980s 432–8; 1980s
    438–56
Hunyadi, L. et al. 450

IAESR 253, 256–8
Impact Project 241, 263, 276, 340
  review of models 242–59
import demands 225–9
import–export ratios 231
import functions 361
import rationing 228, 229
import substitution elasticities 236–7
indeterminacy
  equilibria 145
  in applied intertemporal general equilibrium
    models 111–48
  problems of 135–40
Industries Assistance Commission (IAC) 241–
  51, 255, 259–62, 291–347
information supply 457
input–output models 405, 436
instability problems 136
interest rates 181, 183, 186
International Institute for Applied Systems
  Analysis (IIASA) 197, 354, 455
intersectoral complexes 454–6
intertemporal equilibrium models xi
investment restraint 424–5
IS-LM model 150, 175

Johansen, L. 6–10, 12, 26, 27, 34, 261, 274, 354
Johnson, D. 249, 258, 264, 265
  and Kee, P. K. 248
Johnson, P. D. and Trevor, R. G. 268
Joint Committee on Taxation 62, 105, 107
Jonung, L. 166
Jorgenson, D. W. 20, 21, 22, 27
  and Slesnick, D. T. 22
  and Yun, K.-Y. 22, 26, 57, 58, 106, 107
  et al. 22
Jorgenson–Yun model 22
Judd, K. L. 106

Kalecki, M. 385
Kareken, J. H. and Wallace, N. 111
Karl Marx University of Economics 445
Karlin, S. 23
Kehoe, T. J. 145
  and Levine, D. K. 25, 111–13, 115, 117, 118,
    122, 123, 126
  et al. 112, 113, 118, 140
Kelemen, K. et al. 455
Kemme, D. and Winiecki, J. 400

Keynes–Klein (KK) model 262
King, M. 55
 and Fullerton, D. 54, 107
 and Leape, J. 53
Kis, P. 453
 et al. 26, 405, 453
Klaus, V. and Rudlovcak, V. 393, 401
KLEM model 20
Klijn, N. 244
Kornai, J. 384, 392, 427, 433
Kotlikoff, L. J. and Summers, L. H. 113
Krueger, A. 238
Krueger, A. O. 428

Latin America 210, 211
Lau, L. J. 20
Lawson, A. 250, 254
Lawson, A. *see* Powell, A. A. and Lawson, A.
Leontief model 21
Leontief, W. A. et al. 254
Levine, D. K. 113
 see also Kehoe, T. J. and Levine, D. K.
Lewis, J. D. 429
 and Urata, S. 428
Libura, U. 395
Liew, L. H. 244, 248, 250, 255
Ligeti, I. 434, 454
 and Sivák, J. 434
 see also Ámon, Z. and Ligeti, I.
linear programming models 405, 437
Linneman, H. et al. 215
Lintner, J. 54
Lluch, C. et al. 197
long-run versus short-run closure 269–70
Longva, S. et al. 10
Lucas, R. E. 111
Lundgren, S. 377, 379, 381
 see also Bergman, L. and Lundgren, S.

McKean, R. N. 188
McLaren, Keith R. 272
McLure, C. E. Jr and Zodrow, G. R. 106
MACRO 268
macroclosure 410–12
macroeconomic adjustment 325–30, 424
macroeconomic closure 267–9
macroeconomic models 434–5
macroeconomic theory 411
Madden, J. R. 255
 and Challen, D. W. 246, 255
 and Hagger, A. J. 249, 255
 et al. 244, 246, 248, 254
Malinvaud, E. 169, 266, 384
Mankiw, N. G. et al. 112, 141
Manne, A. S. 23, 427
Mannion, G. R. et al. 250
Mansur, A. and Whalley, J. 55
Mantel, R. 136
manufacturing sector 301
market adjustment process 157–8
Martin, C. 392
Mas-Colell, A. 115
Mathiesen, L. 25
Mauldon, R. G. et al. 336

Meagher, G. A. 248, 256, 275
 and Agrawal, N. 248, 257
 and Parmenter, B. R. 247, 248, 255, 257, 269, 275
 et al. 248, 255
medium-term planning 431–59
Meltzer, B. D. 244, 256
Merrill, O. H. 17
Michel, G. *see* Dewatripont, M. et al.
Mieszowski, P. 18
Ministry of Economic Development 248, 255
MINOS nonlinear programming system 381
Model of International Relations in Agriculture (MOIRA) 215
Modigliana, F. and Miller, M. H. 188
Monash University Centre for Policy Studies 257
MPS-GE 25
Muellbauer, J. 392
 and Portes, R. 384, 387, 388
Muller, W. J. and Woodford, M. 145
multisectoral growth (MSG) models xi
 extensions of Johansen's approach 10–12
 Johansen's 6–22, 25, 354
 later versions of 10
 Norway 261
Mundlak, Y. 197, 216
 and Hellinghausen, R. 215
Murtagh, B. and Saunders, M. 381
Musgrave, R. A. 107
Muth, J. F. 395, 397

National Farmers' Federation (NFF) 257
Neary, J. P. and Roberts, K. 220, 225, 226, 237
Neumann-type quasi-dynamic model 453
New Zealand 259
nonstationary models 143–5
Norman, N. R. 247, 256
 and Meiklei, K. P. 247, 254
Norman, V. D. and Haaland, J. 27
Norway 261
nuclear power discontinuation policy 373–9
numerical multisectoral economic models 4
Nuti, D. M. 400

Offerdal, E. 26
oil price changes 197, 215, 262, 364–73
ORANI model
 Australian Industries Assistance Commission 291–3, 298–300, 325, 330–6, 340–4, 346
 development 10–14, 26
 policy work 241–3, 251, 253, 255–9, 262, 264–7, 273–5
ORANI-CHEM 311–12, 331, 333, 337, 343, 345
ORANI-MACRO 269
ORANI-MILK 11, 302–3, 331, 343, 344
ORANI-ORES 254
ORANI-TCF 343
Organization for Economic Cooperation and Development (OECD) 197, 216, 217
Organization of Petroleum Exporting Countries (OPEC) 197, 215, 262
overlapping generations model 111, 145

Pagan, A. R. and Shannon, J. H. 242
Palmer, E. E. 159
Pareto-efficient equilibria 132
Pareto-efficient steady state 118
Parikh, K. S. et al. 209
Parmenter, B. R. 244, 247, 249, 257
  and Meagher, G. A. 242, 244, 247, 248, 255
  et al. 11, 244
Parsell, B. F. 248
Patinkin, D. 188, 267
Pearson, 262
Pearson, K. R. 251, 275, 335
Pechman, J. A. 107
Pfajfar, L. and Mencinger, J. 427
Phillips–Bergstrom (PB) models 262
Piggot, J. 248
  and Whalley, J. 17, 247, 275
Pindyck, R. 54
plan adjustment model (PAM) 383, 393–400
planned economy models *see* centrally planned
  economy models
plastics industry 301, 311–13, 333, 342
policy analysis 111, 330–6
policy modeling 241–90
  future 273–6
Por, Andras 355
Portes, R. 384, 386, 387, 388, 391, 392
  and Winter, D. 393, 395, 401
  et al. 401
portfolio selection 36, 47, 153, 155–8, 171
Poterba, J. 53
Poterba, J. M. and Summers, L. 107
Powell, A. and Gruen, F. 238
Powell, A. A. 242, 244, 245, 247, 251, 259,
  260, 261, 264, 267, 269, 272, 342
  and Lawson, A. 241, 267
  and Parmenter, B. R. 244, 246
price and income (PRIN) model 450
price models 410–12, 437–8
price revision rules 170, 172
Prices Justification Tribunal 249
production functions 407
PROGPLAN model 450, 452
PRONOSIS model 449
public inquiry process 294–5

quantity rationing model (QRM) 383, 385–93,
  399–401
Quiggan, J. D. and Stoeckel, A. B. 249, 253

Rattigan, A. 259, 260, 261, 273
Rattso, J. 428
reaction coefficients 170, 184
regulation model 438
regulation system 457
  coordination 448
resource use efficiency 335–6
Rimmer, R. J. 246, 247, 259
risk aversion 153
Rivlin, A. M. 259
Robinson, S. 428, 429
  and Dewatripont, M. 238
  and Tyson, L. D. 220, 238, 406, 407, 427,
  428, 429

Robinson, S. (*cont.*)
  et al. 406, 412, 427
  see also Kis, P. et al.
Robinson–Tyson (RT) model 220, 222–3
Roley, V. V. 150
RUNS 196–201, 205, 207, 208, 210, 214, 216
Rutherford, T. F. 25

Sams, D. and Williams, P. 276
Samuelson, P. A. 111, 144
Sandee, J. 264
Sandmo, A. 53, 106
Santos, M. S. and Bona, J. L. 144
Scarf, H. E. 6, 14, 17
  and Hansen, T. 17
Scheinkman, J. A. and Weiss, L. 113
Schreiner, P. and Larsen, K. A. 27
SCLP 25
Selective growth structure 448
Selmrod, J. 150
Shapley, L. S. and Shubik, M. 118
Sharpe–Lintner–Mossin capital asset pricing
  model 38
Shephard's lemma 358–9, 366, 368, 369
Shoven, J. and Whalley, J. 34
Shoven, J. B. and Whalley, J. 6, 16, 17, 18,
  264, 427
Shoven–Whalley model 17
Siriwardana, M. 244, 260
Smith, G. and Starnes, W. 53
SNAPSHOT 264, 5
social accounting matrix (SAM) 14, 231
social rates of return 97
socialist economies 405–30
Solomon, E. 163
special purpose industry models 299–300
steady state conditions 113–20
Stiglitz, J. 53, 54
Stockholm School of Economics 354
Stoeckel, A. B. 246, 253
  and Cuthbertson, S. 245
Stolper–Samuelson theorem 259
Sugden, C. 248, 256
Summers, L. 34, 47, 53, 106
Swan, T. W. 256
Sweden, energy policy 351–82
synthetic material balance 433

Tax Act
  1981 62, 66
  1982 66
tax capitalization effects in assets markets 33–
  57
tax-CAPM 33
tax debt 169
tax distortions, welfare effects 102
Tax Equity and Fiscal Responsibility Act 1982
  (TEFRA) 66
Tax Law 1986 62–7, 72, 74–7, 81, 89, 93, 95,
  96, 98, 101, 103, 104
tax modeling 39
tax preferences 74

tax rates 63, 73–93
  and distortionary impacts of capital income
    taxation 86, 90
  president's proposal 85–9
  Treasury proposal 81
tax reform 93–104
  alternative approaches to 96
  president's proposal 71–3
  Treasury proposal 67–71
  welfare effects of 95, 101–4
Tax Reform Act 1986 26, 58, 59, 61–75, 89–
    109
tax shelter 77
tax system, effects of indexing 47–52
tax wedges 76, 77, 81, 97, 98, 100, 101, 103
Taylor, L. 27
  and Black, S. L. 264
textiles 334, 343
Three-period-lived consumers 126
Tobin, J. 33, 35, 150, 151, 153, 163, 187, 189
trade incentives 218–40
trade policy 408
Truong, T. P. 250, 275
Tyson, L. D. 428
  et al. 428
  see also Kis, P. et al.

Uhrig, J. 343
United States 213
Uruguay Round negotions 201
US Department of the Treasury 105, 106

value of quantity rationing (VQR) 410
Varian, H. R. 118
Viktorinova, B. 401
Vincent, D. P. 243, 245, 246, 249, 250, 275,
    291, 345
  and Ryland, G. J. 249

Vincent (*cont.*)
  et al. 246
virtual prices 225–9

Waelbroeck, J. *see* Burniaux, J. M. and
  Waelbroeck, J.
wage illusion effect 396–7
Walras–Johansen (WJ) models 262
Walrasian model 13, 405, 426
Walrasian theory 4, 354
Walras's law 114, 116, 117, 119, 123, 129, 150
Warr, P. G. 245
  and Lloyd, P. J. 245, 256
  and Parmenter, B. R. 244, 256
Weitzman, M. 398
welfare impacts of tax reforms 101–4
Welfe, W. 386, 392
Werin, L. 25, 149
Whalley, J. 106
  and Mansur, A. 19, 20
Wharton Econometric Forecasting Associates
  262
Whitlam, G. 259
Wilcoxen, P. J. 276
Winiecki, J. 400
Wonjnilower, A. M. 189
World Bank 199–200, 209, 213, 406, 427, 428
Wright, and Cowan, 244

Ysander, B. C. 353
Yugoslavia 218–40, 406
  economic planning 405–30
Yun, K.-Y. *see* Jorgenson, D. W. and Yun,
  K.-Y.

Zalai, E. 427, 453
zero energy growth 355–64